MAJOR AMERICAN SOCIAL PROBLEMS

MAJOR AMERICAN SOCIAL PROBLEMS

Robert A. Dentler

Teachers College, Columbia University
and
Center for Urban Education, N.Y.

Rand McNally & Company   Chicago

RAND MᶜNALLY SOCIOLOGY SERIES
Edgar F. Borgatta, Advisory Editor

To

CHARLES DAVID KEPNER, JR.

Master Teacher, Sociologist, Friend

PREFACE

Books often find their own way to special audiences, yet authors usually write them with certain groups in mind. I wrote this book for the person interested in social problems or social issues — especially for the student enrolled in a course in social problems or social issues. My conviction throughout has been that what all people have in common is a preference for *readable* books. To this extent, I have tried to transcend any one audience, just as the determination to be somewhat understood has led me to counter certain practices common to higher education. For one, readings from works by other social scientists and authors are provided as part of each chapter; this avoids the necessity of purchasing a separate book of readings. Moreover, most of the readings reprinted here are presented in full, not as excerpts.

There are other small innovations. Each chapter, for example, states my sociological point of view about a contemporary national social problem. Each chapter also summarizes much that is known about the problem through the work of others. Yet I have made no pretense of summarizing, let alone surveying, all that is known. The aim of each chapter is rather to provide a *perspective* about a substantial, widely acknowledged, often ill-understood social problem. Features of the perspective are in each instance then qualified and amplified by the work of other authors, presented in the reprinted articles. Then too, for the reader who seeks to go beyond this book and beyond its source materials, I have included a bibliography in each chapter, selections being made against standards of relevance, scholarship, recency, and accessibility.

My hope is that this book also counters some priorities established in many books in the field of social problems. This book emphasizes war, poverty, and intergroup conflict, for example, and neglects vice, gambling, prostitution, and divorce. This departs notably from many books and other materials. My reasoning is that some social problems are greater in magnitude and severity, and hence in consequences, than others. And, some social problems are more deeply embedded in the social structure and thus more likely to generate additional problems. My notion is that gambling is far less significant a problem than poverty; that it is more an effect than a cause of related problems; and, that gambling may not be socially problematic at all under some conditions, where poverty is likely to be under most!

I also hope this book may counter a trend toward the treatment of social problems and issues of national policy as the province of any particular academic discipline. I have maintained that, while social problems are amenable to disciplined inquiry, no one theory or method can claim the merit of being scientific in its analysis of social problems. Moreover, this book does assert that the study and solution of social problems is the 'engineering' phase of sociology (or any other academic department).

The present volume is also very *contemporary* in emphasis. It aims to contribute to the reader's understanding of current social problems, in the belief that sociological perspectives about current problems will sensitize the reader and thus equip him to confront social problems in the future.

This book contains no formal theory of social problems. It is a book *about* social problems, particularly about ones selected for attention because of their national scope, their contribution to the production of other problems, and their duration. If theories *of* social problems are to develop, they ought to come out of philosophy, politics, and social ethics, I believe. Sociology, social psychology, and political science, the main contributing disciplines involved in the writing of this book, are empirical sciences with empirically grounded theories which may or may not be used in the analysis of a given human difficulty.

Chapter One contains a definition, a conception, of the nature of social problems, to be sure. The same chapter presents theories about the origins of social problems in the social structure and its processes of change. But the problems selected for analysis have been chosen pragmatically. In this sense, no formal theory of problems has been applied. My reason for this comes in part from a belief that no scholar anywhere has developed a useful theory of social problems, and in part from a sense of obligation to the reader. I believe that the reader, as a citizen, knows of the existence of group-defined and major social problems. He needs the means for understanding the source, nature, and possible resolution of the problem. This need calls for the application of sociological analysis to problems which go beyond the confines of sociology or any combination of social scientific disciplines.

I have written this book around the premise of an objective—but not *value-free*—interpretation of society. Every effort was made to work under the canons of objectivity and empirical accuracy. But conflicts of value are themselves a common source of social problems, and some problems are interpreted in the light of how little we know that is factual, and how this ignorance itself compounds the social problem. In short, this book admits to the very imperfect state of knowledge about the problems it treats; and I admit to having been swayed by passions and by what Lewis Dexter calls selective inattention. As a result, this book has the virtue of candor and the vice of bias.

ACKNOWLEDGEMENTS

The study of social problems is not the exclusive province of any one intellectual approach or scholarly discipline. The readings reprinted after each chapter in this book testify to this fact. I am especially grateful to the thought and work of the sociologists, political scientists, economists, social critics, and journalists who allowed us to reprint their writings and thus enrich and diversify the points of view developed in each chapter.

I am equally grateful to the many students — high school youths at Camp Columbia, undergraduates at Dartmouth College and Wesleyan University, and graduate students at Columbia University and at Rutgers University — who have strengthened and modified portions of this book through classroom and seminar discussion and examination, and whose reactions to various readings have helped to improve the basis for selection.

While all flaws are mine, what virtues the book reflects are also the result of the help and encouragement of many colleagues, including Phillips Cutright and Donald Pilcher. Peter Morrison served well in helping to collect documents, and David Johnson assisted with bibliography. To Helen Dentler, my wife, my thanks for that most essential help of all: loyal support and sympathetically productive attention to style and point of view. Louise Stearns and the late Therese Barmack gave great help in the preparation of the manuscript, and Marianne Clark of Rand McNally improved the English and eliminated errors with grace and skill.

R.A.D.

CONTENTS

PART I NATURE OF SOCIAL PROBLEMS

1

A POINT OF VIEW

What Is a Social Problem?

Suppose you live in Los Angeles, California. You wake up to a clear, bright morning in February. Two hours later a thick film hangs over the landscape; by noon it is dense enough to filter out the sunlight. At lunch, your eyes smart and you hear the people around you coughing and sneezing. In the evening, at home, you notice that the flowers in your garden are discolored; some of the vegetables are brown and dying. The newspaper reports that five people in your city died from lung ailments. The next day's paper carries letters to the editor that note that the city has a problem of air pollution.

But what *is* the problem? Something is in the air that seems damaging to animal and plant life. This 'something' is an event (or an increasingly common impression of an event) that is thrust upon your attention. No doubt, the first few times the morning air filled with this something, few persons, yourself included, noticed it. It was the recurrent appearance, and the subsequent connection you and others began to make between the appearance and effects such as irritated eyes, that made up

what more and more people in Los Angeles came to call 'the air problem.' The essence of the problem is an event, then, that becomes fixed in the attention of an observer. It exists before it is perceived, but it is the attending to that makes the event into a problem.

An event becomes a problem when the attention given it leads to a somewhat common *definition* of the event as problematic. In this sense, a problem occurs whenever we become conscious of events that stand between the way things are and the way we think they ought to be. A visitor from another planet, landing in Los Angeles at noon on a smog-filled day, might define the lower atmosphere as damaging, *if* his air intake requirements were the same as ours, but he would call this problematic only if he had some sort of objective, such as settlement or colonization. Otherwise, the smog, in his report to headquarters, would represent simply a condition of the atmosphere.

Your aim is to continue to live in Los Angeles; to live there without chronic irritation or lung damage and with the prospect of being able to grow colored flowers and green vegetables in your garden. The conflict between these goals and the stuff in the air constitutes the problem.

Notice, however, that you have already made a connection between the smog and damage to life. This definition, this identification of a correlation, is necessary before the smog takes on significance to humans. A problem may be real and omnipresent, but for human beings its reality depends on the act of definition. A definition classifies and connects an event with other phenomena. The problem is as real as your symbolic definition makes it. Your ability to define it meaningfully makes the problem relevant, hence real; and the definition precedes remedy.

For example, is the stuff in the air smog? Smog means a combination of fog and smoke. Chemists in Los Angeles captured bags of mid-morning air and studied the composition of the stuff with meticulous care for years before they concluded it was not smog, but something much more complicated. The pollutant, as they defined it, contained organic residues from automobiles, incinerators, industries, and other sources, with exhaust fumes from automobiles and trucks contributing the greatest portion. The stuff was predominantly a number of oxides of nitrogen which, through a combination of certain weather and topographic conditions, remain in the atmosphere above the city for extended periods. But these ingredients, they found, did not cause eye irritation or damage to vegetation by themselves! Only after irradiation by intense sunlight did the mess react to produce the murk that causes damage to animals and plants. And, after a decade of scientific study, chemists and engineers failed to define precisely the nature and causes of air pollution in Los Angeles. Complete remedial action awaits more complete definition of the chemical process.

In this instance, the major response to the event has been *scientific*. But if you listened to the Los Angeles radio or read the letters to the editor or heard the sermons in some of the churches fifteen years ago, you would know that the stuff in the air was defined in other ways. Vivid imaginations reported it as poison disseminated by spacemen in flying saucers. Clergymen from obscure sects uncontaminated by the thoughtways of science saw the stuff as a judgment on an evil city. Political hacks thought they saw the stuff most clearly and simply: It was dirty gas from the private utility plants. The hidden hand of greed was discovered in the smokestacks of some, but not all, private industries. Other voices insisted that there was nothing in the air above Los Angeles other than what God and nature intended should be there; that it was dangerous to find problems where none existed.

Human problems come into being when standard expectations are threatened: Eyes should not smart, people should not cough and sneeze in restaurants, flowers should have color, and vegetables should grow in our gardens. When more than a small group of persons see standards being threatened, the outlines of a problem are created by common symbolic action. A problem springs from information, from a report, about a difficulty. Something is not operating as expected, the messages assert; and as the report comes to be shared commonly, the outline of the problem is consolidated.

The definition we give to the difficulty that threatens our standards has to be put into language. In an industrial society such as the United States, the language employed is most likely to be *scientific* — in fact, claim, or intent. The symbolic definitions attended to most widely and seriously are those that people associate with science.

The nonscientific definitions of the stuff in the air over Los Angeles persist, but the resources of the community have long been invested in a single approach, the one shared by chemists, physicists, biologists, and engineers. There may be costly lags in the process, yet when a scientific explanation of air pollution in Los Angeles has been perfected, it will be only a matter of time before local resources are authoritatively allocated to fit a remedy to the cause. At the very least, pressures toward this end will be formidable.

Pulling the strands of this argument together, we have suggested that a problem is any condition or event that is perceived as interfering with the fulfillment of a need or standard. The essential ingredients of a problem include perception and definition of the condition; a standard against which the hindering character of the event may be evaluated; and the implication that the condition can be treated, eliminated or accommodated to more effectively.

There are *social aspects* to virtually every problem, but that is not what we mean by social problems. Air pollution is a social problem, for example, if we agree that the purity of the air people breathe is a necessity for life or welfare — not of some one person or group but of the community or society. Maintenance of purity then becomes a matter of collective responsibility. Air pollution since the late 18th century has been a consequence of industrial technology and, as such, is a technical problem. But when thousands of Londoners died in the black smog of 1952, and when thousands died through technologically caused air pollution in Poza Rica in Mexico, the Meuse Valley in Belgium, and in the Donora Valley in Pennsylvania, the standard of purity of air took on heightened social importance. The standard was also threatened from 1955 to 1962 with the advent of frequent nuclear weapons tests. Nuclear fallout is a pervasive, lethal sort of air pollution that involves all living things over the long term of history.

Culture specifies what is appropriate. It provides expectations about how people ought to behave. Air pollution, at first a nonsocial difficulty, becomes social when groups of people view it as threatening or damaging to their health, well-being, or way of life. Here, the application of a common standard makes a problem social. Pollution by nuclear testing has become a social problem in Japan where effects have been experienced widely and markedly enough to disrupt family life and employment. The Japanese have tasted fallout. For them, and for those who share their standard, fallout is a social problem.

Difficulties and changes in the environment, in technology and in population become social problems, then, when their effects are widely defined as disrupting or violating important expectations. Major social problems come into being when more than a single expectation is obstructed; when damage to a total system or to entire subsystems of expectations is perceived. From this point of view, *a social problem is a condition that has been defined by significant groups within a population as a deviation from, or breakdown of, some social standard these groups believe must be upheld if human life or the order of activities and events that maintains and gives meaning to life is to continue.*

Origins and Locations of Social Problems

Social problems originate in the network of relations between social structures, population processes, and the nonhuman environment and material techniques used by men to survive. The social problems that exist at a single point in time are problems of structure. This means, for example, that certain groups within a national labor force are unemployed on a given day. One group may consist of workers absent from their jobs because severe weather and a breakdown in transport facilities left them stranded at home; moreover, the structures they live and work in, in fact, divide residence from place of work. Another unemployed group consists of families who own and operate very small marginal farms, whose cash crops command no place on the current market, making further planting and harvesting futile.

The social problems that persist over periods of time are matters of dynamics or process. Consider air pollution again. In the case of Los Angeles, damaging stuff *accumulates* in the air because of imbalance in the relation between level and quality of industrial technology (including transport) and the ability of the natural environment to absorb and diffuse foreign stuff in the atmosphere. The process of noxious accumulation triggers a series of human physiological reactions, and so forth.

A scientist may make an early identification of a social problem by virtue of his special knowledge about relations between social structure, population, environment, and technology. The combined knowledge of the student of population (formally known as a demographer) and the student of agricultural economics may, for example, forewarn other publics that a particular population is growing at a rate that will outstrip available food reserves.

No one expert and no one discipline is adequate to the task of identifying the origin, location, and nature of a series of social problems, however. Man's ability to develop reliable and valid predictions about some aspects of most social problems does mean, though, that we are not wholly dependent upon the chance perceptions of human actors in coping with problematic social conditions.

While social problems originate ultimately in the relations between society, culture, and ecological setting, it is important to note that these relations vary in scale and complexity. Major social problems may be located in the relations between societies; in the relations between institutions within a society; in some local communities or local institutions within a society, but not in others. An 'American social problem' may therefore be a problem in foreign relations between the United States Government and the Government of Communist China. It may be an American problem that has major social significance but which is located strictly in an imbalanced relation between residential land use practices and the housing needs of minority groups. Or the problem may be extremely severe, yet restricted to but one or two local communities.

We have suggested the very general structural and historical origins of national and local social problems, and we have suggested the general way in which the problems may be identified. Two parts of the procedure for analysing social problems may be combined at this juncture, therefore.

A social problem has objective origins, according to this point of view, but its definition depends upon socially subjective labeling by vocal groups. A problem develops in *real* space and time and within or between *real* human institutions. Its reality may be verified by disinterested scientific inquiry, and its outcomes predicted. On the other hand, the reality of the problem depends upon its identification by interested, nonscientific participants, who not only prophesy outcomes but also propose remedies which may work solely because people think they work.

This extremely complex process cannot be separated into objective analysis and public action, for the two interact. Scientists themselves are part of the problem-forming and solution-proposing process. They cannot be thoroughly disinterested in public matters which involve their own lives so intimately.

Given this complexity, and given the fact that we have no theory of society which would supply a basis for a theory of breakdowns and maldevelopment within society, it must be understood that *no coherent scheme of classification, analysis, prediction, and control of contemporary social problems, is possible.* But the lack of theory and of scientific method for studying social problems does not invite us to conclude that the partial theories and methods we do have cannot prove helpful. There may be other routes to knowledge of social problems and other bases for social action, but the quest for scientific fact grounded in theory offers a valuable basis for common knowledge and for consensus in action.

If the scientific study of social problems is necessary and desirable, is it also feasible? The burden of proof for this rests with this book's content as a whole. This introduction suggests the conceptual basis upon which a claim to feasibility rests, however. The sections below advance three organizing concepts: social disorganization, deviance,

and value conflict. A section that follows discusses the idea of incompatible rates of change, a more general and abstract principle which helps to integrate the three concepts of social problems. Scientific study of social problems is feasible, from the point of view of this book, to the extent that these concepts sensitize students to relevant events, offer a basis for intelligent inquiry, and help to synthesize otherwise divergent facts.

Social Disorganization

A society is a population settled within a more or less well defined territory, whose members depend on each other for survival and for the realization of common goals. Note how this definition includes the elements of social structure, population, environment, and technology, discussed earlier.

The social structure of any society builds up primarily around two features: interdependence and common expectations. Interdependence arises from the fact that human beings are useful to one another. Individuals ordinarily face too many demands to be able to fend for themselves; hence, specialization around certain tasks is essential. The resulting division of labor distributes and defines a series of work roles which provide the structural cement of society.

As men cooperate, compete, and conflict with one another, they build up histories of reciprocal expectations. They come to know what they want of themselves and of others, as well as what they can expect. These expectations are embodied in beliefs and rules, or values and standards of action, which are transmitted across generations. Thus a society becomes a territorial population which is more or less *organized,* through interdependence and culture, around activities that contribute to survival, maintenance, and fulfillment of other goals.

Implicit in this brief definition is the idea that the key social characteristic of a human society is social organization: the partially systematic *arrangement* of human activities and relations between activities. This arrangement offers groups of humans the possibility of *adapting* to the environment and to other populations. This arrangement also supplies symbolic meaning and satisfaction in the same sense in which the playing of a game according to its rules provides symbolic rewards.

When the arrangement of ongoing activities that makes up the organized framework for life in society is disrupted, damaged, or destroyed, the student of social problems defines the disruption or damage as one type of social disorganization. For example, a public school is mainly an institutional arrangement intended to transmit the cultural heritage. If for any reason, the public schools in a local community are closed for several years (as in Prince Edward County, Virginia) the social scientist defines the situation as one in which a problematic type of social disorganization has occurred. This may be the case for the county residents generally, but it does not describe the situation as it holds for the local educator. He may be employed as a private tutor or instructor, after all, under more advantageous terms than he enjoyed when the public schools were open. Thus, when we speak of disorganization, we must specify exactly what arrangement, and what groups operating under this arrangement, have been disrupted, damaged, or destroyed.

At one extreme, of course, as under severe nuclear bombardment, an entire society may suffer total disorganization. As we move down the scale from this extreme, it is essential to identify the level of the disorganization. For example, many households may break up each year within the United States without damaging or destroying the institutions of marriage and family life. To define divorce, desertion, and separation as generally disorganizing, we would need to be able to estimate the point at which the volume of these practices influence significantly the various rates of marriage, household formation, childbearing and the like.

Deviant Behavior

Social disorganization, or the impairment or destruction of the arrangements under which people depend on each other, whether to cooperate or compete or conflict, is one form of social problem. Another type is most often referred to by social scientists as deviant behavior. *Deviance is action taken by individuals or groups that violates the cultural standards that regulate life and give life meaning within a society.*

Deviant behavior may be socially disorganizing, for many of the arrangements under which people cooperate and compete depend for their continuation upon conformity to rules of conduct. But there is a difference in the character of the two forms of social problems. A child may stay away from school without permission and so act deviantly in the role of truant, but this behavior will not impair significantly the ongoing activities of his school, classmates, and teachers. If virtually all the children of Harlem and their parents in New York City boycott the public schools for a long period of time, public education throughout the city may be disorganized as a result of collective deviance. Disorganization and deviance are thus not the same thing but, depending on the scope of events, one may create the other or its opposite.

Conflict of Social Values

We have suggested very briefly that a society is organized around a cultural as well as a general social structure, and that the two structures intersect completely. The cultural structure is embodied in symbols that prescribe behavior and give it meaning. Among the many types of symbols, we may identify *social values* as those symbols which refer to what is desired by a person or a group; specifically what is desired for self and others and can be obtained only in collective action or through shared agreement. A social value is not a thing or a specific goal. Rather, it is an idea of the good, the desirable, the right.

Social values are communicated through symbols. They are embodied in and sanctioned and pursued through institutions; but they are expressed by and acted upon by individuals and groups. The values a person or his group holds are, in a complex industrial society, usually contradictory as well as diverse. By contradictory, we mean that a white Southerner, for example, may value the social ideal of equality *and* the ideal of racism inherent in the notion of segregation. Other value orientations may be diverse in the sense that they operate for groups in some situations but not in others, or that priorities change for groups under varying circumstances.

The student of social problems may approach certain problems as manifestations of value conflict. Although any substantial problem will involve more than value conflict alone, a local community or a whole society's population may be split into antagonistic camps of opinion which build up around the symbolic particulars that represent each opposing value emphasis. Racial conflict may be understood in this fashion, obviously, but so, too, may various types of problems surrounding crime and delinquency or other forms of deviant behavior. Value conflicts are also often involved when social disorganization occurs. We are not maintaining, then, that value conflict is a conceptually exclusive type of event. Instead, we have singled it out because we believe it is a distinctively significant source of social stress in complex, highly developed societies.

Incompatible Rates of Change

The concepts of disorganization, deviance, and value conflict may be integrated into the larger principle of incompatible rates of change. Underlying this principle is the axiom that a society is a complex arrangement of elements-in-process; an ongoing system of relations between parts. If these parts are related to one another and in process of change within themselves and through these relations, then we may talk about them as having *rates of change*.

A rate of change is simple enough to comprehend in the case of population. A population grows or diminishes in size. Over time, it shows a rate of change in size. A set of technics for utilizing the environment changes constantly if irregularly in the same readily understood sense. New procedures are developed; new designs are invented; new equipment and materials come into play. We may employ the same idea of rate of change to components of social organization. We may say, for example, that attitudes change as the situation of a group changes in response to other processes in the system.

One of the earliest applications of this notion came in the form of *cultural lag*. Here, the gist of the idea was that technological elements are among the fastest changing parts of a high-energy modern society, and that the rate of technological change is often incompatible with the rate of change in other human institutions. The lag between mass production of the automobile and the slower introduction of effective traffic control procedures typifies what was meant by the concept of cultural lag.

Every student of social problems has confronted this idea in a hundred different guises. What we wish to do in this book is advance the notion that the idea of incompatible rates of change can be applied to any set of relations within an ongoing society. A conflict of values may be interpreted as a conflict between a group that has responded to social changes in one way and a group that has responded differently, in a situation where they must cooperate yet where this difference makes compatibility impossible.

If total racial equality is a value orientation held by one part of a population, and total racial inequality is a value maintained by another, under certain societal conditions this difference will not lead to significant problems. Indeed, whole institutions may build up around the disparity to help maintain the positions of both groups. Changes in other values, or changes in technology, population size or distribution, or even changes in rates of conformity, however,

may obligate a change in the relation between racial integrationists and racial segregationists. The problem that results, the stress that builds up around the conflict of values when each group is pressured to accommodate to or to cooperate with the other, is the social outcome. The rate of change in value orientation will have been incompatible with the rate of change in other parts of the social system.

Note that this is not the same interpretation as the normative concept of common values. For example, some writers on race relations have the notion that there is but one 'acceptable' value orientation — say, the ideal of racial equality and complete integration. In this position, the interpretation is that some groups deviate from this norm, and that others fail to fit actions to values. The principle of incompatible rates can be fitted to this normative conception equally well. We might argue that the rate of change in intergroup attitudes in the United States has not kept pace with what is required by the rate of change in other parts of the system, such as the rate of migration of Negroes from the Deep South to cities of the North. Our conviction about the value of the principle of rates of change is derived from the impression that the principle fits empirically both the normative and the somewhat more value-free style of problem analysis. It is a principle that accommodates both the subjective and the objective characterization of major social problems, in other words.

Not all incompatibilities in rates of social change are problematic, though most are stressful. We shall maintain in this book that social problems can be identified somewhat objectively when the combined number of strains resulting from incompatible rates of change becomes high relative to population expectations; or when the incompatibilities jeopardize survival; or when a particular combination of strains increases abruptly in intensity and is therefore experienced sharply.

Special Considerations

In this book, we concentrate on *national* social problems. This means that social problems are viewed as instances of extensive social disorganization or as rates of deviance that have consequences for the survival or maintenance of American society as a whole. We want to fix the spatial locus of our attention. Mental disorder is problematic from this perspective, for instance, *if* the rate of individual deviance is great enough, or increasing rapidly enough, to impair the organization of the national system. Impairment would include a condition in which a substantial number of citizens were denied their customary rights by virtue of being defined as ill. Or mental disorder is a national social problem if the existing arrangements for coping with it are impaired or seriously inadequate.

By this standard, many difficult problems within the United States are neglected in this book. For example, one of the most painfully dramatic events (domestically) of 1962 was the case of James Meredith versus the Governor and the University of Mississippi. Viewed from the desk of a northern sociologist, this crisis seemed intensely problematic. The crisis appeared to be disorganizing for organized race relations. The crisis was precipitated by the deviant conduct of the Governor, who defied the rulings of the Federal courts. Viewed from within Oxford, Mississippi, the harmony of campus and community life was disrupted by James Meredith's violation of the mores surrounding admission to the University! The interpretation of this case thus depends on the angle of vision of the interpreter and on the social level of his interpretation.

Taken nationally, the Meredith incident symbolized the general persistent yet ever changing relations between ethnic groups within the population. The rules of the state designate such acts as preventing Meredith's admission to the University as unlawful and prescribe a penalty. Yet the actions taken are part of the constitutive order. We shall treat only disorganized, that is, inequitable, relations between ethnic groups in contemporary America as a critical social problem. The Meredith crisis was one of severe social conflict. It did not, however, disorganize American society.

Other forms of disorganization entail national significance. We shall give emphasis to the social problem of disorganized intergroup relations, for intergroup conflict of a severe type exists in contemporary America. It is socially and ecologically determined. While phases of such conflict may be inevitable, much of the conflict can be identified and coped with. Thus the Meredith crisis points to a broad, underlying, national social problem of extreme ethnic inequality.

In addition, this book is concerned with the effects on American society of rapid population growth and redistribution. And, without subscribing to simple notions of cultural lag, we believe that since the late 18th century, American society has made its primary adjustments in response to changing imperatives of a *technological* sort; that many types of social disorganization in American life result from the pace of technological change.

The idea of cultural lag is that elements of a society change at different rates; and that material, particularly technical-industrial, elements change fastest. A social problem of disorganization often arises, according to this concept, out of the lag between changes in technology and the rates of change in appropriate social institutions. The lag between mass production of the automobile and the development of traffic control practices typifies what is meant by the concept. We shall treat a variety of social problems ranging from unemployment and poverty to community disorganization partly in terms of the notion of lag.

Among the forms of deviant behavior most commonly studied by sociologists are crime, delinquency, mental disorder, drug addiction, suicide, alcoholism, and prostitution. Against the criteria set forth in this chapter, only *some* aspects of crime, delinquent acts, and mental disorder, represent social problems. A criminal act, such as burglary, may not be a social problem if the *rate* of stealing has not increased more rapidly than the means of control. The rules of law may be violated, but there exist social agents of prosecution, penalty, and rehabilitation to deal with burglars. A problem may develop where the rate changes notably, or where the agencies of justice are insufficiently organized to maintain the expected balance with this type of criminal activity. Or the social problem may involve the society's means of dealing with convicted burglars.

What is suggested by this, however, is that *crime in general is not a social problem.* Nor is mental illness. It may be problematic that significant groups in the society do not understand that, like physical ailments, many mental disorders are generally best defined as a health problem. It may also be problematic that groups ranging from small families to whole institutions of employment do not know how to recognize disordered behavior; or that experts fail to treat the mentally ill intelligently or successfully. But while much of the behavior of mentally ill persons may deviate from social standards and prove critically disruptive to group life, *mental illness* per se *is not a social problem.*

One final illustration must suffice. Family breakdown is frequently approached as a contemporary American social problem. There is no question but that marriages often end in divorce; families are dissolved by desertion or death. Other families break down informally but maintain a veneer of unity. Other families suffer the difficulty of lacking legitimacy in the first place. These events occur at a social level that need not affect the continuing stability of the larger society, however. Painful and personally damaging as marital and family disorganization may be, they are not in themselves a social problem. If rates of family disorganization increase significantly, however, or if rapid changes in population composition, environment, and technology have so affected life situations as to reduce the general likelihood of marital or family satisfaction, the conditions of family life are problematic.

Similarly, the social problem of family life, if one exists, may result from the response the community or the state makes to evidence of family breakdown. The response to illegitimacy, for example, is a social problem if the life chances of the illegitimate child and the unwed mother are reduced by punitive judgments of outsiders. Or a social problem exists if contemporary American society has failed to develop agencies for extending effective services to family groups suffering remediable stress.

Must a Social Problem Be Remediable?

Most students of social problems add to their definition the stipulation that a social problem exists only when influential groups believe that they can do something to resolve or remedy the condition. Two things are implied by this stipulation: First, that a social problem is something that an individual or small group cannot cope with alone; that organized effort is required. Second, influential groups must view a condition as something that can be eliminated or controlled before the condition justifies the term social problem. In other words, among other things, a social problem is a difficulty that is viewed socially as treatable and that requires collective effort in the treatment process.

We accept the idea of collective effort, but discard the idea that the reality of a social problem depends on its being defined as remediable. For action on a problem to occur, a belief in remedy may indeed be necessary. This belief itself may, however, become a social problem, as the connection between abolitionism and the Civil War suggests. The belief may also be manufactured, or it may be an article of social invention. We may find it necessary to behave toward burglars *as if* we can imagine a world in which burglary has been reduced to a rare, hence sensational, event. But that may simply be part of the 'game' of conduct.

Societies vary in the extent to which their members view conditions as subject to deliberate change or improvement. These views affect the way in which social problems come into focus. But the belief in solution or treatment is a by-product, not a condition necessary for the existence of a social problem.

All sociologists agree that we must be aware of the recurrent, perhaps incorrigible, forms of social problems. Improvements in health care have reduced infant mortality (an old old social problem) to a relatively rare event in the United States. The resulting growth in the population, or the speed of that growth, has created a host of new social problems. Traffic congestion is new, for example, but central city overcrowding in housing, a problem as old as the earliest waves of European migration in the 19th century, has been stimulated by population growth.

From the point of view of this book, a social problem must be tackled collectively, but its solution may be expected to release new social problems. The pattern is highly similar to the pattern of the history of the fight between medicine and disease. Every great achievement contains within it the prospect of contributing to a new disease. The organism remains vulnerable and mortal in spite of progress in treatment of present problems.

Other Problems In Defining Social Problems

Our definition leads to some absurd conclusions. Does it make sense, for example, to assert that if a sizeable or influential public is unaware of a threatening or damaging condition, there is no social problem? Does the reality of a social problem depend upon public recognition? Has air pollution become a social problem in Los Angeles because every influential group from the Ladies' Garden Club to the City Health Department has come to define it as such? Or was it a social problem when only the Garden Club had made the alarming connection between colorless flowers and smog?

To define a social problem in terms of social recognition is to err on the side of extreme subjectivism and to raise the question of precisely *whose* recognition is determinative. With this definition, any problem would appear desirable, hence unproblematic, for some influential groups, and problematic for others. One man's meat is another's poison. Pressing this point to an ugly yet logical extreme, the program of racial genocide in Nazi Germany was a social problem for the Jews. Nazi 'statesmen' built the program deliberately as a purification of the national population. They called it the 'final solution.' Was genocide a problem for millions of Germans who later claimed they never heard of the program?

Common, or limited but influential, recognition of a condition as violative or damaging *does not* provide a sound definition of a social problem. We shall guard against this partially absurd definition by maintaining awareness of its pitfalls. But we shall often be forced to apply it for lack of a comprehensive and scientifically detached knowledge of the operating requirements of societies apart from the opinions of their human participants.

The contrast between technical and social problems is in an important degree a contrast in the state of what is *known*. Space engineering, for instance, proceeds from a firm if sometimes crude set of estimates of what is possible and of what is required to achieve the possible. A flight to the moon must be carried out before the space engineer knows with certainty that his hypotheses were correct. The possibility of a flight is not a matter of group definition, however, but something estimated as having a specific probability of success.

Social scientists lack verified and related hypotheses which would release them from dependence on social judgments, their own or those of influential groups. (And, as pointed out earlier, unlike nonhuman systems, society is organized around such judgments.)

To diagnose the genocide of Jews in Germany in 1939 as a social problem, we would have to have had a verified hypothesis about the effects of the practice on the national society. One could have concluded (as too few influential observers did, tragically) by any moral standard common to western civilization, that ethnic genocide was terribly, horribly wrong; hence, certainly, problematic. The 'Final Solution of the Jewish Problem' posed by Nazi leaders violated the cultural integrity of German society. If this were true, German citizens should have felt the force of a moral imperative to combat the policy. But this means that they would have had to assume that their revulsion reflected reliably the average opinions of fellow citizens; or that they were persuaded that their moral diagnosis deserved dissemination to others. Was it rule by terror, or the will of the majority, that made genocide possible?

Apply the same questions to the lynching of Negroes in the United States in pre-Depression America. Here was a practice sanctioned by white Southern mores, something conducted according to cherished standards. Indeed under certain circumstances, failure to lynch would have violated the *local* social standard! Would lynching or the failure to lynch have constituted a social problem in Mississippi in 1920? Here, national law provides a clear solution.

Nor are public definitions sound

guides to the magnitude of social problems. Some events are perceived out of context. For example, great advances have been made in the prevention of transportation accidents since 1930, particularly in air safety. Yet airplane crashes are treated, one by one, as disasters by the press. Influential publics, moreover, have little if any basis on which to *compare* the relative seriousness—extent and effects—of problems. Juvenile delinquency is greeted with greater alarm today than is nuclear testing in the atmosphere.

This definition of social problems explores certain absurdities. Public recognition is in nearly all respects a bad basis for collective judgment. If subjectivism, the problem of differences between publics, conflicts of standards, and ignorance about the relative importance of conditions are all severe qualifications, to these should be added the fact that individuals cannot see themselves clearly. They cannot identify reliably the connections between their problems and infinitely larger, less personal, social trends.

Even in circumstances where peculiarly sensitive observers can spot such connections, most of us are prevented from responding sympathetically by the constraints of culture. *Things as they are*—that is, established practices—embody a form of inertia. They often tend to to be self-justifying and, over the long run, to become expected as appropriate. The judicial doctrine of 'separate but equal' carried just such force in American interracial life between about 1890 and 1954. *Things as they are*, when they do seem problematic, are often accepted by most of us as unwanted but inevitable in the scheme of things. They seem to be the price that must be paid, for instance, for other sorts of desirable changes. Attitudes toward traffic congestion are a case in point. Is the traffic problem merely a by-product of the much wanted achievement of 'a car in every garage'?

A Return to Definition

In spite of these difficulties, the definition stands: A social problem is a condition that has been defined by significant groups as a deviation from some social standard, or breakdown of social organization. Even if our knowledge of society were improved, group definition and the element of the standard could not be eliminated. What is possible in space travel, for example, depends on what can be done with nonsocial phenomena. What is possible in society depends on what members of the society strive for. Men *make* standards, though they are also controlled by them.

In the social as in the technological case, however, there are limits and necessities. Societal survival and maintenance, like the standards that contribute to them or detract from them, probably depend on the continuation of certain activities. If we remain alert to these—even though our knowledge of what we shall call those things that are functional for society may be grossly incomplete—we may find a basis for defining and treating social problems which is partly independent of the vagaries of opinion.

We do not have a good definition of a social problem in part because we lack knowledge of *how* societies operate and persist. We have only a sketchy outline of what the outer limits are, within which a system may flourish. If a problem is an obstacle in the path of a traveller, knowledge of the thing called an obstacle would depend on knowledge of the traveller, his path and destination.

All of this makes the sociology of social problems a *pre-scientific* excursion. For the specialist, this is a limiting situation. His utility depends on his ability to point out trends, to predict future social problems. Unless we can *predict* social problems, or identify them prior to public awareness, we have no science about them except by aspiration. We can be as scientific as the circumstances allow, however. One way of achieving this is to focus attention on the most throughly documented of American social problems; those that have a long history of definition and about which considerable expert consensus has been achieved. For the beginner, this is enough, though he should understand what is missing, namely, an analytical procedure for identifying, measuring, and making predictions about forthcoming problems. Our corrective for the weakness of our definition of social problems shall be awareness of our intellectual limits, or avoidance of the arrogance of ignorance.

References

Becker, Howard S. *Outsiders: studies in the sociology of deviance.* New York: The Free Press of Glencoe, 1963.

Bernard, Jessie Shirley. *Social problems at midcentury; role, status, and stress in the context of abundance.* New York: Dryden Press, 1957.

————Social problems as problems of decision. *Social Problems,* Vol. 6: No. 3 (Winter, 1958-59), pp. 212-221.

Bredemeier, H. C. and J. Toby. *Social problems in America.* 5th Printing. New York: Wiley, 1963.

Brogan, Dennis William. *The price of revolution.* New York: Harper, 1951.

Broom, Leonard. *Sociology; a text with adapted readings.* Evanston, Ill.: Row Peterson, 1961.

Cuber, John Frank. *Problems of American society: values in conflict.* New York: Holt, 1960.

Elliott, Mabel Agnes and Francis Merrill. *Social disorganization.* New York: Harper and Row, 1961.

Fox, Byron. American social problems in a world setting: the role of U. S. government spending. *Social Problems,* Vol. 6: No. 2 (Fall, 1958), pp. 99-107.

Horton, Paul B. and Gerald L. Leslie. *The sociology of social problems.* New York: Appleton-Century-Crofts, 1965.

Landis, Paul Henry. *Social problems in nation and world.* Chicago: Lippincott, 1959.

Lee, Raymond Lawrence (Ed.). *Contemporary social issues.* New York: Crowell, 1955.

Lemert, Edwin. *Social pathology.* New York: McGraw-Hill, 1951.

Lindesmith, Alfred R. Social problems and sociological theory. *Social Problems,* Vol. 8: No. 2 (Fall, 1960), pp. 98-102.

McGee, Reece. *Social disorganization in America.* San Francisco: Chandler Publishing Co., 1962.

Merton, Robert K. and Robert A. Nesbit (Eds.). *Contemporary social problems.* Second edition. New York: Harcourt, Brace and World, 1966.

Merrill, Francis E. The self and the other: an emerging field of social problems. *Social Problems,* Vol. 4: No. 3 (January, 1957), pp. 200-208.

Neumeyer, Martin H. *Social problems and the changing society.* New York: D. Van Nostrand, 1953.

Nordskog, John Eric, Edward C. Mc-

Donagh, and Melvin J. Vincent. *Analyzing social problems*. New York: Dryden Press, 1950.

Raab, Earl and Gertrude J. Selznick. *Major social problems*. New York: Harper and Row, Second edition, 1964.

Rose, Arnold. Theory for the study of social problems. *Social Problems*, Vol. 4: No. 3 (January, 1957), pp. 189-200.

Rosenberg, Bernard, Israel Gerver, and F. William Howton. *Mass society in crisis: social problems and social pathology*. New York: Macmillan, 1964.

Schnore, Leo F. Social problems in the underdeveloped areas: an ecological view. *Social Problems*, Vol. 8: No. 3 (Winter, 1960-61), pp. 182-201.

———Social problems in an urban-industrial context. *Social Problems*, Vol. 9: No. 3 (Winter, 1962), pp. 228-240.

Walsh, Mary Elizabeth and Paul H. Furfey. *Social problems and social action*. Englewood Cliffs, N. J.: Prentice-Hall, 1958.

Weinberg, S. Kerson. *Social problems in our time*. Englewood Cliffs, N. J.: Prentice-Hall, 1960.

SOCIOLOGICAL THEORY AND SOCIAL PROBLEMS
Richard C. Fuller

I

At some risk of stirring up ghosts of sociology's controversial past, it may be suggested that there is now, more than ever, a pressing need for rethinking the relationship between sociological theory and social problems. This need is keenly felt by those who are engaged in teaching general social problems courses to undergraduates.

Sociology departments have inherited social problems courses from their forebears who began teaching them before the turn of the century when the complexion of "sociology" was far more reformative than at the present time. Since the other disciplines were too specialized to bother with social problems, sociology entering the academic curriculum through the back door of the so-called "social science" courses filled up the void by sponsoring discussion of the current societal evils. Subsequently there has been a commendable trend toward specialization in the teach-

From *Social Forces*, Vol. 15, no. 4 (May 1937), pp. 496-502. Reprinted by permission of The University of North Carolina Press. (Several footnotes have been omitted.)

ing of social problems. We now have in the place of such catchall subjects as "Dependents, Defectives, and Delinquents" somewhat distinct and separate courses in Criminology, Poverty and Dependency, Race Problems, Population Problems, Immigration, Family Disorganization, and the like.

Yet there remains a need in most curricula for the offering of a general service course to the many students who are not concentrating in sociology but who desire at least one semester's study of the major social problems of our society. Nor can we escape the fact that by far the great majority of students who "want a sociology course" are interested primarily in the social problems aspects of our field and only secondarily or not at all in what we have been inclined to call "pure sociological theory." What then has sociology to contribute?

II

An examination of social problems literature published over the last two or three decades suggests *two* philosophies of approach:

1. Most of the early texts make no effort to orient the problems discussed to a systematic framework of sociological theory. Each problem is considered more or less at random with reference to heterogeneous factual material, biological, psychological, or political in nature. No attention is given to interrelationships or classification of problems.

Implicit in this procedure is the old assumption that sociology must and should function as the "cap-stone" science. So far as social problems are concerned this means that sociology draws its generalizations from the data of all the other sciences, physical and social, and seeks to integrate or synthesize the contributions of these special sciences insofar as they are pertinent to the particular problem under consideration. Hence, our knowledge of unemployment is not strictly sociological, but is based on the findings of economics, psychiatry, medicine, social work, and the like.

2. The tendency of more recent texts is to posit a sociological frame of reference as background material for the discussion of particular social problems. The logic of this approach is that sociology has outgrown much of its synthetic or "capstone" nature and has a core of theory of its own relating to personality, groups, and institutions.

This viewpoint affords a raison d'être for the inclusion of social problems as legitimate subject matter for sociological inquiry. Nevertheless a prime consideration persists, and that is whether social problems may be described, analyzed, and solutions proposed within the theoretical framework of sociology or any one other discipline. To this question the remainder of this paper is devoted.

III

To what theoretical systems have the sociologists resorted? There are at least *three* characteristic types:

1. *The general conceptual approach.* This is by far the most popular. Social problems are pictured as normal or natural emergents of the social process. They are described against the relief background of social organization, social change, and social disorganization. The situation which constitutes the social problem develops out of the impact of social change on existing behavior patterns. Technologies, folkways, and institutions have been worked out in adjustment to life conditions of the past; although such conditions have subsequently changed, change in the adaptive culture is painfully slow. Since traditional groups and institutions addicted to obsolete patterns cannot effectively cope with the change, the social problem emerges. The result is social disorganization in the units affected; group influence on individual behavior declines, often accompanied by personal demoralization in the individuals concerned.

This broad approach is often used strictly as background material. After preliminary chapters defining social problems and their characteristics, the student is presented with an historical sketch of the major social changes which have disturbed our culture. These changes are usually technological or economic in nature. The impact of inventions on industrial and corporate life is shown to penetrate into other spheres of social organization such as government, law, family, church, and school. The weakening of sacred group sanctions and the consequent individualization of life ensue. These trends are conceptualized in terms of mobility, cultural lag, social disorganization, personal disorganization, and other current sociological theory. The remainder of the text is occupied with a treatment of specific social problems.

Another procedure is to build the entire text around a very general theory of social disorganization, differentiating it with reference to certain units of sociological inquiry such as personal disorganization, group disorganization, institutional disorganization or personal disorganization, family disorganization, community disorganization. The various specific social problems such as unemployment, crime, mental disease, and divorce are discussed within one or another of these conceptual compartments.

The general conceptual approach has as its chief asset the linking of problem situations with the social process of which they are a part. Instead of a haphazard, piecemeal discussion of seemingly unrelated problems, a point of view is offered the student; interrelationships stand out.

Yet there are inherent weaknesses. In the *first* place such concepts as social disorganization, cultural lag, mobility, and the like are at the present stage of development of sociological theory more in the nature of hypotheses than scientifically validated generalizations. They are rather loose descriptive symbols, not precise tools of analysis. Hence when the student comes to apply the theory to specific problems he is at a loss to see its exact bearing though he has a vaguely better understanding than he would have without such theory.[1] In

[1] Is, for instance, delinquency always a function of some phase of social disorganization, i.e., breakdown of group controls over individual conduct? May it not often be a phenomenon of closely-knit, equilibrated, and definitely patterned group behavior, i.e., operation of a boys' gang?

the *second* place this approach is more applicable to certain social problems than to others. It is more or less adequate for those problems the essence of which is a rapidly changing technological culture and a slowly changing adaptive culture. Accordingly, it fits quite readily the description of such problems as economic insecurity, crime and family disorganization; but when the student focuses upon other problems such as physical and mental disease, population pressure, and race conflict, it is by no means clear that the general theory is workable. In the *third* place, since this approach is essentially cultural, there is a tendency to overlook the significance of biological and physical inadequacies in individuals which contribute to the social problem. Not all insanities are induced by cultural strain, not all poverty is traceable to the collapse of ecomonic institutions, not all crime is without reference to hereditary or physiological deficiencies.

2. *The single concept approach.* Somewhat of a variation of the general conceptual approach is the use of one sociological concept as the core around which the discussion of particular social problems is centered, as for instance social conflict.

This approach has the obvious deficiency that no one social problem can be stated completely in terms of any one concept, no matter how inclusive it may be. Furthermore, a given concept such as social conflict is more illuminating for describing certain problems than for others. Finally, since the concept is a process, it cuts through many or all problems and the student tends to find himself studying the process rather than the problem.

3. *The community approach.* A third approach is from the standpoint of community organization. Here the

frame of reference is the community with its ecological structure, economic division of labor, social agencies and institutions. Problems such as health, housing, recreation, and Americanization are discussed from the point of view of practical questions of community control. Community action is the theme.

This approach is promising insofar as the student learns to conceive the problem in terms of the groups, social classes, and institutions of which he is a part. The problem is brought home to him realistically; he thinks it out with one eye on the situation in his own community. However, the unit of reference is somewhat too narrow for many social problems, various phases of which transcend the community as a point of focus. The social and economic organization of wider regional areas and the forces of social change operative within them must be considered as well as the more specific aspects of community readjustment.

IV

The difficulty with the first two conceptual approaches discussed above is not one of applying the theory to problems in general but to problems in particular. This is clearly evidenced by the fact that once the theory is stated as an introduction to the problem the specific operative facts of the problem are discussed without reference to the theory. The interest in the discussion of a particular problem becomes an interest in concrete facts and the broad processes of sociological theory are forgotten. That is to say, the theory serves merely as window dressing for the real goods which make up the problem.

This condition is traceable to at least *two* fundamental truths concerning the nature of social problems which are often overlooked:

1. *All social problems are not alike.* If we select at random the problems of divorce, race conflict, and mental disease, we find as their only common elements of interest to the sociologist: they constitute social situations which the group has come to regard as inimical to its collective welfare; they are very complex and have multiple not single causation; they are relative in time and space; if they co-exist in the same social group there may be some interrelationship between them. Beyond these common factors we cannot go. Any attempt to force all of these problems into one theoretical frame of reference courts a strained artificiality which even the most facile sociological imagination cannot avoid.

2. *A knowledge of the causes of a social problem does not solve the problem.* Many sociologists are preoccupied with describing the causal patterns or sequences which underlie the problem. It is true that social problems often defy solutions because we do not know enough about their causation. But it is also obvious that in many instances even where we do know the causes the difficulty is in removing them without upsetting accepted values and institutional practices. The same institutional folkways which create the problem many times hinder its solution. Thus, the social scientist may explain adequately the causes of seasonal unemployment and employee and employer may predict accurately when it will come and how severe it will be. The most direct remedy would be to quash the profit motive as the sine qua non of our competitive economy and induce employers to carry their men without pay reductions during slack periods.

The rub is that the profit motive is basic in our mores and cannot be erased with a wave of the hand. Though we recognize the social threat of unemployment we are unwilling to alter fundamentally the traditional values of our economy. Hence, the core of the problem is not in most cases the enumeration and classification of causes but rather the working out of remedies which will succeed though they may have no relation to causal sequences. Accordingly a scheme of unemployment compensation or a public works program is not concerned with causes but with solutions.

This failure to distinguish between the causes of social problems and their solutions means a confusion between the theoretical analysis of the problem and considerations of policy involved in the treatment of the problem. Since in dealing with social problems we are in the realm of social values and not the laboratory of the natural scientist, solutions do not follow from analysis of causes. Solutions do follow from a free-for-all discussion of political, moral, and ethical questions inherent in policy determination. *For this latter element in the discussion of social problems it is indeed doubtful that there can ever be a scientific frame of reference.*

V

In the discussion of social problems we are concerned with three kinds of facts: those relative to scientific research, those relative to policy, those relative to efficiency of administration.

1. *Facts relative to scientific research.* The scientist's interest in social problems is in large measure different from that of the public's interest. His concern is with untangling the cause and effect sequences underlying the problem. He is supposed to be free from emotional and reformative considerations. He must gather data, define and test his hypotheses, and if practical offer generalizations which contain some possibilities of prediction. The social scientist's findings are often available to the general public and in this way may find their course into popular discussions of policy. Research may also serve the function of pointing the way to more efficient administration of agencies and programs concerned with the solution of the problem.

Yet in the final analysis the solution of any social problem involves more than scientific generalizations. Whether or not pertinent scientific theory based on careful research is available and known to the citizens, their discussion of solutions goes on in a world of competing values and conflicting social interest among which they must make some selection.

2. *Facts relative to policy.* The public is only incidentally concerned with causes and the attention it gives them is usually ancillary to its concern with solutions. People ask, "What ought to be done?" This question is only partially answerable by reference to scientific theory of causation. Solutions primarily involve questions of policy. And discussion of policy takes one far from the area of dispassionate scientific consideration into the area of cultural predilections, prejudice, and stereotype. A sphere of cultural limitations within which the social problem is imbedded controls the talking over process. To borrow an illustration from Frank, the housing problem is easily solved on paper. When there is a housing shortage what is more logical than to build more houses! There is no dearth of good architects, builders, technological materials, land,

and skill. Yet if we listen in on a group of citizens discussing this problem we find them preoccupied with working out solutions which will not antagonize various groups who have vested interests in the culture complex housing. A reasonable profit must be preserved for the real estate operator and contractor, labor union and banker must be conciliated, government building projects must not unduly interfere with private enterprise. Thus the scheme which is eventually adopted for financing low cost housing must not be so radical as to overturn existing economic mores.

Consequently when social problems are discussed by the sociologist from the point of view of public policy he cannot remain entirely within the framework of scientific theory. If he is realistic he must get across to his students an appreciation that a given social problem is a problem not only because of the difficulty of ascertaining its causes but further because a dangerous social situation must be changed, yet in such fashion as not to imperil cherished values.

3. *Facts relative to efficiency of administration.* A third aspect of the social problem which involves a third type of factual data for discussion is that of the administration of corrective or alleviatory programs. Once policy is decided and reform begun, the social problem dissolves into a number of specific technical problems for the solution of which technical experts with specialized training are necessary. Agencies and institutions are established and functionaries appointed for the administration of techniques of reform. Thus we have our juvenile courts and probation departments, our public works commissions and social security boards, our community fund agencies and social case workers. Problems of

administrative efficiency arise within these units which directly concern neither the social scientist in his study of causal sequences nor the public in its determination of general policy. Such problems must be settled by personnel professionally trained to deal with them. Yet any well-rounded course in social problems must at least state some of these problems of administrative efficiency. If the topic is crime, the activities and problems of the parole board should be discussed. If it is unemployment, the intelligent administration of public works is as worthy a topic for consideration as erudite research into the causal roots of the business cycle.[2]

VI

If this analysis of the three-fold factual character of social problems is sound, how can such facts be most effectively presented to the student? The following suggestions are in summary of the points made in this paper:

1. The student should be given a general point-of-view. Discussion of problems must not be hit or miss. Insofar as the textbook is concerned this may be accomplished by:

(a) An introductory chapter or two dealing with the general nature of social problems and indicating such elements as are common to all problems.

(b) Since social change, social disorganization, and personal disorganization are processes which make up the background of many current social prob-

[2]As previously indicated the application of available scientific knowledge and techniques may facilitate efficiency in carrying out programs of reform: witness the Tennessee Valley Authority project and the social as well as physical engineering involved.

lems, a general symbolic approach built around these concepts gives a systematic, coordinated perspective from which to view the specific problems. But an effort to fit rigidly the discussion of all social problems into this theoretical mold means a confused and strained interpretation.

2. Inasmuch as all social problems are not alike, some classification of general types must be worked out and within these subdivisions there should be some differentiation of theoretical approach. Granted that all social problems overlap to some extent in content and process, yet a more discriminating differentiation of theory according to types should dissipate much of the current confusion between sociological theory and social problems.

3. Insofar as a particular problem can be stated in terms of group, personality, and institutional factors, the sociologist is in position to offer any purely sociological generalizations available and pertinent to the problem. If he chooses he may even devote his principal attention to these sociological phases of the problem. After all, that is his specialty.

4. However, the problem as a whole cannot be presented adequately with resort exclusively to sociological data and generalizations. So long as social problems courses are offered in sociology departments we cannot escape the synthetic function of considering the pertinent generalizations of any science, physical or social, which help to shed light on the problem. After all, sociology is still a very broad discipline committed to the study of human behavior in all its group relationships. Our generalizations are of necessity still quite dependent on spade work in the other sciences. We may not like this situation, but so far as the teaching of social problems is concerned we might as well face it. If there is any distinctive sociological contribution in performing this integrative function, it is the decription of the *total situation* involved in the problem and an avoidance of one-sided particularistic emphases, economic, biological, psychological, or whatnot. In the writer's opinion this is a valuable aid to the student of social problems and a service no sociologist need shrink from.

5. Since scientific research yields but one type of fact relative to the solution of social problems, sociologists cannot escape discussion of facts pertaining to social policy and the administration of reform. Such discussion inevitably leads into ethical, moral, and political issues. This does not mean that discussion need be emotionally biased and completely subjective. It does mean that only through such talking over can students intelligently evaluate the cross currents of conflicting mores and ideologies which in some way must be compromised or dissipated before the talking over process can go on to community action and reform. The classroom is a proper forum for airing these social value aspects of the problem. Scientific theory is only the point of departure for such discussion. It is a guide, not a formula for the solution of the problem.

SOCIAL PROBLEMS IN AN URBAN-INDUSTRIAL CONTEXT

Leo F. Schnore

A review of the literature on social problems points to an inescapable conclusion: the vast majority of social phenomena identified as "problematic" are themselves correlates, concomitants, or consequences of urban-industrialism.[1] A weaker corollary that emerges is that even the relatively ubiquitous problems—those found within societies at all levels of urbanization and industrialization, and within both urban and rural sectors of the same society—assume a different shape and present themselves in more complicated form in the context of the city. Equally striking is the fact that the same conclusion is forced upon us whether we confine ourselves to the domestic scene or take a broader comparative view, i.e., whether we examine only our own highly urbanized and industrialized society or extend our perspective to permit the consideration of societies only beginning to undergo these processes.[2] The problems encountered in the American urban setting have been relatively well explored, however, and we are in a better position to see them as indigenous to the urban *milieu*. As a consequence, the following discussion will be narrowly focused on the United States.

Social Problems in the United States

Confining ourselves to the American scene, it strikes us rather forcibly that most of the major internal concerns facing the United States are connected in a rather direct and intimate fashion with urbanization. We may take the more dramatic problems first of all. Certainly the "race problem" must be

Reprinted, with permission of author and publisher from *Social Problems*, 9, No. 3, Winter, 1962, 228-240.

The review undertaken here was made possible by a grant from the Ford Foundation to the University of Wisconsin for the support of urban studies, and this aid is gratefully acknowledged.

[1]Marshall B. Clinard, *The Sociology of Deviant Behavior* (New York: Rinehart, 1957); Marshall B. Clinard, "The Process of Urbanization and Criminal Behavior," American Journal of Sociology, 48 (September, 1942), pp. 202-213; and Marshall B. Clinard, "A Cross-Culture Replication of the Relation of Urbanism to Criminal Behavior, American Sociological Review, 25 (April, 1960), pp. 253-257.

[2]See Lyle W. Shannon (ed.), *Under-developed Areas* (New York: Harper and Brothers, 1957); United Nations, *Report on the World Social Situation* (New York: United Nations, 1957); and Paul H. Landis, *Social Problems in Nation and World* (Chicago: J. B. Lippincott, 1959).

understood as one of the less happy by-products of a certain degree of upgrading of the Negro's position in the long course of urbanization. Although its roots were established in an agrarian setting, the "problem" is obviously magnified by the tendency of Northward migrants from the South—both Negro and white—to concentrate in cities, for both bring with them a heritage of hostility. In the South itself, recent and rapid strides in the direction of urbanization and industrialization have made old patterns of racial etiquette obsolete; in addition, the new and direct form of competition between the races in industry has apparently compounded the difficulties. It is a compelling fact that all of the recent manifestations of race conflict—whether over schools, buses or lunch counters—have appeared in the *cities* of the South. The lower-status white's response to threat from his rival from a back-country share-cropper's cabin is understandable, even if it lacks the elements of common humanity. Unfortunately, education can hardly be trusted to ameliorate the problem when the school itself has become the institutional focus of discontent. In any event, urbanization can be seen as a kind of triggering mechanism in this process.

Other social problems seem to be found most prominently displayed in the urban context, even if urbanization cannot be regarded as their genesis. It can be argued, for example, that rather high rates of crime and delinquency are the natural concomitants of rapid urbanization, if only transitional phenomena.[3] Even if this bald statement is regarded as unacceptable, it is clear that, at the very least, they are most dramatic and costly in the crowded city. The housing problem, and the appearance of slums and blighted areas, can be more directly tied to the great shifts in distribution of population that our country has witnessed in the course of urbanization. Many metropolitan areas are suffering a chronic and long-standing shortage of housing, while the housing stock of the older city core is clearly obsolescent.[4] The contributions of crowded living conditions to deviant behavior and to racial strife are still inadequately understood, but it remains a striking fact that the most deteriorated areas of our large cities are the main sites of race riots, vice, crime and deviant behavior.

With an appropriately broad conception of "social" problems, one can begin to approach the full range of problems that are often more narrowly defined as "economic" and "political," and that tend to be ignored by sociologists. Economically, one of our greatest difficulties—and certainly an ironic symbol of our level of development—is the recurrence of agricultural overproduction. (We will have occasion to discuss this literal embarrassment of riches more fully in another context.) A closely related issue, however, is the constantly climbing cost of living. The well-known "spread" between prices received by farmers and prices paid by consumers usually serves as a topic for invective; still to be adequately explored is the extent to which the rising cost of living is to be attributed to the mounting expense of distribution in a "metropolitanized" society, where the residential population lives widely dispersed throughout an area that is served by a traffic-clogged center. Both dispersal throughout the peripheral zone and

[3]See Ronald Freedman, *et al, Principles of Sociology* (New York: Henry Holt, 1952), Chapter 13.

[4]Edgar M. Hoover and Raymond Vernon, *Anatomy of a Metropolis* (Cambridge: Harvard University Press, 1959).

congestion in the metropolis itself—still the site of the major warehouses and produce markets—appear to be increasing continuously, and their joint contribution to rising costs has still to be measured carefully. Supplying these same metropolitan areas with housing, highways, and schoolhouses are also economic problems of the first magnitude, although they are usually discussed in a political context. More clearly "political" problems are those arising out of the persistent rural-urban imbalance in political power, with farm areas exercising influence far out of proportion to their populations.[5] One intriguing possibility that occurs to the unbiased observer is that the much-maligned "drift to federalism" is at least partially a consequence of the effective disenfranchisement of American urbanites—a direct product of the traditional actions of the very same advocates of "States' Rights" who so vigorously deplore the growth of a massive federal bureaucracy. In any event, changes in population distribution are not without immediate consequences for political and economic life.

In order to give more coherence to our argument from this point onward, we will employ the "ecological complex"—a set of rubrics comprising population, organization, environment, and technology—as a convenient means of outlining a series of interrelated social problems that seem to deserve sociological attention.[6]

[5]Gordon E. Baker, *Rural Versus Urban Political Power* (New York: Doubleday and Company, 1955).

[6]Here we borrow upon the conceptual scheme outlined by Otis Dudley Duncan in "Human Ecology and Population Studies," in Philip M. Hauser and Otis Dudley Duncan (eds.), *The Study of Population* (Chicago: University of Chicago Press, 1959), pp. 678-716. A similar usage may be found in Leo F. Schnore, "Social Problems in the Underdeveloped Areas," *Social Problems*, 8 (Winter, 1960-61), pp. 182-201.

Technological Problems

First of all, the main *technological* problem with which we are currently faced is a familiar one: the progressive displacement of men by machines. It must be recognized, of course, that this process is one of considerable duration in the West, that it has been solved in the past with only minor disruptions, and that it is a major source of the increases in real income that we have experienced, as well as a principal cause of urbanization *per se*.[7] With the mechanization and rationalization of agriculture, and the heavier capitalization of other extractive industries like oil and mining, the "primary" activities have been long subject to this tendency. We reached the point long ago, in fact, where the declines in the agricultural component of the labor force became not only relative but absolute; not only is the percentage engaged in farming still on the decline, but the actual numbers of farmers and agricultural laborers have fallen off rather rapidly in recent decades. But other sectors of the economy have been subjected to the very same forces; the shrinking of the "unskilled labor" category in manufacturing, for example, bears witness to the replacement of human muscle by mechanical energy. And the most prominent topic in both management and labor circles today is the "automation" of manufacturing. The automatic factory is no mere dream of the future; it is already well established in certain industries, and is certain to spread as present capital equipment reaches obsolescence and requires replacement in other areas of production. To portray this trend as limited to the "secondary"

[7]See Albert J. Reiss, Jr., "An Analysis of Urban Phenomena," in Robert Moore Fisher (ed.), *The Metropolis in Modern Life* (New York: Doubleday, 1955), pp. 5-17.

or fabricating activities, however, would be to mis-state the facts. Electronic computers are already in use in many lines of business, and they promise to show further gains in the "tertiary" sector wherever routine clerical operations are an important component of the cost of doing business. Up to the moment, the limitations on their use seem to lie in their capacity for economically handling more work than many establishments can give them; thus they are mainly confined to the very largest firms. As smaller and cheaper models develop, or as new types of business service oriented to supplying smaller establishments come into being, these machines will probably make even further headway.

Be that as it may, the intimate connections between these technological trends and long-term urbanization itself are only too evident. That we have solved the resulting problems of labor substitution in the past, however, is no guarantee that the threat will be met in the future. In fact, if one projects the secular trend of a labor force increasingly engaged in certain "tertiary" industries into an indefinite future period, a bizarre picture emerges—a population largely occupied with the provision of educational and recreational services for each other. Ridiculous as this may seem, approximating the imaginary population that survived by "taking in each other's laundry," we must be wary of depending upon today's standards in evaluating future trends; one need only read some of the speculative writings of the late nineteenth century to realize just how fantastic the world of the 1960's would appear to a Victorian observer. In any event, the compelling challenge for policy-makers is to deal with the task of shifting large numbers of workers into new pursuits, and in

handling the difficulties that arise out of limited transferability of skills.[8] Since these problems have been with us for a long time—though on a much smaller scale than seems imminent—we have reason to hope that experience from the past may be drawn upon in order to facilitate future adaptation, and sociological research on the subject is sorely needed.

Population Problems

Turning from technological considerations to *population* problems, we are immediately made aware of the demographic concomitants of the foregoing technological trends. Again, they are most visible in the urban context. In particular, the rural-to-urban population shift is far from complete. Many areas—especially in the South—still contain redundant agriculturalists engaged in subsistence production. Most of their output does not find its way into commercial market channels. One may reasonably assume that this marginal farm population will ultimately be drawn into other sectors of the economy.[9] In fact, trends in very recent years indicate that the elimination of this relatively unproductive group is well under way. Nevertheless, a key policy problem persists beneath the surface—a problem that is not ordinarily taken up in the continuing political debates over parity, price supports, and the proper disposition of farm surplus. The hidden issue has to do with the role that government shall play in aiding the adjustment of

[8] See Raymond Vernon, *The Changing Economic Function of the Central City* (New York: Committee for Economic Development, 1959).

[9] Stephen L. MacDonald, "Farm Out-migration as an Integrative Adjustment to Economic Growth," *Social Forces*, 34 (December, 1955), pp. 119-128.

displaced agriculturalists, many of whom become rural-to-urban migrants. Evidence thus far available indicates that under laissez-faire conditions the ex-farmer typically enters the urban work force at or near the bottom of the occupational scale, taking the jobs requiring the least training and receiving the smallest rewards.[10]

A related development that deserves further consideration by both policy-makers and researchers can be seen especially clearly in certain highly industrialized regions where agriculture has been undergoing a long-term decline. We refer here to the pattern of widespread part-time industrial employment by farmers, often accompanied by extensive gardening and small-scale farming by factory workers.[11] Easier commuting has permitted an increased flow of labor between two sections of our economy. (It is an interesting historical sidelight that this pattern has a precedent of many years standing in some parts of Europe, and that Henry Ford actually advocated the adoption of these practices, making it a matter of company policy to encourage off-season work in agriculture.)

Now the significance of this pattern for domestic economic policy arises out of the "marginal" nature of this fluid component of the labor force. In fact, it appears that the affected persons are also physically marginal from the standpoint of local urban labor markets; cutbacks in production seem to strike them first—in part because of their limited seniority—and to contract the areal boundaries of the urban labor market.[12] From one perspective, there are certain undeniable advantages in the situation: gardening by factory workers aids the family budget and may even provide supplementary income, the maintenance of farm residence by ex-farmers guarantees a cushion against urban unemployment, there are no serious problems of adjustment to migration, and there is less need for urban housing. However, the literally marginal status of these workers—both industrial and agricultural, and thereby neither—has obvious disutilities. Among these are the heavy strains of long-distance commuting, for there is evidence that the radius of movement around many plants exceeds 50 miles. "Farm policy," it would seem, is too narrowly defined if it ignores either the plight of cityward migrants or the dilemma of marginality confronting the commuting farmer-factory workers. Their numbers alone demand some attention.

However, the demographic difficulties facing our urban-industrial society are not exclusively distributional in origin. Even a perfect spatial re-allocation of population in accordance with opportunities for livelihood would not solve a number of social and economic problems that arise out of certain trends in population composition. We have had our attention repeat-

[10]Ronald Freedman and Deborah Freedman, "Farm-Reared Elements in the Non-farm Population," *Rural Sociology*, 21 (March, 1956), pp. 50-61.

[11]Walter Firey, *Social Aspects to Land-Use Planning in the Country-City Fringe: The Case of Flint, Michigan* (East Lansing: Michigan State Agricultural Experiment Station, Special Bulletin 339, 1946); Nathan L. Whetten and R. F. Field, *Studies of Suburbanization in Connecticut, 2. Norwich: An Industrial Part-time Farming Area* (Storrs: Connecticut State Agricultural Experiment Station Bulletin 226, 1938).

[12]Roy Gerard, "Commuting and the Labor Market Area," *Journal of Regional Science*, 1 (Summer, 1958), pp. 124-130; Leo F. Schnore, "The Separation of Home and Work: A Problem for Human Ecology," *Social Forces*, 32 (May, 1954), pp. 336-343; William Goldner, "Spatial and Locational Aspects of Metropolitan Labor Markets," *American Economic Review*, 45 (March, 1955), pp. 113-128.

edly called to the "baby boom" that followed the low fertility years of depression and war in this country; in point of fact, a number of combatant nations have undergone the same experience. The result, from a compositional standpoint, is a series of indentations and bulges in the population pyramid that is even more aggravated in the countries that suffered especially heavy wartime losses in particular age ranges (e.g., France and Germany). Even in the United States, however, these peculiarities in age composition have important social and economic consequences.

Stated most simply, we are confronted with the problem of age cohorts of radically different size passing through various age-graded institutions and services.[13] Thus the low rates of accession to the labor market in recent years, which are the result of the limited number of births in the depression years. Our primary and secondary schools have been feeling the impact of the revival of the birth rate for some time; these large numbers are now reaching our colleges, and shortly thereafter, will burst upon our labor and housing markets. At that time the small depression cohorts will be having children, and in such reduced numbers as to lower the crude birth rate and absolute number of births to a certain extent. Only a few years will pass, however, before we will witness the reassertion of higher levels of fertility when the postwar cohorts marry and have children. The overall prospect, then, is for a more or less rhythmic series of delayed reactions to the fluctuations in fertility that

marked the period between the early 30's and the late 50's. The influences upon the housing market, upon educational facilities, and upon industries oriented to the needs of infants and children are perhaps too obvious to require discussion. Moreover, to the extent that population size determines levels of output in an economy closely geared to the market, we may thus anticipate a long-term alternating sequence of expansion and "stagnation" in at least certain industries, with one extreme phase following the other in order.[14]

However, the amplitude of these fluctuations is probably narrow enough to permit relatively easy adjustment for the economy taken as a whole. The problems for policy appear when we consider the *localized* manifestations of these trends, and particularly when we give simultaneous attention to both population distribution and composition. Any resident of a mushrooming suburb will testify to the costs of providing minimal school facilities and adequately trained personnel for a rapidly expanding child population.[15] One disturbing possibility that many local authorities have failed to consider is that of an equally sudden shrinkage in the demand for educational services that will eventually follow the completion of suburban families; newer suburbs with heavy concentrations in a narrow parental age range are particularly vulnerable. This is a form of elasticity of localized demand that may

[13]Norman B. Ryder, "Variability and Convergence in the American Population," *Phi Delta Kappan*, 41 (June, 1960), pp. 379-383; see also Robert J. Lampman, "Paying the Price of Higher Fertility," in *Problems of U.S. Economic Development* (New York: Committee for Economic Development, 1958).

[14]Alvin H. Hansen, *Full Recovery or Stagnation* (New York: W. W. Norton, 1938); William B. Reddaway, *The Economics of a Declining Population* (London: G. Allen and Unwin, Ltd., 1939).

[15]Robert G. Burnight, *Suburban Migration and the Cost of Education*, "Connecticut Population Report No. 2" (Storrs: University of Connecticut, College of Agriculture, Agricultural Experiment Station, 1956).

have very serious ramifications, for our age-graded community institutions and local facilities apparently do not have the flexibility that the situation will require.[16]

Somewhat greater difficulties come into view if we shift attention from schools to housing; housing has been traditionally conceived as a "private industry," and not as an area of primary responsibility for government, and there is still little disposition to interfere with the workings of blind market forces. This is despite the chronic shortages of living space that have plagued many metropolitan areas since the depths of the depression, and the acute undersupplies of housing that have affected a number of the newer areas that grew very rapidly during war years, when private construction dropped to very low levels. Even older and slow-growing areas do not escape, however, for they face the problem of an increasingly obsolescent housing stock.[17] Perhaps the "obvious" solution is an expanded governmental program aimed at undertaking the risks that private capital seems reluctant to assume. The federal government, of course, is already involved in housing on many fronts, as it is in education, if only indirectly. There would seem to be a limited appreciation of the extent of the needs, however, and of the localized nature of these demands. What seems sorely needed is a program of action-oriented research that is based on a sound understanding of

how both compositional and distributional trends tend to intersect in a way that produces real crises in certain local areas while other nearby areas are relatively unaffected. Thus despite the fact that we have long avoided the Malthusian dilemma, modern urban-industrial communities are still subject to powerful demographic forces. The resulting socio-economic problems would seem to demand our closest attention and our most carefully considered responses in the form of policy.

Organizational Problems

When we turn from technological and demographic issues to *organizational* matters, it might appear that we move nearer to a set of solutions. After all, the obvious and natural response to marked technological change is and always has been some kind of structural adaptation. In particular, our long practice in accommodating to the substitution of machines for manpower would seem to bode well for the future. Similarly, there are obvious organizational responses to population growth and redistribution and to variations in demand for housing, schools, and other services. The assimilation of the present marginal labor force, and the provision of physical facilities might seem to be problems almost made for joint solution by private industry and government. But it must be recognized that there are deep-rooted organizational resistances to the easy resolution of many of these matters. We possess a "political economy"—to use the full connotations of this old academic label—that is marked by a fragmentation of political power and a parallel decentralization of economic power. We must be careful not to overstate the case at this point,

[16]The Compleat Planner might suggest that the under-used schoolrooms of the future may be employed for re-training workers displaced by technological trends.

[17]Glenn H. Beyer, *Housing: A Factual Analysis* (New York: Macmillan Co., 1958); Richard U. Ratcliff, *et al, Residential Finance, 1950* (New York: John Wiley, 1957); Glenn H. Beyer and J. Hugh Rose, *Farm Housing* (New York: John Wiley, 1957).

but comparative governmental studies seem to suggest that the United States divides a far higher proportion of major activities between private and public agencies than most other democracies, where one or the other typically reigns alone, and certainly far more than any totalitarian state, where effective power over decision-making is centralized.[18] The result is often a series of coalitions of powerful vested interests—interlocking private and public bureaucracies between which flow a vast amount of information and even personnel, all of it serving the function of maintaining a working relationship in a particular sphere of activity.

Added to this complicated picture, moreover, is a large and ramified network of rival *centers of power* that has developed in a context of a federation of sovereign states, and with a background of "free" enterprise. The resulting "private governments" made up of industrial and labor giants, and the effective power of the states, create another set of organizational resistances that make structural adaptations far less perfect than any mechanistic interpretation would predict. (The extent to which these "private governments" are involved in the affairs of the separate states has been remarked by a number of observers of the political scene.) A further complication is the fact of *cleavages* within both private *and* public sectors of our political economy. The struggles between sister agencies in government sometimes rival the titanic contests between industrial giants and

[18]William Anderson, *The Units of Government in the United States* (Chicago: Public Administration Service, 1949, rev. ed.); William Anderson, *The Nation and the States: Rivals or Partners?* (Minneapolis: University of Minnesota Press, 1955); John M. Gaus, *Reflections on Public Administration* (University: University of Alabama Press, 1947).

the bitter jurisdictional battles of trade unions. To the extent that these public and private corporate entities become functionally similar, they become potential competitors; the result is a complex situation in which a rough and tentative equilibrium based upon "countervailing power" begins to emerge in response to the forces of urban industrialism. Fluid coalitions, deep cleavages, and a vast proliferation of centers of power combine to make organizational responses very slow and unwieldy approximations to the kind of structural adaptations that pure logic might dictate.

All this, however, is merely to say that the pressing problems of an urban-industrial society have distinctly organizational as well as technological and demographic aspects. One particular pair of related structural problems deserves special sociological attention, however, because of its bearing upon the foregoing issues. First, we must refer again to the so-called "imbalance" between rural and urban political power. We are only now awakening to some of the implications of the fact that rural areas exercise a degree of influence far our of proportion to population numbers. And one need not formulate any very complicated "lag" theory to account for this phenomenon, for the imbalance serves the interests of more than a minority of rural dwellers, and it especially fits the operating requirements of the "private governments" that dot our political landscape. A rural-dominated state house of representatives is simply easier to influence. But this is not strictly and solely a legislative phenomenon. Executive branches—including the federal—exhibit the same imbalance. To take only one example, the cabinet contains no spokesman for the urban consumer, whose interests are only occasionally represented by the secretaries of Commerce and Labor; in contrast, the rural producer is served by a massive department that has actually continued to grow during the time that the number of farmers has declined appreciably. Yet we have only recently witnessed a serious effort in the direction of creating a cabinet-level Department of Urban Affairs.[19] However, one can already see the strong resistances to rapid governmental adaptation to urbanism, and a quick solution of problems of urban housing, services, and transportation is not to be expected. The fact that so many policy-makers, whether businessmen, industrialists, legislators or governmental executives, must have outright allegiances with, organizational commitments to, or even only emotional sympathies for the rural minority leads to some pessimism regarding a purely rational policy solution of many of the problems we have enumerated. Although it provides a plausible interpretation, no abstract law of cultural lag seems required to explain why we have been so slow to face the hard facts of life in an urban society.

The second organizational problem is to be found at the local political level; we refer here to the familiar question of "metropolitan government." This has been a widely discussed topic among political scientists, as witnessed by a recent and incomplete bibliography devoted to the subject which contains well over a thousand entries.[20] We will take time for only a few passing observations, but it is worth stressing the fact that the "problems" of political organization in metropolitan areas are not unrelated to those enumerated above. Most of them reduce to the question of the most economic provision of certain social and economic services that have become the acknowledged responsibility of local government; it seems obvious to many writers that the duplication and overlapping authority that accompanies the political fragmentation of the metropolitan area leads to "waste" and "inefficiency." The suggested solutions — and there are many proposals that differ mainly in formal detail — usually involve a basic reorganization of local political structure along "federated" lines, and the creation of a new layer of government corresponding to the expanded area of social and economic interdependence. But for the moment, we are more concerned with the causes of the problem than with proposed solutions.

In most discussions of twentieth century metropolitanism in America, one finds special stress given to the new technology of transportation and communication.[21] We must also recognize that demographic factors have been critical, for population growth and concentration comprise an intimate part of the historical trend we have observed. If one gives particular emphasis to technology, however, a rough analogy may be drawn between the metropolitan dilemma and the difficulties faced by the world community of nations. As Staley has pointed out, the logic of modern technology points to a "planetary economy," but political trends only give further support to strictly

[19]The need for such a department has been recognized for decades. See Philip Kates, "A National Department of Municipalities," *American City*, 6 (1912), pp. 405-407; and Harlean James, "Service — the Keynote of a New Cabinet Department," *Review of Reviews*, 59 (1919), pp. 187-190.

[20]Victor Jones (ed.), *Metropolitan Communities: A Bibliography* (Chicago: Public Administration Service, 1956).

[21]R. D. McKenzie, *The Metropolitan Community* (New York: McGraw-Hill Book Co., 1933); Amos H. Hawley, *Human Ecology: A Theory of Community Structure* (New York: Ronald Press, 1950).

national economies.[22] In similar fashion, it might be said that technological developments have created the essential preconditions for area-wide political organization of the metropolitan community, but constituent governmental entities persist in "localism," extremely reluctant to give up any real measure of autonomy. The patent difficulty with this line of analogous reasoning is that it leads to a rather naive interpretation that accepts a certain "lag" as inevitable. Not only is such a view likely to lead to inaction, but it is liable to overlook certain salient structural considerations. In particular, the local coalitions and cleavages that constitute organizational resistances to metropolitan government seem to warrant further attention by sociologically sophisticated researchers, planners and policy-makers. The main demographic trends are fairly well documented; what should now receive concerted effort is an intensive examination of the structural network that has evolved in response to population changes and technological innovations. Once the critical organizational bonds are identified and analyzed, we might have a more workable means of welding together larger structural units.

One final consideration that is worthy of mention in this brief review is more directly derived from research that has been already accomplished. We refer here to the problem of giving spatial definition to the authority of a political entity designed to conform to the functional bounds of the metropolitan area viewed as a socio-economic entity. It has become abundantly clear that different criteria yield different boundaries, and that any particular set of areal limits will be subject to further change in response to shifting circumstances in the future.[23] From a policy standpoint, then, the whole issue must necessarily be approached in a spirit of flexibility.

Environmental Problems

In order not to neglect the *environmental* aspect of urban life, and some of the problems it presents, we must turn to a brief consideration of physical resources. Now the urban-metropolitan *milieu* may well appear to be an environment literally stripped of natural elements—a setting of glass, wire, plastic, concrete, and steel. But everyone is well aware that an urbanized society consumes—and indeed even wastes—an enormous volume of physical materials.[24] At some point along the way, however, it is necessary to remind ourselves of the simple but fundamental distinction between organic and inorganic elements, for they pose radically dissimilar problems. Organic substances are actually defined by their capacity to reproduce and multiply. The reader will recall the interesting flaw in Malthus' original theory of population, whereby the "geometric" series (1, 2, 4, 8, 16, etc.) was taken crudely to represent the human power to increase in numbers, while the organic substances on which men depend for food were said to increase in only "arithmetic" order (1, 2, 3, 4, 5, etc.). The latter series could be more accurately applied, of

[22]Eugene Staley, *World Economy in Transition* (New York: Council on Foreign Relations, 1939).

[23]Hawley, *op. cit.*, Chapter 13; Howard L. Green, "Hinterland Boundaries of New York City and Boston in Southern New England," *Economic Geography*, 31 (October, 1955), pp. 283-300.

[24]John Kenneth Galbraith, *The Affluent Society* (Boston: Houghton Mifflin, 1958); David M. Potter, *People of Plenty* (Chicago: University of Chicago Press, 1954).

course, to the inorganic substances on which men depend, for these have literally no power to increase by reproduction, though the existing stock may be replenished by new discoveries; in some respects, their status is better represented by the "series" 1, 1, 1, 1, etc. In the face of essentially fixed inorganic resources, then, expanding human numbers pose a potential threat to a given level of living; inorganic resources may certainly be increased by new discoveries, or by the utilization of previously unused elements. But however distant in future time, the process must inevitably end when most of the vital materials have been located and extracted from the environment. Thus a considerably modified and re-oriented Malthusian theory may have more than a little relevance for an urban-industrial society.

Now these views have been recently and persuasively restated by a number of writers concerned with the rapid rate at which industrial society uses up exhaustible resources.[25] Although this literature is often charged with emotion, and occasionally has the shrill tone of hysteria, the problems it raises are profound indeed. Some of these same writers, "conservationists" in the fullest sense of the term, go on to develop an equally pessimistic picture regarding organic resources. By pointing to harmful agricultural practices that induce erosion, to wasteful exploitation of timber reserves, and to the encroachment of urban land uses, they attempt to show that even organic resources are in danger of diminution. All in all, this

[25]Fairfield Osborn, *Our Plundered Planet* (Boston: Little, Brown and Co., 1948); William Vogt, *Road to Survival* (New York: William Sloane Associates, 1948); for some needed sociological perspective, see Wilbert E. Moore, "Flora, Fauna, Land, and People," *Population Index,* 15 (April, 1949), pp. 105-114.

literature has tended to be discounted by many economists and demographers, but (interestingly enough) it has had considerable impact upon public policy, if one may crudely measure influence by citations in the Congressional Record and in policy statements by the Departments of Agriculture and the Interior. Most of the conservationist writings are strikingly similar, however, in sharing one implicit sociological assumption: they are all postulated upon an ideal of a self-contained agricultural-industrial system, in which the nation is assumed to be essentially dependent upon only the physical resources lying within its own sovereign territory. One need only glance at import statistics to gain an appreciation of how much we have already departed from this ideal, if indeed it does represent a desirable goal. One may thus laud the admirable motives and the sense of public responsibility that permeates this literature and still judge it to be an unrealistic portrayal of our true situation. Like it or not, urban industrialism is postulated upon a world-wide network of interdependent relations, economic as well as political, and any conception of our environment that confines it to our national borders is unrealistic in the extreme. It follows, too, that any policy based upon this incomplete appreciation of the actual extent and nature of our extended environment is liable to be defective. In short, a truly "ecological" view is absolutely essential, though sociologists have neglected to provide it.

Conclusions

The subject of urbanization, of course, is sufficiently important to warrant examination from standpoints other than those of students interested in the social problems engendered by the process. In point of fact, much of the empirical sociological study of the city ignores the practical problems of "urbanism as a way of life." This phrase—the title of a famous essay by Louis Wirth—suggests a concern with the ways in which the urban setting impinges upon the individual.[26]

In his essay, Wirth began with a conception of urbanization that drew upon Durkheim's views as enunciated in *The Division of Labor in Society*.[27] Wirth took as the hallmarks of urbanism four demographic and organizational features—great size, density, permanence, and heterogeneity, with the latter conceived as both occupational and "biological," in the sense of racial and ethnic diversity. However, the bulk of his analysis was given over to a lengthy specification of the ways in which these gross morphological features bear upon individual personality and behavior in the urban *milieu*. Drawing upon the German idealistic tradition, as modified in the insightful speculative essays by Simmel and Weber,[28] Wirth attempted to spell out the implications of life in an urban setting. Here he saw sophisticated rationalism, a blasé attitude, competitive impersonality, and even a sense of alienation from one's fellow men. A recent attempt by Kolb to apply Parsons' "pattern variables" to the analysis of life in the city yields almost exactly the same image as that more clearly portrayed by Wirth fifteen years earlier.[29] In all of this material, the "pathological" and the problematic loom large, and it is surprising that thirty years of urban research has not supplied a more coherent set of empirically-based propositions referring to the major social problems in urban society. At least part of this deficiency is due to a lack of systematic *comparative* research. As Wirth himself pointed out, "to set up ideal-typical concepts such as I have done ... does not prove that city and country are fundamentally and necessarily different. It does not justify mistaking the hypothetical characteristics attributed to the urban and rural modes of life for established facts, as has so often been done."[30]

It would appear that American sociologists have been too much inclined to deal with the surface manifestations of American cities. Human ecologists, for example, have been content to map the spatial patterns exhibited by urban communities, and have tended to bypass more fundamental questions concerning urban social organization and disorganization. Somehow, very few writers have exhibited any systematic interest in either the determinants or consequences of urbanization, and even fewer manifest a comparative research interest in these broad topics. Far too much "urban research" has been research that incidentally or accidentally has an urban site; to use Meadows' terms, studies of city problems have had an *"intra*-urban" rather than an *"inter*-urban" focus, and urban *society* is

[26]Louis Wirth, "Urbanism as a Way of Life," *American Journal of Sociology,* 44 (July, 1938), pp. 1-26.

[27]Émile Durkheim, *The Division of Labor in Society* (New York: Macmillan Co., 1933); see also Leo F. Schnore, "Social Morphology and Human Ecology," *American Journal of Sociology,* 63 (May, 1958), pp. 620-634.

[28]Georg Simmel, "The Metropolis and Mental Life," in Kurt H. Wolff (translator and editor), *The Sociology of Georg Simmel* (Glencoe: Free Press, 1950); Max Weber, *The City* (Glencoe: Free Press, 1958).

[29]William L. Kolb, "The Social Structure and Functions of Cities," *Economic Development and Cultural Change,* 3 (October, 1954), pp. 30-46.

[30]Louis Wirth, in Elizabeth Wirth Marvick and Albert J. Reiss, Jr. (eds.), *Community Life and Social Policy* (Chicago: University of Chicago Press, 1956), pp. 173-174.

neglected for the sake of the urban *community*.[31] It seems certain that only a genuinely comparative approach to social problems in an urban context will yield the results that have been so long promised but never delivered.

The type of research design that is required is illustrated by a fairly large body of literature dealing with such topics as rural-urban differences in personality, intelligence, and educational and occupational aspirations and achievements.[32] The various "social

problems"—including mental illness, alcoholism, suicide, homosexuality, divorce, drug addiction, etc.—have not been subjected to the same kind of sophisticated analysis, if one may judge from the less substantial literature. In any case, the need is clear. As Bogue has observed, "renewed social research upon the urban community, from an objective point of view, using representative samples of data and modern research techniques, should produce much of the knowledge that social engineers will need in order to handle social problems which, in the nature of the case, will be largely urban problems."[33]

[31]Paul Meadows, "The City, Technology, and History," *Social Forces*, 36 (December, 1957), pp. 141-147; see also Gideon Sjoberg, "Comparative Urban Sociology," in Robert K. Merton, *et al* (eds.), *Sociology Today* (New York: Basic Books, 1959), pp. 334-359.

[32]Earlier American and European studies are summarized in Pitirim A. Sorokin and Carle C. Zimmerman, *Principles of Rural-Urban Sociology* (New York: Henry Holt, 1929). Examples of more recent work include the following: A. R. Mangus, "Personality Adjustment of Rural and Urban Children," *American Sociological Review*, 13 (October, 1948), pp. 566-575; William H. Sewell and Eleanor A. Amend, "The Influence of Size of Home Community on Attitudes and Personality Traits," *American Sociological Review*, 8 (April,

1943), pp. 180-184; William H. Sewell and Bertram L. Ellenbogen, "Social Status and the Measured Intelligence of Small City and Rural Children," *American Sociological Review*, 17 (October, 1952), pp. 612-616; A. O. Haller and William H. Sewell, "Residence and Levels of Educational and Occupational Aspiration," *American Journal of Sociology*, 62 (January, 1957), pp. 407-411.

[33]Donald J. Bogue, "Urbanism in the United States, 1950," *American Journal of Sociology*, 60 (March, 1955), p. 486.

A NOTE ON SELECTIVE INATTENTION IN SOCIAL SCIENCE[1]

Lewis Anthony Dexter

The subjects that scholars persistently avoid studying are worth considering because such consideration may: (a) suggest a reordering of priorities for research and exposition; (b) help in determining whether certain important topics are left out of account for nonrational reasons; or (c) illuminate the ways recommendations and emphases relate to the logic of theory and diagnosis.

It is assumed that persistent avoidance by a group of scholars of *pertinent* topics is not purely or chiefly accidental. The key word here is "pertinent." We are not interested in the fact that social pathologists have rarely discussed frustrated romance amongst cockroaches — despite William James' remark that "the problem of evil remains in the universe in its full force so long as one cockroach is dying of unrequited love."

We are concerned with consistent inattention to fields and problems which, in terms of theory and definition, seem to fit into particular disciplines. Significant advances in science have sometimes taken place when someone has realized that a problem hitherto neglected or excluded does in fact fit into the methods and techniques of his discipline. One recent example is the "sociologization" of health, previously regarded as a purely medical and biological area.

An organized and systematic set of hypotheses about cases of avoidance could be of great value to sociologists of science — and particularly to students of social problems. The present note is a preliminary contribution to the construction of such hypotheses. It arose from the writer's experience as a research consultant, 1949-57, in the area of mental deficiency. He was particularly impressed by the fact that during 1910-25 the literature showed considerable concern by sociologists and social workers with mental deficiency, that by 1935 this concern had diminished almost to the zero level, and that by 1949 there was virtually no interest by sociologists in the topic. A real revival of general scholarly and philanthropic attention to mental deficiency during the recent past has been accompanied or followed by a fainter but

Reprinted, with permission of author and publisher, from *Social Problems*, 6, No. 2, Fall, 1958, 176-182. Lewis Dexter expands the point of view expressed in this article in his book, *The Tyranny of Schooling; An Inquiry into the Problem of Stupidity* (New York: Basic Books, 1964).

[1]This article was prepared under a grant from the Kate Jackson Anthony Trust of Lewiston, Maine, "for the benefit of God's children known as the feeble-minded."

perceptible sociological re-awareness of the social effects and implications of mental deficiency.

Inattention to, or lack of interest in mental deficiency by sociologists has seemed, superficially at least, to resemble the similar lack of concern by sociologists with civil defense and survival plans during recent years. On the other hand, such topics as psychological warfare, "brain-washing," limited war, suicide, and the Stevenson campaigns seem to be regarded by sociologists as more sociological or more exciting.

Inattention has not been a function of money; during 1949-54, indeed, the writer tried to find out how to spend a trust fund of $60,000 on social science research about mental deficiency; yet, if recollection serves, only two sociologists under 65 had any suggestion regarding the study of mental defectives *as such*. Other proposals assumed that one would take the mental defective as a given—something like a geographical fact—and, for instance, determine how his siblings reacted. Or they involved purely statistical analyses of records about defectives. But, most interesting of all, the majority of sociologists—and psychologists—whose advice was sought shifted the conversation, immediately *and apparently unconsciously,* from amentia to neurosis or psychosis.

It may be pointed out that, similarly, during recent years sociologists could have received considerable financial help from the Federal Civil Defense Administration for research, but few have manifested much interest in the central problems of civil defense, concentrating whatever attention they give to the field on peripheral issues of natural disaster, panic in small-scale fires, etc.

It is, of course, possible to suggest *ad hoc* reasons why sociologists show little interest in this or that particular problem. But we need general reasons: explanations would have to be multiplied indefinitely if we developed *one* to explain why prostitution and illegitimacy seem to have attracted more sociological attention than homosexuality, a *second* to make clear why political corruption has occupied more space in social problems texts, and probably time in social problems courses, than military or industrial espionage, a *third* to show why alcoholism lost and regained respectability as a sociological problem, more or less concurrently with mental deficiency, a *fourth* to help us deduce why divorce is much more emphasized in social problems discussions than warfare, and a *fifth* to make plain why sociologists very rarely, if ever, devote systematic attention to the problem of genocide.

There have been attempts to account for the characteristic emphases of social problems discussion, but they are not particularly helpful: Mills asserts that the focus of the social pathologist is "utilitarian . . . in terms of community welfare," (7, pp. 168, 175) apparently implying a Benthamite concern with the reduction of unhappiness. A standard, not particularly extreme, text in social pathology, published in 1927, says of the mentally defective: "The moron constitutes a great social menace [and] furnishes recruits for those who commit brutal murders, incendiarism, rape, and assault. Most serious of all, he leaves behind a large progeny." (5, pp. 151-152) Between 1910 and 1930, many similar statements appeared in literature accessible to sociologists. In utilitarian terms, such statements should have constituted a strong stimulus to the study of mental deficiency. But actually, even then, serious attention and study were rare.

Further, taking again a utilitarian conception of happiness and unhappiness, it seems reasonable to assume that among middle-class families in recent American society, the mixture of shame and worry created by a mentally defective child is considerable; and it is often believed that the same sort of shame and worry exists among many other families with mental defectives. Nevertheless, the topic of mental deficiency was ignored throughout the 1930's and 1940's.

A third sense of "utilitarian," of course, involves the saving of money. Between 1930 and 1950, the cost of public institutions for mental defectives rose considerably; any concern with saving public moneys and taxes should have led to much emphasis on mental deficiency research.

Hobbs states that sociology textbook writers "rely on other sociology texts as the chief sources of information." (6, pp. 9, 175) This seems to be true; but the sociologist of sociology will also want to know what citations in earlier writers are ignored or minimized. Presumably, the same factors tend to operate that affect memory or conversation: we edit out those matters which we find boring or unrewardingly unpleasant. At any rate, the textbook writers of the 1930's and 1940's had available to them not only the earlier sociological treatises which did discuss mental defect but also the original works on the Kallikaks, Jukes, etc. Mental deficiency was nevertheless deemphasized or ignored.

Hobbs also says that sociology tends to include those subjects that are left over, "those aspects of personality not included in the principal foci of psychology, biology, or genetics." Actually, psychologists and students of genetics were concerned with mental defi-

ciency at the same time that sociologists were — roughly from 1910 to 1930 — and their interest in the topic waned as that of sociologists did. On the other hand, the Kinsey studies stimulated interest in sexual behavior in several disciplines; and alcoholism and propaganda were ignored and emphasized in the different disciplines at about the same time.

A more adequate general explanation of the avoidance of specific social problems by social pathologists would seem to lie in the following interrelated considerations:

A. The development of sociology since 1920 has in large measure been guided by considerations of the effect of socio-environmental differences upon personality and intergroup relationships. Topics which did not fit into this approach, no matter how significant *per se*, tended to be neglected or overlooked for at least four reasons:

(1) They are frustrating or puzzling in themselves. Once a theory has become accepted as plausible, true, and above all "natural," we find, to paraphrase Spencer, "substantial facts exiled by elegant theories — or by theories which have all the acceptability of common usage — from respectable consideration." This process is (except where taboos are involved) rarely deliberate and, therefore, if consciously realized, could be taken into account.

(2) A prevailing theory or point of view tends to attract into a discipline those with a particular ideological bent or focus; topics which do not seem compatible with both the methodology and its implicit or explicit ideology tend to be shunted to one side, or overtly ridiculed, by the second or third generation of scholars, if not by the first.

The interpretation of behavior in democratic, egalitarian, anti-genetic terms attracted into sociology between

1925 and 1945 people whose interests, ideals, and values led them strongly to resent any notion of inherent inequality or even of the biological conditioning of behavior. As they have grown older, their own social situation and perhaps greater maturity has made this egalitarian bias *per se* less significant to some of them; at the same time, immanent in the formal pattern of sociological thinking has been a bias against being influenced by one's own biases, and another bias in favor of using one's detection of one's colleagues' biases as a weapon, biases of which this essay is no doubt in part a product and which may aid in obtaining consideration for it.

A hundred years ago, economic orthodoxy left out of account the qualifications and limitations of which Adam Smith himself was probably well enough aware, because of the same tendency of disciplines to select those persons who find the central ideological implications of the methodology most attractive. Perhaps the real hatred and contempt which some scholars feel or appear to feel for extrasensory perception represents the same process; and the fact that there has been little attention paid, except by a few historians, students of rebellion, to the relationship of weather upon behavior or the psyche[2] may indicate not so much the unimportance of the issue as its incompatibility with the preferred world view(s) of social scientists.

The ideology of sociologists in the United States involved defense of, if not identification with, the underdog. Typically, excluding a few serious followers of Sumner and Paréto, American sociologists tried to get students disembedded from "the cake of custom" so

[2] By social scientists; a few physiologists have discussed weather and behavior.

that they might become "less prejudiced" against countermores behavior; "to understand all is to forgive all" or at least "to defend all." But there were, of course, exceptions; even in liberal colleges, in the late 30's or early 40's, sociologists would have found it difficult to defend conservative Republicanism; by the same token, sociologists found it difficult to defend warmongers or mental defectives.

(3) Granted the exciting possibilities which sociological and anthropological interpretations of behavior opened up in the 1930's, it was nevertheless hard to "explain" or "explain away" differences in the mental endowment of individuals without simultaneously questioning the value and validity of the selective institutional processes by which scholars themselves generally acquire their status. That is, in an open society, sociologists acquire status because they are bright; so they receive some deference and are able to dominate some classrooms. In fact, at least until the postwar period of consultantships and research endowments, most sociologists were teachers, in day-to-day contact with students, able to maintain status in that daily environment by intellectual superiority.

To tell these students—or to say anything to them which could be interpreted as telling them—that stupidity and brightness could be interpreted in the same cultural fashion as the difference between "savages" and "civilized men" would have tended to impeach the legitimacy of the sociologists' own treatment of students.

Put another way, skill at manipulating symbols is the capital of men who have become sociologists; it is consequently no "skin off their hides" when someone attacks the 60 families of American capitalism in exaggerated terms: they are sympathetically "objective" to the attackers; but when a McCarthy threatens the possessors of *intellectual* capital in similarly exaggerated language, their involvement is considerable.

The difficulty in being dispassionate in regard to the social role of the mental defective is a related one. Perry (8) and Dexter (1, 2) suggest that, to comprehend the social origins and meanings of mental deficiency in our society adequately, one must be skeptical about the system of universal competition in manipulating symbols and a career open to the talents, with everybody *compelled* to try to manifest talent.

Sociologists, therefore, found it difficult to interpret mental deficiency in sociologistic terms. And they could not, particularly after Hitler came into power in 1933, state that mental defect is related to inheritance; in those days this shocked the liberal conscience. And so the subject tended to be shunted to one side.

(4) Another reason for shunting it to one side is that the exaggerations of one generation may, if detected, cause the omissions of the next. The history of the "debunking" historians and biographers could well be written in terms of this generalization. If one generation has distorted the significance of a subject, anyone who talks about the subject may be suspected—or may be afraid he will be suspected—of endorsing these distortions. In sociology and social science, in general, study of a subject is supposed to involve sympathy with a prevailing viewpoint about it; in the late 30's for example, a graduate student in sociology who studied labor unions might be automatically supposed, even by his instructors, to sympathize with

John L. Lewis, regardless of his actual views.

Hence, the emphasis on "the fruit of the family tree" and the oversimplification of genetic interpretations in the 1920's (carried on by some textbook writers in genetics for another dozen years) led to a de-emphasis of genetic interpretations and of precisely those topics to which the genetic interpretations had been most dramatically and carelessly applied. Somewhat similar developments took place in the field of alcoholism; the overdramatic claims of extreme prohibitionists in the early part of the twentieth century created a climate in which scholars and intellectuals generally ignored the real and significant problems of alcoholism for about twenty years.

B. The countermores emphasis of American sociology generally tends to imply that the discriminated-against are not as bad as they are painted ("Slums have their own social structure," we say), are not as bad as they seem to be on first impression (we point out that higher crime rates in certain discriminated-against groups are either not correctly compared or a function of discrimination), and are really not any worse than the middle or upper classes (sociologists point out that university students usually do not get taken to court, although they do in fact perform all the offenses of which juvenile delinquents are accused). These statements are all frequently true and it is highly desirable they should be realized by ethnocentric human beings; but it is virtually impossible to argue that mental defectives are "really" as intelligent as university students, in terms of those measures of intelligence which sociologists have been constrained to accept until very recently. It is also extremely difficult to deny that there appear to be ineradicable differences in intelligence even between persons of the same general background.[3]

C. Attention by scholars is in part a function of popular attention; for example, people who talk about nuclear physics have a following and a public, whereas other fields of physical study are more or less ignored. In the 1910-30 period, there was an audience for those concerned with mental deficiency. Depression and war diverted the attention of the interested and educated publics from this social problem to others. It was not until things became almost "normal" again, from the standpoint of the educated citizen, that he had time again to concern himself with mental deficiency; fortuitously, the advancement of medical research had during the 1940-53 period kept alive many low-grade mental defectives, born in middle-class families, who would previously have died; and consequently middle-class interest in mental defect has been stimulated.

In any case, from 1930-1950, sociologists, insofar as they were competing for student interest, colleague attention, and the like—and also, more significantly perhaps, insofar as they were influenced by the same factors as the intellectual public at the time—found mental deficiency a losing game, because the audience for it, real or imagined (11), did not seem impressive.

By itself, of course, this is not an adequate explanation. The present interest of some social scientists in rather complex methodological devices (such as "contact nets") stirs little public

[3]Sarason and Gladwin have recently reviewed the literature in such a way as to indicate a way out of this dilemma. (10) The writer has some doubt as to the validity of their solution. (3)

excitement. And if sociologists in the 40's had been simply following the headlines, they would have concentrated on genocide, warfare, etc. But there is a strong anti-military, anti-toughness component in the ideology of American sociologists that makes it difficult for them to believe in or tackle such topics in comprehensive fashion. At any rate, up to the present, sociological theory does not provide particularly helpful clues to understanding the prevalence of massacre in human history.

Aside from Hitler, the savage slaughters by the Ustashi in Croatia, the communal slaying in India and Pakistan immediately after World War II, the activities of such rulers as Trujillo, Stalin, and Ibn Saud, not to mention the present conceivability of supergenocide through a cobalt bomb, lend the issue some practical relevance. But what have sociologists to say about why "man is a wolf to his fellows" even though the problem is presumably a social one? It is personally depressing and discouraging to deal with such a problem anyway; and it is still more depressing when one has nothing to contribute to its solution.

D. It may well be that criteria of involvement can be set up for any given social issue, and that study will usually follow such involvement. These criteria may be: (1) drama (where "the good side" has some chance of winning), (2) the possibility of doing something or recommending something, (3) identification. The subject matter of mental deficiency is not, somehow, very dramatic; genocide is, in an eerie way, but the good can hardly win out. Few sociologists have any reason to identify themselves with mental defectives, and very few would care to put themselves either in the role of perpetrators or victims of genocide. And, from 1925 to 1955, sociologists had little to recommend in their professional role about either mental defect or genocide. Prior to 1925, the emphasis on heredity, sterilization, etc., did give many sociologists a platform regarding mental defect which they could support; in the past three or four years, some sociologists may have found in the writings of Sarason (9, 10), Perry (8), and Dexter (1, 2, 3) a perspective whose adoption they may recommend, although, for the most part, this perspective is as yet lacking in concrete practical implementation. And aside from pointing out that genocide is not very nice, what can American sociologists say about it? Have we any way of making a Rosas or a Caligula, or a March of the Cherokees less likely?

The foregoing is, of course, a speculative essay with some overstatement to make a point, as is not uncharacteristic of efforts to apply the sociology of knowledge to concrete issues. In particular, it should be stressed that the references to sociologists and social pathologists are to a central tendency, to which there are exceptions; for example, although most sociologists probably do acquire their status through intellectual skill, there are some sociologists whose status and self-confidence arise rather from good fellowship, business ability, athletic prowess, religious devotion, a sense of virtue, etc. And it should also be said that whereas the writer has read most of the social problems texts prior to 1950, and much available literature on mental deficiency, civil defense, and genocide, he may have overlooked some highly relevant changes in the emphasis of sociologists in recent years.

A meaningful study of avoidance would inquire into fields other than sociology. Why, for example, have political scientists until recently avoided the study of the government of nonstate organizations? Why is the systematic comparative method so rarely applied to local politics? Why did psychologists for long steer away from such topics as hypnosis and telepathy? Why are economists generally much more interested in the management of businesses than in institutional management?

The justification for presenting this essay is that it does have serious practical implications for teaching, research, and exposition. If it does no more than redirect attention to the possibility that, despite the rationality of our techniques of research, once we have chosen a subject for study, the choice of subjects for study may itself be needlessly and avoidably irrational, it is probably worth while; particularly so, if some of the individual observations in the text may suggest specific ways of increasing rationality in the choice of subjects for study and in determining why avoided subjects are avoided. (4)

References

1. Dexter, L. A., "A Social Theory of Mental Deficiency," *American Journal of Mental Deficiency,* 62 (March, 1958), 920-928.
2. Dexter, L. A., "Towards a Sociology of the Mentally Defective," *American Journal of Mental Deficiency,* 61 (July, 1956), 10-16.
3. Dexter, L. A., two papers read before the *American Association of Mental Deficiency:* "Comparative Politics and the Handling of Social Deviates;" "Research Needs in Mental Deficiency."
4. Dexter, L. A., "The Policy Sciences and Limited Warfare," *Political Re-*

search—*Organization and Design,* I (1958), 17-19.

5. Dexter, R. C., *Social Adjustment,* (New York: Knopf, 1927).

6. Hobbs, A., *The Claims of Sociology* (Harrisburg, Pa.: Stackpole, 1951).

7. Mills, C. W., "The Professional Ideology of Social Pathologists," *American Journal of Sociology,* 49 (September, 1943), 165-180.

8. Perry, S., "Some Theoretic Problems of Mental Deficiency and Their Action Implications," *Psychiatry,* 17 (February, 1954), 45-73.

9. Sarason, S., *Psychological Problems in Mental Deficiency,* 2nd ed. (New York: Harper's, 1953).

10. Sarason, S., and T. Gladwin, "Psychological and Cultural Problems in Mental Subnormality: A Review of Research," *American Journal of Mental Deficiency,* 62 (May, 1958), 1115-1307.

11. Zimmerman, C., and R. A. Bauer, "The Effect of an Audience on What Is Remembered," *Public Opinion Quarterly,* 20 (Spring, 1956), 238-248.

SOCIAL PROBLEMS AND SOCIOLOGICAL THEORY
Alfred R. Lindesmith

Members and friends of the Society: I want tonight to make a brief statement of the reasons which cause me to believe in and support this society and to hope that it will continue to prosper. In doing so I shall perhaps somewhat overstate and oversimplify my case in order to emphasize my point and for the sake of brevity. I trust that whatever this talk lacks in wit and wisdom will be to some degree compensated for by its brevity.

As I see it, there is a sharp and categorical difference between the concern with social problems and the interest in sociological theory. The former involves applied or practical research and the attempt to influence policy. It is almost always a many-sided, multidisciplinary matter, and involves committing oneself on questions of value or morality, as when legal reform is advocated for the sake of justice or when police reform is urged to protect or restore civil liberties.

In contrast, the task of theory construction is, and probably must be, the

Presidential address to the Society for the Study of Social Problems delivered on August 28, 1960 at the Gov. Clinton Hotel, New York. N. Y., reprinted, with permission of author and publisher, from *Social Problems*, 8, No. 2, Fall, 1960, 98-102.

concern of single disciplines which focus their attention on particular aspects of human social behavior concerning which they seek to formulate valid and significant generalizations. To qualify for the honorific designation of "scientific" these formulations must satisfy a number of requirements which, in the study of human behavior, are especially hard to meet. It is not enough that the writer be careful and exact, that he use numbers rather than words, that the generalizations have no practical implications, or that they be couched in complicated and abstruse language. To qualify as scientific, generalizations of the social scientist must measure up to those standards and specifications which are reasonably clearly established and formulated in the tradition and literature of modern Western science.

In this concern with the development of theory it is desirable and inevitable that the sociologist concentrate on sociological rather than social problems. In his scientific role he is concerned merely with what things are, not with what ought to be. He seeks to be detached, dispassionate, objective and impartial. When he has his scientific hat on he avoids the ethical commitments and value judgments involved in social policy and, I am inclined to think, he is usually not qualified as a scientist to speak authoritatively on social problems. I say this because such problems are not exclusively sociological but are compounds of many diverse elements which are not the exclusive concern of any single discipline.

Having said these things it may appear that the argument leads logically to the conclusion that the sociologist ought not be concerned at all with social problems as such. There was a time when I thought that this was so and I am still inclined to agree that, insofar as he is a scientist, the sociologist's central concern is not with social problems. The dilemma of the sociologist who wishes to be a scientist and who is at the same time vitally concerned with matters that are the subject of controversy on the practical policy level, is most properly handled, in my opinion, not by renouncing one's civic responsibilities but by accepting them and keeping them separate from one's scientific responsibilities. There are risks in whatever one does, but I think the risks here are greatest when the sociologist sets himself apart from his society and tries to limit himself, so far as his public functions are concerned, to being a "pure" and "basic" scientist.

This attempt to be "pure" and "basic" is all too often stultifying and leads frequently to hypocrisy, irresponsibility, pretentiousness and sometimes to evasion or outright dishonesty. To use an illustration from a field in which I am especially interested, there are those who do scientific studies of drug addiction and refuse, in the name of science, to commit themselves on the policy question. This seems hypocritical and evasive to me when the individual concerned, from his dealings with addicts, has acquired some ideas

on policy with respect to them. If one has such views and conceals them, this is simply a lack of frankness and has nothing to do with science. The scientific pose that is regularly assumed is that more money should be spent on research before we can know what we ought to do. This attitude tends to maximize the flow of research funds, but it also often puts the investigator on the side of the status quo. The more miserably and ineffectively the drug problem is handled the more money will be spent investigating it. The effects of a change in policy can never be exactly predicted and if reform must wait until we are sure of the future it will wait forever.

Another aspect of this matter is to ask whether the scientific theories for the sake of which sociologists renounce their civic responsibilities are worth it. Despite the optimistic and constructive attitudes which we tend to assume publicly when we face our undergraduate classes or the members of other disciplines which are as vulnerable as we are, I think most of us privately realize that we have not traveled far enough along the path of science to take ourselves too seriously in this respect. Much of what passes as theory is not really that. More often it is common sense dressed up in fancy verbiage and sometimes it is just verbiage. Much of what is taken as progress consists of the substitution of new words for old ones and many allegedly original ideas turn out to be merely a reflection of inadequate familiarity with the contents of libraries.

While I think that progress is being made in creating a more scientific sociology, I also feel that one has only to read our journals to realize that many investigators are trying to join the scientific family by sneaking in the back door without credentials. One feature of this attempt is to make a virtue of the impracticality of what one does, the assumption being that since it is impractical it must be scientific. Much of the research for which such claims are made falls between two stools, and, being neither practical nor scientific, has no significance at all. One wonders if it would not be better to drop the scientific pretension which is not backed up by the substance of science and limit oneself to enterprises which at least have the virtue of practical relevance. I would not go so far as to advocate this as the goal of sociology. All I want to emphasize is that it is not a sin for a scientist to be concerned with the social problems of his community or society; it is closer to a sin for him not to be so concerned.

Another of the diseases of our discipline which is connected, I think, with our attempt to divorce ourselves from the practical concerns of our society is an excessive preoccupation with techniques at the expense of subject matter. This has led to what has been called the "trivialization" of research in which answers having the appearance of great precision are sought for questions which hardly seem to matter, or in which the self-evident is substantiated within an inch of its life. The image of the sociologist from this viewpoint appears to have become that of a clever technician, available for hire, flitting from one problem to another as research subsidies become available. The criteria for the selection of projects appears to be, not the importance of the problem, but availability of funds and of data amenable to certain types of treatment.

The experiences connected with being involved in and concerned with social problems is, I think, an excel-lent counter-irritant to the tendency of academicians to become over-subtle, over-theoretical, over-pretentious and over-confident of their own verbal and numerical formulations. It is a good thing, even vital, for example, for the criminologist who analyzes crime with I. B. M. machines to visit or know about courts, law, prisons and the police and to be actively concerned with the reform of these institutions when they need it. Association with people of diverse backgrounds and professions who share a common interest in social policy tends to keep one humble and gives one roots in the society which nurtures and supports him. Without this touchstone I think there is a tendency for research to come to be regarded as a racket or merely a convenient way to acquire a reputation, get promotions and make a living.

Thus, while it seems that it is the central job of the sociologist to advance theoretical knowledge I will venture that he should, as a protection against the involutional disorders of excessive academic isolation, maintain as an avocation at least an interest in at least one problem area. In this area I think he should be an expert and an activist, seeking to know not only what pertains to his discipline but everything that he can learn and to exert influence on policy. Properly conceived and managed I believe that this kind of an interest serves to correct some of the typical academic diseases and ultimately serves the cause of scientific advancement.

One wonders how long it will be before there will come an academic Day of Judgment when, perhaps, the long-suffering patient subjects who fill out our questionnaires and submit themselves for interviews will get the idea they are being exploited and demand an accounting. Perhaps those who pay the bills will some time add up all the money and man-hours expended in "pure" research, balance it against the results, and wonder whether it has been worth it. Certainly it is reasonable to expect that there eventually will be some kind of pay-off in the form of public disillusionment and disenchantment for the present halcyon days of easy money. When this pay-off comes I am convinced that the sociologist who will come off the best will be the one who has not written exclusively for other sociologists and who has not washed his hands of all practical affairs.

The therapeutic effects of practical interests and activities arise in the main, I think, from communicating with persons who are not sociologists, social scientists or academicians. Scientific results must, after all, be communicated. Just as the standards by which scientific conclusions are judged are not derived from a single discipline, so also must these conclusions be disseminated and judged beyond the confines of single disciplines and beyond the confines of the academic world. It is a valuable but often chastening experience to try to tell the hard-headed intelligent layman or administrative official what the latest sociological discoveries have been in the field of his competence. Not being able to use the specialized language of our discipline we often find that when compelled to resort to straight-away English some of the glamour and originality of the ideas seems to vanish. One would hardly, for example, use that magic French word *anomie* in talking to non-sociologists but when this concept is expressed in ordinary English words, as it can be, it seems to lose much of its charm and much of its explanatory potency. I do not think that it can be contended that sociology is so advanced

today that its solid achievements can not be formulated in language which an intelligent layman can grasp. We need to communicate in this manner with people outside our fields in order to maintain our own health.

One of the unformulated assumptions which we are led to make by the desire to be regarded as scientists even if we are not is that research is an end in itself, and that it is a noble enterprise per se to spend government or foundation money in doing it. This assumption is manifestly false. Carried to its extreme it sometimes leads to the exploitation of human subjects for personal aggrandizement and to the perversion of the scientific spirit. The goal becomes simply that of securing funds. The more problems there are and the more ineffectively they are dealt with, the greater the flow of subsidies. Under such circumstances it is easy to accept the rationalizations which keep one out of controversy, which do not jeopardize the sources of funds and which support the status quo.

To use drug addiction as an illustration again, the greatly increased prevalence of addiction, especially of young persons after the late war, was a blessing for those looking for research funds. By and large the money that has been put into the study of this problem was probably put into it for practical objectives, to further the understanding of addiction in order to improve the methods of controlling and dealing with it. The proper methods of control are, it happens, the subject of bitter controversy between conflicting schools of thought, between those who advocate reform and those who oppose and often have something to lose from it. In the studies of addiction that have been made since it became a popular subject, remarkably little attention has been given to the crucial aspects of the problem which are the issues in this popular debate and on which policy is based. Without in any way disparaging what has been done, it seems more than a coincidence that so few researchers have looked into what might be called the "hot" aspects of the subject.

There is, in short, serious danger of being corrupted by those who give us money, and the danger is increased by the attractiveness of the rationalizations by which this seduction is effected. The investigator who unwittingly, perhaps, comes to put the securing of funds in first place, necessarily thereby loses some of his scientific objectivity and independence and often neglects important aspects of his subject. A vital participating interest in problems is, I think, some protection, at least, against this kind of perversion, and helps to keep us honest and independent by reminding us of our responsibilities to our subjects, our society and our principles. It is in this spirit, rather than in that of an artificial and radical detachment, that the solid accomplishments of the social sciences are likely to be made.

This society represents to me both a protest against some of the trends which I have mentioned and a means of giving organized opportunity to the desire to express oneself freely and participate more fully in controversial matters of public policy. Because I feel that this activity should be kept distinct from the scientific function, I hope that this society does not become simply another sociological society in which these functions are not separated and in which non-sociologists are not at home. This society is an interest group or association of interest groups rather than a professional association. As such I think

it has already had a significant effect as a gesture of protest and in providing an avenue of expression for interests and a point of view that for a time were close to being outlawed by the advocates of "purity."

As I said at the beginning, I have probably overstated my case. I do not wish to imply that there is nothing to be said for pure and basic social science or for sociological theory. On the contrary, I think there is much to be said for them, but there is little point in saying it here because this concern is not currently threatened, and has in fact been oversold. It seems to me that there is perhaps too much energy being expended in this direction on what has been called "grand theory." Some of this seems to me like working on the tower of a structure which still lacks an adequate foundation. In any case, scientific purity is not assured by the negative acts of refusing to participate in community affairs or of not committing oneself on questions of value or public morality. It is more likely to be assured, as I have indicated, by a judicious balancing of the detached theoretical attitude and that of active participation in the process of change, provided that this combination is coupled with an understanding of the differences between these two orientations. Each has its special risks, limitations, abuses and biases and these need to be analyzed and guarded against. To a considerable extent these two perspectives serve as correctives for each other with the practical attitude constantly checking the abuses and excesses of the theoretical, and the theoretical giving depth and historical perspective to the practical.

I think it is futile to renounce the practical concern, because, from the very fact that we live in a society, we are committed to its values and norms. The assumption of a purely detached theoretical attitude means only that one does not recognize this commitment and the responsibilities it imposes, and that without knowing it, one aligns oneself by default with the opponents of reform. I think that this society was established with something like this in mind and I think it represents the views of many more people than its membership might indicate. I trust that it will in the future realize its goals and define its special functions even more fully than it has in the past.

PART II   GENERIC NATIONAL SOCIAL PROBLEMS

2

WAR AND NATIONAL DEFENSE

Defining War and National Defense

War, as we shall use the term in this chapter, is an institutional form of violent conflict between nations. War is a legal condition that 'permits' two or more nations to conduct a violent conflict. This notion of a legal condition is a significant myth: It allows the state-authorized leadership of a society to distinguish between types of conflict—between accident and attack, between planned homicide and mob action. Unlike rebellion, revolution, sabotage and subversion (all of which are events that lead toward or result from war), warfare is an officially recognized condition of state.

This definition of war proved serviceable up to World War I. It is somewhat inadequate for the twentieth century. War has become more than legalized military conflict between states. The kind of warfare suggested by this definition was overt and politically sanctioned. Today we understand this to be but one kind of *conventional* war.

When revolutionaries engage in military conflicts, they are apt to define their engagements as part of a conventional civil war. The government in control, however, often tries to keep the conflict unconventional. In the resulting uncertainty, foreign governments may exploit the internal revolution and so wage war without recognition of this as a legal condition.

Any narrow definition of contemporary warfare is thus inadequate. The modern definition would see war as a comprehensive system of cultural patterns and institutions involving legalized homicide among whole populations.

Nations engage in military conflict in order to meet the requirements of certain types of situations, at least as these are perceived by national leaders. Customarily, these requirements are interpreted as matters of vital national interest (although such a concept is impossible to define) and the relevant situations are those that occur chiefly outside the home territory of the state.

The language used to justify military conflict is couched in terms of *defense* of the national interest. In reporting on changes in military programs and in summarizing annual budget increase, Secretary of Defense Robert S. McNamara wrote that the United States now enjoys:

...a greater range of military alternatives with which to meet threats of aggression. The actions taken have accelerated the size and mobility of limited war forces, and improved the readiness of all units to respond to sudden emergencies. They are not intended for offensive purposes but to deter potential aggressors from pressing their demands to the point of military conflict . . . . The primary purpose of our arms is peace, not war . . . . Our arms will never be used to strike the first blow in any attack . . . . Our defense posture must be designed to reduce the danger of irrational or unpremeditated general war— the danger of an unnecessary escalation of a small war into a larger one, or miscalculation . . . of . . . enemy intention.[1]

Within this framework of policy, American society, in both its public and private sectors, is organized to wage war. The social, technical, environmental, and demographic arrangements for maintaining national interests, especially preserving national security, are the most complex and largest investments made by the society.

War and American History

Of course, the national government and private sectors of American society are and always have been organized to do many things besides wage war. The United States is currently and has been historically invested (unevenly, of course) in maintaining the apparatus for waging war. It is necessary to stimulate awareness of this: otherwise it may be ignored through avoidance of the unpleasant, through nationalism and chauvinism, or merely through lack of understanding of foreign relations, national security, and domestic social policy.

Nor is the historical and social significance of war for the modern nation of the United States—among many other nations—always clearly understood. Wars, and mobilization of the ability to wage wars, have stabilized temporarily the conflicting interests between the United States and other nations. Warfare has been a chief means of change in the domestic social and technological structures of American society. War, or the threat of it, has had a major role in building American national society. Military force has been essential in spreading and developing American civilization, both domestically in the opening of the Western frontier, and internationally, as the occasion for intense exchange between this and other cultures.

The social fact is that war, or simply emphasis on defense, have often contributed powerfully to the stimulation of great national social problems.[2] The functions that war and defense have served in the course of American history have also been profoundly contradictory. The American Civil War came as close to destroying the social structure as it did to fostering a new level of solidarity among the populations of the northern states. American wars, in other words, have fostered solidarity but at the cost of annihilation of groups, as with the American Indian. Wars have negated and otherwise subverted various individual values, moreover; but they have not always had this effect

[1]*Department of Defense Annual Report for Fiscal Year 1961*, U.S. Government Printing Office, Washington, D.C., 1962, pp. 4-5.

[2]See John U. Nef, *War and Human Progress*, Cambridge: Harvard University Press, 1950.

upon the total community. In short, not all aspects of warfare and defense have been socially disorganizing, any more than they represent 'glorious chapters' in the nation's history.

The United States may well be a 'peace-loving democracy,' but it is also a warring country, to judge from the record.[3] Between 1776 and 1941, American soldiers or sailors were actively engaged somewhere in military conflict during all but twenty years. Every reader knows something of the pattern since 1941. No American government has ever waged war from a conviction that armed conflict is mystically or intrinsically beneficial; but wars have been waged as a continuation of politics by other means, as well as for strictly defensive reasons.

The frequency and intensity of American military involvement cannot be over-emphasized as the basis for the authority of this interpretation. From 1776 to 1900, for example, American army units participated in more than 9,000 battles and skirmishes, and naval units engaged in more than 1,100 episodes of violent conflict. This is an average of about 90 violent conflicts with military weapons of state per year over the first 125 years of national life. This, exclusive of all military conflicts *since* 1900!

Like most other powerful and emerging nation states, then, the United States has engaged fairly continuously in war in efforts to maintain, defend, and, on occasion, to extend, its territory and its population. War has also been conducted to fulfill treaty obligations and sustain international alliances and to change the place of America in the

[3]Facts in this section derived from Quincy Wright, *A Study of War*, Chicago: University of Chicago Press, 1942.

hierarchy of international power. To this mode of conflict, and to our ability to mobilize it as a threat, we owe many cherished accomplishments and values, including territorial integrity, self-government, and the maintenance of the democratic forms of vital institutions.

War and Defense As American Social Problems

In view of these social and historical facts, how do we come to regard warfare and the potential for waging war which constitutes the national defense establishment, as a major national social problem? Is not the ability to wage war simply a major characteristic — indeed, a crucial precondition — of *national* society, or the nation-state?

War has become a social problem for twentieth-century America because war has ceased to serve the functions it once served. Its continuation under contemporary conditions can prove lethally disorganizing for the national society.

As with other Western nations, the pattern for war in the United States prior to 1916 was cyclical. The United States would fight a major war, and then let its military manpower and hardware erode while it rebuilt its domestic economy. After that, it again built up a war force. When this force has reached a certain point, the perfected instrument has been tried in a minor war which, after another fifteen or twenty years, has been followed by another major war.

War, prior to this century, exhibited a periodicity. The cycle correlated with changes in domestic technology, international trade, and with changes in foreign relations between states. Only since 1917, has the cycle itself changed drastically so that the United States has been deeply involved in armed warfare on a major or a minor scale during every decade except that of the Great Depression.

Just as the cycle was contained, so was the magnitude of warfare restricted prior to World War I. Not until the 1870s did the size and cost of armies and navies in the United States begin to exceed a small proportion of the population and the national income. In this century compared to the nineteenth, size, cost, and civilian mobilization adjunct to the American war potential each increased by more than twenty times, relative to population and income.

Investment is paralleled by extent of economic and social costs. In but 200 days of combat, 115 thousand American soldiers (Army only) died from battle-wounds and disease in World War I. Another 206 thousand were returned to the States as wounded and handicapped survivors. In World War II, 315 thousand Americans were killed, 152 thousand listed as missing, and 678 thousand wounded. Wars in any century are prodigious wasters of life, but the critical change in the history of war as an institution occurred in the twentieth century. Two times as many men were killed in battle during World War I, for example, than were killed in all the major wars from 1790 to 1913.

American participation in the two world wars is also less a military fact than a general history of increasing national mobilization. As President Wilson remarked, "It is not an army that we must shape and train for war, it is a nation." In both conflagrations, a previously unfettered national economy was reorganized into a military machine. (Under the impress of mobilization for World War I, for instance, the American railroad system broke down. The gov-

ernment took it over, together with the telephone and telegraph and express companies. In manufacturing, ordinary peacetime products all but ceased to be produced. For two years, the War Industries Board served as virtual economic dictator.)

Moreover, the new wars have no clear ending. In the fall of 1945, after more than six years of total conflict in which more than sixty million persons met their deaths, the beginnings of the Cold War were apparent. Then the Council of Foreign Ministers ended its first postwar meeting in London without agreement on any important issue and with sharp wrangling between Soviet and Western representatives.

World War II, in short, had catastrophic effects upon international stability. This total conflict 'ended' with groups of participants more fully organized than ever to continue violent conflict. The present Cold War is a consequence of political possibilities that developed during World War II, just as World War II was an outcome of World War I. A thermonuclear World War III, moreover, is a possibility rooted in the Manhattan Project and the Hiroshima bombing.

Twentieth-century warfare differs in other basic respects from previous patterns as well. Changes in military technology and in the extent of forces mobilized has meant a critical increase in the length of battles over time, in the number of battles engaged in during each year of conflict, and in the number of countries involved in each war. In other words, twentieth-century war is totalistic in increasing intensity and extensity. Vastly more energy, human and material, is invested, and the conflict rages across entire continents. Half of all the nation states in the world were drawn into World War I, for example, between 1914 and 1917. No more than a handful of nations enjoyed military neutrality during World War II.

Total war ceased to be a controllable instrument of national policy as of 1914.[4] In this sense, the continuing likelihood of total war has become a new kind of social problem for America. When we treat war as a social problem, we refer to a problem that emerges into the future. Extreme military preparedness and the Cold War are immediate expressions of the continuing problem. They are symptoms of future possibilities, of a more cataclysmic phase in the cycle of the 'war system.'

No society can prevent or avert violence. Men, and groups of men will always take the law into their own hands, for example. By twentieth-century total war, however, we mean a case in which the government of one nation mobilizes its population to try to kill off the population and destroy the facilities of some other nation. This type of war is a special type of institutionalized phenomenon. War has occurred everywhere and at all times in world history, but total war involving entire populations is a twentieth-century institution. The problematic feature of total war is not that it is a violent way of settling or waging conflicts, but that it has become an institution that implicates every facet of a national society.

Total war between nations, moreover, is *not caused*. There is no merit in the assumption that if one could isolate the causes of past wars, wars could be controlled in the future. Wars between modern nations result from disputes over interests or intentions that develop into violent controversy and then into total war. The range of possi-

[4]See Raymond Aron, *The Century of Total War,* New York: Doubleday, 1954.

ble types of disputes is infinite; hence the causes of total war are infinite in number.

Technology and the Problem

Over the entire history of the rise of nation states, war was institutionalized as a particular kind of violent contest, as a game that could be won. It is only since 1914 that this game has broken down. As a game, war prior to 1914 was disorganizing to the loser and painful *but enhancing* to the winner.

One brief reference to the new situation of World War I will convey the sense in which the game itself broke down: In the land fighting of World War I the machine gun and the practice of using barbed wire brought the war game to a quick stalemate. The machine gun so increased firepower that the defense was immensely strengthened. As a result of this, the trench system developed. Neither side could dislodge the other. For a year both sides wallowed in muddy trenches. The stalemate of the trenches was broken by the innovation of the tank. The breakdown of the war game is not a one-time affair. Each disorganizing stalemate is overcome, temporarily, by a technological change. By late in World War II, for example, the anti-tank gun proved a match for the tank. And by 1960, distinctions between offensive and defensive weaponry had tended to disintegrate.

The institution of total war has become a race between mutually and continuously *deterred* weapons systems. The concept of deterrence represents the deterioration of war as a contest. Nuclear deterrence, for example, is not an idea that concerns the application of force. It is not a practice of violent coercion. It is rather a notion about how to exploit *potential* force politically. Deterrence is concerned with persuading the enemy that he should in his own interest avoid certain courses of activity. Deterrence in theory is the skillful *non-use* of war.

Types of War: Limited War

There are *types* of war and *stages* of development and disintegration of the war institution. Among these, limited war and total war are the objects of current American concern.[5,6]

Only five years passed between the surrender of Japan and the progressive involvement of the United States in limited wars. Korea (1950-1953) was followed by Indochina (1951-1954), Guatemala (1954), the Congo (1960), Cuba (1961), Laos (1961), Vietnam (1962), the Dominican Republic (1965), and assorted partial operations in other areas. The political merits of each limited action are of no concern here. What is important is that modes of military, paramilitary, and nonmilitary conflict have evolved that have become a standing practice of the United States

[5]J. K. Zawodny, special editor, *Unconventional Warfare*, Philadelphia: Annals of the American Academy of Political and Social Sciences, 1962.

[6]Limited war has evolved during the twentieth century on the model of the Spanish Civil War. Two regularities are worth noting. The myth of national sovereignty has been exploited and abused. Internal strains and conflicts are used as the grounds for intervention. Local revolutions are fomented where they do not already exist or seized upon where they do as occasions for larger-scale power struggles. This may be deliberate, as in Korea or Cuba, or an outcome, as in the African Congo. Secondly, as in the Spanish model, the local conflict becomes a staging area for war games by the larger powers. This suggests an evolutionary feature: local wars since Hiroshima have stopped short of the use of nuclear weapons. See Klaus E. Knorr, *The War Potential of Nations*, Princeton, N.J.: Princeton University Press, 1956.

as well as of all other major powers in the postwar world.

Limited war is financially very costly. Its political outcomes are hard to determine in advance. And its risk as a stimulus to total war is ever present. Yet limited war has evolved as an institution of international conflict that stops short of total war. It is a type of extremely hard bargaining. It involves forms of mutual recognition and communication, as the Cuban crisis demonstrated. It is now used when two nations cannot or will not negotiate, or when neither would trust the other in any agreement reached through diplomacy.

Limited war is an institutionalized adjustment to total nuclear war. For example, consider the strategic position of the forces of the North Atlantic Treaty Organization. In case of a Soviet land attack on a moderate scale in Europe, NATO could choose to fight a limited war, in type of weapons and extent of territory. Such resistance on a small scale would require the Soviet Union to retreat from a military stalemate or to take a step toward increased violence and, therefore, total violence. The sequence of decisions in this example shows that limited war becomes possible primarily against a backdrop of total war. Both sides bargain with their backs against a threat that total war might occur. There is an interval of decision between conflict and holocaust that springs from this new form of warfare.

Limited war fits another special consideration: it is adapted to influencing events within the third of the world—Southeast Asia, Africa, and parts of South America—where basic social and power structures are highly unstable. Thus it is an instrument that fits the difficulty of hard bargaining short of total war between the major powers, and the periodic involvement of the major powers in the pursuit of interests in these unstable areas.

None of this is intended to give approbation to limited war, nor is this a short course in the evolution of military strategy. Military men would distinguish sharply between the forms of limited war, for example. What is suggested here is that, since 1946, war considered as an American social problem has come to mean the prospect of total nuclear war's resulting from either the *policy* of nuclear deterrence or the fact of the growing world *arsenal* of nuclear weapons.

The utility of limited conventional war is reflected in the speech of United States Under Secretary of State George Ball to the NATO Parliamentarians' Conference in November, 1962: "Because we had clear superiority of conventional forces, we were not confronted with the awful dilemma of having to utilize major nuclear weapons or to retreat from our objective." The Cuban Crisis, Ball claimed, "proved the wisdom, indeed the necessity, of the measured response." Immediate resort to military force "might have led the United States and the Soviet Union up an ascending scale of violence."[7]

Nuclear War

The truly problematic facet of the present American security problem is thus the ever-present possibility of a total, a thermonuclear war. This potentiality is an outgrowth of the theory of deterrence upon which the United States has based its security and its for-

[7]The purpose of this speech was to emphasize that what NATO needs is expanded *conventional* forces to meet localized political and military pressures in the future.

eign relations for 20 years. The core tenet of nuclear deterrence is that total war is avoided only when each of the potential enemies can produce a devastating blow to its opponent. It constitutes a strategy for avoiding total war through a power standoff.

The United States has actively pursued nuclear deterrence in an effort to prevent a future thermonuclear war. The twin problems of this policy are first, that the policy carries no guarantee that total war will not start and that if it does, that the entire society will not be destroyed; and second, that the long-term costs of maintaining a nuclear deterrent — financial and social — are corrosive in their influence upon the character of the national society.

The first danger is that, given the means to wage total war, something will occur which will result in the commitment of nuclear stockpiles to such an all-out war. The *something* here has numerous variants. To list but a few, consider what military experts call 'false preemption'; a false warning of an impending attack is received by the Soviet Union or the United States. The warning triggers the delivery of offensive forces against the alleged aggressor. A second form is simple accident: Men in command of offensive weapons lose control and give an unauthorized command to fire; or mechanical failures occur in any one of the hundreds of inter-related control systems that make up the vast, intricate machinery of nuclear weaponry. Another form is escalation. A limited conventional war is fought by commanders who have access to atomic weapons and who cross the ambiguous line between two types of artillery explosives.

Other types present equally horrible possibilities. Diplomatic threats in the game of brinksmanship might have to be carried out, or they might be taken seriously by the enemy. The Soviet Union could miscalculate its position and, out of ignorance or overconfidence, initiate a nuclear attack. A third country could touch off a nuclear conflict, with even an extremely limited nuclear capability of its own, by capitalizing on the extreme distrust between East and West. The source of the initial blast, for example, could be disguised.

These are but a few of the ways in which total nuclear war could begin; in which deterrence, the application of potential force, could — without or with intent — become the application of penultimate violence. The first major problem then is not that such a war could begin. It is that a nuclear war could destroy the national society.

Under nuclear deterrence, each nation is a standing *hostage* to the other. Each is a hostage because the possibility of lethal reprisals is unaffected by the deathblow of a substantial first strike. Either side has in reserve a store of deliverable weapons that make a second strike — a final revenge — possible. Victory is impossible, in the gross or in matter of degree. Mutual annihilation is the totally persuasive prospect in the event of an attack by either side.

The United States and the Soviet Union are both more than amply prepared to wage immediate, total, nuclear war. Newly developing weapons systems like the Army Nike Zeus antimissile missile, or the Air Force proposal for a nuclear armed satellite system, may provide in the future some small measure of defense against ballistic missiles. It remains technologically inconceivable, however, that an effective defense will *ever* evolve. A percentage of nuclear missiles would get through. Even if the percentage is reduced substantially, the United States presently has a nuclear capability at least 50 times greater than that required to destroy the city populations of any major society on the globe. We assume that the Soviet Union maintains an equivalent retaliatory capacity. There is far more than enough killing power to go around, to be shared between military and civilian-industrial targets.

Two Other 'Total' Deterrents

It should be evident to most Americans within a few years, if it is not already, that large-scale nuclear warfare could obliterate this society and others. The obliteration extends beyond the bulk of the civilian population to include destruction of the physical environment and extreme disorganization of the national social order. The same understanding, however, must extend to the chemical and biological capabilities for societal annihilation.

Chemical warfare (commonly referred to as CW) and biological warfare (BW) are thoroughly developed weapons available to both the Soviet and the American governments. Technical development of these weapons has followed the inexorable line of growth common to all other types of twentieth century armaments. For example, about 40,000 tons of war gases were used on the battlefield during World War I by Germany alone. By 1942, Nazi Germany was stockpiling war gases at the rate of 184,000 tons a year. In addition, the Nazis produced two new gases, Tabun and Sarin, both more lethal and more readily deliverable than anything used in World War I, at a rate of thousands of tons annually. The German production plant for generating Tabun was captured by the Russians and moved to the Soviet Union in 1946, where it was reassembled and set in operation. The United States has adopted the other German gas, Sarin, as one of its standards. Both gases, together with a third, Soman (which has even greater lethal strength), are stockpiled in various countries today.

The Sergeant Missile, built under contract for the United States Department of Defense, contains a 1,600 pound warhead designed to carry not only conventional explosives or nuclear charges, but, alternatively, chemical or bacterial payloads. BW capabilities include not only a wide variety of viruses lethal to humans but many that could destroy the environment and thus the human economy through attacks on animals and plants. Taken in combination, nuclear, BW, and CW weapons offer an array of devastating modes of warfare.

There are limits on each. Both BW and CW, for instance, cannot be delivered effectively without accurate meteorological forecasting over wide areas of the environment. Errors could recoil upon the attacking power. But in combination, there is no adequate defense against total war. Just as the specific yield of a 1961 nuclear bomb is 1,000 times that of the yield of the atomic bombs dropped on Japan in 1945, so a total World War III *could* be absolute in its destructive power. Even if millions of persons were to survive such a total war in the United States, the scope of BW alone has consequences that reach far beyond the issue of short term survival.

Return to the Social Problem

The United States has reached a point in a world situation where defense of its own population and territory is an impossibility. There exist technological and military forces that cannot only damage and impair, but can destroy, more or less completely, the national community. Chapter One defined a serious national social problem as a condition that has been defined by significant groups within a population as a deviation from or breakdown of, some social standard these groups believe must be upheld if life or the order of activities that maintains life is to continue. Total war is therefore the gravest social problem confronting the society. Its future dimension as a problem is that the entire society can be destroyed. Its present dimension is that the society is extremely vulnerable: its territory and members cannot be protected from annihilation, hence its continuing survival as a national society is threatened. The past dimension is a century of progressively more and more efficient application of the scientific method to the technology of war.

The Future Dimension

The social problem posed by the threat of total war has been described. We have not tried to assess the likelihood of the threat's becoming a reality, except to detail the various ways in which events, political, military, or mechanical, could conspire, intentionally or unintentionally. Because we are dealing with a possibility located in the future, we must analyze the past and present conditions that shape this future.

The concepts that best explain the social conditions underlying the threat of total war are disorganized relations between nations, and the application to these unstable relations of a technological-military force that is radically incompatible with the requirements for survival. That inter-nation relations will be unstable, and that they will disorganize periodically toward violent conflict, is more than a historical fact: It is generic to the institutional design of a world community built around nations whose governments must behave as if they are sovereign. In this respect, the total wars of this century as well as those of the nineteenth century are products of nationalism.

Total war does not become absolutely problematical, however, except by virtue of technological change. It is for this reason that we emphasize the way in which war is a major social problem: *The obliterative potential of total war today is the core of the problem.* This potential results from the pace of technological change. For example, before World War I, there were no deaths from bombing raids. If the rate of civilian deaths from bombing in World War I is taken as base one, the rate in World War II was 120 times greater. If a line is drawn across these points and is projected into the future, we should expect total population annihilation to be the case in any future world war. This forecast, made by sociologist Hornell Hart, does not include any deaths from nuclear bombs or other atomic weapons, incidentally. Thus nuclear, bacterial, and chemical weapons are not even necessary to the achievement of absolute destructiveness in any future total war. They are but high points in the accelerating growth of military technology generally.

The organization of foreign relations, while far less tangible than the instruments of war, is also a matter of cultural inventions. We can talk about the technology of inter-nation politics, so that the concept of incompatible rates refers to differences in the rate of change in the weapons system versus the system of foreign relations.

The main instrument of modern nation states for handling foreign relations is alliance to maintain a balance of power. This device is as old as the Greek city-state. It uses the maxim that aggressors are less likely to attempt conquest if they face the mobilized war potential not only of a single victim but of a number of states which have joined together to maintain the existing order.

The invention is intended to serve several objectives. Rivalries and conflicts between states are controlled, usually, by preserving the peace. The independence of participating allies is preserved by preventing any one state from dominating all others. And, the looseness of the alliance frees states to try to change their individual positions in a hierarchy of relative power without impairing the overall balance.

These functions sometimes contradict one another. Stability may be sacrificed to independence or power. Worse yet, international communication is weak; perceptions of regimes within the balance differ and change. Generally, there are countless possibilities for disorganization to set in. War may be waged for no purpose whatever, so far as many of the participating allies are concerned.

There are features of a system of balances that render the scheme weak under any circumstances. Nevertheless, the scheme worked effectively once. From the victory over the Spanish Armada until roughly a century after Waterloo, England successfully dominated the non-European world commercially and militarily, and prevented total war in Europe. A variety of forces undermined this balance. Foremost were changes in military technology. Steam navigation, the screw propeller, iron hull, armor plate, rifled naval guns, and finally, the invention of the airplane transformed the war potential of European nations. By 1910, England was unable to hold this balance of power. The invention of new military instruments led (as it had in efforts at conquest reaching back to the phalanx of Alexander) to disorganization of the balance. Stability under a balance of power depends upon defensible territorial frontiers. World War I and the new weapons it revealed eliminated security through alliance. Small states were conquered in a few days, before the support of allies could be mobilized.

The current situation repeats this pattern. Nuclear weapon systems, the North Atlantic Treaty Organization, the Warsaw Pact, and similar current arrangements constitute efforts by West and East to reconstruct a balance of power. Nuclear striking power and conventional military treaties, with degrees of integration of the schemes, now provide the equivalent of British naval supremacy within the nineteenth-century balance of power. The idea of nuclear deterrence is the notion of a power standoff. In the two decades since World War II, the Western world has stablized around a military stalemate.

Like other balances attempted in this century, however, the nuclear stalemate is vulnerable to changes in weapon technology. Too great a nuclear force on one side could trigger a desperate offensive on the other. Antimissile missiles may develop to a point where one power estimates (however incorrectly) that it can attack without danger of national suicide. And as the entire system elaborates, ever larger, more specialized weapons, technical accidents, and miscalculations of intent become more likely. The existing balance has worked. The problem is that there are no guarantees that the political and other organizational machinery regulating a balance grounded in weapons technology can continue to preserve the peace.

A second cultural invention intended to control relations between states is *collective security* through international organization. The United Nations represents the present peak of development in the evolution of this institution. Even among the Western nations that have fostered collective security most assiduously, however—and this includes the United States—the United Nations has been defined as complementing, not replacing, the conventions of the power balance.

The persistent attitude is this: The United Nations is a promising step toward a goal of collective security. The goal, according to this attitude, may not be reached for a hundred years, or a hundred generations. The United Nations is viewed as worth working through so long as it contributes something to security. When its activities do not correspond with national security activities; when its powers seem insufficient for realizing national objectives; or when its goals conflict with national goals, a state should retain it as a "splendid experiment," but should resort to more direct means for national security.

There are thus points at which power balances and international organization conflict. The two institutions may reinforce one another, but only until the balance is threatened by events not controlled by the United Nations. When national policies necessary for maintaining the balance of power are antagonistic to the conditions of membership in the United Nations, it is the younger weaker obligation to the world organization that is sacrificed.

Equally crucial to our conception of war is the lag between the war potential of states and the war potential of the United Nations. Since its formation, the United Nations has increased its ability to mount armed force against an aggressor nation and to prevent inter-nation warfare. Evolution in the integration of political with technological force in the United Nations has been demonstrated in Israel, Korea, and the Congo, in particular. But there remain great deficiencies in this development. There exists no member state consensus about the police powers of the international organization, nor are there means to secure the weapons and soldier-power for coercive action.

A third institutional invention, the combining of isolationism with neutrality, persists as a means of coping with conflict. The United States and other countries of the Western hemisphere employed these devices with some success on occasions prior to World War I. The notion that isolation was a viable strategy continued until Pearl Harbor, when it became apparent that neither isolation nor neutrality were possible any longer; not for large and influential nations, at least, and not for any country caught in the path of the vastly extended areas of combat during total war.

Problem and Remedy

The gravest threat to American society during the remainder of the twentieth century is total war. The rate of development of technics of warfare has outstripped the political means available for preventing war or for employing warfare in the solution of political conflicts. The national environment and its population and social structure are now ultimately indefensible. At the same time, $50 billion a year, the bulk of the entire public economy, is given over to support of the war (or defense) system.

Many experts view the sources of this problem differently. Many see the conflict between East and West less as an extension of power conflicts as old as nation states themselves and more as a value conflict between totalitarianism and freedom. In this view, the United States is engaged in a life and death struggle to preserve freedom. Others view the tension and dangers of the Cold War as constituting the price nation states now pay for their unwillingness to resort to total war to resolve conflicts of diametrically opposed interests. In this view, each side arms and participates in the arms race which neither side wants but which neither side knows how to stop without sacrificing its threatened interests.

Differences in interpretation of the present conflict and its sources lead to different conclusions, certainly; but only in matters of political degree! Few experts maintain that the United States or any other major power in the world today could fight a total war *and* survive. It is in this sense, that weapons technology has brought American society, and all others, to a point where the national territory is indefensible. There are many ways in which 'pre-ultimate' defense continues to be possible. Therefore, we refer only to total war and to the fact that all other forms of twentieth-century warfare contribute to the possibility of total war.

This gravest problem before American society stems from extreme disorganization in international relations. The existing balance of power does not protect a single participating country on either side of the Iron Curtain from the possibility of extermination, grounded as the balance is upon weapons designed to deter war which can only be used to wage war. The organizational mechanisms of alliance offer no guarantee against obliteration. Yet they cannot be scrapped without intensifying instability. No scheme suggests itself for disengagement from overseas obligations or dangers.

Institutions of collective security through the United Nations and related agencies *are* evolving. Before this century, the Western democracies had begun to develop these institutions with some success, and this represents a change in conditions. There is little serious fear, for example, that any of the leading nations in the present Western alliance will wage war against any other member. And, even with the tensions generated by the Cold War, the United Nations has expanded its scope of control. Without hot war, there are good prospects for extending peace indefinitely.

To secure this interval of peace so essential to strengthening of these institutions, the arms race, that is, the high rate of technical change and expansion in weapons systems, must be stopped or slowed significantly. If there is a remedy for the major problem of the twentieth century—total war—it must involve arms control at the least, and military disarmament at best.

This chapter offers a sociological perspective on war viewed from within the United States in this century. If a problem of this magnitude is to be solved, its gross elements must be isolated. We have given emphasis to three of these crucial features: conflict between nations, weapons technology, and mechanisms of international control. All solutions proposed for avoiding total war must be assessed against their treatment of the three elements. Even with weapons control and improved international organization, for example, a remedy to total war must suggest means for reducing the *sources* of conflict.

References

Aron, Raymond. *The century of total war*. New York: Doubleday and Company, Inc., 1954.

Baldwin, Hanson W. The new face of war. *Bulletin of the Atomic Scientists*, 12: 153-158 (May, 1956).

Bernard, L. L. *War and its causes*. New York: Henry Holt and Company, Inc., 1944.

Blake, Robert R. Psychology and the crisis of statesmanship. *American Psychologist*, 1959 (February), *14*, 87-94.

Cantril, Hadley (Ed.). *Tensions that cause wars;* common statement and individual papers by a group of social scientists brought together by UNESCO. Urbana, Ill.: University of Illinois Press, 1950.

Cooper, Joseph B. Psychological literature on the prevention of war. *Bull. Res. Exch. Prevent. War*, 1955, 3(3), 2-15.

Deutsch, Morton. Some considerations relevant to national policy. *Journal of Social Issues*, 1961, *17*(3), 57-68.

Dunn, Frederich Sherwood. *War and the minds of men*. New York: Published for the Council on Foreign Relations, by Harper, 1950.

Dyer, Murray. *The weapon on the wall: rethinking psychological warfare*. Baltimore, Maryland: John Hopkins Press, 1959.

Farber, Maurice L. Psychoanalytic hypotheses in the study of war. *Journal of Social Issues*, 1955, 11, 1, 26-35.

Fox, Byron L. The cold war and American domestic problems. *Social Problems*, 1953, 1, 1, June, 10-12.

Frank, J. D. Emotional and motivational aspects of the disarmament problem. *Journal of Social Issues*, 1961, *17*(3), 20-27.

Gross, Feliks. *The seizure of political*

power. New York: Philosophical Library, 1958.

Horowitz, Louis Irving. *War game: studies of the new civilian militarists.* Ballantine Books, Inc., 1963.

Janowitz, Morris. *Sociology and the military establishment.* New York: Russell Sage Foundation, 1959.

Kahn, Herman. *On thermonuclear war.* Princeton, New Jersey: Princeton University Press, 1960.

Klineberg, Otto. *Tensions affecting international understanding.* Social Science Research Council, Bulletin No. 62, New York, 1950.

Knorr, Klaus Eugen. *The war potential of nations.* Princeton, New Jersey: Princeton University Press, 1956.

Milburn, T. W. The concept of deterrence: some logical and psychological considerations. *Journal of Social Issues,* 1961, *17*(3), 3-11.

Mills, Charles Wright. *The causes of World War Three.* New York: Simon and Schuster, 1958.

Millis, Walter, Reinhold Niebuhr, Harrison Brown, James Real, and William O. Douglas. *A world without war.* New York: Washington Square Press Book, 1961.

Nef, John U. *War and human progress.* Cambridge: Harvard University Press, 1950.

Noel-Baker, Philip. *The arms race: a programme for world disarmament.* New York: Oceana, 1958.

Osgood, C. E. An analysis of the cold war mentality. *Journal of Social Issues,* 1961, *17*(3), 12-19.

Osgood, Charles E. *An alternative to war or surrender.* Urbana, Ill.: University of Illinois Press, 1962 (paper, $1.45).

Pear, T. H. (Ed.). *Psychological factors of peace and war.* New York: Philosophical Library, 1950.

Reves, E. *The anatomy of peace.* New York: Viking Press, 1963.

Reynolds, Q. J. and R. Leckie (Eds.). *With fire and sword.* New York: Dial Press, 1963.

Routhoul, G. *War.* New York: Walker and Company, 1963.

Schelling, Thomas C. *Strategy of conflict.* New York: University of Oxford Press, Inc., 1963.

Schneider, Joseph. On the beginnings of warfare. *Social Forces,* 1952, *31*, 68-74.

Tiryakian, Edward A. Aftermath of a thermonuclear attack on the U.S.: some sociological implications. *Social Problems,* 1959, *6*, 291-303.

Wallace, Victor Hugo (Ed.). *Paths to peace; a study of war, its causes and prevention.* With a foreword by Jawaharlal Nehru. Melbourne University Press, 1957.

Wright, Quincy A. *A study of war.* Chicago: University of Chicago Press, 1942. (2 vols.)

Wright, Quincy. Some reflections on war and peace. *American Journal of Psychiatry,* 1950, *107*, 161-169.

Wright, Quincy, William M. Evan, and Morton Deutsch (Eds.). *Preventing World War III: some proposals.* New York: Simon and Schuster, 1962.

Zawodny, J. K. Special Editor. American Academy of Political and Social Sciences, Philadelphia. *Unconventional warfare.* Philadelphia, 1962.

Znaniecki, Florian. Impact of war on personality organization. *Sociology and social research,* 27: 171-180, January, 1943.

SOCIAL EFFECTS OF NUCLEAR WAR: ON PEOPLE, ON DEMOCRATIC SOCIETY— LESSONS OF THE LAST WAR

Robert A. Dentler and Phillips Cutright

Studies of the effects of nuclear war which deal primarily with the physical damage to be expected from such a conflict tend to leave us with a picture of a surviving society composed of fewer individuals with reduced physical resources but with the same basic democratic institutions and relationships that characterize our present society. We are concerned here with the *social* damage to be expected from nuclear war; with a series of major social problems, defining these generally as breakdowns in relations between the main elements of the social system (e.g., population, social organization, technology, and physical environment) so severe as to threaten the survival of the system. Many features of each element are neglected, including medical technology, communications, and the administration of justice, not because these are insignificant, but because we are better equipped professionally to assess the

Adapted from Robert A. Dentler and Phillips Cutright, Hostage America, Boston: Beacon Press, 1963. Copyright 1963 by Robert A. Dentler &Phillips Cutright, reprinted with permission.

problems selected. Our criteria were pragmatic; namely, our competence as sociologists and those problems on which evidence could be obtained.

Some Effects on the Population

Two studies by the Office of Civil and Defense Mobilization (OCDM) on the effects of thermonuclear war upon civilians in the United States have been released to the public. A partial text of these reports has appeared in official government documents (1). Each of the limited attacks discussed by the OCDM assumed a strike directed both at military installations on the continental United States and at certain cities whose industries or locations near military bases would make them targets in a thermonuclear war.

The principal difference between the two studies is in the size of the attacks assumed. The 1957 study was based on a hypothetical attack of 2500 megatons, the 1959 study on one of 1500 megatons (Figure 1). 1500 and 2500 megatons of explosive power do not represent the actual capability of the weapons stockpiles and delivery systems of either the U.S. or the U.S.S.R. However, the number and size of bombs likely to be committed in an attack and the number of missiles or planes that would succeed in delivering their payload on target cannot be known. As missiles replace planes, and as the accuracy of missiles increases, the tendency might be in the direction of less megatonnage (2).

On the other hand, as missile bases are hardened, the tendency might be toward more megatonnage. Every study of the consequences of nuclear war must begin with an assumption about the size of the attack, and the targets against which it is directed, but all such assumptions are subject to many uncertainties. It must be understood that in adopting the assumptions of the OCDM studies, we are using only one hypothetical attack pattern.

The Office of Civil and Defense Mobilization selected 71 metropolitan areas as the most likely targets in their 1959 exercise. In our re-examination of the 1959 study we used every Standard Metropolitan Area with a manufacturing labor force of 40,000 or more and all of the 53 largest areas (1950 census). This gave us a total of 70 urban areas, and inspection revealed that they are virtually identical with those chosen by the OCDM. The results of our study are not changed by our omission of a few areas included in the 1959 OCDM report.

We differ with the assumptions of the OCDM study in a few respects. We assume, first, that nuclear weapons can utterly destroy any city if the weapon is delivered and, second, that if the enemy wanted to destroy a city he could and would deliver a bomb large enough to do the job. (Unlike the OCDM study of 1959 which, for reasons unexplained in the testimony, pictured the Chicago urban area as escaping with 70 per cent of its population completely uninjured.) We assume that a thermonuclear war is a war with no holds barred. Thus it is realistic to assume that everyone within each of these 70 areas would be killed by blast, firestorms or radiation. We do not, however, include in our estimates a single person outside of these areas; nor do we include the deaths resulting from attacks on military installations located in areas remote from these cities, such as the ICBM bases in the western and midwestern states. We are concerned only with what might happen to the people of the United States if 70 of its largest urban areas were destroyed.

Who Would Be Annihilated? The purpose of our re-examination of the OCDM study is to enable us to see the deaths not only in terms of numbers, but in terms of *who* is being annihilated. Only by understanding the probable selective effect of nuclear war on our labor force can we begin to appreciate the economic problems of recuperation. Only by viewing the dead as individuals with particular skills, religious beliefs and political outlooks can we begin to understand how such an attack would affect the present fabric of our society.

Such an attack on 70 urban areas would result in the death of 68,755,000 persons — 46 per cent of all the people in the United States. Of the 74 million church members, one of every two would be killed. One of every three Protestants would be killed, two of every three Roman Catholics, and nine of every ten Jews (Figure 2). On the basis of recent election figures, it can also be shown that more Democrats than Republicans would be killed, and more northern than southern Democrats, affecting a change in the political balance of our two-party system.

The same attack would kill 72 per cent of all industrial and mechanical engineers; 73 per cent of the architects; an undue proportion of the men and women with the very skills most in demand after such a disaster would perish in the attack. (Table I).

What the social effects of these

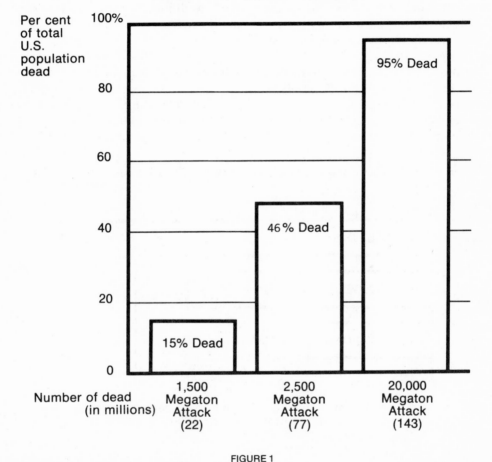

Two Government Studies of the Effect Upon the U.S. Population of Nuclear Attack
(Based on the 1958 population: 150,699,000)

FIGURE 1
Both the 1,500 and 2,500 megaton attacks were "mixed," that is, both military and industrial centers were included. Both were discussed in considerable detail at Congressional Hearings. The 20,000 megaton attack estimate comes from an article by Everett and Pugh, also part of the record of the Hearings. (1959 study, pp. 847, 876; 1957 study, p. 118).

62 per cent of the physicians; 79 per cent of the foremen in the metals industry and 76 per cent of the tool and die makers. Comparing this with the overall death rate of 46 per cent, we can see that population changes would be, is difficult to envision. Even in World War II no nation experienced sudden population losses of this kind or of this magnitude. But whatever their nature, we

must face the possibility that these effects would be serious, if not calamitous.

Social relations between persons and groups in an advanced industrial society like the United States are based upon elaborate and delicately balanced forms of interdependence, reflected in a complex division of tasks and in social standards. Even the most intimate relations between family members are affected by subtle population factors such as the size, age and sex composition and distribution of the population within local communities.

A society maintains certain margins of reserves that allow it to survive fairly

tion breaks down. First-line stresses ramify throughout the system. Surface disorder penetrates the deeper levels of the structure, bringing upheavals in standards and expectations and making older divisions of activity irrelevant. Even if the system somehow manages to recover a balance, the new society is both a different entity and a permanently *scarred* arrangement.

The Effect of Preparation

The foregoing studies do not take into consideration the possibility of civil defense protection. What would be the

Effects of a 2,000-Megaton Attack on 70 Urban Areas Upon the Religious Composition of the U.S.

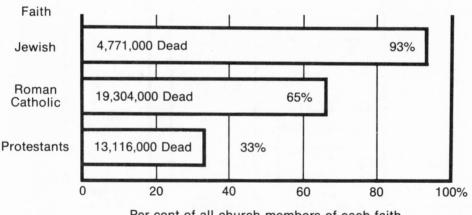

Per cent of all church members of each faith
in the United States, 1950

FIGURE 2

An additional 31 million residents in these areas were not listed as belonging to a church, but must be added to the total death list. The total number of residents, members and non-members was 68,755,000 in 1950. This was 46 per cent of the total U.S. population.

sharp changes in population and to accommodate to natural and economic disasters of a limited magnitude. When these margins are exceeded, reorganization becomes too difficult to achieve and, for an indefinite period, organiza-

difference in the impact of an attack if we had built shelters and prepared for war?

In the 1959 hearings of the Joint Committee on Atomic Energy on "Biological and Environmental Effects of

Nuclear War," is an article by Hugh Everett III and George E. Pugh (3), both of whom are employed by the Weapons Systems Evaluation Division of the

TABLE 1
PER CENT OF TOTAL UNITED STATES POPULATION AND SELECTED OCCUPATIONS THAT MIGHT PERISH IN A MIXED INDUSTRIAL-MILITARY ATTACK OF 2,000 MEGATONS ON 70 URBAN AREAS (1950 POPULATION DATA)

Population Group	Per Cent Dead
Total U.S. Pop.	46
Accountants	73
Architects	73
Authors	77
Chemists	69
Dentists	61
Draftsmen	73
Editors	68
Engineers:	
technical	68
aeronautical	86
chemical	69
electrical	72
industrial	72
mechanical	72
metallurgical	76
mining	34
other	73
Lawyers	65
Natural scientists	66
Physicians	62
Nurses, female	57
Social scientists	78
Salaried managers:	
construction	54
manufacturing	64
communications	48
wholesale trade	58
transportation equip.	79
Clerical, male	65
Clerical, female	65
Compositors, printers	67
Electricians	55
Cranemen	62
Foremen:	
metals	71
machinery	64
Machinists	64
Structural steel workers	64
Tool and die makers	76

Source for population data: *County and City Data Book,* 1952. Source on occupations: U.S. Census: "Characteristics of the Population, 1950" Vol. II, Part 2 (Washington: U.S. Government Printing Office, 1952).

Institute for Defense Analysis, Washington, D.C., called "The Distribution and Effects of Fallout in Large Nuclear-Weapons Campaigns."

Everett and Pugh studied different kinds and sizes of attacks and compared their probable effects on prepared and unprepared populations. An unprepared population was assumed to have had a few hours' warning that an attack was coming. It is given emergency instructions to remain under shelter during and after the attack, but it has only improvised shelters to go to. In contrast, a prepared population has had six months of full-time preparation for an attack. The effectiveness of six months of intensive activity to provide, prepare, build and stock shelters was then calculated. Figure 3 compares the effects of thermonuclear attacks ranging from one hundred to fifty thousand megatons on a prepared and on an unprepared population. Only deaths during and for the first sixty days after the attack are included. If the sick and wounded were added, the figures for each group would increase by an additional ten to fifteen per cent.

Two important things are shown in this chart. A rather steady increase in the number of deaths occurs with each increase in the number of megatons dropped. And the difference in the death rate between a prepared and an unprepared population can be eliminated simply by dropping more megatons.

It would take 5,000 megatons to kill about 75 per cent of the total unprepared population; about 16,000 megatons would kill 75 per cent of the prepared population. Remember that we are not talking here about the cities alone: these figures apply to the population of the nation as a whole.

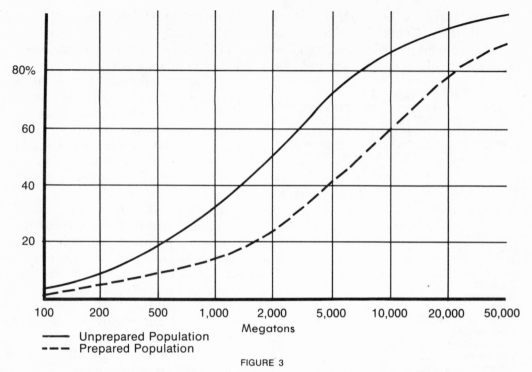

FIGURE 3

Estimated deaths in prepared and unprepared populations from nuclear attacks of various sizes, 60 days after the attack. A prepared population is assumed to have had six months of intensive work building and stocking shelters. The bombs dropped are assumed to be two-thirds fission, which produces fallout.

Source: 1959 Hearings: "Biological and Environmental Effects of Nuclear War," Fig. 9, p. 876.

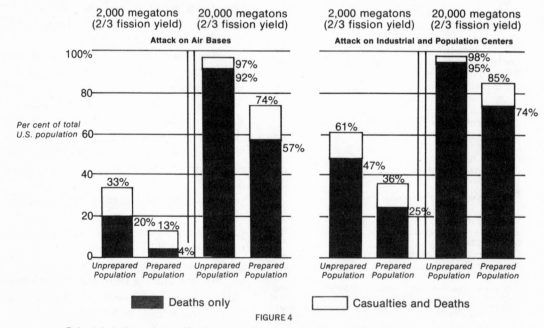

FIGURE 4

Estimated deaths and casualties for prepared and unprepared populations. Attacks assumed are 2,000 megatons (on the left) and 20,000 (on the right). Two types of attack are considered: one on air bases (left) and one on industrial and population centers.

Source: Same as Figure 3.

An actual attack on a large scale would probably be directed at both military and industrial targets, as assumed in the mock attacks of the OCDM in 1957 and 1959. The calculations of Everett and Pugh did not take into account a mixed attack on both industrial and military targets. Their figures are based upon attacks that are *either* industrial or military, not both.

The 2,000 megaton attack on military air bases shown in Figure 4 indicates that with several hours' warning time an unprepared civilian population would have about 33 per cent deaths and casualties, while a prepared population would have a 13 per cent death and casualty rate.

Under the assumption that we continue to "harden" our bases, that is, that we place our offensive and defensive weapons underground in an attempt to make them invulnerable, then the enemy would be forced to use more megatonnage to destroy our air bases. If we had already dug in, then it is conceivable that an enemy would deliver 20,000 megatons instead of 2,000. In the event of a 20,000 megaton attack the death-casualty rate could eliminate three-quarters of the civilian population of the nation, even though the targets were purely military.

The building of an extensive civil defense program would also tend to require increased megatonnage from an aggressor in an attack on industrial centers, for if the purpose of the attack was destruction of our industrial capacity, the labor force would have to be destroyed as well as the factories.

If 20,000 megatons were directed against a prepared population, shelters would be of no use to 74 per cent of the people (Figure 4). They would be dead within 60 days after such an attack. An additional eleven per cent would

be casualties. This would leave fifteen per cent of the people alive and in some sort of physical condition to rebuild the nation. Whether we think in terms of this fifteen per cent, or of the 54 per cent survivors projected in the 2,000 megaton attack, or of some other number, the end of a nuclear war would be the beginning of many problems.

Rebuilding our Society

There is a difference between staying alive somehow through a period of six weeks to six months, and surviving for a decade. One difference is that continued existence depends on renewed opportunity for economic and social cooperation among individuals and groups. Any society contains a handful of citizens who might be able to go it alone against great odds and a strangely hazardous environment. Some form of human or subhuman life would persist beyond even the most cataclysmic of all thermonuclear wars. As the poet Kenneth Patchen concludes in a poem entitled "O Take Heart, My Brothers:" "Life is in no danger of losing the argument! — For after all . . . (As will be shown) She has only to change the subject."*

But extended human survival, particularly survival at a level above that of the primitive folk community, depends for most of us on the prospects for rebuilding certain institutions, certain life-sustaining forms of social and technical organizations. The long-term existence of any human community depends on the presence of adaptive traditions that require generations for their establishment.

*Quoted with the permission of New Directions Publishing Co.

We know something about the minimal requirements for the survival of even the most fragmented societies. Among these, most social scientists would include health and safety standards (however high or low), population supply, and a complex of economic and political resources and regulations. There must also be institutions that motivate men or give them meaningful goals to strive toward. There are others, such as ways and means of rearing and educating the young, that we shall not consider here. But, to survive, these institutions must be built and put into sensible coordination, for they depend on each other just as man depends on them. Where the lives of more than random persons are at stake, health and safety, an economy, political controls, and life goals must take form—and not as independent cards in a game of chance but as features of a synchronized system.

The Economy. One economic analysis, prepared for the Defense Department in the late 1950's (4), examined the chances for recovery from an attack in which 45 per cent of the population is killed and all military and metropolitan targets are obliterated. The economists concluded that such an attack would destroy 80 per cent of the instrument, 77 per cent of the transportation equipment, 77 per cent of the electrical machinery and primary metal industries; as well as three-fourths to two-thirds of these other production systems: rubber, printing and publishing, cloth and garments, general machinery, petroleum and coal. Not only would production capacity in these industries be destroyed but equivalent proportions of all capital goods as well.

These economists concluded that recuperation of the industrial economy was possible in a period of from five to twenty years, *if* a number of vital conditions could *all* be met. First, they reasoned, the money and credit system would have to be intact and investment would have to proceed as usual. Government and corporate credits would have to come to hand that would make new, begin-again contracting and purchasing systems come to life. In order of importance, the other conditions they cited were these: The nation would need a favorable political environment —presumably a stable, energetic government. The surviving labor force would have to get back on the job full time as promptly as radiation conditions permitted, and the momentum of the preattack economy would have to be maintained. Bottlenecks in the technical organization of production and distribution resulting from the dislocation of population and the material ruin of the attack would have to be overcome with speed. The surviving labor force would have to accept reduced standards of health and safety. The balance of nature could not be destroyed by such effects as the wholesale decimation of mammals and subsequent multiplication of insect populations, or the death of forest cover through radiation.[1]

The economists said their estimates depended on assuming that government welfare programs would be cut back quite severely, that military spending would be kept to a minimum, that bacteriological and chemical warfare would not be used, and that no third country would follow up the initial small attack.

Economic recuperation within a decade or two, according to this anal-

[1]The effects of radiation on plant, animal and insect life and consequently on the balance of nature will be discussed in a forthcoming issue of *Nuclear Information.*

ysis, requires that most or all of these conditions be met. A single failure — say, for example, that all soft wood forestation is destroyed by low-yield radiation — and the forecast of recovery in five to fifteen years cannot be maintained. The conditions also must occur at more or less one and the same time: economic momentum depends on the prevention of production bottlenecks; energetic governmental regulation depends on the acceptance by the surviving labor force of lowered standards of health and safety, and so forth.

The nation must get the economy going in reasonably short order after an attack, or it may not get it going at all. The stimulation of momentum requires a usable transportation system, the swift restoration of power and communications apparatus, and provision for long-term shelter, food and clothing for the working population. If momentum is achieved, it must be maintained across a ten-year period. Raw materials, critical inventories, stockpiled resources and equipment must be at hand. These economists concluded that food in sufficient quantities to feed the surviving populace for two to four years must be deposited in advance of any attack.

This economic analysis is perhaps a classic in view of the chain of *if-type* assumptions that must be made before the estimate of recovery is reached. The size and kind of bombs used and the altitude at which they were exploded, as well as the targets selected are all choices for the attacker, not for the agents of recuperation. Yet such assumptions as these, as well as assumptions mentioned above about human behavior and political organization are all closely linked in reaching the estimate of recovery. A change in any one of these assumptions would require an entire restudy of the hypothetical post-attack situation before one could say whether or not the previous recovery estimate could be justified in the changed situation. (For a critique of the method used by this and similar studies, see [*Nuclear Information*], May 1963).

These economists were interested in whether we could recover economically to a point of material well-being that was something like our preattack existence. Suppose we are less demanding and we concern ourselves with the question of economic survival at a bare subsistence level something like that of contemporary Iran. One need not ask, after all, for the best of all possible economic worlds. Here our understanding is helped by the examples of the U.S.S.R. and Germany and their progress in recuperating from the effects of World War II. One eminent economist, Oscar Morgenstern, argues that we could not regain past levels of living, but that the experience of the Soviet Union illustrates the great resilience of industrial economies. And Herman Kahn presents the Soviet case as partial evidence that the United States could face great destruction, yet recover.

Soviet and German Experiences. The Soviet Russian economy absorbed the shock of the German invasion and in 1945 was operating at about the same level as in 1940. By 1950, production had nearly doubled over 1945 (5). Far from experiencing the obliteration of their factories and capital, the Soviets were in relatively complete industrial operation throughout the 1940's.

How could this be? It is true that about twenty million Russians were killed during the war, or about twelve per cent of their 1940 population. But those who died were not strategic for the maintenance of the economy. The

Soviets anticipated the routes that would be followed by a German *land* invasion (a kind of anticipation that is impossible in missile warfare). They relocated their industries and labor force before the main invasions occurred. In addition, most of the invasion routes ran through nonindustrial rural terrain, and the German air offensive could not reach the inland industrial centers of the economy. If Russian experience documents anything, it shows how an industrial economy may be defended against a *land* and a short-range air attack.

The Allied attack on Germany extended over several years and (unlike the Nazi invasion of Russia) was directed at critical industrial sectors — with important exceptions such as the destruction of Hamburg and Dresden. Thus, several months were given over to concentration on the bearing industry, then the transport system was attacked, and then the petroleum and nitrogen refineries were destroyed. This offensive had great effects, yet sectors of the economy that were not selected continued to produce at high levels until land invasion wiped them out.

Is this an argument for the resilience of a modern economy? If our problem for comparison is a nuclear attack, it is essential to recall that the devastation of German industry took place across a two-year — not a two-day or two-week — period. It must be recalled that although Hamburg and Dresden were leveled more completely than any other cities in history except Tokyo, German civilian deaths from Allied bombings during the entire war totaled about 500,000, or less than one per cent of the German civilian population. If the German experience, for all its horror, is to be compared with a nuclear attack of similar proportions on the United States, we must assume no more than two to five million deaths. Such an attack would amount to the dropping of one ten-megaton bomb on New York City. That is a long way from 46 per cent of the nation's population dead from a 2,000-megaton attack (Figure 2). In actual explosive power, about three megatons of bombs were dropped on Germany in the entire course of World War II.

There are other crucial differences. The German labor force was not shattered by the bombing program. The German machine tool industry was only lightly affected by direct attacks; it maintained its level of output throughout the war (6). The final collapse of production was due to the destruction of transport routes and equipment and to the occupation.

If we go ahead with an imaginary comparison despite these differences, we are struck not with the recuperative power of the German economy but *with the time and wealth it took to rebuild in spite of many favorable conditions.* Governmental stability was achieved through the machinery of the Allied occupation. The Allies had fresh memories of the political chaos in Germany after World War I that made the rise of Hitler possible. Health and safety problems were generally resolved within one year through massive outside aid. A substantial civilian labor force was at hand, trained and properly located, and disposed to resume work. Most sectors of the economy were intact (except for postwar dismantling by the Russians in East Germany). Given these favorable circumstances, *why were three billion dollars of direct economic aid from the United States alone necessary to German economic recuperation?* In spite of massive outside assistance, economic recovery was not achieved even in West Germany until three years after World War II. No economist on record anticipates massive outside aid to the United States following a nuclear World War III. What nations would be standing by with a Marshall Plan?

If comparisons have any worth whatever (and the lack of comparable events suggest they do not), they indicate *not* that modern industrial economies are resilient, but that recuperation depends on ability to anticipate the type of attack, on what remains intact after the attack, on the extent of destruction of *people* as well as industry and capital, and on the availability of outside help.[2]

Social and Political Problems. To get an inkling of some of the social and political problems involved in rebuilding, let us look briefly at the case of Hiroshima.

Hiroshima, a delta city accustomed to disastrous floods and well organized to handle crises, was not rebuilt primarily by its own citizens but by migrants from the hinterlands who surged into the ruins in the aftermath of the bombing (7). Those who had lived through the attack suffered from extreme

---

[2]The narrowness of much American disaster research is reflected in Charles E. Fritz' "Disaster," Chapter 14 of *Contemporary Social Problems*, Robert K. Merton, and others, eds. (New York: Harcourt, Brace & World, 1961). After a fine resume of social reactions to natural disasters, Fritz cites the many mechanisms that aid in unifying and energizing groups and communities in post-disaster situations. He shows "why societies rebound so dramatically from the disruptive and destructive effects of disaster." He concludes by referring to the recuperation of West Germany, Russia and Hiroshima, and to the Rand Study (Ref. 4). "Disaster studies show that human societies have enormous resilience and recuperative power . . .". But such studies *also* show the conditions necessary for recuperation, very few of which occur in nuclear warfare.

shock and fatigue that lingered for a year. Although American occupation authorities issued food for a year, the May Day "festivities" of 1946 took the form of hunger demonstrations and the week-end holiday was spent by most city dwellers in the search for weeds and edible barks. The mayor himself reported that a year after the attack he attempted (under an agreement with occupation authorities) to renounce the black market, but that faced with starvation he resumed private purchases. A judge committed suicide when faced with a choice between breaking the law and starvation.

Demoralization was so extreme that industrial alcohol was sold as a substitute for saki; many citizens died or went blind from drinking it. The narcotic, Hiropon, that kills the appetite and induces a torpor of well being flourished on the black market. As late as the 1950's, Japanese sociologists reported after studying orphans of the bombing that a fear of forming attachments and producing children was very prevalent among a majority of youthful survivors.

Hiroshima's reservoirs were filled soon after the attack, but thousands of shattered pipes had to be replaced in order to build up the pressure to start the water system. For every hole the engineers plugged by day, more were dug by citizens at night to steal a drink. Gangsters organized the sale of water as a profitable racket. They fought so effectively to prevent repairs to the system that engineers had to work at night in carefully policed shifts to put the water system in order.

After the first nightmare month of locating the living and removing the dead, the struggle was resumed to keep damaged body and battered soul together. Reconstruction did not begin for five months after the attack. No gas mains operated for six months. Four months after the attack, ten buses were in operation to take more than 42,000 workers to and from points in the rubble each day. And four months after the bomb, the number of crimes reported in Hiroshima and its suburbs for one month was as high as the figure for all criminal activities throughout the entire war. Crimes of violence and theft were particularly prevalent.

Ten to twelve months after the attack, administratively undirected reconstruction efforts got underway. The city was bombed in August 1945. By early 1947, amusement districts, gambling dens, brothels and theaters had resumed operations. Without housing aid from the government, people began to erect wooden or corrugated iron huts.

Catastrophic as it was, the attack on Hiroshima did not level the entire metropolitan area of the city. A few weeks after the explosion, the area numbered 130,000 inhabitants compared with the 390,000 who had lived there previously, if garrison troops were included. This, in short, was a miniscule attack by the standard of present-day possibilities. There is another sense in which Hiroshima, for all its unforgettable horror, is but a faint indication of future possibilities: part of the city and part of its highly skilled labor force survived. There were engineers at hand to repair the water mains. An attack on America might obliterate such urban resources. Although 120 Japanese cities were devastated by bombing and incendiary attacks, total casualties did not begin to approach what a modern thermonuclear attack would yield. *When Hiroshima began its reconstruction, there was a domestic society and an invader at hand to bring aid.*

There should be no fantasy on the question of outside help in the event of a thermonuclear war. The questions "How many people will die in the first attack?" and "How many people will survive the first two years?" pale before the question, "How will the war come to an end?" There is nothing in history to suggest that either side would cease attacking until there was nothing left with which to attack. The cost of total holocaust would be the sacrifice of help from the surviving corners of the globe where the less industrially developed nations would themselves be struggling to survive in an environment contaminated by radioactivity. Even in the event of a "limited attack," what remaining nations would be able, let alone disposed, to come to the rescue?

Survivors in the U.S. would face the problems of Hiroshima multiplied many times, and would have to solve them with little or no outside help. Could they do so through existing American democratic institutions?

Could Democracy Survive? Martial rule is the most likely form of government control to be exercised during the first year or two after a nuclear attack. It matters little whether martial law is implemented by civilian or military defense authorities; patently, some officials from each group would survive. Both have developed procedures for cooperation. We suggest that older cultural distinctions between military and civil authority would prove immaterial in any extreme crisis, just as the traditional representative functions of local, state and federal governments would be sacrificed, however indefinitely, to the necessities of survival through authoritative control.

Depending on prevailing winds and the chance-like pattern of rainfall, certain states might survive a nuclear attack quite intact. Under the assumptions we made, North Dakota, Idaho and Montana would survive a small attack more or less completely.[3] Consider the political situation, then, in terms of regulatory centers—federal, state and local. Washington, D.C., and all pertinent centers of federal authority including military units would have been eliminated. The federal cortex of our political system and virtually all its pertinent regional extensions would be gone, as would federal communications exclusive of a fragmented civil defense radio system. National Guard units would serve under state civil defense authorities in the patches of intact society in the central northwest, and in smaller sectors of a handful of widely dispersed states. Local governmental authorities would survive in a much broader yet even more widely dispersed range of communities. In lieu of a pyramid of authorities there would exist a scatter of regional, state and municipal enclaves, only a few of which could be expected to be in contact with more than a handful of others, for a time. Under these conditions, the stress to reconstruct a centralized political system, though deferred for a time in the face of physical problems, would be tremendous.

New goals, with new procedures for achieving them, including control over all remaining national resources, would require extreme centralization. Central authority would be limited in that the survivors would be dispersed in remote rural sectors. But for an intermediate

[3]However, an attack on military bases in the future might well change this picture, as a large Incontinental Ballistic Missile base is being built in Montana and another in North Dakota (*Nuclear Information*, Oct.-Nov. 1962).

period, responsibility for survival and reconstruction would rest with a uniquely authoritative few, a quasi-military elite, in each enclave.

Without social order men are lost; and that social order presupposes law. A system of standards regulating relations between men is essential for human existence at every level, from death camp to democratic society. The novelist's notion of the modern survivor tucked away from disaster in his northern Minnesota shelter is wholly fictitious. The so-called primitive through all periods of history has clung to his laws more tenaciously, more unthinkingly, than anyone else.

For this reason, a Hobbesian choice between chaos and surrender to a central authority would eventually confront a postattack America. Hobbes was wrong in thinking that the one thing that holds men together and makes survival possible is erection of a power able "to over-awe them all." Hobbes ignored the informal ties that bind men together. But Hobbes was wrong *only for the case of a society in balance.* In the extremes of crisis, where these ties are shattered by terror, death, and uncertainty, law and order, to exist at all, require allegiance to a strong central authority.

Extreme national crises have always placed democracies at the mercy of whatever clique acquires most efficiently the techniques of gaining power. That the United States military and civilian defense elites would constitute dispersed, competing and eventually conflicting cliques is simple enough to demonstrate. All the resources crucial for survival would be in unprecedented short supply. We might expect cooperation and coalition of authority to develop in the North Dakota-Idaho region, where mutual assistance between rural states could be to the advantage of all parties. But surviving, isolated communities might depend on their quasi-military leadership for defense against inroads from towns suffering even more extreme shortages. The altruistic generosity that characterizes aid in time of natural disasters springs from the fact that surpluses are available to communities and states located away from the disaster area. In an extended period of extreme, relatively universal scarcity and deprivation, the altruism of emergency aid would contradict short-run group interests.

When would quasi-military rule end and democratic political reorganization begin? This would depend on reconstruction of the economic and social structure. Democratic institutions depend on political parties that come into being to mediate between community and governmental authority. Party loyalties vitally depend in turn on combinations of economic and social incentives—upon *routine* expectations within family, work, ethnic and religious groups. In crisis, these routines would be broken up. The economic and social bases of interest groups would be dislocated. Even the pattern of two-party composition itself would be badly fragmented by a nuclear attack.

To terminate the period of martial law, individuals must have resources, including political morale, to reform voluntary associations, interest groups and political parties. They must have access to power and influence to affect decisions of their regime. The physical security of the individual and his family, for example, must not be threatened by economic collapse. Dependence on the state must be reduced.

The survivors of a substantial nuclear attack would be strung out across the most isolated rural backwaters and backlands of the country. Our discussion of the effects of a nuclear attack on the population makes it clear that the composition of the postattack population would be so different from that of today's population that this factor alone would make for differences in the post-attack society. To the interminable hazards of fallout, water and food contamination, forced relocation of families and labor assignments to individuals, therefore, must be added the obstacles of weak communications and heterogeneity. That new community and interest and party associations which would fit the new life situation could be built under these obstacles, is doubtful. Without such intermediate networks of attachment, the individual would have to choose indefinitely between the chaos of anarchy and surrender to the military or quasi-military state.

An extended period of martial law would further undermine the structures essential for the rebuilding of democracy. If the economy were to resume operations the new government would have to expand its powers and activities dramatically. This would challenge existing protections of individual freedom to dissent from government decrees or to test the constitutionality of governmental acts. Safety and health regulations, like schedules for decontamination and construction, would have to be so rigid as to place the regime in the position of dictating personal hygiene, diet, control over residence, material resources, professional services and the movement of labor.

Although demoralizing despair might run deep, the prospect of a public reaction against the new leadership is slim. The scope of the crisis would be so grave that only the most stupid and inept exercise of authority would be likely to be attacked. Those charged with the administration of martial law would be seen as effective, and accepted as legitimate, by the surviving population. If the case of Hiroshima applies, the new regime would also tend to incorporate within itself all forms of emergent, informal leadership.[4]

There are powerful constraints, then, that would be set in motion by the scope of the disaster to maintain undemocratic leadership by a quasi-military elite. That the quest for democratic reconstruction might eventually assert itself also seems likely. But realization of the goal would have to await major rehabilitation of the social structure and the economy.

Conclusion

We have discussed the effects of thermonuclear wars of varying levels on the population, economy, political organization and certain aspects of the physical environment of the United States. An attack of 1,000 to 2,000 megatons on urban targets would have a staggering impact on the major components of the American social system. *To kill the society you do not have to kill all the inhabitants.*

Our review of the post-World War II recovery experience of Germany and the Soviet Union forced us to conclude that no reasonable parallel can be drawn between the level of economic disorganization that followed World War II and the effects of a thermonuclear war

[4]Robert Jungk (7) describes vividly the emergence of an obscure young Japanese official, Shimzo Hamai, who by finding ways to provide emergency food and clothing "became overnight the most important man in Hiroshima."

on the American economy. Further, devastation of vital sectors of the labor force, yet unknown mass ecological effects of radiation, the unpredictable reaction of the surviving population to the holocaust, and the chance that a political order adequate to the challenge would not emerge force us to conclude that recovery of American society would be unlikely (8).

The difficulty of recovery from relatively minor devastation was illustrated with the case of Hiroshima. As we found in the German case, recovery was dependent upon the amount of aid given by surrounding population and American military forces, and the existence of a stable political order. Only if favorable conditions are present do we have evidence that modern interdependent societies are capable of recovery from what would nowadays be called a very limited attack. There is little reason to believe that such favorable conditions would exist in the United States following a thermonuclear war.

References

1. Material from the 1957 study is taken from the Special Subcommittee on Radiation of the Joint Congressional Committee on Atomic Energy, "The Nature of Radioactive Fallout and Its Effect on Man," Washington, D.C.: U.S. Government Printing Office, 1957.
   Data from the 1959 OCDM study was taken from the Hearings of the Special Subcommittee on Radiation of the Joint Committee on Atomic Energy, 86th Congress, "Biological and Environmental Effects of Nuclear War," Washington, D.C.: U.S. Government Printing Office, 1959.

2. "Strategic Weapons of Nuclear War," *Nuclear Information*, July 1962, p. 10.

3. "Biological and Environmental Effects of Nuclear War," *op. cit.*, pp. 859-881. The article is reprinted from its original source, the journal *Operations Research*, Vol. 7, No. 3 (March-April 1959).

4. This study by the Rand Corporation is summarized in Herman Kahn, *On Thermonuclear War* (Princeton: Princeton University Press, 1960), pp. 82-5. See also, *Report on a Study of Non-Military Defense* (Santa Monica, Calif.: Rand Corp., 1958).

5. Thomas Fitzsimmons, and others, *Russian Soviet Federated Socialist Republic*, I (New Haven: Human Relations Area Files, 1957), 65-66. Harry Schwartz, *Russia's Soviet Economy*, 2nd ed., (New York: Prentice-Hall, 1954), p. 127.

6. *United States Strategic Bombing Survey:* Overall Report (European War), September 30, 1945, pp. 85-6. Data on the effect of the air offensive on the German population and economy are taken from this Government report.

7. Jungk, Robert, *Children of the Ashes: The Story of a Rebirth,* N.Y. Harcourt, Brace and World, 1962. Our account of Hiroshima depends heavily upon this book, which is based on both first-hand social research and intensive coverage of secondary sources.

8. Bureau of Research and Survey of the National Council of Churches, *Churches and Church Membership in the United States: An Enumeration and Analysis by Counties, States and Regions,* New York 1956-58.

A POSSIBLE FUTURE

Walter Millis and James Real

"The goal," according to the agreed American and Soviet statement of principles, is to "ensure that disarmament is general and complete and war is no longer an instrument for settling international problems." Both parties may profoundly distrust the motives of the other in proclaiming this goal, but the fact remains that there is no other practicable or possible resolution of the modern dilemma. With all the various military and military-political solutions doomed almost demonstrably to failure in the future (as all have consistently failed so far), one is forced to the only remaining alternative – a demilitarized world, necessitating the abolition of the war system and the end of organized international war.

It is intellectually easier and more comfortable to continue to play with ideas of an indefinite stabilization of the war system, of a reduction in its levels of terror and destructiveness; but no long-term policy can be constructed out of these concepts, while unless and until the demilitarization of the global system is consciously and earnestly accepted as the ultimate goal, it is unlikely that much interim progress can be made with them. The choice, which has been narrowing over the past century, has narrowed sharply with the nuclear revolution; until we can now say with confidence that it is a choice between the ultimate demilitarization or the ultimate destruction of our civilization. The Soviet-American statement of principles means that on this the two powers are agreed; and perhaps this is a good deal. Unfortunately, it is obvious that they are agreed on almost nothing else.

The very way in which the statement is phrased – "to ensure that disarmament is general and complete and war is no longer an instrument for settling international problems" – conceals a critical difference in approach. This is like saying: "Our goal is to ensure that eggs are eliminated and that chickens are no longer to be instrumental in meeting international food problems." Which comes first? If chickens are dispensed with, there will be no difficulty about eliminating the eggs; if the eggs are eliminated, there will be no difficulty about dispensing with chickens as a food resource. The Russian position is

Reprint, with permission of authors and The Macmillan Company, from *The Abolition of War* by Walter Millis and James Real. Copyright © by The Fund for the Republic, 1963.

that if all agree to abolish the chickens (war), all problems as to the armament eggs—inspection, compliance, control, international police, and so on—become easily manageable. The Western position is that if you agree gradually to abolish the eggs (armaments), the chickens of war that hatch from them will gradually disappear in the process, and the war problem will become manageable.

Of the two views, the Russian is, superficially, much the more logical. There can really be little doubt that it is the great weapons systems themselves —with all the fears and ambitions that they engender—that are the major "causes" of war between modern, highly integrated states. The only way to get rid of war is to get rid of it— entirely—and once this has been done, actually or prospectively, the new sociopolitical situation that must result will be self-sustaining and self-perpetuating. In an arresting paper, David F. Cavers has argued that once the process of general disarmament to police-force level had been started, it would set up a kind of political chain reaction, each step hastening and reinforcing the next, in which the presently insuperable problems of inspection and compliance would dissolve of themselves. Leo Szilard's amusing and satiric fantasies of the future usually show a much harder grasp of the realities than can be found in the stodgier and more "realistic" discussions of disarmament experts. Szilard's imaginary disarmament conferences of 1987-1988 have little difficulty with problems of inspection and complicance under conditions of virtually complete disarmament; the hard problem, in his imaginary future as it is today, is in getting the movement toward total disarmament started.

The Russians would abolish war in order to make disarmament possible; the West would start a process of gradual reduction of armaments in order to make the abolition of war possible, meanwhile clinging at every step to all the supposed safeties and securities of the war system, until finally assured that war is no longer necessary to it. That this is bound to be self-defeating it should hardly be necessary to argue, though the point is beautifully illustrated by the long wrangle over a ban on nuclear testing. As originally conceived, the test ban had an admirable directness and simplicity. Since air bursts of nuclear weapons are in at least some degree dangerous to all humanity, and since they are quite readily detectable, an agreement to discontinue them would be simple and self-enforcing. With both the American and the Soviet governments favorable to the idea, one might suppose than an agreement could have been written in an afternoon. Years afterward, there is still (at the end of 1962) no agreement.

To raise the idea was to focus attention upon the possible military advantages of further testing. Then it appeared that even if air bursts were banned, undetectable underground (and possibly outer-space) tests might still be conducted. The Russian view was that there should be a general undertaking to discontinue all tests, detectable or undetectable. The American view was that the United States could not bind itself to discontinue all forms of testing unless it had assurance that the Russians were not violating their corresponding undertaking by conducting undiscoverable underground tests. Matters thus proceeded until it was found that a system for certainly monitoring small underground tests would be far more difficult and expensive to establish than had at first been supposed. By this time, the question of security against possible violation by the other side had been raised beyond all proportion to the practical military-technical issues involved.

American policy was, in effect, confronted with a choice. It could have a Soviet undertaking to halt any further testing of any kind, in return for a similar undertaking by the United States. This would put an effective, self-enforcing, end to the dangerous air bursts; it would engage the Soviet Union not to conduct underground bursts, but would give no positive assurance that the Soviet Union would honor its engagement. Or the United States could reject the Soviet offer, in the hope of forcing the USSR into accepting a hugely expensive and politically dangerous inspection system that would guarantee USSR performance of the undertaking not to conduct underground experiments. Presumably, this choice must have been weighed by American policy-makers, in the AEC or the National Security Council or elsewhere. If so, no intelligible account of the argument has ever reached the general public. On what grounds, military, political, or technical, it was determined that the very great advantages of a joint agreement to conduct no further testing at all were outweighed by the military advantages the Russians might gain by conducting clandestine underground tests was never explained. Yet such was the determination.

A fantastic interlude ensued in which the Americans sought to force the Russians to accept their completely controlled test ban by threatening to resume testing if the Russians did not accept. The Russians similarly sought to put pressure on the Americans to accept their uncontrolled test ban. This was centainly fatuous on the American side,

since the last thing the Americans wanted was a resumption of any sort of testing. Russian motivation is less clear. Whether, if the Americans had accepted the uncontrolled ban (which would have effectively ended air testing) the Russians would have stood by it, or whether, for military reasons, they were anxious to resume air testing and were simply maneuvering the Americans into a position in which the Americans could not prevent a resumption of such tests, we do not know. The result, at any rate, was the massive series of Russian air bursts in the fall of 1961. These were of far greater importance to weapons development than concealable low-yield bursts underground, they could have been prevented by our agreement to a general ban; and they were soon being anxiously scrutinized by our technical experts to find whether they had given Russian weaponry an important "lead" over our own. Whether they did or not, the Americans had been maneuvered or had maneuvered themselves, into a position that made the usual riposte (resuming air bursts on our own part) difficult and embarrassing.

The public argument for resumption of American testing rested on the familiar "arms race" arguments, those which contended that the Russians had used the informal moratorium period for intense preparation of tests that might lead to an overwhelming "breakthrough" that would hopelessly shatter the deterrent balance. There was considerable technical and emotional force to these contentions. Men such as Hans Bethe appear to have been sufficiently shaken by the possible implications of the Russian series to have made dramatic shifts in their previously held positions against American test resumption. Fortified by outside opinions such as these, influential technical groups within the Department of Defense and the Atomic Energy Commission joined with a majority of the members of the Joint Congressional Committee on Atomic Energy in urging the President to resume atmospheric testing. He proved unable to resist these persuasions for long, and entered the Geneva disarmament negotiations in March with a position that made their breakdown virtually inevitable. American tests were resumed in May.

By attempting in this instance to cling to the supposed protections of the war system while endeavoring to reduce its impact, the United States made the worst of both worlds. A broader approach to the test-ban problem, capable of taking political and psycholgical as well as crassly military considerations into account, might have led to happier results. This is commonly said to have been impossible because the United States cannot "trust" the Russians. But this is a mistaken way of looking at the matter. No nation, of course, ever can or does trust another beyond the limits to which mutual self-interest extends; and confidence cannot be pushed beyond those limits by even the most perfect systems for proving the other side to be cheating. The point is not that the United States should have put greater "trust" in the USSR, but that it should have made a shrewder analysis of the factors of self-interest involved on both sides. This would, it is believed, have indicated that it was improbable that the Russians would violate a general test ban and that even if they succeeded in doing so without detection the military gains to them would not really have been of major importance, and certainly far less than the military and political gains for the United States through securing the general ban on all further testing. But the

test-ban negotiations, by the very fact that they focused all attention on the weapons systems themselves, to the exclusion of all the human and political factors surrounding them, rendered this sort of analysis virtually impossible. At the end of 1962 there was evidence of some second thoughts on both sides, suggesting that such analysis might not be so impossible after all. But the episode remains as one more of many illustrations of the truth that one cannot reduce or suppress weapons systems by negotiatory processes that must attach maximum, rather than minimum, political and cultural values to the military power of the weapons one is trying to suppress.

The Russians are quite right in their argument that the only way to disarm is to abolish war. Certainly, a gradual disarmament program, which clings tenaciously to all the supposed values of the war system as it proceeds, is most unlikely to proceed at all. The obvious defect in the Russians' position is, however, that it gives no indication of how they propose to abolish war, of what contributions they propose to make to this consummation, or of how they anticipate that the resultant demilitarized world will operate. Disarmament proposals predicated, in effect, upon the prior abolition of the war system, and which can proceed only as there is general agreement that the war system be laid aside, are equally unlikely to proceed at all unless they can give some hint as to how this agreement might be brought about. It is all very well for Khrushchev and Kennedy to adopt a common goal of general and complete disarmament and the elimination of war as an instrument of national policy. But so long as neither statesman can really face the implications of his own position, the goal will almost certainly remain, in the practical contexts of international affairs, of only propagandist significance.

If it is true that the modern choice is between demilitarization and destruction, something more than all this is desperately needed. It is here argued that two things, specifically, are needed. The first is a reasonably clear and persuasive picture of how a demilitarized world could be expected to operate — what institutional arrangements it would require, how these institutions would function, what fundamental cultural changes it would demand or would itself produce, what securities it would guarantee and what sacrifices it would exact. And — most significant of all — how it would resolve the power issues that are inherent in human life, national or international, which in the past have normally been confided to the arbitrament of organized war, and for which a demilitarized world would have to find some other means of resolution.

The second thing that is needed is some idea of how the process of general demilitarization can in fact be initiated. It will be argued here that (as has already been suggested) the process once started will prove self-sustaining and that the end result — a demilitarized world — should be highly stable. But to get the process under way would seem to call for profound changes in present-day political and cultural concepts. How far these changes must extend, and what the possibilities are that they may begin to be of effect before we are overtaken by thermonuclear extermination, are questions demanding careful attention now. Indeed, the two requirements — a clear and persuasive picture of how the demilitarized world would operate, and a clear concept of how such a world might in fact be generated — are so closely interrelated that there may be a certain artificiality in attempting to separate them. For the purposes of the present discussion, however, this division appears to assist in clarifying the argument, and it is here adopted.

The design of a demilitarized world is, it is believed, a good deal less difficult, and much less Utopian, than is usually assumed. For one thing, we already have large working models of effectively demilitarized international societies, providing us with concrete experimental material in this area, the significance of which seems often overlooked. It is true that none of these models successfully bridges the chasm between the Communist and the non-Communist worlds, but they do provide important data upon the actual behavior of the highly integrated modern sovereign nation-state under conditions of effective demilitarization. And they are data that dispute many of the more generalized fears as to the consequences of a global demilitarization as well as some of the more elaborate notions as to what would be required to effect and sustain a global demilitarization.

The most useful and important of these working models is the North Atlantic Treaty Organization. There can be little doubt that the fourteen sovereign states who are members of NATO (together with some others, such as Sweden, Switzerland, Ireland, Spain) are effectively demilitarized as regards each other. These are the states that have waged among themselves (at times, to be sure, with outside assistance) almost all the important wars in modern history. Today, a war ranging any of them against one or others in the group seems as near to an impossibility as anything in the future can be. For present purposes it is unnecessary to ask how this situation has arisen; it is enough to ask how the relations of this community of mutually demilitarized sovereign states are in fact conducted, how the "disputes" that continue to arise between them are settled, what institutional devices have or have not seemed prerequisite to the maintenance of peace and order among them.

If one examines the North Atlantic Alliance and its associated states from this point of view, a number of suggestive conclusions emerge. There can be little doubt in the first place that they are mutually demilitarized. Most of them maintain large military establishments, but these establishments are not designed or organized to fight each other. For many reasons it would be technically difficult for them to do so — because large portions of their forces are earmarked for the NATO unified command, because of their common weapons systems and logistic bases, because of the complications surrounding the joint control of the tactical nuclear weapons. These technical disabilities are immensely compounded by the overweening political and economic control of the United States, upon which the whole military system depends. Thus another war like those of 1914 and 1939, involving France, Germany, Britain, Italy, and the United States, has been rendered as impossible as another war like that of 1861 involving the several states of the American Union.

This effective demilitarization has been accompanied, whether as cause or effect, by other suggestive developments. They have brought profound changes in the political and cultural attitudes of Western Europeans. Frenchmen and Germans today do not regard each other with anything like the prejudices that obtained on both sides of the border in 1914 and in 1939. There continue to be differences and disputes,

some of a major character, among the members of the North Atlantic system, but no one imagines that they could be usefully resolved by resort to organized war. There are serious practical issues, such as those surrounding the question of British association with the European Common Market and American trade and tariff policies in respect to it, but no one has suggested that war would be a usable instrument of policy in such issues; and they are being gradually worked out by negotiatory processes that can proceed, fundamentally, because the negotiators do not have war as a possible alternative to adjustment. There are even issues of abstract "power" within the alliance — issues of the kind that has always seemed unsusceptible to resolution except by the trial at arms — which no one expects to eventuate in war. There are European resentments against the abstract "power" of the United States; there are American resentments against De Gaulle's attempt to acquire the nuclear symbols of "power" — which cannot for a long time, if ever, be turned into an operable power on the actual world stage. Such contests over "power" and "glory" within the alliance may be expected to continue, but no one thinks that battle either must or can be the "payoff." Within the alliance, the power balances will shift, but it will not again take a bloody inter-NATO war to record the change.

Another cliché that experience calls in question is that which assumes that a prerequisite to a demilitarized world is a developed system of global law, capable of resolving all international "disputes" by juridicial means backed by coercive powers of enforcement. Such institutions, not merely of international but of supranational juridical authority, appear to be developing within the

North Atlantic complex—the Court of Justice of the European Coal and Steel Community is an example—but they are developing as a consequence rather than as a cause of demilitarization. They enjoy supranational authority in those areas where it is clearly in the interests of the participating states to accord it; but they have no supranational coercive or police powers. When the NATO Treaty was ratified in 1949, it made no provision for a supranational government, no provision for an inter-NATO judiciary to "settle disputes," and no provision for an inter-NATO police force with coercive powers. Even the unified NATO military command was not developed until later, when the developing power relations in the Western world made both the necessity for and the fact of effective intra-Western demilitarization apparent. Such institutional changes and developments as were requisite to take account of this fact have tended to appear as they are needed. When global power relations make a global demilitarization both possible and unavoidable, the institutional modifications will follow in due course.

A similar model of a demilitarized international system appears to be provided by the Western Hemisphere. There has not been an international war between or among any of the twenty-two sovereign states within the Hemisphere for the past thirty years or so. While all but one (Costa Rica) maintain formal military establishments, most of them actually amount to little more than the national police forces envisaged by all proposals for general disarmament. They have been used only as such police forces would be; they do not plan or prepare war against other members of the group and have not been employed by their governments to back up mil-

itary threats against other states. The defection of Cuba to the Communist camp and its extensive armament with Communist weapons may alter this situation, but it does not seem to have done so as yet. So far Castro has in fact confined his aggressive and expansionist tendencies to the nonmilitary methods of propaganda and subversion. Until the discovery of the Soviet missiles and bombers in Cuba, it was these methods, rather than the Castro armaments, that alarmed other members of the group. Too little is known about the reasons for the Soviet export and subsequent withdrawal of the weapons to estimate the ultimate significance of this episode. But so far it has led to no move toward re-armament on the part of the other American states. Most of them are struggling with severe social and economic problems; but to none has it occurred that they could be resolved by resort to organized war. Like others among the smaller nations, they may even see that the vast debilitation of the giant states by the war system only denies to them the resources that could and should go into their own social and economic rehabilitation.

All this has come about without even as rudimentary a structure of international governance as is provided in the NATO system. Differences and disputes of course arise among the members of the group, but they are not susceptible to resolution by war—as the United States discovered when confronted with the Castro problem. In fact, wars do not really proceed from "disputes"; they proceed from underlying power issues that specific disputes do no more than catalyze. The power relations in the Western Hemisphere are not such, even after the intrusion of the struggle between the Communists and the non-Communists, as to make organized war a practicable instrument of policy. Even in the weapons crisis the United States, while using military force to police the situation, was very careful to avoid threatening war in order to secure the removal of the missiles.

These situations, of course, present models only; and it may be argued that they are not models applicable to the full-scale global structure. It may be said that it is only the overriding power struggle between the Communists and non-Communists that has made possible the development of the power structures within NATO or the Western Hemisphere that have permitted these examples of international demilitarization. It does, indeed, seem obvious that the processes of global demilitarization —of general and complete disarmament —cannot be initiated without a *détente* in the struggle between Communists and non-Communists, and our models do not throw much light—they may throw some—on how this can be brought about. For the moment, however, this is another question. The immediate concern is with the design of a world demilitarized, not with the more difficult problem of its construction.

Since demilitarization is apparently impossible without it, one is justified in beginning by assuming the existence of a *détente* among the four or five great centers of military power—the United States, the Soviet Union, Western Europe, Great Britain (or Britain with Western Europe), and China—extending at least as far as that which exists today among the NATO powers or those of the Western Hemisphere. It would have to include a final liquidation of the Second World War (much as the former Western Allies have liquidated their differences with Germany, Italy, and Austria) and the effective resignation of any serious irredentist or territorial claims by one power against another. It would have to include an operative understanding among all (like that which exists within the North Atlantic grouping) that whatever differences might arise among them could not be settled by resort to organized war and would have to be resolved by other means. It would have to include a realization on the part of each of the great power centers that the others were permanent parts of the landscape of the age; that it was hopeless to dream of resolving conflicts between them by the destruction of one or another. These are the minimum conditions for a demilitarized world. But they are not Utopian. Urged on by the nuclear terrors, we are not impossibly far from them even today. Since 1945 the great powers have at least been acting as if such a *détente* already existed, even when they have not talked as though it did.

It is assumed, therefore, that the demilitarized world begins with an effective, even if more or less tacit, agreement of this kind among the four or five major power centers. Each has the size, in land area and population, and the industrial and economic development to make it a viable system of human organization in itself—largely self-contained, and if not fully "autarchic" at least with no unappeasable demands upon the peoples, territories, and resources of the others that would seem to it a rational cause of war.[1] Each

[1]The assumption here is that China will develop along much the same lines as the Soviet Union has done. She has not done so as yet, and the combination, in the Chinese case, of an enormous and growing population with a backwardness of industrial development which may fail to overtake it admittedly raises a question as to the assumption. Will not "population pressure" drive the Chinese into aggressive expansion into the less populated areas of Siberia or Australasia? To many, this question is enough to dispose at once of any question of a warless world. I do not think the

will be disarmed to police-force level. It is believed that there has been no very serious study of just what "police-force level" means. But it must mean at least that the war offices, general staffs, military mobilization and reserve systems will have been dismantled; that all heavy weapons systems, nuclear and non-nuclear, will have been discarded and war industries converted to nonmilitary uses. The great powers will thus be reduced substantially to the present position of the great majority of sovereign states today, few of which have significant war industries of their own and not many of which maintain heavy weapons in important numbers even when they are available from foreign suppliers. The military establishments of the smaller powers are for the most part not really capable of foreign war; generally speaking, their equipment and organization give them little more than the capability of maintaining internal order and controlling their frontiers against border raids or in matters of customs and immigration. The great-power police forces in a demilitarized world will have to be capable of this much. For the purpose they will doubtless require more than nightsticks and

answer is so simple. The relation of "population pressure" to war may be obvious in the case of the ancient migratory tribes; its relation to the modern wars of the modern highly integrated states is anything but obvious. Though Hitler's demands for *Lebensraum* were among his most powerful propaganda weapons, few would seriously attribute the Second World War to the pressure of German population; nor, conversely, argue that it was the population pressure on the Soviet Government that dictated its resistance, its repulse of the Germans, or the extensions of its political power in 1944 and 1945. The border warfare between China and India cannot, certainly, be attributed to population pressures. It is strategic, not demographic. There is little reason to suppose that Chinese, any more than Indian, leaders will conclude that a disparity between population and resources can be cured by war, when many more efficient means are available.

pistols; but even if their equipment includes such things as light tanks, machine guns, or patrol airplanes, their organizational and command systems will not be conducive to their use for aggression upon their neighbors. Such national police forces, moreover, having laid aside their intercontinental rockets, bomber fleets, naval carrier forces and submarine fleets, can have effect only upon their immediate neighbors. In general, the five giant power centers are not contiguous. There is a common border between the Soviet Union and China, but most will probably feel that this is already as completely demilitarized, by political and power factors, as the border between the United States and Canada. The Communist and the Western systems meet in Central Europe, but only in a complex of satellite states. This border is dangerous and unstable as long as the major centers can overleap it for direct attack upon each other; but if their potential hostilities can be worked out only through local operations of a police-force type, the frontiers are likely to become as stable as those in Latin America.

The demilitarized world will thus start with a great-power *détente* and a general reduction of armaments everywhere to a police-force level. What is striking about this assumed situation is the very large measure of stability it will contain. It is often argued that even general and complete disarmament cannot abolish war; even if all nuclear weapons are destroyed, this will not eliminate from the human brain the knowledge of how to rebuild them; even if all military forces are reduced to lightly armed police, they will go on fighting each other (even with "sticks and stones") as did the little armies of the seventeenth and eighteenth centuries, with nothing more than their smoothbore muskets. What this totally overlooks is the rapidly developing change in the international power structure that both makes demilitarization a possibility and will tend to conserve it once it is achieved. It is, of course, impossible to eradicate the knowledge of how to make nuclear bombs; it is not impossible to inculcate the realization that it is pointless to make them. The knowledge of how to revive a war system will remain; it is any reason for doing so that will disappear, as it has already begun to disappear today.

The stability of a demilitarized world would resemble the present stabilization of Western Europe under NATO much more than the attempted stabilization of Europe under the war system after 1918. The power organization of the modern world has in fact progressed enormously—taking the globe as a whole, there is actually more "law and order" and less violence in it than ever before in human history—and for a demilitarized future one need not posit the relatively primitive power organization that made wars frequent in Latin America in the nineteenth century and incessant in Western Europe in the eighteenth and seventeenth centuries. In a demilitarized world each of the four or five highly stabilized great-power governments would be committed, not simply in regard to each other but with their own peoples and taxpayers, to the abolition of war. In each, the large fraction of the Gross National Product now going into war and the war industries would have been converted to other and more desirable uses. The economic costs of a rearmament policy would appear to all of them to be enormous— especially when police arrangements had eliminated any need for it—while the risks it would entail would seem wholly incommensurate with any end

that could probably be attained by it, much as the political-military risks of actually resorting to nuclear arsenals today seem incommensurate with anything that could thereby be gained. When Hitler launched Germany on the paths of rearmament and military "power," there were probably few if any Germans who thought the objectives were mistaken; today, a new Hitler would be excoriated in his own country first of all, and in a generally demilitarized international society this would be true in all countries. In many states today the leaders are those who benefit in power and wealth from the war system; in a world demilitarized, the leaders would be those who had benefited from the process of demilitarization, who were committed to it and who would be the first to denounce any effort at its revival.

The four or five great stabilized, industrialized, and self-integrated power centers in fact offer a firm foundation on which to construct a demilitarized world power structure. If they were all, the problem would perhaps have been solved by now. But beyond their borders perhaps a third of the human race is found in the "uncommitted" or "underdeveloped" or "neutralist" world. That either the Western democratic-capitalist system or the Sino-Soviet Communist system can wholly or successfully organize this vast segment of humanity, with all its complex internal power issues, seems most unlikely. The "domination of the world" is as ephemeral a bogey for one side as for the other; and if the "cold war" has indicated anything it has indicated that "world domination" is as far beyond the power of the Soviet-Communist system as it is beyond the power of Western "capitalism." The comparative disorganization of the "uncommitted world" will doubtless continue to invite the great-power centers to rivalry for influence and control over its development. But rivalry need not, as the "cold war" again suggests, take the form of organized war. The great-power organizations themselves cannot be assumed to have been fixed for all eternity. One must expect conflict of interest, with resultant change and flux both within the great-power systems and among them, as well as in the uncommitted areas; and one must, we believe, expect a fair amount of riot, local violence, and guerrilla war in the process. In a generally demilitarized world such episodes need be no more disruptive to the underlying power balance on which the demilitarization rests than was, for example, the Irish guerrilla war for independence against Great Britain. But to keep such problems within limits, it already seems necessary for the demilitarized world to develop at least a minimal form of supranational authority.

The necessity, not merely for an international but for a genuinely supranational authority, has long been felt; and men have restlessly looked for its source in many places, from the "collective security" of the League of Nations down to "world opinion" or "moral authority," or a development of "natural law," uniformly without avail. We have many international authorities, but few sources of supranational authority have become available to us. Of course, the time may come when it is derived from a genuinely supranational global government, exercising over all states and groups and individuals within them powers, backed by a global "monopoly of force," comparable to those exercised by the federal government over the American states and their individual citizens. Until that obviously far distant time, it is believed that where supranational authority is needed, it can be derived only from the principle that underlay the United Nations charter— the principle of great-power unanimity.

In the United Nations charter it was hoped to secure great-power unanimity through the device of the great-power veto. This did not work. A supranational authority, if it is to be an *authority* at all, must be veto-free within the limits of its empowerment. The avenue to unanimity is not to be found through a veto, but through limiting the empowerment strictly to those areas in which all parties will recognize that it is to their own interest to accept what is in effect compulsory jurisdiction. In designing a demilitarized world, the question is what is the very minimum of supranational authority that it will necessitate. It is believed that this minimum, given the existing power structure in the world, can be put at a very modest level.

Once the world has been demilitarized, supranational authority will be needed primarily to ensure that rearmament does not take place; that the national police forces do not gradually develop into military threats against each other; and to exert in the less stable areas of the globe the kind of police power the UN has already been called upon to supply in Palestine and Africa. That it would have to establish compulsory enforceable jurisdiction in the settlement of "disputes" between the great powers seems doubtful. Once the enormous weapons systems, with the fears and the insoluble issues of abstract power that surround them, have been eliminated, differences that will continue to arise between the great-power centers will surely be susceptible to resolution by existing negotiatory and arbitral processes, as they are now within the Western community.

For all these purposes the supranational authority will have a modicum of armed force under its own veto-free command. It would not need and could not have a great supranational nuclear military force capable of coercing any of the great states — upon whose assent its own existence and effectiveness would depend. The whole success of a demilitarized world turns upon the *abolition* of military coercion as a means of adjusting the relations of states, and one cannot hope to abolish it on the national level if one is simply to reassemble it on the international level. The international police force, which appears in all plans for disarmament, must be just that —a police force and not an army. In the prevention of rearmament, most of the political and psychological factors will be, as has been suggested, on the side of the authority, and its useful instruments will be those of investigation, intelligence, and report, not of armed might. Once the world has been demilitarized, it is believed that it will be possible to define certain kinds of incitations or conspiracies looking toward clandestine rearmament or weapons development as international crimes, and to give the supranational police rights to intervene against such actions similar to those the American federal police organs enjoy within the several states. But by and large the great, highly organized powers can be relied upon to police themselves, as we now rely, for example, upon the great powers in NATO.

The functions and empowerment of the supranational police in the less stable areas of the globe are less easy to envisage. Since Theodore Roosevelt's claim to a "police power" in the Caribbean, if not long before, the idea of an international, or at least great-state, police control over "the little bandit nations" has been prominent in the dis-

course; but it has never been logically developed, and attempts to give it practical expression have rarely been happy. Khrushchev has cavalierly cut through the dilemma by saying that it will be the function of the international police to prevent all wars "except those of national liberation." The indignation with which this has been received in the West conceals the fact that the West (unless it really proposes to establish an iron *status quo* upon the globe) has no better answer for the riots, rebellions, and guerrilla wars that would be fairly certain to continue in a world generally demilitarized. Where the limits of supranational authority (and supranational armed power) in such situations are likely to lie is a problem that calls for much more study than it has been given.

One can only say that we have, on the one hand, been learning by experience (for proof one need only compare the "UN police action" in Korea with those in Palestine and the Congo); while, on the other hand, the problem of local violence, rebellion, and guerrilla war will lose much of its dangerous significance in a generally demilitarized world. Local power conflicts may be anything but bloodless (though we tend to forget how many problems have been solved since 1945, how many vast changes have been effected, by substantially bloodless means) and may, as in Algeria or the Congo, present appalling pictures of injustice, cruelty, and disorder. But they are not "causes" of major war; they can at most only trigger a major war already prepared by other military and power factors. The notion that armed violence or even small-scale international war anywhere represents a kind of center of infection, capable, unless immediately suppressed, of spreading into a Third World War, stands the real processes of international politics on their head. The small war cannot explode into a great one unless the great one already stands ready for detonation. The small war is like the dynamite cap. The dynamite cap is in itself by no means harmless, and has to be handled with care to avoid local damage. But unless and until the dynamite is attached to it, the damage will remain localized.

For the time being, at least, the great powers have been effectively demilitarized by their own weaponry; a great war seems as of today impracticable, and is not in preparation. The great powers have eschewed direct military intervention in African issues, and the police problem has fallen more or less by default to the UN. The forces it has deployed are very small; they have not attempted to resolve the political and power issues involved, but have mainly tried only to limit the violence. This situation, it would seem, would be the same whether the great powers are temporarily demilitarized by fear of their own weaponry or permanently demilitarized by a *détente* and disarmament. The working results, in the Congo and elsewhere, have been disagreeable in the extreme; but they have not been catastrophic. It is hard to doubt that this experience provides a model for the probable function of a supranational police force in dealing with the remaining violence in a world generally disarmed.

The demilitarized world will not and cannot eliminate the infinite variety of power struggles inherent in the nature of man. What it can and must do is to eliminate the war system, under which all these struggles "head up," both needlessly and catastrophically, into a giant military struggle between four or five great centers of organized power. Mortal combat (especially mor-

tal combat raised to levels of mass destruction hitherto practiced only in the ancient world) is not the only, it is not the usual, and it is not the final or even effective test of power in the modern world. There are many other ways besides organized war available today for resolving the almost infinite variety of power issues with which humanity must struggle. It is impossible to say with any precision just how these many issues would be dealt with in the absence of the great weapons systems; it is not impossible to prophecy that they would be dealt with much better than the weapons systems are likely to do. It is enough, for the moment, to point to the essential viability of a global system built upon the four or five great national power centers that now exist, these being mutually demilitarized to police-force levels and provided with a modicum of supranational force to ensure that no remilitarization took place and to provide for at least a minimum of order in the less stable areas of the world.

In many discussions of international peace, the "sovereign state" appears as the great villain in the drama. But this is to overlook what a really remarkable achievement in human organization the great modern industrial state—like the United States, the Soviet Union, the Western democracies, and potentially Communist China—really is. Its contributions toward human productivity and welfare are immense; so are its potential contributions toward peace and a reasonably just order. It is true that in its Communist and Western forms it has arisen out of somewhat different historical backgrounds; the two enshrine different concepts of "freedom"; the justice of one is not the justice of the other. Both have, however, proved themselves operable ways in which to organize the infinite variety of men in creative cooperation. Their rise has already brought to the world as a whole a far greater measure of "law and order" with far less actual violence or bloodshed than history has ever previously known. The world as it exists today is a tolerable one—"better" by most standards than any that previously existed—and it is only the fears of what the great weapons systems will do to it in the future that prevent our cheerful acceptance of the modern power structure.

Here is a large measure of working world organization already attained. If the great power centers can refrain from tearing each other to radioactive rubble, they can become in themselves an adequate base for a world system that, while not perfect, not static, not completely nonviolent, can, with only small additions to the institutional arrangements we now have, work at least far better than the war system ever has toward the betterment of man.

WORLD GOVERNMENT AND SUPRANATIONALISM
Amitai Etzioni

National Security: A Cracked Shell. Like turtles in their shells, human groups have shielded their members from outsiders since the beginning of history. But with time, these shells tend to expand to counter the increasing range of weapons outsiders employ.[1]

The medieval castle, for example, protected behind its walls the peasants of the surrounding estate from bandits and other lords' armies. (In exchange, the peasant supplied the lord and his knights with goods and services.) The cannon made the castle too small; it hopelessly cracked the "shell" of the medieval security unit.

The new protective shell was provided by the nation-state. Even the largest cannon could not reach its core unless the border fortifications were first cracked. Typically, World War I was fought along trenches that separated France and Germany, protecting the national borders and the populations behind them.

The introduction of the bomber in

Reprinted, with permission of the author and Collier Books, from *The Hard Way to Peace* by Amitai Etzioni. Copyright © by The Crowell-Collier Publishing Company.

[1]John Herz, *International Politics in the Atomic Age* (New York, Columbia University Press, 1959).

World War II made the national security unit too limited. The bomber could fly above the land-bound shell and hit the civilian population in the heart of the nation. But because of the limited range of bombers, an enlarged security unit could supply protection, if not to one country, then to the core of a group of them. Thus, for instance, even at the worst period of World War II, the United States—the industrial core of the allied forces—did not stand in serious danger of being bombed; most of the United States did not even experience a "black-out" in the midst of the most furious fighting.

The development of long-range bombers and missiles turned the whole globe into two security units organized on a bloc basis, each covering half the earth. The Western shell ranges over more than 20,000 miles, from Alaska to New Zealand, from Berlin to Tokyo, and from Hong Kong to Spitzbergen. It includes four military alliances interlocked by the leadership of the United States—NATO in Europe, CENTO in the Middle East, and SEATO and ANZUS in the Far East—as well as several two-country alliances. The Communists have a similar chain of alliances, centering around the Soviet Union.

All these military alliances started as strictly intergovernmental arrangements. War plans were coordinated, ammunition and weapons standardized, communication procedures formulated, and so on. But the tendency is to *merge* the national military organizations into a supranational military force (although it still might have national *units*). Thus a supranational commander-in-chief is appointed; a central, unified headquarters, to command the national units directly, is founded, and units of different nations are thrown together into shared military maneuvers. Thus, the problem of security calls for multination military cooperation, which in turn calls for a supranational military authority and organization.

It is questionable whether supranational military organizations grant security and whether the old conception of security through shells is still valid, in view of the range of the new weapons and their potency. Obviously, the author thinks that the days of man's security under a shell have passed, while most nations still act as if they can put their trust in their newly augmented shells. The main point about supranationalism, and the most widely accepted, is this: The days of *national* security have passed.

The Payoff of Economic Union. There is only one way to eat your cake and have it too — and that is by increasing international trade. The increase in the volume of exchange generates an improved division of labor among the participating countries, each nation producing what it is best suited for rather than straining to supply by itself all or most of its manifold needs. The result is that *all* countries will have a larger national income without any increase in investment or effort. Hence, from a strictly economic viewpoint, removing all national restrictions on trade, so as to establish a free global market, would be the most desirable arrangement.

Actually, the removal of national trade barriers progresses gradually; sometimes it even goes one step backward before going two steps forward. There are no big jumps, such as the opening up of a continent to free trade. Like the expansion of the security unit from the castle to the nation-state, the free market expanded from the sphere of one feudal lord to that of the national market. Germany, the United States, Italy, and so on, become not only integral security units but also integral markets.

Now, with the formation of supranational security units, we find serious efforts to establish supranational markets, to coordinate and even integrate the economies of several nations, the way their militaries are integrated. The best-known supranational market was formed by six countries — France, West Germany, Italy, Belgium, the Netherlands, and Luxembourg — in 1957. It requires each member to reduce its tariff barriers against other members by 10 per cent each year. So far, not only have the tariffs been reduced ahead of schedule, but working conditions of the countries are also in the process of being made uniform: social security levies and working hours are matched, to create equal conditions for free competition; investment and monetary policies are coordinated; transportation and energy development plans are synchronized; and many other areas of economic activities are becoming truly supranational. England and six other countries (Sweden, Norway, Denmark, Switzerland, Austria, and Portugal) formed their own "common market" in 1960. It is quite likely that the two groups will form a combined common market in the near future. Seven Latin American countries formed a common market in 1961. Attempts are also being made to put into effect two such unions in West Africa.

The Communist bloc's economic integration is also gradually advancing. There are no tariff barriers among Communist countries, and the five-year plans of various Eastern European countries are reported to be coordinated to develop a division of labor among them, to avoid duplication, and to encourage each to produce what it is best able to.

Like supranational security, supranantional economies are first regulated by meetings of representatives of the various governments concerned. As the intercountry economic flow increases, statewide regulation of the economies is reduced. As the demand for a new regulatory agency is stepped up, the tendency is to pool some economic sovereignty and to establish a supranational authority that has some direct control over multinational economic processes. The European Coal and Steel Community, for instance, installed a High Authority that by-passes the six member governments and deals directly with management, unions, banks, and parties in the six nations, in order to regulate policies concerning investment, wages, working conditions, transportation, and other related matters. It can even impose fines on the corporations that do not observe the agreements and regulations, though in case of refusal to pay the fine, the police of the various states would have to collect it. Thus, supranational economies involve the gradual creation of supranational sovereignty the way supranational security does.

Political Integration: Power for Pygmies. Though it receives little pub-lic attention, one of the strongest reasons for the pooling of national sovereignty is the desire of small nations to countervail bigger ones. Each small nation alone has little weight, but when a number of them act in unison, they are heard. Of the six European countries that are forming the supranational community, two—West Germany and France—are more powerful than the others. Hence we are not surprised to learn that the three smallest members have an additional strong integration of their own; Belgium, the Netherlands, and Luxembourg are integrated into Benelux. True, Benelux existed before the European community and has other reasons for its being, but since the European community developed, Bene-lux has found an additional reason for its integration, and the process has been accelerated.

Newly independent nations in Africa have been expected to be hyper-nationalistic (just as converts are often the most ardent supporters of a cause). Many otherwise acute political observers feared a Balkanization of Africa, the emergence of a continent full of many small, weak states, in continual conflict with each other. But the fact is that Africa has more planned, attempted, and budding nation unions than any other continent.

The underlying motive for political unification in Africa seems to be similar to that of smaller nations in Europe. African expert Immanuel Wallerstein points out that these nations seek independence not just to be free, but also to be equal.[2] As each realizes that it cannot gain such status alone, its supranational endeavors increase. Similarly, Latin American unification movements are

[2]*Africa: The Politics of Independence* (New York, Vintage, 1961), Chapter 6.

encouraged in part by the desire of these countries to countervail the influence of the United States in the Western hemisphere. The Scandinavian unification movement has similar overtones, in its effort to balance the power of Great Britain. It is as if they all acted on the maxim: united we stand, divided we fall.

Cultural Bridges. Many other less weighty factors operate in the same direction; each on its own would not move the mountain of nationalism, but as they are added to military, economic, and political efforts at unification, they ease, contribute to, and accelerate the process.

Science demands more and more manpower and becomes more and more expensive. Tests tubes are still used, but much modern research requires a multimillion-dollar cyclotron. Binoculars are still of help, but important breakthroughs in astronomy are made with mammoth telescopes and highly expensive research rockets. Hence nations now tend, as do universities within their respective countries, to specialize in some branches of science, leaving the other branches to other members of the international community, thus creating a scientific supranational division of labor. In addition, joint institutions are formed to serve the whole communities. UNESCO has established two centers for social studies — one in Brazil, the other in Chile — both serving all Latin America. The East European countries have a joint institute for nuclear research, located in Moscow. A joint school of journalism for the Scandinavian countries is attached to Arhus University in Denmark, and its board is elected by the press organizations in all Scandinavian countries.

The international flow of scientific information, the meetings with colleagues in other nations, and the shared projects, all strengthen the supranational community of scientists and scholars. These communities tend to be free from many of the nationalistic stereotypes and form a natural pro-supranationalism interest group. They also provide groups of experts who see matters in a comparatively objective light and are competent in cross-cultural and supranational communication.

A similiar function is fulfilled by the increasing *"international civil service,"* composed of white-collar employees and professionals who find their career in the various supranational and international organizations. Geneva, Brussels, and Paris are full of thousands of such people, constituting an international community that meets at social parties, follows the careers of its members, and respects and encourages those who overcome national bias in their work. This provides for the necessary atmosphere for a neutral, supranational administration.

Of special interest are regional *educational* institutions, where young intellectuals and political leaders of various nations gain a similar outlook and come to know each other intimately and which train an increasing number of the members of the "international civil service." The College de Europe in Brussels, the International Seminar in Salzburg, Austria, and the European University in Florence, Italy, play this role. Such institutions will eventually supply more supranationally-minded leaders and more supranational ties among the elites of the various countries.

More common are the many educational exchange programs that bring students, professors, businessmen, and leaders from various countries into close contact. Supranational summer camps, work camps, and song, dance, and sports festivals lend some support to the formation of supranational sentiments.

The revolutionary advances in *transportation* of goods and people have shrunk the earth. The airplane reduces the social size of a supranational community to that of a large city. This makes cross-national contact easier and more common, and this in turn supports a feeling of community.

Revolutionary progress in *communication* further shrinks the globe. Regional networks of radio and television are well underway. Eurovision carries television programs from a large number of Western European countries into the homes of millions of citizens of this supranational community. East Europe and Scandinavia have their own supranational networks of television and radio. Such communication networks make foreigners less alien and allows nation-communities to share events that range from the opening of a supranational research institute to a multination festival.

While these factors are often viewed as "international," affecting members of all nations, they are actually "supranational," affecting chiefly smaller nation-communities. While interbloc cultural, scientific, and educational exchange programs gain much public attention, such exchanges among the members of the same nation-community are much more common. Moreover, interbloc exchanges not only are less frequent but also have much less effect on international relations, because, while such exchanges can accelerate and support an ongoing process of unification, carried by more weighty factors in the military, economic, and political spheres, they can neither initiate nor carry on a unification process, as

some enthusiasts of interbloc organizations and exchange programs believe.

The Expansion of the Moral Community. The existence of an effective government on the local, state, or national level is predicated on the citizens' not using violence against each other. To some degree the government can force observation of the law, but if the citizens are basically wolves, no government will have enough force to control them. Hence, a moral commitment by the citizens not to exercise violence toward each other is an essential requirement for the existence of a shared viable government. It is this moral community — the communities of those to whom we do not apply violence even when differences of interests and opinions are large, and whom we expect not to use violence toward us — that provides the moral foundations for peace.

The scope of this no-violence community has gradually expanded throughout history. It included only a few hundred people in man's primitive stage; outsiders were literally free game. The Greek polis extended the no-violence status to all its citizens, but "barbarians" and slaves were at best partially covered. With the emergence of the nation-state, the no-violence moral community expanded greatly — though, again, not all social groups were included.

Over the last hundred years, the moral community has gradually expanded to include all groups within one nation: first, women and children, then the laboring classes; most recently, racial minorities are gaining their place. The redefinition of the insane and the criminal as not morally bad but as mentally ill, hence as entitled to treatment and rehabilitation, rather than segregation behind bars, is an expression of the same basic trend. We are close to the day when all those who live within the boundaries of a nation-state will be treated as members of its moral community, entitled to the basic human rights and freedom from violence that such membership involves.

Many religions have declared the moral community to be universal, to encompass all created in the image of God. But until recently, such pronouncements had only a limited effect on the behavior of mortals. While many subscribe in principle to universal expansion of the moral community, they rarely act accordingly. The best way to become a national hero is still by killing as many citizens of another nation as possible.

But in recent years there has been a growing tendency to truly extend the moral community beyond national boundaries. More and more neighboring nations are included, especially when other supranational ties are already shared. A simple but central indicator is that we find war with those nations "inconceivable" (so long as they do not apply violence to us, which we believe they will not). An interesting case is the slow evolution of a European no-violence community whose members include Germany and its arch enemies of yesterday. France and Germany fought each other, with much bloodshed and abuse, three times in less than a century. Between the wars, the level of animosity was high, both on the national and interpersonal levels. The idea of revenge, of redeeming the national pride from the last defeat, was a conception on which the post-1871 and post-World War I generations were nourished. Not so after World War II. West Germany and France are now intimate allies, supporting each other's demands in the political arena; West German and French towns declare themselves "sister" cities; children of the two nations spend time together in summer resorts, and German soldiers could recently use French soil for their military exercises, with next to no protest.[3] It seems that in the near future Frenchman and German will find war with each other, as well as with other members of the European community, "inconceivable." This provides the moral fiber for the evolving supranational community.

Similarly, the Scandinavian countries, which used to fight each other bitterly, now not only constitute a peaceful community, but they also delete past bloody incidents from their history textbooks, so that the younger generation will grow up on brotherhood, not hatred.

[3]Even England, which is at best on the verge of joining the European community, is already changing its attitude to West Germany, and not only on the official level. The *Guardian* (Manchester) of August 15, 1961, reports:

"The commanding officer of the 84th Panzer Battalion, West German tank battalion, that will train on the firing range at Castlemartin, Pembrokeshire, next month, flew back to Germany from Wales delighted with the facilities at the camp and with the way he was received.

"Lieutenant-Colonel von Kleist said: 'My reception was much better than I expected.' There had been no hostility towards him during his two-day visit to Pembroke, where he paid a courtesy call on the Mayor, Alderman J. Sidney Rees.

"Colonel von Kleist, who did not wear his war decorations, which include the Iron Cross, in a press conference placed some emphasis on the greeting that is already being extended to his men.

"Several British girls wanted to strike up pen friendships. There had also been several offers to spend weekends in British homes.

"Colonel von Kleist, a relative of the wartime Panzer general, was asked how he felt in bringing uniformed Germans to Britain, where he was a war captive for two-and-a-half years. 'We feel guilty for the last war, but we are now integrated fully in NATO,' he said."

The British Labour party, however, passed a resolution in October, 1961 to deny British training facilities to West German troops.

Supranational expansion of the no-violence community often follows the formation of other supranational ties, such as those of the economic, political, and military spheres. It benefits from the expansion of communication networks, tourism, cultural exchanges, and shared educational institutions, which add their influence to the more basic bonds. While the extension of economic, military, and political ties often precedes the expansion of the moral community, these ties are greatly strengthened once the moral community catches up with them. Violence among the member nations is now considered not only against the interests of each nation, but also immoral.

From Nation-Union to Global Society

One or two generations from now, the earth will probably be populated with a score or two of supranational communities, instead of the present multitude of nations. Many of the supranational communities will be united in supercommunities, or blocs. How much closer will this bring us, though, to a global society and a stable peace? Will not these supranational communities be nations writ large, fighting each other with the same venom but with more strength than the nation-states? While this possibility cannot be excluded, it seems to me that nation-unions both in the long and short run brighten the outlook for evolving a stable peace.

Nation-Unions and Nonwar. Most contemporary supranational communities are less than ten years old. Many, in fact, are only at the beginning stage, and only a few of the new nation-unions have developed to the point where strong loyalties to the nation-community have been firmly established. But even in this short period, some not insignificant contributions to peace have been made.

The most immediately apparent one is the absence of wars among member nations *within* supranational communities. Archenemies of yesterday are now sharing a union and are extremely unlikely to fight one another again. Not only have all border fortifications and troop positioning been abolished, but their military organizations are also gradually integrating into one supranational organization and their citizens are beginning to include each other in a moral community.

3

POVERTY

Meaning of Poverty

Poverty means the relative inability to subsist. It denotes the inability of an individual or household to provide (through its own means or the transfer of resources from others) the necessities of life. We say *relative* inability because what people regard as necessary varies across time and place.

At one pole, poverty signifies death by starvation or exposure through lack of clothing and shelter. In the Great Potato Famine in Ireland in the 19th century, intense poverty killed thousands of families in a single decade. In India and Russia, until the 20th century, poverty was a way of life for most people for hundreds of years. Yet it did not become a social problem in either place until aggravated by other crises such as war, rapid technological change, and ideological conflict.

At the other pole, what one means by necessities of life can be so enlarged through economic and cultural change that poverty may not mean biological inability to survive. It may mean the lack of a share, however modest, in the goods defined socially as necessary for a subsistence level of living.

Poverty is indicated by a ratio of needs to resources. But this ratio is complicated. Needs vary with changing standards and requirements. Types and amounts of resources are changed by economic and technical changes in the society. And the ratio of needs to resources for any individual or household may rise and fall over the period of the life cycle.

The Price System

In the nature of competition, if some win, others must lose. The process presumes *scarcity* of what is valued most. Status, for example, reflects ability to command scarce resources. Competition for resources is regulated in the United States and throughout Western civilization, through the use of *price*.

A modern price system *mediates* values, thereby regulating their exchange. A price system sets a money value, a common expression of worth or exchange potential, upon most resources.

Some values remain outside the price system; for example, family love, friendship and patriotism. Others once in the price system have been eliminated, such as titles and slaves. With economic growth and changing technology, however, most values come to be mediated through the price system. The larger and more complex the system of technology, social organization, and population composition, the more the price system becomes a common denominator.

Price, or the setting of dollar terms on matters of value, has the advantage of flexibility and universality. A price system allows different groups to seek different kinds of gratifications. It converts competition and conflict between groups for scarce values into partial cooperation through negotiation over rates of exchange. The commonality of prices makes orderly competition possible.

Price measures scarcity as well as value in common terms.[1] It allows us to quantify life conditions for different groups of persons in the national society. Because of common rates of exchange, we can decide what it costs in terms of dollars to subsist, to subsist and then some, and to live comfortably. In an advanced industrial economy, many vital facets of the social situation can be translated into dollar terms of what we shall call *level of living*.

Today, people go to the market to buy goods they need or want. Goods are

[1]With the increasing variety of values that fall *inside* the price system in American society, pricing facilitates equality of opportunity. For those who want a good or service, for example, its availability on the basis of price alone eliminates barriers to access. The unequal availability of restaurants, hotels, and motels, and housing between Negroes and whites in the United States illustrates the case where price fails to guarantee equal availability, of course.

anything that people believe have the power to satisfy a need or want. Goods may be marketed whether they are material or nonmaterial, as when the buyer purchases a phonograph (material) to listen to a recorded piano concert (nonmaterial). Here, only the pleasure of listening, and not the skill of performing, can be bought with the record. (Goods of both sorts are produced and consumed without money and without recourse to the market, but these are rare.)

Income System

So precise is the price system today (exclusive of those goods that remain separated from the price system) that we can quantify in dollars nearly all of the material and nonmaterial goods that a person or household obtains for use in a given time. This is called *real income*. Real income embraces income obtained through any source: investment, labor — including work done apart from the labor force conceived as away-from-home occupations — and wages, and cooking food and making or caring for home furnishings and equipment. Contributions to real income include public provision of schools, streets, water and related services, the services of durable goods such as houses and automobiles. We can, in brief, estimate real income whether the consumer buys apples from a store or raises them on a tree in his own yard.

A person's *level of living* is set by his real income. One's *standard of living*, or the way one wants to live, is not as fixed. It varies with changing needs and wants. The two are seldom interchangeable. In this framework, level of living has real income as a denominator. A below-subsistence level of living would be one at which real income is not great enough to permit survival. A subsistence level would be survival without margin for contingencies.

Real income, the total of all commodities and services obtained from any source for use by an individual or group, shrinks or extends with quality of care in the choice of goods, and with the division of money outlay and work outlay, that is, with quality of income management. Real income is further affected by whether a person or group produces goods at home for private use.

There is a difference between annual cash income and annual real income, but earned cash income is the main factor in the American income structure. First, the two are highly correlated. Second, among the poor, nonwage income sources are irrelevant. People who are poor or pinched can save very little, even when they are educated toward wise consumption behavior (which they rarely are). Lack of savings results in limited capital for medical insurance and housing, for example, which might enable them to earn more real income. Limited capital also freezes one to a job, prohibiting participation in a fluid labor market.

According to surveys conducted by the U.S. Department of Commerce in 1959, roughly 20 million out of 45 million families earned less than $5,000. This included the dollar value of food and fuel produced as well as cash income. Of these 20 million, about 5 million were without assets, in dollar savings, insurance, home payments, or otherwise. About 9 million of the 20 million had total assets of less than $1,000. For low income families and individuals in the United States, then, the most relevant factor in level of living is annual cash income.

Level of Living and Poverty

What is a subsistence scale of living? It is the level a family or an unattached person must attain in order to subsist across a year. Subsistence denotes only existence, but its connotation is existence at a bare minimum. What is a subsistence level when translated into annual income? Obviously, the level varies in time and place. The condition of poverty constitutes an absolute problem for the person experiencing it, but to understand it socially we have to think about it as a condition relative to history and country. Even if it is absolute for the impoverished person, it may take a lifetime to reveal itself. Families do not ordinarily fail to subsist all of a sudden. The absolute effect of poverty accumulates through disadvantage, malnutrition, psychic deprivation, and disease.

Subsistence and poverty vary in time in the sense that less may have been required to help insure survival in times when the scale of society was less enlarged, when families and individuals faced less complex demands and opportunities. Certainly, subsistence levels vary across countries, though to what extent we are not at all certain. And levels differ according to size of family, age of children, and ability to consume intelligently.

A path may be struck through this thicket of qualifications if we use established, empirically set estimates of what it costs in annual income to subsist, modestly but adequately, as the consumer economists put it, in this decade in the United States.[2] For nearly a

[2]Much of this and the following information derives from: Conference on Economic Progress, Poverty, and Deprivation in the United States (Washington, D.C.: Conference on Economic

quarter of a century, the Bureau of Labor Statistics of the U.S. Department of Labor studied costs of living for families of different ages and sizes and for individuals in different communities across the United States. From these, economists concluded that a four-person family needs an annual income of $6,624 to live modestly but adequately in Seattle, Washington (1959). The same family could limp along at the level of subsistence for $5,696 in Atlanta, Georgia. The same surveys and analyses suggest an annual income for unattached persons of between $2,300 and $3,000 for the same year. The range of subsistence incomes for 1959 goes from $2,300 to a high of $9,397 for families containing six or more persons.

If we use this information to set an *average*, we need only two additional pieces of data to describe poverty crudely. We need to know that roughly two thirds of all families in the United States contain four or more persons. Therefore, the subsistence budget for the four-person family provides a meaningful crude average for households. And we then have to decide where subsistence ends and poverty begins.

Economist Robert Lampman used $2,500 as the poverty line for an urban family of four. Adjusting for size of family, and for urban versus rural loca-

tions, he concluded that *19 per cent* of the American population was impoverished. With a slightly higher definition of less than $3,000, a 1958 study reached an estimate of *24 per cent* of the population. Using a higher ceiling of $4,000 for two-or-more-person families and $2,000 for unattached individuals, economist Leon Keyserling used 1960 data and identified 34 million persons in families and 4 million individuals as impoverished, or a total of *21 per cent*.[3]

Economic Deprivation

The significance of this goes beyond explaining similar results from dissimilar studies. It suggests the presence of plateaus along the curve of income distribution. It gives us a basis for considering the idea of *deprivation*.

For example, if $6,000 stands as the subsistence level budget for average size families, as the Labor Department work suggests, we have taken standards that range from roughly $2,000 to $3,500 *below* this level as representing below-subsistence budgets. This led to a conservative estimate of one in five American families as impoverished.

Progress, 1962) [The main author of this analysis is Leon Keyserling, and it is known as the Keyserling Report]; Michael Harrington, *The Other America: Poverty in the United States* (New York: Macmillan and Company, 1962); Gabriel Kolko, *Wealth and Power in America* (New York: Frederick Praeger, 1962); Robert J. Lampman, *The Share of Top Wealth-Holders in National Wealth* (Princeton, N.J.: Princeton University Press, 1962); and James N. Morgan, et al., *Income and Welfare in the United States* (New York: McGraw-Hill Book Co., 1962). See also John Kenneth Galbraith, *The Affluent Society*, (Boston, Houghton Mifflin Co., 1960.)

[3]What is most dramatic about these estimates is their consistency, regardless of the income level used as a ceiling. For the total population, very different ceilings and different ways of handling family size and location yield remarkably uniform results. Available national estimates cluster between one fifth and one fourth of the population as living below subsistence, or in poverty.

What accounts for this consistency regardless of cutting point? It results from the fact that families cluster in the $2,000 to $3,999 income interval, and unattached individuals cluster in the "under $2,000" interval, when the income distribution from less than $1,000 to $5,000 — the lower half of the income structure — is considered. Another way of conveying this is to note that the bulk of low income families fall in the $2,000 to $3,000 interval, just as most low income individuals fall in the $1,000 to $1,500 interval.

What of the families and individuals who fall between this subsistence budget line and the conservative poverty line? Take family incomes first and, with Keyserling, take $6,000 as the upper subsistence level. Then, we would regard as deprived the families who fell between $4,000 and $6,000. His analysis finds 37 million family members are deprived, or 10.3 million out of 45 million family groups. The number of deprived households is equal to the number of impoverished. Two out of five American families appear to be impoverished or deprived.

Closer Looks at Three Levels of Living

We have distinguished three types of low income living: subsistence (or modest but adequate), deprived (or pinched), and poor. In gross terms, even when all qualifications are considered, there is evidence that about 20 per cent of the total population lives within each of these categories. Depending on where the ceilings are set, moreover, the groupings are fairly distinctive. That is, the subsistence group clusters at and just below the median annual income for the country. The deprived group falls in between subsistence and poverty.

The impoverished make up a separate category indicated by a plateau in the income curve that runs from $1,000 to about $3,000 a year for families. About 60 per cent of the national population, at least, secures a level of income which just reaches the minimum needs estimated for contemporary living or which at worst falls short of this minimum twice over. These three income groups make up 60 per cent of the population, but they receive only 30 per cent of the income attained by the population each year.

This tells us only that income is very unequally distributed in the United States. It does not signify any particular social problem except by way of suggesting that large numbers of persons are economically insecure, hence vulnerable to serious life difficulties.

What is the magnitude of the insecurity? What differences do income inequalities make in the lives of persons at the several levels? The entire income and price system of the economy is so arranged that there are constraints on families and individuals to live up to standards that far exceed realistic levels of income. What are the true patterns of expenditure and relative need among the lower income groups?

Consider first our subsistence-level group. What kind of living is provided for a family of four living in a large metropolitan area with an annual income, as of 1960, of about $6,000?

Let us imagine a wage-earning husband of about 40, his house-keeping wife, and their two children, a boy of 13 and a girl of 8. They live in a rented private apartment of four rooms, plus a kitchen and private bath. The dwelling has hot as well as cold running water, central heat, electric lights, gas cookstove, and an electric refrigerator. The apartment building is within walking distance of city schools, libraries and other public services, including bus transportation.

This family can afford to pay the high rent it must for an apartment with these amenities and in this good location. In fact, they pay a rent of more than $100, if not much more. They can also pay for utilities, supplies of soap and cleaning materials, and for periodic purchases of furniture, sheets, towels and cleaning equipment, all of which are included in the $136 shown in the estimate chart below.

appliance is a five-year-old television set.

The quality of food consumed by this family is nutritionally sound. With

BUDGET ESTIMATES FOR SUBSISTENCE, DEPRIVED,
AND IMPOVERISHED FAMILIES*

Item	Monthly Cost		
	Subsistence	Deprived	Impoverished
Food	$160	$106	$70
Clothing	48	32	32
Housing	136	90	54
Transport	20	15	15
Medical	32	21	20
Personal	12	10	10
Recreation, Education, Communication, & Tobacco	30	20	20
Life Insurance	10	7	4
Dues, Gifts, Contributions	20	13	0
Social Security	12	8	5
State Tax	5	2	0
Federal Tax	38	25	0
Total monthly	$523	$349	$230
Total yearly	$6,276	$4,176	$2,760

*Estimated for four persons, husband-wife family residing in New York City. Data not exact but adapted for illustration from the work of the New York City Budget Standard Service and U.S. Department of Labor Budgets, 1954-1959.

Mr. Subsistence travels to work by bus. His family may have a car if it is located on the edge of the city. The car was purchased second-hand and is now at least eight years old, and is not used for more than 6000 miles each year. The father buys his lunch very cheaply at the cafeteria of his company; all other meals are prepared by the mother at home except for a once-a-month treat of eating out.

Mrs. Subsistence cleans and launders without paid assistance. She could save money by doing her dry cleaning at home, but she has been tempted into using the bulk dry-cleaning machines at the corner laundromat. Moreover, she has enough income at her disposal to own a washing machine, electric iron, and vacuum cleaner. The favorite family

great care given to skillful buying and preparing, the mother could save as much as $150 a year over what she currently spends on food, *if* the incentives for doing so were stronger.

There is also enough money so that the family members are decently clothed. For example, Mr. Subsistence buys a topcoat about every 4 years, and one suit, a pair of trousers, 5 shirts, 2 pairs of cheap shoes and 12 pairs of socks each year. His wife has enough to buy a coat every 2 years and one hat, 4 dresses, 2 pairs of shoes, and 10 pairs of nylon stockings a year. They spend about $48 a month from their gross monthly income of $523 for clothing.

The Subsistence family has enough income to cover haircuts from barbers and home hair treatment equipment for the mother and daughter. Their $12 a month, or $144 a year, for personal care covers this and such items as toilet soap, toothbrushes, toothpaste, shaving and sanitary supplies, although clearly the amounts will always be limited and in short supply.

Their $384 a year reserved for medical care gives them enough to make four visits annually to physicians and two visits to dentists, and to have enough left to maintain membership in a hospital insurance plan and to pay for drugs and diagnostic services. Chronic illness or a costly accident would of course break this limit. But for routine care, even over several years when costs are higher for this family than in other years, the amount is adequate.

The $30 a month for recreation, education, communication, and tobacco, pays for two cartons of cigarettes, one neighborhood theater movie admission, one weekly magazine and one daily newspaper subscription. The $15 that remains after this set of entertainments must cover all school fees — supplies, athletic events, social affairs, and leave enough over so that parents and children operate and maintain their TV. They usually also visit a diner for a supper once every month. No beer or alcoholic beverages can be maintained except in place of something else. Similarly, this family can afford to belong to but *one* organization aside from the father's union.

The term, subsistence-level of living, remains meaningless without these empirical particulars. Once the model is sketched in, we can see that the level is adequate by way of food, clothing, and shelter, yet the family is short on long-term security, health care, education and recreation, and participation in the life of their community. *Subsistence means, for the modern American urban*

family, a life style of respectable, cautious living. It is at variance with the themes emphasizing consumption that surround the family in its daily living in the city.

The subsistence level is possibly frustrating or dulling. It is *not* disorganizing or threatening to life, however. Any number of conditions, if present, could impoverish this subsistence-level family, however. Unwise management of credit, drinking or alcoholism, chronic illness, or loss of employment are among the personal crises that convert subsistence into deprivation and poverty. Larger economic crises have the same effect. Many poor families of today were the children of parents impoverished by the Great Depression in the 1930s. The subsistence family or individual is vulnerable; its adaptive resources are limited.

Contrast the budget for the subsistence family of four with that of the impoverished family. Call them the Poor family. The Poors have 60 cents per person per day (or $2.40) to spend on food. Without high skill dietetics and food management, hunger and malnutrition are inevitable at this level. Housing is restricted to slum tenements, with crowding into two or three rooms. No medical expenses, other than occasional trips to free hospital clinics, can be handled.

The personal care budget of the Poors provides only minimum toilet and sanitary supplies at home, and an occasional haircut. The $10 a month must somehow cover purchase of home permanents, shampoo, bobby pins or wave lotions, face powder or cleansing cream, lipstick or rouge, shoe polish and brushes, or spot removing fluids for dry cleaning. Few urban Americans will do without most of these items. They will sacrifice other necessities in order to remain minimally groomed. (Personal care items for a single, at-home, adolescent girl, for example, average $55 a year.)

For recreation, education and communication, the Poor family is like the Subsistence family except that *no* money can be spent on magazines or eating out. There is enough for a used TV set, a radio, one local movie a month, and a family paper, but nothing for magazines, books, sports, plays or concerts. No telephone can be maintained; even letter writing is expensive. With care, enough money may be available for gifts at Christmas, but not at any other time in the year. The Poor family has no money for membership dues, gifts, or contributions. Its insurance budget will pay for burial insurance, nothing more.

This is poverty because this level of living fails to provide for subsistence, however minimal, over the long term. For example, the expenditure for food will guarantee malnutrition in all but the most skilled of kitchens. The malnutrition may be concealed in prenatal illness of mothers, maternal and infant mortality, or infant morbidity. The clothing budget cannot provide shoes that fit growing feet, or outer wear that is protective in cold weather. Nor can clothing be kept clean or in repair.

Housing in a big city, at a rental of $45 a month for four, will involve vermin, rodents, exposure to contagious diseases, overcrowding, and friction or restrictions on child development, unless it is a public project. Most of all, it will require constant movement from place to place: rents change, tenements burn down or are demolished, and types of occupancy change. Finally, medical and personal care and recreational outlets are fixed below a level that provides for any kind of change in the life situation, including crises of illness and unemployment. This does *not* mean that the Poor family will fail to survive. It means that this level of living, under American urban conditions, stacks the odds against survival.

Likely Causes of Poverty

In interpreting poverty, many irrelevant factors have been overemphasized in the past. One fallacy was to attribute poverty to whatever undesirable qualities appear to be correlated with very low income. Usually this fallacy takes two forms, individual and societal: Uninformed commentators for years have interpreted poverty as the result of sin, 'bad' genes, laziness, or vice, whether alcohol, sex or gambling. The societal counterpart to this nonsense is the notion of poverty as caused by some single condition in the economic or political order, such as unequal taxation, war, discrimination, or immigration.

Modern economic and social research offer better information about the correlates of American poverty. One recent and most careful study, done by social scientists at the Survey Research Center of the University of Michigan,[4] found the following categories to be the most common attributes of poverty among families (that is, exclusive of single, unrelated individuals): Where the head of family is *nonwhite* (47 per cent were in poverty); physically or mentally *disabled,* whether fully or partially (46 per cent); *single* and has children (45 per cent); *65 years* or older (39 per cent); usually employed, but *unemployed* for all or part of 1959 (27 per cent); or where the head of the

[4]James N. Morgan, et al., *op. cit. Income and Welfare in the United States, ibid.*

family is a self-employed farmer or businessman (21 per cent). Among the 13.8 million families estimated to be in poverty by this study, 11.4 million (83 per cent) fell into one or more of these six groups.

The groups overlap, of course. Half of the families with aged fathers or mothers were disabled and/or non-white, for example. Two fifths of the broken families were nonwhite. Keyserling found that of all persons living in poverty in 1960, 57 per cent were in households whose heads had eight years or less of education. More than 40 per cent were clustered in the South; and most poor southerners with low educational attainment were Negroes.

The correlates of poverty are substantially the same for individuals, with higher proportions of the *aged* and of unemployed young adults as the chief difference.

These correlates can be called the major 'likely causes' of poverty, but it must be understood that this reasoning is circular. For instance, many families have very low incomes because the main wage earner is handicapped by limited formal education; yet, poverty often produces deficiencies in education among children in poor families. In the same way, it means little to say that being Negro 'causes' poverty. Rather, being Negro causes restricted opportunity, which in turn often produces impoverishment. Older persons are unable to find work or are limited in their ability to work, as are the disabled. The heads of broken families must care for children and earn a living at the same time. Their double burden reduces their earning power. Self-employed persons are vulnerable to sudden changes in market demands for their products and services. *In these ways only may we speak accurately of*

the correlates of poverty as 'likely causes.'

Impersonal Causes of Poverty

These correlates must be objectified as to their bases in the economy and the social structure if we are to understand poverty. For example, half of all of the nation's poor families are Negroes, or persons over 65, or both. Nearly one fourth are temporarily unemployed or disabled, or both. Why is this? The first general reason is relative scarcity in the economy. The second, which reinforces the first, is the character of contemporary American social organization.

The rate of economic growth since World War II, while sufficient to improve the level of living of most of the population, has not been enough to insure that employment opportunities will keep pace with population growth. As with other social problems, the source of strain lies with incompatible rates of change. A shortage of employment opportunities among unskilled and semi-skilled workers results not merely in job and wage insecurity through unemployment for many, but in intensified discrimination through conflict and competition for scarce jobs.

Without high rates of economic growth, consumer purchasing power and, therefore, ability to move toward new opportunities, improved health, and education among consumers, is restricted. In the same way, federal and state programs of welfare assistance, vocational rehabilitation for the disabled, and programs of unemployment insurance, are limited by lack of sufficient revenues from taxes.

Political incentives for legislating programs against poverty are also restricted to periods of gravest crisis, making innovation and reorganization of defenses against poverty unlikely. This was true, at least, until 1964. In a period when four out of five Americans are subsisting, and five out of ten live better than ever before, who cares politically about the impoverished few?

Historical patterns also reinforce this condition. There was real concern among American colonial leaders for the 'deserving poor,' for example. Those who deserved help were colonists who conformed to current religious and political beliefs and moral codes and who exhibited a 'keenness to work.' Charity was further limited to local residents who were *not* poor at the time they were accepted into the immediate community.

These historical traditions have changed only a little. The Michigan survey group found, for example, that in spite of elaborate and expensive local, state, and federal provisions for public welfare, less than one fourth of the poor families in their national sample received public assistance of any kind. In fact, 40 per cent of the disabled and 38 per cent of the broken families received *no public help* during 1959! The greatest single source of public, indirect aid came, in fact, from the lighter tax burdens imposed on these families. In keeping with colonial tradition, no present American welfare program aims to eliminate poverty by placing a real income floor under those unable to earn enough to subsist. Instead, each program is designed to help out, but to fall intentionally short of adequate assistance in order not to undermine the recipient's 'motivation' to work hard. The amount of assistance also falls short in order to avoid competition between private and public sectors of the economy.

Some Other Aspects of Poverty

Poverty in the United States differs markedly from poverty in the underdeveloped nations of the world. There, the great majority must defend themselves against starvation each day and severe hunger is a general way of life. American poverty is more a state of relative material deprivation. One in five Americans suffers relative to the other four in five. Americans are also poor relative to what is possible as a general level of living relative to the total economy.

Once, we could think of poverty as a function of scarcity of resources. General economic growth in this country once depended mostly upon the abundance of resources. In the last fifty years, however, resources, while still vital, have played a diminishing role in determining economic growth. Factors other than resources, such as the business cycle, the maintenance of demand and employment, the development of technology, the shift in consumption toward services, and changes in the level of net government expenditures are the chief active determinants of growth today. The resource base of the American economy is now adequate. It will continue favorable for the remainder of this century. Threatening shortages can be remedied through foreign markets, substitute materials, or the science of reuse of formerly wasted materials. *We do not have poverty in American because of scarcity.*

Alternate economic forces deserve illustration. Consider unemployment. Short-term and periodic unemployment results from seasonal factors. In 1960, there were about 4 million more jobs in midsummer than there had been in midwinter. Such expansion disappears again the following winter. In the same way, short-term unemployment varies with swings in the business cycle. The economy has slumped every three to four years during the past two decades. During each recession, workers are laid off. When an upswing resumes, production goes up but re-employment lags for a while. These and other causes of periodic unemployment are partly compensated for by unemployment insurance. This has operated in this country, with federal support, since World War II.

Long-term unemployment reflects the main *untreated* sources of poverty (although unemployment insurance provisions also fall short of what would be required to defend adequately against even temporary joblessness). Long-term poverty from unemployment results from interaction among several economic and social processes. First, there is the annual growth of the labor force, which expands at a rate of about one million workers a year. (From 1950 to 1962, the average expansion was about .8 million annually. By 1965, this rate increased to more than one and a half million new workers per year.)

Expansion of the labor force interacts with automation (or the mechanization of processing and distributing) to intensify unemployment. *Alone,* automation creates new jobs as well as displaces workers. The new machines substitute for workers, but machine construction and operation require workers, and their maintenance and repair create new jobs. Lower production costs also stimulate output; economic growth, hence expanding opportunity for work through new demand, results. Automation does not occur in a vacuum, however. Instead, workers are laid off in one plant in one community, while jobs of a different kind are created somewhere else. The newly unemployed cannot transfer easily from place to

place. Even if they could, skill requirements are changed. Thus, an increasing number of workers are laid off annually, and an increasing number of new jobs are slow in being filled.

Economists refer to this as *structural unemployment.* By itself, structural unemployment caused by automation would be insignificant in determining poverty. When it is compounded with an expanding labor force, however, the extent of economic insecurity and its annual growth becomes a major national social problem.

The seriousness is illustrated by these figures: In 1953, the number of employable adults who reported being out of work for more than 6 months was less than 100,000. In 1956 (a year of prosperity, incidentally) it was about 250,000. In 1960, it was 500,000. And by 1962, it had reached 1,000,000. These are, for the most part, long-term unemployed who are neither too old nor too disabled to work, but who have been displaced by an expanding labor force, changing technology, geographic shifts in job opportunities, and inability or unwillingness to retrain for higher and different types of skills.

There are thus important reasons for poverty within the current American economy. *Among the 13.8 million families estimated by Morgan as impoverished, these economic reasons apply, however, to not more than one third of the total.* They relate, at most, to poverty as caused by unemployment, premature retirement, and the risks of self-employment among farmers and small businessmen. To these groups, we may add perhaps half of the nonwhites —those barred from jobs through discrimination, a discrimination that would be less effective if structural unemployment were less severe. Theirs are the low-skill jobs hit hardest by automation and labor force expansion.

Politics of Poverty

The character of poverty in America can be understood only culturally and politically. For example, every individual and family in the nation now below a subsistence income could be lifted to the subsistence level at a cost of about $10 billion a year, according to Morgan. This is about one fifth the annual cost of national defense. The elimination of economic poverty, if not the elimination of the sources of poverty in the economy, is a ready possibility. We know roughly how much poverty exists today, roughly what the causes of each sort are, and how these could be attacked. Poverty *could* be abolished, given the political will.

But what is the 'political will' in a national democracy? Why, in this instance of poverty, is the will to eliminate the problem lacking? Again, are there structural as opposed to superficial reasons?

Impoverished Americans are underrepresented politically. That is, they cannot communicate their needs or press their cause with the same forcefulness as other groups. They do *not* make up a political group; and collectively they lack the means to do so. Only the racial minorities have more than poverty in common among the major groups of economically deprived citizens.

Government, unions, and many producers *are* positively committed to treatment of the problem of poverty, however. By a problem in 'political will,' we do not mean that influential groups have not taken up the issue of poverty and its elimination. Rather, the issue was treated—at least until 1964—as if there is no solution other than continued growth in the economy. The common assumption is that employment is the only way in which most adults can and ought to receive income. Sources of poverty other than lack of work are treated as subject to rehabilitation toward employment or as objects of medical care, public or private.

The mention of one among many alternatives, should amplify this interpretation. Suppose that, hypothetically, we refused to link incomes to work. We could in principle establish an *economic floor* under every individual in the society, without implying personal inadequacy or undeserved rewards. We could thus extend the present concept of social security to all population groups.

The Old-Age, Survivors and Disability Insurance system (OASDI) in the United States has expanded since its creation in 1935 until today it covers, in a limited way, more than 90 per cent of the population. Among those not covered—for example, federal government employees, certain self-employed professional groups, and members of religious orders—many are explicitly protected by other programs of retirement benefits. Near-total coverage of all relevant sectors of the population will be achieved soon. Other forms of public and private assistance are designed to cover disabilities and temporary unemployment, and to protect the children of vulnerable parents, especially in poor, single-parent families.

Take an alternative suggestion. The federal government could act to guarantee jobs for all employable citizens, including the prematurely retired aged population. Where no work is available, new industries and public works could be subsidized or initiated directly by the government. We have, nationally, the fiscal ability to set a limit on how low incomes should be permitted to drop, or the ability to make work where none exists privately.

The Deeper Source of the Problem

These and other "utopic" suggestions are advanced by Herbert Gans in his paper reprinted in this chapter. Why are economic floors and full employment programs, among other solutions, seldom taken seriously?

We come, with this question, to the root of American poverty, at least as this author interprets them. The root cause is the political and economic organization of the society, designed as it was for conditions of scarcity and the ethics of work and profit. As one economist puts it:

> We do not wish to achieve full employment at the expense of serious inflation, or at the cost of impaired incentives, reduced productivity, or restrictions on one's freedom to move to another job. We do not wish to alleviate the distress of a stranded community by permanently subsidizing its industries or its workers. Nor do we wish to provide opportunity for some by preventing the entry of others into an occupation or industry.
>
> Thus Federal responsibilities to low-income families must be exercised within important limitations. We must exercise care, in attempts to assist such families, that we do not adversely affect our political institutions and that we do not conflict with economic objectives which are of equal or greater importance than assisting disadvantaged groups within the population.[5]

The basis for American poverty is, in short, the grounding of the economy

in private initiative and competition, regulated only indirectly and impersonally through political institutions. Any proposal for solving the problem of poverty will be tested, in the political arena, against this historic criterion: Are private incentives and open competition left intact under the proposed change? Even in the midst of the Great Depression, the first social security legislation faced great misgivings. Many Americans feared that social security would destroy the initiative and desire of individuals to take care of themselves. Only the severity of the national emergency overrode this reservation.

Since 1936, the *forms* of federal service, in grants-in-aid to the states, and in funds for assistance, have multiplied. Social insurance for the aged, survivors, and the disabled, continues as the keystone of the protective structure. But one must also include anti-poverty programs, public health services and medical facilities, special educational aid, vocational rehabilitation services, school lunch and surplus food programs, aid to dependent children, the blind and the aged. All of these impinge upon the conditions of poverty, deprivation and dependency.

The federal contribution has become more diversified and has grown in total amount from $3 billion in 1935, to $22.6 billion in 1959. *It has not grown relative to the gross national product, however:* 4.4 per cent in 1935 (the height of early expenditures) versus 4.9 per cent in 1959. Patterns of state and local protection are similar: 5.4 per cent in 1935 versus 5.8 per cent in 1959.[6]

Poverty is therefore a condition of institutional design. There is a point to which the American public seems pre-

---

[5]Howard B. Myers, Statement at *Hearings Before the Subcommittee on Low-Income Families*, the Joint Committee on the Economic Report, Eighty-Fourth Congress, Government Printing Office, 1955, p. 60.

[6]Annual reports in the Social Security Bulletin, U.S. Government Printing Office, Washington, D.C.

pared historically to go in order to cope with poverty and the health and welfare problems that poverty produces. This extent may be summed up as roughly 10 per cent of the productive resources of the society. If the 10 billion dollars a year cited by Morgan and associates were added to resolve this fiscal limit, the commitment would expand to about 12 per cent a year.

The determinants of poverty, then, are cultural and organizational. Each institutional means for coping with poverty has grown up around a particular disadvantage, handicap, or vulnerability. No comprehensive system for preventing and eliminating the problem has evolved.

The cultural basis for this is the tradition which divided the needy into the deserving and the undeserving poor. Under the colonial ethos, poverty was suspect until its bearer gave evidence of adversity. Under the puritan ethic, in fact, poverty was a sign of spiritual disgrace, of inner evil. It was to be shunned, unless it had resulted from misfortune. Thus, blindness could be treated as a sign of evil, as could mental illness or mental retardation. Unemployment was a sign of laziness, itself a serious vice, just as many people today regard the refusal of a worker to relocate in a new community as a lack of initiative.

Each form of need experienced by Americans has had to undergo social redefinition, historically.[7] Changing concepts of health, welfare, and economics have transferred groups of citizens from the class of the undeserving to the class of the deserving poor. The root construct has not changed in the

process. With the exception of social insurance for the retired worker, public and private assistance has remained a matter of 'helping the needy who are worthy.' Today one speaks of *eligibility* rather than worth, however. This cultural formula may be expressed this way: From each — within the limits of help and without any discomfort to the giver — to each according to his needs, where these are judged as misfortunes.

Concomitant with this formula are organizational arrangements for providing for transfer of income. Of these, welfare expert Evaline Burns has written:

> The simultaneous operation of several different social-security techniques, the practice of providing against different risks by separate programs, and the financial and administrative participation of several levels of government all make the American social security system a highly complicated structure. This complexity is to some extent a mirror of the fact that America is a country characterized by great diversity of living conditions, economic interests, social attitudes and customs, and by a Federal form of government. It reflects, too, the fact that the different circumstances which occasion interruption of private income present different types of economic and social problems. Yet it is equally relevant that so great a number of programs and authorities create many problems. The situation creates possibilities of both gaps in, and overlapping of, protection. It raises questions of equity among the different population groups. It makes heavy demands on the mutual tolerance and cooperation of different levels of government.[8]

[7]For a good history, see Robert H. Bremmer, *From the Depths: The Discovery of Poverty in the U.S.*, New York University Press, New York City, 1956.

[8]*The American Social Security System*, Houghton Mifflin Co., Boston, 1949, pp. 60-62.

This is a careful way of saying that no system has yet emerged, given the diversity of demands and the character of the political and economic structures. In the absence of a system (using system to refer to arrangements that persist coherently), the means for coping with poverty are inadequate. They result in gaps, duplication of services, and inequities in help.

Poverty as a National Social Problem: Overview

In this chapter we have viewed poverty as a deficit in the relation of consumer resources to the need for consumer expenditures. Taking cash income as the mainstay of consumer resources, we said that one fifth of the American population takes in less than one half of what is needed to subsist. Another one fifth approximates the income required for basic subsistence.

Most individuals and households suffering from low income are persons too old to work, the mentally or physically disabled, unemployed but experienced workers, or single parents who cannot both care for children and earn wages. The single largest group consists of nonwhites barred from jobs or decent wages through racial discrimination. These groups overlap greatly.[9]

We also described concretely the levels of living referred to as poverty and deprivation, with their implications for malnutrition, exposure to the envi-

[9]Our way of looking at poverty has controlled statistically the differences due to variation in needs as opposed to income. Differences in size of family or numbers of other dependents, for example, are built into the analysis made by Morgan and associates. We have neglected differences resulting from illness, damage from disaster, and such important but numerically limited things as addiction to narcotics or alcohol.

ronment, lack of medical protection, and pervasive restriction on family life and individual development. The psychological and social correlates of life at this level—discrimination, low self-confidence, and ultimate despair or frustration—are cited as tragic and obvious outcomes.

In interpreting the causes of modern American poverty, we considered the failure of the rate of economic growth to keep pace with population expansion and automation. Particular emphasis was given to structural unemployment and its effects. We noted that, fiscally, the problem could be eliminated if it were not for the historic character of the relation of social organization to the national economy. We considered further the cultural and organizational limitations that exist at present on the provision of security against poverty.

We have reserved for this final section any proposition that defines poverty as a national social problem. Poverty is clearly objectionable on general humanitarian groups. We seek to eradicate it because it is a sign of personal as well as collective distress. But this is a sociological analysis. And we have posed sociological criteria for the presence of major national social problems in Chapter One. How does poverty relate to these?

Poverty meets several criteria, at least in the American case. Poverty contributes powerfully to disorganization of the national social structure. It disrupts the otherwise normal lives of its victims. It threatens to impair the lives of those who never become poor:

So long as poverty is allowed to exist, it is possible that anyone may some day be in want. The continued existence of poverty, therefore, leads to insecurity and fear, even on the part of many who may never themselves become destitute. The elimination of poverty for the few thus adds to the security of the many.[10]

Serious, extensive poverty is a disorganizing force in other ways. It induces anxiety; failure; illiteracy and ignorance; morbidity and premature mortality; and blighted communities. The pathology it generates absorbs public and private services and transfers funds that could otherwise be diverted to more productive ends. Its pathologies, such as crime and disease, victimize the innocent. In short, poverty impairs the normal functioning of social relations.

In another sense, in an affluent society, it is a very problematic form of social *deviance*. The impoverished adult bears the stigma of his low social and economic status in his dress, his diet, and often his speech and job skills. Little is expected of him at work. Less is expected of his children at school. And low, differential expectations are vicious if silent forms of discrimination.

The impoverished individual may be deviant in a more fundamental cultural sense, however:

> Not all people who are poor necessarily live in or develop a culture of poverty... The Jews who lived in poverty in eastern Europe did not develop a culture of poverty because their... literacy and their religion gave them a sense of identification with Jews all over the world... (but some) people in ... poverty have a strong feeling of marginality, of helplessness, of dependency, of not belonging. They

are like aliens in their own country, convinced that the existing institutions do not serve their interests and needs. Along with this feeling of powerlessness, is a widespread feeling of inferiority, of personal unworthiness.[11]

If poverty becomes for many Americans a way of life characterized by a psychology of alienation and despair, then the social deviance that results will be a matter of political conflict and social miscommunication rather than of crime and deliquency. *New* social organization will then be required as well as new fiscal policies in any future system of social and economic security.

Poverty is a major national social problem in other respects. It may result from insufficient economic growth, but it also reduces levels of demand. It involves an under-utilization of labor and consumption resources which ought to be put to full use if economic growth is a common goal of the society.

The future survival of American society depends as much upon developments in the world at large as upon internal conditions. Among these, one must include the views of foreign elites, including government officials. They can learn, for example, that the national wealth of the United States, exclusive of military hardware, has increased from about $575 billion in 1945 to about $1,700 billion in 1948, an increase in wealth *per head* from about $5,600 to $7,100 in these three years alone. They can learn that in 1959, the poor one third of the United States population owned but one per cent of all this wealth. The next one fourth owned five per cent.

[10]Howard R. Bowen, Statement Before the Subcommittee on Low Income Families, *op. cit.*, p. 31.

[11]Oscar Lewis, "Further Observations on the Culture of Poverty," Mimeographed essay, 1962, Department of Anthropology, University of Illinois, Urbana.

The top two per cent of the income recipients owned about one third of all the wealth.

They can see that, with less national wealth, countries such as Denmark, Sweden, France and Holland maintain superior programs of economic and social security, judging from extent and magnitude of benefits and coverage. Foreign observers will, in short, discover in America gross poverty and extensive economic deprivation in the midst of greater national wealth than is available to any other modern society. Some will be tempted to draw the ideological conclusion that American political and economic institutions make poor models to adopt, or even poor bases for international alliances. The persistence of poverty in the midst of affluence is thus a powerful trump card for anti-American interests.

References

Anderson, Nels. *The hobo: the sociology of the homeless man.* Chicago: Phoenix Books, University of Chicago Press, 1923, 1961.

Back, Kurt. *Slums, projects, and people.* Durham, North Carolina: Duke University Press, 1962.

Bayley, Monica, "Efforts to solve the problem of dropouts," *School Life,* December 1963.

Bendix, Reinhard, and Seymour M. Lipset (eds.). *Class, status, and power.* Glencoe: The Free Press, 1953.

Bowman, Mary Jean and Warren W. Hynes, *Resources and people in east Kentucky: problems and potentials of a lagging economy.* Baltimore: Johns Hopkins, 1963.

Bremner, Robert Hamlett. *From the depths; the discovery of poverty in the United States.* New York: New York University Press, 1956.

Burgess, M. Elaine and Daniel O. Price, *An American dependency challenge.* American Public Association, 1963.

Caplovitz, David. *The poor pay more; consumer practices of low-income families.* New York: Free Press of Glencoe, 1963.

Caudill, Harry M., *Night comes to the Cumberlands: a biography of a depressed area.* Boston: Atlantic Little, Brown, 1963.

Centers, Richard. *The psychology of social classes.* Princeton, New Jersey: Princeton University Press, 1949.

Conant, James B., *Slums and the suburbs,* New York: McGraw Hill Book Co., Inc., 1961.

Conference on Economic Progress, Washington, D.C. *Poverty and deprivation in the United States; the plight of two-fifths of a nation.* Washington, D.C.: 1962. ("The Keyserling Report.")

Duhl, Leonard J., (Ed.). *The urban condition: people and politics in the metropolis.* New York: Basic Books Inc., 1963.

Economic Report of the President, Transmitted to the Congress, January 1964, together with *The annual report of the council of economic advisers.*

Epstein, Lenore A., "Unmet need in a land of abundance," *Social Security Bulletin,* May 1963.

Evans, G. *War on want.* Pergamon Press, Macmillan Company, 1963.

Galbraith, John K. *The affluent society.* Boston: Houghton Mifflin Company, 1960.

———Approach to poverty; address, June 3, 1962. *The Department of State Bulletin,* 46:1024-7, June 25, 1962.

Gabriel, Kolko. *Wealth and power in the United States.* New York: Frederich Praeger, 1962.

Ginzberg, Eli, assisted by Anderson, Bray, and Smuts; *The Negro potential.* New York: Columbia University Press, 1965.

Greenfield, Margaret, *Social dependency in the San Francisco bay area: today and tomorrow.* Institute of Governmental Studies, University of California, Berkeley, 1963.

Hanlin, Oscar. *Uprooted.* Universal Library, Grosset and Dunlap, Inc.

Harrington, Michael. *The other America: poverty in the United States.* New York: The Macmillan Company, 1962. Penguin Books, Inc. 1963.

Henderson, Vivian W., *The economic status of Negroes: in the nation and in the South.* Atlanta, Georgia: Southern Regional Council, 1963.

Hollingshead, A. B., and F. C. Redlich, *Social class and mental illness,* New York: John Wiley & Sons, Inc., 1958.

Johnston, Helen L., "Major health problems," *Extension Service Review,* August 1963: Reprinted by U.S. Public Health Service.

Lampman, Robert J. *The share of top wealth-holders in national wealth.* Princeton, New Jersey: Princeton University Press, 1962.

_____*The low income population and economic growth.* U.S. Congress, Joint Economic Committee, Study Paper No. 12 86th Congress, 1st. Session, December 1959.

Lewis, Oscar. *Further observations on the culture of poverty.* Mimeographed essay, 1962, Department of Anthropology, University of Illinois, Urbana.

Luck, James Murray. *The war on malnutrition and poverty; the role of consumer co-operatives.* New York: Harper and Brothers, 1946.

MacDonald, Dwight. *Our invisible poor.* Reprint No. 23, Sidney Hillman Foundation, 1963.

May, Edgar, *The wasted Americans.* Harper and Row, February 1964.

Miller, S. M., "Poverty and inequality in America: implications for the social services," *Child Welfare,* December, 1963.

Morgan, James N.; H. David Martin; Wilbur J. Cohen; and Harvey E. Brazer; *Income and welfare in the United States.* New York: McGraw-Hill Book Co., Inc., 1962.

Orshansky, Mollie, "The aged Negro and his income," *Social Security Bulletin,* February 1964.

_____, "Children of the poor," *Social Security Bulletin,* July 1963.

Passow, Harry A. (Ed.). *Education in depressed areas.* New York: Bureau of Publications, T.C., Columbia University, 1963.

Perkins, Ellen J., "Unmet need in public assistance," *Social Security Bulletin* April, 1960.

Pond, M. Allen, "Interrelationships of poverty and disease," *Public Health Reports,* November 1961.

Schorr, Alvin L. "Filial responsibility and the aging." *Journal of Home Economics,* 54:271-6, April, 1962.

_____, *Slums and social insecurity: an appraisal of the effectiveness of housing policies in helping to eliminate poverty in the United States.* U.S. Department of Health, Education, and Welfare; Social Security Administration; Research Report No. 1, 1963.

Sexton, Patricia. *Education and income.* New York: The Viking Press, Inc., 1961.

Srole, Leo; Thomas S. Langner; Marvin

K. Opler; Thomas A. C. Rennie; *Mental health in the metropolis; the midtown Manhattan study.* New York: McGraw-Hill Book Co., Inc., 1962.

The President's Task Force on Manpower Conservation, *One-third of a nation: a report on young men found unqualified for military service.* January 1, 1964.

U.S. Attorney General's Committee on Poverty and the Administration of Criminal Justice. *Poverty and the administration of federal criminal justice, report.* Washington, D.C., 1963.

U.S. Department of Commerce, Bureau of the Census; "Income of families and persons in the United States: 1962" *Consumer Income,* Series P-60, No. 41 of *Current Population Reports,* October 21, 1963.

White, Gladys O.: Alberta D. Hill; and Edna P. Amidon; *Improving home families.* U.S. Department of Health, Education, and Welfare; Bureau of Family Services; BFS No. 736, May 1962.

Wilson, Charles Morrow, *The landscape of rural poverty: corn bread and creek water.* New York: Henry Holt and Company, 1940.

POVERTY IN THE UNITED STATES

Wilbur J. Cohen and Eugenia Sullivan

President Johnson, in his State of the Union message on January 8, 1964, pledged the Administration to "unconditional war on poverty in America." In this message, the President focused national attention on the paradox of millions of Americans living in poverty and deprivation in the midst of the rising prosperity enjoyed by the majority of citizens.

Mass poverty, as it once existed in this country and still exists in many parts of the world, has been eliminated in the United States due to the combination of steadily rising productivity, higher levels of educational attainment, and an improving network of private and social insurance and assistance. But progress in melting the hard core of poverty that still afflicts a sizeable group of Americans has been far too slow.

Poverty is costly not only to the individual but also to society. Physical and mental disease, delinquency and crime, loss of productive capacity—all of these are part of the environment of poverty.

Reprinted with permission, from *HEW Indicators*, Spring, 1965, published by the U.S. Dept. of Health, Education, and Welfare.

Mr. Cohen is the Assistant Secretary (for Legislation), U.S. Department of Health, Education, and Welfare, and Miss Sullivan is a Program Analysis Officer on his staff. Selected references are given at the end of this article.

But the most fundamental reason for declaring war on poverty is a moral one. This Nation and its institutions are founded upon the belief that each individual should have the opportunity to develop his capacity to the fullest. Those who are born into the world of poverty are not only deprived of most of the material comforts of life, but are also stunted in their emotional, intellectual, and social development, and thus effectively prevented from realizing their human potentialities. Past accomplishments in reducing the extent of poverty have been the result of combined efforts of all levels of government and of private groups. Similarly, the eventual elimination of poverty will call for a national effort involving a wide range of public and private measures to stimulate economic growth, wipe out discrimination, and increase opportunities by raising the educational, skill, health, and living levels of those Americans who have heretofore failed to share in the fruits of economic progress.

In order to attack the problem of poverty, it is essential to know who are the poor and what causes their poverty.

TABLE 1
SELECTED CHARACTERISTICS OF ALL FAMILIES AND OF POOR FAMILIES, 1962

Selected characteristic	Number of families (millions)		Percent of total	
	All families	Poor families	All families	Poor families
Total	47.0	9.3	100	100
Age of head:				
14-24 years	2.5	.8	5	8
25-54 years	30.4	3.9	65	42
55-64 years	7.3	1.4	16	15
65 years and over	6.8	3.2	14	34
Education of head:[1]				
8 years or less	16.3	6.0	35	61
9-11 years	8.6	1.7	19	17
12 years	12.2	1.5	26	15
More than 12 years......................	9.3	.7	20	7
Sex of head:				
Male.....................................	42.3	7.0	90	75
Female	4.7	2.3	10	25
Labor force status of head:[2]				
Not in civilian labor force	8.4	4.1	18	44
Employed	36.9	4.6	78	49
Unemployed	1.7	.6	4	6
Color of family:				
White....................................	42.4	7.3	90	78
Nonwhite	4.6	2.0	10	22
Children under 18 years of age in family:				
None	18.8	4.9	40	52
One to three	22.7	3.3	48	36
Four or more	5.5	1.1	12	11
Earners in family:				
None	3.8	2.8	8	30
One	21.1	4.3	45	46
Two or more	22.1	2.2	47	23
Regional location of family:[3][4]				
Northeast................................	11.5	1.6	25	17
North Central	13.1	2.3	29	25
South	13.5	4.3	30	47
West	7.0	1.0	16	11
Residence of family:[4][5]				
Rural farm	3.3	1.5	7	16
Rural nonfarm	9.9	2.7	22	30
Urban	31.9	5.0	71	54

[1] Based on 1961 income (1962 prices).
[2] Labor force status relates to survey week of March 1963.
[3] Based on 1960 residence and 1959 income (1962 prices).
[4] Data are from 1960 Census and are therefore not strictly comparable with the other data shown in this table, which are derived from *Current Population Reports.*
[5] Based on 1959 residence and 1959 income (1962 prices).
Note.—Data relate to families and exclude unrelated individuals. Poor families are defined as all families with total money income of less than $3,000.
Sources: Department of Commerce and Council of Economic Advisers.

The Size and Nature of Poverty in the United States

The question of how many people live in poverty depends upon the definition used. The poor are those whose basic and irreducible needs exceed their means to satisfy them. A number of factors affect a family's needs—size of the family, the ages of its members, health conditions, and place of residence. Income to satisfy these needs may come from a number of sources including earnings from work, public and private transfers, utilization of past savings, ownership of a home or other assets, and ability to borrow. There is no clear and unvarying standard of the total of goods and services that constitute a minimum level of living.

What Is Poverty? Welfare agencies, public and private, have established various minimum family budgets for use in determining eligibility for assistance payments to the needy. A recent study reported in the *Social Security Bulletin* defined a "low-cost" living plan for a nonfarm family of four and found its cost in 1962 to have been $3,955. The same study priced an "economy" living plan at $3,165. Other studies of family income have used different demarcations to separate poor families from those with adequate incomes. On balance, these studies provide support for using as a demarcation of the poverty line an annual family income of $3,000. Since budgetary needs vary among different geographic areas and among families of different sizes and age composition, the use of this cutoff point will provide at best only a rough approximation of the numbers of poor families.

Certainly this simple measure of poverty would not be suitable for determining eligibility for particular benefits or participation in particular programs.

This definition of poverty does however serve as a benchmark for measuring the dimensions of the task of eliminating poverty, setting the broad policy goals, and measuring past and future progress toward the achievement of these goals.

Number and Characteristics of the Poor. Of the 47 million families in the United States in 1962, some 9.3 million or *one-fifth of these families—containing more than 30 million* persons—had total *money incomes below $3,000* (Table 1). Over 11 million of these family members were children. More than 1.1 million families were raising four or more children on incomes below $3,000. Some 5.4 million families, containing more than 17 million persons, had money incomes below $2,000. More than 1 million children were being raised in very large families (six or more children) with incomes of less than $2,000.

A large percentage of persons living alone or living with unrelated persons in units such as boarding houses are found in the low-income groups. In 1962 about 45 percent of these unrelated individuals—5 million persons—had incomes below $1,500, and 29 percent, or more than 3 million persons, had incomes below $1,000 (Table 2). In total, between 33 and 35 million Americans were living in poverty in 1962—nearly one-fifth of the population of the United States.

Substantial progress has been made since World War II in reducing the extent of poverty in this country and lowering the numbers of families whose incomes are inadequate. A high level of economic growth during the decade 1947-57 resulted in the decline in the number of poor families (with incomes below $3,000 in terms of 1962 prices) from 11.9 million to 9.9 million, or from 32 percent to 23 percent of all families.

TABLE 2
NUMBER AND MONEY INCOME OF UNRELATED INDIVIDUALS, BY SELECTED CHARACTERISTICS, 1962

Selected characteristic	Number (millions)	Percent with income	
		Less than $1,500 (1962 prices)	Less than $1,000 (1962 prices)
All individuals	11.0	45	29
Age:			
14-24 years ...,.........	1.1	51	40
25-54 years	3.5	27	19
55-64 years	2.3	37	25
65 years and over.........	4.2	64	37
Sex:			
Male	4.3	35	21
Female..................	6.8	51	34
Color:			
White	9.5	43	27
Nonwhite................	1.5	59	41
Residence:			
Farm....................	.4	67	50
Nonfarm	10.6	44	28
Nonearners................	4.3	75	49

Note.—Unrelated individuals are persons (other than inmates of institutions) who are not living with any relatives.
Sources: Department of Commerce and Council of Economic Advisers.

TABLE 3
MONEY INCOME OF FAMILIES, 1947 AND 1950-62

Year	Median money income of all families (1962 prices)		Percent of families with money income	
	Dollars	Index 1947 = 100	Less than $3,000 (1962 prices)	Less than $2,000 (1962 prices)
1947	4,117	100	32	18
1950	4,188	102	32	19
1951	4,328	105	29	17
1952	4,442	108	28	17
1953	4,809	117	26	16
1954	4,705	114	28	17
1955	5,004	122	25	15
1956	5,337	130	23	14
1957	5,333	130	23	14
1958	5,329	129	23	14
1959	5,631	137	22	13
1960	5,759	140	21	13
1961	5,820	141	21	13
1962	5,956	145	20	12

Sources: Department of Commerce and Council of Economic Advisers.

A slower rate of growth between 1957-62 and higher levels of unemployment contributed to a slowdown in the reduction of poverty, as the number of poor families declined to 9.3 million, or 20 percent of all families (Table 3).

It is interesting to note that the *progress in reducing poverty since World War II has been effected without any major change in the percentage distribution of income by size of income.* The lowest income quintile of families received five percent of the total income in 1947 and five percent in 1963. The highest quintile of families received 43 percent of total income in 1947 and 42 percent in 1962. Thus it is apparent that the reduction in poverty since World War II has been the result of a general rise in incomes rather than of a change in distribution of the total.

In order to attack poverty successfully, it is necessary to have facts about the incidence of poverty among various groups and in various geographical areas. While it is true that certain groups — the inadequately educated, the aged, and the nonwhite — have a high incidence of poverty, it is also true that poverty is widely diffused among all major groups in the population and in all parts of the country (Table 1). Nevertheless, for purposes of pinpointing an attack upon poverty, the income data do reveal substantial concentrations of poverty among certain groups. For example, families headed by persons age 65 and older comprise 34 percent of poor families but only 14 percent of all families. Similarly, 22 percent of poor families but only 10 percent of all families are nonwhite; 25 percent of poor families and 10 percent of all families are headed by females (Chart 1). Other types of families with a high risk of poverty are those headed by persons

with a grade school education or less, families headed by persons not in the labor force, families with no wage earner, and rural farm families. To be sure, some of these groups overlap considerably, but these categories do help identify some of the sources of poverty.

Sources of Income. Wages, salaries, and self-employment income constitute nearly four-fifths of total personal income in the United States. Thus poverty is most closely associated with absence of earned income or low earning power. What are the reasons for low earnings? Obviously, a family with no wage earners is likely to be poor — three-fourths of the families in this category had incomes below $3,000 in 1962. It has been estimated that about half of the families headed by part-time workers are poor. Withdrawal from the labor force or part-time employment may result from a number of causes: age, disability, premature death of the principal earner, need to care for children or disabled family members, lack of any saleable skill, lack of motivation, or simply heavy unemployment in the area.

There is another group of poor families whose poverty is due not to lack of employment but rather to the low rates of pay found most commonly in certain occupations. For example, 45 percent of farm families and 74 percent of families headed by domestic service workers are poor (Table 4). The low rates of pay in these occupations generally reflect low productivity. Other factors include discrimination, low bargaining power, and exclusion from minimum wage coverage. The failure of many workers to move out of these low paying occupations may reflect lack of education or training, physical or mental disability, poor motivation, inadequate knowledge of other opportunities, or unwillingness or in-

CHART 1: CHARACTERISTICS OF POOR FAMILIES
Compared With All Families

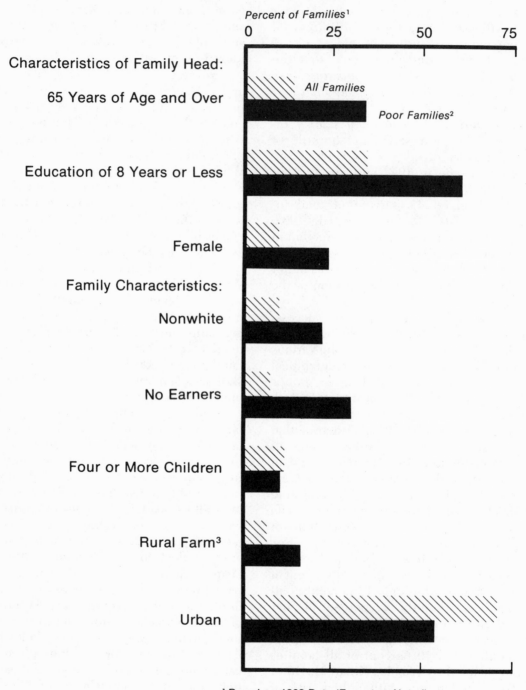

Percent of Families[1]

Characteristics of Family Head:

65 Years of Age and Over

All Families

Poor Families[2]

Education of 8 Years or Less

Female

Family Characteristics:

Nonwhite

No Earners

Four or More Children

Rural Farm[3]

Urban

[1] Based on 1962 Data (Except as Noted).
[2] Families With Income of $3,000 or Less.
[3] Based on 1959 Data.
Source: Department of Commerce.

ability to move away from familiar surroundings.

The decline in the numbers of
unskilled and semi-skilled jobs and the
increasing premium placed on skills
and training intensify the importance of
educational deficiency as a factor in
poverty. Three out of eight families
headed by persons with a grade school
education or less are poor. Where nonwhite status and rural residence are
added to educational deficiency, there
is an even higher incidence of poverty.
Typically, nonwhites earn less than
whites with the same education even
when they practice the same occupation
(Table 5).

Property income and use of savings
may provide the difference between
inadequate and adequate incomes. For
the elderly in particular, savings are
important. The 1962 Survey of Consumer Finances found that over half of
the aged with incomes below $3,000
had liquid assets of $1,000 or more.
About 18 percent had assets of $5,000 or
more.

Generally though, families with
low earnings do not accumulate a large
amount of assets. The assets they do
have are most often in the form of
owner-occupied homes. Although home
ownership lowers housing costs, it does
not provide money income that can be
used for other current expenses.

Because low incomes are chronic
for most families living in poverty, the
majority are unable to accumulate savings. A study of family income in 1959
by the Survey Research Center of the
University of Michigan[*] found that
more than one-half of the aged poor had
less than $500 in liquid assets and less
than one-fifth of all poor families had

[*]James N. Morgan, Martin H. David, Wilbur
J. Cohen and Harvey E. Brazer, *Income and
Welfare in the United States*, McGraw Hill Co.,
1962.

accumulated savings of more than $500.
Only 23 percent of the poor families
used money savings at all in 1959, and
the mean amount used was $120.

Thus, it is clear that for most families property income and savings do not
constitute a buffer against poverty.

Transfer payments are a much more
significant factor in the total income of
low income families. Although transfers
constituted only 7 percent of total family
income in 1960, these payments comprised 43 percent of the total income of
low income spending units.

Public transfer programs include
social insurance, such as unemployment
compensation, workmen's compensation, and old-age survivors and disability insurance; veteran's benefits and
public assistance programs, such as Old-
Age Assistance (OAA) and Aid to Families with Dependent Children (AFDC).
Insurance-type programs are aimed essentially at preventing poverty, with
eligibility based on past employment
and benefits on past earnings. Assis-

TABLE 4
INCIDENCE OF POVERTY, BY OCCUPATION OF
FAMILY HEAD, 1962

Occupation of head[1]	Incidence of poverty (percent)
Total civilian workers	12
Professional and technical workers.	3
Farmers or farm managers	45
Clerical workers	7
Sales workers	9
Craftsmen	5
Operative workers	11
Domestic workers	74
Service workers other than domestic	22
Farm laborers or foremen	56
Laborers, except farm and mine . . .	23

[1]Occupation in March 1963.
Note.—Data relate to families and exclude unrelated individuals.
Poverty is defined to include all families with total money income
of less than $3,000; these are also referred to as poor families.
Incidence of poverty is measured by the percent that poor fam-
ilies with a given characteristic are of all families having the
same characteristic.
Sources: Department of Commerce and Council of Economic
Advisers.

tance programs ordinarily are aimed at alleviating the conditions of those who are already poor or handicapped. Eligibility for assistance benefits may or may not be based on current income but neither eligibility nor the size of benefits typically bears any direct relationship to past income.

By sustaining incomes when earnings are interrupted or terminated, pub-

lies were covered by social security or other government pensions in 1959, as contrasted with 93 percent of all families. Forty percent of all families were covered by private pensions and annuities but only 11 percent of poor families had such protection.

Transmission of Poverty Between Generations. Since low incomes are chronic for most poor families, the ques-

TABLE 5
EARNINGS OF ELEMENTARY SCHOOL GRADUATES,
BY COLOR AND OCCUPATION, 1959

Occupation	Average earnings of elementary school graduates		Earnings of nonwhites as percent of earnings of whites
	White	Nonwhite	
Craftsmen, foremen, and kindred workers[1]	$5,300	$3,800	72
Machinists	5,500	4,300	79
Painters and construction and maintenance workers	4,200	3,100	73
Plumbers and pipefitters.........................	5,600	4,000	71
Operatives and kindred workers[1]	4,800	3,600	75
Truck and tractor drivers	4,900	3,300	68
Other operatives and kindred workers	4,800	3,800	80
Service workers (including private household workers)[1]	3,900	2,900	75
Farm laborers and foremen........................	2,400	1,500	62

[1] Over-all average for group includes some occupations not shown separately.
Note.—Elementary school graduates are persons who completed 8 grades of school but not more.
Sources: Department of Commerce and Council of Economic Advisers.

lic insurance type transfer programs have played an important role in preventing poverty among those whose past earnings have been adequate. Insurance programs are of least help to those whose earnings have never been adequate.

Public assistance programs are an important support to low income and handicapped persons. Nevertheless, the Survey Research Center study found that less than one-fourth of poor families received public assistance during 1959. The findings also showed that poor families are less likely than others to have social security and private pension coverage. Only 84 percent of poor fami-

tion of transmission of poverty between generations arises. The evidence points to the conclusion that poverty breeds poverty. Education and occupational status are correlated with economic status. The University of Michigan study showed that low educational attainment tends to perpetuate itself between generations.

Among poor families, 64 percent were headed by a person who had less than an eighth grade education. Moreover, fewer than two-fifths of the heads of poor families had gone beyond the educational level of their fathers. Similarly, only 45 percent of the children of poor families completed high school or more, as compared to 65 percent of the children of all families. Poor families also have substantially lower aspirations for sending their children to college—31 percent of poor families expected their sons to go on to college as compared to 66 percent of all families. Particularly alarming is the fact that one-third of the children of poor families have less than a grade school education. Unless measures are taken to provide them with further education and training, they will probably perpetuate the poverty of their parents.

The poor earning power of the present generation of the poor is corre- lated with the earning power of their fathers. The Michigan study found that the fathers of heads of poor families are more likely to be farmers or unskilled laborers than are the fathers of all family heads. Moreover, the heads of poor families show much less upward occupational mobility than all family heads. In fact, it appears that a number of the heads of poor families moved into less skilled jobs than their fathers had.

The findings of the President's Task Force on Manpower Conservation, released in January 1964, attest to the transmission of poverty between generations and the effects of the environ-

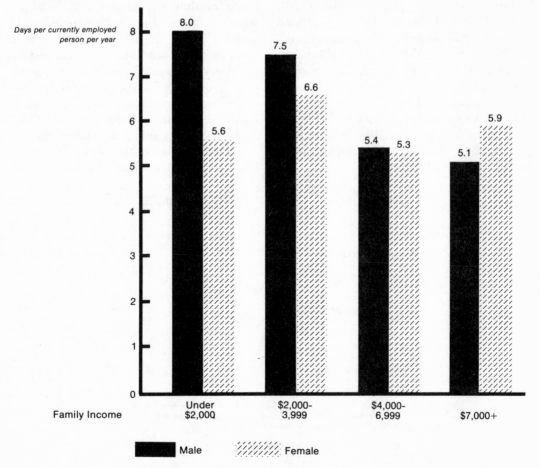

CHART 2: NUMBER OF WORK-LOSS DAYS PER CURRENTLY EMPLOYED PERSON PER YEAR, BY SEX AND FAMILY INCOME.

Days per currently employed person per year

| Family Income | Under $2,000 | $2,000-3,999 | $4,000-6,999 | $7,000+ |

Male / Female

ment of poverty on youth. The Task Force found that one-third of the Nation's youth would fail to meet the standards for military service established by the Selective Service System and that poverty is the principal reason for their failure to meet those physical and mental standards. About one-fifth of the youth rejected on mental grounds come from families which have received public assistance in the previous five years. Almost half come from families with six or more children. The fathers of more than half of these rejectees never completed grade school and four out of five of the rejectees were themselves school dropouts.

Other data highlight the social and economic costs of poverty. The U.S. National Health Survey has found that persons with low incomes are more likely to suffer disabling effects of injury or illness than persons of higher income (Chart 2). Similarly, studies of mental illness in New York City and New Haven, Connecticut showed that severe, disabling mental illness is more prevalent in low-income groups than among the more affluent.

Similarly, infant mortality and prematurity rates are higher among low-income mothers. Among nonwhites—almost half of whom are poor—infant mortality is twice as high as for whites and maternal deaths are four times as frequent.

Nevertheless, despite these factors that tend to perpetuate poverty, the proportion of poor families and the proportion of American children exposed to poverty has been smaller in each succeeding generation. But in recent years, at least, the reduction in the ranks of the poor has not been equal for all types of families. The notable exceptions to the general progress have been families with no earner, with head not in the civilian labor force, with head 65 years of age or older, with female head, and on farms. Of all these categories, only the farm families are declining in numbers; therefore, these high risk poverty groups—which also include the nonwhites—have come to constitute a larger proportion of the poor over the past 15 years (Table 6 and Chart 3).

The increasing prominence of certain handicapping characteristics among

TABLE 6
SELECTED CHARACTERISTICS OF POOR FAMILIES,
1947 AND 1962

Selected characteristic	Percent of poor families with characteristic	
	1947	1962
Family head:		
65 years of age and over	20	34
Female......................	16	25
Nonwhite families................	18	22
Rural farm families	30	'20
No earners in family	16	30

[1] Data are from *Current Population Reports* and are for 1959, based on income in 1962 prices. See Table 7, footnote 4, for comparability problem.

Note.—Data relate to families and exclude unrelated individuals. Poor families are defined as all families with total money income of less than $3,000 (1962 prices).
Sources: Department of Commerce and Council of Economic Advisers.

CHART 3: INCIDENCE OF POVERTY

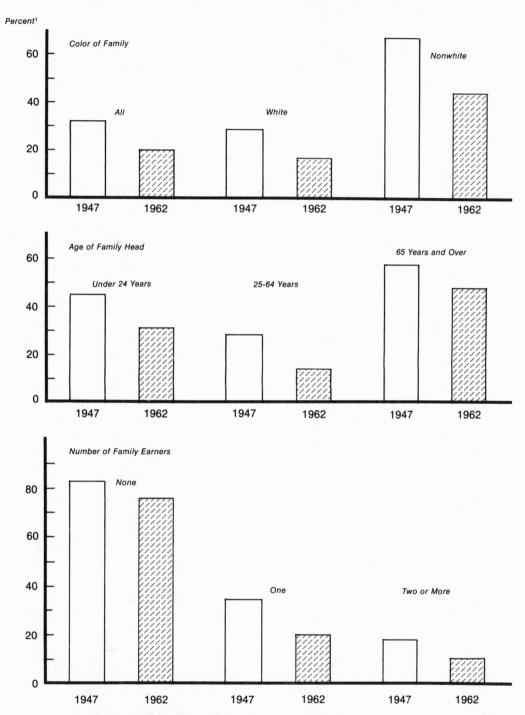

[1] Percent of families with given characteristic that are poor. Poor families are defined as all families with total money income of less than $3,000 (1962 prices).

Sources: Department of Commerce and Council of Economic Advisers.

the poor population point to the need to focus more sharply on these handicaps and to devise methods to overcome them. Clearly, future economic growth alone will not provide exits from poverty for many families with one or more special handicaps.

It is important to remember, however, that one-third of the present poor are children. The greatest hope for eliminating poverty in the future is to improve the availability and quality of education for the poor children of today.

Strategy Against Poverty

While a high rate of economic growth with a resulting high level of employment is a powerful force for the reduction of poverty, economic growth will not in itself eliminate poverty. As the analysis of the composition of poor families shows, many have no members in the labor force and thus are unaffected by fluctuations in the business cycle and corresponding changes in employment levels.

Beyond the need for maintaining a healthy economy, there is a need for a broadscale attack on poverty and its causes from many different directions. Such an attack should include a broad program of education and training, income maintenance to meet basic needs, expanded health and housing programs and other services to improve the physical and social environment, an equitable and efficient tax system, and a constant effort to maintain the optimum use of resources and manpower.

Increasing Opportunities for Nonwhites. As the Census income data shows, the burden of poverty falls to a disproportionate degree on the nonwhite population. A program to end racial discrimination is essential to improving the economic well-being of Negroes, Indians, Spanish-Americans, Puerto Ricans, and other minorities. Discrimination in employment is reflected in lower median incomes for nonwhites, higher rates of unemployment and underemployment, and a greater concentration in occupations particularly susceptible to unemployment—unskilled farm and nonfarm labor, semi-skilled production jobs, and service occupations.

Discrimination in employment is reinforced by discrimination in other areas, particularly education. The median number of school years completed for nonwhite persons age 25 and over is 8.2, compared to 10.9 for white persons of the same age group. About 47 percent of adult nonwhites had less than eight years of schooling in comparison to 17 percent for other groups. Special efforts—including the provision of basic education—must be made to train the unskilled and upgrade the skills of semi-skilled Negroes. Implementation of the recent vocational education legislation and the manpower training amendments will be a part of such efforts.

Improving the Environment of the Poor. Improvement of the physical and social environment in which poor families live is another essential of the attack on poverty. Poor physical environment is associated with poor health and lack of energy and drive. The feelings, aspirations, and behavior of the poor are affected by dilapidated, unsanitary, unsafe housing—whether in congested city slums or depressed rural areas, such as Appalachia. Better housing programs, increased urban renewal, and improved recreation facilities—all help to raise aspirations and improve motivation, particularly among the youth. For it is among the youth of today that the greatest effort must be made to break the cycle of poverty and dependency.

In addition to adequate housing, there is a need for hospitals, parks, libraries, schools and community centers. There is a growing need to provide facilities for the care of children of working mothers. Many of these working mothers are heads of families and their incomes generally are low (Chart 4).

the effects of poverty and deprivation. The Department of Health, Education, and Welfare and the Housing and Home Finance Agency have cooperated in a *Joint Task Force on Health, Education, and Welfare Services and Housing.* The Joint Task Force is conducting several projects to demonstrate ways of bringing community health, education, and welfare services to residents of public housing through a cooperative effort of

CHART 4: INCOME OF FAMILIES WITH FEMALE HEAD AND OWN CHILDREN UNDER 18, 1959

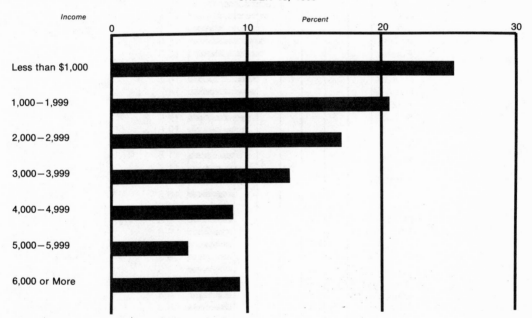

Greater availability of *day care facilities* would not only be of great direct benefit to the children involved but would also make it possible for some mothers who now receive public assistance to be trained for employment and thus become self-supporting.

More than physical buildings are needed to change the environment of poverty. Imaginative new approaches are called for to bring needed health, education, and welfare services to low-income families to help them overcome

Federal, State and local action. Expansion of this and similar efforts would be a significant step in the direction of helping provide urgently needed services to hard-core slum and rural poverty areas.

Recognizing that early and preventive action is vital in preventing the perpetuation of poverty, there must be greater emphasis on prenatal care and on the medical care and nutritional needs of the young. Protection of children in low-income families must begin

CHART 5: PERCENT OF FAMILIES WITH INCOME BELOW $2,000, CALENDAR YEAR 1959.

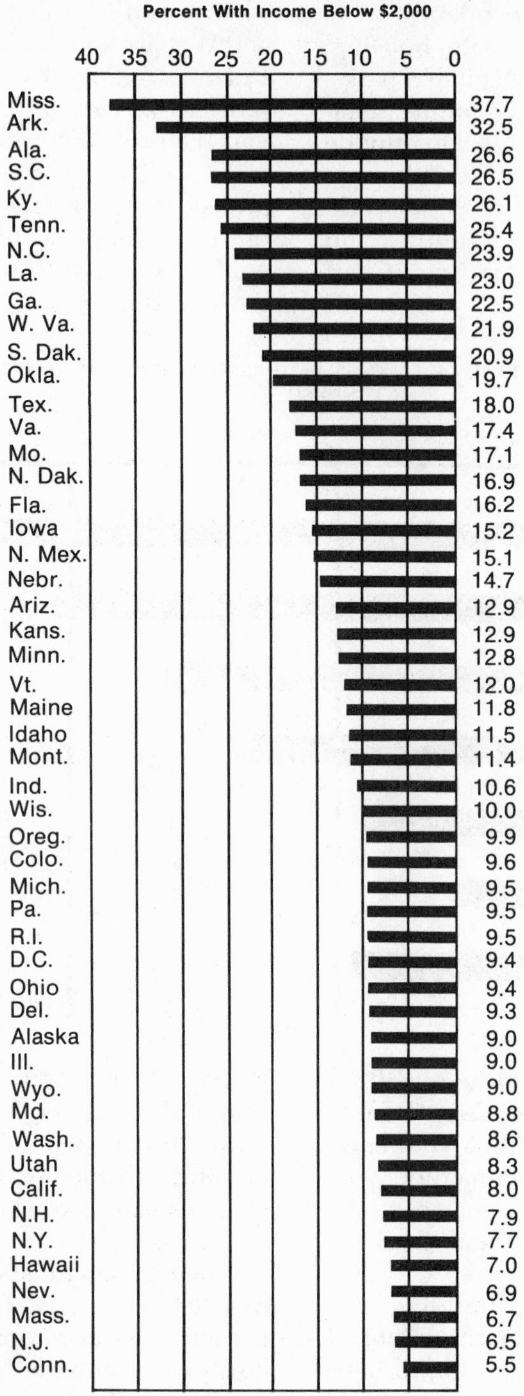

Percent With Income Below $2,000

	40 35 30 25 20 15 10 5 0	
Miss.		37.7
Ark.		32.5
Ala.		26.6
S.C.		26.5
Ky.		26.1
Tenn.		25.4
N.C.		23.9
La.		23.0
Ga.		22.5
W. Va.		21.9
S. Dak.		20.9
Okla.		19.7
Tex.		18.0
Va.		17.4
Mo.		17.1
N. Dak.		16.9
Fla.		16.2
Iowa		15.2
N. Mex.		15.1
Nebr.		14.7
Ariz.		12.9
Kans.		12.9
Minn.		12.8
Vt.		12.0
Maine		11.8
Idaho		11.5
Mont.		11.4
Ind.		10.6
Wis.		10.0
Oreg.		9.9
Colo.		9.6
Mich.		9.5
Pa.		9.5
R.I.		9.5
D.C.		9.4
Ohio		9.4
Del.		9.3
Alaska		9.0
Ill.		9.0
Wyo.		9.0
Md.		8.8
Wash.		8.6
Utah		8.3
Calif.		8.0
N.H.		7.9
N.Y.		7.7
Hawaii		7.0
Nev.		6.9
Mass.		6.7
N.J.		6.5
Conn.		5.5

Source: "Characteristics of Families Receiving Aid to Families with Dependent Children, Late 1961," Bureau of Family Services.

with adequate prenatal care of mothers to reduce infant mortality and prematurity. *The 1963 amendments to the Social Security Act* are designed to expand and improve maternal and child health services, especially for the medically indigent, with the objective of reducing infant mortality and prematurity rates among the high-risk, low-income population.

The problem of rural pockets of poverty is particularly challenging. In many of these areas, depletion of national resources or technological changes have destroyed the economic base of the region. Lack of local resources results in inadequacies in school systems and in health and other community services. The high incidence of poverty in the South largely reflects rural poverty (Chart 5). The *Area Redevelopment Program* initiated in 1961 makes available a wide range of Federal financial assistance to urban and rural areas of severe and chronic unemployment. This assistance includes loans to create new private enterprises and expansion of existing firms, financial aid for public facility improvements that will increase employment, and technical aid to help develop new products, markets and resources. This type of effort is essential to restoring a viable economy to such regions.

Education and Training Needs. Because both the urban and rural poor are likely to suffer from the handicap of lack of education and skills, training and retraining programs are an important factor in combatting poverty. *Recent amendments to the Manpower Development and Training Act* address themselves to some of the "problem" unemployed—the functionally illiterate and the young worker. The 1963 Amendments to MDTA lowered the age limit for training allowances from 19 to 17 and increased the funds available for training youth under age 22. Also, the new law provides for up to 20 weeks basic education for functionally illiterate workers to enable them to qualify for and benefit from educational training.

The educational deficiencies of many of the adult poor point up the need to provide the children of poor families with skills and motivations needed to compete in the labor market of today and tomorrow. The failure to provide every individual with the opportunity and incentive to develop his capacities to the fullest extent bears heavy costs in terms of unemployment, chronic dependency, loss of productive power, and an increase in tax-supported benefits.

It is increasingly recognized that effective education for the children of poor families must be tailored to their special needs and must compensate for intellectual and social deficiencies in the home environment. Such education is necessarily more expensive than that for children from homes that are more secure economically and socially. Children from poor and deprived neighborhoods are far more likely to be served by inadequate schools and instruction than are children of more affluent neighborhoods. Demonstration projects conducted at schools located in deprived neighborhoods have made it clear that children from poor backgrounds are just as capable as other children of acquiring the skills, motivations, and attitudes necessary for productive life. Improvement and expansion of school health and school lunch programs will benefit the health and education of children living in poverty.

Conclusions

One-fifth of the Nation's families live in poverty, yet the poor are not a homogeneous group. They are made up of young and old, disabled, able-bodied, white and nonwhite, urban and rural dwellers. Generally though, they are unemployed, underemployed, or seasonal workers. Many, of course, are too old, too young, too sick or disabled to work. But for the able-bodied adult poor, jobs must be found to provide these workers and their families with sufficient income to maintain an adequate standard of living. Greater economic growth would undoubtedly put many of the unemployed to work. But for a distressing proportion of the unemployed, education and training, even basic literacy training, are needed before they can find gainful employment in our increasingly complex technology. Disabling physical and mental conditions of many of the poor must be combatted by provision of social, medical, rehabilitative and other services required, before they can become self-supporting members of our society. The many health, educational, welfare, and income maintenance programs that already exist in this country must be focused on the problem of eliminating poverty. The expansion and redirection of these programs under a purposive policy aimed at eliminating poverty and dependency is now the urgent need.

An anti-poverty program should aim at lifting people out of conditions of poverty and raising their educational, health, and skill levels to increase their opportunities. The war against poverty must not only be a national effort, but must be carried out through community action. This will call for coordination and cooperation among the departments and agencies of the Federal Government, participation of State and local agencies, and full participation by the private sector of the community.

SOCIAL SECURITY
Sigmund Diamond

It is a commonplace to state that, in its modern forms, social insurance was born of the necessity to provide government assistance to help meet the hazards of industrial life—industrial accident insurance, workmen's compensation, health insurance, old age and survivors' insurance, unemployment insurance, widows' and orphans' pensions, family allowances, minimum wage legislation and the like. In these forms, modern social insurance programs had their origin in Bismarckian Germany. Long before the enactment of this legislation, however, there was in the United States—and elsewhere—a program for handling the problems of the unfortunates of society, a program which, while it mitigated some of the harshness of modern social problems, established certain traditions which made more difficult the adoption of a nationwide program of social insurance on the model that had been developed in Europe.

What follows below is not a résumé of the history of social insurance; that can be found in any number of excellent books. We shall begin with (1) a brief

statement of the origin of modern social insurance programs in nineteenth century Germany; consider (2) the early history of the English Poor Law system, which provided the basis for the system of handling social unfortunates in the United States; and then turn briefly (3) to a discussion of the development of poor relief in colonial Massachusetts, as an example of how these problems were handled in early American history.

I. The Origins of Social Insurance

Modern social insurance is the result of the industrialization of the world, but conceptions for the handling of the weak and the poor long antedate industrialism, of course. All societies at all times develop ideas concerning the "value" and the "importance" of their constituent elements, notions concerning the degree of responsibility—if any —that society should have for these constituent elements, and a set of beliefs concerning what is responsible for social misfortune and catastrophe. The particular answers that a society gives to these questions affect, obviously, whether the "poor" or the "aged" or the "disabled" will be perceived as social groups, whether their plight will be seen as the result of their own weakness or failure or the result of the operation of broad social forces, and, finally, whether they will be considered as having any "claim" on society to help them in their plight.

In the history of Western Europe, long before industrialization, certain ideas existed that influenced decisively the degree to which society felt responsible for the welfare of its members and, indeed, whether it felt that misfortune arose from social causes which established a claim on society or was the result of personal weakness or failure which deserved nothing more than scorn or contempt.

A pervasive theme of Hebraic social thought, for example, was the idea of social justice; the unequal distribution of wealth—at least among the prophets—and lack of compassion for human suffering were condemned. These same ideas were carried over into early Christianity and had a kind of fruition in the Middle Ages, with the interest of the Church in the providing of charity and with the organization among the craftsmen's gilds of all forms of mutual benefit funds. Again, during the nineteenth century, the acceptance or rejection of ideas of social security was influenced by the great debate over whether social betterment resulted from the action of individuals or, at least in part, from the activity of the state; by the gradual broadening of the "natural rights" to which men were held to be entitled; and, perhaps perversely, by increasing fear that failure to mitigate the misfortunes of industrialization would increase the hazard that a disaffected people would come to feel that society was responsible for their plight and so would move against it. In broad perspective, then, the growth of ideas of social security may be seen as involving a constant redefinition of the value of its constituent elements to a society, expanding ideas of what might be considered as the valid claims that an individual has against society, and growing realization that the hazards of industrial society are too great to be successfully met by the resources of individuals or even of large-scale organized groups outside the government.

Industrialization—or, more precisely, the hazards of life under industrial conditions in the late nineteenth century—was the major impetus that led, in Germany and elsewhere, toward social insurance. Long before Bismarck, the industrial workers, following the example of medieval artisans, had formed mutual aid societies, but these were voluntary, reached only relatively small groups, and were not strong enough to offer sufficient protection. For that, state intervention was necessary.

Before Bismarck's legislation, the protection of working people in Germany was provided from three different sources. One of them was the employer's liability for compensation in case of accidents, but in most cases the protection was illusory because it required suit for damages by the employee and proof that the injury was due to the negligence of the employer. In 1838, when the first railroad was built in Prussia from Berlin to Potsdam, a law was enacted requiring the payment of compensation for accidents unless the company could prove negligence on the part of the employee. After the unification of Germany in 1871, the same law was extended to mines, quarries, and factories. Welfare institutions of an entirely different kind were the mutual benefit societies, which provided sickness, disability and funeral benefits, and pensions to widows. By a Prussian statute of 1854, membership in such a benefit society was made compulsory; contributions (amounting to a percentage of wages) were deducted by the employer who had to contribute an amount equal to one-half the employee's contribution. Finally, another group of welfare measures — poor relief — was vested in the State. This was a matter of public charity, not of legal right, and the recipient was deprived of civil rights.

As early as 1849, Bismarck had said: "The social insecurity of the worker is the real cause of their being a peril to the state."

When he decided to remove that peril by the organization of a system of social security, there was already much in German history upon which he could draw for support. In 1883, the Sickness Insurance Act was passed and finally, in 1884, an Industrial Accident Insurance Act. In 1889, these were supplemented by Old Age and Invalidity Insurance, in which the principle of employer-employee contributions was supplemented with government subsidies.

Though several European countries accepted the principle of old-age insurance in the years after it was adopted in Germany, they did so with a difference. Denmark, Great Britain, Australia, and New Zealand, for example, instead of compelling persons to save for their old age — which is the essential principle of the contributory system — instructed the local authorities to pay a regular pension to "worthy" persons over the age of 60 who were in need of assistance. The weakness of the system was that the applicant had to prove his need; the public began to look upon the pensions as a form of charity and the self-respect of the recipients was undermined. By the 1920's, most of the countries of Europe adopted or converted to the compulsory contribution system, leaving only the United States, India, and China as major countries without a national system of old-age security.

II. The Early History of the English Poor Law System

Beginning in the late 15th century, the English economy underwent a basic transformation. Men who had supported themselves and their families by tilling the open fields now found themselves without employment — and without legal remedy — as a result of their eviction from the land as the land was converted from tillage to pasture for the raising of sheep. The older economic system had assumed adequate employment for all; indeed, its great problem had been to find labor to meet the demand. By definition, an able-bodied wanderer was a ne'er-do-well; all that was necessary was to punish him and to encourage the hand of charity in the relief of the sick and the infirm. But now, for the first time, there was a surplus of labor; many who were willing and able to work could not find employment, and took to the highways to seek bread and work.

The problems created by the enclosure movement — involving the transition from arable to pasture land for grazing — were exacerbated by a transition of another kind. In the Middle Ages, charity was largely a function carried on by the church and its institutions; by 1531, for example, there were in England several hundred foundations of a religious nature, some of which maintained hospitals for the sick and cared for the aged. With the coming of the Protestant Reformation to England, all such religious foundations were abolished and their estates confiscated. A vast swarm of retainers and hangers-on was, therefore, added to those made unemployed by the enclosure movement.

How, then, were the unemployed and the poor to be taken care of? In the 16th century, there were four main sources of relief for the indigent:

1) In all ages the monasteries gave to the poor, and as the poverty created by the enclosure movement increased, so did alms-giving by the monasteries.

2) The hospitals, which began as foundations for the relief of the sick and housing of the poor, supplemented the work of the monasteries.

3) All of the important gilds maintained funds for the relief of poor members. With the passage of time, the practice of providing shelter in the gilds for the poor reached the point at which they had become veritable alms-houses.

4) The fourth major source of alms was private charity from rich persons. Prior to the great rise in poverty as a result of the enclosure movement, the efforts of the government to handle the problems of mendicancy and poverty were characterized by extreme repression. By the Statute of Laborers (1349), the asking of alms by "valiant beggars" was forbidden; furthermore, "every man and woman, of whatsoever condition, free or bond, able in body, and within the range of threescore years, not living in merchandise, nor exercising any craft, nor having of his own whereof he may live nor proper land about whose tillage he may himself occupy, and not serving any other, shall be bound to serve him which shall him require, and take only the wages, livery, meed, or salary which were accustomed to be given in the places where he oweth to serve." In the Statute of 1388, the attempt was made to bind the poor to the place of their birth; it was directed that "beggars impotent to serve shall abide in the cities and towns where they be dwelling at the time of the proclamation of this statute." These acts were followed by a series of such measures characterized for the most part by the repressiveness of forced labor at fixed wages and by attempting to force the poor to remain in a fixed locality.

Many of the leading English municipalities developed their own programs for the solution of the problem of vagrancy considerably before the enactment of Poor Law legislation by Parliament. Such a series of measures for example was adopted in London between 1514 and 1524. All able-bodied tramps were forbidden to beg; and citizens were forbidden to give alms to unlicensed beggars. These provisions, however, did not take care of the meritorious poor. The second stage, therefore, was to issue licenses to all persons entitled to beg. The poor were classified into helpless poor children, sick and impotent persons, and sturdy vagabonds. Christ Hospital was selected for the care of the children; licenses were issued for the second group; while a plan was devised for the third group of bringing them together in one place —the mansion house of Bridewell— and forcing them to work. The key element in this system was the idea of classification. The beggar was separated out from the body of the poor, while the poor, an increasing part of the community, came to be regarded as a necessary public burden instead of an object of individual charity. But this latter idea of community responsibility carrying through the London scheme, for example, continued to be raised as a matter of private charity, not as a result of taxation. Furthermore, since the problem of the poor was perceived as a local, not a national, one, the solution was local in the sense that only the poor belonging to a particular town were entitled to relief. Others were "warned out," that is, driven away from the towns in which they were not legally resident.

The earliest national Poor law legislation was remarkably similar to what we have described for London. The object of the Act of 1536 was that none should "go openly begging." To this end, the authorities were charitably to receive, and then to "succor, find and keep" all the "impotent poor" belonging to their district. The necessary means were to be provided by alms in the church, and the clergy were instructed to exhort their flocks to be charitable. "Common and open doles" were forbidden, and no person was permitted to give money in alms except in church. "Valiant beggars" were, of course, whipped and sent away.

Despite all efforts to obtain funds for the relief of the poor, they remained insufficient. In 1572, the second of the Elizabethan Poor Laws provided for the appointment of collectors and overseers as civil officers with power to compel men to serve in these positions for one year, or to forfeit the sum of ten shillings. The Act of 1576 empowered the Justices of the Peace in every county to purchase or hire buildings to be converted into houses of correction. They were to provide a stock of wool, hemp, flax, or iron for the unemployed "to the intent that they might be accustomed and brought up in labour and then not like to grow to be idle rogues . . ."

By new legislation at the end of the 16th century, the poor were classified into three groups: the able-bodied poor, for whom work was to be furnished as in the Law of 1576, with refusal to be punished by imprisonment; those unable to work—the "impotent poor"—were provided for in almshouses; dependent children—unless they had parents or grandparents who could be compelled to support them—were to be cared for by apprenticing them, the boys until age 24, the girls until age 21 or until they were married. The source of income was a tax levied and collected weekly by overseers of the poor from every possessor of lands, houses, or tithes in the parish "in such competent sums as they shall think fit." Locally-elected overseers of the poor supervised administration of the system. This law, together with one enacted in 1662 that provided relief in any locality only to those who held legal residence in it, provided the basis for the English system of poor relief until well into the 19th century. By the time of the Elizabethan Poor Laws, then, the basic principles for providing aid to the helpless had been worked out. The relationship of the state to the individual, as contemplated by the Poor Laws, was that the citizen who could not help himself should be helped by the community, and that every citizen enjoying the advantages of civil government should be obliged to contribute for the relief of the distressed.

III Development of Relief in the United States

The governing principle in the development of a system of charity in 17th century New England was the idea —born in England but sharpened by existence under frontier conditions—

that the community (in this case, the town) could restrict undesirable persons. For the most part, the reasons for closing the gates of the town on newcomers had to do with (1) incompatibility of religious belief, and (2) likelihood of early public dependency. The pressures for exclusion of undesirables increased with the practice adopted early in the history of the colonies of shipping paupers and convicts to them.

Between 1617 and 1619 one hundred dependent children were shipped from London for Virginia. In 1622 and again in 1635, vagrants were kept in the Bridewell in London pending deportation to Virginia. The ports of Massachusetts frequently witnessed such arrivals, but after the American Revolution deportations were organized on a systematic basis. An 1835 report of the City of Boston indicates that "the exportation of paupers had become in England a well-known and regular business, and certain American vessels were called the 'Work-house Line.'"

The laws of Plymouth Colony relating to the problem of settlement may be taken as characteristic of all New England's early legislation on the subject. In 1642, laws were adopted forbidding bringing into the community, without consent, persons who were likely to become a charge on the settlement; making importers of persons who were likely to become chargeable responsible for them while dependent; and making all masters of servants responsible for them during the period of their dependency. Despite all these deterrents, the numbers of those in distress increased, particularly the widows of men killed in the various colonial wars. Accustomed to English law and practice, the colonists attempted to meet the situation by making each township responsible for its own dependents, as

the parish had assumed such responsibility in England. To reduce their own liability, the towns resorted to the practice of "warning out" those who were likely to become public charges, that is, evicting from the town those likely to become dependents who had not acquired legal residence. Even with respect to those to whom the town had a legal responsibility to provide relief, the basic concern of the town during at least the first 150 years of New England history was to try to avoid liability, even where that worked tremendous hardship on the dependent, hardship to the point of the dispersal of the dependent's family. There was little hesitation, for example, in closing up a household, placing the children by indenture, or putting the parents out in service in order to prevent a public expense. The Boston Town Records for March 25, 1672, for example, state:

"It is ordered that notice be given to the several persons underwritten that they within one month after the date hereof dispose of their several children (herein nominated or mentioned) abroad for servants, to serve by Indentures for some term of years, according to their ages and capacities; which if they refuse or neglect to do the magistrates and selectmen will take their said children from them, and place them with such Masters as they shall provide according as the law directs. And that they do according to this order dispose of their children do make return of the names of the Masters and children so put out to service, with their indentures to the selectmen at their next monthly meeting. . . ."

The records of the town of Gardner, Mass., for January 5, 1789, state:

"To see what method the town will come into to take care and provide for Oliver Upton and his family; to vendue them out to the lowest bidder, or to take some other method, as the town shall think best when met. Voted, to vendue them to the lowest bidder. Voted, to choose a committee to draw the condition of sale. The condition of sale of Oliver Upton and wife are such, that the lowest bidder have them until March meeting, with their household stuff, and to provide victuals and drink, convenient for them; and to take care of them. The Selectmen to take a minute of his household stuff. Also the children to be let out to the lowest bidder until the selectmen can provide better for them; and to provide victuals and drink for them. Oliver Upton and wife bid off by Simon Gates, at one shilling per week. Oldest child bid off by Simon Gates, at one shilling per week. Second child bid off by John Haywood at ten pence per week. Third child bid off by Andrew Beard at one shilling, two pence per week. Fourth child bid off by Ebenezer Bolton, at one shilling, nine pence per week."

In short, scant consideration was shown for the unfortunate; the problem was to get rid of the burden of dependency and, if it had to be borne, to distribute it equally upon the townsfolk. The town of Hadley, Mass., boarded Thomas Elgarr, "a town's poor," with 32 persons for a period of 65 weeks prior to January, 1685. He remained from one to three weeks with each host. In 1687, the widow Baldwin was removed from house to house, "to such as are able to receive her," and ordered to remain two weeks in each house. Under the circumstances, "going on the town" — with the stigma it involved and with its harshness of terms — was an unmitigated disaster.

It became the custom in Massachusetts and elsewhere to "bid off" the support of the town's poor at public auction, usually at the village tavern on a Saturday night following the annual town meeting. At the table were the town fathers and those who could estimate accurately the value to them of the labor of unemployed men, widows, and children. The records of the town of Fitchburg report the name of each pauper, the name of the successful bidder, and the amount the town had to pay each week ranging from nothing to full support, depending upon the bidder's estimate of the value of the labor of the person whose service he had just won at the auction.

The system of auctioning the poor eventually lost ground; protests forced the development of the system of providing for the unfortunate — the aged, the sick, and the poor — in almshouses. Indeed, the system of placing the poor in almshouses grew especially rapidly in the larger cities, where the number of the poor was so large that the almshouse could be administered with greater economy and efficiency than the auctioning of the poor. Though the first of these public almshouses was erected in Boston in 1660, it was not until 1735 that some system of classification of the poor was adopted. Until that date all dependents — aged persons, widows, dependent children, the sick, the insane — were kept under the same roof. Under legislation adopted by the General Court of Massachusetts in 1735, the town of Boston was authorized to erect a house in which the poor could be put to work; offenders were not to be admitted and the decrepit were to remain in the almshouse.

The system developed for the handling of dependent children requires special attention.

The first child placed out by public authority in Massachusetts was apparently Benjamin Eaton, indentured in

1636 by the governor and assistants of Plymouth Colony to "Bridget Fuller, widow, for 14 years, she being able to keep him at school 2 years, and to employ him after in such service as she saw good and he should be fit for; but not to turn him over to any other, without the Governor's consent."

The policy of the early New England community was that each person —even young children—should be attached to a family and have some occupation. In 1657, for example, the town records of Boston report: "It is agreed upon the complaint against the son of goodwife Sammon living without a calling, that if she dispose not of him in some way of employ before the next meeting, then the townsmen will dispose of him to some service according to the law."

When an abandoned child was found, the first effort was to place it with some family. In 1645 in Plymouth, an infant was left with a family by a father who promised to pay board, but who instead left the community. The child was indentured to the party to whom it had been left until age 24. In Massachusetts Bay Colony, the attachment of each child to some family, in a self-sustaining occupation, was required by law as early as 1642. ". . . all parents and masters" were required to "breed and bring up their children and apprentices in some honest lawful calling, labour or employment, either in husbandry or some other trade, profitable for themselves and the Commonwealth, if they will not or cannot train them up in learning, to fit them for higher employments." In this early period, indenture was the only method of disposing of dependent children. The following contract from the records of Malden, Mass., in 1745, is typical:

"This indenture witnesseth that Jo-seph Lynde, Thomas Wait, John Dexter, Stephen Pain, and Joseph Wilson, Select-Men, Overseers of the Poor of the town of Maldon . . . by and with the consent of two of His Majesty's Justices of the Peace for said county have placed and by these presents do place and bind out John Ramsdell a poor child . . . unto Edward Wait . . . Yeoman and to his wife and Heirs and with them after the manner of an apprentice to dwell and serve from the day of the date of these Presents until the fifth day of April . . . 1762 at which time said Apprentice if living will arrive at the age of 21 years during all which said time or term the Said Apprentice, his said Master and Mistress well and faithfully shall serve their Secrets. He shall keep close their commandments lawful and honest everywhere; he shall gladly obey; he shall do no Damage to his said Master nor suffer it to be done by others . . . ; he shall not waste the goods of his said Master nor lend them unlawfully to any; at Cards, Dice or any other unlawful game or games he shall not play; fornication he shall not commit; matrimony he shall not contract; taverns, ale houses, or places of gaming he shall not haunt or frequent. From the service of his said Master by Day or Night he shall not absent himself. . . . And the said Master doth hereby covenant for himself, his wife and Heirs to teach or cause the said Apprentice to be taught the Art and Mystery of a Cord Wainer and also to read write and cypher. And also shall and will well and truly find, allow unto and provide for the said Apprentice sufficient and wholesome Meat and drink, with washing, lodging, and apparel and other necessaries meet and convenient for such an Apprentice during all the time or term aforesaid. And at the end and Expiration thereof shall dismiss the said Apprentice with two good Suits of Apparel for all parts of his Body, one for the Lords-Day, the other for working Days, suitable to his quality. . . ."

The basic method of public child care in the colonial period was as we have seen, the indenture, but the almshouse, too, played its part. It was characteristic that in the almshouse and in whatever correctional institutions existed, children were not separated from adults. Not until 1825 was Boston authorized to use its House of Industry or establish a House of Reformation for the custody of "all children who live an idle or dissolute life, whose parents are dead, or, if living, from drunkenness or other vices, neglect to provide any suitable employment, or exercise any salutary control over said children." Elsewhere children continued to be kept together with adults in the almshouse until the 1840's. Not until 1882 did the state of Massachusetts adopt a system of placing dependent children with families, paying the costs of the board of such children.

In general, the need of assistance for children lay in the same social disorganization that gave rise to the other 19th century welfare movements. Industrial accidents deprived children earlier and more frequently of their parents. The mobility and anonymity of industrial society meant that orphans were often left among strangers. Low wages and simplification of work drew children into factories. Employment of mothers was often followed by less than adequate supervision and care of children.

Historically, care of orphans devolved upon the Church. The first children's institution in America was connected with the Ursuline Convent in New Orleans. The immediate occasion for its opening was a massacre by the Natchez Indians in 1729, which left many orphans in Louisiana. In 1738, the celebrated Methodist preacher George Whitfield established the Bethesda Orphan Houses in Savannah. These appear to have been the only pre-Revolutionary orphanages in America, but after 1800 the number grew rapidly, reaching 75 by 1850 and 600 by 1890. In the first half of the 19th century, most of these orphanages were "congregate," that is, a considerable number of children were brought together in a single institution, where they usually slept in dormitories and ate in common dining rooms. In the latter part of the century, these tended to be replaced by orphanages on the "cottage plan," where the children lived in relatively small groups and had something approximating family life. In addition, in the second half of the century the whole idea of segregating children into asylums came under attack and the practice of placing them in private homes increased. The first organization in America to adopt "placing-out" as a definite policy was the New York Children's Aid Society founded in 1853. Both the purposes and the methods of work of the Society can be seen in its first circular:

"This society has taken its origin in the deeply settled feeling of our citizens that something must be done to meet the increasing crime and poverty among the destitute children of New York. Its objects are to help this class by opening Sunday meetings and industrial schools, and gradually, as means shall be furnished, by forming lodging houses and reading rooms for children and by employing paid agents, whose sole business shall be to care for them. . . . We hope, too, especially to be the means of draining the city of these children, by communicating with farmers, manufacturers, or families in the country, who may need such employment. When homeless boys are found by our agents, we mean to get them homes in the families of respectable persons, and to put them in the way of an honest living."

Parallel with the growth of the Aid Society and humane societies for children was the development of public child-caring agencies. Before the 19th century, the only public provision for needy children was in almshouses and through the provision of "outdoor relief." The public care of children in the United States seems to have begun with the establishment of municipal orphan asylums; one was opened in Charleston, S. C., in 1794 and one in Philadelphia in 1820. These rapidly developed into the "county homes" so characteristic of the 19th century. Not until 1911 was a significant new step taken in the care of needy children; this was the so-called "mother's pension," first developed in Missouri in 1911.

The United States has consistently lagged behind Europe in most forms of social protection. Though most of the states of the Union had adopted workmen's compensation laws just before World War I, that was fully a quarter century after they had been introduced in Europe. With other forms of social insurance the lag has been even greater. Old-age pensions have long existed in the United States, but they were traditionally reserved for war veterans. The first bill for general pensions, introduced in Congress in 1907, sought to build on that tradition by creating an "Old Home Guard" to include all elderly people in need of assistance. Four years later, Congressman Victor Berger, a Socialist, introduced a bill providing a pension of $4 a week for all persons over 60 whose income was less than $10 per week. During the next 20 years many more such proposals were made in Congress, but none was ever reported out of committee.

Efforts to obtain state action were somewhat more fruitful. Arizona was the first state to enact old-age pension legislation; but its act, passed in 1914, was declared unconstitutional. Nine years later similar laws were enacted by Montana, Nevada, and Pennsylvania. By January, 1935 — on the eve of the adoption of the Social Security Act — 28 states had old-age pension laws, but none was satisfactory. In every case, the applicant had to prove that he was in need and that he had no close relatives upon whom he could call for aid. The age limit was usually high — 70 years in 13 states, 68 in North Dakota — but far more serious were the stringent residence requirements. Arizona, for example, required that a person live 35 years in the state before receiving a pension: only Arkansas and Delaware granted pensions to persons who had not made their home in the state for at least 10 years. Finally, the amount of the pension was usually low. North Dakota did not allow anyone to receive more than $150 a year; the limit $15 a month in Indiana, $250 a year in Kentucky, and $25 and $30 a month elsewhere. Of approximately 7,500,000 persons in the United States who were over 65 on January 1, 1935, only 231,000 — or about three percent — were actually receiving old-age pensions.

Although unemployment benefits were granted by American labor unions more than 100 years ago, no systematic attempt was made to establish a public unemployment insurance system until World War I. In line with American traditions, the early efforts along these lines were confined mainly to state legislatures. An unemployment insurance bill modeled after the British scheme was introduced in Massachusetts in 1916. Five years later an attempt was made in the Wisconsin legislature to adopt the law drafted by Professor John R. Commons, the distinguished labor economist, and it came within one vote of being adopted. Not until the coming of the depression, however, was it possible to obtain sufficient support for such legislation in the states; and even then only Wisconsin adopted such a law. In 1931, unemployment insurance bills were introduced in 17 state legislatures; in 1933, there were 65 such bills introduced in 24 states. Still, Wisconsin was the only state to adopt such a law.

As we have already seen, early American welfare practice — based upon experience with the English Poor Laws — placed primary responsibility on local units of government. During the 19th century, state government emerged as the major instrument of social welfare — mental asylums, schools for the deaf, juvenile reformatories, and the like. More recently, other functions have been added: corrections, mental health, various medical services (crippled children, care of the tubercular), unemployment insurance (with federal financial aid), workmen's compensation (since 1948 in all states), vocational rehabilitation, veterans' services, public recreation, school social services.

Federal welfare activity, held back by dominant laissez-faire attitudes, was far slower in coming. The need for such federal intervention was stated by the United States Supreme Court in the decision upholding the constitutionality of the Social Security Act: "Needs that were narrow or parochial a century ago may be interwoven in our day with the well-being of the nation.... Only a power that is national can serve the interests of all."

Utilizing constitutional provisions giving the federal government power to tax, provide "for the common defense and general welfare," and "regulate commerce among the several states," the federal government more and more was pressed into service to meet the problems of industrial society. Small and traditional programs — care of veterans and Indians, the Children's Bureau — were now joined by the massive new insurance programs — old age and survivors' insurance, unemployment insurance, public assistance. The major welfare functions of the Department of Health, Education and Welfare include the following: 1) old-age, survivors', and disability insurance (completely federal; amended since 1935 to cover nine-tenths of the working force); 2) public assistance (financial aid for state-administered programs of old-age assistance, aid to the blind, aid to the disabled, aid to dependent children); 3) child welfare (grants-in-aid to the states for crippled children, maternal and child health, general child welfare programs; Children's Bureau); 4) vocational rehabilitation; 5) public health. In addition, other major federal welfare programs include: 1) veterans' services; 2) unemployment insurance and employment service; 3) federal court social services; 4) Indian welfare services; 5) housing programs; and 6) income-security programs for railroad workers.

SOME PROPOSALS FOR GOVERNMENT POLICY
IN AN AUTOMATING SOCIETY *
Herbert J. Gans

At a recent conference on the problems of the low income populations, one of the participants proposed this assignment: What measures for coping with poverty and unemployment could the Administration develop if it wanted to—or had to—formulate a crash program resembling that of the First Hundred Days of the Franklin D. Roosevelt Administration?

The seventeen proposals that follow stem from this assignment. They are a set of individual—and often unrelated—ideas, and should not be considered as parts of an integrated program. Partly for this reason, I take little cognizance of what is already being done or proposed, for example, in schemes for depressed area redevelopment, occupational retraining, public works programming, the revision of welfare and unemployment benefits, the education of non-middle class children, and in the struggle against racial discrimination. Nevertheless, few of the proposals are original.[1]

Some of the proposals are suitable for a crash program; others are longer-range schemes. Most of them are, however, "patchwork" ones that assume the continuation of the present economy and society, and seek only to institute needed reforms. Even so, many are probably not politically feasible at present. My assumption is, however, that in a crisis—and I think such a crisis may be on the way—new political alignments develop which quickly redefine political feasibility. The important criterion is whether the proposals are workable and rational; that is, whether they achieve the intended ends without unanticipated consequences deleterious to these ends.

I would be the first to admit that

Reprinted, with permission of author and publisher, from *The Correspondent*, 30, Jan.-Feb., 1964, 74-82.

*I am indebted to a number of people for critical comments on an earlier draft, especially Stanley Aronowitz, Robert Dentler, Christopher Jencks, Donald Michael, Ralph Showalter and Melvin Webber.

[1] I owe an obvious debt to Donald N. Michael's seminal paper, "Cybernation—The Silent Conquest" (Center for the Study of Democratic Institutions, Santa Barbara, 1962). Moreover, some of the proposals were undoubtedly first suggested by friends and colleagues with whom I have discussed this topic informally over the past months.

most of the proposals are not fully thought out and do not at present meet this criterion. Indeed, I have written this paper in the hope that they will be subjected to critical comments, and that these will ultimately produce some workable schemes.

I — The Proposals

The proposals are based on the assumption that in the coming decades automation, the use of computers, and other technological-economic trends will lead to continuing increases in productivity and concurrent decreases in employment. The shrinkage of jobs is thus becoming a major problem in American society, and no longer a problem only for unskilled workers.

There are three major types of problems with which the society — and its economy — must deal: the upgrading and shifting of workers and potential workers into the skilled jobs, including not only blue collar, but also white collar and professional ones, that will be available; the creation of more jobs, especially for unskilled and semiskilled workers; and the elimination of poverty, a problem left over from the past. Proposals 1 to 4 deal with the first; 5 to 15, with the second; and 16 to 17, with the third.

The Shift to Skilled Jobs. The movement of workers from unskilled to skilled occupations essential to the economy is necessary for the employment of those left jobless, and to fill the unfilled jobs that even now exist in considerable number. These aims might be aided by the following:

1. Incentives to Encourage Entry into Unfilled Jobs. Recruitment for presently unfilled jobs might be increased by the federal certification of individual occupations as "Unfilled," and by the concurrent development of programs that eliminate the causes of their being unfilled. Higher salaries, better working conditions, and the like should be encouraged within these occupations, training programs and financial incentives for new recruits outside them. (See also 3 and 4.)

Among the unfilled occupations which need workers most urgently are the service professions: teaching, social work, public health, medicine, nursing, psychiatry; but openings exist also in many other kinds of work.

2. The Creation of Helping Technicians or Subprofessionals. Perhaps even more important than additional recruitment into the service professions would be the creation of an entirely new occupational stratum: people who work in these professions but on a "subprofessional" level. The needed skills could probably be taught in one or two-year programs, or slightly longer ones combining apprenticeship with formal instruction. Recruitment into this stratum should be encouraged among high school or college students who do not — or do not yet — feel themselves ready for professional training, and among adults who want to change occupations.[2] By calling them technicians or subprofessionals, opposition from the established professions would be reduced, and new curricula could be developed which would avoid some of the lengthy instruction which has become entrenched in these professions.

[2]There may be adults who, whatever their jobs, want to be teachers or social workers, but who are too old to start professional training. They might be attracted to the subprofessions — assuming of course that the work could be made financially and socially rewarding.

The greatest need is for technicians of working and lower class origin who could help the low-income population attain the social and cognitive skills required to become part of the larger society.[3] Others are needed in almost all health, welfare, education and other public service programs which suffer from a shortage of staff.

Recruitment into unfilled jobs and the creation of a subprofessional stratum are by far the most important proposals made here. Both can be implemented fairly quickly and easily and can add many new jobs to the economy. Indeed, Frank Riessman has estimated that as many as four to six million helping technicians could be employed in the next decade.[4] Moreover, both proposals encourage the kind of work that will be important in the society of the future, as well as dignified and rewarding for the jobholder. In addition these proposals could reduce the workload which is rapidly becoming an overload in the existing professions, thereby halting the stratification of American society into an overworked professional minority and an underemployed majority, a trend that has many undesirable social and political consequences.

3. Incentives to Encourage Occupational Shifts. Many economic and social obstacles now prevent people

[3]For more detail, see Herbert J. Gans, *The Urban Villagers* (Free Press of Glencoe, New York, 1962), Chap. 12 and pp. 273-278, and especially Frank Riessman, "The Revolution in Social Work: The New Non-professional" (Mobilization for Youth New York, November, 1963, mimeographed).

[4]Riessman, *op. cit.* Programs to implement this proposal are now being developed in a number of places, for example, in the Urban Studies Center at Rutgers and by Arthur Pearl of the Center for Youth and Community Studies, Howard University. Individual agencies, notably the Chicago Area Project, have used helping technicians for a number of years.

from making career or even job-type changes once they are adults, although this applies more to white collar workers than blue collar ones. Some of these obstacles can perhaps be overcome by a grant program which would allow adults to leave the labor force temporarily without loss of income so as to retrain themselves for new jobs. A grant, modelled on the G. I. Bill and equivalent to a going salary or wage, could be made available to anyone wanting to undertake training for an "Unfilled" job. This scheme might be more successful than current retraining efforts, because it would recruit people who want to be retrained for an occupation of their own choice.

Eligibility to participate in this grant program could also be available to adults who left school in adolescence, and want to complete their high school and college education. This would attract dropouts who have realized their mistakes, as well as people who are dissatisfied with their initial career choice and would like to get more education for an as yet unspecified job change. Of course, wherever possible, specific jobs which can serve as a target for them must be available.

4. Incentives for Earlier Entry into the Skilled Occupations. Another way of encouraging people to train themselves for skilled work—especially those not planning to go to college—would be a combined apprentice-education program which starts in high school and allows students to enter an occupation of their choice while still in school. This proposal, suggested by Arthur Pearl, might appeal to youngsters who are unhappy in high school, as well as those who cannot afford to go to college at present. If the grantees are satisfied with their job choice, the apprentice-education program could be continued through college, thus allowing them to obtain a free college education while earning some pay. Income grants, such as those suggested in 3 above, might have to be added as students marry.

The Creation of New Jobs. The second, and in some ways the most important problem is to create new jobs, especially for the unskilled and semi-skilled. This is extremely difficult, given the trends of the economy, and the norm that such jobs should not be of the make-work type. Although some proposals for the creation of new jobs can be suggested, equal priority ought to be given to another approach, the reduction of work-time (either in hours or weeks or months) to spread existing jobs among a larger number of workers. Although this approach has so far been rejected by the Administration — and justifiably so because it will hurt America in international market competition — it is likely to become more necessary in the years to come, and more feasible also, as foreign wage rates begin to resemble American ones.

5. *Industry Incentives to Develop a Secondary Work Force.* One way of reducing work hours would be for the government to subsidize industry to adopt a standard work week of 25-30 hours — at present pay — and to eliminate over-time. This would encourage the creation of a secondary work force, which would hold the same job the other 15-20 hours a week. This force might hire young people — especially in connection with 3 and 4 above — or older people who want to work fewer hours. Tax reductions and income incentives, such as suggested in 16 and 17 below, might be necessary to encourage people to shift to the secondary work force, and similar incentives must be available to industry to cope with added production costs.

This proposal is likely to become more feasible as automation progresses. Since automated machinery must run all the time, the three shift work force now found only in some industries is likely to be needed in many others, and secondary or even tertiary work forces can be created.

6. *Incentives to Workers to Reduce Work Hours.* Another approach, suggested by Christopher Jencks, would be to encourage people who want to work fewer hours to do so. This could be done by taxing overtime work, or by reducing taxes for those who want to work fewer hours — thus tying taxation to the number of work hours — or by giving income grants to reduce the differences in pay between full-time and less than full-time work.

This scheme, like the previous one, would, of course, encourage moonlighting. It should be noted, however, that moonlighting is possible only when extra jobs are easily available, and then primarily because wages are too low to permit workers a decent standard of living from one job. This can be resolved only by raising wages. Moreover, moonlighting could be discouraged by taxing second jobs at a higher rate than first ones. Finally, a study should be made to see whether moonlighting is clearly undesirable, or whether it does not also create jobs that would otherwise not exist. Since moonlighting jobs generally require fewer than forty hours of work per week, they might be the kinds of jobs suitable for the secondary work force proposed above.

7. *Elimination of Involuntary Workers from the Labor Force.* Another way of spreading the work would be to make it profitable for people who do not really want to work to leave the labor force. This would include older people and mothers who work for income

rather than job satisfaction. In addition to permanent departures, it might be desirable to encourage temporary departures from the labor force for those who want to take time off to travel or to loaf, although this is not likely to create permanent new jobs.

Some day it may even be necessary to discourage anyone other than the breadwinner in each household from working, either by raising taxes for second and third workers, or by giving allowances to wives and mothers to stay home. Women who want to work and pursue careers should not be discouraged, but those who do not really want to work should be kept out of the labor market as much as possible.

8. *Grants for Currently Unpaid Volunteer Work.* One way of discouraging women from taking jobs would be to pay them for volunteer work. Many women —and men—work hard in voluntary organizations and derive the same satisfactions as others do from a job. Indeed, being an officer in an important local voluntary association can be a full-time job. Paying such officers from government funds would not only encourage them to stay out of the labor market, but it might also attract more people into community service, especially those who cannot afford to do it now.

9. *The Professionalization of All Occupations.* In the future, the service occupations are likely to play the dominant role in our economy. One way of creating more jobs in them is to speed up the rationalization and professionalization of these occupations, so that work in personal services, repair and maintenance, and even domestic service becomes more attractive and rewarding. This proposal, suggested by Thomas Gladwin, would also raise the level of service in the society. Needless to say, considerable changes in job definition

and in the status relationship between worker and customer are required.

In addition, the already ongoing professionalization of other occupations should be encouraged, and with it, the extension of the temporal fringe benefits —or job interruptions—available especially in the academic world. There is no reason why eventually, most workers should not be able to obtain long vacations, sabbaticals, travel grants, periodic return to school, "visiting" appointments in other places, and the like. This would not only enhance the job, but would also help to spread the work.

10. *Export of Surplus American Consumer Goods.* Private enterprise and the government could cooperate in the export—at low cost or absolutely free—of some of our surplus consumer goods to the developing areas, not only to raise their standard of living, but also to build up the demand for such goods, and thus to create new jobs in this country.

This is a variant of Seymour Melman's scheme to export machine tools, and David Riesman's "Nylon War," the idea of sending consumer goods to Russia to reduce cold war tensions. It could cover yet other items that would be of mutual benefit. Emphasis in such a giveaway should be on those goods not already produced—or not likely to be produced in the near future—in the developing areas.

11. *"Export" of American Skilled Workers.* Another way of opening up jobs would be to encourage workers whose skills are in oversupply here to work overseas in the developing areas, where such skills are in demand, either on the job, or for training the domestic labor force, with the federal government paying their salaries or making up the difference between American and foreign wage scales. This scheme may

falter because of the reluctance of settled blue collar workers to leave this country or even the locality where they grew up, but it might be possible to encourage young blue collar workers to spend some time overseas as part of their apprenticeship, perhaps in a kind of Peace Corps stressing their skills.

Jobs for the Unskilled. The most difficult task is to expand job opportunities for the unskilled. The best solution is to make certain that as many young people as possible are trained for marketable job skills and the number of unskilled workers is reduced to a bare minimum by the next generation. Thus, providing jobs for the unskilled should be a temporary need, and if so, some policies may be justified as short-range solutions that would not be desirable on a permanent basis, *e.g.* Proposal 13.

12. Employer Incentives for the Hiring of the Unemployed. One solution would be to discourage private enterprise from resorting to those types of automation which sharply reduce jobs, either by incentives to hold back automation or by taxes which would reduce the cost advantages of automating. Another approach would be to offer tax reductions and more direct financial incentives to employers to hire those who suffer most from unemployment: the very young and those in late middle age. Such incentives would have to be awarded in such a way that no one of adult working age would be released in order to hire them, and that new jobs would be created as a result. It is doubtful, however, that this could create any significant number of jobs.

13. Temporary Adjustment of the Minimum Wage Law. Another method for creating new jobs might be to cut back the legal minimum wage to, say, 75 cents an hour, and have the difference between it and an adequate wage made up by federal payments to the affected wage-earners. This cutback might lead to the development of new businesses, and with it an expansion of job opportunities for the unskilled. Since such a proposal would in effect mean a government subsidy for marginal firms — where working conditions are often the poorest — and since it would also imply a regression from the wage levels for which unions have fought over a century, such a proposal might have dangerous consequences. Therefore it would need careful study, perhaps through some pilot experiments, in order to see whether the benefits in terms of the number of new jobs would outweigh the social and political costs. If the experiments were successful, the scheme could be tried on a wider scale. The dangers in this proposal might be ameliorated by making it a temporary device; that is, to permit wage reduction only until the new business is on its feet, after which it would be required to pay the going wage. This scheme would be useful only in enterprises not likely to be automated once normal wages were paid.

14. Encouragement of New Businesses Using Unskilled Labor. A more positive approach to the same problem would be to encourage the formation of new businesses, especially in the area of services, by a low cost loan and loan-insurance scheme — the latter somewhat like FHA — which would facilitate the starting of the business and eliminate a large part of the risk. Early mortality would not necessarily be prevented, but the costs of failure would be borne in part by the government. Market studies and imaginative social invention might indicate a number of feasible new businesses and services, especially those which supply the demand created by increasing leisure time and rising taste levels. For example, farmers near urban areas might transform their farms into resorts providing low-cost vacations for city dwellers. Dormitories where people can leave their children for an evening, car rental agencies which rent out used cars at low cost and lawn care companies might be profitable.

15. *A Blue Collar National Service Corps.* One of the best ways of employing the unskilled is a public works program. In addition, it might be desirable to set up a National Service Corps — somewhat like the new CCC suggested by Sen. Humphrey and others — which would carry out those additional public works and municipal service functions that are too expensive or of too low priority to be financed from local revenues or a federal public works program. This Corps would also train youngsters in marketable skills. It could be an expansion of the proposal by the Kennedy Administration for a Corps which stresses mainly white collar and professional skills.

Among the most important projects to be carried out by such a Corps would be the rehabilitation of preservable substandard urban housing to bring it up to a livable level. This is suggested by the failure of slum clearance to improve the housing conditions of the poor and by the possibility that current rehabilitation programs, to be carried out by subsidizing private enterprise, will raise rents beyond the occupants' ability to pay. If rehabilitation were carried out by a service corps, guided by skilled workers, many people might be employed, and housing conditions could be improved immeasurably. Since the crucial feature of rehabilitation is the reduction of overcrowding within slum apartments, the construction of additional low-cost housing for those displaced is also necessary. This can be accomplished by government sub-

sidies to either tenants or builders, and would provide more jobs for the building industry. In addition, the Corps might also help in the provision of municipal services that can stand improvement, for example, mail delivery, garbage removal, street cleaning, and the care of open recreational space and public buildings.

The Elimination of Poverty. Poverty is of course intimately related to unemployment, and would be reduced if the previous proposals were carried out. In addition, the raising of substandard incomes could be accomplished by the following:

16. *The Elimination of Income Taxes among the Low Income Population.* This measure, which has been proposed many times in recent years, should be tried out to determine whether it would significantly reduce poverty and increase purchasing power. But by itself it is probably not enough.

17. *Direct Income Grants to the Low Income Population.* If tax abatement is insufficient, it will be necessary to resort to direct grants, based on the conception that everyone is entitled to a standard minimum income, whether obtained from work or other sources.[5] People who are earning less than this minimum (perhaps $4000 for an urban family, somewhat less for a rural one and for people without children) should be eligible for federal grants — not welfare payments — awarded on the same equalization principles now used in allocating grants to the states. Costly as such a scheme would be, the great spur to purchasing power that would result would be likely to reduce the net cost to

[5]This proposal has recently been presented in greater detail by Robert Theobald, "Abundance: Threat or Promise," *The Nation,* May 11, 1963, entire issue, and in his book, *Free Men and Free Markets* (Clarkson Potter, New York, 1963).

the government. There is of course a danger that such grants would discourage some from working, but experience with welfare payments has made it clear that most people would prefer to earn their income from work. When the day comes that work is no longer available to everyone, an income grant—financed in part from the "profit" of automation— is likely to be considered a less visionary or irresponsible scheme than today, and I can visualize a future era in which all members of society will be eligible for such a grant. Since every radical idea requires years of consideration and repetition in order for it to become acceptable, serious discussion of this type of proposal is highly desirable even now.

II – The Problem of Implementing the Proposals

All of the aforementioned proposals stem from the assumption that normal methods of job formation, either in private enterprise or in government, will not be enough in the future, and that new approaches have to be found. Moreover, these approaches require that job formation be planned with other than present criteria, and that efficiency, profit and cost-price ratios must sometimes be superseded by social benefit considerations. Although many of the proposals can—and should—be carried out by private industry, they do require more extensive government involvement in the economy and in the planning of that economy.

Since the initial and sometimes permanent costs of creating new jobs will require considerable new outlays of public funds, new sources of such funds must be found. One obvious source is a diversion of some of the money now spent for missiles and lunar exploration. Another would be an "automation tax," so that a proportion of industry's savings in production costs would be turned over to the government to pay for the social and economic consequences of automating. Whether or not these sources are sufficient must be determined. If they are not—and this seems most likely—the rest of the funds would have to come from increased income and other taxes levied against the general public, especially since many of the proposals call for tax reductions for some parts of the population. Whether or not the economy can tolerate a sharp rise in taxes without serious downturns in productivity is an important question. How to persuade people that taxes must rise is another.

Middle class people could probably pay more taxes than they now do without having to make serious cutbacks in their private expenditures, but this would not be sufficient to gain their assent. One drawback is that Americans believe government spending is almost always wasteful and infringes on their freedom to make their own spending decisions. This belief can only be altered by demonstrating to people that they need the government services for which they pay, and one method of demonstration is to raise a part of the cost of government by user charges, rather than by taxation. This would enable people to see what they are paying for, although it would also allow them not to use services for which they do not want to pay. It might, however, help to create a new climate of opinion about taxation.

Another way to lighten the psychological burden of taxation is to reduce the multiplicity of taxes, and find a way to collect all of them, federal, state and local, in a lump sum income tax.

Another would be to find a way of levying taxes in relation to expenditures, so that they would be low during those periods of the lifecycle when home purchases, raising children, etc. create the greatest pressure on the family budget, and high when these pressures abate. But whatever the method of increasing taxes, it will require a redistribution of income from the haves to the have-nots, which is likely to be met by intense resistance from the former and by the inability of the latter to exert political pressure on our political institutions.

The federal government has so far been quite unresponsive to the needs of the low income population, and has not felt any real urgency about the state of the economy. Congress is especially insensitive to the problem. One reason is that unemployment affects only a portion of the country and of the society. Not only are the depressed areas highly concentrated geographically, but as Eric Larrabee and David Riesman have pointed out, the economy is a dual one, consisting of affluent and poor sectors, in which the latter are powerless. Congress represents primarily the affluent sector, and the funds which finance election campaigns come almost entirely from a very small portion of that sector. This imbalance might be ameliorated if political campaigns were financed from taxes, rather than by contributions, for this would increase the dependence of senators and representatives on a larger number of voters. Even so, it is not likely to produce a legislature that will be favorable to any scheme involving income redistribution or large scale change in the economy.

The real difficulty is that the people in the poor sector of the economy are neither numerous enough, nor unified in area—or even self-interest—nor effective in making their needs felt.

They vote less often than others, but even when they vote, their ballots carry little weight because they live in Northern cities or Southern states with one-party political machines, or in districts which have been effectively gerrymandered to reduce their influence within the political structure. Until this population can demonstrate the power of numbers at the ballot box, and make its needs felt vocally in other ways, neither Congress nor the Administration will have much political incentive to act in its behalf. Political action by the poor and unemployed, be this in the form of picketing, protest marches, political organization, unions of the jobless, or all of these, will also be necessary.

Even so, no major changes in the economy, nor in government intervention in the economy, will probably take place until unemployment increases even further, and until automation swells the ranks of the jobless with more of the now stably employed blue and white collar workers. At that time, the have-nots will not only be more numerous, but they will include people who have some political strength. Moreover, when the corporate giants begin to discover that continuing automation creates unemployment among their customers, and deprives these of the money to purchase their goods so that sales decline seriously, private industry will also demand government intervention in the economy. Since by then, the economic crisis will have already resulted in a high toll in human misery, it would be desirable if government intervention could come early enough to prevent this.

III—Work and Social Worth

Even if the government can initiate changes in the economy to increase job opportunities, a considerable amount of unemployment is probably here to stay. If present trends continue, most of it will affect an ever-growing minority of permanently jobless people, who will be sacrificed to a life of suffering in order to maintain the existing socio-economic arrangements.

Many of the proposals presented above seek to prevent the creation of such a group and to share the work equitably. Yet even if this can be achieved, it is quite likely that in the future there will not be enough full-time employment for everyone who wants it. While the negative economic consequences can perhaps be handled through income grants, there are also social and psychological ones that cannot be dealt with as easily, particularly the loss of social usefulness that accompanies unemployment.

This consequence stems from a traditional American — and Western — culture pattern: that man acquires his social worth and thus much of his self-respect and ego-strength from his job. If that job is not available, widespread anomie resulting from uselessness is likely to follow, and ways must therefore be found to enable people to be — and feel — socially useful, in other, nonwork activities.

Now it is true that for many people, especially blue collar workers, the job has never provided much satisfaction, being primarily a source of income to finance the search for satisfaction elsewhere. But even people who do not identify with their work feel useless if they do not have a job, a feeling which affects their role in the family — visible especially in the marital difficulties of Negro men who have suffered so long from instability of employment — and their entire life. Eventually, joblessness can lead to despair, total apathy, and mental illness.

Criteria of social worth will of course change somewhat as employment opportunity decreases, but they will probably not keep pace with the latter. Even the Great Depression did not do away with the attitude that unemployment is a personal failing. Consequently, it becomes necessary to discover which institutions, old or new, can enable people to feel socially worthy when they are jobless or only employed part-time. The ideal target is a society in which nonwork institutions are more important than work, and in which the departure from the labor market is anticipated rather than feared. This ideal has been proposed in many utopias, past and present, but so far it has been mainly a dream of overworked intellectuals which has not been shared by the rest of society. Now the dream may have to become a reality.

At present, the problem is conceived largely as the availability of extra spare time which must somehow be filled with leisure activity — the so-called threat of leisure. As a result, education for leisure is being advocated again, as it was during the Depression. I am skeptical that this is a solution. For one thing, most people, especially in the middle class, do not lack leisure ideas, but rather lack the time and money with which to carry them out, and of course, the ability to depart from the labor force. Moreover, a considerable amount of leisure training is already being offered as part of the college experience. Leisure training for the noncollege population may help some people, especially among the most poorly educated, although studies of the low income population suggest no dearth of leisure time activities at present, at least among people who can pursue sociability with relatives, friends and neighbors.

But the main drawback of education

for leisure is that if fails to come to grips with the real problem. As Depression era studies show, people become less interested in leisure activities when unemployed, because job loss deprives them of social and personal worth. Leisure activity is no substitute because much of it is by definition socially useless.

I have not so far seen any feasible solutions to the problem. The professionalization of jobs, the interruption of work by long vacations and sabbaticals, and the upgrading of rewards for community service (see 8 or 9 above) will help a little. So would a concerted attack on the rejection of leisure, especially of "non-constructive" leisure activity, still embedded in the Puritan ethic, and a recognition of the virtues of spontaneous socializing and loafing that still exist in the cultures of the lower, working and lower middle classes.[6] Still, these proposals are not enough.

Social planning and social research must begin to find ways of revising the institutional arrangements and beliefs that provide social and personal worth. Such planning might begin with the study of societies and groups in which worth is not measured by work, including the leisure classes of the past in Western society, adolescents, bohemians, hoboes and Skid Rowers of our own, and especially those preindustrial and preliterate societies which cherish no concepts of work and job. Not that such findings can be easily transferred to the modern situation. The three institutions which in the past have been most effective in instilling belongingness—the small community, the tribe, and the extended family—play a minor role in a large urban-industrial society, while hoboes and bohemians have been despised for their deviant ways. The only hopeful feature of this problem is that there is still some time—perhaps a generation or so—to find a solution.

[6]It is ironic that these cultures are under attack by upper middle class critics, reformers and caretakers who seek to instill their own work priorities and Puritan-like leisure attitudes at a time when they are in danger of becoming anachronistic.

4

ETHNIC RELATIONS

Introduction

Conflicts between majority and minority groups in the United States are today so severe as to damage the organization, stain the world image, and impair the adaptive functioning of the national society. More than legally defined inequalities and human and economic costs are involved. The conflicts are symptoms as well as causes of a disorganization that threatens the survival of the society, for survival requires the ability to change, as writer and Negro American James Baldwin says: "It is the responsibility of free men...to apprehend the nature of change, to be able and willing to change." Segregation can result in the nation's destruction through "the abdication by Americans of an effort really to be free. The Negro can precipitate this abdication because white Americans have never, in all their long history, been able to look on him as a man like themselves."[1]

[1]Quoted in *Time*, May 17, 1963, p. 27.

Definitions

Ethnicity refers to a social characteristic of a population. Its root, *ethnikos*, means nation, and writers originally employed the term to describe behavior and attitudes associated with country of origin. Today, however, an ethnic group includes persons who, by virtue of commonly perceived physical and cultural traits, are self-conscious of special group membership and subject to differential treatment by persons outside the group.

The term ethnicity is akin to, yet broader, intellectually more accurate, and politically more responsible, than the idea of race. Race is fundamentally a biological concept. It grew out of the untested assumption that the human species consists of branches which are biologically distinct from each other. The shortcomings of the concept of race are so great that most social scientists prefer to work with other more exact conceptions of group characteristics which are essentially social and cultural.

Biological principles for defining

and identifying races vary. They cannot be applied consistently—that is, scientifically. In real life, people classify one another through location, language, style of life, and other criteria that have nothing to do with biology. These popular distinctions are often thought of as racial. There are thus two reasons for eliminating the idea of race. The biological delineation is poor; and even where it may have relevance, it does not correspond with common social usage.

This is especially true in interpreting social conflict. Ethnicity, not race, arises out of contact between historically separate human groups. Physical differences are initially of little importance in this process. Skin color, stature, body type or hair texture, among other features, may be singled out in the course of contact between groups and used to make distinctions. But physical appearances by themselves seldom if ever lead to the establishment of group differences. Proof of this comes directly to mind: Within many socially homogeneous populations there are substantial differences in physical appearance that do not lead to cleavage or differential treatment.

When two groups meet for the first time and there stand between them differences in history of location and degree of previous isolation as well as differences in language, values and behavior, ethnic distinctions are likely to develop. Differences in physical traits—real, imagined, or attributed—may then be identified and used to reinforce the sense of difference. The term ethnic signifies that this process of differentiation may be singled out analytically from among other manifestations of the same process. Groups, after all, develop from many bases. Ethnic differentiation alone, however, springs from group distinctions grounded in place and culture of historical origin.

Two or more ethnic groups do not automatically conflict when their members meet along a new frontier. They may cooperate; they may compete in some ways and merge or assimilate one another in others; or they may make contact but for a time remain independent of one another.

The nature of the *initial* contact between groups is often a determinant of the form of the relation. Conflict is apt to become the form of relation between the groups when one of them is dominant in size, technology, or resources, and when the subordinate group has something that is coveted by the dominant one. For example, in the white European settlement of North America, a technologically dominant European group invaded and conquered native Indian territory. Indian life and culture was severely damaged and in some areas destroyed as the territory was absorbed by whites and the margin left for Indian resettlement. Extreme conflict between white settlers and the Indians raged for a century and a half after the period of initial contact.

White Americans invaded Africa and employed a superior weapon and transport technology to secure, in this case, manpower rather than territory. Large numbers of captive Africans were thus imported into the newly established American society under terms of exploited subordination. (As apologists of slavery and, later, of segregation put it, Africans were 'saved from savagery' by capture.)

As a third case, from the War of Independence until after World War I, voluntary migrants from a host of very different settings and cultures entered the now-occupied territory of the new

America as economically subordinate, socially marginal members.

In these three cases of the Indian, the African, and the late-coming European and Asian immigrants, the initial terms of contact stimulated conflict: the terms were territorial conquest, enslavement, and economic exploitation. In all three cases, conflict was minimized when the subordinate groups accepted a deprived status. Conflict with the Indian was as much the result of refusal to be stripped of his territory as it was of the white European's determination to expand his frontier. Conflict is thus greatest when members of the subordinate group resist the aims of the dominant group; or when later they attempt to change their social status, political power, or economic prospects.

There are enormous complexities involved in the analysis of ethnic group relations, but these need not obscure the axioms we have advanced here. The hierarchy of relations between ethnic groups, for example, is fixed initially by fairly simple considerations. For the United States, white European supremacy was established by the goal and the means of the transatlantic migration. Taking the chief goal as the pursuit of economic livelihood, one sees that the earlier the arrival and settlement in the new territory—given effective means for invasion and continued control—the greater the advantage over all subsequent migrants. Other factors affect the place each population group carves for itself in the social pecking order; but in the American case, the main event was economic competition in which crucial advantage accrued to the earliest arrivals.

If important advantages derived from ethnic dominance are to be consolidated, they must be sanctioned and the sanctions must become implicit. A society will thus organize more or less entirely around the inter-ethnic hierarchy and around the system of beliefs that develop to explain, to make legitimate, and thereby maintain the hierarchy. When such a system is well developed, it operates effectively for the subordinate as well as the dominant groups, though it always results in disadvantage for the subordinated.

Prejudice is a socially learned *readiness* to behave differentially and unfavorably toward members of particular ethnic groups. Prejudice is a disposition to discriminate. The disposition may be expressed in overt acts; it may be blocked by competing attitudes; or it may remain inert for lack of situations which present an occasion for its expression.

Discrimination differs from prejudice. Discrimination is an act of differential treatment of persons defined as belonging to a particular group. Logically, it could occur in the absence of prejudice on the part of the actor. Actually, the unprejudiced actor who discriminates is behaving under the influence of other prejudiced persons.

The key term is thus neither prejudice nor discrimination, but 'differential treatment.' Everyone discriminates between persons and groups, and differentiation is a universal human activity. The differential treatment that underlies ethnic relations and discrimination, however, is differentiation on grounds that violate important institutional standards of the society.[2]

[2]As sociologist Robin Williams puts it, "Except for the probable deviations around such social norms, it is expected in our society that occupational opportunity will be available on the basis of merit or ability, that all citizens are entitled to specified legal rights, that economic transactions will be carried out according to the

Modern Americans learn their prejudices as they grow up. They discriminate on the basis of them, or out of conformity to the prejudices of others around them, when the situation is most fitting for the manifestation of this special type of differential treatment. Discrimination thus grows out of arrangements for maintaining certain features of social organization, yet it involves the violation of precious standards of other features of that organization! Hence, the disorganization that results springs from inconsistencies deep in the social order. It is the great prototype of a total social problem, for ethnic discrimination is at once conformity and deviance; a basis for consensus and a basis for value conflict; a source of support for social organization, and a great force for disorganization.

Segregation and discrimination are this complex, for one thing, because the standards of the national society are not only not always upheld; they are not consistently applied either. The American who discriminates may act from a position of national authority, but his acts are rooted in localities. Until recently, for example, the codes of the Federal Housing Authority were consistently discriminatory. Those who obeyed them—government officials, bankers, realtors, and home owners—worked deliberately and formally to the disadvantage of ethnic minorities.[3] Even these codes were used inconsis-

tently: there were communities in which discrimination in the provision of federally insured purchases of housing was applied much more emphatically than in others.

When an ethnic hierarchy of social relations has been established, and when the hierarchy is reinforced by systems of beliefs through which individuals are educated into prejudice and discrimination, the image that the dominant groups hold of the subordinates also tends to control the behavior of the latter.[4] The American Negro is not only held in place, for example, he learns to *preserve* this place.

The American Negro

There are many ethnic minorities in the United States: groups who are the object of prejudice and discrimination and whose members think of themselves as different. If Roman Catholics are *not* considered, however, the many minorities break very readily into two groups: Negroes and all others. All but 1 per cent of the census-defined nonwhite population is Negro. About 19

rules of the market. Discrimination may be said to exist to the degree that individuals of a given group who are otherwise formally qualified are not treated in conformity with these nominally universally institutionalized codes." Robin M. Williams, *The Reduction of Intergroup Tensions.* New York: Social Science Research Council, 1947, p. 39.

[3]U.S. Civil Rights Commission Report on Housing. Gov't. Printing Off., 1961.

[4]In James Baldwin's words, "One's hair was always being attacked with hard brushes and combs and Vaseline; it was shameful to have 'nappy' hair. One's legs and arms and face were always being greased, so that one would not look 'ashy' in the wintertime. One was always being mercilessly scrubbed and polished, as though in the hope that a stain could thus be washed away . . . . The women were forever straightening and curling their hair, and using bleaching creams. And yet it was clear that none of this would release one from the stigma of being a Negro; this effort merely increased the shame and rage. There was not, no matter where one turned, any acceptable image of oneself, no proof of one's existence. One had the choice, either of 'acting just like a nigger' or of *not* acting just like a nigger —and only those who have tried it know how impossible it is to tell the difference." Quoted in *Time, loc. cit.*

million out of roughly 20 million non-white Americans were Negroes in 1960. Other minority groups defined socially as white as a whole constitute but 7 per cent of the population. Negroes constitute more than 10 per cent.

All ethnic minorities are increasingly well dispersed across the country, yet among the larger groups all save the Negro remain concentrated in particular regions and communities within these regions. American Jews are predominantly centered in the New York City metropolitan area. Spanish and Mexican Americans are heavily concentrated in the Far West.

One third of all Negroes reside in the Deep South, and another third continue to live in the border states between the South and North. The remainder, more than five million, have migrated since 1900 to the ten largest cities of the industrial North.[5] The Negro minority is thus much larger and more widely dispersed nationally than any other minority group.

Negro-white relations are distinctive in yet another way. Discrimination against Negroes has been more systematic, uniform, and intense, than discrimination against other groups. Only the treatment of the American Indian (and, during World War II, of the Japanese-American) approaches the scope and depth of anti-Negro practices.

The reasons for this are historical and social. Under slavery, the dispossession of the Negro minority was total. The elimination of slavery through war, while improving the status in fundamental ways, also strengthened

[5]These *central cities* contained about four and a half million Negroes in 1960: Los Angeles, San Francisco, Chicago, Detroit, Milwaukee, Cleveland, Philadelphia, Boston, and New York. An additional one million live in Washington, D.C., Baltimore, and St. Louis—border cities.

the psychological bases of racism in the South. And, the size of the Negro population and its great migratory movement northward since 1900, has made contact, hence conflict, between whites and Negroes more frequent throughout the nation. At worst, the institution designed historically to preserve the status of the Negro as inferior and allegedly subhuman is stronger than those devised to maintain advantages over any other group in the society. At best, and with few exceptions, this institution has undergone significant modifications only within the last twenty years.

Consider a few features of this institution, beginning with formal education. At the close of the school year in 1962, eight years after the Supreme Court school integration decision of 1954, only 2,725 of the 2,482,170 Negro pupils in the public grade schools of the South (about .001 per cent) were attending classes with whites, according to the reliable Southern Education Reporting Service of Nashville. If the South's rate of compliance with the Supreme Court directive of "all deliberate speed" continues at this pace, school desegregation in the South will be completed in about 7,000 years.

We lack comparable figures on school segregation for the North, but conditions have been documented for a number of industrial cities. In Gary, Indiana, for instance, 54 per cent of the public school population were Negro in 1961, and 97 per cent of these children attended all-Negro schools. Gary's schools were officially segregated from 1922 to 1947, but later changes in the local law did not lead to changes in practices.[6]

[6]Max Wolff, "Segregation in the Schools of Gary, Indiana," *Journal of Educational Sociology*, February, 1963, pp. 257-261. Vol. 36, No. 6.

More crucial are institutional barriers to the right to vote, for a voice in government is a necessary prerequisite to equal opportunity in American society. As of 1960, in some one hundred counties in eight Southern States, Negro citizens were prevented from exercising the right to vote. Few Americans deny the fact of this abridgement. Even Senator Allen J. Ellender of Louisiana acknowledged on television in 1963 that Negroes are denied voting rights in parts of Louisiana and Mississippi.

Disenfranchisement through gerrymandering and malapportionment is common for Negroes in some of the states where they are not directly prevented from voting through vigorous local enforcement of barriers. Gerrymandering is a form of political districting in which district lines are drawn in such a way as to put particular groups of voters into, or out of, particular districts in order to limit or heighten the effectiveness of their votes. The Alabama Legislature in 1957 changed the boundaries of the city of Tuskegee, for example, so that all but five out of 400 Negroes who voted previously in local elections were placed outside the city limits. (This particular case was so glaring as to lead to court nullification. Others are more subtle.)

In malapportionment, political districts are so arranged that one district has greater strength than others in the same state. In legislatures of border and Southern states, rural counties are frequently 'over-represented,' thus *reducing* the impact of urban Negroes and more moderate urban whites upon racially affected political issues.

Among the important clues to the status of the American Negro is his place in the economy. Barriers to employment and equal income influence not only material well-being but mobility, style of life, and in a money culture, self-image.

Of the two thirds of the Negroes who live in the South and the border states, about one third of these live on farms, most of them as tenant farmers and hired hands. Discrimination is at its peak in the marginal farm counties of the rural South, a region that has been distressed economically for whites and Negroes for many decades. There, Negroes own the smaller, poorer farms or they are prevented from buying land at all. Bank credit is differentially supplied. Mortgagors make more severe demands on Negroes; farm owners cheat their Negro laborers by maintaining a credit rather than cash payment system. Through collusion between county law officials and landowners, a kind of legalized peonage is not uncommon.

Many forces have softened this condition. The Great Depression, the mechanical cotton picker, the extension of cotton planting into West Texas, the opening of industrial job opportunities during World War II, and the increasing urbanization and industrialization of the South itself, have emptied hundreds of rural deep southern communities of their Negro tenant farmers and farm laborers. This great migration is an extension of the movement begun during World War I, but it has meant a modest improvement in southern rural economic conditions for those Negroes who have remained.

Negroes first entered urban industries in large numbers in World War I, but even after demonstrating competence in the factory environment, Negroes remained the last to be hired and the first to be fired. During the Great

Depression, they lost the gains they had made: The proportion of Negroes in manufacturing, for example, was lower in 1940 than it had been in 1910. Only employment in domestic service remained steady.

World War II was the next turning point, as under the double impress of severe manpower shortages and expanded production, and with the marginal influence of fair employment directives and legislation by states and the federal government, the number of Negroes in skilled and semiskilled jobs *doubled* between 1940 and 1945. Some of the industrial unions gave Negroes full membership during this period. Others afforded Negroes auxiliary or second-class status. Most of the trade and craft unions remained segregated, officially or tacitly. The employment patterns established among Negroes during World War II have continued substantially into the present decade. In recessions, Negroes are among the first to lose their jobs, and Negro unemployment in any current year is nearly twice that of white unemployment.[7]

A 1957 study of Negro membership in construction trade and craft unions in 32 cities reflected a uniform pattern of exclusion from certain occupations, including electrical workers, ironworkers, plumbers, steam-fitters, and sheetmetal workers. Lower paying trades, such as the hod carriers, are more commonly open to Negroes. Where Negroes do gain union membership, they are far less likely to get jobs through union referrals.

[7]A study made by the Connecticut Commission on Civil Rights concluded that in that state, the average income of Negro families whose members had completed high school or college was about equal to that of white families whose members had not gone beyond grade school.

In its 1961 report, the United States Commission on Civil Rights concluded:

The depressed economic status of Negroes is the product of many forces, including ... discrimination against Negroes in vocational as well as academic training. Discrimination against Negroes in apprenticeship training programs. Discrimination against Negroes by labor organizations — particularly in the construction and machinists' crafts. Discrimination against Negroes in referral services rendered by State employment offices. Discrimination against Negroes in the training and employment opportunities offered by the armed services, including the civilian components. Discrimination by employers, including Government contractors and even the Federal Government.... The Negro is denied, or fails to apply for, training for jobs in which employment opportunities have traditionally been denied him; when jobs do become available there are consequently few ... qualified Negroes available to fill them; and often, because of lack of knowledge of such newly opened opportunities, even the few who are qualified fail to apply.[8]

When Negroes do secure appropriate education, job training, employment, and an income equal to what any worker would earn for the same work, their *material* difficulties are far from over in a national society that has been organized intricately to sustain discrimination against Negroes in all domains. Consider housing, described in the 1959 report of the United States Civil Rights Commission as "the one com-

[8]1961 Report on *Employment*, Vol. 3, pp. 153-154.

modity in the American market . . . not freely available on equal terms to everyone who can afford to pay."

Until the formal terms were changed by presidential directive in 1962, residential segregation in the United States was so consistently practiced as a policy by sellers, realtors, banks, and related money lenders, that not only local institutions but the Federal Housing Administration, the Veterans' Administration, and the Federal National Mortgage Association pursued clearly discriminatory policies in the financing and management of real property. As of 1962, the formal policies were changed. State laws have been similarly altered or improved since 1950, so that many northern states prohibit discrimination in housing. It will be many years before the crucial changes in *informal* practices by which neighborhoods, parts of cities, and white communities are kept strictly segregated, are likely to take place.

Northern Negroes are, by and large, restricted residentially to ghetto housing. Before World War I, many midwestern communities refused openly to allow Negroes to live within the city limits. Before 1920, Elmwood, Indiana, boasted a sign that read, NO NEGROES ADMITTED HERE: and another in this Ku Klux territory read, NIGGERS, READ AND RUN. Restrictive covenants flourished in the larger cities and their suburbs which made sale of land or houses to Negroes illegal.

The constitutionality of such discriminatory laws was challenged by Supreme Court action in 1948, yet in Chicago and Detroit, race riots continued to flare into the early 1950s as a result of the settlement of Negroes in previously all-white neighborhoods. In Cicero, Illinois, in 1951, one Negro family caused such a commotion that

the Illinois National Guard was ordered to restore order. Harvey Clark and his wife, both college graduates, and their young children were prevented from moving into a rented apartment by the Cicero Chief of Police. With the help of a federal injunction, the Clarks moved in, but a white mob made a shambles of the apartment building while the police made no arrests and even permitted the mob to throw Clark's piano into a bonfire of personal furniture and effects.

Very little has changed since 1947, when Baltimore's Negro population, amounting to 20 per cent of all residents, occupied only 7 per cent of the city's housing. In Harlem, the population density remains so severe that if the same average of nearly four thousand persons per block were maintained for the entire American population, 180 million Americans could be housed within the five boroughs of New York City!

The costs of deprivation and injustice in white treatment of the American Negro are not difficult to calculate sociologically. The infant mortality rate for whites in the nation was 25.8 per thousand in 1959; for Negroes, 50.2. The maternal death rate for whites was 2.6 per ten thousand; for Negroes, 10.2.

Expressed in terms of life prospects instead of death rates, the median income for urban white families in 1961 was $6,433, compared with $3,161 for urban Negro families. The income gap, which narrowed substantially during the period from 1941 to 1950, was even greater among rural nonfarm workers. In this group, whites had a median family income of $4,981 in 1960, compared with $1,917 for nonwhites. Slightly more than 4 per cent of all white families earned less than $1,000 in 1960, contrasted with more than 15 per cent of all nonwhite families.

Birmingham and the Future

Birmingham, Alabama, became in 1963 a national symbol of a new phase in Negro-white relations. Negro leaders, determined to reveal the depths of racism and to demonstrate their growing ability to counter its effects, selected Birmingham in the late 1950s as a bastion of racial inequality. Between 1957 and 1963, there were 18 racial bombings and about 52 cross-burnings in Birmingham. In spite of Negro efforts during these years, the city remained totally segregated, from schools to restaurants, drinking fountains, and toilets.

Then in May of 1963, Birmingham Negroes, stimulated by the leadership of the Reverend Martin Luther King, intensified a campaign of negotiation with local white commercial, professional, and political leaders for minimum concessions by greatly expanding public, nonviolent demonstrations.

Public prayer sessions, parades, and church-centered rallies came to include as participants elementary and secondary school children and youth. White police counter-actions were equally intense as Negro demonstrators were 'controlled' by police dogs, powerful firehoses, and mass arrests and jailings that included six-, seven-, and eight-year-old children.

Minor concessions were achieved within ten days of campaigning, but these were overshadowed by a national public reaction of shock. Americans, long conditioned to ethnic conflict and campaigns for civil rights, were stunned to discover, on the one hand, the depths of white southern intransigence and official white brutality, and to grasp, on the other, the ultimacy of Negro intentions. Speaking about equal rights, Martin Luther King commented that three words expressed a universal Negro disposition: "all," "here," "now." The Birmingham conflict demonstrated that Negroes were disposed to sacrifice their personal security to eliminate racial discrimination, and that they were now organized to achieve this goal.

The Birmingham conflict also clarified the limits of governmental, public action. Presidential speeches, congressional legislation, court decisions, and administrative directives, while ameliorative, were revealed conclusively as inadequate. The political slogan embraced by federal officials became: the transfer of racial conflict from the streets to the courts. Actually, Birmingham signified the extent to which judicial remedies had already been tried and found wanting by Negro action groups.

As ethnic relations move from uneasy accommodation, to controversy and frustration, to open conflict as they have in both the North and the South, and as the Birmingham conflict signified, old attitudes stiffen, groups are polarized at extremes, and the means for solution appear to diminish.[9]

Some formerly flexible Southern whites are constrained by intensified conflict toward greater inflexibility. Negroes who are less militant than others before Birmingham must henceforth become more so or suffer loss of influence in the growing race for leadership among competing groups.[10]

[9]New federal laws offering new protections of civil rights contribute to solution. But in the advanced stage of conflict, the prospects for passage of new laws through a representative Congress have diminished. (Even to so much as prevent Southern filibustering in the United States Senate, for example, 67 out of 100 votes are needed to invoke cloture. To secure this number, a Democratic Administration would have to attract roughly 25 Republican votes. This is of course what took place after long debate in the passage of the Civil Rights Bill in the early summer of 1964.)

[10]Roy Wilkins, Executive Secretary of the National Association for the Advancement of Colored People, for example, went to Jackson, Missis-

Birmingham revealed that there is no direct way of eliminating ethnic inequality or racial tension. Laws and court directives based on their application are far from sufficient. More than twenty states have fair employment practices commissions, for instance, and yet fail to insure fair employment practices. The machinery for gradual resolution of inequities exists, but Birmingham offers testimony that Negroes are now unwilling to wait. Gradualism is increasingly abhorrent to more and more Negroes. Even cooperation with white leadership has come to be avoided as a sign of lack of militancy.

Negro-White Relations

The American Negro is set upon transforming the *status quo* in race relations that has been maintained for more than sixty years. Over the remainder of the present decade, all evidence points to greatly intensified interaction around all issues bearing on race relations. The changes that have accumulated since World War II (and chiefly because of changes in opportunity resulting from labor shortages during that war) are leading rapidly toward significant and potentially cataclysmic changes.

In spite of all the limitations on what federal and state governments can do, the most significant of these changes occur through legislative and executive decisions. Until the 1950s, most interaction on matters of prejudice, discrimination, and civil rights, took place between northern white liberals and southern whites. In the new phase which culminated in Birmingham, Negro leadership came into its own and will henceforth shape its own strategies.

sippi, and was arrested for picketing, less than a month after the Birmingham incidents.

New social forces have been released. Negro interest groups will parry and thrust for dominance, and the two major political parties will make new accommodations to changing coalitions. Much of the visible process will be played out between Negro leaders and within the two national parties. Clearly, we may expect increasing alignment of the federal government's powers with Negro interests, with resulting counter-pressures from other special interest groups.

So far as enacted standards go, legal supports for total desegregation will continue to be extended and implemented for the remainder of this century. Between 1900 and 1950, roughly 38 federal Supreme Court decisions and legislative and executive orders were delivered to eliminate discrimination in public accommodations, transportation, education, recreation, job opportunities and voting. More than twice this number have been formulated and passed between 1950 and 1963, and we may expect to see the legal network consolidated within the decade. An omnibus bill became the Civil Rights Act of 1964. Several sections of this Act have had strikingly immediate effects. Provisions guaranteeing voter registrations in particular are already shifting the electoral balance of power from white to Negro in more than a dozen counties in the Deep South.

Yet ethnic discrimination will persist. It is reinforced primarily by custom and mores, informal standards, rather than by the law.

The boycott, the picket, the freedom ride, the sit-in, and related nonviolent direct action by Negroes are designed to challenge *informal* elements of the *status quo*. Direct action has marked social effects that lead to unmistakeable changes. First, the organized actions themselves are not in essence conflicts; the tension and controversy revealed through them existed prior to the direct action. But in taking the action, 'frozen conflict' is melted. The tacit consent of the Negro to the *status quo* is broken. Customs and mores of both Negroes and whites are challenged. Alternative ways of behaving unfold. Secondly, a previously demoralized Negro minority is redefined by its own efforts. Acceptance of the self as inferior is diminished; courage and confidence are generated.

Viewing future trends, then, there exist mechanisms, legal and informal, for changing dramatically the *status quo*. As rights receive improved protection, and as means for challenging old styles emerge, diffuse racial prejudice will decline; Negroes will become stronger politically and psychologically; and those who now stand to gain from discrimination will lose their advantage.

What is missing, and what is therefore socially problematic, are the kinds of changes in the economy, national technology, and social structure that will reinforce these changes in ethnic relations. Vast shortages in the labor force during both world wars represent the sort of change most necessary to erect a new, more equitable, more stable, *status quo*.

The issue fundamental to ethnic group relations in the United States is equality of competitive conditions. There is good reason to expect that under the national standard of open, fair competition, Negroes will remain severely disadvantaged. Social liberals, white and Negro, have advanced such concepts as compensatory education and benign quotas in housing and school districting. Compensation and quotas, like favoritism, violate the norm of equal competition. Americans may

have to choose in the near future between free competition and desegregation, in which case new social tensions will develop.

The American Indian

There were fewer than 524 thousand American Indians counted in the 1960 census, in contrast to 18.9 million Negroes. Among all racially designated ethnic minorities, however, the Indians comprised the second largest group in the nation. In spite of their relatively small number, Indians are almost as widely dispersed as Negroes across the states. Half of the fifty states contain sizeable Indian groups.

The situation of the American Indian illustrates the social history of discrimination as vividly as does that of the Negro. But it is not a duplication of the Negro situation. The historical character of Indian-white relations is unique, as we showed earlier in this chapter, and the economic bases of white exploitation of the Indian are different.

Just as the determinants are different, so the remedies, if and when they are applied, will differ. The Negro minority is large enough to exert political force, for example. Indians (despite long training in political negotiation) have narrowly limited political resources. The problem of Indian-white relations is unique because many Indians are unable either to abandon or to revive their tribal-communal life. Their partially broken yet influential cultural heritage stands between them and assimilation. At the same time, it offers an incomplete alternative to assimilation.

The American Indian is neither a vanishing population nor a member of a dying culture. Yet, until very recently, it seemed otherwise. By purchase, treaty, theft, treachery, and genocidal gun-power, Europeans, in pressing the Indian across the Appalachians, then beyond the Mississippi, and then into the wastelands of the Far West and Southwest, reduced the Indian population from about one million in 1700 to a quarter of a million by 1900.

Not until this century, were the deliberate as well as unintended forces of the white expansion — disease, warfare, impoverishment, and dependency — relaxed and partially corrected. Until 1934, federal policies oscillated between varying forms of deprivation and unplanned programs, most of them designed to break up tribal lands and reservations and to enforce assimilation. Significant attempts at amelioration began under the New Deal.[11]

In 1961, federal policy shifted once again. The practice of termination of trusteeship was reversed. Emphasis went to programs of economic development of tribal groups. In the current phase, reservations are left intact (more than three fourths of the Indian population remain on the old reservations), and the United States Department of the Interior attempts to create employment

[11]The Indian Reorganization Act (IRA) of 1934 authorized the expenditure of $2 million a year for the purchase of land to be held in trust for Indians by the Federal Government and prohibited future allotments of Indian lands. It also provided for tribal government, tribal incorporation for credit and other business purposes, and preferential employment of Indians by the Indian Bureau. In the twenty years since, many Indian communities were stabilized economically. Education and health services improved, and the magnitude of the general problem was reduced socially. The financial costs were considerable, however. Thus in 1953, the IRA was eliminated. Federal policy was reversed. The policy of protecting tribal lands was replaced by legislation designed to terminate federal trusteeship. Between 1953 and 1957, about 12 per cent of all tribal lands were sold, nearly all of it to whites. (U.S. Civil Rights Commission — Report, *Justice*, p. 123, 1961.)

and to improve living conditions within the reservations.

Take the Pine Ridge Reservation of the Sioux, for example. As a result of the new effort, more Indians at Pine Ridge are employed gainfully than in any year since the days of the Civilian Conservation Corps of the New Deal in 1935. A Denver firm (owned by non-Indians) sends bare fishhooks to Pine Ridge, where the Sioux workers tie leaders on them. A mimimum wage of $1.15 an hour has enabled roughly 400 Sioux workers at Pine Ridge to earn about $46 a week. Although only this 400 among the 1900 heads of Sioux families at Pine Ridge are employed, 51 families have been able to leave their canvas tents and log shacks to move into cheap homes financed by federal assistance.

Inevitably, perhaps, with increased income, the employed families began to dress their children and to feed them more effectively. School attendance became more regular. And 74 families removed themselves from the relief rolls during the first year of the program. Increased job opportunities are obviously central to remediation of the Indian as well as to the Negro situation.

Note the limitation on the 'fishhook solution,' however: The Pine Ridge project began late in 1961. By mid-1962, the Denver firm was over-stocked with Sioux-tied fishhooks. Of the 388 Sioux workers employed in 1962, 164 were laid off by the end of that year.

New legislation calling for federal funds for Indian loans for economic development and for white investment in reservation industries has been before the Congress since 1962. A significant modification in the economic prospects of reservation Indians would be expensive. To date, insufficient political stimulus has been marshalled to induce serious federal investment in a solution.

In spite of a changing surface in inter-ethnic attitudes, in other words, no adequate program of aid has been undertaken *and* maintained.

Just as the Negro minority has its rural southern contingent and its urban northern growing edge, so the Indian population has begun to move out of the tribal reservations during the last 25 years and to migrate toward the larger cities of the Southwest and California. In spite of federal educational programs, most Indian newcomers to the big cities carry with them the scars of poverty, cultural estrangement, and illiteracy. The Indian is torn between two very unsatisfactory prospects: reservation dependency and apathy with some federal protection against starvation, versus unequal competition on the metropolitan labor market in an alien white society. There is seldom a middle ground. Prejudice against the Indian is strongest in the small communities of whites that surround reservations. Discrimination is least severe in the large but distant cities, where the way of life is most strange and where any social support structure of kin is thinnest.

Other Minority Groups

Many other ethnic groups continue to experience handicapping discrimination in modern American society. Among those confronting the gravest barriers to equal opportunity today, apart from Negroes and American Indians, are Latin Americans and French Canadians. Among the former are three substantial groups: Puerto Ricans, Cubans, and Mexicans, and one might also include the Spanish Americans (Hispanos) of Colorado and New Mexico, who have been citizens of the United States for several generations.

Puerto Ricans and Cubans are concentrated fairly exclusively along the eastern seaboard, the former mostly in the New York metropolitan area, the latter in Miami. These groups face every facet of the pattern of prejudice: color, language, religion, dress, and life styles. Hispanos and Mexican-Americans in the Southwest face even more carefully calibrated modes of discrimination. Several states deny these Latin Americans their citizen's right to serve on juries, for example. And—because they have been residents in the Southwest for many more years than Puerto Ricans and Cubans have resided in the East—formal as well as informal devices have been mobilized to preserve their low status in the inter-ethnic hierarchy.

French Canadian immigrants to the United States are clustered along the Canadian-American border, primarily in Maine, New Hampshire, and Vermont. This group has been migrating slowly for decades, and it has achieved some political weight in sectors of these three states. Discrimination against newly arriving French Canadian families is therefore not a matter of formal violations of civil rights but of intense economic deprivation and rigid social exclusion from the 'native' New England population.

Other portions of the United States contain clustered minorities ranging from the large Jewish community of the New York metropolitan region, to the Mennonites and Hutterites of the Middle West, to the Oriental groups of the Far West. These are relatively small population groups, centered in particular regions. Most of them came to this country with vigorous, intact cultures. Thus none of them constitutes a *national* social problem as does the Negro or the Indian.

Taken as a whole, these diverse

minorities face grave obstacles to civil, economic and social equality. The well being of individual members of each of these minorities is unjustly tied to the modes of acceptance and rejection by which their larger group is received. These modes are subject to changes over which neither the minority group nor its members have control.

The fate of Japanese-Americans in World War II illustrates this. When Japan declared war on the United States, all Japanese on the West Coast were incarcerated in relocation centers (concentration camps) inland. They were not allowed to vote, and local matters in the camps were decided by non-Japanese authorities. Japanese inmates were released after the war, but before they could vote they had to re-establish residence and register.

Japanese-American experience since the relocation also exemplifies the favorable side of conditions for many of the smaller minority groups, however. In spite of extensive, persistent discrimination against them (all forms of which were intensified by the hostility and pain released by the war), thousands of Japanese families managed not only to resume their normal lives during the 1950s, but to *assist one another* toward improved job opportunities and upward mobility through education. There were strong features in their cultural heritage which could be fitted effectively to the American urban setting, including mutual aid, strong valuation of study and schooling, and occupational self-discipline.

The National Social Problem

For two centuries, the regional concentration of most ethnic minorities in America obscured any delineation of the national social problem of inter-ethnic relations or of the national policies which evolved to handle this problem. Since the group most discriminated against varied from locality to locality, the national implications of the problem were left undefined.

Since World War II, the outline of the national policy, in mores and in law, has become clear: Immigration barriers, relocation camps, disenfranchisement, residential ghettoes, and separate, hence unequal educational facilities, have begun to fuse logically into variants on a single theme of discrimination through segregation. Social exclusion of the French Canadian in northern Vermont differs from Jim Crowism in Alabama only in the completeness of the barriers to comprehensive equality.

Improvement in the lives of all ethnic minorities is thus increasingly perceived by a majority of Americans as a problem of a single kind. As the Negro struggle for full citizenship unfolds, the much smaller minorities will gain or lose by the successes or failures of this largest, least privileged minority.

In spite of the national core of this social problem, the unique situation of each group, and the special regional locus of each, will require flexible, diversified remedies. One may interpret the present phase of the ethnic problem as one in which the culture of America has begun to achieve a new integration. Social, economic, and political inclusiveness will be broadened, however slowly and painfully. But in the process, we shall discover that between ethnic groups in each locality, some form of competition and conflict will persist. No *national* program will eliminate the infinite forms of local injustice toward and exploitation of minorities.

After World War II, a Social Science Research Council study called "the rapid discovery and application of practical effective techniques for the control of intergroup tension and hostility ... one of the crucial needs of our time."[12] Such techniques have not been found over the years since that call was sounded. Human relations experts know more about building liaison between groups, and police more about riot control, than they did in 1947, but there is no evidence to suggest that intergroup problems are generally soluble.

Is progress made on intergroup problems? Lynchings of Negroes have diminished, yet murder from ambush may be a new equivalent in the South. Indians are not slaughtered by cavalry charges as they were as recently as 1890, but Navajo babies die regularly from malnutrition. Nevertheless, in protection under law and court action, in representation through interest groups, in the reduction of matter-of-fact, everyday violence directed against minorities, and in a reduction of segregation, a new level of national cultural integration may be seen. Antisemitism and anti-Catholicism, the more virulent forms of religious discrimination which flourished for a century, have diminished substantially.

The outline of a manifold yet single national social problem, discrimination against ethnic minorities expressed through prejudice, denial of rights and equal opportunities and embodied in systematic segregation, has emerged, been defined and stripped down to factual particulars. A general softening of the problem has been achieved. But particular solutions and fully effective remedies have yet (if ever) to be attained.

[12]Robin M. Williams, *The Reduction of Intergroup Tensions*. New York: Social Science Research Council, 1947, p. vii.

References

Abrams, Charles. *Forbidden neighbors.* Harper, 1955. A history of the slums.

Allport, Gordon. *Nature of prejudice.* Garden City, New York: Doubleday Anchor books, 1954.

Ashmore, Harry S. *The Negro and the school.* Chapel Hill: University of North Carolina Press, 1954.

Baldwin, James. *Notes of a native son.* Boston: Beacon Hill Press, 1955.

Baldwin, James. *The fire next time.* New York: Dial Press, 1963.

Baldwin, James. *Nobody knows my name: more notes of a native son.* New York: Dell Publishing Company, 1961.

Barron, Milton L. *American minorities: a textbook of readings in intergroup relations.* New York: Alfred A. Knopf, 1957.

Berger, Monroe. *Equality by statute.* New York: Columbia University Press, 1952. Chapter 5.

Bernard, Jessie. *American community behavior.* Dryden, 1949. Chapters 16 and 17.

Berry, Brewton. *Race relations.* Boston: Houghton-Mifflin Company, 1951.

Bibby, Cyril. *Race, prejudice, and education.* New York: Praeger, 1960.

Blaustein, Albert P. and Clyde Ferguson Clarence. *Desegregation and the law.* New Brunswick: Rutgers University Press, 1957.

Botkin, B. A. (Ed.). *Lay my burden down: a folk history of slavery.* Chicago: Phoenix Books, University of Chicago Press, 1945.

Bradley, Mary Hastings (as told by Reba Lee). *I passed for white.* New York: Longmans, Green and Company, 1955.

Brink, William, and Louis Harris. *The Negro revolution in America.* New York: Simon and Schuster, 1964.

Brown, Ina Corinne. *Story of the American Negro.* New York: Friendship Press, 19 .

Clark, Kenneth. *Prejudice and your child.* (2nd Ed.) Boston: Beacon Press, 1955.

Clayton, Horace and St. Clair Drake. *Black metropolis: a study of Negro life in a northern city.* New York: Harper Torchbooks, 1945. (2 vols.)

Cooper, Robert L. "The frustrations of being a member of a minority group: what does it do to the individual and to his relationships with other people?" *Mental Hygiene,* 29:189-195, April, 1945.

Cox, Oliver Cromwell, *Caste, class, and race.* Garden City, New York: Doubleday and Company, Inc., 1948.

Daedalus, The Journal of the American Academy of Arts and Sciences. *The Negro American,* Vol. I. Boston: Fall, 1965.

――――― *The Negro American,* Vol. II. Boston: Winter, 1966.

Davie, Maurice R. *Negroes in American society.* New York: McGraw-Hill Book Company, Inc., 1950.

Davis, Allison and Dollard, Charles. *Children of bondage.* Washington, D. C.: American Council on Education, 1940.

Dollard, John. *Caste and class in a southern town.* (3rd Ed.) New York: Doubleday Anchor Books, 1949.

DuBois, W. E. Burghardt. *The souls of black folk.* Greenwich, Conn.: Fawcett Publications, Inc., 1953.

Franklin, J. H. *From slavery to freedom.* New York: Alfred A. Knopf, Inc., 1947.

Frazier, E. Franklin. *The Negro in the United States.* New York: Macmillan Company, 1949.

――――― *Race and culture contacts in the modern world.* New York: Alfred A. Knopf, Inc., 1957.

――――― *Black bourgeoisie: the rise of a new middle class in the United States.* New York: Collier Books, 1957.

Gittler, Joseph B. (Ed.). *Understanding minority groups.* New York: Wiley, 1956.

Griffin, John Howard. *Black like me.* New York: Signet Book, 1960.

Hager, Don J. "Housing discrimination, social conflict, and the law." *Social Problems,* Vol. 8:No. 1 (Summer, 1960), pp. 80-87.

Herskovits, Melville J. *The myth of the Negro past.* Boston: Beacon Press, 1941.

Hughes, Everett C. and Helen M. Hughes. *Where peoples meet.* Glencoe, Ill.: The Free Press, 1952.

Johnson, Charles S. "Social changes and their effects on race relations in the south." *Social Forces,* 23:343-348, March, 1945.

Journal of Social Issues, Vol. 8:No. 1 (1952). Intergroup contact and racial attitudes.

Vol 9:No. 1 (1953). Trade unions and minority problems.

Vol. 9:No. 4 (1953). Desegregation: an appraisal of the evidence.

Vol. 10:No. 1 (1954). Human problems in the changing south.

Vol. 13:No. 4 (1957). Race relations in private housing.

Vol. 14:No. 1 (1958). Interpersonal dynamics in a desegregation process.

Vol. 15:No. 4 (1959). Desegregation research in north and south.

Kardiner, Abram and Lionel Ovesey. *Mark of oppression: explorations in the personality of the American Negro.* New York: The World Publishing Company, (Meridian Books), 1951.

King, Martin Luther. *Stride toward freedom.* New York: Harper and Brothers, 1958.

Lincoln, Eric C. *The black muslims in*

America. Boston: Beacon Press, 1961.

Lind, Andrew W. (Ed.). *Race relations in world perspective.* Honolulu: University of Hawaii Press, 1955.

―――― *Negro revolt.* New York: Signet Books.

―――― *When the word is given.* New York: Signet Books, 1963.

Marden, Charles F. *Minorities in American society.* New York: American Book, 1952.

McDonagh, Edward C. and Eugene S. Richards. *Ethnic relations in the United States.* New York: Appleton-Century-Crofts, 1953.

McKee, James B. "Community power and strategies in race relations: some critical observations." *Social Problems,* Vol. 6: No. 3 (Winter, 1958-9).

Miller, Warren. *The cool world.* Greenwich, Conn.: Fawcett Publications, Inc., (Crest Book), 1959.

Mitchel, Glenn and William Peace, (eds.). *Angry black south.* New York: Cidadel Press, 1962.

Montagu, A. *Race, science, and humanity.* Princeton, New Jersey: Van Nostrand, 1963.

Myrdal, Gunnar. *An American dilemma.* New York: Harper and Brothers, 1944.

Negro year book. Tuskegee Institute, 1952.

Nordholt, J. W. Schulte. *The people that walk in darkness.* New York: Ballantine Books, 1960. Translated by M. B. Van Wijngaarden.

Ottley, Roi. *Black odyssey.* New York: Scribners', 1948.

Patterson, Haywood and Earl Conrad. *Scottsboro boy.* New York: Bantam Books, 1950.

Peck, James. *Freedom ride.* New York: Grove Press, Inc., 1962.

Pettigrew, Thomas F. *Profile of the Negro American.* Princeton, New Jersey: Nostrand Press, 1964.

Raab, Earl (Ed.). *American race rela-*
tions today. Garden City, New York: Anchor Books, Doubleday and Company, Inc., 1962.

Rose, Arnold. *The Negro in America.* New York: Beacon Press, 1944.

Rose, Arnold M. (Ed.). *Race prejudice and discrimination.* New York: Knopf, 1951.

Rose, Arnold M. "Inconsistencies in attitudes toward Negro housing." *Social Problems.* Vol. 8:No. 4 (Spring, 1961), pp. 286-93.

Saenger, Gerhart. *The social psychology of prejudice.* New York: Harper and Brothers, 1953.

Simpson, George E. and Yinger, J. Milton. *Racial and cultural minorities.* New York: Harper and Brothers, 1958 (rev. ed.).

Snyder, Louis L. *Idea of racialism: its meaning and history.* Princeton, New Jersey: Anvil Books.

Social Problems. Vol. 2:No. 4 (April, 1955). Devoted to a symposium on desegregation in the public schools.

Trager, Helen G. and Marian R. Yarrow. *They learn what they live.* New York: Harper and Brothers, 1952.

Tumin, Melvin M. "Exposure to mass media and readiness for desegregation." *The Public Opinion Quarterly,* Summer, 1957, pp. 237-251.

―――― *Segregation and desegregation.* New York: Anti-Defamation League of B'nai B'rith, 1957.

―――― Paul Barton, and Bernie Burrus. "Education, prejudice and discrimination: a study in readiness for desegregation." *American sociological review,* 23:41-49, February, 1958.

Wakefield, Dan. *Revolt in the south.* New York: Evergreen Target Book. 1960.

Walker, Harry J. "Changes in the structure of race relations in the south." *American Sociological Review,* 14: 377-383, June, 1949.

Wallace, Robert. The background of segregation. *Life*, part I: pp. 41, 43-64, September 3, 1956; part II: pp. 41, 96-108, September 10, 1956.

Williams, Robert F. *Negroes with guns*. New York: Marzani and Munsell, Inc., 1962.

Woodward, C. Vann. *Strange career of Jim Crow*. New York: Galaxy Books, Oxford University Press, 1957.

Zimmer, Basil G. "The adjustment of Negroes in a northern industrial community." *Social Problems*, Vol. 9:No. 4 (Spring, 1962), pp. 378-386.

See the following periodicals: *Phylon, The Crisis, Commentary, Journal of Negro Education, Journal of Negro History.*

A SOCIETAL THEORY OF RACE AND ETHNIC RELATIONS

Stanley Lieberson

"In the relations of races there is a cycle of events which tends everywhere to repeat itself."[1] Park's assertion served as a prologue to the now classical cycle of competition, conflict, accommodation, and assimilation. A number of other attempts have been made to formulate phases or stages ensuing from the initial contacts between racial and ethnic groups.[2] However, the sharp contrasts between relatively harmonious race relations in Brazil and Hawaii and the current racial turmoil in South Africa and Indonesia serve to illustrate the difficulty in stating—to say nothing of interpreting—an inevitable "natural history" of race and ethic relations.

Many earlier race and ethnic cycles were, in fact, narrowly confined to a rather specific set of groups or contact situations. Bogardus, for example, explicitly limited his synthesis to Mexican and Oriental immigrant groups on the west coast of the United States and suggested that this is but one of many different cycles of relations between immigrants and native Americans.[3] Similarly, the Australian anthropologist Price developed three phases that appear to account for the relationships between white English-speaking migrants and the aborigines of Australia, Maoris in New Zealand, and Indians of the United States and Canada.[4]

Reprinted, with permission of author and publisher, from *American Sociological Review*, Vol. 26, No. 6, December, 1961, pp. 902-910.

[1] Robert E. Park, *Race and culture*, Glencoe, Ill.: The Free Press, 1950, p. 150.

[2] For example, Emory S. Bogardus, "A Race-Relations Cycle," *American Journal of Sociology*, 35 (January, 1930), pp. 612-617; W. O. Brown, "Culture Contact and Race Conflict" in E. B. Reuter, editor, *Race and Culture Contacts*, New York: McGraw-Hill, 1934, pp. 34-47; E. Franklin Frazier, *Race and Culture Contacts in the Modern World*, New York: Alfred A. Knopf, 1957, pp. 32 ff.; Clarence E. Glick, "Social Roles and Types in Race Relations" in Andrew W. Lind, editor, *Race Relations in World Perspective*, Honolulu: University of Hawaii Press, 1955, pp. 243-262; Edward Nelson Palmer, "Culture Contacts and Population Growth" in Joseph J. Spengler and Otis Dudley Duncan, editors, *Population Theory and Policy*, Glencoe, Ill.: The Free Press, 1956, pp. 410-415; A. Grenfell Price, *White Settlers and Native Peoples*, Melbourne: Georgian House, 1950. For summaries of several of these cycles, see Brewton Berry, *Race and Ethnic Relations*, Boston: Houghton Mifflin, 1958, Chapter 6.

[3] Bogardus, *op. cit.*, p. 612.
[4] Price, *op. cit.*

This paper seeks to present a rudimentary theory of the development of race and ethnic relations that systematically accounts for differences between societies in such divergent consequences of contact as racial nationalism and warfare, assimilation and fusion, and extinction. It postulates that the critical problem on a societal level in racial or ethnic contact is initially each population's maintenance and development of a social order compatible with its ways of life prior to contact. The crux of any cycle must, therefore, deal with political, social, and economic institutions. The emphasis given in earlier cycles on one group's dominance of another in these areas is therefore hardly surprising.[5]

Although we accept this institutional approach, the thesis presented here is that knowledge of the nature of one group's domination over another in the political, social, and economic spheres is a necessary but insufficient prerequisite for predicting or interpreting the final and intermediate stages of racial and ethnic contact. Rather, institutional factors are considered in terms of a distinction between two major types of contact situations: contacts involving subordination of an indigenous population by a migrant group, for example, Negro-white relations in South Africa; and contacts involving subordination of a migrant population by an indigenous racial or ethnic group, for example, Japanese migrants to the United States.

After considering the societal issues inherent in racial and ethnic contact, the distinction developed between migrant and indigenous superordination will be utilized in examining each of the following dimensions of race relations: politi-cal and economic control, multiple ethnic contacts, conflict and assimilation. The terms "race" and "ethnic" are used interchangeably.

Differences Inherent in Contact

Most situations of ethnic contact involve at least one indigenous group and at least one group migrating to the area. The only exception at the initial point in contact would be the settlement of an uninhabited area by two or more groups. By "indigenous" is meant not necessarily the aborigines, but rather a population sufficiently established in an area so as to possess the institutions and demographic capacity for maintaining some minimal form of social order through generations. Thus a given spatial area may have different indigenous groups through time. For example, the indigenous population of Australia is presently largely white and primarily of British origin, although the Tasmanoids and Australoids were once in possession of the area.[6] A similar racial shift may be observed in the populations indigenous to the United States.

Restricting discussion to the simplest of contact situations, i.e., involving one migrant and one established population, we can generally observe sharp differences in their social organization at the time of contact. The indigenous population has an established and presumably stable organization prior to the arrival of migrants, i.e., government, economic activities adapted to the environment and the existing techniques of resource utilization, kinship, stratification, and religious systems.[7] On the basis of a long series of migration stud-

---

[5]Intra-urban stages of contact are not considered here.

[6]Price, op. cit., Chapters 6 and 7.
[7]Glick, op. cit., p. 244.

ies, we may be reasonably certain that the social order of a migrant population's homeland is not wholly transferred to their new settlement.[8] Migrants are required to make at least some institutional adaptations and innovations in view of the presence of an indigenous population, the demographic selectivity of migration, and differences in habitat.

For example, recent post-war migrations from Italy and the Netherlands indicate considerable selectivity in age and sex from the total populations of these countries. Nearly half of 30,000 males leaving the Netherlands in 1955 were between 20 and 39 years of age whereas only one quarter of the male population was of these ages.[9] Similarly, over 40,000 males in this age range accounted for somewhat more than half of Italy's male emigrants in 1951, although they comprise roughly 30 per cent of the male population of Italy.[10] In both countries, male emigrants exceed females in absolute numbers as well as in comparison with the sex ratios of their nation. That these cases are far from extreme can be illustrated with Oriental migration data. In 1920, for example, there were 38,000 foreign born Chinese adult males in the United States, but only 2,000 females of the same group.[11]

In addition to these demographic shifts, the new physical and biological conditions of existence require the revi-

[8]See, for example, Brinley Thomas, "International Migration" in Philip M. Hauser and Otis Dudley Duncan, editors, The Study of Population, Chicago: University of Chicago Press, 1959, pp. 523-526.
[9]United Nations, Demographic Yearbook, 1957, pp. 147, 645.
[10]United Nations, Demographic Yearbook, 1954, pp. 131, 669.
[11]R. D. McKenzie, Oriental Exclusion, Chicago: University of Chicago Press, 1928, p. 83.

sion and creation of social institutions if the social order known in the old country is to be approximated and if the migrants are to survive. The migration of eastern and southern European peasants around the turn of the century to urban industrial centers of the United States provides a well-documented case of radical changes in occupational pursuits as well as the creation of a number of institutions in response to the new conditions of urban life, e.g., mutual aid societies, national churches, and financial institutions.

In short, when two populations begin to occupy the same habitat but do not share a single order, each group endeavors to maintain the political and economic conditions that are at least compatible with the institutions existing before contact. These conditions for the maintenance of institutions can not only differ for the two groups in contact, but are often conflicting. European contacts with the American Indian, for example, led to the decimation of the latter's sources of sustenance and disrupted religious and tribal forms of organization. With respect to a population's efforts to maintain its social institutions, we may therefore assume that the presence of another ethnic group is an important part of the environment. Further, if groups in contact differ in their capacity to impose changes on the other group, then we may expect to find one group "superordinate" and the other population "subordinate" in maintaining or developing a suitable environment.

It is here that efforts at a single cycle of race and ethnic relations must fail. For it is necessary to introduce a distinction in the nature or form of subordination before attempting to predict whether conflict or relatively harmonious assimilation will develop. As we shall shortly show, the race relations cycle in areas where the migrant group is superordinate and indigenous group subordinate differs sharply from the stage in societies composed of a superordinate indigenous group and subordinate migrants.[12]

Political and Economic Control

Emphasis is placed herein on economic and political dominance since it is assumed that control of these institutions will be instrumental in establishing a suitable milieu for at least the population's own social institutions, e.g., educational, religious, and kinship, as well as control of such major cultural artifacts as language.

Migrant Superordination. When the population migrating to a new contact situation is superior in technology (particularly weapons) and more tightly organized than the indigenous group, the necessary conditions for maintaining the migrants' political and economic institutions are usually imposed on the indigenous population. Warfare, under such circumstances, often occurs early in the contacts between the two groups as the migrants begin to interfere with the natives' established order. There is frequently conflict even if the initial contact was friendly. Price, for example, has observed the following consequences of white invasion and subordination of the indigenous populations of Australia, Canada, New Zealand, and the United States:

> During an opening period of pioneer invasion on moving frontiers the whites decimated the natives with their diseases;

occupied their lands by seizure or by pseudo-purchase; slaughtered those who resisted; intensified tribal warfare by supplying white weapons; ridiculed and disrupted native religions, society and culture, and generally reduced the unhappy peoples to a state of despondency under which they neither desired to live, nor to have children to undergo similar conditions.[13]

The numerical decline of indigenous populations after their initial subordination to a migrant group, whether caused by warfare, introduction of venereal and other diseases, or disruption of sustenance activities, has been documented for a number of contact situations in addition to those discussed by Price.[14]

In addition to bringing about these demographic and economic upheavals, the superordinate migrants frequently create political entities that are not at all coterminous with the boundaries existing during the indigenous populations' supremacy prior to contact. For example, the British and Boers in southern Africa carved out political states that included areas previously under the control of separate and often warring groups.[15] Indeed, European alliances with feuding tribes were often used as a fulcrum for the territorial expansion of whites into southern Africa.[16] The bifurcation of tribes into two nations and the migrations of groups across newly created national boundaries are both consequences of the somewhat arbitrary

---

[12]See, for example, Reuter's distinction between two types of direct contact in E. B. Reuter, editor, *op. cit.*, pp. 4-7.

[13]Price, *op. cit.*, p. 1.

[14]Stephen Roberts, *Population Problems of the Pacific,* London: George Routledge & Sons, 1927.

[15]John A. Barnes, "Race Relations in the Development of Southern Africa" in Lind, editor, *op. cit.*

[16]*Ibid.*

nature of the political entities created in regions of migrant superordination.[17] This incorporation of diverse indigenous populations into a single territorial unit under the dominance of a migrant group has considerable importance for later developments in this type of racial and ethnic contact.

Indigenous Superordination. When a population migrates to a subordinate position considerably less conflict occurs in the early stages. The movements of many European and Oriental populations to political, economic, and social subordination in the United States were not converted into warfare, nationalism, or long-term conflict. Clearly, the occasional labor and racial strife marking the history of immigration of the United States is not on the same level as the efforts to expel or revolutionize the social order. American Negroes, one of the most persistently subordinated migrant groups in the country, never responded in significant numbers to the encouragement of migration to Liberia. The single important large-scale nationalistic effort, Marcus Garvey's Universal Negro Improvement Association, never actually led to mass emigration of Negroes.[18] By contrast, the indigenous American Indians fought long and hard to preserve control over their habitat.

In interpreting differences in the effects of migrant and indigenous subordination, the migrants must be considered in the context of the options available to the group. Irish migrants to the United States in the 1840's, for example, although clearly subordinate to native whites of other origins, fared better economically than if they had remained in their mother country.[19] Further, the option of returning to the homeland often exists for populations migrating to subordinate situations. Jerome reports that net migration to the United States between the midyears of 1907 and 1923 equalled roughly 65 per cent of gross immigration.[20] This indicates that immigrant dissatisfaction with subordination or other conditions of contact can often be resolved by withdrawal from the area. Recently subordinated indigenous groups, by contrast, are perhaps less apt to leave their habitat so readily.

Finally, when contacts between racial and ethnic groups are under the control of the indigenous population, threats of demographic and institutional imbalance are reduced since the superordinate populations can limit the numbers and groups entering. For example, when Oriental migration to the United States threatened whites, sharp cuts were executed in the quotas.[21] Similar events may be noted with respect to the decline of immigration from the so-called "new" sources of eastern and southern Europe. Whether a group exercises its control over immigration far before it is actually under threat is, of course, not germane to the

[17]Witness the current controversies between tribes in the newly created Congo Republic. Also, for a list of tribes living on both sides of the border of the Republic of Sudan, see Karol Józef Krótki, "Demographic Survey of Sudan" in *The Population of Sudan*, report on the sixth annual conference, Khartoum: Philosophical Society of Sudan, 1958, p. 35.

[18]John Hope Franklin, *From Slavery to Freedom*, second edition, New York: Alfred Knopf, 1956, pp. 234-238, 481-483.

[19]Oscar Handlin, *Boston's Immigrants*, revised edition, Cambridge, Mass.: The Belknap Press of Harvard University Press, 1959, Chapter 2.

[20]Harry Jerome, *Migration and Business Cycles*, New York: National Bureau of Economic Research, 1926, pp. 43-44.

[21]See, George Eaton Simpson and J. Milton Yinger, *Racial and Cultural Minorities*, revised edition, New York: Harper & Brothers, 1958, pp. 126-132.

point that immigrant restriction provides a mechanism whereby potential conflict is prevented.

In summary, groups differ in the conditions necessary for maintaining their respective social orders. In areas where the migrant group is dominant, frequently the indigenous population suffers sharp numerical declines and their economic and political institutions are seriously undermined. Conflict often accompanies the establishment of migrant superordination. Subordinate indigenous populations generally have no alternative location and do not control the numbers of new ethnic populations admitted into their area. By contrast, when the indigenous population dominates the political and economic conditions, the migrant group is introduced into the economy of the indigenous population. Although subordinate in their new habitat, the migrants may fare better than if they remained in their homeland. Hence their subordination occurs without great conflict. In addition, the migrants usually have the option of returning to their homeland and the indigenous population controls the number of new immigrants in the area.

Multiple Ethnic Contacts

Although the introduction of a third major ethnic or racial group frequently occurs in both types of societies distinguished here, there are significant differences between conditions in habitats under indigenous domination and areas where a migrant population is superordinate. Chinese and Indian migrants, for example, were often welcomed by whites in areas where large indigenous populations were suppressed, but these migrants were restricted in the white mother country. Consideration of the

causes and consequences of multiethnic contacts is therefore made in terms of the two types of racial and ethnic contact.

Migrant Superordination. In societies where the migrant population is superordinate, it is often necessary to introduce new immigrant groups to fill the niches created in the revised economy of the area. The subordinate indigenous population frequently fails, at first, to participate in the new economic and political order introduced by migrants. For example, because of the numerical decline of Fijians after contact with whites and their unsatisfactory work habits, approximately 60,000 persons migrated from India to the sugar plantations of Fiji under the indenture system between 1879 and 1916.[22] For similar reasons, as well as the demise of slavery, large numbers of Indians were also introduced to such area of indigenous subordination as Mauritius, British Guiana, Trinidad, and Natal.[23] The descendants of these migrants comprise the largest single ethnic group in several of these areas.

McKenzie, after observing the negligible participation of the subordinated indigenous populations of Alaska, Hawaii, and Malaya in contrast to the large numbers of Chinese, Indian, and other Oriental immigrants, offers the following interpretation:

> The indigenous peoples of many of the frontier zones of modern industrialism are surrounded by their own web of culture and their own economic structure. Consequently they are slow to take part in the new

[22]K. L. Gillion "The Sources of Indian Emigration of Fiji," *Population Studies,* 10 (November, 1956), p. 139; I. M. Cumpston, "A Survey of Indian Immigration to British Tropical Colonies to 1910," *ibid.*, pp. 158-159.

[23]Cumpston, *op. cit.*, pp. 158-165.

economy especially as unskilled laborers. It is the individual who is widely removed from his native habitat that is most adaptable to the conditions imposed by capitalism in frontier regions. Imported labor cannot so easily escape to its home village when conditions are distasteful as can the local population.[24]

Similarly, the Indians of the United States played a minor role in the new economic activities introduced by white settlers and, further, were not used successfully as slaves.[25] Frazier reports that Negro slaves were utilized in the West Indies and Brazil after unsuccessful efforts to enslave the indigenous Indian populations.[26] Large numbers of Asiatic Indians were brought to South Africa as indentured laborers to work in the railways, mines, and plantations introduced by whites.[27]

This migration of workers into areas where the indigenous population was either unable or insufficient to work in the newly created economic activities was also marked by a considerable flow back to the home country. For example, nearly 3.5 million Indians left the Madras Presidency for overseas between 1903 and 1912, but close to 3 million returned during this same period.[28] However, as we observed earlier, large numbers remained overseas and formed major ethnic populations in a number of countries. Current difficulties of the ten million Chinese in Southeast Asia are in large part due to their settlement in societies where the indigenous populations were subordinate.

Indigenous Superordination. We have observed that in situations of indigenous superordination the call for new immigrants from other ethnic and racial populations is limited in a manner that prevents the indigenous group's loss of political and economic control. Under such conditions, no single different ethnic or racial population is sufficiently large in number or strength to challenge the supremacy of the indigenous population.

After whites attained dominance in Hawaii, that land provided a classic case of the substitution of one ethnic group after another during a period when large numbers of immigrants were needed for the newly created and expanding plantation economy. According to Lind, the shifts from Chinese to Japanese and Portuguese immigrants and the later shifts to Puerto Rican, Korean, Spanish, Russian, and Philippine sources for the plantation laborers were due to conscious efforts to prevent any single group from obtaining too much power.[29] Similarly, the exclusion of Chinese from the United States mainland stimulated the migration of the Japanese and, in turn, the later exclusion of Japanese led to increased migration from Mexico.[30]

In brief, groups migrating to situations of multiple ethnic contact are thus subordinate in both types of contact situations. However, in societies where whites are superordinate but do not settle as an indigenous population, other racial and ethnic groups are admitted in large numbers and largely in accordance with economic needs of the

[24]R. D. McKenzie, "Cultural and Racial Differences as Bases of Human Symbiosis" in Kimball Young, editor, *Social Attitudes*, New York: Henry Holt, 1931, p. 157.

[25]Franklin, *op. cit.*, p. 47.

[26]Frazier, *op. cit.*, pp. 107-108.

[27]Leo Kuper, Hilstan Watts, and Ronald Davies, *Durban: A Study in Racial Ecology*, London: Jonathan Cape, 1958, p. 25.

[28]Gillion, *op. cit.*, p. 149.

[29]Andrew W. Lind, *An Island Community*, Chicago: University of Chicago Press, 1938, pp. 218-229.

[30]McKenzie, *Oriental Exclusion, op. cit.*, p. 181.

revised economy of the habitat. By contrast, when a dominant migrant group later becomes indigenous, in the sense that the area becomes one of permanent settlement through generations for the group, migrant populations from new racial and ethnic stocks are restricted in number and source.

Conflict and Assimilation

From a comparison of the surge of racial nationalism and open warfare in parts of Africa and Asia or the retreat of superordinate migrants from the former Dutch East Indies and French Indo-China, on the one hand, with the fusion of populations in many nations of western Europe or the "cultural pluralism" of the United States and Switzerland, on the other, one must conclude that neither conflict nor assimilation is an inevitable outcome of racial and ethnic contact. Our distinction, however, between two classes of race and ethnic relations is directly relevant to consideration of which of these alternatives different populations in contact will take. In societies where the indigenous population at the initial contact is subordinate, warfare and nationalism often — although not always — develops later in the cycle of relations. By contrast, relations between migrants and indigenous populations that are subordinate and superordinate, respectively, are generally without long-term conflict.

Migrant Superordination. Through time, the subordinated indigenous population begins to participate in the economy introduced by the migrant group and, frequently, a concomitant disruption of previous forms of social and economic organization takes place.

This, in turn, has significant implications for the development of both nationalism and a greater sense of racial unity. In many African states, where Negroes were subdivided into ethnic groups prior to contact with whites, the racial unity of the African was created by the occupation of their habitat by white invaders.[31] The categorical subordination of Africans by whites as well as the dissolution and decay of previous tribal and ethnic forms of organization are responsible for the creation of racial consciousness among the indigenous populations.[32] As the indigenous group becomes increasingly incorporated within the larger system, both the saliency of their subordinate position and its significance increase. No alternative exists for the bulk of the native population other than the destruction or revision of the institutions of political, economic, and social subordination.

Further, it appears that considerable conflict occurs in those areas where the migrants are not simply superordinate, but where they themselves have also become, in a sense, indigenous by maintaining an established population through generations. In Table 1, for example, one can observe how sharply the white populations of Algeria and the Union of South Africa differ from those in nine other African countries with respect to the per cent born in the country of settlement. Thus, two among

[31]For a discussion of territorial and tribal movements, see James S. Coleman, "Current Political Movements in Africa," *The Annals of the American Academy of Political and Social Science*, 298 (March, 1955), pp. 95-108.

[32]For a broader discussion of emergent nationalism, see Thomas Hodgkin, *Nationalism in Colonial Africa,* New York: New York University Press, 1957; Everett C. Hughes, "New Peoples" in Lind, editor, *op. cit.,* pp. 95-115.

the eleven African countries for which such data were available[33] are outstanding with respect to both racial turmoil and the high proportion of whites born in the country. To be sure, other factors operate to influence the nature of racial and ethnic relations. However, these data strongly support our suggestions with respect to the significance of differences between indigenous and migrant

TABLE 1
NATIVITY OF THE WHITE POPULATIONS OF SELECTED AFRICAN COUNTRIES, CIRCA 1950

Country	Per Cent of Whites Born in Country
Algeria	79.8
Basutoland	37.4
Bechuanaland	39.5
Morocco[a]	37.1[c]
Northern Rhodesia	17.7
Southern Rhodesia	31.5
South West Africa[b]	45.1
Swaziland	41.2
Tanganyika	47.6
Uganda	43.8
Union of South Africa	89.7

Source: United Nations, *Demographic Yearbook*, 1956, Table 5.
[a]Former French zone.
[b]Excluding Walvis Bay.
[c]Persons born in former Spanish zone or in Tangier are included as native.
Note: Other non-indigenous groups included when necessary breakdown by race is not given.

forms of contact. Thus where the migrant population becomes established in the new area, it is all the more difficult for the indigenous subordinate group to change the social order.

Additionally, where the formerly subordinate indigenous population has become dominant through the expulsion of the superordinate group, the situation faced by nationalities introduced to the area under earlier conditions of migrant superordination changes radically. For example, as we

[33]United Nations, *Demographic Yearbook,* 1956, Table 5.

noted earlier, Chinese were welcomed in many parts of Southeast Asia where the newly subordinated indigenous populations were unable or unwilling to fill the economic niches created by the white invaders. However, after whites were expelled and the indigenous populations obtained political mastery, the gates to further Chinese immigration were fairly well closed and there has been increasing interference with the Chinese already present. In Indonesia, where Chinese immigration had been encouraged under Dutch domain, the newly created indigenous government allows only token immigration and has formulated a series of laws and measures designed to interfere with and reduce Chinese commercial activities.[34] Thompson and Adloff observe that,

Since the war, the Chinese have been subjected to increasingly restrictive measures throughout Southeast Asia, but the severity and effectiveness of these has varied with the degree to which the native nationalists are in control of their countries and feel their national existence threatened by the Chinese.[35]

Indigenous Superordination. By contrast, difficulties between subordinate migrants and an already dominant indigenous population occur within the context of a consensual form of government, economy, and social institutions. However confused and uncertain may be the concept of assimilation and its application in operational terms,[36] it is

[34]B. H. M. Vlekke, *Indonesia in 1956,* The Hague: Netherlands Institute of International Affairs, 1957, p. 88.
[35]Virginia Thompson and Richard Adloff, *Minority Problems in Southeast Asia,* Stanford, California: Stanford University Press, 1955, p. 3.
[36]See, for example, International Union for the Scientific Study of Population, "Cultural As-

important to note that assimilation is essentially a very different phenomenon in the two types of societies distinguished here.

Where populations migrate to situations of subordination, the issue has generally been with respect to the migrants' capacity and willingness to become an integral part of the on-going social order. For example, this has largely been the case in the United States where the issue of "new" vs. "old" immigrant groups hinged on the alleged inferiorities of the former.[37] The occasional flurries of violence under this form of contact have been generally initiated by the dominant indigenous group and with respect to such threats against the social order as the cheap labor competition of Orientals on the west coast,[38] the nativist fears of Irish Catholic political domination of Boston in the nineteenth century,[39] or the desecration of sacred principles by Mexican "zoot-suiters" in Los Angeles.[40]

The conditions faced by subordinate migrants in Australia and Canada after the creation of indigenous white societies in these areas are similar to that of the United States; that is, limited and sporadic conflict, and great emphasis on the assimilation of migrants. Striking and significant contrasts to the general pattern of subordinate immigrant assimilation in those societies, however, are provided by the differences between the assimilation of Italian and German immigrants in Australia as well as the position of French Canadians in eastern Canada.

French Canadians have maintained their language and other major cultural and social attributes whereas nineteenth and twentieth century immigrants are in process of merging into the predominantly English-speaking Canadian society. Although broader problems of territorial segregation are involved,[41] the critical difference between French Canadians and later groups is that the former had an established society in the new habitat prior to the British conquest of Canada and were thus largely able to maintain their social and cultural unity without significant additional migration from France.[42]

Similarly, in finding twentieth century Italian immigrants in Australia more prone to cultural assimilation than were German migrants to that nation in the 1800's, Borrie emphasized the fact that Italian migration occurred after Australia had become an independent nation-state. By contrast, Germans settled in what was a pioneer colony without an established general social order and institutions. Thus, for example, Italian children were required to attend Australian schools and learn English, whereas the German immigrants were forced to establish their own educational program.[43]

similation of Immigrants," *Population Studies, supplement,* March, 1950.

[37]Oscar Handlin, *Race and Nationality in American Life,* Garden City, New York: Doubleday Anchor Books, 1957, Chapter 5.

[38]Simpson and Yinger, *op. cit.*

[39]Oscar Handlin, *Boston's Immigrants, op. cit.,* Chapter 7.

[40]Ralph Turner and Samuel J. Surace, "Zoot-Suiters and Mexicans: Symbols in Crowd Behavior," *American Journal of Sociology,* 62 (July, 1956), pp. 14-20.

[41]It is, however, suggestive to consider whether the isolated settlement of an area by a racial, religious, or ethnic group would be permitted in other than frontier conditions. Consider, for example, the difficulties faced by Mormons until they reached Utah.

[42]See Everett C. Hughes, *French Canada in Transition,* Chicago: University of Chicago Press, 1943.

[43]W. D. Borrie assisted by D. R. G. Packer, *Italians and Germans in Australia,* Melbourne: F. W. Cheshire, 1954, *passim.*

Thus the consequences of racial and ethnic contact may also be examined in terms of the two types of superordinate-subordinate contact situations considered. For the most part, subordinate migrants appear to be more rapidly assimilated than are subordinate indigenous populations. Further, the subordinate migrant group is generally under greater pressure to assimilate, at least in the gross sense of "assimilation" such as language, than are subordinate indigenous populations. In addition, warfare or racial nationalism—when it does occur—tends to be in societies where the indigenous population is subordinate. If the indigenous movement succeeds, the economic and political position of racial and ethnic populations introduced to the area under migrant dominance may become tenuous.

A Final Note

It is suggested that interest be revived in the conditions accounting for societal variations in the process of relations between racial and ethnic groups. A societal theory of race relations, based on the migrant-indigenous and superordinate-subordinate distinctions developed above, has been found to offer an orderly interpretation of differences in the nature of race and ethnic relations in the contact situations considered. Since, however, systematic empirical investigation provides a far more rigorous test of the theory's merits and limitations, comparative cross-societal studies are needed.

References

Brewton Berry, *Race and Ethnic Relations*, rev. ed. Boston: Houghton Mifflin, 1958.
A good textbook, containing in Chapter 6 a summary of the idea of race relations cycles.

Leonard Broom and John I. Kitsuse, "The Validation of Acculturation: A Condition to Ethnic Assimilation." *American Anthropologist*, 1955, 57: 44-48. Reprinted in Kimball Young and Raymond W. Mack, *Principles of Sociology: A Reader in Theory and Research*, 2nd ed. N. Y.: American Book, 1962, pp. 117-120.
A study of access to participation in the dominant institutions as a precondition for the assimilation of minorities.

William M. Kephart, "Negro Visibility." *American Sociological Review*, 1954, 19:462-467. Reprinted in Young and Mack, *op. cit.*, pp. 161-165.
A research project relating minority population concentration, visibility, and law enforcement.

Seymour M. Lipset and Reinhard Bendix, *Social Mobility in Industrial Society*. Berkeley and Los Angeles: U. of California Press, 1960.
A discussion of the mobility ethic in American society and a comprehensive, well-documented comparative analysis of the rates of social mobility in industrial societies.

Raymond W. Mack, Linton Freeman, and Seymour Yellin, *Social Mobility: Thirty Years of Research and Theory.* Syracuse: Syracuse U. Press, 1957.
An annotated bibliography of scholarly work on social mobility.

ECONOMIC STATUS OF NONWHITE WORKERS, 1955-62

Matthew A. Kessler

The gradual movement of nonwhite workers (over 90 percent of whom are Negroes) into higher skilled and better paying jobs has continued since the mid-1950's. However, despite these recent gains, large gaps continue to exist between white and nonwhite workers, as measured by most indicators of social and economic well-being.[1]

Nonwhites continue to be concentrated in less-skilled jobs and are subject to more unemployment than whites. The jobless rates of nonwhites are still at least one and one-half times higher than for whites in every age-sex grouping, and for some age groupings are three times as high. Unemployment

Reprinted, with permission from Special Labor Force report No. 33, Monthly Labor Review, July, 1963, Dept. of Labor Statistics, U.S. Dept of Labor. Matthew Kessler is a member of the Division of Employment and Labor Force Analysis, Bureau of Labor Statistics.

[1]This article reviews recent trends (1955-62) in the employment status of nonwhites in the United States, with particular emphasis on occupational shifts, manpower utilization, income, and educational attainment. The analysis of the two most recent business cycles, 1957-59 and 1960-62, uses seasonally adjusted quarterly average unemployment data not previously available. This article updates and complements a series of studies on the economic status of the Negro by the Bureau of Labor Statistics; the last previous BLS study in the series was *The Economic Situation of Negroes in the United States*, rev. 1962 (U.S. Department of Labor, Bulletin S-3).

bears disproportionately on the nonwhite worker whatever his industry or occupation. Not only is he subject to more frequent spells of unemployment; once out of a job, he has tended to remain jobless for a longer period of time.

After achieving relatively substantial gains in money income during the early postwar period, nonwhite families have failed to keep pace with the rise in average income of white families since the mid-1950's, despite the continued shift of nonwhite workers into higher paying jobs.

During the past two decades, nonwhites have narrowed the educational gap that had historically existed between themselves and white persons, a development which has helped to foster their steady but slow movement up the occupational skill ladder. Since the mid-1950's, however, differences in the level of educational attainment between whites and nonwhites have remained essentially unchanged.

Industry and Occupation Changes

Throughout the postwar period, there has been a dramatic shift of nonwhites out of agriculture. In 1962, 12 out of every 100 employed nonwhite workers were employed in agriculture, compared with 16 out of 100 in 1955 and 21 out of 100 in 1948.[2] (See table 1.) The precipitous fall in this proportion throughout the postwar period is a result of the exodus of nonwhites from sharecropping and marginal farms, particularly in the South, as well as the growth of alternative employment opportunities in other sectors of the economy.

In this quest for a higher money income, however, many nonwhites who shifted to nonfarm employment paid the price of greater job insecurity. As they often lack education and vocational training and are limited by discriminatory hiring and layoff practices, their employment opportunities are restricted to relatively unskilled and semiskilled occupations. These are the very lines of work that are particularly sensitive to the business cycle and are vulnerable to large-scale reductions through automation. Although professional and clerical occupations have provided a major source of both white and nonwhite employment growth since the mid-1950's, nonwhites continue to be overrepresented in such occupations as domestic servants, laborers, and semiskilled operatives.

White-Collar Occupations. Between 1955 and 1962, an increasing number and proportion of nonwhite workers entered the higher skilled and better paying white-collar occupations. In 1962, however, only 17 percent of all employed nonwhites were in white-collar occupations, compared with 47 percent of white workers (table 2). White

[2]Differs slightly from occupational totals shown in table 2 since the industry classification includes some occupations not classified as farm workers in the classification by occupation (e.g., agronomists, veterinarians, and bookkeepers).

workers in this group outnumbered nonwhites 28 to 1, in marked contrast to their comparative representation in the civilian labor force (9 white for each nonwhite worker). The number of nonwhites in white-collar jobs has risen by 50 percent since 1955, about the same rate of increase as noted during the early postwar period and two and one-half times the increase for whites. However, unless there is a substantial acceleration of these trends, the percentage of nonwhite workers in white-collar employment will still be substantially below that of white workers for many years.

Nonwhite workers have been entering the professional, technical, and clerical fields faster than other white-collar occupations. These occupations have risen by 60 percent since the mid-1950's, reflecting expanded job opportunities, particularly in public administration. The largest concentration of nonwhite workers in the white-collar group (almost 1 out of 2) is employed in such clerical occupations as office machine operators, bookkeepers, typists, secretaries, stenographers, and filing and recording clerks.

The largest relative gains posted by nonwhites between 1955-62 were in professional services (such as hospital, medical, and other health services, welfare and religious institutions) and business and repair services—all of which grew nearly 70 percent in the 7-year span. This approximated advances noted in the earlier postwar period and compared with about a 35-percent increase for whites since 1955. Nonwhites also recorded relatively sharp gains in the growing field of educational services—up by 60 percent compared with a 50-percent rise among whites. Governmental policies assuring nondiscriminatory employment practices may

TABLE 1
EMPLOYED PERSONS, BY INDUSTRY AND COLOR, 1948, 1955, AND 1962[1]
[Percent distribution]

Industry	White			Nonwhite		
	1962	1955	1948	1962	1955	1948
Total employed:						
Number (thousands)	60,749	56,698	53,434	7,098	6,496	5,944
Percent	100.0	100.0	100.0	100.0	100.0	100.0
Goods-producing industries	41.4	46.2	48.6	36.2	41.5	47.5
Agriculture	7.2	10.1	12.6	11.7	15.7	21.1
Mining, forestry, and fisheries	1.1	1.4	1.5	.4	.7	3.0
Construction	6.4	6.5	6.0	5.7	5.3	4.4
Manufacturing	26.8	28.2	28.5	18.4	19.7	18.9
Service-producing industries	58.6	53.8	51.4	63.8	58.5	52.5
Transportation and public utilities	7.0	7.4	8.3	5.4	6.0	6.4
Trade	19.8	20.2	20.1	13.8	13.5	11.5
Service and finance	26.8	21.5	18.5	39.1	34.7	31.4
Private households	2.6	2.2	1.7	15.8	16.3	16.1
Educational services	5.5	4.0	2.8	4.4	3.0	2.1
Professional services, except education	6.9	5.3	3.9	7.4	4.9	3.3
Business and repair services	2.8	2.5	2.4	2.2	1.4	1.0
Other services, including entertainment	4.3	3.5	4.2	7.2	7.2	7.4
Finance, insurance, and real estate	4.7	4.0	3.5	2.1	1.9	1.5
Public administration	5.1	4.6	4.6	5.4	4.2	3.3

[1]Data for 1948 and 1955 not adjusted to reflect changes in definition of unemployment adopted in 1957.
Note: Because of rounding, sums of individual percentages may not equal 100.

account for the continued gains registered by nonwhites in public administration since the mid-1950's — up 40 percent compared with an 18-percent rise among whites.

Nonwhite employment in the professional and technical fields has increased at a somewhat faster rate than for whites since the mid-1950's. Yet in 1962, only about 5 percent of all employed nonwhites were engaged in these occupations compared with 12½ percent of all white workers. While teaching provides a major source of professional employment for both whites and nonwhites, a higher proportion of nonwhite than white professional workers (mainly women) were employed as elementary and secondary school teachers in 1962 — nearly two-fifths and one-fifth, respectively. Indicative of nonwhite recent progress in the professional field is the fivefold increase in their employment in the growing engineering occupations during the 1950's compared with a two-thirds rise for the occupational group as a whole. Nevertheless, nonwhites accounted for only 1½ percent of all professional engineers by 1960.[3]

Only 4 of every 100 nonwhites were employed as managers, officials, and proprietors and as sales workers in 1962, a somewhat higher proportion than in 1955 and 1948. The proportion of white workers in these occupations in 1962 was much higher (19 percent).

Blue-Collar Occupations. After registering small gains in the early postwar

[3]U.S. Bureau of the Census, *U.S. Census of Population, 1960, General Social and Economic Characteristics, United States Summary*, PC(1)-1C, table 88; and *U.S. Census of Population, 1950, Characteristics of the Population, United States Summary*, Vol. II, Pt. 1, table 128.

period, the proportion of nonwhites employed in blue-collar occupations fell slightly between 1955 and 1962, returning to levels prevailing in 1948. Blue-collar jobs have accounted for two-fifths of total nonwhite employment throughout most of the postwar period. During the more recent 7-year period, the proportion of white workers in these occupational categories also declined moderately.

demand for this type of labor has diminished steadily during the postwar period as a result of automation and other technological developments.

Service Occupations. Nonwhites are still seven times as likely as white workers to be employed as private household workers (including maids, babysitters, housekeepers, chauffeurs, laundresses). During the earlier postwar period, the number of nonwhite private

TABLE 2
EMPLOYED PERSONS, BY OCCUPATION GROUP AND COLOR, 1948, 1955, AND 1962[1]
[Percent distribution]

Major occupation group	White			Nonwhite		
	1962	1955	1948	1962	1955	1948
Total employed:						
Number (thousands)	60,749	56,698	53,434	7,098	6,496	5,944
Percent	100.0	100.0	100.0	100.0	100.0	100.0
White-collar workers	47.3	42.1	39.1	16.7	12.0	9.0
Professional and technical workers	12.6	9.8	7.2	5.3	3.5	2.4
Managers, officials, and proprietors, except farm	11.9	11.1	11.6	2.6	2.3	2.3
Clerical workers	15.8	14.2	13.6	7.2	4.9	3.3
Sales workers	7.0	6.9	6.7	1.6	1.3	1.1
Blue-collar workers	35.4	39.0	40.5	39.5	41.8	39.7
Craftsmen and foremen	13.6	14.1	14.6	6.0	5.2	5.3
Operatives	17.5	20.2	21.0	19.9	20.9	20.1
Laborers, except farm and mine	4.3	4.7	4.9	13.6	15.8	14.3
Service workers	10.6	9.0	7.9	32.8	31.6	30.3
Private household workers	2.1	1.8	1.5	14.7	14.8	15.6
Other service workers	8.5	7.2	6.4	18.1	16.8	14.7
Farm workers	6.8	9.9	12.4	11.0	14.5	21.0
Farmers and managers	4.0	6.0	7.8	2.7	5.0	8.5
Laborers and foremen	2.8	3.9	4.6	8.3	9.5	12.5

[1] See footnote 1, table 1.
Note: Because of rounding, sums of individual percentages may not equal 100.

More than 8 of every 10 nonwhite workers in blue-collar jobs (compared with 6 out of 10 white workers) continued to be in either the semiskilled or unskilled occupations. These jobs tend to be concentrated in those goods-producing and related industries (such as transportation) which are quite sensitive to the business cycle. Moreover, the

household workers remained virtually unchanged, while nonwhite employment in other service occupations, such as hospital attendant, barber, and cook, rose significantly (25 percent). During the 1955-62 period, this trend appears to have continued, with little change in nonwhite private household employment and a substantial gain (18 percent)

TABLE 3
UNEMPLOYMENT RATES, BY COLOR, 1947-62[1]

Year	White	Nonwhite	Nonwhite as percent of white	Year	White	Nonwhite	Nonwhite as percent of white
1962	4.9	11.0	224	1954	4.5	8.9	198
1961	6.0	12.5	208	1953	2.3	4.1	178
1960	5.0	10.2	204	1952	2.4	4.6	192
1959	4.9	10.7	218	1951	2.8	4.8	171
1958	6.1	12.6	207	1950	4.6	8.5	185
1957	3.9	8.0	205	1949	5.2	8.2	158
1956	3.3	7.5	227	1948	3.2	5.2	163
1955	3.6	7.9	219	1947	3.3	5.4	164

[1] Data for 1947-56 not adjusted to reflect changes in definition of unemployment adopted in 1957.

in the number of nonwhites entering other service jobs. Among white workers also there was a steady rise in the proportion of service workers outside of private households throughout the postwar period—up between 20 and 25 percent in each of the two periods. In 1962, as in the earlier postwar period, proportionately twice as many nonwhite as white workers were in these rapidly expanding but still relatively low-paying and low-to-moderately skilled service occupations.

Manpower Utilization

Unemployment. Throughout the postwar period, unemployment has consistently fallen most heavily on the nonwhite worker. Comprising only a tenth of the civilian labor force in 1962, nonwhites accounted for two-tenths of the jobless total. This disparity was evident among both men and women.

The unemployment rate for nonwhites, at 11.0 percent in 1962, stood at its third highest level in the postwar

TABLE 4
UNEMPLOYMENT RATES, BY COLOR, AGE, AND SEX, 1948, 1955, AND 1962[1]

Age and sex	White			Nonwhite		
	1962	1955	1948	1962	1955	1948
Males, 14 years and over..	4.6	3.4	3.1	11.0	8.2	5.1
14 to 19 years	12.3	9.6	8.3	20.7	13.2	7.6
20 to 24 years	8.0	6.3	5.8	14.6	11.2	10.6
25 to 34 years	3.8	2.5	2.4	10.5	8.0	4.2
35 to 44 years	3.1	2.4	1.9	8.6	7.4	4.5
45 to 54 years	3.5	2.8	2.2	8.3	5.8	3.1
55 years and over	4.1	3.7	2.8	10.1	7.8	3.5
Females, 14 years and over	5.5	3.9	3.4	11.1	7.5	5.2
14 to 19 years	11.5	8.2	6.9	28.2	16.2	10.4
20 to 24 years	7.7	4.5	3.6	18.2	11.4	8.9
25 to 34 years	5.4	3.8	3.2	11.5	9.1	6.1
35 to 44 years	4.5	3.4	2.3	8.9	4.9	3.3
45 to 54 years	3.7	2.9	2.5	7.1	4.6	2.4
55 years and over	3.5	2.8	2.6	3.6	4.4	2.2

[1] See footnote 1, table 1.

period (table 3) and was only slightly lower than rates recorded in the recession affected years of 1958 and 1961. Their 1962 unemployment rate was double the jobless rate of white workers. This relationship has persisted throughout the postwar period, and in fact tended to increase in the latter part of the postwar period. In the years 1947-49, the nonwhite unemployment rate averaged about 60 percent higher than for white workers, whereas in each year from 1954 through 1962, it was consistently twice as high.

Nonwhite boys and girls 14 to 19 years of age continued to have one of

25-34 and 35-44 age brackets (primarily family breadwinners) recorded unemployment rates about three times as high as for white men (about 9 and 3 percent, respectively). A differential of similar proportions was recorded in 1955.

Even within the same major occupation group large differences in unemployment rates persisted, with rates for nonwhites generally substantially exceeding those of white persons. Among both white and nonwhite workers at the lower end of the occupational hierarchy, both nonfarm laborers and operatives usually have relatively high

TABLE 5
UNEMPLOYMENT RATES OF EXPERIENCED WORKERS,[1]
BY COLOR AND MAJOR OCCUPATION GROUP, 1955 AND 1962

Major occupation group	White		Nonwhite		Nonwhite as percent of white	
	1962	1955	1962	1955	1962	1955
All occupation groups[2]	4.9	3.5	11.0	7.7	224	208
Clerical and sales workers................	3.8	3.2	7.7	7.0	203	219
Craftsmen and foremen..................	4.8	3.9	9.7	8.8	202	226
Operatives	6.9	5.5	12.0	8.4	174	153
Private household workers	3.1	3.0	7.1	5.6	229	187
Other service workers...................	5.3	5.2	10.8	8.8	204	169
Farm laborers and foremen	3.9	3.0	5.8	6.3	149	210
Laborers, except farm and mine	11.0	9.8	15.8	12.1	144	123

[1]The base for the unemployment rate includes the employed, classified according to their current jobs, and the unemployed, classified according to their latest civilian job, if any; excludes the unemployed persons who never held a full-time civilian job.
[2]Includes the following groups not shown separately: Professional and technical workers; managers, officials, and proprietors; and farmers and farm managers.

the highest jobless rates of any age-color group. (See table 4.) In 1962, the unemployment rate of nonwhite teenagers remained near 25 percent, compared with about 12 percent for white youth of the same ages. Since 1955, the jobless rate of nonwhite teenagers has increased faster than for white youngsters—up about 60 percent among nonwhites compared with a 30-percent rise for white youth.

In 1962, nonwhite men in both the

unemployment rates; however, differences are not (and have not been) as great as in most other occupation groups (table 5). This may reflect a high proportion of such workers in highly unionized mass-production industries, some of which provide for nondiscrimination clauses in their collective bargaining agreements.[4]

[4]See "Antidiscrimination Provisions in Major Contracts, 1961," *Monthly Labor Review,* June 1962, pp. 643-651.

Differences in overall unemployment rates by color are partially explained by the higher concentration of nonwhites at the lower rungs of the occupational skill ladder. Even assuming there were no differences in the occupational distribution of both groups, however, nonwhites still would have had a higher unemployment rate than whites in 1962. But assuming that the experienced nonwhite civilian labor force had the same occupational distribution as the experienced white civilian labor force, and applying actual jobless rates of nonwhites to this adjusted occupational distribution, the difference in the overall jobless rate between whites and nonwhites in 1962 would have been cut in half. Under these assumptions, the unemployment rate for nonwhites would have been 8.1 rather than 11.0 percent of their number in the labor force, compared with an actual rate of 4.9 percent for whites.

Nonwhites workers not only have higher rates; they are also subject to more frequent spells of unemployment. For persons experiencing any unemployment throughout the year, the chances are much greater that nonwhites rather than whites will have repeated spells of unemployment during the year. About 3 of every 10 nonwhite men who had been unemployed sometime during the year were subject to 3 spells or more of unemployment in 1961, compared with 2 of every 10 white men who had some unemployment. Moreover, nonwhite workers spend a considerably longer period of time on layoff or looking for work between jobs. Since 1954 (earliest year for which these data are available), nonwhites have consistently accounted for 20 to 30 percent of both long-term unemployment of 15 weeks or more and very long-term unemployment of 27 weeks or more, as the following tabulation shows:

	Nonwhites as a percent of total unemployed for—	
Year	15 weeks or more	27 weeks or more
1962	25.9	28.4
1961	22.5	23.6
1960	24.9	26.0
1959	24.3	26.2
1958	22.0	23.0
1957	22.4	23.8
1956	21.8	21.6
1955	20.0	21.5
1954	20.4	24.0

Since the peak of the 1957 cycle (on a seasonally adjusted basis), nonwhites have consistently had a higher proportion of their total unemployment concentrated in the group out of work 15 weeks or more than have the white unemployed (chart 1).

In the 1957-59 cycle, after seasonal adjustment, unemployment among both whites and nonwhites rose by about 70 percent between the third quarter of 1957 (prerecession peak) and the second quarter of 1958 (recession trough). (See chart 2.) During the downturn phase of the most recent cycle (1960-62), the number of jobless white and nonwhite workers both increased by similar proportions from prerecession peak to the recession trough—up 30 and 25 percent, respectively. In the upturn of the 1957-59 cycle (four quarters after the trough had been reached), differences in the rate of decline in unemployment among whites and nonwhites were not significant. There was, however, a relatively sharper drop in the rates for whites in the 1961-62 recovery period. During this later period, whites recorded a 25-percent decline in joblessness, compared with only a 10-percent dip among nonwhites. By the subsequent quarter, however,

TABLE 6
EMPLOYED PERSONS IN NONAGRICULTURAL INDUSTRIES, BY FULL- OR PART-TIME STATUS AND COLOR, 1956 AND 1962
[Percent distribution]

Full- or part-time status	White		Nonwhite	
	1962	1956	1962	1956
All employed persons:				
Number (thousands)	56,388	52,661	6,267	5,733
Percent	100.0	100.0	100.0	100.0
At work—				
On full-time schedules[1]	85.7	88.4	78.6	79.5
On part-time for economic reasons[2]	3.2	3.0	10.3	9.0
Usually work full-time	1.6	1.8	2.8	3.3
Usually work part-time	1.6	1.2	7.5	5.7
On part-time for other reasons; usually work part-time..................	11.1	8.6	11.0	11.5

[1] Includes persons who actually worked 35 hours or more during the survey week and those who usually work full-time but worked 1 to 34 hours during the survey week because of noneconomic reasons (bad weather, illness, holidays, etc.).

[2] Includes persons who worked less than 35 hours a week because of slack work, material shortages, job turnover, inability to find full-time work, etc.

Note: Because of rounding, sums of individual percentages may not equal 100.

the improvement from the trough was about the same for both groups.

Part-Time Employment. In every year since 1956, a higher proportion of nonwhite than white persons were working at part-time jobs. In 1962, 21 percent of all employed nonwhites, compared with 14 percent of all white workers, were working less than 35 hours a week; however, the rate of "economic part time" continued to be three times as high for nonwhites as for white workers—10 percent of total nonwhite employment as compared with 3 percent of total white employment (table 6). In 1962, as in previous years, nonwhites accounted for about one-fourth of all nonfarm workers on part time for economic reasons while constituting only 10 percent of nonagricultural employment.

Nonwhite workers in 1962 accounted for 16 percent of those on reduced workweeks because of economic reasons (such as slack work and material shortages), while comprising 35 percent of those on part time because they were unable to find full-time jobs.

This latter category is likely to have a high proportion of young workers and adult women, many of whom are employed in private household and other service occupations.

The proportion of nonwhite workers on part time for economic reasons has risen significantly over the past 6 years, while that of white workers has remained about the same. On the other hand, the entire rise in voluntary part-time employment was among white workers.

The difference in the proportion of white and nonwhite workers who work at year-round full-time jobs is appreciable. Only one-half of nonwhite men compared with two-thirds of white men with work experience were reported to have worked steadily at full-time jobs in 1961.[5] This difference has persisted since the late 1940's when such data first became available. During the post-war period, nonwhite women made sizable gains in full-time year-round

[5] See "Work Experience of the Population in 1961," *Monthly Labor Review,* December 1962, pp. 1347-1358.

CHART 1: UNEMPLOYMENT 15 WEEKS OR MORE AS PERCENT OF TOTAL UNEMPLOYMENT, BY COLOR, 1955-62
(Seasonally adjusted quarterly averages)

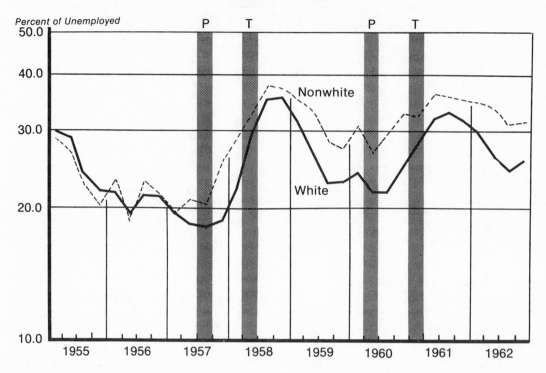

Note: The quarters indicated as peaks or troughs (P and T, respectively, in the chart) include the months designated by the National Bureau of Economic Research as the turning points in the general business cycle.

jobholding, while the proportion of white women in this category remained relatively stable. This improvement among nonwhite women has resulted in part from their shift away from farm occupations—jobs where work schedules tend to be unstable. In 1961, there were proportionately almost as many nonwhite as white women with full-time year-round jobs (32 and 38 percent, respectively).

Labor Force Participation. A salient development in labor force activity of nonwhite workers in recent years has been the sharp decline in labor force participation rates of teenage boys and older men (table 7). In 1962, rates for nonwhites in these groups were below those of white men in the same ages. The especially sharp decline for nonwhites continued a secular trend, including the long-term decline in agriculture, increased years of schooling, and liberalized retirement programs — developments which have also affected whites greatly in recent years.

During the 1950's, at least 70 percent of the net migration from farms consisted of young people under 20 or who reached 20 during the decade.[6] In general, farm youth, whether in or out of

[6]See *Current and Foreseeable Trends in Rural Population,* paper presented by Calvin L. Beale, Economic Research Service, U.S. Department of Agriculture, at the 40th Agricultural Outlook Conference, Washington, Nov. 14, 1962.

school, tend to be an integral part of the farm labor force. Their rates of labor force participation are usually higher than those of nonfarm youngsters of the same ages. In view of the continuing decline in the proportion of nonwhites employed in agriculture between 1955

percentage points, respectively. Probably because of the trend toward earlier retirement, participation has also been declining (although to a much smaller extent) among men 55 to 64 years of age, with the nonwhites again showing sharper declines.

CHART 2: UNEMPLOYMENT RATES, BY COLOR, 1955-62
(Seasonally adjusted quarterly averages)

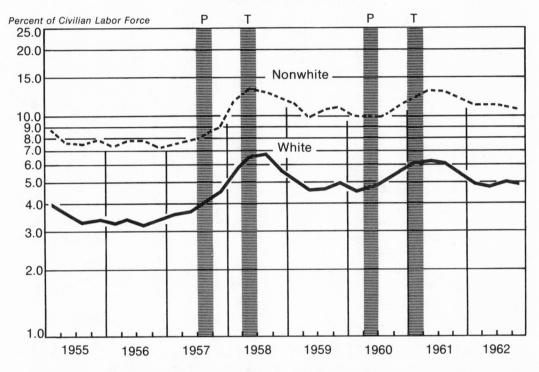

Note: The quarters indicated as peaks or troughs (P and T, respectively, in the chart) include the months designated by the National Bureau of Economic Research as the turning points in the general business cycle.

and 1962, it is reasonable to assume that many of these young farm leavers were nonwhite. A sharp rise in the number of youngsters enrolled in school, as well as unusually high jobless rates which have prevailed in recent years among nonwhite teenagers, may have contributed to their drop in participation.

Participation rates of both white and nonwhite older men (65 and over) dropped very significantly between 1955 and 1962 — down about 9 and 13

Among men in the central age group 25 to 64 years, where participation rates tend to be the highest, nonwhite men continued to have somewhat lower rates than whites. This may be due to a higher incidence of disabling illness and injury among nonwhite men, associated with their concentration in manual, more hazardous occupations.[7]

[7]See *Current Population Reports, Employment of White and Nonwhite Persons: 1955* (U.S. Bureau of the Census), Series P-50, No. 66, p. 2.

TABLE 7
CIVILIAN LABOR FORCE PARTICIPATION RATES,
BY AGE, COLOR, AND SEX, 1948, 1955, AND 1962

Age and sex	White			Nonwhite		
	1962	1955	1948	1962	1955	1948
Both sexes	56.1	57.1	56.7	60.0	61.9	63.5
Male	78.6	82.8	84.2	76.4	81.8	84.8
14 to 19 years.........	40.8	45.6	50.7	38.4	48.8	58.4
20 to 24 years.........	86.5	86.5	84.4	89.3	89.7	85.6
25 to 34 years.........	97.4	97.8	96.0	95.3	95.8	95.3
35 to 44 years.........	97.9	98.3	98.0	94.5	96.2	97.2
45 to 54 years.........	96.0	96.7	95.9	92.2	94.2	94.6
55 to 64 years.........	86.7	88.4	89.6	81.5	83.1	88.4
65 years and over......	30.6	39.5	46.6	27.2	40.0	50.3
Female............	35.6	33.7	30.6	45.6	44.4	44.4
14 to 19 years.........	29.7	30.5	32.8	24.0	25.3	30.4
20 to 24 years.........	47.1	45.8	45.1	48.6	46.7	47.1
25 to 34 years.........	34.1	32.8	31.3	52.0	51.3	50.6
35 to 44 years.........	42.2	39.9	35.1	59.7	56.0	53.2
45 to 54 years.........	48.9	42.7	33.3	60.5	54.8	51.1
55 to 64 years.........	38.0	31.8	23.3	46.1	40.7	37.6
65 years and over......	9.8	10.5	8.6	12.2	12.1	17.3

Nonwhite women historically have participated in the labor force in greater proportions than white women. The postwar rise in labor force participation rates of adult women has occurred both among white and nonwhite women. Despite these changes, only about two-fifths of all white women 25 to 64 were in the labor force in 1962, compared with nearly three-fifths of nonwhite women of the same ages.

Income and Education

Income. Nonwhites tend to have a somewhat larger number of wage earners per family unit and higher rates of labor force participation than whites, which tend to reduce white-nonwhite differentials. A partially offsetting factor is the relatively high concentration of nonwhites in agriculture, where income received in kind is excluded. Family income is nevertheless a useful criterion of socio-economic wellbeing since many expenditure patterns relate to the family unit as a separate entity.

The average (median) income of both white and nonwhite families has increased quite substantially in dollar amounts during the past two decades. Very notable income advances by non-whites were made particularly during World War II and the early postwar period as a result of wartime induced shortages of unskilled workers and governmental action designed to raise the income level of lower paid workers. The family income of nonwhites climbed from less than 40 percent of white family income in 1939 to nearly 60 percent in the early 1950's. Although since then nonwhites have continued to raise their money income, they have failed to bring about a further narrowing of income differentials between the two groups. In fact, on a relative basis, nonwhite family income as a percent of white family income has shown little change since 1952-53 (table 8). This phenomenon seems to be due to the fact that during the past decade, professional, technical, and managerial workers (where nonwhites are still very underrepresented) showed much larger relative income gains (up nearly 70 percent) than workers at the lower rung of the occupational skill ladder (where nonwhites are still disproportionately concentrated). The incomes of laborers

in that category (45 percent). At the upper end of the income scale — $10,000 or more — 6 percent of nonwhite families were in this group in 1961, in sharp contrast to their negligible proportion in 1948 and 1955 (about 0.5 percent in both years). Despite recent employment gains made by nonwhites, which is reflected by their movement into higher money income groups, a substantial gap continues to exist, with proportionately three times as many white families in the $10,000 or more bracket.

TABLE 8
MEDIAN FAMILY INCOME, BY COLOR, 1948-61

Year	White	Nonwhite	Nonwhite as percent of white	Year	White	Nonwhite	Nonwhite as percent of white
1948	$3,310	$1,768	53.4	1955	$4,605	$2,549	55.4
1949	3,232	1,650	51.1	1956	4,993	2,628	52.6
1950	3,445	1,869	54.3	1957	5,166	2,764	53.5
1951	3,859	2,032	52.7	1958	5,300	2,711	51.2
1952	4,114	2,338	56.8	1959	5,643	2,917	51.7
1953	4,392	2,461	56.0	1960	5,835	3,233	55.4
1954	4,339	2,410	55.5	1961	5,981	3,191	53.4

Source: *Current Population Reports, Income of Families and Persons in the United States* (U.S. Bureau of the Census), Series P-60, Nos. 6-39.

and service workers rose by only 40 percent during this same period, compared with an increase of about 180 percent during the forties.[8]

In 1948, nearly 8 of every 10 nonwhite families had money incomes of less than $3,000. (See table 9.) This proportion had dropped to 6 out of 10 by 1955 and to 5 out of 10 by 1961, but it was about 2½ times the proportion of white families in this relatively low income category. Since 1955, the proportion of nonwhite families in the $5,000 to $10,000 category had increased one and one-half times (to 23 percent), but was still well below the comparable proportion of white families

Educational Attainment. Very large strides have been made during the past two decades in reducing the persistent educational gap between nonwhite and white persons. By 1962, the average white person 25 to 29 years of age had completed 12.5 years of schooling, compared with 11.2 years of schooling completed by the average nonwhite person in the same age bracket.[9] For nonwhite men, this represented a gain of some 4½ years of school since 1940; for whites, the average gain was 2 years. This narrowing of the educational gap during the postwar period can be largely attributed to the rising proportion of nonwhite youngsters who have

[8]See Herman P. Miller, "Is the Income Gap Closed? No!" The New York Times Magazine, November 11, 1962, pp. 50-58.

[9]See "Educational Attainment of Workers, March 1962," pp. 504-515 of the *Monthly Labor Review*, May 1963.

TABLE 9
TOTAL MONEY INCOME OF FAMILIES, BY COLOR, 1948, 1955, AND 1961
[Percent distribution]

Family income	1961		1955		1948	
	White	Nonwhite	White	Nonwhite	White	Nonwhite
All income classes .	100.0	100.0	100.0	100.0	100.0	100.0
Under $3,000	18.6	47.5	25.7	57.3	42.6	78.1
$3,000 to $4,999	19.4	24.4	30.3	28.3	35.2	16.3
$5,000 to $9,999	44.7	22.8	36.6	13.7	19.1	5.3
$10,000 and over......	17.1	5.6	6.5	.6	3.1	.4
Median income	$5,981	$3,191	$4,605	$2,549	$3,310	$1,768

Note: Because of rounding, sums of individual percentages may not equal 100.

Source: *Current Population Reports, Income of Families and Persons in the United States* (U.S. Bureau of the Census), Series P-60, Nos. 6, 24, and 39.

TABLE 10
MEDIAN INCOME OF FAMILIES IN 1961,
BY COLOR AND EDUCATIONAL ATTAINMENT OF FAMILY HEAD

Years of school completed	Total	White	Nonwhite	Nonwhite as percent of white
Elementary.................	$4,074	$4,378	$2,539	58.0
Less than 8 years	3,279	3,656	2,294	62.7
8 years	4,772	4,911	3,338	68.0
High school	6,032	6,186	3,863	62.4
1 to 3 years	5,644	5,882	3,449	58.6
4 years	6,302	6,390	4,559	71.3
College	8,210	8,288	6,444	77.8
1 to 3 years	7,250	7,344	5,525	75.2
4 years or more	9,264	9,315	7,875	84.5

Source: *Current Population Reports, Income of Families and Persons in the United States: 1961* (U.S. Bureau of the Census), Series P-60, No. 39.

been enrolled in school. At the elementary school level, the differential has been markedly reduced. But at the high school level, despite some narrowing of differentials during this period, the percentage of nonwhites attending school falls appreciably below that of white students.

Since the mid-1950's, however, the gap has essentially remained the same, with both groups showing a rise of about 1 full year in median school years completed, which departs from previous longrun trends. Recent income data by color and educational attainment of the head of the family also support conclu-

sions found in other studies[10] that the income gap between whites and nonwhites is not completely closed even when educational levels of both groups increase (table 10). However, the differential is substantially reduced at the college level, with the family income of nonwhite college graduates in 1961 about 85 percent of that of white college graduates.

[10]See Herman P. Miller, *Income of the American People* (New York, John Wiley & Sons, Inc., 1955), pp. 42-48; and *Current Population Reports, Income of Families and Persons in the United States: 1956* (U.S. Bureau of the Census), Series P-60, No. 27, pp. 10-11.

ATTITUDES TOWARD DESEGREGATION

Herbert H. Hyman and Paul B. Sheatsley

Nearly eight years ago—in December, 1956—we summarized in these pages the main findings of 14 years of investigation by the National Opinion Research Center at the University of Chicago on the attitudes of white Americans toward Negro Americans. Those findings showed that a majority of white persons in the North favored racial integration of public schools, believed there should be no racial discrimination in public transportation and said they would have no objection to living near Negroes of their own income and educational status. In the South a majority of whites opposed each of these views.

Another finding, however, was that since 1942, when the studies had begun, white opinion in both the North and the South had moved steadily and in some cases strikingly toward the acceptance of integration. Underlying this long-term trend, it appeared from the surveys, were fundamental changes in old beliefs about the Negro—such as that he is innately inferior to whites—and a continued influx of better-educated and more tolerant young people

into the population of white adults.

A retrospective look now makes it seem that at the time of our earlier article the pace of events in the area of race relations was slow, at least compared with the pace of events since 1956. Even then, however, school-integration conflicts in small communities such as Clinton and Oliver Springs in Tennessee, Clay and Sturgis in Kentucky and Mansfield in Texas had led to episodes of violence and drawn national attention. Since then developments have come frequently and dramatically: in 1957 the Little Rock conflict, the first Civil Rights Act to be passed by Congress since the Reconstruction and the first demands for school integration in the North; in 1960 the first "sit-in," which was conducted by Negro college students in Greensboro, N.C., and led to a wave of similar demonstrations in both Southern and Northern cities; in 1962 the riots at Oxford, Miss., and last year the march on Washington.

The pace and scope of the Negro protest movement have provoked intensified resistance to integration in some quarters and may even have alienated many whites who are basically sympathetic to the aspirations of Negroes. The surprisingly strong showing of George C. Wallace, the segregationist governor of Alabama, in several Presidential primaries this spring has been interpreted by some analysts as reflecting just such a reaction.

In the light of these developments it is reasonable to to ask if the generally optimistic conclusions we drew in our 1956 article are still tenable and if the long-term trend toward the acceptance of integration has been halted or perhaps even reversed. We have a basis for providing some answers to those questions. Last year the National Opinion Research Center, aided by a grant from the Whitney Foundation, was able to make three surveys (in June, November and December) repeating some of the questions asked in the surveys on which the 1956 article was based. The new findings provide a measure of two significant things: the actual shifts in the attitudes of white adults as a result of the eventful developments in race relations since 1956, and the trends of opinion on integration over a span of more than two decades.

Before we discuss these findings we shall briefly describe how the surveys were made. Each survey was designed to include a representative sample of the nation's adult white population and for that purpose involved interviews with 1,200 to 1,500 individuals. The interviewers were white people trained for the task and living in the sample areas. Each interview resulted in a punched card containing the answers and pertinent information about the person interviewed: age, sex, education, place of residence and so on. In this way the National Opinion Research Center was able to compare the opinions of various groups, such as the elderly and the youthful, the highly educated and the poorly educated, and many others.

In discussing the findings we shall use the terms "South" and "North." "South" refers to three regions as defined by the Bureau of the Census: the South Atlantic region (Delaware, Maryland, the District of Columbia, Virginia, West Virginia, North Carolina, South Carolina, Georgia and Florida), the East South Central region (Kentucky, Tennessee, Alabama and Mississippi) and the West South Central region (Arkansas, Louisiana, Oklahoma and Texas). "North" refers to the rest of the country except for Alaska and Hawaii, where no interviews were conducted. Finally, we wish to emphasize that what we have sought to investigate over these 22 years is the trend of white opinion on racial integration. That is why the findings we shall discuss pertain only to the opinions of white adults and do not include the views of the more than 10 million Negro adults in the nation.

The dramatic changes throughout the nation are illustrated by the findings about school segregation, based on the question "Do you think white students and Negro students should go to the same schools or to separate schools?" In 1942 fewer than a third of all whites favored the integration of schools. The attitudes of Southern whites at that time were about as close to unanimity as one ever comes in surveys of the U.S. public: only 2 percent expressed support for integration. Among Northerners in that period integration also represented a minority view, endorsed by only 40 percent of white adults.

By 1956, two years after the Supreme Court decision against racial segregation in public schools, national approval of integrated schools had risen to approximately half of the total white population; in the North it had become the majority view, endorsed by three out of five white adults. Even the South was far from immune to the changing situation. Earlier only one person in 50 had favored school integration; in 1956 the proportion was one in seven. The most recent figures now show not only that the long-term trend has continued but also that in the South it has accelerated. Today a substantial majority of all white Americans endorse school integration. In the North the figure has continued its steady climb and now stands at approximately three out of every four adults. But whereas in the 14 years from 1942 to 1956 the proportion of Southern whites who accepted this principle rose only from 2 percent to 14 percent, the proportion has now risen to 30 percent in just seven years since that time.

That these are real changes rather than accidental results reflecting unreliability of the sampling method is indicated by other findings. In spite of the errors inherent in all sampling procedures, which may run as high as three or four percentage points in samples of the size used in these surveys, the figures for the total white population, in three separate surveys in 1956 and in three other separate surveys last year, did not vary by more than one percentage point. Even the findings for the separate regions, based on smaller numbers and therefore subject to an even larger sampling error, are highly stable.

The surveys repeated in 1956 and 1963 also establish that the changes in national opinion on this question represent long-term trends that are not easily modified by specific—even by highly dramatic—events. The survey last November was conducted within a week after the assassination of President Kennedy, but the national findings remained unchanged in spite of any soul-searching that may have been occurring in the North or the South. In 1956,

between the June and September surveys, the attention of the nation had been focused on the first violent crises over school integration in a number of small towns in the border states and in Texas. Again the figures showed no change. The overall picture is thus one of a massive trend, unbroken by the particular news events of the day.

What accounts for the steady and strong rise in support for school integration? One important factor would seem to be the conversion of segregationists. The size of the "Don't know" vote in opinion surveys can be taken as a crude but fair measure of the intensity of the public's views. If large numbers report themselves as undecided, the opinions of the remainder are often lightly held Conversely, if almost everybody has an opinion on the issue, it is probable that opinions are strong.

It could have been expected that in 1942 — 12 years before the Supreme Court decision and long before the great ferment in civil rights—a considerable number of Americans would have been undecided on the question of school integration. On most issues put to the U.S. public in surveys it is common to find that 10 percent or more of those interviewed are undecided. Yet in 1942 the "Don't know" group on the question of school integration amounted to no more than 4 percent of the total.

That group has remained at about 4 percent since 1942. Therefore the increased support for school integration cannot have come significantly from the ranks of the undecided, leaving the number of staunch segregationists virtually unchanged; nor can it be argued that a number of segregationists have become doubtful of their position and have moved into the ranks of the undecided. The greatly increased support for integration must have come mainly from segregationists who switched to the opposite camp.

There are other indications of the public's strong involvement in the issue of race relations. In last December's survey, prior to any specific questions about integration, respondents were asked: "What, in your opinion, are some of the most important problems facing the United States today?" More people mentioned civil rights and race relations than mentioned any other problem. Similarly, when respondents were asked to rate their degree of interest in a number of public issues, there were more people reporting themselves "very interested" in Negro-white relations than in Cuba or the forthcoming Presidential election.

In sum, the long-term trend toward school integration seems to be moving with considerable force. It has not been reversed even by highly dramatic events. Moreover, integration has been achieving its gains by converting persons with strongly held opposing views.

The problems of Negro-white relations involve many issues other than the integration of schools. For two of these —the integration of neighborhoods and of public transportation—detailed data are available on the trend of public opinion over the 22 years. The question asked concerning neighborhoods was: "If a Negro with the same income and education as you have moved into your block, would it make any difference to you?" The question was asked in this way to eliminate the factor of social class from the discussion and leave the respondent confronted only with the issue of his potential neighbor's color. Since the answer "It would make a difference" could include people who would positively welcome a Negro neighbor, supplementary questions clarified any ambiguity in the matter. The question asked about transportation was: "Generally speaking, do you think there should be separate sections for Negroes on streetcars and buses?"

On these questions the same funda-

Year	Event
1954	Supreme Court decision against school segregation
1955	Court ruling on school integration "with all deliberate speed" Federal order barring segregation in interstate transportation
1956	School integration conflict, Clinton, Tenn.
1957	First Civil Rights Act since Reconstruction; Little Rock conflict
1958	First use of Civil Rights Act in Negro voting case
1959	Closing of public schools in Prince Edward County, Va.
1960	Second Civil Rights Act; Start of "sit-in" movement, Greensboro, N.C.
1961	Freedom rides
1962	James Meredith at University of Mississippi
1963	March on Washington
1964	Congressional debate on third and strongest Civil Rights Act Supreme Court order on reopening Prince Edward County schools

MAJOR EVENTS in the field of race relations during the past decade are listed chronologically. They indicate the background against which opinions of whites were formed.

mental trends and underlying processes appear as in opinions on school integration. Opinion has remained highly crystallized, with fewer than 4 percent unable to decide. And although these questions were asked in only one of the 1956 surveys, so that it was not possible to judge the impact of short-run events at that time, the fact that there was little change between June and December of last year again suggests that attitudes are not greatly modified by such events.

North has been consistently less amenable to residential integration than to integration of public transportation, and the shift in the North over the 22 years has been smallest on the residential issue. Presumably these attitudes reflect the fact that in most of the North whites maintain a social distance from Negroes, although allowing them the legal right to use the same public facilities. This social pattern has contributed to the existence of *de facto* school segregation

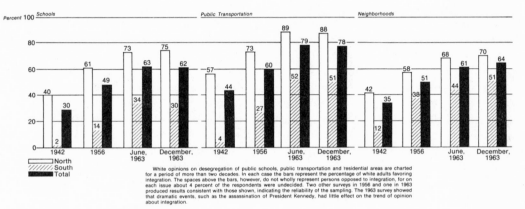

White opinions on desegregation of public schools, public transportation and residential areas are charted for a period of more than two decades. In each case the bars represent the percentage of white adults favoring integration. The spaces above the bars, however, do not wholly represent persons opposed to integration, for on each issue about 4 percent of the respondents were undecided. Two other surveys in 1956 and one in 1963 produced results consistent with those shown, indicating the reliability of the sampling. The 1963 survey showed that dramatic events, such as the assassination of President Kennedy, had little effect on the trend of opinion about integration.

The main findings, which are presented in more detail in the illustration below, are that support of residential integration rose from 35 percent in 1942 to 64 percent at the end of last year among all whites; that for Northern whites the increase was from 42 percent to 70 percent and for Southern whites from 12 percent to 51 percent, and that during the same period of more than two decades approval of integrated public transportation rose from 44 to 78 percent among all whites, 57 to 88 percent among Northern whites and 4 to 51 percent among Southern whites.

The uniformities in the long-term trends in both the South and the North should not be allowed to obscure certain regional differences in the pattern of opinion on schools, neighborhoods and transportation. For example, the

in the North, even though the great majority of white Northerners are now opposed to school segregation in principle. The pattern is illustrated by the comment of a retired mason in a town in eastern Pennsylvania. After expressing approval of integrated schools and transportation, he said he would object if a Negro of equal education and income moved into his block. He added: "I believe in equality, but not that much."

Having discussed the broad findings of the surveys of the National Opinion Research Center since 1942, we turn to some interpretive remarks and to certain aspects of the findings, particularly as they pertain to views about the integration of schools. We shall first discuss the validity of the responses on which the findings are based. Then we shall examine in some detail opinions about the intelligence of Negroes; the correlation between the support of school integration and the degree of school integration existing in the community; the views of Northerners who have lived in the South and of Southerners who have lived in the North; the correlation between degree of education and support for integration, and the attitudes of different age groups.

It is sometimes argued that in public opinion surveys the respondents do not always reveal their true opinions but instead tend to give the answers they think are expected of them. According to this argument some of the opinion supporting integration is of this character because integration is now fashionable. In our view it is unlikely that such factors inhibited many of the respondents in the surveys we are discussing. The surveys show a substantial number of individuals, even in the North, who express opposition to integration, and the magnitude of the opposition is highest in just those spheres where independent evidence would lead one to expect it: the schools in the South and housing in the North.

On many other questions asked in the most recent surveys white respondents freely expressed opposition to full integration or voiced criticism of Negroes. An example is provided by a question asked last December: "Do you think there should be laws against marriages between Negroes and whites?" To this 80 percent of Southern whites and 53 percent of Northern whites answered affirmatively.

Furthermore, many of the respondents seem to take full account of the moral issues involved and still end up on the segregationist side. For example, a mother in North Carolina gave this response to the question about school integration: "I have mixed emotions. I

think they deserve the right, but when I think of my own children going with them, I don't know. . . . Well, I guess I'd say separate schools."

That the demonstrated decline in support of segregation reflects changes in fundamental beliefs is suggested by the long-term trend in white opinion about the inherent intelligence and educability of Negroes. On several occasions since 1942 the National Opinion Research Center has asked the question: "In general, do you think that Negroes are as intelligent as white people — that is, can they learn things just as well if they are given the same education and training?" In the responses to that question there has been a striking change. In 1942 only 50 percent of Northern whites answered "Yes." Today the figure has risen to 80 percent. In the South today a substantial majority credits Negroes with equal intelligence, in contrast with only 21 percent in 1942.

This revolutionary change in belief goes far to explain the increased acceptance of school integration over the past two decades. It has undermined one of the most stubborn arguments formerly offered by whites for segregated schools. The illustration shows the relation between belief in the educability of Negroes and the support of integrated schools in the 1956 and 1963 surveys. As one might expect, those who regard the Negro's intelligence as equal to the white's are much more likely to favor integrated schools than those who regard the Negro as inferior in intelligence. There is more than this, however, to be said. Belief in the equal intelligence of Negroes, after rising steadily for 14 years, leveled off in 1956 and has remained stable since then. Support of integrated schools, however, has continued to rise. Plainly there are forces at work in the growing support for the integration of schools other than belief in the educability of Negroes.

Attitudes on school integration vary according to the degree of integration existing in a given area. This becomes apparent when one looks at particular Southern areas instead of regarding "the South" as a homogeneous region, as we have in this discussion up to now. The occurrence of racial crises in some Southern communities but not in others and the varying degrees of official

ents living in those areas constitute a tiny fraction of the total, and the sampling error of this particular statistic could be substantial. To give greater strength to the findings we have pooled the results of the surveys in June and December, 1963, and as another check we have compared responses made when the Gallup Poll, at our request, asked Southern whites the question on school integration in June, 1963.

In Southern districts where consi-

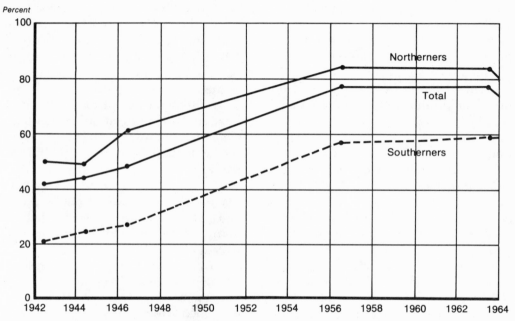

Intelligence of Negroes in the opinion of whites is the subject of this chart. A series of polls in which whites were asked if they believed Negroes to be as intelligent and educable as whites produced the percentages of affirmative responses shown here.

compliance with Federal law suggest that there are large differences within the region. Our surveys bear this out. We divided our sample of Southern localities into three groups according to the amount of integration in the public schools: those with considerable integration, those with token integration and those that remain completely segregated. Since few Southern communities fall into the first classification, respond-

derable integration of schools has taken place 54 percent of white adults favor integration; in districts where token integration has occurred, 38 percent express favorable attitudes, and in segregated districts 28 percent favor integration. There is obviously some parallel between public opinion and official action, but which came first? In the desegregated areas did integration come about in response to a more favorable public opinion or did the more favorable public opinion develop only after the official act of desegregation?

Close analysis of the current findings, compared with those of the 1956 surveys, leads us to the conclusion that in those parts of the South where some measure of school integration has taken place official action has *preceded* public sentiment, and public sentiment has then attempted to accommodate itself to the new situation.

In the 1956 surveys of those Southern districts that had already achieved some integration of schools only 31 percent of white adults expressed approval of the idea. By 1963 the number of such communities had been increased by those districts that only belatedly and reluctantly accepted a measure of integration; in our current sample more than half of the Southern respondents living in communities now classified as integrated to any degree experienced such integration only within the past year, and none of those in areas of considerable integration were exposed to such a level of integration before 1962. One might expect as a result that the proportion approving integration would be even lower than it was seven years ago. Instead approval of integration has risen in such areas from less than a third in 1956 to more than half of their white population today.

Similarly, it was found in 1956 that only 4 percent of white adults in Southern segregated districts favored the integration of schools. Since then some of these communities have reluctantly adopted a measure of integration, so that the segregated districts that remain might be described as the hard core of segregation. Within this hard core, however, approval of school integration has now risen to 28 percent of the white public. Thus even in the extreme segre-

gationist areas of the South the tides of opinion are moving toward integration, and in the more progressive areas it seems that official action in itself is contributing to the speed and magnitude of popular change.

In this connection it is relevant to cite the results of the following question, asked repeatedly over the years by the Gallup Poll and included in the National Opinion Research Center survey of June, 1963: "Do you think the day will ever come in the South when whites and Negroes will be going to the same schools, eating in the same restaurants and generally sharing the same public accommodations?" In South and North alike, whether the community has segregated or integrated schools, more than three-quarters of the white adults believe that integration is bound to come. In contrast, only 53 percent of the respondents felt that way in 1957. Apparently the pattern is that as official action works to bury what is already regarded as a lost cause, public acceptance of integration increases because opinions are readjusted to the inevitable reality.

Data from the 1963 surveys also enable us to compare opinions in Northern communities that vary in the extent to which Negro and white children attend the same schools. As we have noted, such segregation in the North stems largely from patterns of residential housing rather than from law, but the comparisons with the South are nonetheless of interest. Again we find greater support for integration where integration actually exists and greater support for segregation where there is no integration. In both types of community, however, the overall level of support is much greater in the North than in the South. Among Northern whites living in districts that have segregated schools 65 percent favor integration; in Northern areas where schools are considerably integrated 83 percent favor the policy.

A similar pattern of support for integration growing with exposure to integrated situations appears in the findings about people who have moved between North and South. The top illustration compares the opinions of four groups: Northerners who have never lived in the South, Northerners who once lived the South, Southerners who have never lived in the North and Southerners who did at one time live in the North. From the comparison it is apparent that Northerners who once lived in the South differ very little in their views from Northerners who have never been exposed to Southern life. They are only slightly less favorable to integration. In striking contrast, those Southerners who have previously lived in the North differ greatly from those who have always lived in the South. Except on the issue of school integration, the attitudes of Southerners with a history of earlier residence in the North

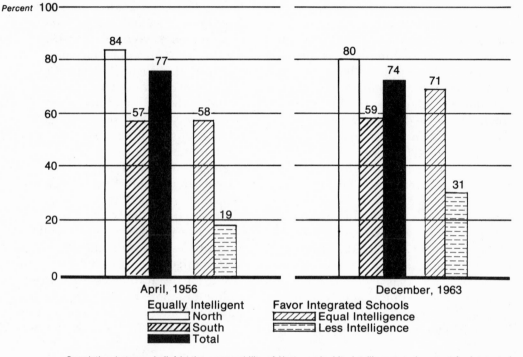

Correlation between belief in the comparability of Negro and white intelligence and support for integrated schools is indicated. The three bars at left in each set show details from chart on opposite page; colored bars, show support for integration of schools varies according to opinion of Negro intelligence.

are much closer to those of Northerners than to those of their fellow Southerners. Even on school integration the difference is substantial.

The influence of geographical mobility on Southern opinion may well account for a considerable part of the gross change in Southern attitudes over the recent decades. Although the rate of movement from South to North exceeds the rate from North to South, the Southern migrants represent a relatively small proportion of the Northern population, whereas among Southerners today a considerably larger proportion have had some Northern exposure. Thus the net effect of migration is to strengthen support for integration.

As for the relation between amount of education and support of integration, both the 1956 and the 1963 surveys showed that the better-educated groups, North and South, were more favorable to integration of schools and public transportation than people of less education were. Between the two surveys, however, all subgroups have become more favorable to integration. Since the number of cases in the South is small, and since the subgroup estimates, are subject to a larger sampling error, we have pooled the two recent surveys.

The most dramatic change of opinion has occurred in the best-educated segment of the Southern white population, where the proportion in favor in integration has increased from only about a fourth to almost half. Lest formal education appear to be a decisive factor, however, note that in 1963 the best-educated white Southerners were not as favorably inclined to integration as the least-educated white Northerners, and that by 1963 those Southerners had not yet reached the level of opinion already exhibited in 1956 by poorly educated Northerners.

In 1956 it was found that the segment of the white population represented by people 65 and older, in both the North and the South, was least favorable to integration, and the same finding is documented in the recent surveys. One would expect this result on the basis of education alone; inasmuch as the expansion of educational opportunity is a development of recent decades, the oldest adults are less likely than the younger ones to have had advanced schooling. Indeed, some of the long-term trends in attitudes toward segregation may simply represent the passing of the oldest generation and its replacement in the population by younger individuals of greater tolerance. The persistence of the difference in attitudes between the oldest group and younger groups would help to account for the further changes in public opinion in more recent years and would augur still more change in the future.

Since the analysis of differences

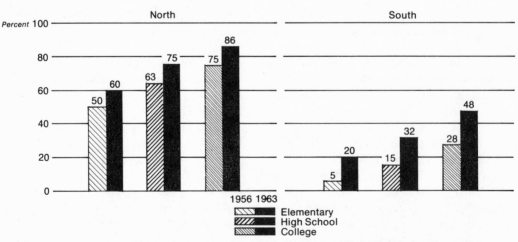

Degree of education and attitudes toward integration of schools are compared. Each bar shows the percentage of whites in that category supporting integration of public schools. Although support for integration rises with degree of education and has gone up in all categories, even college-educated Southerners have yet to attain the level of support for integration of public schools shown in 1956 by Northerners of grammar school education.

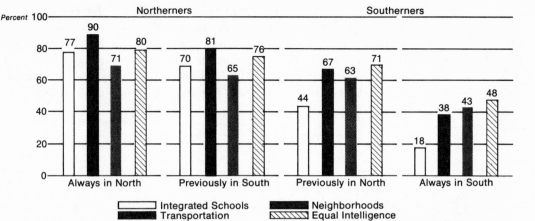

Percent 100

Northerners   Southerners

Always in North — Integrated Schools: 77, Neighborhoods: 90, Transportation: 71, Equal Intelligence: 80

Previously in South — Integrated Schools: 70, Neighborhoods: 81, Transportation: 65, Equal Intelligence: 76

Previously in North — Integrated Schools: 44, Neighborhoods: 67, Transportation: 63, Equal Intelligence: 71

Always in South — Integrated Schools: 18, Neighborhoods: 38, Transportation: 43, Equal Intelligence: 48

☐ Integrated Schools   ■ Neighborhoods
■ Transportation   ⬚ Equal Intelligence

Exposure to integration appears to increase white support for integration. Northern whites who previously lived in the South show nearly as much support for integration and as much belief in the comparability of Negro and white intelligence as whites who have always lived in the North. Southern whites with previous Northern residence show a markedly higher support for integration and belief in the equality of white and Negro intelligence than Southerners who have never lived outside the South.

between age groups is so relevant to an understanding of long-term opinion trends, the sample in last December's survey was designed to double the number of interviews with the youngest adults—those from 21 to 24. These extra interviews were not included in the tabulations except for this particular analysis, but by using them here we can place greater confidence in our findings for this age group, which otherwise would account for only a small portion of the national sample. In this way we are able to provide more evidence for a new finding that appeared in the survey of June, 1963, but then could be regarded only as suggestive. The finding, which is reflected in the illustration on this page, is that whereas in 1956 the youngest adults were the most favorable to school integration, by 1963 the pattern—at least for the South—seemed to have changed. Although they were never as prosegregationist as the older age groups, the 21-to-24-year-olds appeared in the recent surveys to be less favorable to the integration of schools than the adults aged 25 to 44. The difference is admittedly small and could

conceivably be due to sample variation. But the finding appeared in all of last year's surveys; unless it is disproved by subsequent studies one must accept as valid the evidence that the youngest adults are relatively less tolerant than formerly, in spite of the fact that on the average they are more highly educated.

The members of the youngest group in 1956 have, of course, now aged sufficiently to be included in the present 25-to-44 group and have added their earlier quantum of tolerance to that older group's attitudes. Those who are now in the 21-to-24 group were still children in 1956 and so were not included in the surveys of that time. But why, having arrived at the status of young adults, do they not exhibit the larger measure of tolerance characteristic of the equivalent age group in earlier years?

That the phenomenon is clearly evident only in the South suggests an explanation, because this newest group of young Southern adults has lived through experiences quite different from those of the generation of young adults studied in 1956. They have spent their high school and college years in the stormy decade since the Supreme Court decision, and it is they who have been most closely associated with the crises and dislocations that have ac-

tion race relations as the biggest problem facing the country today. The youngest Southerners are more likely than the next older group to express themselves as believing the Negro protest movement is "violent" rather than

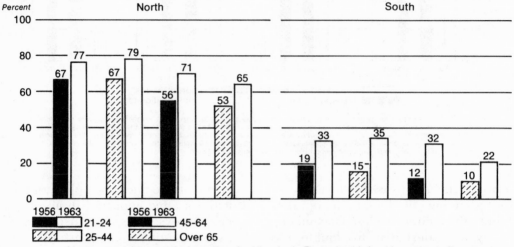

Age groups vary in support for integration of public schools. The tendency is for older persons to show more opposition to integration. A different trend may be appearing, however, among Southerners of the youngest group. In 1956 that group showed more support for integrated schools than the next older group; it now shows less. Such a tendency might be attributable to the direct involvement of the youngest Southerners in the clashes of recent years over school and college integration.

companied the transition to integration in various communities. Actually few of them appear to have suffered directly from these events. They were asked "In what ways have you or any members of your family been affected by integration?" More than four-fifths reported no effects. It is noteworthy, however, that not a single Southerner of this age group spontaneously reported any kind of favorable effect, whereas among Northerners of the same age 5 percent volunteered an answer describing the personal effects of integration in favorable terms.

Plainly the conflicts of integration have had a great immediacy for the young Southerners. The issue of civil rights is more salient for them than for the older groups in our Southern sample. More of them spontaneously men-

"peaceful" and to voice the opinion that demonstrations and protests have "hurt the cause" of Negroes.

Other questions substantiate the likelihood that a change of attitude has occurred among young Southern adults. When asked if their views have remained the same in recent years or have become more favorable or less favorable to integration, it is this youngest group that is more likely than others to report both a change in attitude and a shift away from a favorable opinion. For example, the youngest adults in the South say they have shifted almost two to one against integration in recent years. The older groups report less change of attitude, and when it occurs, the shifts are about equal in both directions.

Apart from this tendency, about the

extent or permanence of which we cannot yet be sure, it appears that the attitudes of white Americans of both the North and the South are continuing to shift toward greater acceptance of integration. We cannot be certain that future events will not reverse the course. But the unbroken trend of the past 20 years, and particularly its acceleration in the past decade of intensified controversy, suggest that integration will not be easily halted. In the minds and hearts of the majority of Americans the principle of integration seems already to have been won. The issues that remain are how soon and in what ways the principle is to be implemented.

THE CHANGING COLOR OF OUR BIG CITIES

Leo F. Schnore and Harry Sharp

It is no exaggeration to call the growth of nonwhite population in our major cities one of the truly outstanding social trends of the twentieth century. In 1900, when 43 percent of the white population was living in urban communities, only 22.7 percent of the nonwhite population lived in cities. At our most recent census in 1960, 69.5 percent of all whites and 72.4 percent of all nonwhites were urban dwellers, making the nonwhites more urbanized than the rest of the American population.

The concentration of nonwhites in very large cities is even more dramatic. The central cities of our twelve largest metropolitan areas contained 13.2 percent of the United States population in 1960. At the same time, these cities held over 31 percent of American Negroes. (These cities are New York, Los Angeles-Long Beach, Chicago, Philadelphia, Detroit, San Francisco-Oakland, Boston, Pittsburgh, St. Louis, Washington, Cleveland, and Baltimore. In the California cities there are substantial numbers of persons of Chinese and Japanese ancestry, who are also treated as "nonwhites" in census statis-

tics; but the nonwhite population in most cities is almost entirely Negro.)

Actually the rapid influx of nonwhites is not confined to a handful of very large places. Every one of the fifty largest cities in the continental United States — each containing at least 250,000 inhabitants in 1960 — showed increases in their proportions of nonwhites between 1950 and 1960, our two most recent censuses. This trend was evident in all sections of the country, North and South, East and West. In some cases (e.g., Minneapolis, St. Paul, and El Paso), the increases are modest, with a difference of only one or two percentage points. In other instances, however, the changes are substantial; for example, Newark changed from 17.2 to 34.4 percent nonwhite, and Washington's proportion of non-whites rose from 35.4 to 54.8 in 1960.

There were regional differences, however, in the experience of metropolitan areas. Fully 70 percent of the 212 Standard Metropolitan Statistical Areas currently recognized showed increasing proportions of nonwhites between 1950 and 1960, but this figure conceals an important difference between the South and the rest of the country. Outside the South, nine out of every ten metropolitan areas showed

Reprinted, with permission of author and publisher, from *Trans-Action*, January, 1964.

nonwhite increases over the decade. In the South itself, the trend was radically different, for only 35 percent of the southern metropolitan areas (27 out of 77) experienced relative gains in numbers of nonwhite. *In other words, six out of every ten southern metropolitan areas had lower proportions of nonwhites in 1960 than in 1950.* In general, it was only the larger southern metropolitan areas that gained large numbers of nonwhites.

Dark Core

The twelve largest metropolitan areas listed earlier now contain almost a third of the American Negro population. The proportion of whites in the United States who lived in the twelve central areas has fallen slightly but steadily since 1930, while the proportion of nonwhites has consistently increased, doubling in the thirty-year interval. Between 1950 and 1960 these central cities lost over two million whites while gaining 1.8 million nonwhites. In addition, although the white population has become progressively more concentrated in the suburban "rings" around these cities, the relative number of nonwhites in these rings (only 3 percent in 1930) has grown by just two percentage points in thirty years.

The collective pattern described above is generally reproduced in each of the twelve areas taken individually. *The total population increased rather slowly in the depression decade of 1930-1940, then grew faster over the last two decades, with the nonwhite populations growing at rates from two to four times greater than those of the white populations.*

In fact, the only central area of the twelve which did not experience an absolute loss in number of whites between 1950 and 1960 was Los Angeles-Long Beach; and in this case the rate of growth of whites fell off during the last decade while that for nonwhites continued to rise at an extremely rapid rate. As a result of these trends, eight of the twelve central cities have considerably fewer whites within their borders now than they did thirty years ago. New York, San Francisco-Oakland, and Washington have approximately the same number as in 1930. Only the Los Angeles-Long Beach area can show a noticeable *absolute* increase in the number of whites in 1960 as compared to 1930 and a substantial proportion of its central growth must be attributed to annexations.

Whites Leave Washington

Thus the *relative* number of whites in every one of the twelve large central cities has decreased drastically over the last thirty years. This trend started slowly in the 'thirties, gained momentum in the 'forties, and became most pronounced during the 'fifties. The experience of one central city—Washington, D. C.—touches on the dramatic. In 1930 almost three-quarters of the inhabitants living in the city of Washington were white; currently, more than one-half of the residents of this city are nonwhite.

In contrast to the sharp drop in the proportion of whites in the central cities, the most common pattern in the suburban rings is one of near stability in racial composition. Thus despite the rapid absolute growth of the ring area, and despite the fact that the nonwhite *rate* of growth in the ring often is higher than that of the whites, the proportion of whites in eight of the twelve suburban rings changed by less than three percentage points between 1930 and 1960. In Washington, D. C., and in Baltimore, the relative number of whites in the ring actually *increased* substantially during these thirty years.

White Rings

Since 1930 the nonwhite population has expanded rapidly in every one of the large central cities; correspondingly, the central city white population has remained relatively stable or has substantially declined. This process of racial turn-over reached a peak of intensity between 1950 and 1960. The population decline of our largest cities would have been much more pronounced if increased numbers of nonwhites had not partially compensated for the loss of the white population. As we have noted, the flow to the rings was even greater over the last ten years than it was earlier.

But this "decentralization" movement involves a distinct color line. While the cities are becoming more and more nonwhite, the rings maintain an amazingly high and constant proportion of white residents; without exception, from 93 to 99 percent of the population in the rings of our twelve largest metropolitan communities are white and this situation is basically unchanged since 1930.

Continuation of the trends documented here would certainly have tremendous implications for the future of the metropolitan community in the United States.

● What are the reasons for these massive shifts?

● How far will the population redistribution by race continue?

● Will our largest metropolitan areas eventually consist of white rings surrounding nonwhite cities?

Why The Population Shifts

One reason why the central city is losing its white population is that whites in the city are older and have higher death rates. More importantly, under-developed city land for the building of new homes is in very short supply. Those dwellings that are available often are not as attractive to young white families as comparably priced homes in the suburbs. Finally, for a number of whites, fears of various kinds —threats of possible physical violence, hazards of declining property values, concern over the color composition of schools—begin to operate when nonwhites become neighbors.

The ring population is increasing at a tremendous rate not only because of movements into them but also because suburban areas have a high proportion of young couples who are producing children at a very rapid pace. They are "baby farms" in an almost literal sense. Additional factors which have contributed to the accumulation of population in the ring include the greater ability of American families to pay the higher costs of transportation; the decentralization of industrial and commercial enterprises; and the construction of vast suburban housing tracts and massive expressways which lead into the heart of the city.

Nonwhites are increasing in the larger cities because of the higher birth rates of central city nonwhites and because of the "pull" of a more favorable political-economic climate. The big cities have the jobs to which nonwhites can aspire, even though they may not pay well.

Why have nonwhites clustered near the center of the city and avoided the outer city and the ring? Part of the explanation is certainly the low economic status of the nonwhite and his inability to afford a new home in a more expensive neighborhood. *Most observers would agree, however, that the major factors in residential clustering by race are restrictive selling practices which ultimately create separate housing markets for whites and nonwhites.*

Forecast for Chicago

In any case, the trend is one of long standing and is not likely to be reversed in the near future. A series of population projections by two University of Chicago sociologists, Donald J. Bogue and D. P. Dandekar, is instructive. The city of Chicago lost almost 400,000 white residents between 1950 and 1960 and gained 328,000 nonwhites in exchange. Part of this was due to "natural increase" on the part of nonwhites, for births exceeded deaths by almost 171,000. (The other 157,000 new nonwhites were migrants.) Nonwhite fertility was higher than that of the white population; in fact it increased 17 percent between 1950 and 1960, while white fertility went up by only 9 percent. The projections by Bogue and Dandekar assumed that the volume of Negro in-migration will remain about the same as in recent decades, but that Negro fertility will decline.

On this basis, the population of Chicago in 1990 would consist of 1,941,000 whites and 1,777,000 nonwhites, or a bare majority of whites. This compares with the 76.4 percent white population counted in the 1960 census. If the exact trends of the 1950-60 decade were to be extrapolated into the future, however, Chicago nonwhites would achieve a majority as early as 1975.

We can anticipate that the rest of the twentieth century will be marked by a continuation of the established trend toward concentration of the American Negro in large cities and a continuation of the accompanying social upheavals that have captured the attention of the nation in recent years.

RACISM IN THE UNITED STATES
Lewis M. Killian and Charles M. Grigg

Has Biracial Cooperation Worked?

If preservation of an external appearance of "racial harmony" in the community is taken as the measure of success, then the community we studied was indeed successful "in preserving good race relations during a period of statewide and internal tension. Moreover, the biracial committee seems to have made some contribution to this success, especially through its 'safety-valve' function. But by another measure . . . race relations had not improved significantly during the life of the biracial committee. The fundamental problems of the Negro community remained unresolved, affected little by token desegregation of the golf course and the schools. If school desegregation, housing, employment, and use of public recreational facilities had explosive potentialities, these potentialities were still there and no preparation had been made to cope with them. In this sense the cooperative approach symbolized by the biracial committee could be deemed a failure. Why? . . .

Reliance on 'improving communi-

Reprinted, with permission of authors and publishers, from *Racial Crises in America: Leadership in Conflict*, Copyright © 1964 by Prentice-Hall, Inc., Englewood Cliffs, N.J., here reprinted as exerpted in and with permission of *Current*, June-July, 1964.

cation' through such a device as the biracial committee implies an ameliorative approach to race relations. To the extent that the committee is expected to bring about change, its function is to stimulate and guide social change through the collaboration of leaders of the white and Negro segments of the community. By the same token, even if it does not itself initiate programs of change, it is expected to forestall conflicts which may arise as the result of demands for change. Race relations are thereby to be taken out of the context of power and placed in the realm of peaceful cooperation. But it is in exactly this respect that such an approach is unrealistic.

What does the analysis of attempts of leaders to engage in inter-racial communication and cooperation suggest as to why the cooperative, consensual approach is so unproductive of change? One reason that emerges is the reluctance of top-level white leadership to become actively involved in ameliorative efforts. . . . It has been shown that, by their own definition, the majority of the white members were not from the top echelon of influential citizens in the community. Some of the more influential but also more conservative leaders had been on the first biracial committee; they had hastened its demise by their adamant defense of the status quo. One of the most influential of these conservative leaders had been asked to serve on the new committee and had declined. The orientation to the general white power structure of those white leaders who were on the committee, and their fear of sanctions for going too fast for both the most influential leaders and the white community in general, were evident.... Their orientation was fundamentally toward preserving the status quo. While even the most conservative members recognized that change would come about in the community as a result of Negro pressure, they perceived their function as that of containing the force of the Negro pressure and at the same time protecting the community from undesirable publicity or economic loss.. . .

The dilemma of the Negro negotiator. Negro leaders, with the exception of a few of the most militant, do not desire racial conflict, nor are they unwilling to accept an atmosphere of harmony in the community as a goal. Their willingness to support and serve on a biracial committee reflects the hope that change may come about in the community without the ordeal of nonviolent resistance and demonstrations, with all the risks that they entail. Hence, *the preservation of racial peace* becomes the superordinate goal for which both white and Negro members of the biracial committee can work. But this creates a serious dilemma for the Negro leader, particularly the militant leader who, if forced to, would choose progress over peace. The dilemma arises from the fact that peace does not serve as an effective superordinate goal *unless there is some threat to this peace.*

The Negro leader cannot simultaneously serve as a guardian of the peace of the community and at the same time threaten this peace by invoking the power of the Negro community. The more militant Negro leaders on the committee under consideration here recognized this. One of them pointed out that the committee operated in such a way that it could take no action unless an issue was created in the community to be referred to the board. If the leader who is on the biracial committee takes the leadership in creating such an issue he is likely to be rejected as a member of the team by the white members.... This threatens the very existence of the committee, because his fellow Negro members are then placed in the position of joining the whites in their rejection of him or of drawing together as a solid racial bloc in his defense, thereby alienating themselves from the white portion of the team.

The other alternative is for the Negro members of the committee to relinquish the dynamic leadership role in the Negro community to people outside the committee. If they themselves represent the top leadership in the Negro community, this means that they leave the field open for reckless parvenus who may, for a variety of reasons, be anxious to challenge their position. Furthermore, when issues created by such free-lance leaders do come before the committee for resolution, the established leaders whose job it is to negotiate may appear in the role of the Uncle Tom who does not negotiate with whites, but compromises in slowing down change to a pace acceptable to the white power structure. But, again, if the Negro member of the committee refuses to negotiate, but instead supports whatever Negro demands come before the team, he takes the risk of destroying the cooperative venture. In optimistically accepting the flattering and seductive premise that, as a member of a biracial committee, he becomes a partner with the white leader in a generalized community leadership, the Negro leader eschews his role as an antagonist in a power struggle.

The dilemma of the white negotiator. Ironically, the more the white representative on such a body sympathizes with the plight of the Negro team member and defines racial problems in the same terms as do the Negro leaders, the more he finds himself confronted with a similar dilemma. In this community and others, city officials have had difficulty persuading white leaders to serve on such boards because they feared that the mere fact of membership might cause them to be branded by their fellow whites as 'integrationists.' If the white leader, having agreed to serve, advocates change in race relations without a prior application of power by the Negro minority, he may be perceived by both his fellow white members and by his peers in the white community as having failed to support the white interests which he is supposed to represent. . . .

If 'better race relations' signifies the achievement of fuller participation in American society by the Negro along with the reduction of intergroup conflict, then the picture presented here is a dark one. The biracial 'team' approach produces only a superficial type of communication. The changes this approach is likely to produce are insignificant in comparison with the results of independent, aggressive action by militant Negro leaders who approach the white power structure with threats, not petitions.

But even militant tactics often win only token victories. White Americans will not voluntarily sacrifice their advantages unless they are confronted with power that threatens other values. The prospect is that most of the Negro's gains will continue to come through conflict.

Is Conflict Better Than Negotiation?

It is evident that the concept of conflict used here implies something broader than merely 'violence' or 'force.' It includes any form of interaction in which the parties attempt to achieve their objectives by demonstrating that they possess superior power. It might be described simply as 'a relationship in which somebody has to lose.' Submission, not consensus, is the 'pay-off.' Power may be manifest as force . . . or it may consist of the threat of force—'the ability to employ force, not its actual employment, the ability to apply sanctions, not their actual application.' Hence the conflict relationship may range from violence, in which physical force is applied (and sometimes resisted) through the invocation of nonviolent forms of force, such as boycotts, demonstrations and legal sanctions to verbal threats of the use of force. . . .

In such a context as this, the establishing of communication between whites and Negroes in no way means that conflict has been terminated. It does not even mean that a minimum of consensus has been reached on the issues involved. It is more likely to signify that the white men of power have found the conflict so costly that they wish to limit it, moving it from the streets, the stores, and the courtroom into the conference room. In actuality the white and the Negro leaders gathered around the conference table do not constitute a biracial team. They are two 'truce teams' representing the still antagonistic parties to a conflict. Realism demands that they concentrate not on their points of agreement but on the issues which underlie the conflict. Limitation of the conflict will result from the strategic use of threats and the reciprocal assessment of the balance of power, not from mutual protestations of goodwill. . . .

This suggests that communication and negotiation between white and Negro leaders can be effective only if the relationship is recognized as a conflict relationship. The communicators are antagonists, not partners. When the negotiators are freed from the obligation of playing the dual role of arbitrator and antagonist, each is free to state his position clearly, in a way that will preserve his solidarity with the group which he represents. But each is also free, having stated his position, to retreat strategically in the process of negotiation.

An important corollary of this proposition is that such negotiations can be effective only when the Negro community can muster enough power to require white leaders to negotiate. In some communities Negro leaders have demonstrated the improved power position of the Negro minority by invoking economic or political sanctions. Another significant source of Negro power is intervention from the federal level, either by judicial order or executive action. Appeals to the moral sensibilities of the white community through demonstrations are not likely to be effective unless used in combination with these other sources of power. Demands on the white community, unsupported by power, result only in the display of force to show the superior power of the white community, whether under the guise of law or not.

The effectiveness of the white liberal as a member of the white truce team is limited. He agrees with representatives of the Negro community to an extent that is not typical of the white power leaders. But it is the ability of a negotiator to influence the people whom he represents that is crucial to his success, not his agreement with the opposition. The white liberal is of greatest use in the negotiation process in a role resembling that of an 'intelligence officer,' who is able to take the role of 'the enemy' and interpret the Negroes' position to the other members of the white power structure. He may also be effective as a 'liaison agent,' who speaks the language of both sides and is trusted by both. In this role he can also be something of a mediator, assessing the relative power positions of the two parties at various stages of the negotiation and summing up the progress that has been made. To play these roles effectively, however, he must remember that he is still a member of the white team and avoid giving the appearance of having 'gone over to the enemy.'

How Conflict Works in a Southern Town

Can an approach which so frankly recognizes the conflict relationship and deliberately exposes the opposed attitudes of the two sides have any integrative effect? Will it not simply widen the rift between the two racial groups?" Lewis Coser's theoretical analysis in his book, *The Functions of Social Conflict*, suggests that recognition of conflict may not only limit the conflict but may also have integrative effects for the community as well. Our actual observation of such a relationship between white and Negro leaders supports his conclusions.

The city in which this was observed is much more typically 'southern' than is the Florida city in which the biracial committee approach was tried. Its roots go much further back in southern history but, like many other southern cities, it is in the process of shifting from a commercial to an industrial center. Its city officials have explicitly rejected proposals for an official biracial committee, and they have fought a vigorous and highly effective legal delaying action against attempts to desegregate public facilities. Nor has it been able to avoid racial violence. It is one of several southern cities in which nonviolent 'sit-ins' were met with violent opposition by segregationist elements in the local population and from surrounding counties.

But it was this violence which provided the impetus for a long process of communication and negotiation. While the Negro demonstrators did not gain an immediate victory, they demonstrated their ability to invoke the sanctions of notoriety upon the community, as national newspapers, radio and television broadcast descriptions of mob violence on the city's main streets. A group of economically powerful white leaders became convinced that this sort of notoriety could be extremely harmful to the city's industrial growth, as the experience of Little Rock had demonstrated. They were also convinced that the Negro community had the power to bring this sort of bad publicity to the city again. . . . In this episode of conflict, these white leaders saw that militant Negroes could be subdued by force but only at a price they did not care to pay.

The uses of racial antagonism. They did not, however, attempt to form an unofficial biracial committee on which a group of 'reasonable' or 'moderate' Negro leaders would attempt to speak for the Negro community. Instead, they constituted themselves as a white committee and, through a Negro intergroup relations worker, invited Negro leaders to form a committee of their own. The Negro liaison agent was able to persuade the top officers of a wide range of Negro organizations, including the leaders of the recent demonstrations, to attend an initial meeting with the white leaders. The two

groups met in an atmosphere of hostility; no words were minced by either side in condemning the other for its 'extremism.' But a sufficient number of the white leaders were convinced of the power and determination of the Negro leaders, and a sufficient number of the Negro leaders were impressed by the willingness of even conservative white leaders to listen to them, to allow the negotiations to continue. Within a few months desegregation of some, although not all, of the establishments around which the violence had erupted was accomplished peacefully.

The militant Negro leadership had won. But as so frequently happens in institutional desegregation, it was only a token victory, for only a small proportion of the Negro population profited from the change. One Negro leader declared, 'I'm getting ulcers from eating in desegregated restaurants just to prove that they're really desegregated!' The conflict did not end at this point. In fact, many months later a Negro leader would declare to a white leader, 'Desegregating eating places is not important —not many Negroes will eat in them; it's creating employment opportunities that is important!' So the negotiations continued.

Token desegregation, creating exceptions to a predominantly segregated pattern, never provides the enduring satisfaction to Negroes that seems in prospect while they are struggling to achieve it. It does not remove the larger, underlying causes of Negro dissatisfaction. Thus each token victory is followed in time by new demands and intensification of the conflict. Moreover, the militant Negro leader cannot long remain a leader if he rests on his laurels after a limited victory. He must define new issues and initiate new struggles. . . .

Negotiating from strength. So, over

a period of two years, Negro leaders in this southern city have selected new issues and marshaled their forces for more demonstrations. During this period, however, they have found the committee of white leaders insisting upon a confrontation over the conference table at the first hint of 'trouble.' Using the language of the international cold war, some of the white leaders have described these as 'eyeball to eyeball' conferences. The results have varied. The Negroes have sometimes won most of their demands, as in the case of the desegregation of additional eating places. Always, agreements reached have been effective because the white leaders are sufficiently high in the power structure to influence business men. Equally important, they represent enough power to cause city officials to be as alert in preventing breaches of the peace by white segregationists as in breaking up demonstrations by Negroes. In all of these settlements, the superordinate goal has been 'keeping the peace' and avoiding notoriety....

It must be emphasized that if this is a committee of white 'moderates,' they are 'moderate segregationists.' They have never initiated action to bring about any desegregation except in response to pressure from the Negro community. They make it quite clear that, in their roles as members of the committee, they are only incidentally concerned with segregation as a moral issue. Their primary concern is the image of the community as it affects their economic interests. In meeting with their Negro counterparts, all realize that they are assessing their current power position in a continuing conflict relationship. As a result, there is no resentment of the fact that each group habitually holds a 'council of war' before confronting the other. This is ex-

pected; in fact, the white leaders urge the Negroes to be sure that all the Negro leaders who might take action with reference to the issue at hand either be represented at the conference or consulted beforehand....

These white leaders understand that an agreement reached with a segment of a disunited Negro leadership group may be nullified quickly by other segments of the group. The effectiveness of this approach, from the standpoint of the white leaders, was clearly demonstrated when the Negro group pressured one of its most militant members who threatened to violate the terms of agreement accepted by the entire group.

Can conflict break down prejudice? Paradoxically, this interaction within a conflict relationship seems to produce positive changes in the attitudes of the individuals involved. The phenomenon of developing respect for an able antagonist who pursues his objectives with candor, courage, and integrity is not an uncommon one. White Americans may have to learn respect for Negro Americans as opponents before they can accept them as friends and equals.

In a conflict relationship, moreover, stereotypes can be broken down through personal confrontation. Comments of members of these two leadership groups indicate that they have come to perceive previously unnoticed differences in members of the opposite group. They have developed an awareness of the structural restrictions upon the behavior of each side, so that neither appears quite as unreasonable as before. And even in concentrating on their points of disagreement, they have found areas of agreement and likeness.

In this process, which is still going on, neither whites nor Negroes have achieved dramatic victories. In a very real sense, both have won and both have lost. The white leaders have 'given in' to some demands for desegregation, as their critics are quick to charge. But they have achieved their goal of protecting the city from notoriety. The Negroes have achieved only token desegregation, but they have done so without going through the costly and painful process of battling on the streets in order to achieve the same result. Both parties have left the 'never-never land' of believing that racial conflict in 20th-century America is temporary and will disappear with the settlement of any single controversy. They realize that if conflict in their community is not limited by negotiation it will break forth in the streets.

But this is only one level of the conflict relationship. So far these two 'truce teams' have concentrated on symbolic manifestations of the Negro's inferior position, not the underlying problems of educational deficiency, lack of job skills, unemployment and substandard housing. The truce will endure only if drastic action is taken to alleviate these conditions. Otherwise Negro leaders of the type represented here will increasingly find themselves negotiating about token desegregation for the 'black *bourgeoisie*'

while the Black Muslims or nationalistic Negro politicians speak for the Negro masses. . . .

But why should the white American, particularly the segregationist, help the Negro to achieve greater equality when inequality is one of the major bulwarks against integration? Here the American creed and the dream of government by consensus, not by force, become relevant. It has become painfully evident in the past few years that, unless the nation begins to take longer strides on the first mile of the long road to equality and integration, the Negro revolt will change from a nonviolent to a violent one.

The white community will have to fight those Negroes who have too much spirit to submit any longer, and it will have to support with its charity those who are too apathetic to fight. The only other alternative will be increasingly repressive measures which would change the nature of the republic and destroy the image of American democracy in the eyes of the world. There is no easy way out. The battle has been joined. The question is whether the conflict will rend American society irreparably or draw its racially separated parts together in some yet unforeseeable future.

PART III   PROBLEMS OF PLACE

5

RURAL PROBLEMS

Introduction

American society originated in rural settings. The earliest institutional features of government, economics, religion, recreation, family, and community were adapted to rural life. The main setting has changed, however. The American people are now predominantly urban. A changing population distribution and a technological revolution have relocated the American scene from the rural village to the metropolitan area in the course of fifty years.

This chapter inquires into the effects of this relocation upon the older, rural America. The national dimensions of these changes are these: Has the older form of rural social organization been adapted to the new conditions, or disorganized by them? How much stress has occurred in rural communities, and with what strains and disruptions upon the society as a whole?

The Rural Farm Population: Demand Has Been Outrun

The historic ideal of agriculture in the United States is the family-sized, owner-operated farm. Colonial land policies, with few exceptions, allowed each settler as much land as his wealth, promise, or influence seemed to permit. Most rural land went to farmers with moderate means or established reputations. They, in turn, depended upon family labor. The assumption was that land-owning family farmers would pursue their best interests, and that these would coincide with the best interests of the larger society: For two centuries, with few exceptions, political and economic leaders behaved as if what was good for the family farmer was good for the nation as a whole.

Connected with the ideal was the concept of a ladder of agricultural success:[1]

> According to the idea of the agricultural ladder, a farm youth climbs to owner-operatorship through a succession of all or most of these steps: (1) Working on his parents' farm to get his initial farming experience; (2) working as a hired hand on a neighbor's farm to get more

[1]Frank H. Maier, et al., "The Tenure Status of Farmworkers in the United States." Technical Bulletin No. 1217, U.S. Dept. of Agriculture. U.S. Government Printing Office, July, 1960, p. 5.

farming experience and to accumulate enough capital to set himself up as a tenant; (3) renting a farm on his own for several years ... for a down payment on a farm; (4) buying a mortgaged farm; and (5) eventually achieving unencumbered farm ownership, by paying off the mortgage over a number of years.

For several reasons, the ideal has never been accomplished. "Considering the entire adult male agricultural work force ... in 1950, the proportion of owner-operators was ... at its 1880 level —54.7 per cent of all male farm-workers aged 20 and over."[2] For decades, the odds of becoming a farm owner, if one was a farm worker, have been only 50-50. In the Deep South, the odds are about 80 to 20 against ownership. Nationally, ownership declined to 47 per cent in 1900, and to 41 per cent in 1940, and did not rise to 54 until 1950. As for the ladder, a rural farm youth who tried to climb it was most likely to remain on the rung of tenant, sharecropper, or hired hand, at least until he was in his fifties.

The ideal of the self-owned family farm has been little more than a dream ever since the closing of the frontier. The forces that produced this, moreover, explain how the rural farm basis of American society has been not only in transformation but in demise for a century.

What are these forces? Frontier land after the Civil War was neither free nor accessible to all. Land in America has been abundant compared to many other nations, but the level of farm technology has been such that only the most arable land has been needed to meet the demand for products. Where a single farm family can produce what is needed

for several families, as in the United States, there is no commercial point in working inferior land. And, competition for the best land will be keen.

Rapid changes in farm technology also made farming an increasingly costly enterprise. "In 1950, the average value of implements, machinery, and work stock per farm was 7 times the 1870 figure ..."[3] The same revolution in technology reduced the number of man-hours needed per unit of crop output. It caused an annual shrinkage in the required farm labor force. In 1900, one farmworker produced enough for seven consumers. By 1957, he produced enough for 24 persons. The same farmworker, moreover, took fewer hours per year to produce for 24 than he took to produce for seven in 1900.

The long-term forces undermining the rural dream also include the ceiling on domestic demand for farm products. The market expands with population growth, yet each person in the society can eat only so much. Farm output first exceeded population requirements in 1910. By 1944, with wartime demand, output far exceeded growth. No stable foreign market has developed for this surplus. "During the last 50 years, agricultural exports have tended to absorb a declining share of U.S. farm production."[4]

The ideal of the family farm involved not only the ladder of success but the ideal of the large family. Children were, for the self-owned farm household, the cheapest, potentially most abundant source of labor. Net reproduction for the rural farm population in 1905 was two times that of urban families. In 1950, long after farm children ceased to serve as prime economic assets, rural farm net reproduction was

[2]*Ibid.*, p. 6.

[3]*Ibid.*, p. 37.
[4]*Ibid.*, p. 43.

about 1.8 times as great as the urban rate.

Under these forces (to which one should add the magnetism of the expanding urban way of life), the rural farm population has shrunk. One in three Americans were farmers in 1910. Only one in ten lived or worked on farms in 1960.[5] And for every one hundred farms in 1944, there were 82 in 1954.[6]

So extreme has this shrinkage been that the definition of farmer has changed for the United States Bureau of the Census. In censuses through 1950, the farm population was defined to mean all persons living on farms, as determined by the question, "Is this house on a farm (or ranch)?" Under the current definition, however, a farm must be a place of ten or more acres from which at least $50 worth of agricultural products were sold in the last year, or a place of less than ten acres which sold at least $250 worth of farm produce. This change resulted principally from the fact that "an increasing number of families whose livelihood is not gained directly from agriculture are now living in the open country (many of them in former farm houses.) These families tend to report themselves as living on farms."[7] The farm remains, but it is neither farmed nor lived in by farmers. In half a century, the rural but nonfarm population has grown from 19 per cent (1910) to 24 per cent (1958) of the national population.

What stresses have urbanization, industrialization and a changing farm technology produced? In the words of Secretary of Agriculture Orville Freeman:

> There are not enough jobs to go around ... There is enough underremployment each year among workers ... who live on farms to equal a full year of unemployment for 1,400,000 workers. If we did not have so many people underemployed in agriculture, the Nation would have roughly 1,400,000 more unemployed workers than are currently reported.[8]

In other words, even though the population housed on farms declined from 32 million in 1910 to 21 million in 1960; even though there are but half as many operating farms today as there were in 1940; and even though many workers living on farms have not migrated but have found alternate types of work in rural business and industry, the rate of change is insufficient. The nation sustains too many farms and too many farm workers and their families, relative to market demand. The result is a rural form of unemployment-underemployment.[9] "Demand," says the Secretary, "has been outrun." The lag reveals itself in poverty and deprivation.

Fate of the Family Farm Ideal

The rural ideal survives despite this transformation. Most of the farms that have disappeared have been the least

[5]*Farm Population.* U.S. Department of Agriculture Marketing Service, AMS-80, February, 1960.

[6]*Family and Larger-than-Family Farms,* Agricultural Report Number 4. U.S. Department of Agriculture, Farm Economics Division, January, 1962, p. 2.

[7]*Farm Population, op. cit.,* p. 11.

[8]Statement on the Area Redevelopment Bill, before the House Banking and Currency Committee, February 27, 1961.

[9]A gigantic reorganization of the society has been under way for half a century. Today, farm families obtain a third of their net incomes from *non*farm sources. Of every one hundred farm operators, 45 did some work off their farms in 1959. About one third worked more than one hundred days off their farms in 1959. Yet the reorganization has not taken place fast enough.

adequate, most marginal units. The better, bigger family farms continue to flourish. They neither disappear nor become absorbed into larger-than-family size farms, contrary to popular impression.[10] The rural family unit of production, where it is large and efficiently operated, remains compatible with the new machine economy. Indeed, the research of social scientists in the Department of Agriculture suggests that only the feature of *ownership* in the basic agrarian ideal is endangered by current trends. New types of tenancy, in which farm families become not sharecroppers but industrial managers and executives of property owned by large corporations, have emerged.

The shrinkage of the rural farm base, poverty and deprivation, and the movement of ill-equipped rural peoples into the cities, are processes which in themselves do not automatically change an institution. Those who leave or suffer are the small marginal farmers, the tenant and the sharecropping families, hired hands, and their children. The ladder of agricultural success remains open for most children from the profitable family farms, although the top rung for them may be farm management rather than ownership.

A 'shaking-down' is in process. Farm families with technical skills, good land and enough of it, and other capital holdings, can remain in place. They are like the advantaged managerial, executive and professional classes in the urban society. At best, their children, if they stay in farming, can expect to expand the family business. At worst, they can expect to manage the combined holdings of some corporate investor or producer. The one in three farm families who earned less

[10]*Family and Larger-than-Family Farms, op. cit.*, p. 30.

than $2,000 in 1959 can expect to be forced out of farming. They are the people with few prospects.

The Rural Village

How has the change in the agricultural economy affected rural community organization? Unlike European villages, villages in the United States have never been communal, nor did they build up as citadels or walled places. American rural communities have instead developed chiefly as *agencies* of farming, mining, lumbering, limited manufacturing, and trade. Farm families have not lived in them so much as used them commercially and socially. An American village is usually one of three things: an assembly and shipping center of raw materials; a retail center for distributing goods received from cities; or a center of settlement in which various social institutions may be clustered, such as churches, lodges, clubs, schools, and fairs. In each function, villages obviously depend upon the nearest urban settlements and upon the rural population around them for their maintenance.

If we think of agricultural villages as incorporated places of not more than 2,500 residents located amidst a cluster of farms and serving farm families, we can gain a sense of the impact of agricultural change upon rural community in the United States during this century. Roughly three fourths of all American villages formed up to 1930 were agricultural villages. In 1920, 20 per cent of all Americans lived in rural villages. This declined to 5 per cent by 1960. Nor was this the result of changing definitions, for there were 12.8 thousand such incorporated villages in 1920, compared with 13.3 thousand in 1960. Few new villages developed during these years; and most of them became ghost towns in fact or in function.

Rural communities have thus been losing people and functions year by year throughout this century. After World War I, village businesses began to fail en masse. Property values declined severely, families left homes they had been settled in for generations, and local institutions—churches, schools, and voluntary associations in particular—were dissolved. The forces at work were identical to those causing shrinkage of the farm labor force. They were impersonal and gradual in influence. Most were beyond the control of village residents and nearby farmers.

Some of the forces undermining rural village communities were distinctive. The functional relation of villages to cities is so intimate in the American case that villages have been unable to maintain their autonomy. For example, population in the 1800s was more or less evenly spread throughout the country. Even the smaller towns enjoyed local ownership of production and distribution and were therefore somewhat independent of the large cities. With the expansion of the great metropolitan areas, control was absorbed into the urban centers. Smaller cities changed into subcontracting agencies for the big cities. Detroit came to control towns as distant as Muncie, Indiana, where General Motors parts were made under contract. Markets for farm produce, lumber, and minerals also came under the control of the big cities. Sociologists call this *metropolitan dominance*, but the influence is exerted not so much by metropolitan municipalities as by nationwide corporations. Some functions of the rural community were absorbed. Others were obliterated by this change.

The more social functions of rural communities were further undermined by the advent of the automobile. As garages, filling stations, cafes, dance halls, motels and other recreation centers have proliferated, commercial strips, along highways, the rural versions of urban sprawl, have eliminated the services of villages as gathering places and transit-points. Villages, towns, and small rural cities have either accommodated to the life of roadways (as they have to metropolitan dominance) or they have disappeared. In either case, *the trend is away from community.*

Few rural communities disappear in any one decade. In fact, villages persist long beyond the need for their functioning. This has certain disorganizing effects. For example, the loss in population in villages, as on farms, is selective as to age, educational attainment, and health. The best educated, most employable, and healthiest, particularly those between 20 and 45, tend to leave. Community institutions and organizations may adjust to this change, but historically they have done so only very slowly. As a result, schools, churches, civic groups, and governmental agencies continue long after the need for service has ended or changed. Medical and other new services often do not develop because of lack of capital or initiative. What is needed by the declining village is missing. What is available functions without competent leadership and with little relevance to local requirements.

Rural Industrialization

Private corporations and public agencies have given increasing attention to the problems of surplus rural labor and declining rural community organization. Rural industrialization is one means by which new opportunities and social reorganization are generated. Rural labor is available for industrial hire.[11] However,

> rural industrialization cannot adequately absorb surplus rural labor. The movement of plants from one area to another often merely transfers economic problems from one to the other.[12]

When rural workers shift from farming, mining, and lumbering to factory work, the groups most subject to poverty and deprivation are seldom directly assisted, however. Older rural workers and others with no previous factory experience or skill fail to obtain employment. For the youngest, ablest, and best educated, rurally situated factories mean substantial jumps in income without residential dislocation. Moreover, factory workers are drawn not from the farms in the open country but from the villages, thereby helping to revive local institutions.[13]

Rural industrialization can infuse capital as well as human hope and vitality into farm and nonfarm localities. But the sources of poverty include the fact that the rate of economic growth for the total society is below population requirements and present living standards. Thus, it may be true that industrial concerns can locate in rural places without disrupting labor markets elsewhere, but it is also true that there are not enough factories to go around.

[11]See bibliography of *Rural Industrialization: A Summary of Five Studies.* Agriculture Information Bulletin No. 252, Economic Research Service, Department of Agriculture, November, 1961.

[12]There is general agreement that the location of industrial concerns can provide a reduction in surplus rural labor without disturbing labor markets in other areas. (*Ibid.*, p. 3.)

[13]Conclusions verified by surveys. See *ibid.*, pp. 1-2.

New industries are in short supply in cities, too. They are not being constructed because new markets for additional products have not developed at a sufficient rate. To this extent, rural factories, however sound in principle, will not eliminate rural underemployment or resuscitate village communities for a long time to come.

When industries are put into the countryside, moreover, control of them remains urban and corporate. The DuPont chemical empire illustrates the point. The DuPont corporation in 1954 owned 72 plants in 25 states. Its central office in Wilmington, Delaware, does not dominate Ellenton, South Carolina, or the adjoining rural townships of Dunbarton, Jackson Bush, and Meyers Mills, but DuPont and several other companies did purchase this area and raze several villages and towns to the ground to build a hydrogen bomb plant. There is work there now, but most of it demands advanced skills. The new development did not revive community. Indeed, Augusta, Georgia, the nearest metropolitan area, *lost* population between 1950 and 1960. Augusta's urban fringe, where bomb-factory workers settled and where new services were needed, boomed with a population increase of 227 per cent! These workers live in the open countryside, in housing and shopping clusters, not in the city or villages.

A solid-fuel factory on the urban fringe of Lawrence, Kansas, provides a different illustration. It is what economists call *footloose industry* — a plant or company that springs up as a result of a government contract, which could be located in any of a thousand places, and which has an uncertain longterm future. The new plant meant new tax revenues for the town of Lawrence, to be sure. But its operation was fully automated, so that a 500-acre factory could be manned by 80 employees. Little new employment opened for local people. Engineers who came from outside the state to work in the plant tended to settle 30 miles away in urban Topeka. In less than two years, the plant lost its contract and was closed, at least temporarily.

What rural industrialization may contribute is deconcentration of resources, production, and distribution. In greater Boston, one can live in a rural New Hampshire village and commute to the industrial fringe that has sprung up around the old Boston. Or, one can live in the core of the city and travel to work in the countryside. In either case, industrialization— for better or worse— severs work from residence and so dissolves community. This is not a 'solution' to rural problems so much as an areal aspect of national change.

Rural Area Development

An advanced industrial society has many more resources to command than dispersal of footloose factories. Capital and skills have been pooled since 1960 to assist distressed rural areas and rural underdevelopment. In 1961, Congress enacted and funded (with a cautious $100 million) an Area Redevelopment Act, for example. The Act provides federal loans and grants for public works, rural industrial development, technical aid, and the retraining of workers. In addition, programs of expanded rural electrification, watershed development for power and recreation, rural housing loans, school improvement, and adult education have been initiated.

The Federal Departments of the Interior, Commerce, and Agriculture,

the land grant colleges with their historic dedication to research and development of rural life, and the many state legislatures disposed to foster rural economic growth, suggest that the capacity to attack the problem of rural lag exists.

Some Residual Problems

In spite of the availability of means to resolve the half-century-old problems of rural decline, grave reservations must be examined. Two are sociological in character: one organizational, the other attitudinal.

The organizational dilemma is this: The groups now addressing themselves to rural development are themselves responsible for maintaining the rural labor surplus. Labor does *not* flow freely out of agriculture at the rate necessary to avoid falling incomes. Rural workers and their families have migrated to the cities or to places of opportunity. But they have done so too slowly for their own welfare or the balance of the national economy.[14]

The Federal Government introduced price supports for farm products in 1948, when prices and farm incomes slumped as a result of a post-war decline in demand and continuing wartime schedules of supply. Under price sup-

[14]Although the exodus from agriculture in the past decade or longer has been large by any standards, it has not been large enough. Two important special factors, in addition to the large scale of the movement required, should be mentioned in explanation. First, the need for movement has been disguised by temporary upsurges of demand for agricultural products, during World War II and the Korean War, and by the price-supporting programs of the government. Second, the excessively high level of urban unemployment ... tended to keep the movement of labor out of agriculture less than it should have been. (Committee for Economic Development, *An Adaptive Program for Agriculture*, New York 22, New York, 1962), p. 19.

ports, the government purchased selected products that could not be sold in private channels at the prices agreed upon under the support program. Federal expenditures under this program grew from about $1 billion in 1948 to $5 billion in 1961. The accumulated surpluses now cost another $1 billion a year to store. Inevitably, the program of price supports has slowed the rate of movement of resources out of agriculture.

Private and public groups are committed both to subsidizing the existing surplus rural economy and to diverting it from farming to other types of resource exploitation. The price support program is but one illustration of how incentives for remaining on the farm are provided with one hand, while incentives for leaving are advanced with the other.

Yet a two-faced policy may be inconsistent logically and feasible politically. Underdevelopment and underemployment in rural America can, after all, be treated in several ways. Surplus production and surplus labor can be diverted and relocated in urban areas; urban production systems, whether through industrial factories or factory-like farms, can be exported to the countryside; or rural workers can be upgraded by changing their level of aspiration and their level of competence to earn a living. We do not yet know in what ways these are mutually exclusive possibilities. Nor do we know whether one or all of them can prove effective only when arrangements supporting the existing situation are eliminated. The paradox of price supports, combined with efforts at industrialization and rural area development, may be only superficially contradictory.

Another social problem at the root of the rural labor surplus is the complex of attitudes. The American rural subsistence economy, after all, builds upon beliefs in careful and low-capital investment, do-it-yourself individualism, and limited productivity. A market economy, on the other hand, reinforces beliefs in capital risk, managerial competence and contractual cooperation between specialized groups. To shift from the one economic pattern to the other, people must change some of their beliefs. In a changing economy, it is not accidental that farmers who value efficiency, science, and change itself generally adopt new ideas more quickly than individuals who value security, conservatism and tradition.[15]

Our rural society has long been adjusted to the presence of what rural sociologists call 'change agents.' These are trained experts whose job it is to stimulate changes in the behavior of farmers. County Extension Agents, soil conservation officials, and other professionals, are employed by government and corporate industry to serve as local helpers charged with transmitting information and guidance which in turn stimulates changes in beliefs and thereby releases the farmer to adopt new practices. Land grant colleges and agricultural high schools function in much the same way.

One task of the change agent is to communicate the fact that there are better — that is, more profitable — ways of employing one's resources. The chance for profits itself stimulates fundamental change, but socially, the information about profitability must, like any other news, be diffused among persons. It is a farmer's perception of profitability that induces change, not an objective

[15]Charles R. Hoffer and Dale Stangland, "Farmers' Attitudes and Values in Relation to Adoption of Approved Practices in Corn Growing," *Rural Sociology*: 23: 112-120, 1958.

force. His perceptions, in turn, depend upon attitudes.[16]

If change agents knew how to improve the situation of the deprived rural families, in short, they would still have to find the way to communicate this knowledge influentially. As it stands at present, two deficiencies exist. First, rural workers most responsive to information about change are those who have already adapted to past changes most successfully. They have gained more formal schooling, they take more frequent and effective advantage of special training facilities, they aspire to increased benefits for themselves and their children.[17] Second, change agents are themselves equipped to stimulate improvements in agriculture. Few of them have new solutions or meaningful alternatives to offer *nonfarm* families. Their information about life beyond the rural county, even for farmers, is limited. They are trained to work within limits that are too narrow for what confronts their many kinds of clients.

Migrant Farm Workers

Migratory agricultural labor exists because there is a surplus of farm labor in some areas when a shortage obtains in others. Variations in crops, growing seasons, and proximity to markets set the economic structure within which a persistent need for short-term labor ready to enter an area in the harvest season is generated. It also exists because alternatives have seldom been sought. The United States economy contained about a million migrants in 1960. About 400 thousand were Americans — members of the native work force. About 150 thousand were their dependents. The remainder were foreign workers, mostly Mexicans, brought in temporarily as contract laborers. About 15 thousand Puerto Ricans were also included.[18]

The movement of each major migration may be viewed as a stream. For instance, an Atlantic Coast stream involves 60 thousand workers, mostly Negro Americans, who begin each year with Florida fruit harvests and work North into New York, New Jersey, and New England. Puerto Rican contract laborers come into the United States each year to join this stream and then return to Puerto Rico. A second route is called the Sugar Beet stream. It originates in Texas and moves up into the Mountain States. It contains about 75 thousand workers, most of them Mexican Americans.

A Midcontinent stream also begins in Texas, and progresses across the Midwest into Canada. This group, composed chiefly of about 50 thousand Mexican Americans, is designed for heavy grain harvesting work and contains few dependents. In the other streams, families of migrants usually travel together.

A fourth is the Cotton Harvest stream, which also begins in Texas, is

[16]Beliefs or "values operate as criteria for making choices between alternative courses of action or between action and no action. . . ." (Eugene A. Wilkening, "Techniques of Assessing Farm Family Values: A Study of Acceptance of Farm Practices as they Relate to Family and Other Group Factors," *Rural Sociology* XIX, 1954, pp. 39-49. See also, A. Eugene Havens and Everett M. Rogers, "Adoption of Hybrid Corn: Profitability and the Interaction Effect," *Rural Sociology*, December, 1961, Vol. 26, No. 4, pp. 409-413.)

[17]Grady W. Taylor, "An Analysis of Certain Social and Psychological Factors Differentiating Successful from Unsuccessful Farm Families," *Rural Sociology*, Vol. 26, No. 3, September, 1962, pp. 303-315.

[18]Janet M. Jorgenson, et al., *Migratory Agricultural Workers in the United States*, Grinnell College, Grinnell, Iowa, Department of Sociology, 1961.

composed mostly of Mexican Americans and Negroes, and which moves across the Deep South. A fifth stream develops annually in Oklahoma and moves north and west to harvest vegetables and fruits. This contains some 30 thousand workers and their families, most of them white Americans. A West Coast stream of some 120 thousand workers and their dependents moves along the western seaboard, harvesting many varied crops and originating in no single state. This large stream contains whites, Negroes, and Mexican Americans.

The farmers who employ migrant workers operate from narrow margins of profit, with large outlays of capital equipment, and with tremendous year-to-year variation in their dollar profits, depending upon the quality of the weather and the ups and downs of markets over which they have no direct control. Labor costs are one of the few economic sectors in which these farmers can budget to reduce their expenditures and maximize their profits.

Migrant workers, while they return year after year, are viewed as strangers and outsiders. Their needs — educational, medical, financial, and social — do not fit the categories which have built up around the provision of welfare. Their well-being cannot be attached conveniently to local village or county enterprises. They come and go, they do not "belong" to the settings in which they work. The cultures they carry with them are alien to the local agricultural community. Economically and culturally, then, powerful forces separate employers from their employees in this work situation. The bases for cooperation as opposed to exploitation are thin.

Income, housing and education, in that order, represent the common American 'rewards' that are always in short supply among migrant agricultural workers. Migrant workers, who make up about one fourth of the total national hired farm worker labor force, often suffer long spells of enforced idleness between jobs. Crop damage from adverse weather often strands them without income, far from their homes. According to the U.S. Department of Labor, 40 per cent of all migrant farm workers were unemployed during part of 1959; and 10 per cent were out of work for six months or more.

When they do find work, they receive the lowest available pay. Migrant workers averaged $6 a day at farm work during 1959. Male workers averaged $1,025 as total cash income for the whole year.[19] This cash must cover family subsistence, transportation, and payment to crew leaders. (Crew leaders make the work arrangements and set the terms for work. They also usually provide transportation. They represent a secondary source of exploitation, of course.) To complete the economic condition, migrant workers are generally excluded from coverage under minimum wage laws, state unemployment insurance, workmen's compensation laws, and laws that protect the right to organize unions for collective bargaining with employers.

Housing conditions for migrant farm workers are equally grim. Half of the states maintain legislated standards for migrant labor housing, and the Department of Labor enforces some protections under the interstate commerce clause of the Constitution. Although ten states which employ more than 10 thousand migrants each year have mandatory

[19]*Hired Farm Workers in the United States,* June, 1961, U.S. Department of Labor, Bureau Employment Security, Washington 25, D.C., p. 32.

housing laws, three of the heaviest users (Texas, Kansas, and Oklahoma) have no housing codes. Moreover, codes vary greatly in enforcement from state to state. Penalties for violation vary from a $10 fine to an average in a few states of $200 fine and/or imprisonment up to 60 days. The most severe penalty is $1,000 and/or imprisonment up to one year.[20] Standards are evolving and improving. Even where they are energetically enforced, however, migrant work camps represent the most substandard shelter facilities available to any group in the American population except perhaps those for minorities in inner city slums and some Indian groups.

There is evidence that agricultural technology can eliminate the problems that attend migratory farming by eliminating the demand for itinerant labor itself:

> At the National Conference to Stabilize Migrant Labor held in Chicago [in] 1959, there were several persons who voiced the opinion that by cooperative planning, crops in most areas of the country could be sufficiently diversified to offer nearly a full year of continuous employment to agricultural workers ... Dr. Varden Fuller, Professor Agricultural Economics at the University of California, Berkeley, and Dr. Theodore W. Smith, Chairman of the Department of Economics at the University of Chicago shared this opinion.[21]

This type of solution has been demonstrated in rural sections of Michigan and California. Two limitations are most pressing: relocation of migrants, and costs. The cultural differences between

migrant families and other farm families can be overstated. A study of migratory workers in Michigan disclosed that, contrary to common stereotypes, few were habitual wanderers or 'hobo types'. Most of the families studied expressed a strong desire to stay permanently in Michigan.

Deep South Negroes and Mexican Americans *do* represent 'different' cultural groups, when the mainstream white farm society of the nation is used as the common standard. Deep readjustments would be involved if migrant families from these groups were settled permanently in villages of the Middle West and the Northwest.

Pockets of Poverty

Migrant farm workers comprise but a small fraction of the rural labor force that is victimized by poverty and deprivation. Rural poverty is concentrated in the South, of course. In fact, incomes of farm families in the South, in both 1950 and 1960, were only about one half as high as incomes of farm families in the Corn Belt.

Underemployment; small, inadequate farms with ruined soil; soil ill adapted to the crops these farmers attempt to grow; and a high proportion of aged persons, are all characteristic of distressed rural areas of the Appalachian South and the Ozarks of Missouri and Arkansas. (The Appalachian strip runs through Virginia, West Virginia, Kentucky, Tennessee, North and South Carolina, and Georgia and Alabama. At any one census, there are between 8 and 10 million persons in this area, and another million who move in and out of it in search of employment.)

Typically, the residents of these

---

[20]*Housing for Migrant Agricultural Workers*, Bulletin 235, November, 1961, U.S. Department of Labor, U.S. Government Printing Office.

[21]Janet M. Jorgenson, *op. cit.*, p. 51.

areas are undereducated, strongly attached to their local territory, and unresponsive to efforts to move out of their areas and take on industrial or service skills. Despair, suspicion, and bitter pride stand as a potent obstacle to attempts to introduce programs of rural development, new local industry, or skill training and relocation.

Health Problems

Mining and farming are two of the most dangerous occupations in the United States. Only the construction industry suffers a higher death rate. The high accident rate for farmers is especially serious, for employment and compensation insurance systems, private or public, do not cover most farm workers.

Rural families in America have greater general medical needs than do urban families, yet they are shortchanged on the care they receive. Distance from facilities, costs, and rural attitudes are all involved. Rural physicians and nurses are generally older, less specialized, less informed about current practices, than urban health professionals. There are also fewer of them per one thousand rural population. In the urban South, the ratio in 1960 was about one physician per 1.2 thousand population, in contrast to a rural ratio of one doctor per 2.5 thousand population. Patterns are similar for dentists, laboratory technicians, and hospital and clinic facilities.

When rural families get improved health services, they are not always disposed to make use of them. The Federal Hill-Burton program has erected hospitals and clinics in about 4 thousand areas, most of them rural. But the oldest and medically neediest rural residents are negative toward health

personnel and facilities. They tend to seek a doctor only in a terminal emergency.[22]

Rural Government

One student of rural social change once remarked that "civilization feeds on the rot of villages." Earlier, this chapter emphasized the deterioration of rural communities as their populations and that most of their functional autonomy, was absorbed by metropolitan areas. As urban areas extend into the hinterland, however, rural counties and villages experience a 'second blow'. As a county's farms are cut up for residential plots to house nonfarm commuters to distant central cities, new controls of zoning and new county and village governmental services are needed.

Characteristically, zoning, the public instrument for the regulation of land usage, is introduced too late to be instrumental in preventing urban sprawl in rural counties. Zoning laws cannot be retroactive. They must apply only to intended future developments. Often farmers sell parts of their acreage bit by bit, in areas where no program of zoning has evolved. The residential transformation is gradual. Only slowly do country lanes begin to look like suburban streets. Gas stations, shops, and later, industrial units, crop up at scattered points. Only when the 'sprawl' is extensive and unplanned and therefore locally threatening, is control introduced.

Zoning is merely symptomatic of this dilemma. Falling water tables, sewage problems, new traffic control difficulties, overloading of school facilities,

[22]Robert L. McNamara, et al., "Contacts with and Conception of the Physician in a Rural Setting," *Rural Sociology*, 1957, Vol. 22, pp. 213-220.

fire protection needs, all crop up within areas which suffered loss of population, revenues, and leadership, only 25 to 50 years earlier.

The mechanisms for rural government are lacking in the midst of pressure toward suburbanization. Counties have not undertaken governmental consolidation. Only three cases of such reorganization among 3 thousand counties occurred in 1956, for example. Townships in the Midwest, the major form of rural authority, were laid out long ago, without regard to village or other community boundaries. In New England, village and township governments in areas of sudden expansion through resort development often undergo conflict and competition for control.

Meanwhile, functioning authority has drifted upward, so that with few exceptions, county commissioners, not village and township political leadership, exert primary authority. Although the authority and responsibility of county officials has increased, their salaries reflect slight change. County government expenditures in Ohio, for example, increased 230 per cent between 1940 and 1955, yet the average salary of an Ohio county commissioner in 1955 was about $3,200; for a sheriff, about $4,100.[23]

The genesis of the problems we have outlined in this chapter is primarily the speed of technical and social change; the disruption of an agrarian society in equilibrium. A balance built around the ideal of the self-owned family farm and the small village community has been tipped by industrial change and urbanization.

The forms of the most pressing of these problems, however, are dictated by cultural norms that prescribe the conditions under which scarce values shall be allocated in the national society. Economic poverty and deprivation, and intergroup exploitation of ethnic minorities, are the most pressing difficulties common to rural America. We have seen in earlier chapters that these stresses are in no way peculiar to the village or the open countryside.

Each specific rural social problem, moreover, is attacked, however soundly or unsatisfactorily, by a series of state and federal programs. Protection under the law and public economic investment are substantial, ranging from housing and health codes for migrant workers, to price supports and soil banks and industrial development programs for distressed rural counties. Most rural social problems, in short, have received observation, definition, and planning. The national investment, private as well as public, commercial and philanthropic, however, has never been great enough to remedy the problems.

References

Agrarian societies in transition, the annals, 305, (May, 1956).

Allen, Frederick Lewis. *The big change.* New York: Harper, 1952.

American Assembly. *United States agriculture: perspectives and prospects.* New York: Columbia University, 1955.

Anderson, C. Arnold. Trends in rural sociology. In Robert K. Merton, et al. (eds.). *Sociology today.* New York: Basic Books, 1959.

Anderson, W. A. High-school youth and the values in rural living. *Rural Sociology,* Vol. 18 (June, 1953), pp. 156-63.

[23]Everett M. Rogers, *Social Change in Rural Society,* Appleton-Century-Crofts: New York, 1960, pp. 393-394.

Belcher, John C. The nonresident farmer in the new rural society. *Rural Sociology,* 19, No. 2 (June, 1954).

Benedict, Murray R. *Farm policies of the United States, 1790-1950.* New York: The 20th Century Fund, 1953.

Benvenuti, B. *Farming in cultural change.* New York: Humanities Press, 1963.

Bernard, Alvin L. Cultural changes in American rural life. In *Rural Education: a forward look, yearbook, 1955.* Department of Rural Education, National Education Association, Washington, D.C., 1955. pp. 306-11.

Bertrand, Alvin Lee, et al. (eds.). *Rural sociology; an analysis of contemporary rural life.* New York: McGraw-Hill, 1958.

Bowles, Gladys, K. Migration patterns of rural-farm population, thirteen economic regions of the United States, 1940-50. *Rural Sociology,* 22 (March, 1957), 1-11.

Brunner, Edmund de S. *American society: urban and rural patterns.* New York: Harper, 1955.

——— *The growth of a science; a half century of rural sociological research in the United States.* New York: Harper, 1957.

——— and E. Hsin Pao Yang. *Rural America and the extension service; a history and critique of the cooperative agricultural and home economics extension service.* New York: Bureau of Publications, Teachers College, Columbia University, 1949.

Butterworth, Julian E. and Howard H. Dawson. *The modern rural school.* New York: Crowell, 1957.

Gee, Wilson. *The social economics of agriculture.* New York: The Macmillan Company, 1954.

Hamilton, C. Horace. The sociology of a changing agriculture. *Social Forces,* 37:1-7, 1958.

Hardin, Charles M. *The politics of agriculture.* Glencoe, Ill.: Free Press, 1952.

Heady, Earl O., et al. (eds.) *Agricultural adjustment in a growing economy.* Armes: Iowa State College Press, 1958.

Higbee, E.C. *Farms and farmers in an urban age.* New York: 20th Century Fund, 1963.

Jorgenson, Janet M., et al. *Migratory agricultural workers in the United States.* Grinnell, Iowa: Grinnell College, Department of Sociology, 1961.

Kaufman, Harold F., Otis D. Duncan, Neal Gross, and William H. Sewell. Social stratification in rural society. *Rural Sociology,* 18, No. 1 (March, 1953).

Kolb, John Harrison. *Emerging rural communities; group relations in rural society.* A review of Wisconsin in action. Madison, University of Wisconsin Press, 1959.

——— and Edmund de S. Brunner. *A study of rural society.* (4th Ed.) Boston: Houghton Mifflin Company, 1952.

Kraenzel, Carl F. *The great plains in transition.* Normal: University of Oklahoma Press, 1955.

Lancaster, Lane W. *Government in rural America* (2nd Ed.). New York: Van Nostrand, 1952.

Larson, Olaf F. The role of rural sociology in a changing society. *Rural Sociology,* 24: 1-10, 1959.

Loomis, Charles P. and Allen J. Beegle. *Rural sociology: the strategy of change.* Englewood Cliffs, New Jersey: Prentice-Hall, 1957.

Malone, Carl C. Appraising farm programs and proposals. *Farm Policy Forum,* Vol. 7 (Winter, 1954), pp. 32-36.

Mighell, Ronald L. *American agriculture: its structure and place in the economy.* New York: John Wiley and Sons, 1955.

National Educational Association of the United States Department of Rural Education. *Handbook on rural education; factual data on rural education, its social and economic backgrounds.* Washington, D.C., 1961.

Nelson, Lawry. *Migratory workers: the mobile tenth of American agriculture.* Washington, D.C.: National Planning Association, 1953.

—— *Rural sociology* (2nd Ed.). New York: American Book Company, 1955.

Rogers, Everett M. *Social change in rural society.* New York: Appleton Century Crofts, 1960.

Rural industrialization: A summary of five studies. Agriculture Information Bulletin No. 252, Economic Research Service, Department of Agriculture, November, 1961.

Schickele, Rainer. *Agricultural policy.* New York: McGraw-Hill Book Company, 1954.

Smith, Thomas Lynn. *The sociology of rural life.* New York: Harper, 1953.

Soth, Lauren. *Farm trouble.* Princeton, New Jersey: Princeton University Press, 1957.

Taylor, Carl C., et al. *Rural life in the United States.* New York: A. A. Knopf, 1949.

Taylor, Grady W. An analysis of certain social and psychological factors differentiating successful from unsuccessful farm families. *Rural Sociology,* Vol. 26, No. 3 (September, 1962), pp. 303-315.

Vidich, Arthur J. and Joseph Bensman. *Small town in mass society.* Princeton, New Jersey: Princeton University Press, 1958.

West, James. *Plainville, U.S.A.* New York: Columbia University Press, 1945.

Wilcox, Walter W. *Social responsibility in farm leadership.* New York: Harper, 1956.

Youmans, E.G. *The rural school dropout.* Lexington, Kentucky: University of Kentucky, Bureau of School Service, 1963.

RELATION OF CHRONIC LOW FARM INCOMES TO MAJOR NATIONAL ECONOMIC PROBLEMS

William E. Hendrix[1]

Relatively low incomes have characterized much of rural America for many decades, and they have been a subject of public concern since at least the early 1930's. Their persistence after the extensive remedial programs and the unprecedented national economic growth of the last few decades makes it clear that many of our ideas as to their causes and requirements for solution are inadequate. Meantime, Federal, State, and local agencies are working harder than ever before to eradicate rural poverty. It is fitting therefore that these problems be considered in our annual meetings, for it is now important that we ask anew about their causes and requirements for solution.

One might hold that rural poverty is only more complex than had been supposed and that it must therefore be treated with larger doses of a much broader complex of remedies than

Paper read before AEA and AFEA, NYC, 1961, and reprinted in the *Journal* of the Farm Economics Division of the Economics Research Service of the U.S. Dept. of Agriculture, used with permission.

[1]The ideas expressed in this paper are those of the author.

previously has been tried. But that problems are complex when they are not understood is a *non sequiter*. Rural poverty is admittedly complex when viewed without adequate analytical frames. It is a function of research, however, to break complex problems into more elemental and easily understood parts, and to show how these parts fit and work together. The ideal is to break the complex into parts so that each has its unique set of causes and its unique set of possibilities and requirements for solution or, in short, its "single hypothesis" explanation.

Enough work along such basic analytical lines has been done to warrant the thesis that a large part of the problem of rural poverty is closely akin in its causes and requirements for solution to involuntary unemployment in the nonfarm economy and is therefore closely related to the Nation's general employment, stability, and growth problems. In this paper, I shall indicate (1) the conceptual and factual basis for this thesis, and (2) some of its implications (a) for alternative explanations of the low-income problem and (b) for policies and programs directed toward its solution.

Basis for Thesis

The conceptual basis for the thesis can be set forth most easily if we first distinguish between two distinct phases of inquiry into the causes of low incomes. The first relates to the current causes of low rural family incomes or to the conditions which in any given year account for the differences between family incomes in chronic low-income rural areas and those in the rest of the Nation's economy.[2] The second phase relates to reasons for the presence, pervasiveness, and persistence of the causal conditions and thereby to reasons for the location and chronic nature of the low incomes.

In this paper, I shall emphasize mainly the former of these phases. The first step in its development is that of showing, on the basis of general income theory, the *possible* kinds of causes of low incomes. The second step is to assess, on the basis of available facts, the relative importance of these possible causal conditions.

An orientation to the former of these steps is provided in the model of an economy fulfilling the conditions needed for the persistence of equal family money incomes. Conditions that need to be fulfilled for this purely hypothetical world are surprisingly few in number. It logically follows that the obverses of these few conditions provide a list of the possible current causes of differences in family incomes that

matches in exhaustiveness the adequacy of the equality conditions listed.

Most of these equality conditions are well known to economists. Briefly stated, all families would receive incomes of the same size if all of these conditions were fulfilled: (1) If the economy were perfectly competitive; (2) if all families were alike in capital wealth, in number and employment capacities of family members, in tastes and values, in income from gifts and other transfer sources, and in the degree to which their incomes were affected by temporary or transitory conditions; (3) if all employments and places of employment were equally attractive; (4) if there were no differences among localities in the purchasing power of money; (5) if there were no buyer or seller discrimination on the basis of factors unrelated to pecuniary worth;[3] and (6) if there were no cost of transfer between kinds or places of employment.[4]

Instead of these income-equality conditions, however, their obverses are common throughout most of the Nation's economy. Hence, differences among regions, industries, occupations, and socio-economic groups in size of family income are to be expected in our society. Low incomes *per se*, however, do not denote economic problems. Rather, in a market economy with large freedom of individual and family choice, all family income differences, and, therefore, all parts of the rural

[2] The rural poverty problem as an income problem pertains merely to differences among families and individuals in the size of their income.

[3] This condition is implicit in the assumption of similar tastes and values.

[4] In an economy fulfilling all of the other equality conditions enumerated, this last condition would insure the persistence of equal family incomes despite rapid economic growth or large geographic differences in industry growth rates or technological progress. Income equality would also be maintained despite either original or later developing differences among products in their supply and demand elasticities.

poverty problem that can be explained within perfectly competitive theory are consistent with what Marshall has called the *equality of efficiency earnings*.[5]

The part of family income differences that cannot be accounted for by one or more of these "efficiency-equalizing factors," however, denotes inefficiency in the allocation or employment of resources. It is to this possible part of the rural poverty problem that the thesis of this paper is directly related.

Inefficiencies can occur in the use of any factor, human or physical. To simplify analysis, however, in the rest of this paper I shall subsume all inefficiencies under the heading of that in employment of the human factor,[6] and I shall refer to this possible part of the rural poverty problem as that resulting from *involuntary underemployment*.

The task of explaining such involuntary underemployment is in effect that of explaining why wage differences occur and persist in the same general labor market among workers equal in ability and tastes. In its most severe form, it is the problem of indicating why, among such workers, some have well-paying jobs while others are involuntarily unemployed.

In earlier economic thought, little attention was paid to the possibility of a low-income problem that could not be explained within competitive theory. Yet, the existence of this kind of low-income problem has been implicitly, if not explicitly, assumed in most economic treatments of American rural poverty during the last few decades. The best known examples, coupled with extensive measurement attempts, are those found in the writings of Schultz and other economists at the University of Chicago.[7]

In measurements adjusted for all major efficiency-equalizing parts of farm-nonfarm income differences except that relating to values and tastes—or to the *voluntary* component of farm underemployment—Johnson has estimated that in 1956, the Nation's farm workers received incomes that were only about 65 percent as large as those received by nonfarm workers of comparable abilities.[8] Glasglow, using the same general measurement techniques but with refinements made possible by the availability of additional data, found that nearly the same size of farm-non-farm income disparity existed in 1959.[9]

I have converted Glasgow's estimates into estimates of underemployment expressed in units equal to a full year of unemployment. If in 1959 the Nation's male farm workers 20 to 64 years of age had earned as large incomes as did workers of comparable abilities in the Nation as a whole, the aggregate income that these farm people received could have been earned with 1.1 million fewer workers. Expressed in another way, underemployment among the Nation's male farm workers 20 to 64 years of age existed in 1959 in an amount equal to a full year of unemployment of 1.1 million workers. In 1959, the Na-

---

[5]Marshall, Alfred, *Principles of Econ.* (8th edition) Macmillan and Co. Limited, London, 1938, p. 549.

[6]This can be done without violence to the objective of efficiency in the use of capital resources by treating each bundle of capital resources used in conjunction with a given labor force as a distinct form of employment.

[7]See especially Schultz, T. W., *Agriculture in an Unstable Economy,* McGraw-Hill Book Co., N.Y., 1945.

[8]Johnson, D. Gale, "Labor Mobility and Agricultural Adjustment," *Agricultural Adjustment Problems in a Growing Economy,* Iowa State College Press, 1958.

[9]Unpublished estimates by Glasgow, Robert B., Farm Econ. Div., ARS, USDA.

tion's male farm workers needed a median net labor and management income of about $3,200 to have received as much as their counterparts in the nonfarm economy. Hence, if they had been as productively employed as were workers of comparable ability in the nonfarm economy, they would have earned in the aggregate an additional income equivalent to about $3.5 billion net farm income. Losses of this size concentrated within a single industry, and heavily concentrated geographically within this industry, suggest major maladjustments between this industry and the rest of the Nation's economy.

Data showing the geographic distribution of these 1.1 million man-year equivalents of underemployment have not been developed. On the basis of other data, however, it is fairly obvious that they are most heavily concentrated in low-income farm areas, particularly in the South. For among regions, areas, and counties in the Nation as a whole, farm-nonfarm income disparities are inversely related to the farm income level, with the disparities in the southern areas substantially larger than in the Nation's higher farm income regions.[10]

Nor do we know how much of the Nation's rural underemployment is *involuntary*. Most economists who have dealt with the rural underemployment problem, however, have implicitly, if not explicitly, placed the larger part of it in the involuntary category.[11] There are good reasons for believing that this diagnosis is correct. As indicated in studies by Schuh, Sjaastad, Bishop, and others,[12] farm people take nonfarm jobs about as rapidly as they become available. In fact, when new industry is developed in most low-income areas, the number of job applicants is often several times as large as the number of new jobs. Low-income farmers have also been highly responsive to new farm opportunities, as indicated by the rapid development of the broiler industry. In fact, even production controls and marketing quotas are widely believed to be as badly needed for commodities like cotton, tobacco, peanuts, and broilers that are grown in low-income areas as they are for the major commodities grown in more prosperous parts of agriculture.

Although most economists admit the fact of large concentrations of involuntary underemployment in rural low-income areas, they differ widely in their explanations of it. At one extreme, a few economists still seek explanations within competitive theory, with some even ascribing involuntary underemployment to a low level of aspirations, seemingly unaware that they are thereby simply jumping into another categorical box. Others ascribe the underemployment to imperfections in labor markets but place these imperfections mainly in conditions affecting rural people as a supply of nonfarm labor. A more recent view holds that the amount of underemployment is a function of the rates of national economic growth *per se*, presumably without any

[10]Glasgow, R. B., *Farm Family Income: Its Distribution and Relation to Nonfarm Income*, Agr. Res. Serv., 43-34, USDA, July 1956.

[11]See especially Johnson, D. Gale, "Functioning of the Labor Market," *J. of Farm Econ.*, Feb. 1951.

[12]Schuh, G. Edward, "Some Dynamics of the Agricultural Labor Market," paper presented at summer meetings of the Econometric Society, Stillwater, Okla., 1961. Sjaastad, Larry, "Trends in Occupational Structure and Migration Patterns in the U.S. With Special Reference to Agriculture," and Bishop, C. E., "Economic Aspects of Migration From Farms in the U.S.," papers presented at conference on Labor Mobility in Agriculture, Iowa State Univ., Nov. 8, 1960.

relation to the competitive structure of markets.[13] My own thesis, first published in the 1958 summer issue of the *Farmer Policy Forum,* has been that involuntary underemployment reflects an excess in the Nation's supply of labor relative to the demand; that this imbalance is in theory impossible without labor policies in nonfarm labor markets that prevent wages from equating the labor supply and demand; that this imbalance can be corrected by growth in the demand for labor relative to the supply; but that given the imbalance, agriculture is highly vulnerable to its incidence because of its own competitive labor market, the bases upon which limited jobs are rationed, and agriculture's declining labor needs and high labor replacement rates.

A recent attempt to explain the excess labor in agriculture within competitive theory is the one relating to the effects of farmer's large longterm investments in forms of capital for which there are large disparities between purchase and resale prices. Such disparities are illustrated by the case of the southern farmer who kept four well-fed mules that he had not worked for 3 years. When asked why he kept them, he replied, "These are $400 mules! The most I've been offered for them is $75 a head." If this farmer had a lower income than he could have earned from the conversion and reinvestment of his farm capital and from a nonfarm job presumed to be available, his underemployment would seem to have been voluntary or rooted in value orientations keeping him "farm bound."

In other words, the "sunk-capital" theory of underemployment and excess capacity when set within competitive frames is a variant of the oldest of all theories of underemployment and low

incomes among employable workers, that ascribing their poverty to their own special preferences and values. It probably explains a part of the Nation's low-income problem but not the part fitting the term "involuntary underemployment."

The best known view ascribing involuntary underemployment to supply-oriented labor market imperfections is the one that ascribes the failure of farm workers to move into more remunerative jobs to their lack of enough capital with which to move. Rural workers are limited in their knowledge of job alternatives and capital wealth. But these conditions, instead of being primary impediments, appear to be the symptoms or the results of much more basic impediments to farm-nonfarm labor transfers. For if nonfarm labor markets were fully competitive, the mere existence of involuntary rural underemployment would itself induce employers to engage in enough labor recruitment and procurement activities to correct the underemployment. For with large underemployment, employers could reduce labor costs by recruiting the underemployed workers. Their failure to do so strains the assumption of a fully competitive labor market.

In short, without labor policies that permit the number of workers available to employers in more advantaged sectors of the economy to exceed the number of jobs they have to fill, there could be no involuntary underemployment. It is this resulting excess in the supply of labor over the demand that is the definitive characteristic of involuntary underemployment wherever it occurs and whatever its extent.[14]

[13]Schuh, *op. cit.*

[14]For a fuller development of this thesis, see Hendrix, W. E., "Income Improvement Prospects in Low Income Areas," *J. of Farm Econ.,* Dec. 1959, pp. 1065-1075.

Given large labor supply-demand imbalances in the Nation's general economy, agriculture, especially agriculture in low-income areas, is highly vulnerable to its incidence for these reasons: (1) Agriculture is a highly competitive industry with respect to the ease and freedom of entry by workers who cannot readily find non-farm jobs. (2) Underemployment permits increased selectivity in the hiring of workers, which militates against the older, the poorly educated, and other handicapped workers whose members are relatively more numerous among the Nation's underemployed farmworkers than among the major competitors of farmworkers for new nonfarm jobs. Farmworkers are also disadvantaged relative to their nonfarm competitors for jobs because of their greater distance from the jobs available. (3) As a result of technological progress and limited markets, agriculture is declining in its needs for labor and meantime its natural population increase greatly exceeds its replacement needs.[15]

Implications of Involuntary Underemployment for the Origins of Impoverished Areas

Involuntary underemployment heavily concentrated in a rural area means that too many families are trying to make a living on the area's present market and resource bases. For an agriculture organized on a family-farm basis, this means small, inadequately equipped and often poor-land farms. Hence, farming in such an area, compared with that in the Nation's better farm areas (where high capital requirements to begin farming close easy entry), seems very inefficient. The causes of this inefficiency, however, lie in the structural and growth characteristics of the larger general economy that account for the involuntary underemployment.

In short, the farm people to whom we ascribe such inefficiency are themselves merely the victims of inefficiency in the functioning of the Nation's general economy. They are victims because they are so situated among the Nation's population and occupational groups that they are among the most vulnerable to the incidence of the general economy's labor supply-demand imbalances.

Moreover, even the Nation's low-income farmers operate within an agriculture that is highly dynamic in its markets and technology. Hence, like farmers in more prosperous parts of agriculture, they too are caught upon a technological treadmill[16]—one requiring them to use ever more and more capital merely to maintain their present incomes.[17] To meet these capital needs from their meager incomes, farmers in areas with large concentrations of underemployment have often mined and depleted their land resources; let already inadequate housing, farm buildings, fences, and machinery run down; gone without needed medical services; curtailed the private expenditures needed for their children to use public education facilities; and in other ways reduced levels of living below the needs for social and economic efficiency. Moreover, communities with large numbers of such people have lagged behind most of the rest of the

---

[15]Without "imperfections" in labor markets none of these conditions could cause agriculture, or any of its parts, to be any more subject to underemployment than other parts of the economy.

[16]Cochrane, W. W., *Farm Prices: Myth and Reality,* University of Minn. Press, Minneapolis, 1958.

[17]Brewster, J. M., "Long Run Prospects of Southern Agriculture," *Southern Econ. J.,* Oct. 1959.

Nation in their investments in roads, schools, hospitals, recreation facilities, and other forms of social overhead capital of the kinds that have undergirded this Nation's economic growth from its early beginnings.

We, therefore, find in farm areas with large concentrations of underemployment small, inadequately equipped and often severely eroded farms; people living in crowded dilapidated houses; farm machinery in poor repair; a high incidence of remedial physical defects; a high level of school dropouts; inadequate community facilities; notable cultural lags; and other conditions all combining to impoverish people and the communities in which they live. These conditions are the incidences of large involuntary underemployment persisting over decades of time. Rural areas with large concentrations of such underemployment are in a situation roughly equivalent to that faced by an urban community with average unemployment per worker of 4 to 5 months per year above the normal levels, a level of unemployment that occurs not once in every 4 or 5 years but annually over decades of time—this without the benefits of unemployment compensation.

In brief, this is the way in which large concentrations of involuntary underemployment persisting over a long period of time have helped to account even for parts of the low-income problem that in a short-run context are consistent with the efficient use of resources. In this century, we have seen these patterns of retrogression closely approximated in much of the Nation's low-income agriculture except when they have been reversed because employment has increased faster than growth in the Nation's supply of labor,

or because large governmental and business investments have created many new jobs.[18]

Implications for Policies and Programs

The presence in rural low-income areas of large concentrations of involuntary underemployment obviously has important implications for possible solutions of the low-income rural problem. Such underemployment is not indigenous to low-income people or to the areas in which they live but, like involuntary unemployment in urban areas, it results from the structural and growth characteristics of the Nation's general economy. In particular, it results from a labor supply-demand imbalance that can not be explained apart from conditions that impede intersector transfers of resources at the rates needed for their optional allocation.

Within an agriculture organized on a family farm basis, large concentrations of involuntary underemployment and farming patterns that appear to be highly inefficient usually, if not always, occur together. Since the latter is a product of the former, however, it can-

[18]The main elements of this thesis can be found in several treatments of problems of chronically depressed industries, particularly in those by economists interested in the problems of general equilibrium in a mixed market economy. J. S. Bain's chapter on "Excessive Competition" in his recent *Industrial Organization* (John Wiley and Sons, New York, 1959) is an excellent example. Another closely parallel treatment is that found in K. E. Boulding's *Economic Analysis* (Harper and Brothers, New York, 1941). In Boulding's treatment, however, this thesis can be easily overlooked because it is presented in two separate sections spaced 155 pages apart, one "on mixed market systems" beginning on page 523, and the other on the "unprofitability of industries faced with inelastic demands," beginning on page 778.

not be corrected apart from reducing the associated underemployment.

Three general ways have been suggested for reducing the economy's involuntary underemployment as opposed to measures that merely shift its incidence to other population groups. These include (1) job retraining to help underemployed workers to qualify for jobs in labor-scarce occupations, such as are normally found even in periods of large unemployment; (2) competitively induced downward adjustments in wages to bring the labor supply and demand into balance, as suggested in competitive economic theory; and (3) increases in the aggregative national demand for labor relative to the supply.

In recent months, considerable attention has been focused on the opportunities for correcting underemployment through the job retraining route. How large such opportunities will be, however, will depend upon (a) the size of the labor shortages in the economy's labor-scarce sectors and (b) the effectiveness of retraining programs in bridging the gaps between the education, skills, and other personal qualities required in labor-scarce occupations and those now possessed by underemployed workers. If labor-scarce sectors need only chemists, physicists, mathematicians, engineers and the like, and if the underemployed workers have not gone beyond high school, elaborate retraining programs with offerings equivalent to those of our colleges and universities will be needed to correct their underemployment. If the requisite skills in the labor-scarce occupations can be quickly and easily learned, the persistence of large labor scarcities in these occupations in the face of large involuntary underemployment and unemployment is so much an economic paradox that it warrants careful investigation.[19]

In recent years, considerable attention has been given to the relation of wage and price policies to the level of employment[20] and in recent months the President and the Secretary of Labor have emphasized the needs for labor and management to restrain their demands for higher wages and prices lest such increases lead to larger unemployment. The possibility of reducing underemployment and unemployment through competitive job bidding, however, is now given little attention by economists, for in much of the economy, wages are set through contracts for advance periods of 2 or more years. In most industries other than agriculture, wages are downwardly inflexible in response to individual job bids, probably because of the influence of such things as public opinion, custom, minimum wage laws, and employers' desires to forestall the organization of their workers.

Despite limited wage competition, however, some communities with large concentrations of underemployment have been able to devise plans for securing new industry and jobs with results that are in the direction of those postulated in competitive theory. These plans involve giving back to nonfarm employers paying standard wages a sizable amount of their wage bill, or its equivalent, as site, plant, and development subsidies raised through taxes. With their workers unable to engage in wage competition, such communities

[19]The larger value of such retraining probably lies in the uses made of it as bases for the rationing of jobs and in our likely future needs for the improved skills.

[20]*Employment, Growth and Price Levels*, Hearings before the Joint Economic Committee, U.S. Congress, Sept. 22-25, 1959.

have been able through subsidies to defray other production costs with a resulting total cost structure closer to the structure that would result if wages were competitively determined.[21]

The mechanics, if not the economics of such "wage-pay-back plans" have been known and widely used in low-income areas for a long time. Whether at any given period the unexploited opportunities in such approaches to reducing underemployment are ever very large is questionable in view of the large competition by regions, States, cities, and counties for new industries and jobs.

In the main, reduction of involuntary underemployment in rural areas, and of involuntary unemployment in urban sectors, as well, will require increases in the rates of national economic growth sufficient to absorb such underemployment and unemployment in the face of rapid technological progress and large increases in the labor force.

How to achieve such growth in the Nation's economy is outside the scope of this paper. Whether the Nation will reduce its large underemployment and unemployment substantially in the 1960's remains to be seen.[22] Without such reductions, however, that part of the Nation's low-income problem caused by involuntary underemployment can be alleviated in only these ways: 1) The low income can be raised through income-transfer measures and 2) the incidence of the underemployment itself can be shifted to other population groups.

Examples of the former include aid

to the indigent aged, the blind, and dependent children and a large part of unemployment compensation benefits to the unemployed. Most of the Nation's involuntarily underemployed farm people, however, are eligible for little such assistance.

Many of the things that have been done in the past and that are still commonly recommended for solving the low-income problem are actions that achieve their objective mainly by shifting the incidence of the economy's underemployment from one population group to others. Within agriculture, this can be done by giving farmers in low-income areas enough special assistance in improving their comparative farm advantages to intensify agriculture's supply problems and to widen still further the farm-nonfarm income gap. In the nonfarm economy, this can be done by measures that help selected areas with large underemployment to divert factories and jobs from other areas, including those that also have large underemployment.

The fact that measures for correcting the low-income problem must achieve their objectives mainly through a redistribution of employment opportunities is not in itself a valid criticism of these measures. It is important, however, that we know in what ways remedial measures work to achieve their objectives so that, if the redistribution route needs to be taken, measures that will shift the incidence of the economy's underemployment to those sectors that are most able to bear it can be chosen.

Improvements in educational levels of people in areas with large underemployment appears to be one of the better ways of helping to distribute job opportunities more evenly and thereby

[21]Moes, John E., "The Subsidization of Industry by Local Communities in the South," *The Southern Econ. J.*, Oct. 1961.

[22]Levine, Louis, "Economic Security for Agricultural Labor," paper presented in this session.

the incidence of the economy's under-employment. Such means are available because of the uses of years of schooling to ration jobs in our less than full-employment economy. Interesting data bearing on such uses are those on South-North (meaning all of the non-South) income disparities for population groups standardized by race, sex, and age. It is generally accepted that the South has larger underemployment, or a larger supply of labor relative to demand, than does the North. Yet among white male workers in each census age group from 25 to 54 years of age, those in the South in each educational group from the completion of 4 years of high school to the completion of 4 or more years in college had about as large a median money income in 1949 as did those in the North.[23] In groups with less than 4 years of high school training, however, the South-North differentials increased substantially with each decrease in school grade level. Hence, among white males 35 to 44 years of age, the median earnings of the South's high school graduates was $1,101 more than that of those completing only the eighth grade. In the North however, a high school education made a difference of only $630, or $571 less than in the South. That this difference reflects more the use of a high school diploma to ration the South's more limited job opportunities, rather than the superiority of southern over northern high school training in increasing labor capacities, seems to be a tenable hypothesis.[24]

[23]*Education*, Special Report, PE No. 58, 1950 U. S. Census of Population, U. S. Dept. of Commerce, 1953.

[24]For an interesting treatment of a southern buyers' market with respect to education, see Ginzberg, Eli and Bray, Douglas W., *The Uneducated*, Columbia Univ. Press, New York, 1953.

Improvement in educational levels in low-income areas is important, but so is the need for a higher national level of employment to make fuller use of the labor capacities the Nation now has. Over time, the correction of involuntary underemployment (and unemployment) can be an important means of enabling the Nation's low-income areas and people with the use of only their own resources and incomes to narrow existing educational gaps.

Conclusion

In summary, since passage of the Employment Act of 1946, the task of opening up and creating the new jobs needed to put unemployed workers back to work has been recognized as a national responsibility. In our approach to involuntary underemployment in rural areas, however, we are still plagued by the view that an underemployed worker ought himself to create the job needed to correct his underemployment. We have come close to institutionalizing this view in what is now widely called "operation bootstrap." We need to recognize that the problem of involuntary underemployment is as much a national problem as is that of large-scale urban unemployment; that it needs to be taken account of in our national employment statistics and in our national employment policies; and that programs extending to rural areas, little more than pep talks and slogans coined from time-worn cliches, are feeble instruments for the correction of large involuntary rural underemployment.

SOCIOECONOMIC ASPECTS OF MANPOWER ADJUSTMENTS: LOW-INCOME RURAL AREAS

William H. Metzler

Technological and economic development has spiraled in those areas in the United States that are at the crossroads of cultural exchange. On the other hand, cultural patterns of subsistence farmers in hill areas have changed very slowly.

The cultural values in subsistence farming differ fundamentally from those in commercial agriculture. They stress getting along on small resources, staying out of debt, and being content with what you have, as contrasted with a special skill, high productive methods, and ambition to get ahead.

The opportunity of subsistence farmers to shift into commercial farming is limited. The shift in values is most difficult; furthermore, as farm technology increases, a continuous flow of manpower out of agriculture is necessary. Local nonfarm work opportunities are increasing, but the major shift

This paper was presented at a joint meeting of the American Sociological Society and the Rural Sociological Society, Seattle, Washington, August 27, 1958. The views expressed are those of the author and do not necessarily represent those of the Farm Economics Research Division, ARS, or of the Department of Agriculture.

Reprinted, with permission of author and publisher, from *Rural Sociology*, 24, No. 3, Sept., 1959, 226-235.

is to employment in large urban centers. The habits and values of these people are a strong handicap in their adjustment to the responsibilities of urban life. [*]

Economic and cultural development has progressed at highly variable rates in the United States as well as in the rest of the world. Cultural growth has pyramided at the crossroads and the market places — at the places where people exchange new information and ideas. Meanwhile many people remote from the areas of cultural cross-fertilization have continued in the routines of life that have been impressed upon them from generation to generation. Cultural interchange has been particularly slow in cases of families and groups that strongly emphasize moral, religious, and other basic cultural values differing from those in society as a whole. In spite of our highly developed means of communication, cultural disparities in our society are still so great that one group is quite unable to comprehend another. We would like to believe that all rural families are now being reached by modern ideas and ways of thinking. Workers at the grassroots level, however, still find it most difficult to bring new ideas about farming, homemaking, or community activities to people who are still outside the round of our general community life and cultural development.

New tools, new products, improved methods of production, and higher standards of living have been part of the cultural growth in the rapidly developing sectors of the economy. These have resulted in a spiraling of production, consumption, capital, and employment opportunities in the urban centers of the nation. This expansion has been particularly great during recent years and has attracted to it people from the less developed parts of the economy. During the last two decades, movement from small unprofitable hill farms has snowballed, and we now have the problem of adjusting our most independent, unsophisticated citizens into a highly complex fabric of group activities and responsibilities.

Technological development and commercial organization in agriculture are now matching that which had previously begun in industry, and farming is becoming completely integrated into the commercial economy. Producers in such an economy must gauge their production to match market demands, or they may become impoverished by glutting the market. Consequently, as farm technology advances, there must be a continued movement of manpower out of agriculture if farm prosperity is to continue.[1]

Manpower performs a very different role in a subsistence, as compared to an exchange economy. Ordinarily, a subsistence economy is characterized by low capital investment, do-it-yourself methods, and low levels of produc-

tivity. Production for self does not lead strongly in the direction of increased efficiency.[2] A market economy, however, puts a high premium on managerial skill, proficiency in using capital and labor, and the ambition to get ahead. People who shift from subsistence to commercial farming must go through a marked transformation of values.

Cultural Values

This paper deals particularly with low-income people in the hill and mountain area in the southeastern part of the country. The statements apply neither to all low-income people nor to all hill people. They do apply, in part at least, to subsistence farmers generally. A major purpose is to stress the fact that manpower adjustment in many low-income areas involves cultural patterns that have been handed down for generations and which strongly affect the ability of low-income farmers to make a good adjustment either in agriculture or outside it.[3]

Among the first settlers in the hill areas of the Southeast were hill farmers from England, Scotland, and other countries, who already had a heritage of subsistence living.[4] The hunters, adventurers, and wage-workers who also came to the area had simple, but more flexible, cultural standards. So there has been some cultural growth, but our

[1] See Joint Economic Committee, *Hearings before the Subcommittee on Agricultural Policy* (79th Congress, 1st sess., Dec., 1957).

[2] Harald A. Pedersen, "Cultural Differences in the Acceptance of Recommended Practices," *Rural Sociology,* XVI (1951).

[3] Somewhat similar problems in cultural adjustment are underway in many parts of the world as newer cultures come into contact with old ones. See Arden R. King, "A Note on Emergent Folk Cultures and World Culture Change," *Social Forces,* XXXI (1953).

[4] Edwin White, *Highland Heritage* (New York: Friendship Press, 1947).

concern here is with those people who took their cultural values most seriously and looked on the ways of life of outsiders with suspicion.

We have difficulty in understanding the culture of these hill people because we think of them as living in a system of economic and social values similar to our own. For example, we refer to them as farmers. Actually, they have a way of life which is more appropriately termed the subsistence in contrast to the agricultural complex. Their basic motivation, however, is neither economic nor agricultural, so the term is too narrow. The term "folk culture" or "peasant culture" comes much closer to describing the complex of values in which they live.[5] Some aspects of this complex are directed toward subsistence, but family, moral, and spiritual values are also among the primary bases of this culture.[6]

Their traditions include only incidental production for the market, and they are not geared into our commercial way of life. Their interest in agriculture tends simply to be functional rather than professional or commercial. Their lack of interest in the accumulation of business profits through agriculture, and their accompanying lack of desire to ascertain the most profitable use of their land and labor, fit into production for their own use but would be fatal in commercial agriculture.

Commercial farmers, who conclude that these people lack the entrepreneurial point of view, are right, because

it is not an element in their way of life. As a commercial farmer who moved into the Ozark hills put it, "Why, these people don't know what farming is! When they get a couple of cattle they are completely satisfied." To function adequately in their type of economy, that was all they needed. Actually, they live according to a system of values that is quite sound in a subsistence economy. Generations of small-scale farming and living have developed a complex of life in which satisfation with simple living is a chief element.[7]

These people not only lack the entrepreneurial point of view; they also lack experience in the use of money. Operating with a minimum amount of money is almost an ingrained complex. They are very conscious of the fact that money is hard to obtain and that a small amount must be made to go a long way. On the other hand, the use of any large sum of money is outside their complex of understanding, and they are at a loss to know how to handle large amounts wisely. The first salesman they meet may take the entire amount for an automobile that is unsuited to their needs even though the children may have inadequate clothing and dozens of minor needs should have been met.

These families try to avoid indebtedness but borrow small amounts in order to meet their cash expenses. Owning a farm is one of their life goals, but they cannot afford to go deeply into debt, because subsistence farming does not yield large amounts of cash.[8] As the

[5]Robert Redfield, "The Folk Society," *American Journal of Sociology*, LII (1947); also C. P. Loomis and J. A. Beegle, *Rural Social Systems* (New York: Prentice Hall, 1950).

[6]Popular accounts of customs of hill people have been quite numerous; e.g., see Wayman Hogue, *Back Yonder* (New York: Minton, Balch. 1932), Vance Randolph, *Ozarks* (New York: Vanguard, 1931), and C. M. Wilson, *Backwoods America* (Chapel Hill, N.C.: University of North Carolina Press, 1934). But scientific students seem to have neglected this field of study.

[7]Robert Redfield lists as peasant values "an intimate and reverent attitude toward the land; the idea that agricultural work is good and commerce not so good; and an emphasis on productive industry as a prime virtue" (Peasant Society and Culture [Chicago, Ill.: University of Chicago Press, 1956], p. 112.

[8]William T. Wilson and William H. Metzler, *Characteristics of Rural Rehabilitation Clients in Arkansas* (Arkansas Agr. Expt. Sta. Bull. 348; Fayetteville, 1937).

Farm Security Administration discovered, they are overwhelmed by any large debt even though it is carefully designed to increase the size of their business. A consuming fear that they might never be able to pay off the debt forces them out of agriculture.

The research worker is incredulous when he enters on his record that families of this type had total cash incomes of around $300, $400, or $600, during the previous year. The man in town who has difficulty in living within his income feels sorry for "those poor devils out in the hills" and concocts programs to help them. Usually, however, the hill people are more completely adjusted into their round of life than he is in his. His demands continue to rise, but theirs do not. The general increase in levels of living has made him regard their ways and levels of life as poor and inadequate.

What the man in town overlooks is the fact that low levels of consumption are also a basic part of the subsistence complex of the hill people. Low levels of economic aspirations are essential to the contentment they feel there. When a hill family forgets the virtues of thrift and becomes attracted to expensive ways of life, its days in subsistence agriculture are numbered, for these other ways of life call for cash outlays that cannot be obtained from the proceeds of such a farm. To get these people to want new gadgets is a good way of getting them to make an economic adjustment. The persuasive salesman can get a much faster result than the county agent who approaches them from the viewpoint of increasing their income from the farm.

These people have a reputation for hard work. Their poor tools and hand equipment mean that some of them work very hard during the planting and harvesting periods of the year. It is protracted work on a regular schedule that fails completely to fit in with their leisurely habits, sociability, hunting and fishing interests, and other aspects of an unregimented life.

The real problem lies among those hill families in which practically all the education and training take place within the family circle. Parents are unable to transmit values, skills, and understandings which they do not have. Hence cultural development occurs at a very slow pace except for the addition of a few of the more obvious gadgets of civilization. Often, these provide an illusion of greater cultural development than has actually occurred. In fact, there is much jealousy of people who take on new ideas or "succeed to such an extent that they are surpassing their kin."[9] Individuals who rise above the level of the family group usually find it more comfortable to live elsewhere.

Excessive familism results in a limited range of community contacts and a low degree of integration into the community. Ordinarily, country schools have few community activities that serve as integrators for either children or adults. Church affiliations of these people are likely to be with dissident rather than with orthodox sects. The families who stay apart from the general stream of community events are the ones that remain in the old folk traditions.

Their way of looking at life puts a rather indifferent value on formal education.[10] In fact, the ideas, facts, and habits learned in school may be regarded as detrimental to the values that the family has made an effort to incul-

[9]James S. Brown, *The Family Group in a Kentucky Mountain Farming Community* (Kentucky Agr. Expt. Sta. Bull. 598; Lexington 1952), p. 33.

[10]M. Taylor Matthews, *Experience Worlds of Mountain People* (Columbia University Contributions to Education No. 700; New York, 1936).

cate. The youth who learns too much may no longer be satisfied to work hard with poor equipment and to live meagerly. Another avenue out of the subsistence way of life then is through the school system. Parents may either open up this avenue or block it, depending on the extent to which they have any vision outside their round of life.

Although the thinking of these people is limited in terms of financial promotion and economic endeavor, it is deep so far as emotions, morals, and religion are concerned. Strong emotional attitudes in regard to morals and religion are central in their cultural complex and buttress them against the desire for wealth, ostentation, and social position. Their thinking on most matters is emotional rather than coldly calculated. Their emotions flare quickly and may involve them in brawls, feuds, romantic irregularities, and more serious offenses.

The mixture of highly moralistic thinking with direct and violent individual action makes them rather uncertain citizens.

Economic Adjustment

The basic values of these people have been presented in more detail than their present cultural situation warrants. A gradual shift away from the tools and devices of a subsistence economy and toward those of a commercial economy has taken place at varying rates among them. These changes are bringing about a slow shift in life values. The important point is that these people now are moving between two cultures which are oriented as a whole in entirely different directions. Each culture constitutes a way of life from the cradle to the grave, but they move along different roads

toward different ends. Acculturation of any group of people is a difficult process.[11]

Adjustment of these people into commercial agriculture in the local area offers only limited possibilities.[12] Commercial agriculture is highly competitive, and few types of agricultural enterprise in marginal areas can compete successfully with farms in the more fertile parts of the country. In fact, many farmers will have to leave these marginal areas in order to permit farm holdings to attain a size that can be operated competitively. Also, the cultural adjustment that these people must make to become efficient commercial farmers is very great. Extension programs only reach them selectively after they have gained some educational background. It would be simpler to assist these families into a carefully designed program of live-at-home farming and to encourage them to add some nonfarm work and a small amount of specialized commercial production to permit them to meet their cash needs.

Fortunately, local industries have sprung up in the low-income areas and have eased the adjustment problem.[13] A

[11]For a review of the role of culture see Howard W. Odum, "Folk Sociology as a Subject Field for the Historical Study of Total Human Society and the Empirical Study of Group Behavior," *Social Forces*, XXXI (1953); also Ruth Benedict, *Patterns of Culture* (New York: Houghton Mifflin, 1934).

[12]Roger J. Woodworth, "Solution of the Problem of Low Income in the South: Farm Reorganization," *Journal of Farm Economics*, XXXIX (1957).

[13]Paul Mehl, *Major Manufacturing Industries as Potential Sources of Employment in Low Income Farm Areas* (U.S. Department of Agriculture, Agricultural Marketing Service, No. 176; April, 1957).

For limitations on local industrialization as a solution, see Rufus B. Hughes, Jr., "Solution of the Problem of Low Income in the South: Industrialization," *Journal of Farm Economics*, XXXIX (1957); also Vernon W. Ruttan, "The Potential in Rural Industrialization and Local Eco-

1956 study in the Arkansas Ozarks indicated that only 18 per cent of the open-country households gained all their livelihood from agriculture. Sawmilling, poultry processing, canning, and other lines of nonfarm work afforded employment to some member of almost half the families in the area (48 per cent). Social Security, other retirement payments, and similar nonwork sources of income were also a more important source of cash income than agriculture.

The exodus of surplus manpower from the Ozark area has permitted local agricultural adjustments that had been held back by too-small holdings. Farms in the Ozarks of Arkansas have increased in size by one-third since 1939, investment per farm has tripled, and there has been a shift from subsistence farming to dairying, livestock farming, and broiler production. Commercial-minded farmers who are moving in are creating a new spirit of enterprise and business. Average income per farm in constant dollars has tripled. In 1956 farmers in the area complained of a shortage of labor to perform tasks on their farms. There still are a number of subsistence farmers there, but most of them have either left the area or shifted to local nonfarm employment.

Surveys made in low-income areas in the Southeast indicate that the under-employed there are interested primarily in nonfarm employment and not in agriculture.[14] In fact, nonfarm op-portunities are not developing fast enough for these people. In local areas around defense and other major installations, farm people have quit full-time farming so rapidly that the only persons left are the women, children, aged, and infirm.

The major manpower adjustment, however, has involved movement away from hill areas to urban industrial centers. This still is the case despite the tendency of industry to decentralize. Adjustment has proceeded largely through natural social and economic processes.[15] As individuals have become aware of greater economic opportunity elsewhere, they have learned through trial and error where to go and how to obtain employment.

The extent to which this avenue of adjustment has been open has varied. During the 1930's, hill farmers erected numerous small cabins on their over-crowded farms. Their own houses were too small, and it was only fitting that their sons and daughters, when they married, should have houses of their own. The manpower calls that accompanied World War II were the most welcome type of relief they had ever received.

The spring of 1958 saw another movement of families from industrial centers back to rural areas in the southern states. This movement serves to remind us that the heavy demand for additional manpower in industry may

nomic Development," a paper presented to North Central Farm Management Committee Conference on Adjusting Commercial Agriculture to Economic Growth, Chicago, Mar. 1957; and Sheridan Maitland and James Cowhig, "Studies of the Effects of Industrialization in Rural Areas: Some Preliminary Findings," a paper presented at the annual meeting of the Rural Sociological Society, Pullman, Wash., Aug., 1958.

[14]W. F. Porter and W. H. Metzler, *Availability for Employment of Rural People in the Upper*

Monongahela Valley, West Virginia (West Virginia Univ. Agr. Expt. Sta. Bull. 391; Morgantown, 1956); William H. Metzler and J. L. Charlton, *Employment and Underemployment of Rural People in the Ozarks* (Arkansas Agr. Expt. Sta., Bull. 604; Fayetteville, 1958).

[15]Lowry Nelson, "Rural Life in a Mass-industrial Society," *Rural Sociology*, XXII (1957); also William H. Metzler, *Population Trends and Adjustments in Arkansas* (Arkansas Agr. Expt. Sta. Bul. 388; Fayetteville, 1940).

not be the normal situation in our economy. It may have been that World War II, foreign aid, national defense, and a backlog of demand following the war created a temporary opportunity for hill-country workers to adjust into the industrial economy.

In recent months, many of the sawmills in the Ozark and Appalachian areas have closed because of lack of demand for lumber and other construction materials. In case of economic trouble, small local industries are usually the first to close. Until we discover a formula for smooth and continuous economic growth, adjustment of manpower from agriculture into industry either locally or in urban centers is likely to be sporadic and uncertain.

Urban Adjustment

Data in regard to the urban adjustment of these people is still fragmentary.[16] Apparently, their occupational adjustment in the cities presents fewer immediate problems than adjustment into commercial farming in the local area. Their lack of technical and managerial background is no handicap when they take a highly routine or specialized job. They are likely, however, to be irked at having to follow instructions or at the regularity of their work. They may quit and be reem-

[16]Lack of adjustability of southern whites in Indianapolis is analyzed by Eldon D. Smith in an unpublished Ph.D. thesis. This is summarized briefly in Eldon D. Smith, "Nonfarm Employment Information of Rural People," *Journal of Farm Economics*, XXXVIII (1956). Numerous recent magazine articles point to difficulty in adjusting the southern mountain white in Chicago, Detroit, Cleveland, Cincinnati, and other northern cities. Less difficulty of adjustment is reported in small cities in the South. See Clopper Almon Jr., "Origins and Relation to Agriculture of Industrial Workers in Kingsport, Tennessee," *Journal of Farm Economics*, XXXVIII (1956).

ployed a number of times before they locate a situation that is tolerable. If they become so maladjusted that they return to the hills, their stay in the empty quietness of the country is likely to be a short one.

The impersonal relationships in the city provide these people with a freedom to follow their own devices that they did not have in the small community. Other members of the family are likely to join them, and eventually they discover other people with backgrounds similar to their own. They gradually establish "cultural islands" which enable them to slow down the pace of social adjustment.

On the other hand, they learn to avoid contacts that are distasteful, and strong lines of social difference may develop. In some neighborhoods, these once-friendly folk may go so far as to say, "We have nothing to do with our neighbors and they don't bother us. That keeps everybody out of trouble."

Yet these are the more superficial aspects of adjustment. These people are not likely to make a complete adjustment in the city. They are not likely to participate actively in such matters as elections, direction of school policies, civic improvement campaigns, or other civic activities.[17] They are likely to remain too uninformed about community responsibilities to be able to function constructively. When they do participate, it is likely to be because of some emotional excitement, and it may be in a wholly undesirable direction. Their tendency to take the law into their own hands is not easily eradicated. The city then has simply inherited the problem of how to make these family-

[17]Roscoe Giffin, "From Cinder Hollow to Cincinnati," *Mountain Life and Work* (Fall, 1956), Berea, Ky.

minded individualists into community-minded participants in the life of the group as a whole. The cities have better tools to work with in the form of better schools, playgrounds, and group activities.[18] But the cities also have better-organized groups of socially unadjusted people who can draw other unadjusted people to them. Any large concentration of these people in our big cities is potentially dangerous until we find ways of substituting rational principles of behavior in place of their traditions of direct action.

Aids to the social adjustment of these people in the cities would include: (1) schools to assume complete responsibility for creating a desire in the children for an education; (2) special guidance programs for youth in how to adjust to urban life and occupations; (3) special churches attuned to their emotional needs but also giving guidance in urban adjustment; and (4) an opportunity to acquire their own homes, so as to develop stability and responsibility.

The adjustment problem in the hill country falls most heavily on youths who have too little to do and who develop attitudes of frustration because of limited opportunities. Now the need for special programs to occupy the time and interests of youth is being transferred to our urban centers.

The binding force of family tradition gradually loses its power when the hill family moves to the city. The close contacts between parent and child are replaced for the child by numerous contacts with youths having different cultural backgrounds. As the old values lose their force, new ones will replace them. If the schools and other community agencies perform their social function, the children from hill families can become soundly adjusted citizens in their new society. If these agencies fail, social maladjustments may multiply indefinitely. Manpower adjustments are coming about automatically, but they are bringing in their wake social maladjustments that do not take care of themselves.

The urgent social problem facing us, then, is not out in the open country. Hill people are slowly building a sound way of life from live-at-home and commercial agriculture plus nonfarm employment. The problem is to reconstruct life values among urban newcomers so that an integrated community life can be maintained in our cities. This reconstruction calls for special programs and methods.

[18]Roscoe Giffin and the staff of the Major's Friendly Relations Committee, *The Southern Mountaineer in Cincinnati* (Cincinnati, O.: 1954); also Ward F. Porter, "The New Urbanites Challenge to Education," unpublished manuscript, 1957.

NO HARVEST FOR THE REAPER:

The Story of the Migratory Agricultural Worker in the United States

Herbert Hill

Mid-Twentieth Century America is an amazingly prosperous land—indeed, the wealthiest nation in the world. In these United States we have proportionately more natural resources, more automobiles, more superhighways on which to drive our automobiles, more refrigerators, more television sets and radios, than does any other country, anywhere.

Yet in the midst of this plenty are two million people comparable in their destitution to feudal serfs, save that they are bound to no land. Their mobility is in many ways their tragedy. For these people must roam ceaselessly, often having no single place to call home. In their wanderings over the face of our country, these nomads hope mainly to stave off starvation for themselves and their children. But their hopes also dwell on a decent home, good schooling for their children, a pleasant journey from one work place to another, as do the hopes of most citizens. Dare they hope for these things, when they must live in abandoned farm houses, shacks, chicken coops, tents, or dilapidated

Reprinted, with permission of author and the National Association for the Advancement of Colored People.

barns, when their children often receive no education at all and must work long hours if the family is to survive?

Who are these people who are so poor and so desperate? They are the American migratory farm workers, and the conditions under which they live and work do not belong in any enlightened nation. Of the estimated some two million, over one-third are native-born Americans, the majority of whom are Negroes. Another one-third are citizens of foreign nations who are brought here to work and then return to their own countries. The remainder are Mexicans who enter the United States illegally to engage in farm labor; these are known as "wetbacks," since they literally wade or swim across the Rio Grande River to enter the United States.

Unfortunately, the general public remains largely ignorant of, or indifferent to, this serious and complicated national problem. Former Senator Frank Graham of North Carolina recently observed that:

"Migrant workers and their children are the most rootless, homeless, churchless, defenseless, and hopeless people of our country. The local communities, the state and nation, churches, schools, health and social agencies all have a responsibility."[1]

And here are the words of migratory farm workers, testifying before a federal commission on migratory labor:

Question: Can you estimate how much work you get ... in a year?
Answer: I think that I work around six or seven months in the whole year.
Question: How much do you make?
Answer: In the whole year we make — well, not over seven hundred dollars.

✳ ✳ ✳

Question: What kind of work were you doing for forty cents an hour?
Answer: Irrigating, and also thinning beets. Once in a while I would drive a tractor.... I have never refused work of any type regardless of wages.
Question: About how much work have you had in the past?
Answer: I worked six, seven months out of the year.

✳ ✳ ✳

Question: Have you got any other suggestions that you want to make?
Answer: Well ... I think a fellow ought to be able to make enough money in order ... that he could school his children ... without having to work them sometime and keep them out of school.[2]

Migratory labor is today employed principally in the harvesting and processing of a great variety of fruits, such as berries, melons, apples, oranges and other citrus products, most vegetables including potatoes, beans, lettuce, cel-

ery, tomatoes and sugar beets; is frequently used for picking cotton, but is seldom employed on dairy farms, livestock farms, poultry farms, or diversified general farms.

The President's Commission on Migratory Labor which was established by executive order in 1950, conducted what is perhaps the most exhaustive and significant study ever made of this national problem. It submitted a historic report to the White House on March 26, 1951 with many recommendations and proposals which have been almost completely ignored by Federal agencies and the state governments up to the present time. The Commission's analysis and conclusions, for the most part, remain completely valid today.

The President's Commission in its report estimated that migratory farm workers are seven per cent of the nation's farm manpower, although they are called upon to perform less than five per cent of the man-day's of work. The Commission drew this conclusion:

> "... migratory farm labor cannot be dismissed as having little significance ... in addition to the human problems involved, the system of migrant labor has implications for our economy and for our culture which we should no longer neglect...."[3]

Since the turn of the century, agriculture in the United States has undergone tremendous changes, as has the status of farm labor. The current development is toward huge "corporation" farms, in contrast to the family farms of a half-century ago. (A "corporation" farm is a big business, and is run like a big business.) Large farms now cover one-third of the land in the United States as a whole and two-thirds of the land in the

[1]Address by Frank P. Graham at the National Sharecroppers Fund Conference, New York City, November 13, 1957.
[2]*Migratory Labor in American Agriculture,* Report of the President's Commission on Migratory Labor, 1951.

[3]Ibid.

western states; a large farm is classified by the census as five thousand or more acres in the West, and one thousand or more acres in the remainder of the country.

Agriculture is rapidly becoming "a factory in the field." In California, citrus fruit is a billion dollar industry, employing a half million wage earners, selling $3 billion worth of products and paying over $500 million in wages. In its packing plants are 130,000 men and women, working on highly mechanized, and in many instances, automated equipment. Even the 400,000 field hands increasingly work with machinery. In lettuce and asparagus harvesting, conveyor belts are used for assembling and packing. The firms that own land include some of the nation's biggest industrial corporations. Standard Oil and Southern Pacific Railroad together own 123,492 acres. The Kern Land Company owns 231,000 acres. In San Joaquin Valley alone thirty corporations own more than 5,000 acres each. A similar development towards industrialized agriculture is rapidly taking place in most other states.

In the past decade the system of cotton land tenancy in the South has greatly diminished. With the virtual collapse of "King Cotton" in the five southeastern states, which in the past supplied a major part of cotton for the United States and the world cotton market, thousands of sharecroppers and agricultural day workers were dispossessed from the land; these people have been uprooted from their homes and work and now they swell the migratory labor stream especially along the Atlantic Seaboard where the majority of these workers are Negroes.

Despite the deplorable conditions under which they are forced to live, the uncertainty of work, and the lack of any normal relationship with an employer and with society, migratory farm workers are productive workers and are absolutely vital to the agricultural economy of many states and the entire nation.

There are now six major streams of migratory farm workers in the United States:

1. Migrants, most of whom are Negroes, who start in Florida and move North along the Atlantic seaboard through Georgia, the Carolinas and Virginia into Maryland, Delaware, New Jersey, New York and Pennsylvania, working in a wide variety of harvesting and food processing operations.

2. Migrants, almost all of whom are Mexican-Americans, who start in Texas and go into the North Central and Mountain States, working mainly in the sugar-beet harvest and also picking vegetables and fruits.

3. Migrants, most of whom are of Mexican descent, who start in Texas and go North to Montana and North Dakota, working in the wheat and small-grain harvests.

4. Migrants, most of whom are Mexican-Americans and Negroes, who start in Texas and then divide into two groups, with one group moving to the Mississippi Delta and the other group moving westward to New Mexico, Arizona and southern California, working in cotton.

5. Migrants, usually whites of early American stock, who start in Oklahoma, Arkansas and western Tennessee, and move North and West, working in fruit and tomatoes.

6. Migrants, of all backgrounds, who work up and down the Pacific Coast, harvesting and processing various fruits and vegetables.

Would these migratory workers be better off were they able to find farm work in one locality and stay there? The

President's Commission on Migratory Labor thought not. It stated:

> "In summing up this comparison of employment and earnings for migratory and non-migratory workers, the similarities are more obvious than the differences. Both are under-employed. In both cases, women and youth are drawn extensively into employment.... Earnings per day are below prevailing standards.... This analysis of the employment and earnings of migratory and non-migratory farm labor suggests that for the migrant to settle down as a non-migratory farm laborer will not help him much financially."

Statistically, about half the migrant workers are women — most of them mothers. The President's Commission found that in the migratory labor force there are as many males fourteen years through seventeen years as there are eighteen years through twenty-four years; altogether, there are as many males under eighteen years as there are forty-five years and older.

Governmental Neglect

As is evident, American Government has neglected the migratory farm labor problem at all levels: Federal, state and county. The United States Farm Placement Service shrugs off responsibility for the working and living conditions of migrant laborers although placing these workers in harvesting and food processing jobs at the request of employers. The Farm Placement Service also uses labor contractors and crew leaders in its recruiting activities, despite the record of these notorious middlemen, and generally appears mainly interested in meeting the labor demands of growers, no matter what the effect may be on the workers. Other branches of the Federal Government are responsible for the foreign contract labor system, and for the poor enforcement of immigration laws which enables thousands of Mexicans — "wetbacks" — to enter the United States illegally. Remiss as it has been in relation to the "wetbacks," the Federal Government has taken more action to relieve that problem than it has toward solving other aspects of the farm labor question.

With the exception of three states migratory agricultural workers are not covered by workmen's compensation laws. This exclusion is significant because farming has the third highest fatality rate of any industry in the United States, exceeded only by mining and construction. During 1956 the total number of men, women and children killed in agricultural work exceeded that of any other industry.

Farm labor is totally excluded from Federal minimum wage and maximum hours legislation. U.S Department of Labor statistics indicate that the average farm worker's hourly pay is sixty-eight cents, as compared to $2.79 an hour for the construction industry or even $1.05 an hour for laundry workers who are among the lowest paid of all non-agricultural occupational groups in the United States.

Farm workers are now supposed to receive certain benefits of the Social Security system. But most employers throughout the country simply ignore the law.

Investigations made by the NAACP along the Atlantic Seaboard and on the West Coast have repeatedly disclosed the widespread illegal employment of children for farm labor. It is all too evident that Federal and state child labor laws are inadequately enforced.

U. S. Secretary of Labor James P. Mitchell recently acknowledged this and stated that: "Agriculture violates the child labor provision more than any other industry."

Farm labor is excluded from all benefits of unemployment insurance coverage, as well as most other protective and labor legislation.

H. L. Mitchell, president of the poor and struggling National Agricultural Workers Union, recently stated that "No law protects the right of farm workers to organize into unions and bargain with their employers. The result is that less than one per cent have ever been members of a union. Up to this point organized labor's concern has been expressed mainly in the adoption of resolutions of sympathy for their plight."

The annual average wage of all farm workers in the United States in 1957 was $892 earned on jobs on and off the farm. The annual wage was $728 for farm work alone. Farm workers were employed an average of 125 days on agricultural labor and 19 days in other types of employment. Measured in terms of real wages their pay was $4.91 per day.

Of the two million migratory workers employed in agriculture, 700,000 worked 150 days or more for the same employer. Over 1,200,000 workers were employed on the larger farms, many of them controlled by powerful corporate interests. Migratory farm labor is so essential to the nation's farming and food processing industry that in addition to recruiting migratory labor in the South and Southwest, through state employment services and private labor contractors, the Federal Government enters into contractual labor agreements with Mexico, the British West Indies, Japan and the Philippines and Puerto Rico.

A member of Congress from a southwestern state described this contract labor system as follows: "100 years ago we owned slaves—today we just lease them."

Municipalities generally are indifferent to the condition of migrant labor camps in their areas, usually choosing to do nothing. Often local residents show a distinct animosity toward Negro farm laborers whenever such workers appear on the village streets. On too many occasions local police have made these workers the victims of police brutality. Illegal search and seizure, detention by police for long periods without arraignment and other violations of due process are often experienced by migratory farm workers throughout the United States.

The NAACP in cooperation with a small number of other groups has been instrumental in securing the passage of remedial state legislation but often even these limited laws are inadequately enforced. Pennsylvania, New Jersey and New York, all heavy users of migratory farm labor, have recently enacted regulatory statutes. Typical is New York State which now has a substantial body of law relating to the use of migratory farm labor in that State. Among the most important of these statutes are:

1. Licensing of labor contractors.
2. A requirement to maintain payroll records and to issue a wage statement indicating monies earned and deductions from wages.
3. Certification of migrant labor camps by the State Health Department.
4. Prohibition of child labor during the non-school period.
5. Licensing of camp commissaries.
6. Revocation of growers' reg-

istration, authorizing the Industrial Commissioner to prohibit the use of migratory farm labor by a farmer or labor contractor who misrepresents conditions of employment.

But recent NAACP investigations have uncovered widespread violations of these and similar laws, in the rural areas of New York State and elsewhere.

The Journey

For most Americans, reaching one's job by a reasonably convenient means of transportation is no problem. For the migratory farm worker, reaching his job may be agony. When he arrives at his destination, he may be so ill from the hardships of the journey that he cannot stand, but has to be carried from the vehicle. This is because migrant workers are hauled long distances in trucks — not through their free choice, but because very often their employer's labor contractor requires such haulage as a condition of employment. Often, too, migrants cannot afford to travel by public carrier, although they are forced to pay a fee for being hauled by truck.

A New York newspaper reporter in 1953, made this observation:

"In the early days of the summer you can stand along the edge of the main highways leading North out of Florida and Georgia and watch the migrant workers on their way to northern fields, packed like animals on the way to market.

"Crowded in trucks equipped with crude benches or orange crates for seats, men, women and children roll through the Carolinas and Virginia, sharing their common misery and exhaustion. Sometimes they stop for a hamburger and a Coke.

Mostly they just keep rolling along.

"The Federal government has established rules for the shipment of cattle. Every so many miles they must be taken from the trucks, allowed to stretch their muscles, drink and eat. If it's hot weather, they must be hosed down with water.

"Migrant workers have no such protection. They just keep rolling along."[4]

Some of the migrants have told of their experience. These were hauled from Texas to Minnesota.

"It rained on us, and we stayed wet for two days."

"We had to travel sitting on a board for three days and nights. I had the baby on my lap the whole way."

"The same driver drove all the way from Texas with no one to spell him. I can't see why he didn't fall asleep and kill us all."

"They treat cattle better. My back aches when I think of it."

"My name is Manuel Martinez. I was one of forty-two people on that truck — me and my wife and three children. The women and children took turns sitting on the planks on each side. The first night, Chuck the Boss drove right through with no stop. I banged on the cab and begged him to stop for the sake of the kids. He yelled, 'Sit down — how are we going to get the beets if we don't get a move on.'"

"When the truck finally reached Minnesota . . . only a few could jump out without help. . . . Some were sick and fell to the ground."[5]

[4]Allan Keller, Series on Migratory Labor, New York *World Telegram and Sun*, week of September 8, 1953.
[5]"Out of Their Poverty" by Joyce L. Kornbluh and Hyman H. Bookbinder.

Trucks used to transport migrant farm workers generally are ancient and unsafe, without any real seats and very much overcrowded. Entire families, including infants and small children, are hauled in this manner for days and nights, with few rest stops or provisions for eating. On many such trips, no rest stops are made for thirty-six hours or more. Numerous accidents have happened which would not have occurred had the truck been in proper mechanical repair. Breakdowns due to mechanical failure can lead to even further misery on the part of the passengers.

On June 6, 1957, farm workers en route through North Carolina for work in Pennsylvania and New York were in an accident in which twenty were killed and others seriously injured. Fatalities and injuries as a result of accidents on the road occur very frequently each spring and summer when the migratory farm workers are moving through the countryside and along the highways.

A *New York Times* editorial on June 10, 1959 headlined "Migrant Workers' Tragedy" stated:

> "The highway smash-up in Arizona that took the lives of sixteen migratory farm workers from Mexico and injured thirty-two others, some critically, seems an unmitigated tragedy.
> "... The 'bus' in which the Mexicans were riding was a medium-sized truck, with canvas sides and no windows, and its only exit, in the rear, was blocked by baggage and a water barrel. Those killed were asleep on the floor or trapped near the front of the bus. The driver had dozed off at the wheel. Evidently the most obvious requirements of safety, both as to the vehicle itself and its operation, were flouted. ..."

The Governor's Committee on Migratory Labor reported the following incident in Pennsylvania in 1958:

> "One morning in York County, the State Police came upon a disabled truck carrying thirty-two migrants en route to Utica, New York from Florida.... The truck was stopped by the roadside with two flat tires. The group had no money to buy tire replacements, and had been for two days without food."[6]

Many food growers have made strenuous efforts to try to block any improvements in the transport of migrants. In May, 1957, the Interstate Commerce Commission held a hearing to consider establishing safety regulations governing the interstate transportation of farm workers. S. H. Butler of the Green Giant Company, Dayton, Wisconsin, testified as follows:

> "We feel that the requirement banning travel from 8:00 p.m. to 6:00 a.m. would work a hardship on the laborers being transported as well as upon employers. It has been our experience that these trucks can complete the trip from Texas to Wisconsin in from fifty to sixty hours, with stops only for meals, gasoline, and general stretching...."[7]

At the same hearing, the Tri-State Packers Association, Inc., of Easton, Maryland, expressed its dislike of a proposal that trucks carrying farm workers be required to have seats. The Packers Association:

[6]Final Report, 1958, Pennsylvania Migratory Labor Program, Harrisburg, Pennsylvania, January, 1959.
[7]"The Forgotten People" by Paul Jacobs, *The Reporter* Magazine, January 22, 1959.

"The floors of the truck in which the persons are transported are normally covered with bedding or sacks of clothing which provide a more suitable resting place than would seats of the type suggested by the Commission. The requirement that seats be provided appears to be extremely undesirable. . . . In addition, these trucks are used to haul produce to the processor; it would be practically impossible to attach the seats securely and still use the vehicle to haul produce."[8]

Journey's End — The Dwelling Place

Migrant labor camps, where workers are housed while employed, generally consist of every type of structure imaginable, except decent housing. The NAACP has made numerous investigations of migrant labor camps in many states over a period of years. Migratory workers have been found living in dilapidated barns, chicken coops, old shacks, barracks, machine storage sheds, and pigpens. Fifteen to twenty persons may share a tiny cabin or a small room; frequently there are no windows, no heat, and no indoor cooking facilities.

Investigations have uncovered camps in which the entire sanitary facilities consist of one outside privy with no door; no running water, no electricity, no beds or old springs with no mattresses, badly leaking roofs, no screening, no refrigeration and on one occasion outdoor privies draining toward a water pump.

In one Pennsylvania migrant labor camp investigated in 1952 the NAACP labor secretary discovered five hundred inhabitants with one privy and one

[8]Ibid.

shower; in this camp, men, women and children lived together in a group of dilapidated barns and in an abandoned farmhouse, with approximately fifteen persons in each small room. In another Pennsylvania camp inspected by the Association there was no running water, no privy, no washing facility of any kind.

In a New York State camp investigated in 1958, the NAACP representative found the housing to consist of a series of attached tar-paper and clapboard shacks; inside, serving as beds, were double rows of wooden planks upon which straw had been placed. Similar sleeping facilities are usually found in migrant labor camps throughout the country.

Many camps have no facilities for the removal of garbage, so that filth is strewn around the area, creating a public health menace.

In Pennsylvania in 1958, state government representatives found "a migrant crew of fifty men, women and children from Florida . . . living in dilapidated railroad boxcars."[9]

But, such facilities are not given gratis; the workers must pay for this "housing." Therefore, a sum for "room rent" is inevitably deducted from each worker's paycheck.

Frequently, migratory workers must live in this employer-owned housing as a condition of employment. If such is not the case, migrants often do not have the money to move elsewhere — even were decent housing available within walking distance of the job.

A California newspaper described the conditions in some of that State's migrant camps in these words:

[9]"Out of Their Poverty" by Joyce L. Kornbluh and Hyman H. Bookbinder.

"Longest slum in the world...village conditions in Pakistan no worse than some of the California camps...migratory families living under conditions similar to refugees in Seoul (Korea)."[10]

In New Jersey, at a meeting described by Newark newspapers as the "rowdiest public hearing in years," four hundred farm owners loudly booed the suggestion that they provide blankets, warm water and electricity for their hired farm workers.[11]

A New York reporter wrote of the migrant labor camps he inspected as follows:

"[The trucks] leave the main roads and bump along over dirt roads until they reach a group of cabins in rows or flimsy barracks or remodeled barns or shanties. Seldom are the labor camps for migrants out on the traveled highways.

"It's better to keep them out of sight. A man's conscience won't hurt him so much if he doesn't see these hovels where fellow Americans must live for twelve or fourteen weeks....

"In the yard outside are great stacks of rusty bed springs or rickety iron cots. It's first come first served, so the workers scramble to pick the best ones.

"Beside the bed springs are bales of straw, and each worker fills a ticking cover with enough straw to give his body ease after nine and ten hours in the fields harvesting what they call 'stoop crops.'

"The picture differs a little here and there. In some camps there are cinder block cubicles instead of shanties. In others there are mattresses, torn, dirty,

and as comfortable as a rock pile to sleep on. But all are alike in absence of running water in the cabins, in reliance on old-fashioned outdoor privies and in their general atmosphere of down-at-the-heels drabness.

"These quarters are provided by the farmer, the grower, or the farmer's cooperative association. But that is about the limit of his interest in most cases."[12]

This experience was recorded by a magazine writer:

"One day early last fall, I drove to Maple Lawn Farms, six miles east of Sunbury, Pennsylvania, where potatoes, tomatoes and beans are grown. Like most migrant camps, the one there was hidden at the end of a dirt road, out of sight from the main highway. (Others are stuck away in swamps, behind warehouses or close to dumping grounds.)

"About forty migrants, with twelve children, were living at the Maple Lawn Camp. Three large families were crammed into a converted chicken coop. The rest shared an unheated barn partitioned into tiny cubicles. One of the cubicles held five cots and an open kerosene stove. Mattress bags were stuffed with straw. Burlap was used for sheets and blankets.

"Outside, ragged children played in a garbage heap. A former cowstall equipped only with a rickety table and a Coke dispenser served as a 'recreation hall'. Doorless latrines with stopped-up plumbing fouled the air.

"At the chicken coop, I talked to a frail, sad-eyed young woman with an infant in her arms who had come up the pre-

[10]San Jose (California) *Mercury,* January 23, 1958.
[11]Newark (New Jersey) *Star Ledger,* January 7, 1959.

[12]Allan Keller, Series on Migratory Labor, New York *World Telegram and Sun,* week of September 8, 1953.

ceding July from Gardenville, Florida.

" 'We've got no lights here', she said tonelessly. 'Electricity is off. We've got no water in the washroom. We all use a pump in the yard.... Why don't we move? Mister, we haven't any money to go nowhere.' "[15]

Several investigations and studies have made clear that the United States Government assumes no responsibility regarding the conditions of work—including housing—for which it is recruiting, either at the Federal or the state level. The following testimony was given before a Federal Commission of Inquiry by the State Supervisor of the Farm Placement Service in Florida:

Question: You say the employment service tries to make sure that there is housing for these people? How do you make sure that there is housing? What do you do?

Answer: That varies greatly. Where it is possible, we inspect....

Question: Of course, you would have no authority if you found . . . any housing . . . to tell the grower, "You have got to fix this up so and so, and put these beds in," and so forth. Would you have such authority?

Answer: No, sir; none whatever....

Question: ... Could you not refuse to refer workers to that farm if, in your opinion, the housing was in bad shape?

Answer: That is right.

Question: Do you do that?

Answer: Yes.

Question: Do you have a standard of housing written up in some way on the basis of which you do that?

Answer: No; no, sir. In other words, it

must be a question of at least *reasonable protection against the weather. That* is about as far as we can go.[14]

And Then—Payday

Payday is just another frustration in the lives of most migratory farm workers. NAACP investigations have revealed that a common practice in many labor camps is to inform farm laborers after several weeks of work that they have earned no money or even that they are in debt because of deductions for food purchased in camp commissaries and for "room rent" and transportation. Under this guise, wages simply are withheld. If migrant families then attempt to leave the camp, they are warned that they cannot depart because of their "debts." Open intimidation and even threats of violence are commonplace at this point, to prevent the worker and his family from leaving the camp site.

An investigation by the NAACP labor secretary in 1958 revealed that the majority of the workers at the Frank Swiercznski labor camp on Route 104, Orleans County, New York, received only one or two dollars at the end of each week's work. Those who complained were informed that amounts had been deducted for transportation, "room rent," food, debts, and unspecified expenses. These workers did not receive payroll statements as required by New York State law, indicating monies earned for a given period and itemized deductions, nor had they been told that deductions would be made for transportation, living quarters, food, and so forth.

[13]"Our Miserable Million" by Theodore Irwin, *Coronet* Magazine, September, 1958.

[14]*Migratory Labor in American Agriculture,* Report of the President's Commission on Migratory Labor, 1951.

Another investigation by the NAACP in 1958 at the Oak Orchard Villa Camp in Genesee County, New York, disclosed that workers' wages were withheld for a three-week period, at the end of which time many workers were informed that they had earned nothing for the period because of deductions. Contrary to the usual situation, some fifteen workers managed to leave this camp and went wandering about the countryside without food or adequate clothing in a search for other employment.

A magazine writer who visited migrant labor camps in New York State reported the following episode:

"At a camp in upstate New York, a tall, emaciated man from Georgia showed me his pay slip for the previous week. He had earned $16.20 picking beans. But $14.40 had been deducted for groceries, rent and transportation, leaving him a net of $1.80."[15]

The fact that the migratory worker is sometimes furnished "housing" and transportation—by his employer, is of little benefit to the worker. The President's Commission on Migratory Labor took note of these matters as follows:

"Farm workers, it is true, have an additional source of income in the perquisites furnished by the employers—usually housing and transportation.... The value of perquisites (transportation and housing) given to migratory workers was estimated by the United States Department of Agriculture to be an average of *thirty-six cents a day*. For the one hundred and

one days of employment per year of the average migratory worker, this would amount to thirty-six dollars."

Migrant workers' wages often are piece rates based on such units as hampers or boxes, or else on such units as acres or thousands of plants. Sometimes, wages are paid by the hour rather than by the piece. It is not at all uncommon for wages to be changed at the whim of the employer. That is, when conditions are favorable for a higher yield, the piece rate may be lowered.

The direct result of extremely low wages and comparatively few days per year when work is available is family work; housewives, young children, and youths must work very long hours for the family to barely survive.

The farmers, large growers and the food processing and packing corporations are responsible for these pitiful wage rates and working conditions, and they have repeatedly indicated their determination that there shall be no minimum wage legislation for agricultural workers.

During the 1947-57 inflationary period, farm workers' wages remained consistently low while the factory workers' wages rose sharply. Specifically, farm workers' average annual wages rose only about $150, while the average yearly earnings of factory workers reached approximately $2,000. In 1958, the average annual earnings for all farm labor was estimated to be $892. This includes wages earned on farms and other employment.

A recent study of the annual earnings of migratory farm laborers who leave Mississippi each year for harvesting work in other states revealed "that 12 per cent of these migrant workers reported that they had no money at the

[15]"Our Miserable Million" by Theodore Irwin, *Coronet* Magazine, September, 1958.

termination of their work period elsewhere."

George T. Dowdy, Sr., Professor of Agricultural Economics, Tuskegee Institute, observed that "the seriousness of this is further aggravated by the fact that 60 per cent of all migratory workers included in this study received a gross annual per capita income of only $667; the remaining 40 per cent earned less than this amount."

Farm workers as a group lack steady work and have extremely low rates of pay and low annual earnings. Among all farm workers, however, migrants are the most exploited, the most marginal and desperate.

From "Cain't" to "Cain't"

To use such terms as working conditions and job standards in connection with migratory agricultural employment is meaningless, because there are no established standards as these terms are understood by factory workers. No limits exist in relation to the hours of work, the days of work, the exact type of work. The only factor of which a migrant farm worker can be absolutely certain is that his wages will be lower than those of other workers in all other occupations. In many localities, a day's work goes from "cain't" to "cain't"—from when you cannot see the sun in the morning until you can no longer see it in the evening.

A migrant worker never knows how many days he will be called upon to work in any particular week. If the weather is unfavorable, he will be left sitting in his shack, and there will be no pay for this period and he and his family will be incurring debts for food and "housing." Other times, he and his family may work seven days a week, sixteen hours a day.

Union Organization

These migratory men and women — and children — who labor in the fields have absolutely no voice in the conditions of their employment. The American Federation of Labor-Congress of Industrial Organizations has neglected the nation's agricultural workers, especially the migrants, although these people more than any other group of workers are urgently in need of union protection and benefits.

Not only has it neglected farm workers, but the American Federation of Labor has in at least one instance actually delivered them to their exploiters. This astonishing incident occurred in Louisiana in 1956. Incredibly, the Louisiana State AFL Labor Council openly supported Act 397 in the state legislature; Act 397 was a "right-to-work" law banning the "union shop" thereby making union organization extremely difficult if not impossible. But Act 397 applied only to agricultural labor, such as sugar-mill and processing workers, cotton-gin and compress employees, and those employed in rice-mill and related processing occupations. In return for its support of Act 397, the Louisiana State AFL Labor Council was awarded the repeal of a more inclusive "right-to-work" law also covering industrial workers which had been enacted in 1954.

So outrageous was this betrayal of agricultural workers in Louisiana, that two representatives of the small National Agricultural Workers Union (an AFL-CIO affiliate) appeared at a quarterly meeting of the AFL-CIO national executive council at Unity House, the summer resort of the International Ladies Garment Workers' Union in Pennsylvania, to protest this shameful "deal." H. L. Mitchell, president of the Union and Dr. Ernesto Galarza, the Union's Secretary-Treasurer, met with the AFL-CIO executive council in August, 1956. AFL-CIO President George Meany appointed a two-man subcommittee to hear the charges and to hear also the Louisiana Labor Council's defense of its behavior. The subcommittee was composed of Joe Curran, president, National Maritime Union, and Richard Walsh, president of the International Alliance of Theatrical, Stage Employees Union. The verdict: a recommendation that the AFL-CIO approve the action of the Louisiana State Labor Council. This approval was voted unanimously. Following the board meeting, President Meany described the Louisiana action as "economic expediency."[16] It is of course interesting to note that the victims of this "economic expediency" were mostly Negroes.

During its extensive investigation of migratory labor utilization, the President's Commission on Migratory Labor was able to discover only one work contract and two collective bargaining agreements covering domestic migrant farm workers.

The one contract was in use by the Blue Mountain Division (Pacific Northwest) of the Green Giant Company. A company representative testified before the Commission that the Blue Mountain Division offers a non-negotiated work contract which it terms an "Offer of Employment" to its migrant employees. Among other features, this contract states the approximate date on

which work will commence, the approximate period of the work, a guaranteed minimum wage of sixty dollars for each two-week period if the worker stays for the entire season, a set charge for board and room arrangements, a description of the housing arrangements, a provision of transportation via truck to the job, and an obligatory group medical insurance at a charge to the worker of seventy-five cents per week. Commenting upon the contract, the President's Commission stated:

> "The employment record which this type of personnel practice has produced is striking. The Texas-Mexicans under this contract turn out to be 'reliable' workers. Other migratory workers referred to as 'white' who work under the same conditions, live in the same housing, eat the same food, but who are not accorded a contract, are found to be 'unreliable. . . . The record of the Blue Mountain Division of the Green Giant Company indicates to us that when a company treats its workers as employees . . . workers respond as employees. . . ."

The two collective bargaining agreements encountered by the President's Commission existed between a local of the Meat and Cannery Workers (affiliated to Amalgamated Meat Cutters and Butcher Workmen of North America, AFL-CIO) and Seabrook Farms — a large grower-processor in New Jersey, and a local of the United Packinghouse Workers of America AFL-CIO and Fellsmere Sugar Producers Association — a cane-sugar producing and processing association in Florida. Concerning migrant labor, the Commission made this interesting observation:

> "In each of these instances . . . collective-bargaining coverage was limited, since the

[16]"The Labor Movement Cripples a Union" by Paul Jacobs, *The Reporter* Magazine, November 1, 1956.

bulk of the seasonal (migrant) field labor was not specifically covered by the agreement. Nevertheless, in both instances, provisions of the agreements afforded a measure of benefit to seasonal and migratory workers because some of the collective bargaining results were extended to them. Principal among these were rights of promotion from field to plant work and seniority in hiring and firing."

Although farm employers have resisted unionization bitterly, the two employers mentioned above commented favorably to the Commission upon their experiences of dealing with a union as the collective bargaining agent for their farm workers. Mr. Seabrook testified:

> "I don't think we have suffered any from it. We happen to be dealing . . . with quite respectable unions that have very reputable leadership, and we haven't been subjected to any wildcat strikes."

The Fellsmere Association representative told the Commission:

> "You have to admit that the union does perform a job for you that [the company] would have to employ people to do for you to maintain labor relations. It makes for more economical operations."

Agricultural workers in the United States are lagging far behind those in Europe from the standpoint of unionization. In Great Britain, Norway, Sweden, Denmark and Holland, one-half to four-fifths of the agricultural workers are members of trade unions, while in West Germany and Austria organizations of land workers have been revived. It must be recognized, however, that unioniza-

tion of migratory agricultural workers in America will be an extraordinarily difficult task because of the extreme mobility of the labor force.

No Help for the Sick

The health of migratory farm workers undoubtedly is the most seriously impaired of any group of people in the nation. Many migratory children suffer from chronic diarrhea, due to fatigue and infection. The lack of sanitary facilities in migrant labor camps presents a constant menace of an epidemic.

Migrants generally have no way of getting from the labor camp to a doctor or a hospital and, even if they were taken for medical care, they ordinarily could not pay for it. Because of residence requirements, migrants generally are not considered eligible for medical care through public welfare benefits. NAACP investigators have found countless migratory workers, of all ages, wandering through the camps with infected sores and other disorders in need of immediate medical treatment.

On February 5, 1959, Dr. Hector Garcia, chairman of the American G. I. Forum, Corpus Christi, Texas, told the National Advisory Committee on Farm Labor about the health and medical problems of farm workers and their families. Dr. Garcia stated:

> "The children of migrant parents are born into a world completely of their own. An anemic mother, and possibly a tubercular father—a life that will take him into his world where he may possibly die within one year, either from diarrhea, tuberculosis or malnutrition. His infancy would be a very close association with his brothers and sisters. Their home

would be [a] one- or two-room shack, with no inside running water and no flushing-toilet facilities. If he lives to be of school age, he could possibly go to many schools on different occasions at different places, but will never average more than three years of schooling in his life time.... His future life will be one of wandering, poverty and more sickness....

"As a migrant, his world will be from the Atlantic to the Pacific—from the Great Lakes to the Rio Grande. It will be his world, however, only in that the only piece of property that he will own will be his grave....

"I may be here because I am still haunted by that remembrance of a day ten years ago when the little boy came to my office to ask me to go and see his mother who was sick. I went to his home—a one-room shack. I found a dead mother with six children lying in the same bed, all covered with blood from the hemorrhage of a dying tubercular mother."

The National Consumers Committee for Research and Education sponsored a research demonstration project among migrant agricultural families in Marquette County, Wisconsin, in 1957. The project report notes:

"Medical care was arranged for such critical cases as a child subject to epileptic seizures, a tubercular father, a man who needed to have a diet for high blood pressure translated into Spanish, a deaf child needing institutional care."[17]

The President's Commission on Migratory Labor found that tuberculosis, infant mortality, maternal mortality,

[17]"Home is Where They Find It," National Consumers Committee for Research and Education, Inc., Cleveland, Ohio, February, 1958.

dysentery, enteritis, smallpox, typhoid, are all "much more prevalent among migratory workers than among the general population."

It is important to note that the diet of migratory farm laborers is not sufficient to maintain health. A physician testifying before the Commission stated:

"I can say from the reports of the the nurses that we do have dietary deficiency diseases ... and cases of that have come to my attention—due to a diet consisting of corn meal and perhaps rice and very little else. *There is also evidence of... ordinary starvation among many of these people....* A survey which I made and photographed in the Mathis, Texas, labor camps showed that ninety-six per cent of the children in that camp had not consumed any milk whatsoever in the last six months. It also showed that eight out of ten adults had not eaten any meat in the last six months.... The reason given was that they could not afford it with the money they were making."

A survey made about 1950 revealed that only about one-sixth of the state and local agencies providing free medical care to the destitute do so without residence requirements. No evidence has since come to light to indicate that this situation has since improved.

Under these circumstances, what can parents do when their baby is dangerously ill? Here is what happened to a migratory farm family in the San Joaquin Valley of California:

Inquest: "... The body is that of a well-developed, moderately emaciated white male infant—approximately four months old...."

Father's testimony: "On November 4th, he started vomiting but stopped and seemed better. About nine o'clock on Sunday, the 6th, he was very bad, and we started for the hospital. We took him to the Coalinga Hospital but we didn't have any money and they sent us to the General Hospital in Fresno. We are not familiar with this area and we stopped at the Wallace Sanatorium. We didn't have any money so they sent us on to the General Hospital. When we arrived they told us the baby was dead."[18]

A few states have made some limited effort to provide medical care for the destitute migrant farm workers, but the situation still is generally wretched. The States of Pennsylvania, New Jersey and New York each conduct a number of medical clinics, and some farm syndicates have begun to maintain clinics, but these are isolated and inadequate.

Excluded from Federal, State Labor and Welfare Laws

Although it is clear that migratory agricultural workers are more in need of the protection and benefits of welfare laws and labor legislation than any other group in our population, these workers are systematically excluded from state and federal welfare legislation — with the exception now of Federal Social Security. This exclusion works an enormous hardship on these workers and is an important factor in the harsh conditions under which migrants live. Usually where there is no specific exclusion of agricultural labor from welfare and labor statutes, the laws simply are not applied or enforced in regard to farm workers.

The following brief summary will illustrate how farm workers, including migrants, are excluded from the very welfare laws which they desperately need. The information given below was compiled from data issued by the Bureau of Labor Standards, U.S. Department of Labor.[19]

Minimum Wages. The wage and hour provisions of the Federal Fair Labor Standards Act do not cover agricultural workers. There are no state laws setting a minimum wage for farm workers as a group; seven states and the District of Columbia have general minimum wage laws covering women and minors only.

It is interesting to realize that Hawaii and Puerto Rico are ahead of the mainland in the matter of welfare laws covering farm workers: the minimum wage laws of Hawaii and Puerto Rico apply specifically to agricultural workers.

Labor-Managemnt Relations (Taft-Hartley) Act. This Federal labor relations law does not cover agricultural workers. Therefore, migrant farm workers cannot make use of the law's provisions for labor union organization and collective bargaining.

Unemployment Insurance. The unemployment insurance laws of every state except Hawaii specifically exclude agricultural labor. Hawaii, while still a territory, passed an agricultural unemployment insurance law.

Workmen's Compensation. (Workmen's compensation pays comparatively modest benefits to workers who are injured on the job; a large number of

[18]*Migratory Labor in American Agriculture,* Report of the President's Commission on Migratory Labor, 1951.

[19]*Status of Agricultural Workers Under State and Federal Labor Laws,* U.S. Department of Labor, Bureau of Labor Standards, Washington, May, 1958.

accidents and injuries occur in agricultural employment.)

Fourteen states have some coverage of agricultural workers, but in eight of these states only farm workers engaged in certain mechanical or power operations are covered. Only Connecticut, Ohio and Vermont cover farm workers in the same manner as others and *only in Ohio is the law compulsory.*

In all but a few states farmers may, if they wish, insure under the compensation law. But few farmers have chosen to protect their workers in this manner.

Wage Collection. In only twelve states are the laws broad enough to cover the claims of farm workers who wish to authorize the Commissioner of Labor to undertake the collection of back wages. In one other state—New York—the Department of Labor and Industry may hold hearings on claims for wages and may make decisions in certain controversies.

Temporary Disability Insurance. (Temporary disability insurance pays certain benefits to workers who have become temporarily disabled.) The four states which provide temporary disability benefits completely exempt agricultural workers.

Transportation of Farm Workers. A 1956 amendment to the Federal Interstate Commerce Act authorized the Interstate Commerce Commission to establish for certain motor carriers of migrant workers reasonable requirements with respect to the comfort of passengers, safety of operation and equipment, and qualifications and maximum hours of service of the operators of such vehicles. Such requirements now have been issued by the Commission; the requirements include regulations for rest stops, meal stops every six hours, the provision of seats with back rests, protection of the passengers from

cold, and so forth. The regulations apply to migrant carriers only if the vehicle travels a distance of more than seventy-five miles and if such transportation is across a state line.

Unfortunately, these highly desirable regulations have not been well enforced, and therefore, have not been particularly effective.

Regulation of Farm Labor Camps. About half of the states have laws or regulations that apply to all labor camps or to camps for migrant farm workers; these laws range from very limited regulation to rather comprehensive regulation covering sanitation, housing and camp location.

However, these laws are so little enforced as to be of little more use than if they never had been passed.

Social Security: Old Age and Survivors' Insurance. Under 1957 amendments to the Federal Social Security Law, a person employed on a farm or working in other types of agricultural enterprise earns social security credit for his work from each farm operator who pays him $150 or more in cash wages in a year. The amendments also provide that if an employee does farm work for an employer on twenty or more days during a year for cash pay figured on a time basis, such pay is covered by the Social Security Law.

However, at the conclusion of an extensive investigation during the summer of 1958 along the Atlantic Seaboard, the author reported to the Social Security Administration that actual coverage for migrant farm labor was "negligible."

Why should farm workers be excluded from those specific welfare laws that they especially need? The reason is that most state legislatures are dominated by powerful agricultural interests, and these same interests have a very strong influence in Congress. The pitifully few laws which have been passed for the protection of farm workers are violated constantly by farm employers who are penalized very lightly or not at all when such violations are exposed.

The National Sharecroppers Fund and the League for Industrial Democracy have given an excellent description of the political operations of the farm interests:

> "The big farm lobby is spearheaded by the American Farm Bureau Federation, a powerful organization controlled by the big farmers, although its membership includes many small farmers. The lobby includes the special crop and industry associations, and works closely with the National Association of Manufacturers.... It is well-financed and effective.
>
> "One of the lobby's most important activities is the prevention of legislation which would extend to farmers and farm workers the benefits of social welfare legislation...."[20]

Because of the grinding poverty in which migrant families are forced to live, mothers and children very often work in the fields along with the man of the family—to earn enough for survival. In 1956, for example, Federal investigators who inspected only a fraction of the nation's farms found some 4,200 children less than sixteen years of age working when they should have been in school.

Two Federal laws control the employment of children in agriculture. The Fair Labor Standards Act establishes a sixteen-year minimum age for agricultural employment *during* school hours. The Sugar Act specifies that

[20]*Down on the Farm: The Plight of Agricultural Labor,* New York, 1955.

producers are not to obtain maximum benefits if they employ children under fourteen years, or permit those of fourteen and fifteen years to work more than eight hours a day; this Act applies to the cultivation and harvesting of sugar beets or sugar cane.

Only six states and the District of Columbia expressly provide a minimum age for the employment of children in agriculture during non-school hours; this age varies from ten years in Utah to fourteen years in several other states. For agricultural work during school hours, a minimum age expressly applies in thirteen states and the District of Columbia; this age varies from fourteen to sixteen years.

A study made by the Bureau of Labor Standards of the Department of Labor notes that:

> "Compulsory school-attendance laws supplement the standards set under the child-labor laws by requiring boys and girls to attend school to a certain age, usually to sixteen. In many states, however, these laws permit children under sixteen, or even under fourteen, to be excused from school to work in agriculture.
>
> "The situation as it relates to migratory children is even more serious, since the school laws often do not apply to them, and travelling from state to state as they do, opportunities for school attendance are often very meagre."

NAACP investigations have shown that child-labor laws simply are not enforced in respect to the children of migratory farm workers; it is common to find children of seven, eight, nine and ten years working in the fields, especially along the Atlantic Seaboard during the height of the harvesting season.

An eight-year-old migrant boy, who

was taught to read and write at a special school for migrant children, told some of his experiences in this little essay:

"Get down on your knees. Then start picking beans. When you get two hampers full then you weigh them. After you weigh them you put them on the truck. But before you put the beans on the truck you must put them in a sack. You must pick beans all day. You go home when the man tells you."[21]

In 1957 many young children were found to be illegally employed as farm workers in California. That same year in California alone, 125 children under sixteen years of age were injured, some of them disabled permanently. Only one California farmer was prosecuted in 1957 for violating child labor laws.[22]

Because they often are working when they should be in school, migrant children have the lowest educational attainment of any group in the nation, according to the United States Office of Education, which has said of migratory children:

"They enter school later than other children, attend fewer days, make the least progress, drop out of school sooner and constitute the largest single source of illiterates.... Every year at least 600,000 [migrant] children are being denied the privileges of a public school education."

When these unschooled children become adults, they will not be equipped to do work which is any more satisfying or financially secure than that in which their parents are trapped. This

[21]"Sweatshops Under Blue Skies" by Sol Markoff, AFL-CIO American Federationist, October, 1957.

[22]Public Hearings, National Advisory Committee on Farm Labor, Washington, February 5, 1959.

is one of the most tragic aspects of the entire problem of migratory farm labor.

On February 6, 1959, Mildred Fairchild Woodbury, chairman of The National Child Labor Committee, presented the following report at the Public Hearings of the National Advisory Committee on Farm Labor:

"Although many states now have laws that protect children from harmful employment, most ignore children who work in commercial agriculture. Twenty states apparently would permit any child of any age to work in commercial agriculture. They have no laws that set a minimum age. Four of the five states that have set a minimum age of 14 permit children to work at an earlier age if they have the consent of their parents....

"Children who work in agriculture do not suffer from the harmful effects of the labor alone. Their whole way of life is deprived. They suffer from poverty, community rejection, inadequate housing and sanitary facilities, poor health, inadequate health services; lack of public services, etc. The one fact about them that is incontestable is that they don't have the opportunities educationally that our country has insisted on for its children. The United States Office of Education reports that migrant children have the highest degree of illiteracy of any group in our nation; they rarely go beyond elementary school. Nothing is done to help them occupationally—to give them the education, preparation, or special help they need to become productive working adults.

"The National Child Labor Committee recommends amendments of the Fair Labor Standards Act to give children in commercial agriculture the same protection it extends to others; minimum-wage coverage for farm workers; allocation of funds for enforcement of present legislation; extension of federal aid to education (including funds for vocational counseling and training); federal aid to depressed rural areas; and extension of desirable employment standards to all agricultural workers — social security, workmen's compensation, unemployment insurance, the rights of unionization and collective bargaining...."

When the mother of the family must work in the fields, infants and young children often are left in the camp during the day with no care or supervision. A New York newspaper reporter described some of his observations of this as follows:

"To feed the children the parents are virtually compelled to work in the fields. And what happens to the children?...I saw them locked in old jalopies to keep them out of harm.... Often there was no one to prepare a midday meal and the babies and little children go from breakfast to supper with nothing to eat....

"A social welfare worker told of finding four children whose mother was in a hospital. There was no food in the shabby cabin.

"'I spoke to the crew leader, and he didn't care,' said the county welfare official. 'I spoke to the farmer and he didn't care. I had a little food in my car and I gave it to the children.'"

The Crew Leader: A Key Figure

The labor contractor or crew leader may well be the most vicious figure in the entire system of migratory farm labor. He is responsible to no one, and his practices too frequently are utterly unscrupulous. Along the Atlantic Seaboard he usually is a trafficker in human misery for profit.

It is the labor contractor or crew leader who arranges for the worker and his family to be hauled in trucks under inhuman conditions, who deducts exorbitant amounts from the earnings of workers or withholds their wages altogether, who attempts to prevent dissatisfied workers from leaving the labor camp under his control and is often engaged in various rackets including prostitution and the sale of liquor. The farmer or grower almost always refuses to take responsibility for the conditions pertaining to his workers although the grower who thinks of himself as a respectable, law-abiding citizen directly benefits from the crew leader's control and discipline of the work force.

NAACP investigations during 1958 have shown that at several labor camps in New York State where state labor and health standards are enforced, the services of the crew leader or labor contractor have been dispensed with entirely; these investigations found that workers were employed directly by the operating companies at the Birdseye Corporation camp, the Quaker Maid Company camp, and the Russo Brothers Muck Farm.

A New York newspaper reporter described succinctly the workings of the vicious labor contractor-crew leader system:

"... quarters are provided by the farmer, the grower or the farmers' cooperative association. But that is the limit of his interest in most cases.

"The middle man is the leader, or labor contractor, and all too often he is the villain of the whole sad business.

"He makes a deal with the

growers to supply a certain number of workers and he rounds them up in the South, transports them North, and often collects the pay for them, doling it out later.

"Greedy for his own share, he usually delivers his workers to the farmer several weeks before the crops are ready for picking. This is one of the worst and most widely-accepted evils of the whole migrant picture.

"Day after day, week after week, the workers sit in their shacks, waiting to go into the fields and earning not a penny. Before they have picked their first bushel of beans or cherries or tomatoes they are in debt to the camp store, run by the crew leader or by someone he has licensed to operate it for him."[23]

A licensed labor contractor in California gave the following testimony before the President's Commission on Migratory Labor:

Question: Do you know what prices these [contractors'] commissaries charge, whether it is reasonable with what the merchants would charge in the village?

Answer: It invariably is unreasonable ... they charge a man two dollars [or] two dollars and a quarter a day for room and board.... That board is really terrible. I mean they really rob them.

[The labor contractor] is in a position to sway the general equilibrium of honesty in any direction he wants.... There are many contractors and solicitors who have camps.... They supply the food, the women, the narcotics—in which there is a heavy traffic within these camps—and beer

and wine and everything else, so they subsequently end up with a large proportion of the payroll.

The same President's Commission indicated deep dissatisfaction with the entire system of labor contractors and crew leaders in migratory farm labor. The Commission asserted:

"The labor contractor system is essentially a means by which the employer of migratory farm workers avoids the responsibilities of obtaining and managing his labor. It is a system in which abuses may flourish.... To the extent that a crew leader or labor contractor recruits labor, he is an employment agent. In this activity are to be found ... malpractices ... such as the misrepresentation of work opportunities, the charging of excessive fees, and sending workers to places where there are no jobs.

"For his services as an employment intermediary, whether as a supplier or as a supervisor of employment, the contractor or crew leader may exact a heavy financial toll....

"The practices and rates for compensating crew leaders and labor contractors are so variable and diverse as to defy convenient classification. In some instances, the farmer pays for the middleman's services which are rendered in his behalf, but all too often the worker pays most of the costs, regardless of whether the services are useful to him or whether the intermediary is only parasitic."

Few states have laws regulating farm labor contractors. Four states require that such contractors obtain licenses, comply with certain regulations as to records, refrain from engaging in certain undesirable practices and, usually, file a bond. New York State has a

[23]Allan Keller, Series on Migratory Labor, New York *World Telegram and Sun,* week of September 8, 1953.

law requiring labor contractors bringing ten or more migrant workers into the state to register with the Industrial Commissioner and to keep records on wages, working conditions and other data; the Commissioner may revoke, suspend or refuse to renew the registration for various reasons, including giving false information to workers as to terms and conditions of employment; employers may not use the services of labor contractors who are not registered. The State of Pennsylvania has issued regulations applying to labor contractors, providing for licensing, and placing upon them certain duties and responsibilities.[24]

Judging by existing conditions, however, these laws are honored more in the breach than in the observance.

Many labor contractors and crew leaders are responsible for a vicious camp atmosphere where sometimes fences or barbed wire prevent workers from getting out and visitors from getting in; armed guards patrol some camp sites in the event the barbed wire is not sufficient to discourage escape.

Foreign Migratory Workers in the United States

During the summer of 1957, together with Dr. Ernesto Galarza of the National Agricultural Workers Union, the NAACP labor secretary observed at first-hand the labor camps and working conditions of farm labor in several areas in California. In the course of interviewing many groups of Negro and white farm laborers and from an examination of statistical data it was determined that

[24]*Status of Agricultural Workers Under State and Federal Labor Laws*, U.S. Department of Labor, Bureau of Labor Standards, Washington, May, 1958.

native American workers, both Negro and white, have been virtually forced out of agricultural employment in California as a result of the importation of Mexican nationals. In addition it was found that the importation of farm labor from Mexico is broadly used to depress wage rates for domestic farm labor throughout the entire West Coast area.

On August 27, 1957, officials of the West Coast NAACP office, in a telegram to California's Governor Knight and Vice President Nixon, reported the "arbitrary refusal of Marysville fruit growers to employ Negro and other minority American agricultural workers in favor of Japanese and Mexican nationals." NAACP representatives reported that their investigations revealed that "many farm workers are extremely destitute and in need of immediate assistance . . . a breakdown in housing and sanitation in migratory labor camps is mounting in severity." Governor Knight was urged "to order an immediate investigation of housing, health and sanitary conditions" and Vice President Nixon was urged to intervene "with the proper federal agencies to alleviate a serious and explosive situation."

The foreign nationals who are themselves the victims of an appalling exploitation and poverty, have today largely displaced domestic workers from farm labor in California and elsewhere in the West and Southwest. In many instances their presence has made the total employment situation for all workers much more desperate.

The Mexican worker or "bracero" now comes to the United States under international agreement; the legal basis for this is U. S. Public Law 78, which was adopted because of acute wartime manpower shortages in agricultural labor.

However, an analysis of the number

of workers brought to the United States under Public Law 78 clearly indicates that there has been a steady increase each year, so that even in a year (1958) of widespread unemployment and recession, over 450,000 foreign nationals were brought to the United States.

Because the agreement is between government and government, many safeguards for the workers are included. But inadequate appropriations for inspection and enforcement have reduced the value of the international agreements although it is necessary to note that imported workers are legally in a superior position to domestic workers who usually have none of these protections.

Other foreign workers, employed under a contract between foreign governments and growers' associations or only between grower and grower, are less well-protected; and worst of all are the most recent programs, such as those involving Japanese and Philippine workers, which are not under Department of Labor supervision, but only under the Immigration Bureau of the Department of Justice which is not equipped for such work.

The President's Commission on Migratory Labor, finding that "alien labor has depressed farm wages, and therefore, has been detrimental to domestic labor," said:

"There is nothing wrong or immoral in employing foreign workers in American agriculture when there are mutual advantages in doing so. Employment of foreign workers is really not the issue. The point is that our Government has an obligation to make certain that these foreign workers do not reduce still lower the wages of domestic farm workers....

"The issue then is job standards. We must raise the standards and conditions of work in migratory farm employment and thereby eliminate the dependence by farm operators on poverty at home and misfortune abroad as the foundation of the recruitment of their labor supply.

"Fundamentally, this means that public policy must encourage farm employers to build reliable jobs for reliable people, not to maintain obsolete and intolerable standards.... We must build toward an agriculture that will yield a decent American income for those who provide labor."

"We Don't Need You Boys Any More"

To understand how the alien labor program has affected native born farm workers on the West Coast one must hear them as they tell their own stories:

"I am Casey Garcia. I am an American citizen and was born in Los Angeles.... We always worked in the crops and travelled from one place to another.... There was a job for everybody who wanted to work.

"Then the big companies started bringing in nationals from Guadalajara, Monterrey and other places. The nationals had contracts to work for wages at fifty cents an hour.... We always made more than fifty cents an hour no matter what we did in the fields.

"In 1950 there were about five thousand nationals brought into El Centro ... the boss would say, 'We don't need you boys any more. The Farmers Association is sending some nationals.... The contract says they must work three-fourths of the time and we can't afford to pay them for not working' ... we couldn't get the Labor Department to send the nationals back to Mexico."

* * *

"I am Raul Aguilar, a farm worker. My home is now in Stockton, California. I started to work in the fields . . . in 1946. . . . We used to work seven days a week.

"By the end of 1947, and the first months of 1948, we started having trouble with the 'wet-backs'. (Mexicans illegally in the United States.) We couldn't find work in the winter months because the labor camps were full of 'wetbacks'. They had first choice in all the work.

"By 1951 there were fewer 'wetbacks', but larger quanti-ties of Mexican nationals. By 1952 and 1953 local families were moved out of the family labor camps and nationals were housed there instead. . . .

"The wages [for lettuce] used to be twenty-five cents a box. . . . Soon these people found themselves out of jobs because the Mexican nationals started working in everything. They dry-packed lettuce in the fields at eighty-two-and-a-half cents an hour and soon the local work-ers started to work fewer hours. . . .

"At first we used to go to the fields and ask the farmers for work but they always said. 'Sorry—we cannot give you work because the work is for nationals only' . . . pretty soon we stopped going. . . .

"In 1958, while the bread-line was on for people without work, busloads of Mexican na-tionals were coming to Stockton to take over our jobs."[25]

More than a half-million foreign farm workers now are brought into the United States under contract each year,

plus many thousands of Puerto Ricans who also are brought in for work under contractual arrangement. In addition farm laborers from Jamaica and the Bahamas are brought to the United States through work agreements nego-tiated directly between American farm employers and the Bahamian or Jamai-can Governments or their agents.

The United States Immigration Ser-vice and Department of Labor have provided the following figures for all of or part of the year 1957:[26]

FOREIGN CITIZENS

Contract workers imported
from Mexico 450,422
Mexican workers illegally in
the United States, who were
apprehended during the year   44,451
Contract laborers imported
from Canada   7,015
Contract laborers imported
from British West Indies . . .   8,244
Contract laborers imported
from Japan   1,000
Contract laborers imported
from French West Indies . . .   32
Contract laborers imported
from Bahamas   3,912

UNITED STATES CITIZENS

Contract workers imported
from Puerto Rico   13,214

Although conditions for migratory farm workers are much the same throughout the United States, condi-tions among foreign nationals may vary considerably because of difference in contractual arrangements and degree of enforcement of labor provisions. Typical of what imported laborers may expect either on the West Coast or along the

[25]Public Hearings, National Advisory Committee on Farm Labor, Washington, February 5, 1959.

[26]*The Condition of Farm Workers in 1957,* Annual Report of the National Sharecroppers Fund, Inc., New York.

Atlantic Seaboard is the poor treatment of Bahamian workers as reported by the Workers Defense League, which described the dilapidated and unsanitary housing facilities for such workers in New Jersey and Virginia. Some of the most scandalous conditions, especially with regard to economic exploitation, were found at the huge apple orchards owned and operated by Sen. Harry F. Byrd of Virginia. The League also quoted a Long Island grower as saying that he preferred Bahamians because, ". . . when I get ahold of their permits, they gotta stay put and they know it. If they make a move, they'll be thrown out of the country."

Mexican Nationals: The Largest Foreign Group

By far the largest number of alien farm workers in the United States are the Mexicans brought to this country under an international agreement. Because this agreement is continuously violated by American farm operators, the conditions of these workers are in most cases about as bad as those of American migrant workers.

Dr. Ernesto Galarza, on behalf of the National Agricultural Workers Union, has made an extensive study of Mexican contract farm workers in the United States. He estimated that since 1942 more than one million Mexican citizens have worked in this country as agricultural laborers, and that they have worked in more than half of the forty-eight states. In his investigations of migrant camps where Mexican laborers are living and working in the United States, Dr. Galarza found blatant and widespread violations of the international agreement under which the Mexicans are brought to this country.

Among the rights of Mexican nationals enumerated in the international Migrant Labor Agreement of 1951 (amended) are the following:

1. A guarantee that the worker can choose the type of farm work he desires.
2. A guarantee that wages at the prevailing rate paid domestic workers for similar work shall be paid the Mexican.
3. A guarantee that the wages paid the Mexican shall be sufficient to cover his "normal living needs."
4. A guarantee that the Mexican will work not less than three-fourths of the work days of the total period of his contract, beginning the day after his arrival at the place of employment.
5. When higher wages are paid for specialized tasks such as operation of machinery or vehicles, the worker is to be paid such higher wages.
6. No deductions are to be made from the worker's wages except those provided by law.
7. A guarantee that the Mexican will be provided with a statement in Spanish and English, at the end of each pay period, showing the rate of pay, total earnings, hours worked, and itemized deductions.
8. A guarantee that when the contractee is not given the opportunity to work at least four hours a day, because of conditions beyond his control — such as weather, he is to receive subsistence from the employer, which is to be noted on his pay record.

It is evident that if such provisions and others relating to living standards were thoroughly enforced, and if they covered American as well as Mexican migratory farm workers, many abuses would be eliminated. However, as far back as 1951 the President's Committee on Migratory Labor scored the laxity in enforcing contractual provisions and stated:

> "...official vigilance for the protection of living and working standards of alien farm laborers was largely abandoned in the post-war phase. Responsible United States administrative agencies practically ceased to exert effective effort to preserve the requirements of national immigration policy.
>
> "The same ineffectiveness or laxity that undermined protective standards in the contract spread also to the official scrutiny of the number of foreign laborers that employers claimed they needed."

Although the provisions in international labor contracts are rarely enforced, the Farm Bureau and the growers' contracting associations have attacked the United States Labor Department for the very existence of regulations covering Mexican contract workers. E. S. McSweeney, secretary of the Arizona Cotton Growers' Association, told a Congressional subcommittee in 1958 that "we as farmers or farm organizations" have "become quite bitter about this constant regulation down to the minimum detail." One of the labor camps operated by Mr. McSweeney's association was described by a Labor Department official as "by far the worst.... Each unit is about ten by twelve. Four men and a kerosene stove are squeezed into each hut.... The door to some of the huts can't be closed from the inside. As a result chickens invade and leave their droppings on the floor.... The garbage is infrequently collected...."[27]

Other housing for Mexican contract

workers has been well described by the workers themselves:

> "I am sleeping in a building that used to be a market. We have to cover the holes in the windows and walls with paper.... Yesterday I asked for another blanket because of the cold. (The camp boss) said: 'No, you are supposed to have only one'...."
>
> ❋ ❋ ❋
>
> "Our camp was without water for a week. The contractor said the pump broke...we could not wash our clothes and we could not take a bath for a week...."
>
> ❋ ❋ ❋
>
> "We are installed in a barn which was used for the cows when we moved in.... The smell inside...is sufficiently repelling. It is strong and fresh cow smell...."

One Mexican national probably expressed the sentiment of the group when he declared:

> "These things have to be tolerated in silence because there is no one to defend our guarantees. In a strange country you feel timid...."[28]

At the lowest point of agricultural activity in California in 1958 (the week of January 3rd), over thirty thousand Mexican nationals were certified for work. Dr. Ernesto Galarza reported that on January 3rd "Braceros" were "to be found in over eighty crop activities. At times the 'bracero' labor force has represented more than 35 per cent of all seasonal farm workers in California. Many crops are now known as 'dominated crops' because the Mexican Na-

[27]"The Forgotten People" by Paul Jacobs, *The Reporter* Magazine, January 22, 1959.

[28]*Strangers in Our Fields,* Based on a Report Made Possible Through a Grant-in-Aid From The Fund For The Republic, Washington, 1956.

tionals have swamped out the domestic workers. In a 'dominated crop' the forces of the free labor market don't operate. It is an area of administered wages."

In the course of his testimony at the Public Hearings of the National Advisory Committee on Farm Labor in Washington, D.C. on February 5, 1959, Dr. Galarza vividly described the current operation of the contract labor system in California as follows:

"The moment the bracero is contracted in El Centro, the Association [of growers] is responsible for his food and transportation. At that moment he becomes a cost item in production. He is therefore hired as late in the day as possible and hustled north by bus so that he can arrive in time to do a full day's work. The trip may be six hundred miles long, so it is made at night, with breakfast served on the double and work starting immediately.

"It has taken a series of tragedies to bring home to the people of California how persistent and widespread is the violation of the state's high standards for the transportation of farm workers. Last year twelve braceros were burned to death inside a flaming truck which was also carrying tools, equipment, and a can of gasoline. Two years before that, eight Mexicans were killed and six were injured when a freight train smashed into a panel truck near the city of Salinas. In this instance, the passenger space was not only carrying men — it was carrying two-and-one-half pound hoes which very likely added to the injuries, if not the fatalities of the crash.

"Braceros are imported to do stoop labor in the fields, so the theory goes. The hard and me-

nial tasks of hoeing and grubbing do not attract domestic workers, not even at 70 cents an hour. But the Mexican National, with his captive ways, has captivated employers in nurseries, poultry farms, cattle feed lots, wineries and packing sheds. He is now commonly used to drive tractors, operate sprinkling systems, pack lettuce, thresh beans and do odd repair jobs, youngster sitting and gardening for his boss in town.... *The California Farmer*, January 3, 1959, reported that '30 Mexican Nationals daily move 150 quarter-mile lines of 4-inch, 30-foot joint aluminum pipe' on the Mettler Ranch near Bakersfield.

"In the winter of 1957, under heavy pressure from the National Agricultural Workers Union, the Farm Placement Service reluctantly denied permission to use Mexican Nationals in vineyards and orchard pruning. Hundreds of jobs were thus made available to domestic workers. The domestic farm labor force proved entirely sufficient and satisfactory, and this was recognized by the Farm Placement Service itself. In the winter of 1958-59 the same domestic labor force was available, but the Farm Placement Service declared a shortage of pruners. Nationals were certified and domestics were displaced.

"Workers who are not free to shop about for the best job available have nothing to say about wage policies. Thus, when the commercial wineries of the San Joaquin Valley studied how to cut their grape harvesting costs, they changed the method of payment. Instead of paying by the box, usually nine cents, they paid by the drum. Grapes were dumped into a drum holding from eight to ten boxes. The rate of pay reported by some Nationals was 45 cents a drum — a loss of 50 per cent in wages.

"Agriculture is a hazardous occupation. Both workers and employers in other industries must make persistent efforts to lessen the hazards and form work habits of safe performance. But in the flexible, ever-shifting Mexican farm labor force, conditions work in the opposite direction. For in the last analysis what the [growers'] associations want is an unstable labor force, whose members constantly change. Thus the bonds of common interest, experience, and cooperation are kept at a minimum, even though part of the price is paid in limb and life.

"This was brought out in an incident in a strawberry field three years ago. A crew of six Nationals was spraying the plants with a deadly insecticide called Parathion. None of them had masks. They were asked if they knew what they were doing. One of the men replied that they were 'putting a little powder' on the field, adding that 'it is somewhat molesting' because 'it provokes us to cough sometimes.' The poisons reduce the cholinesterase count in the blood which in turn reduces nerve impulses in such functions as breathing, causing death."

Nationals had even been used, he continued, as strike breakers when domestic workers had organized to improve their conditions.

"We have seen Mexican Nationals taking the places of striking domestic workers, under armed guard, in the cotton country of the Central Valley and in the tomato fields of Tracy and Stockton.

"With respect to union breaking, the classic example is the strike of the melon pickers of the Imperial Valley, which my Union organized and directed in 1925. We saw there the spectacle of five thousand Mexican Nationals certified by the secretary of Labor during the critical phase of the strike. We found the Mexican Consul advising his government that the certification was proper because the strikes affected 'only a few ranches.'"

"The Wetback": A Fugitive

In addition to the Mexicans brought legally to this country, a large number enter illegally each year to be employed by farm operators. These workers have no rights at all, since they are illegally in the United States, and, therefore, they are exploited to the extreme degree. A federal commission has said of the "wetback":

"The 'wetback' is a hungry human being. His need of food and clothing is immediate and pressing. He is a fugitive and it is as a fugitive that he lives. Under the constant threat of apprehension and deportation, he cannot protest or appeal no matter how unjustly he is treated. Law operates against him, but not for him. Those who capitalize on the legal disability of the 'wetbacks' are numerous...."[29]

"Wetbacks" may live along roadside ditches and huddle in shacks with no sanitary facilities, and may work for as little as fifteen cents an hour. They displace domestic workers, of course, and they have been known to bring in

[29]*Migratory Labor in American Agriculture,* Report of the President's Commission on Migratory Labor, 1951.

contagious diseases on occasion because of their illegal entry without a health examination.

Federal enforcement of immigration laws is the sole direct solution to the "wetback" problem in the United States. Such law enforcement has been extremely lax in the past. American aid to rural Mexico to help alleviate the terrible poverty that forces these people over the border in search of a pittance would be of help in solving the "wetback" problem.

Citizens Act

Some examples of positive action are to be found in Pennsylvania where an effective citizens' committee was organized to bring about reforms in the treatment of the thousands of migratory farm workers brought into that State. The Pennsylvania Citizens' Committee on Migratory Labor was organized as a result of the extensive investigation of labor camps and working conditions in the State undertaken in 1951 and 1952 by the NAACP and Dr. Cyrus Karraker of Bucknell University. These investigations resulted in a series of dramatic exposés which received widespread public attention. The Pennsylvania Citizens' Committee has been responsible for a number of significant reforms, among them the establishment of day-care centers for the children of migratory workers in Potter County, which has the greatest concentration of migrants in Pennsylvania.

A limited number of special summer schools for the children of migrant workers have been established in Rochester, New York; Oak Center, Wisconsin; Wiggins, Colorado; Bay County, Michigan; and Des Plaines, Illinois.

Enlightened farmers in Kings Ferry and Cutchogue, New York, have attempted to build adequate model labor camps and day-care centers, while some large processors in Maryland and New Jersey have donated money and buildings for child-care centers.

However, these few valuable and constructive projects, which have been the result of work by dedicated volunteer groups, are inadequate and isolated and do not begin to deal seriously with the basic issues which are clearly the responsibility of State and Federal Governments.

Administrative Action

Secretary of Labor James Mitchell recently acknowledged that even without any new legislation, "there are five things the Government can do within the limits of existing authority which would contribute substantially to alleviating the plight of the American farm worker.

"*First*, the Government can return to the grower the responsibility for recruiting and retaining a labor supply. The Government has in effect guaranteed the grower a supply of labor, and in many instances this guarantee has been given without adequate consideration of the wages and working conditions offered by the grower. . . .

"*Second*, it can restrict the use of the public employment office facilities of the Federal-State Employment Service system to the use of growers whose wages, working conditions, housing and other arrangements are not substandard. . . .

"*Third*, the Government can revise its procedures, eliminate the loop-holes, and substantially tighten up its enforcement of the provisions of Public Law 78 so that the present adverse effect of the importation of Mexican Nationals can be minimized....

"Fourth, the Government can apply to other foreign workers such as British West Indians, Bahamians, Filipinos, Japanese, and Basque sheep herders, the kind of protection and standards that the Congress has already prescribed with respect to Mexican nationals. In doing so the Federal Government should adhere to the recommendations on this subject of the International Labor Office—recommendations which our Government helped to formulate but which as yet it has not followed, at least insofar as they apply to those other categories of foreign workers....

Fifth, those State Governments which have already established the machinery for licensing and regulating labor contractors and crew leaders could apply the same standards to them as should be applied to the operations of the Federal-State Employment Service system with reference to serving growers...."

But when the U.S. Department of Labor held public hearings in Washington on September 10 and 11, 1959 on proposals to establish wage, housing, transportation and other standards for migratory farm workers, the powerful agricultural interests assisted by Secretary of Agriculture Ezra T. Benson sharply attacked any Federal action on behalf of farm labor.

As a result of widespread protest, the U.S. Department of Labor, in September, 1959, proposed minimal requirements for growers using Government employment facilities in recruiting migratory farm workers. "Benson Opposes Farm Job Rules" was the headline of a New York Times report appearing on September 12, which quotes the Secretary of Agriculture's request to "avoid or delay the promulgation of regulations and other action relating to farm labor...." Representatives of the Farm Placement Service from several southern states, including Virginia, denounced the Labor Department's proposals as an "interference with State's Rights."

However, support came from several religious groups and other organizations. The Very Rev. Msgr. George C. Higgins, director of the Social Action Department of the National Catholic Welfare Conference asserted:

"Those who oppose the regulations apparently have left no stone unturned in their efforts to kill the regulations. It is a matter of public knowledge that they have instigated a flood of mail—they have gone to the Congress and to the White House."

Necessary Legislative Action

The responsible national and local organizations concerned with migratory farm labor in the United States have agreed on the following 14-Point legislative program as realistic and vitally necessary:

1. The use of the public employment facilities of the Federal-State Employment System should be restricted to growers whose wages, housing and working conditions meet minimum standards.

2. The protections and standards currently recognized as necessary in Puerto Rican and Mexican National

contracts should cover all migrant workers, foreign and domestic. Such standards should not be lower than those recommended by the International Labor Office.

3. The Fair Labor Standards Act should include farm workers in its provisions, particularly in the minimum wage provisions. It should be amended to extend child labor protection to children outside as well as during school hours. Complementary state legislation is needed.

4. The Labor Management Relations Act should protect the right of farm workers to organize and bargain collectively. The organization of farm workers should be encouraged.

5. Crew leaders and labor contractors should be licensed on a national basis.

6. Ways of extending the Unemployment Compensation Act to cover farm workers should be studied.

7. Federal aid should be extended to help states in encouraging improvement of housing migrants and extension of health and welfare services to cover migrants. Federal financial aid should be made available specifically for the construction and renovation of migrant farm labor camps. Congress should direct the Department of Health, Education and Welfare to supplement existing grants to the several states, making available money for direct relief grants to migrants, with eligibility for such grants not dependent upon the recipient's residence status in any particular state.

8. State legislation should be enacted to carry out the recommendations of the President's Committee on Migratory Labor in the fields of housing and transportation, and to extend compulsory Workmen's Compensation to cover farm workers.

9. The states should be encouraged to provide adequate education and child care for migrant children. Federal aid should be supplied where necessary to make this possible.

10. Congress should authorize an investigation of the foreign-labor program by a responsible committee representing the public, employers and labor.

11. A program for rural redevelopment should be enacted by the Congress with broad scope to wipe out "depressed areas" through land conservation, natural resources and industrial development, together with education, vocational guidance and training for people living in rural communities.

12. Interstate Commerce Commission regulations affecting the transportation of migrants should be amended to include an "out-of-service" provision to prevent a vehicle transporting migrants from operating if its mechanical condition is to be a likely cause of an accident or breakdown.

13. Congress should direct the United States Department of Labor to establish and operate, in cooperation with the several states, a federally financed interstate system of highway rest stops for migrants.

14. Congress should direct the Department of Labor to establish a Bureau of Migratory Farm Labor. It should assign to this Bureau primary responsibility for raising the living standards of migratory labor. Such a Bureau should have a clear directive as to its responsibilities in housing, transportation, child labor, minimum wages and other worker protections, child care, registration of crew leaders, health, welfare, and all other matters relating to agricultural labor.

The enactment of these recommendations into law and vigorous enforcement would result in basic changes in the intolerable conditions which characterize migratory labor in the United States.

Every local branch and state conference of the National Association for the Advancement of Colored People, as well as churches, trade unions, civic organizations and all other groups with a commitment to social justice must vigorously work for the adoption of these proposals by the Congress and, where indicated, also by state legislatures.

It is necessary to mobilize broad public support for these recommendations and to make American citizens aware of the social conditions which prevail in the most neglected part of the national economy.

There have been innumerable studies and fact-finding commissions; committees of the Congress and of various state legislatures have conducted untold investigations; and eight years ago a Presidential Commission made a comprehensive report to the White House. There have been interminable conferences, discussions, speeches, monographs and articles and pious statements by public officials.

What is clearly needed now is broad and effective action. Action by Government; action by enlightened growers and the management of the vast food processing and packing corporations of this country; action by organized labor; action by all the responsible elements in American society to effect fundamental changes in the recruiting, organization and allocation of the nation's agricultural manpower resources, and to secure a basic reorganization of the system of migratory farm labor which will be in the interests of the entire community.

6

URBAN SOCIAL PROBLEMS

Meaning of Urbanism

Throughout the world, new cities are forming. The fringes of old cities, especially large ones, are growing at their fringe at rates faster than the population at large. This heightened growth in cities has been going on for more than a century. In 1800, nearly two per cent of the world's population lived in cities of 100 thousand or more. By 1950, 13 per cent had moved into the largest, most crowded settlements.

This urban trend will continue well beyond the remainder of the 20th century. It represents one of the major ecological adjustments in the history of man: a revision of the milieu, a relocation of the population, an adoption of different ways of life, all in response to the forceful imperatives of industrial technology.

The United States has always been prompt in its urban response to industrial change. In less than 100 years, the nation has relocated from the hinterlands into the metropolitan areas. By 1960, more than one half of all Americans lived in 213 urban areas. Among these, the largest contained 52 million inhabitants, or nearly one third of all Americans.

American cities grew primarily through migration from rural areas and from abroad. Their natural increase through net reproduction in a stable population is small. Americans make up an uprooted population; mobile within states in response to changing job opportunities; migratory between states and regions in response to changing locations of industrial and other commercial development. Of the 159 million Americans five years old and over in 1960, for example, only half had lived in the same place for five years or more. About a third moved, but within the same county; 16 per cent had moved to a different county — half of them to a place in a different state.

Regions and states of high economic growth show the highest mobility and in-migration. Nearly 75 per cent of the residents in the Northeast stayed in place from 1955 to 1960, in contrast to 40 per cent for the West. In the West, one out of every six residents had moved in from another state between 1955 and 1960.

The main route of migration has

been movement away from rural farm areas and toward metropolitan areas. This is reflected in occupational change. The emerging occupational pattern is distinctively urban. For example, persons in professional and technical occupations increased from 6 to 12 per cent of the civilian labor force from 1940 to 1960. Other rapidly growing categories included sales and service, and clerical workers. Farm and mine laborers, and operators—blue collar industrial workers—have decreased substantially.

Two types of population movement go on simultaneously in American metropolitan areas. Migration into the areas from the hinterlands, a movement of urban concentration, is determined mainly by differential rates of economic growth and job opportunity. Sixteen out of 213 metropolitan areas, between 1950 and 1960, increased in population size by at least 55 per cent. The Fort Lauderdale Metropolitan area grew by 264 per cent; Las Vegas, Nevada, by 123 per cent, and Midland, Texas, by 109 per cent, between 1950 and 1960.[1] There were areas of new industrial expansion. The Fort Lauderdale area, for example, includes the space program site at Cape Kennedy.

The second pattern of movement is *suburban dispersion* within each metropolitan area. There were 29 counties with net migration increases of 100 thousand or more from 1950 to 1960.[2] Of these, 16 were suburban counties adjacent to the largest cities. Los Angeles County and Nassau County near New York City, headed the list. This mobility

[1]U.S. Bureau of the Census, *Current Population Reports*, Nov. 1962 Series P-23, No. 7. Net migration excludes natural increases, or the difference between number of births and deaths. It represents solely the difference between the number migrating into an area and the number who leave.
[2]*Ibid.*

is made up of hinterland and in-migrants *and* of people leaving the large central cities. The nine counties with the greatest net out-migration for 1950 to 1960 were all parts of central cities, with Brooklyn, Manhattan, and Philadelphia leading the group. *The old central cities have generally not grown in net population since 1930,* except outside their political boundaries.

The older central city settlement does not thin out much. Businesses stagnate and buildings age, but the American central city grows to a high density at its core, achieves a certain size, and maintains it for decades. Residents who leave for the suburbs are replaced by lower-income migrants from without.

Real net growth occurs around the perimeter of the older central city. With the spread of automotive transport since 1920, suburbanization has been so rapid that the Bureau of the Census has come to treat major cities and their environs as *urbanized areas.* An urbanized area contains at least one city of 50 thousand or more as well as all surrounding, closely settled incorporated places and unincorporated areas.

In 1960, six out of ten inhabitants of these urbanized areas resided in central cities. Among the 40 per cent living in the urban fringe, one in three lived outside of villages or towns—in open country which must be regarded as urban rather than rural in character. The urban fringe is growing three times faster than the central cities. The growth invades old established suburbs, creates new towns and villages, and moves beyond them into abandoned farm fields.

Has the population growth of urbanized areas meant the development of a way of life different from that of the rural villager or the farmer in the open country? Population size, density and heterogeneity differ, to be sure. But do they affect the values, social relations and life styles of Americans? Does urban concentration stimulate interdependence between a greater number of people, yet reduce dependency on particular persons? Do cities offer freedom from personal and sentimental controls? Does an urban person belong to many groups, without experiencing close allegiance to any one of them?

Similar concepts of urbanism suggest that as place of work is separated from residence, as services necessary to life become specialized and clustered in particular parts of the urbanized area, relations between people also become specialized. Urban persons are not friends so much as contractually associated for a limited undertaking, whether at home or at work. Or so some ideas on urbanism suggest.

The population of the urban settlement is not only vast. It is highly diverse as well. City dwellers come from extremely varied backgrounds. Once in the city, they continue to seek different ends. Common values are uncommon. Social controls depend upon laws and their enforcement as opposed to informal pressures. Routines, like goods and services, while highly differentiated, become standardized.

There is *no* empirical verification for this view of urbanism as a social psychological way of life. The notion of the city as a way of life determined by the conditions of size, density and heterogeneity, was advanced in the 1930s by sociologist Louis Wirth and schematized later by others.[3] Not only do we lack evidence: *The evidence that is at hand contradicts the view.* Every close empirical look at city dwellers suggests that neighborliness is widespread; family ties are close for a majority of persons; and that even where people move within the city, they retain active friendships throughout several neighborhoods. Furthermore, informal pressures flourish to reinforce standards of social conduct—even in slum neighborhoods.

The conception of urbanism as a social psychological state of being bogs down further when we see that urbanization transcends place. The goods, services, information, and tastes of the city are communicated throughout the interland. Whatever is psychological about city living can be transmitted. What, then, *is* the significance of urbanism for the study of social problems? *Is* urbanism a matter of place or of psychology?

Metropolitan Functions

The urbanized areas, particularly the cities at their centers, are more than dense population settlements. They are differentiated parts of a national society. They operate as specialized points where the elements of the national communications and transportation systems intersect. Big cities are points within which the stability and change common to processes in the national society are controlled, negotiated and ordered.

As headquarters for work, markets and decisions, metropolitan areas serve as control centers for maintaining a continental society. As physical and organizational crossroads, as innovators, and as mediators of law for the nation, metropolitan communities are nuclei of integration.

[3]Louis Wirth, "Urbanism as a Way of Life," *American Journal of Sociology* 44: 1-24, July, 1938; also see E. Shevky and W. Bell, *Social Area Analysis,* Stanford, Calif.: Stanford University Press, 1955, pp. 7-8.

When we think about urban social problems, we refer, not to the problems of one segment of the national population which happens to live in a certain type of environment, but to the functions these environments serve in the larger society. There was a time when we could talk about rural *versus* urban American life. That time has passed. There are so many kinds of communities, both rural and urban, that generalization is impossible. Urbanization is a process, moreover, which can be detached from place: it is exportable, such that the prosperous Indiana farm family today has more in common with the suburban family on the fringe of Indianapolis than with the rural family on a submarginal farm in neighboring Kentucky.

A single modern American urban environment contains many possibilities, from suburban estate to factory slum. Urban institutions, practices, and styles penetrate the furthest reaches of the rural hinterland. It is even common for rural migrants to inhabit the urban core and to retain nonurban patterns of behavior for two generations.

Problems of metropolitan structure and function impinge on the entire national population. As control centers in the network of the larger society exert influence, so cities and their suburban surroundings influence all phases of change and stability in that society.

There is a way in which the city as an *imaginary place* continues to constitute a social issue in America. This is in the conflict between nostalgia for the 'good and simple life of the village,' and the alienation associated with the great metropolis. Rural nostalgia, however influential, is invalid and misplaced. Neither type of American settlement is better suited to human needs than the other. The village is no center of cooperation, hope and goodwill. Nor are cities fumey, sick gluts of anti-natural existence. The social problems of urban American communities do *not* spring from anything intrinsic to metropolitan life. Nor is there a rural idyll to which to return.

Urbanism and Urban Life Reconsidered

Today, a city is the geographic nucleus of an area distinguished from other areas demographically and organizationally. As population, a city is larger, denser, and more heterogeneous. Organizationally, cities perform distinctive economic and political functions. Social relationships within them are not different in kind from those in other areas; rather there is greater *variety* in types of places and forms of organizations.

The word *urbanism,* intended to refer to a way of life exported by the culture of cities, has ambiguous content in modern American society. Cities provide for greater diversity of cultural forms and therefore for greater freedom for creativity than do rural areas. Cities are centers of technological change, which include sanitation and the prevention of disease. In this respect, urbanism is a vague term referring to the changing aspects of civilization, both good and bad, which tend to be generated in metropolitan communities and to be transmitted outwardly.

Cities and their suburban environs are thus not in themselves problematic. The attributes of American cities in particular are not socially problematic except in the eyes of those who hold to the myth of the rural idyll. It is true that great population diversity, a complex division of labor, and differences in life styles stimulate divergent standards and conflicting values. Ethics dictating personal relations may become obscured so that city dwellers lack norms for 'right conduct.' The same obscurity means, however, that there are fewer standards to which one must conform. Freedom is the result. Whether the increase in freedom that can result from urban population characteristics and social organization is functional or demoralizing depends not upon the goodness or badness of urban society, but upon the uses of this freedom.

A city and its environs are also designed to facilitate changes in standards. Modes of family life are 'released' to vary tremendously. Age groups are more fully differentiated. Greater mobility between places and up and down the income and job ladders facilitates changes in ideas and exchanges in beliefs and skills. But there is nothing intrinsically good or bad about change, or about institutional diversity and social mobility, or even about conflict. In the same way, city dwellers are free to be more or less materialistic and more or less individualistic than were Americans in 19th century towns and villages.

We emphasize this because so much that is false has been written about the *disorganizing* properties of urbanization. *The problems we treat in this chapter are urban social problems in that they arise from differences in the rates of change between elements in the urban situation, not because there is something wrong with cities per se, with urbanized areas, or with urbanism.*

Housing Supply

Housing is not a 'city problem' in America. Housing is demonstrably less adequate in rural areas than in cities. But the migration of workers and their families into cities, and the movement of central city inhabitants out into the suburbs, puts a continuous stress on the supply of dwelling units in urban areas. As areas of the most rapid growth, American cities and suburbs face a constant shortage of housing. Not until 1950, in fact, did the nation begin to meet the fiscal demand, let alone the more comprehensive human need for urban housing. The gap was stimulated by immigration from Europe, migration from the South to the North, migration from the Middle West to the West, and lags in building during two world wars and the Great Depression.

Take, for instance, the volume of urban residential construction in relation to the rate of new urban household formation from 1910 to 1950. Construction fell far below the growth of households during every ten-year period, save that from 1920 to 1929, when prosperity and postwar regrouping of families combined to create a great boom of building in the outer rings and suburbs of cities. This boom was cut short during the Great Depression and was not resumed until after 1945 because of material and labor shortages during World War II. Thus, American cities entered the second half of this century with a substantial accumulated shortage of dwelling units, even when the matter of mobility is ignored!

In spite of the ups and downs of the urban construction market, the industry surged forward to fill the gap between need and supply between 1949 and 1955. Since then the industry has erected roughly 1.2 million new nonfarm dwelling units each year, where it never exceeded .9 million units a year previously.

For several reasons, including the cumulative backlog of shortages, this surge has never been adequate for urban shelter requirements. Estimation of urban housing needs is a dreadfully complicated business. In 1957, Glenn H. Beyer, Director of the Housing Research Center at Cornell, and a pioneer in making such estimates, made a careful projection of housing needs for the nation between 1956 and 1965. His low estimate was 1.3 million, and his high, 1.9 million.[4]

On this gross basis, the gap between need and supply was lower in 1963 than at any time in recent history, except perhaps 1925. Yet a shortage persists, and it is concentrated wholly within the urban areas. Moreover, the homes being built are not consonant with the income levels or types of households of those with greatest need. The decade has been a period of erecting single family suburban dwellings, where the earlier boom in the 1920s was evenly divided between rental apartment constructions and suburban family homes. In the 1950s and 1960s, three fourths of all urban construction was of single family homes. Also, the costs of housing have risen faster than

other consumer prices ever since 1948.[5] The supply, in type and volume, remains unsuited to the requirements and to the demand; that is, to ability to pay.

What is the genesis of this problem? Part of the explanation rests in the history of performance of the housing industry, as this has been shown to be handicapped by recession, depression, and wartime shortages. But is this explanation sufficient? What else must be taken into account to interpret why the world's most affluent, most urbanized society cannot supply domestic needs for city and suburban shelter?

The sociological answer is that a *system* of housing has never developed in the United States. A *national urban system* would have included private and public control centers capable of estimating accurately needs as well as supply and demand; (1) adequate research and planning functions; (2) an industry capable of responding effectively to population changes in areal location, age and income groupings, and household combinations; and most of all, (3) a technology capable of surmounting wide differences in patterns of land use, terrain, and material and labor costs.

None of these exists, except in prototype. The outlines are showing through, but the form of the system remains far from delineated. Economic studies of housing have been pursued vigorously since World Was II. Yet research in housing lags behind what has been undertaken in agriculture, manufacturing, medicine, and many other realms of applied science and technology. Corporate industry has not responded broadly to the benefits it

---

[4]*Housing: A Factual Analysis*, New York: Macmillan, 1958, p. 285. This estimate takes into account the rate of household formation, net migration, building and unit conversions, losses from weather and fire and the like, vacancy fractions, and loss through slum clearance. It is possible to revise his estimate, using 1960 Census data not available to Professor Beyer in 1957. One discovers that even his high estimate understates the rate of household formation and the rate of slum clearance now involved not only in clearance projects but in renewal programs and in highway construction. Certainly, his low estimate is too low. On the other hand, we find certain of his other data are compensatory, and using the new housing and population reports, we reach an estimate of 1.85 million units needed per year, or roughly what Professor Beyer made as a *high* projection.

[5]Housing and Home Finance Agency, *Housing in the Economy, 1955*, Washington: Government Printing Office, 1956, pp. 22-25.

might derive from housing research and planning, and "the Government has been excessively concerned with both the attitudes of Congress and industry" (which it considers its client, rather than the public).[6]

Nor is there a systematic relation between supply and demand in urban housing. Unlike other commodity markets, housing markets are local. Buyers and sellers, builders and investors, compete within sections of single metropolitan areas. Construction of new housing proceeds through the competitive activities of about 125 thousand builders. The codes which regulate their operations and use of materials are also local. Credit is a function of practices and economic prospects *within* metropolitan areas, rather than across the nation.

The effects of the housing industry are national in scope, but decisions and operations are local. The industry does between $20 and $23 billion worth of business annually. It employs 5 million workers and creates markets for dozens of other industries. The entire economy reacts to rises or declines in the housing business. Yet it has not centralized in any important way.

It operates similarly to the way the automotive industry would operate if cars were built in local garages, rather than in Detroit or in plants controlled from Detroit. Therefore, the relation between needs and actual supply for the national urban housing market as a whole is meaningless. New York City supplies luxury apartments in excess of area needs, while Phoenix, Arizona (a metropolitan area with explosive growth), builds too few apartments and too few tract houses to meet local demands.

Urban housing has been compared

[6]Beyer, *op. cit.*, p. 286.

here to the automotive industry. But the two are not comparable. Their differences go a long way toward explaining the *unorganized* state of the housing industry. A car is mobile, while a house is settled into an environment in which are implicated all the other institutions of the metropolitan community: land and the regulation of its use, the physical services of streets, sewers, water and fuel systems, and the relation of the setting to schools, transportation, retail outlets, churches, and the like.

Even if all homes and apartment buildings were mass produced—say, prefabricated—they would have to be assembled at the site. Each structure becomes a local assembly plant. Houses endure for years, and we have yet to develop means of demolishing them as we do old cars.

There are also important internal differences between the industries. Builders do not control their material suppliers as does Detroit. Perhaps most crucial—Americans think of dwelling places as tailored to their individual preferences, while cars are acceptably standardized commodities. Only the low and low-middle income households accept highly standardized housing, as in public housing projects, and then only because the price has been substantially reduced.

If the remainder of the urban housing system were intact, the industry itself would represent, under both historic and current conditions, major organizational lag compared with any other *basic* American enterprise. There are some 125 thousand builders at work on urban plots, exclusive of the many persons who build their own (25 per cent in 1950!). About 125, or one per cent, have built 35 per cent of the nation's urban housing since 1950. These are the big, usually most efficient contractors, like

Levitt and Gerholz. They cut labor and material costs through small-scale versions of mass organization and production. Most builders erect only one or two houses a year. Needless to say, they use the same handicraft techniques that are employed by´do-it-yourself enthusiasts.

Because of the organization of labor, urban dwellings are not erected by builders but by subcontractors from independent firms. Conversion to authentic mass production would mean deep restrictions in the large labor force now engaged in construction. Construction workers get good wages relative to workers in comparable industries, but their dependence upon seasonal weather means that their annual wages are low. Mass production would further reduce the manhours required and would eliminate most semi-skilled positions.

The construction trades have resisted technological development of the housing industry for decades. They have also resisted opening their ranks to recruitment on the basis of merit. Typical resistances are these: Plumbers often require that most of their work be done on the site, a barrier to use of prefabrication: painters have organized to prevent the use of spray guns; mechanical trowels are prohibited by the masons.

In many communities, construction trades use closed programs of apprenticeship, thus preventing different ethnic groups from entering the trade. In other situations, building trade unions have sought to fix rates of output, and have worked to upgrade jobs so that lower order tasks must be executed by more skilled, hence more highly paid workers. In the long term, these are signs of a labor force struggling to consolidate a stronghold in trades that will

be dissolved through changing technology. In the short term, such practices increase housing costs and thus reduce demand.

A residual technology has been available for transformation of the housing industry for many decades. Inventors and engineers in the manufacturing and processing industries have provided a tidal wave of synthetic materials, fabricating techniques, and modifications in assembly and design operations which await wide application. Since the late 1930s, prefabricated construction of housing has grown from 4 to 10 per cent of the urban residential contruction market. The techniques are available. Engineers know how to mass produce whole floor, roof, and wall sections, which can be lined up and connected swiftly. Sectioned interior partitions can also be shipped conveniently and then dropped into place. Plumbers may be among the first skilled laborers to decline into a repair and maintenance capacity, for the complete plumbing needed in a single-family dwelling can now be packaged and sealed into bathrooms. William Levitt uses only small parts of this new technology, yet with a permanent, trained work force, he built decent suburban houses for about $9 a square foot in 1963, compared with $13 a square foot for the average, nonengineered home.

Two other types of resistance to innovation and technical change are more influential than any of the others, however. These are public lack of interest in mass-produced housing, and the limited state of development of metropolitan housing ordinances.

Urban shelter is an ostensible symbol, a manifest reward. One's house or apartment announces his social rank, which is itself a function of occupation, income and educational attainment.

One's house is also a stage upon which to dramatize the distinctive life style of one's family, taking life style to refer to aesthetic preferences, consumption practices, and combinations of task and recreational activities. If one social function of city living is social as well as high individual differentiation, there is little reason to expect shelter consumers to be drawn toward inexpensive but relatively uniformly constructed dwellings.

Even where techniques of mass production liberate rather than freeze builders — and modern prefabrication potentially opens a wider than usual range of plans and housing details — there are subjective resistances to attitude change. Economy construction is attached attitudinally to the image of cheap, dull, factory-made products. And this image is reinforced by some realtors and mortgage speculators who stand to gain from rising costs and inflation. Mass production in housing remains a program tailored pretty exclusively to low income public housing in cities, to tract suburbs in the low middle income category, and to a few midwestern towns where prefabricators have succeeded in their campaign.

If the housing industry is fragmented and local in character, city ordinances are adapted to this pattern. Even the Federal Housing Agency employs a code in assessing homes for mortgage insurance that is adapted to materials specifications rather than to materials performance. A performance code is one which allows for variations and changes in the material and technology used in construction, but which maintains standards about weight loadings and usage tolerances. A code based on materials specifications is one that says what sorts of materials must be used and what sizes and qualities must be employed. A performance code says that a pipe must withstand x pounds of pressure, where a specification code names the metal and diameter of the pipe that must be used for each type of building.

Existing codes are implemented by building inspectors. The opportunities for mutual reinforcement of building trades interests and retention of certain codes, however outmoded technologically, is obvious. Masons can exert political force to insure that bricks continue to be a main source of construction material in a given locality. Electricians can influence city administrations to prevent changes in codes that might allow the use of prewired systems. Finally, local codes differ tremendously, so that materials specified for use in one community are prohibited in another. Under these conditions, centralization and automation of this industry will be very slow in developing.

Housing Blight in Cities

Ecologists have found that the dollar value and physical quality of housing in large cities are more than a system of rewards: The value is distributed along a gradient, so that most of the best housing is located in the newest, most distant sectors of the community, and the worst is clustered, for the most part, in the oldest, most central sectors. While there are many problems associated with the general incompatibility of rates of change within the urban housing market, major social concern centers upon the low end of the housing gradient: the dilemma of the housing slum.

All housing affects family and social relationships. Very poor housing frequently helps to reduce self-respect and induces pessimism and passivity.

Frustrations and stresses to which persons might otherwise adjust are intensified by poor housing.[7]

A city slum is characterized by deteriorated houses densely occupied by economically impoverished and deprived people whose way of life is often at variance with those of higher income groups. The term slum has many connotations. It sometimes signifies something about both housing and occupants. At other times it connotes a neighborhood of decay and transition; a physical setting inhabited by the down-and-out, the marginal, and the disadvantaged among all groups.

So much attention has been given to such slums by planners and social scientists that more neutral and precise definitions have been developed. For example, a planner would refer to a housing slum as a *blighted area*. If he worked for the Chicago Plan Commission, he would classify an area as blighted if the buildings were at least half residential; if half of its buildings were built before 1900; if half the dwelling units were substandard in quality; and if at least a fifth of these were substandard by reason of being unfit for use. For him, substandard would mean

[7]Alvin L. Schorr, *Slums and Social Insecurity*, Research Report No. 1, Social Security Administration Division of Research and Statistics, U.S. Government Printing Office, 1963, writes that poor urban housing may produce "Pleasure in company but not in solitude, cynicism about people and organizations, a high degree of sexual stimulation without legitimate outlet, and difficulty in household management and child rearing; and relationships that tend to spread out into the neighborhood rather than deeply into the family. Most of these effects, in turn, place obstacles in the path of improving one's financial circumstances. Obstacles such as those presented by poor health or inability to train children are obvious. Those presented by having ties centered in one's neighborhood rather than in one's wife and children are less direct, but significant. Such a family . . . is less likely to move if a better job requires it."

unfit for use (lacking heat, light, or private toilet, or lacking repairs), or seriously overcrowded. Overcrowded, in turn, would mean occupancy by as many or more than 1.5 persons per room, plus an extra family of two or more persons (e.g., doubling up of households).

He would go further and distinguish between degrees of blight. No matter how refined his definition, however, his approach overlooks old structures which may be desirable residences. He also works with averages for a neighborhood, which neglects the fact that an area may contain much good housing mixed with some very substandard, aging structures.

Slums may be demolished and cleared for public purposes, such as housing projects or commercial redevelopment. After a half century of social and medical interest, American courts accepted as valid the notion that housing blight is correlated with contagious diseases and epidemics, high mortality rates, high crime and delinquency rates, police and fire hazards. This correlation is not necessarily a matter of cause and effect, but it indicates that the kind of housing people live in can restrict their behavior and thus impair their life prospects.[8]

Slums have also been shown repeatedly to be costly. A blighted area in Indianapolis, for example, contained 10 per cent of the city's population, but it accounted for 24 per cent of the venereal disease clinic cases, 19 per cent of the patients at hospitals for the insane, 30 per cent of all city hospital services, and 25 per cent of the costs of arrests and imprisonment annually. About one third of the city population of the

[8]Jay Rumney, "The Social Costs of Slums," *Journal of Social Issues*, 7: 77-83, 1951.

United States lived in blighted areas in 1930, but this third furnished nearly half of the major crimes and juvenile delinquency, half of the tuberculosis and 45 per cent of the total city service costs for that year. Economically, the same third yield 6 per cent of the total city tax revenues on real estate.[9]

Although slum housing is linked with high social and economic costs, removal of slum housing and rehousing in better structures does *not* lead to sufficient improvements in social welfare. Housing reform alone fails to deal with the range of problems imbedded in slums. For a slum neighborhood is a blend of difficulties produced by a wide range of larger national problems.

Consider the major causes of residential urban slums. A city is an ever-changing form of human settlement. Its changes involve continual, fairly open economic competition for favorable sites by business, industry, and realtors. Land at the city center, especially land surrounding the central business district, is subjected to continual changes in use, or so its owners expect. Over the short-term, property owners of core locations find commercial advantage in squeezing maximum rental revenues from their holdings. If land uses and maintenance standards are generally uncontrolled, economic competition will automatically produce physical deterioration. Economically, a slum is a high-yield, short-term investment; a warehouse of property for future speculation; and a supply depot for people en route from the outside in search of a stopping place.

The blighting process is compounded by aging. Core areas of large

[9]Gist and Halbert, *Urban Sociology*, New York, Crowell, p. 466.

inner cities are older than other urban sectors. The structures in the core, apart from the new office buildings in the very center, are usually 50 to 150 years old, depending on the age of the city itself. The land these aging structures occupy is valuable; the structures are worthless save as temporary rental apartments.

New buildings are contracted and built in areas where net dollar returns promise to be highest. These are areas which are perceived as most desirable socially and commerically. In ordinary investment transactions, slum properties are bypassed as new residential locations. Roughly a quarter of a million new residential units a year are built within American central cities. But this is only a few thousand more than the number removed each year through demolition, condemnation, or conversion to commercial and industrial use.

If it were not for the exodus to the suburbs, the pressure on city housing would get progressively worse. As it is, the blight spreads. Housing ages and deteriorates and is subdivided internally. As expensive new 'luxury' buildings and new suburban tracts go up, the borders of the slum expand from the core across the inner ring. *There is nothing in the natural commercial housing supply process to prevent extending blight.*

In many cities, moreover, there is genuine pressure for slum housing. Ethnic minorities are prevented by realtors, mortgagors and property owners from living elsewhere. Other low-income adults and families do not know where else to look, or cannot afford to sign a lease, or find that only blighted housing is located near their place of work or potential sources of employment. For socially and economically deprived persons, American cities are short on housing, public and private, and long on rent for slum properties.

Rent is not low in many blighted dwelling units, however. Ethnic segregation and the shortage of units induce pressure toward further crowding into slums. Slum landlords count on this pressure to maintain their profits. Large, aging apartments can be cut into one- and two-room units and let out at stiff prices. A one-room unit in a Puerto Rican neighborhood in Manhattan may be priced at $100 to $170 a month. For the landlord, this means a return on his initial investment of as much as 60 per cent, or up to four times the average return for city rentals.

Governmental efforts to cope with this blight are often hamstrung. One example is the Baltimore experience.[10] A law enforcement drive to make slum landlords bring properties into line with housing codes and to help owners of dwellings in blighted neighborhoods rehabilitate their homes and apartments began in 1947 and was tried out in one neighborhood in 1950.

The Pilot Program intensified housing pressure. It undertook demolition of Negro housing at just the time when Negro families were pouring into Baltimore from the South. So great was the demand that

> Speculators could rent or sell slum housing at prices that would have provided decent quarters in a white neighborhood. In 1951 ... the quarters rented by Negroes in the Pilot Area were 19 per cent worse ... than the units rented by white families. Yet the Negroes' rent averaged $10 a month

[10]Martin Millspaugh and Gurney Breckenfeld, *The Human Side of Urban Renewal*, Baltimore, Md., Fight-Blight, Inc., 1958, pp. 6-15.

higher. A Negro had little choice but to pay. His ramshackle apartment in the Pilot Area was likely to be the only one he could find.[11]

And the rehabilitation and enforcement program undermined directly one of the ways slum dwellers had of making ends meet. It prohibited subletting that would overcrowd the apartment or home. At the same time, when slum landlords were forced to make repairs, they also raised rents. Median rent jumped 18 per cent for the Pilot Area in 18 months. Others refused to make repairs, knowing they could gain a delay of six months to a year in court, and knowing that the fines could be cheaper than repair bills. The average fine for the Baltimore Pilot Area, for example, was $22.17.

Housing the Aged

A poorly coordinated housing supply in most metropolitan areas, and a greater extent of blight, make up two dimensions of the problem of congested urban settlement. Others deserve mention to illustrate how inclusive and ramified are issues of urban housing.

One of these is the housing of the aged. The proportion of persons 65 years of age and over in the United States increased from 4 per cent in 1880 (1.7 million) to 9 per cent in 1960 (16.2 million). About 11 per cent, or 25 million, will be aged by 1980. A recent study of Old Age and Survivors Insurance beneficiaries by the United States Social Security Administration showed that the median income of married couples was about $183 a month. For re-

[11]*Ibid*, p. 11.

tired unattached men it was about $97. One fourth had no support apart from social security insurance payments. As our chapter on poverty indicated, most aged persons in our society are severely pinched if not impoverished.

The problem of housing the aged in urban communities is an extension of this more general support problem. By retirement age or several years thereafter, older persons ordinarily revise their shelter arrangements. All but about one fifth lack the income and physical strength to maintain the shelter they may have inhabited for many years. Internal deterioration often combines with neighborhood change, often blighting, to leave aged persons with depreciated housing that does not fit their needs or their levels of living. Cities lack the types of housing and the supply that would be required to meet the increasing aggregate need for this special population.

Where housing for the aged is dispersed through the community, it is usually not designed for aging persons. Exclusive of Florida retirement housing programs, few steps have been taken to design shelter to meet the realities of the much extended lifespan of most Americans. Some older, less physically able persons require group housing, where housekeeping functions are centralized. These are available only for the financially most solvent 20 per cent. Few aged persons want to be institutionalized in nursing homes or hospitals, but many who require such intensive medical and custodial care cannot afford to get it. Many others are institutionalized for want of alternative types of available housing. Not all aged persons are disposed, regardless of incentives, to leave their metropolitan area homes and migrate to sunny southern

centers of private housing development.

The National Housing Act of 1956 contained provisions to cope with this problem by making it easier for older persons to purchase homes; by financing nonprofit rental housing projects for the elderly; and by expanding the supply of low-rent public housing for older people. Under this section of the Housing Act, somewhat less than 5 thousand such dwellings had been erected by 1960. At the rate set during the first four years of operation, the total amount of construction for this purpose — nearly all of it within cities — will not exceed 10 thousand by 1965. Experimentation and demonstration of housing possibilities are flourishing, especially with support from large private foundations. But no concerted public attention and no clear means of meeting this need has yet crystallized.

The Homeless Man on Skid Row

The need for housing for the aged in cities represents a problem resulting from population dynamics: the life span has expanded faster for more persons than have the social mechanisms for responding to the change through diversified housing, to mention but one lagging response. Skid Row men represent a relevant contrast, for this metropolitan group, which is as old as the Middle Ages, is *diminishing* in number.

A homeless man is a city-dweller who is separated from family, kin, and friends. Lacking resources, he settles into the cheapest backwaters of the nation's largest central cities, in blighted blocks which specialize commercially in housing these men. Such a sector is usually termed a Skid Row or Skid Road, a place where men on the way down and out of the social structure congregate.[12]

Historically, Skid Rows have not served a specific type of man. They have rather operated as repositories for a variety of persons. These ranged from those workers whose jobs depended upon the seasons—harvesters, lumberjacks, fruit-pickers, and ice-harvesters— to those who were ill and destitute. The number and variety of men congregated in a city fluctuated with the seasons and with times of depression and prosperity. The Chicago Municipal Lodging House provided nearly half a million lodgings in 1914, for example, but in 1919, the same welfare agency closed its doors for lack of applicants. Wartime prosperity was the cause.[13]

As the size of this homeless population has diminished, the *toughness* of solving the social problem, the life condition of these men, has increased however. For in place of the bulk of migratory workers and temporarily unemployed men, Skid Rows now harbor, for the most part, the physically disabled, the aged, and chronic alcoholics. While programs of planned solution have been proposed, *no* major city in the United States has, as of 1963, instituted an attack on this special problem. Some five cities are conducting small experiments.

Public Initiative: Preface

In emphasizing urban problems of habitation, we have neglected a variety of severe strains peculiar to urban institutions — religious, educational, medical, and commercial — which are fixed physically in place but which must adapt to rapid social changes that threaten to leave them outmoded or misdirected functionally. This order of problem is symbolized by the Lutheran Church that was the one structure to be left standing in an urban renewal project in Philadelphia. The denomination fought effectively to retain its edifice. Now, its minister and staff are left to await the effects of a marked change in the locality and its population. Will old programs of this church have any relevance for the new neighborhood residents? Will old members who fled to the suburbs continue to be attracted back into the city to attend this church? Does this edifice have functions to perform in its presently indeterminate milieu?

We might take another tack, however, and lump churches, schools, stores, streets, power lines, telephone systems, gas lines, and water mains together as services. In composite, these are the networks of facilities produced by the interplay between technology, the environment and the social structure, that supply the *context* within which housing and transport problems take on significance. Modern living without adequate services is not merely inconvenient; for a given city neighborhood or a new tract development in the suburbs, inadequate services can spell disorganization and a collapse of land and other values basic to local community maintenance.

Most technical aspects of providing adequate services have been solved in the United States. Very complicated and costly planning is required, but the knowledge and experience are available. Indeed, communities within a large metropolitan area can be planned physi-

---

[12]See H. Warren Dunham, *Homeless Men and Their Habitats,* Wayne University, 1953. Also, Tenants Relocation Bureau, *The Homeless Man on Skid Row,* City of Chicago, September, 1961.
[13]*The Homeless Man on Skid Row, ibid.,* p. 5

cally and developed comprehensively so that services as well as housing and transportation can be rather uniformly packaged. This technical knowledge liberates services from place. A church may serve not a local parish but a radius of Sunday commuters as wide as an entire metropolitan area. A store is not rooted to its street-corner, with truck deliveries and telephone orders and storage and preparation systems.

Characteristically, the mid-century urban American entering a metropolitan area buys or rents more than housing. With his housing come services which he purchases through cash and taxes. The quality and style of these is for the most part a matter of the level of living the individual consumer can afford financially to maintain.

In this respect, the bases of community life are severely refracted. A community has until recently been a relatively local population of interdependent groups. Under this new technology, proximity in location is rendered irrelevant. One may buy more or less of it, as he chooses. He can purchase a package of shelter and all related services built into a single complex within the city, or he can purchase their dispersed equivalent in the suburbs.

A local population was once interdependent through its division of labor. Under the new urban condition, one may sleep in one place and work in another, have kin in a third, and maintain friendships with people dispersed through a dozen surrounding localities. There is an elaborate division of work in modern cities, but it does not depend very deeply upon proximity. Rather, places are set apart for special activities, and people travel to them. Similarly, public services may be centralized in a place, with their functions being transported to consumers.

Community interdependence was also once a result of relative cultural unity. Communities were experienced as communities because their social structures embodied standards of social conduct, ways of doing things, and reasons for doing them that way.

Urbanization liberates persons and groups from such cultural unity. We must not, however, regard this force as therefore disunifying or disintegrative of social structure or its cultural patterning. What seems to result under the new condition is a variety of bases for shared standards of conduct. One chooses his 'cultural envelope' from a baffling, perhaps dazzling, array of alternatives.

Why, then, in the face of these dramatic changes, have we singled out the problem of housing? It is not that housing is the most challenging strain. Rather, the development of the governmental complex around housing contains, we believe, the outline of the future city as it unfolds on many other dimensions of activity and need, including the dimension of change in the character of community.

Public Initiative

Federal leadership in urban affairs has, for political reasons, been comparatively slow in developing. The Department of Agriculture was founded more than a century ago (1862), and has exerted Cabinet-level influence on rural social and economic issues for decades. The irony is that cities exert enormous political and economic influence over their hinterlands; yet in government legislatures, their needs were not voiced in persuasive organized fashion until the Great Depression era.

Federal leadership during the New Deal was stimulated less by an urban orientation (although it is true that there were vital linkages between the Roosevelt Administration and local Democratic Party strength concentrated in large central cities) and more by an effort to help commercial activity by priming the housing industry. Sheriff sales and mortgage foreclosures were so frequent, for example, that the Roosevelt Administration designed the Home Owners Loan Corporation in 1933, ostensibly to relieve the distress experienced by home owners. Actually, housing was a promising arena within which to cultivate urban political support among voters *and* to increase employment and reduce local relief costs. Again, the Federal Housing Administration was set up in 1934 to reinvigorate private construction. These and other primarily urban housing agencies were consolidated into a National Housing Agency in 1942.

During World War II, the federal government got even more deeply involved in financing and managing the housing economy. Military housing, civilian shelter for war workers, and programs of rent control, were erected to mobilize the population and its resources for warfare.

Intensified industrialization for war stimulated in-migration to the cities and, by 1946, the nation was confronted by a severe metropolitan housing shortage. The emergency housing agencies and their programs which grew first from the Depression and, second, from the War, were therefore renewed and elaborated to attempt to meet national postwar housing requirements. A Veterans Emergency Housing Program was passed in 1946, and the National Housing Agency projected mechanisms for stimulating new construction through private builders.

The postwar thrust of federal leadership declined, however, as private sectors of the economy exerted new influence against further incursions. Congress refused to enact price controls on building materials, new houses, and building lots, as several bills proposed in 1946 and 1948. Programs for financing low-cost public housing in cities were also defeated.

Relations between federal programs and housing as the single domain of urban life to receive concerted attention remained uncertain until 1965, when a Cabinet-level Department of Housing and Urban Development came into being, for example. At stake are extensive and complicated private economic interests and enterprises and, of equal significance, issues of state as well as municipal political authority.

The postwar housing shortage was so pressing that in spite of counterforces, federal programs were further enlarged in 1949. Since that time, public housing programs have remained intensely controversial. But the Housing and Home Finance Agency, the present unit which houses all continuous programs for housing, has extended its role year by year until it has become the major financial agent in most domains of urban housing.

The Federal Housing Administration illustrates this. It has survived since the Roosevelt Administration. It does not itself lend money for building, but by insuring the loans of money by local lenders it affects the amount of new private construction. Because it operates as an insurance system, it is designed to reinforce soundness in the housing economy. To guarantee 'good risks,' it maintains building standards and so affects the quality of the industry and its products. For private homes and, to a lesser extent, for commercial rentals, the Federal Housing Administration in effect manages a national mortgage system, a program of monthly amortization payments, schedules for repayment of debts, and influences interest rates. In any given year, the FHA covers about one fourth of the mortgages extended on new nonfarm dwellings. In less than 25 years, therefore, its policies have come to exert tremendous indirect force upon urban life.

Urban Renewal

The Housing and Home Finance Agency (HHFA) engages in many programs other than the underpinning of the private single-family dwelling industry. It operates a program of research and statistical reporting which centralizes knowledge of the urban scene. It provides money and skill for local municipal planning, including planning for relations between public and commercial services and transport systems, as well as programs of housing. It makes loans to colleges for building programs, loans for improving public facilities in smaller communities, loans for housing projects and programs for the aged, home repair and improvement loan insurance, and related enterprises.

In his Housing Message in 1961, President Kennedy asserted, "Unless we increase the supply of low-rent (public) housing, our communities cannot rid themselves of slums, provide adequate community facilities, and rehouse low-income families displaced by clearance operations." The assertion reflected the interest of his administration in improving the legislative basis for federal financing of public housing projects in central cities.

This basis is incomplete, but the Housing Act of 1961 authorized the Public Housing Administration of HHFA to contract with local government authorities to erect roughly 100 thousand new public housing units. Reflecting the controversial character of

public—which means governmentally subsidized—housing this Act, like previous ones, requires municipalities to make prompt and full repayment to the federal government on loans for this purpose.

In spite of the impressive array of federal programs just catalogued, in other words, housing blight and the larger problem of imbalances between urban development and growing population requirements are *not* attacked directly by any one or all of the HHFA programs. Urban housing and related services are not public facilities to date, nor are they subsidized substantially through public federal means.

The exception to this pattern, and what we consider the chief prototype for future development in national approaches to solutions of urban social problems is the Urban Renewal Program of the HHFA. Since 1949, the Congress has enacted provisions for loans, grants, technical assistance, and special mortgage insurance to so-called urban renewal areas, "Taken together these represent a 'kit of tools' making possible a partnership among local governments, private enterprise, citizens, and the Federal Government in mounting an offensive against slums and the causes of urban blight."[14]

Central to the Urban Renewal Program is the concept of *capital grants*. Many other forms of assistance are available, but the crucial feature of the program is that federal monies are provided for as much as three fourths of the net costs for acquisition, demolition and clearance, and rebuilding of urban buildings and whole neighborhoods.

Contract authority totalling about two billion dollars was arranged for

[14]*The Urban Renewal Program Fact Sheet,* HHFA, February, 1962, Government Printing Office, p. 1.

urban renewal projects between 1949 and 1961. Slum clearance and renewal projects relocated or displaced more than 85 thousand households during that time. By 1970, an estimated one million persons in cities will be displaced by renewal and related local and federal development activities. To an ever-increasing extent, then, this program will have the greatest effects on the living environment of metropolitan households of any activity engaged in by the Federal Government.

This program has struggled to exert public influence within a structure that involves all levels of government and crucial sectors of the private economy at the same time it impinges intimately upon the life settings of individual citizens. Nothing short of foreign affairs requires more intricate development and sensitive political timing.

The entire program has grown up around the objective of supplementing rather than supplanting private markets and local and state authority. Therefore, when a subcommunity has been acquired and most of its structures demolished, local agencies typically place the cleared land on the market for use by private developers. Where rehabilitation rather than demolition is the end, federal monies have been introduced to enable private markets to become active with properties that would otherwise have proved unprofitable for investment. A portion of the cost is written off as a loss.

Characteristically, it takes a city four years to put together the outlines of what HHFA calls a *workable program*. It then takes another two or three years to negotiate changes in the plan and to move it through each part of each level of government. For a single neighborhood filled with overcrowded and obsolete residential and service structures, then, as much as a decade is needed to

so much as approach fiscal, technical, and political consensus around a project.

At this point, a city may exercise eminent domain: It may acquire at fair market prices the structures and properties to be demolished or rehabilitated. Because ownership is so complicated, markets are so sensitive to change, and the politics of acquisition and human relocation are so treacherous, a neighborhood or larger inner city area may be the focus of massive public and private energies as well as dollars for fifteen years before one neighborhood has been reduced to the rubble that signifies a cleared space.

There is no direct route to the exertion of force, financial or political, upon this single city problem of blight. Yet we select the residential slum and the operation of the federal renewal program upon it as an example of the single public activity occurring on the contemporary urban scene. The delay between the promise and the realization of redevelopment is echoed in the statistics of urban renewal operations. Of the 2.7 billion dollars committed for such projects as of May, 1962, less than $600 million were actually disbursed.

On the surface, it seems as if two new neighborhoods of blight take form during every decade within which one is redeveloped. Beneath this discouraging impression, however, is the fact that the mere availability of federal monies and their commitment to redevelopment results in powerful stimulation of local metropolitan reconstruction. The structure of the situation is such that support is channeled and expended only slowly and cautiously. But its existence induces private investment, local political reorganization and revitalization, and ramifies in programs of health, education, and welfare institutions not directly attached to housing.

Urban Transport

Aggravating the urban housing problem is the urban population expansion, described at the outset of this chapter. We review the salient facts here in order to apply them to transportation as a problem as pressing, and probably more complex with regard to solutions, than the problem of housing: The metropolitan areas of the United States grew four times faster than all the remaining combined territory of the nation from 1950 to 1960. Of the urban increase of 23 million persons in this decade, 18.1 million occurred in the suburban and nonfarm areas surrounding the central cities.

Population increases fastest in those areas where automobile ownership is most dense. Indeed, urban outer ring and suburban growth has been made possible by extension of ownership of automobiles. The tremendous redistribution—the concentration in cities and deconcentration from their center into suburbs—is a function of automotive transport as it has evolved since 1910.[15]

Some experts think of this as a

[15]Thomas J. Seburn and Bernard L. Marsh, *Urban Transportation Administration,* Bureau of Highway Traffic, Yale University, 1959, pp. 4-16. So powerful is this technological thrust that: "The demand for new transportation facilities increases independently and at a faster rate than the population. One factor is the continuing shift to the use of the private automobile which is a prominent characteristic of urban society today ... Rural land is presently being converted to urban use at the rate of a million acres per year. New suburbanized industries and other traffic generators required added facilities to meet new travel desire lines ... A complicating factor for the central city is that many of the residents of the outlying jurisdictions work in the central city. The street system of the central city is overloaded by traffic generated in areas outside its control. This requires heavy expenditures for controls, improvements, maintenance, enforcement, and parking. The central city finds little opportunity for extracting tax revenues from those creating the need for these expenditures."

single urban problem of *congestion.* They lump noise, air pollution, residential, pedestrian and automotive crowding, and traffic snarls into a single box. The central city is viewed as a kind of sinkhole down which the effects of crowding in traffic and housing, generated by the large metropolitan area, are poured. This ignores the scope and detailed complexity of the several problems.

For example, traffic congestion and transport control problems are not limited to the inner city. As new suburbs develop, new local streets are built. Arterial routes are generated by suburban residential and commercial development. Most of these are built and regulated by state and county governments. They intersect and in other ways strain the larger expressway system of interstate defense highways.

The financial and managerial tasks of keeping pace with all forms of highway expansion interact with programs of renewal in the central cities. Renewal stimulates new growth and maintains central city population levels (although overconcentrations in blighted sectors may be changed). National policy is committed to retaining the form of central cities as centers of work and housing. Systems of mass transit must therefore also be maintained, especially rail and subway and bus operations, if ease of public movement, so crucial to economic integration and vitality in the city, is to be maintained. Yet automotive transport competes so effectively with mass transit that the financial position of the mass transit is undermined. Central cities must have public transport systems, but such systems no longer pay their own way. In the same way, the automotive transport undermines the value of housing and commercial facilities in the inner ring of the city.

These are two sides of the urban

transport problem: the demands upon metropolitan resources and government to keep pace with the requirements of metropolitan areas for automotive transport, and the effects of this demand upon the central city. A third facet is a by-product of the same automotive revolution: traffic accidents.

According to the Interstate Commerce Commission, passenger deaths in 1961 in automobiles and taxis (on roads other than turnpikes) occurred at the rate of 2.2 per one hundred million miles driven, compared with rates of .16 for buses, .10 for trains, and .69 for domestic airplanes (scheduled commercial). Of the 91 thousand accidental deaths of all types in the nation in 1961, 38 thousand, or more than one third, were caused by motor vehicle accidents. As a killer, the motor vehicle, and primarily the private automobile travelling in metropolitan areas, ranks as follows:

Cause of Death — 1961	Rate per 100,000 Population
Major heart diseases	514.0
Malignant cancer	147.5
Early infancy diseases	36.6
Flu and pneumonia	29.8
Accidents, other*	30.2
Motor vehicle accidents	20.5
	778.6
All other causes, residual	151.7
Total rate, all causes	930.3

*These include falls, burns, drownings, railroad, firearm, poisons. Source: Public Health Service, U.S. Department of Health, Education and Welfare.

Motor vehicle accidents and deaths are major destructive forces in American life. Death by motor vehicle is difficult to evaluate in absolute terms, however dreadful and common it is. It is hard to know whether to compare it with death by disease, or only with other sources of accidents. The social component of mortality from early diseases in infancy suggests that disease comparisons are relevant. The nonwhite infant mortality rate, for example, is nearly twice that of the white — an unmistakable but less visible form of unjust jeopardy. It is hard to know whether to say the death rate for motor accidents was 'only' two thirds the total rate for "Accidents, other," or to consider this evidence of excess. Moreover, the death rate for motor vehicles has declined slightly, yet steadily, during the past 20 years.

Automotive transport threatens human health as well as life by indirect as well as direct if accidental means. Take air pollution as a single case in point:

In the Los Angeles Basin's 4000 square mile area, public transport is relatively nonexistent. The inhabitants, to a man, use the automobile to move about the area. Some three million internal combustion engines puff along streets, byways and freeways pouring almost 6000 tons of pollutants per day (68% of the total) into the air over Los Angeles County, while power plant stacks in the area contribute a mere 256 tons, or three per cent of total air contaminants. Remaining 29 per cent is attributed to miscellaneous sources.[16]

We know that this pollution is irritating and in all respects undesirable as a feature of contemporary urban life. We do not yet know whether the inhalation of air polluted by automotive exhaust 'produces' cancer of the lungs, although many physicians assume this to be the case. All authorities agree that private cars contribute very heavily to current

[16]"Air Pollution," Special Report Issue of *Power,* December, 1960, p. 102.

levels of urban air pollution, and that this pollution is a grave *potential* hazard to human health, expecially for persons with chest, lung, or heart disorders.[17]

Urban Automotive Transport as a Social Problem

We have set out the features of the situation, but we have not identified a distinctively social aspect to the problem. Urban Americans clearly *want* to travel by car, even if such travel is costly, hazardous, and extremely demanding upon the planning and control functions of government. What, then, makes this a social problem?

The new automotive and highway systems of transportation, and the effects of this system, transcend the old pre-auto boundaries of taxation and governmental control. Roads were once a *local* affair. Their construction and management, like operation of the housing industry, could be handled locally. This has become a major national political and economic subject. With the passage of the Federal Aid Highway Act of 1956, Congress pledged its support for the construction of 41 thousand miles of the National System of Interstate and Defense Highways. About 24.8 billion dollars for this system are federal, matched by 2.6 billion dollars in state funds. By about 1972, this new system will connect 48 of the states and link all but 23 of the nation's 212 metropolitan areas into one integrated circulatory pattern.

As this national network unfolds and stimulates further urbanization and suburbanization, local road construction and control must keep pace or risk

extreme imbalance. Yet, metropolitan areas are not integrated politically. No government agency is in a position to pass and enforce laws for such areas, or to tax and spend for such areas. Indeed, a typical metropolitan area contains between one thousand and 1.5 thousand governments and roughly 100 autonomous municipalities.[18]

Under this condition, it is impossible to plan an orderly local road system, to share policing of the roads and inspection of vehicles, to distribute the burden of traffic costs equitably, or to manage rational location of residential and commercial facilities within the transport network.

If one ignores the norm of quality of the system, if one settles for some confusion and mismanagement, the sheer rate of growth of auto traffic will require change. Nearly 70 per cent of all automobiles are concentrated in the urban areas, and the number of motor vehicles in the United States has grown from 32.5 million in 1940, to 78.6 million in 1962, and may exceed 100 million by 1975.

If this were a matter of simply investing more money in the transport system, we might view this as an economic, not a social, problem. *But the money is available:*

> This is the root of the metropolitan financial problem: How to divert a larger share of resources to government use, or more simply, how to get more funds than existing revenue systems will produce, without unduly impinging on private production... Metropolitan financial problems [stem] primarily from the lack of adequate machinery rather than from any lack of capacity... Today's large

[17]John R. Goldsmith and Lewis H. Rogers, "Health Hazards of Automobile Exhaust," *Public Health Reports*, June, 1959, Vol. 74, No. 6, pp. 551-558.

[18]Robert C. Wood, *Suburbia, Its People and Their Politics*, Boston: Houghton Mifflin, 1959.

urban communities, being typically the focal points of wealth and income, have the resources to meet their urban needs.[19]

Urban transport is a social problem, therefore, because Americans are constrained to choose expanding deficiencies, inefficiencies and life and health hazards in their movement through their metropolitan settings, or to choose increased governmental taxation and authority. Unlike the problem of urban housing, no controversy between public versus private responsibility haunts the traffic problem. All aspects of roads and their use, save the manufacture and sale of vehicles, have been in the public domain for centuries. But the scope and uniformity of that domain have changed. They must change faster if automotive transport is to continue at current levels of operation.

Solutions to urban traffic problems are available technically. Highway design, traffic volume control, safety appliances, exhaust fume appliances, and police coverage are examples of resources available through social as well as mechanical engineering. But to opt for these, Americans must want higher levels of taxation and greater centralized authority over land use, police, and institutional activities! Whenever American citizens are asked to choose by vote between expanding and limiting urban government, with rare exceptions they choose limitation.

As with approaches to urban housing, therefore, the attempt at solution 'drifts upward.' Federal and state highway programs are legislated without *direct* electoral choice. The inter-urban road system is put into place and locali-

ties struggle to adapt after the fact. The federal highway program, designed as it is to meet interstate and defense requirements, also contradicts the federal urban housing and renewal programs at many points. The highway program intensifies deconcentration, for one thing, while the central city renewal effort reconstructs the holding power of the central business district. Articulation of the two federal activities is left, for the most part, to state and local planners and engineers who lack the fiscal means or political authority to cope with discrepancies.

Summary

The point of view of this chapter has been that the major contemporary social problems of cities result from incompatible rates of change between growth in technology, an expanding and redistributing population, outmoded forms of settlement and habitation, and the availability of political mechanisms for regulating relations between them.

Several types of urban housing problems—total supply versus need, central city blight, and dilemmas of the aged and the homeless—illustrate these incompatibilities. The impact of metropolitan area growth and deconcentration upon local community organization was treated as a second demonstration of the overall situation. Social aspects of urban transportation—insufficient metropolitan governmental authority and money to implement this authority—were then considered as effects of imbalance in diverse rates of technical and social change.

Attention to federal initiatives in housing and transportation suggested that it is at this *national level* that the society is coping with its varied and

[19]Lyle C. Fitch, "Metropolitan Financial Problems," *Annals* of the American Academy of Political and Social Science, November, 1957, Vol. 314, pp. 66-67.

contending urban problems. The national public programs were viewed as partly controversial and partly indirect in character. Efforts to cope with the most pressing urban problems center today in the Congress and the federal executive agencies. These efforts have not been integrated organizationally, nor is the magnitude of the federal activity apparent to the citizen at the local level. As federal urban renewal and highway construction enter the coming decade, the main problem in urban society may become the reorganization and improvement of local-to-federal and federal-to-local communication, control, and expenditure.

References

Anderson, Nels, *The hobo: the sociology of the homeless man*. Chicago, Phoenix Books, University of Chicago Press, 1923, 1961.

Back, Kurt. *Slums, projects, and people*. Durham, North Carolina, Duke University Press, 1962.

Bendix, Reinhard, and Seymour M. Lipset (eds.). *Class, status, and power*. Glencoe, The Free Press, 1953.

Bogue, Donald J. *Skid row in American cities*. Community and Family Study Center, University of Chicago, 1963.

Boskoff, Alvin, *The sociology of urban regions*. New York, Appleton-Century-Crofts, 1962.

Bremmer, Robert Hamlett. *From the depths: the discovery of poverty in the United States*. New York, New York University Press, 1956.

Caplovitz, David. *The poor pay more: consumer practices of low-income families*. New York, The Free Press, 1963.

Caudill, Harry M. *Night comes to the Cumberlands*. Boston, Little-Brown, 1963.

Centers, Richard. *The psychology of social classes*. Princeton, New Jersey, Princeton University Press, 1949.

Conference on Economic Progress, Washington, D.C. *Poverty and deprivation in the United States: the plight of two-fifths of a nation*. Washington, D.C. 1962 ("The Keyserling Report").

Evans, G. *War on want,* Pergamon Press: New York; Macmillan Company, 1963.

Gabriel, Kolko. *Wealth and power in the United States*. New York, Frederich Praeger, 1962.

Galbraith, John K. *The affluent society,* Boston, Houghton-Mifflin, 1958.

———— "Approach to poverty": address, June 3, 1962, *The Department of State Bulletin,* 46:1024-7, June 25, 1962.

Handlin, Oscar. *Uprooted,* Universal Library, Grosset and Dunlap, Inc.

Harrington, Michael. *The other America: poverty in the United States*. New York, Macmillan Company, 1962 Penguin Books, Inc, 1963.

Hunter, David. *The slums: challenge and response*. New York, The Free Press of Glencoe, 1965.

Lampman, Robert J. *The share of top wealth-holders in national wealth*. Princeton, New Jersey, Princeton University Press, 1962.

Lewis, Oscar. *Further observations on the culture of poverty*. Mimeographed essay, 1962, Department of Anthropology, University of Illinois, Urbana.

Luck, James Murray. *The war on malnutrition and poverty: the role of consumer co-operatives*. New York, Harper and Brothers, 1946.

MacDonald, Dwight, *Our invisible poor*. Reprint No. 23, Sidney Hillman Foundation, 1963.

Miller, S. M. "Poverty and inequality in America: implications for the social services." *Child Welfare*, December, 1963.

Morgan, James N., et al., *Income and welfare in the United States.* New York, McGraw-Hill Book Company, 1962.

Passow, Harry A. (ed.). *Education in depressed areas.* New York, Bureau of Publications, T. C. Columbia University, 1963.

Schorr, Albert L. *Slums and social insecurity.* U.S. Government Printing Office, Washington, D.C., 1963.

—— "Filial responsibility and the aging." *Journal of Home Economics,* 54:271-6, April, 1962.

Sexton, Patricia. *Education and income.* New York, Viking Press, Inc. 1961.

U.S. Attorney General's Committee on Poverty and the Administration of Criminal Justice. *Poverty and the administration of federal criminal justice, report.* Washington, D.C. 1963.

Wilson, Charles Morrow. *The landscape of rural poverty: corn bread and creek water.* New York, Henry Holt and Company, 1940.

URBANIZATION—CHANGING PATTERNS OF LIVING
Kingsley Davis

If we look broadly at the history of the United States, we can discern certain geographical shifts of population which tell a fairly complete story. In broad outline, there are perhaps five major shifts. First, is the well-known westward migration of our people, which has continued with amazing persistence since the founding of our nation, and seems destined to go on for some time yet. Second, the less publicized but nevertheless impressive movement from South to North. Third, the continued movement of people from rural lands to major urban aggregations, which has already made this nation what I call an urbanized society. Fourth, the greater participation of one-tenth of our population, the Negroes, in all three of these movements—in the South-to-North, the East-to-West, and the rural-to-urban movements. Fifth, the accelerating deconcentration of the populations in our big and growing metropolitan areas.

I shall not go into detail on the South-to-North movement, except to note that in 1950 there were two million more people who were born in the

Reprinted, with permission of author and publisher, from *The Changing American Population*, Arden House Conference, Institute of Life Insurance, 1962, pp. 59-68.

South but living in the North than vice versa. In other words, over roughly a lifetime there was a net residue of two million migrants from South to North.

Connected with the five geographical shifts in the United States are two other trends—the sustained growth of population in the nation, and the rising level of living. These long-run persistent factors are partly responsible for and partly the result of the geographical shifts.

Let me deal briefly with the westward movement and its urban implications. As indicated already, its most distinctive feature is its persistence. The historian, Frederick Jackson Turner, thought of the moving frontier as the dominant force in American history, and he described that frontier as essentially being gone by 1890. It turns out that Turner was thinking altogether too heavily in terms of the role of agriculture, and hence of free land, in the westward movement. There is no indication whatever that the westward movement diminished after 1890.

If we take the block of states grouped as the West, and compute the ratio of their population growth to that of the nation as a whole, we find that the West never gained in population less than one and a half times, or more than three and a half times, what the entire country gained. The advantage of the West in population growth in the 1940-50 decade was higher than it was in any but two previous decades. The 1950-60 advantage was below average, but still above what it was in the 1910-to-1930 period. In the decade of the 1950's the West added eight million to its population. One state, California, added more than five million, more people than any but six states had in 1950. Of this additional five million in California, 62 per cent can be estimated to be due to net in-migration and only 38 per cent to natural increase. Since Californians reproduce at about the national average, their greater growth in population is due to in-migration.

Why this continued movement from East to West, long after the frontier was closed? Undoubtedly the answer lies in greater economic opportunities, but not solely or even chiefly in agriculture. In 1960 only 5.3 per cent of the population of the West was classified as farm. In California in 1950 only 5.5 per cent of the state's population was classified as rural farm, and of the five and one-tenth million increase in the state's population between 1950 and 1960, 92.1 per cent occurred in the urbanized areas. These urbanized areas constituted only 1.9 per cent of the total area of the state.

The East-to-West migration is overwhelmingly a movement to cities and to urban occupations, and not into agriculture. The continuance of the movement has been due to the lateness and hence the greater modernity of economic development in the West. The Eastern Seaboard was settled in a pre-industrial era, under an old-line, only partially modernized European-type agriculture; and it was fairly densely settled under that kind of an economy. It was not easy, therefore, for this area to rationalize its economic activities. It did rationalize them in part, especially in the northern part of the Eastern Seaboard, under the stimulus of its tremendous trade and commerce with Europe. As population moved into the Midwest, it moved at a time when the industrial revolution was already under way, so that the new economic activities, including agriculture, were pursued on a more rationalized economic basis.

As a consequence, the Midwest never acquired the high ratio of people to land that the Eastern Seaboard exhibited. Especially in the western part of the Midwest, an extensive, highly rationalized agriculture developed which used relatively little manpower. It looked for a while as if the Midwest—from Minnesota and the Dakotas on down—would develop in much the same way as the New World nations arriving late in the industrialization process did (Argentina, New Zealand and Australia, for example), with tremendous urbanization and highly rationalized agriculture using very scant manpower. The only trouble was that this western part of the Midwest was not itself a whole country. The main market cities for its products and sources of its manufactures were not there in its own territory but on the seaboard where the commerce was. And so, there came a brake to the development of the Midwest, which slowed it down and caused it to remain more agricultural than most of the other areas. The region was too remote from international commerce and trade.

The Far West came still later in its development and hence started at a yet more modernized level. Being more rationalized from the beginning in its economic development, it could pay higher wages and could thus exert a tremendous pull on migrants. Some areas of the Far West never went through an agricultural phase at all. California, for example, had most of its people in mining at first, and they shifted very quickly to urban occupations. The state never had more than 23 per cent of its labor force in agriculture. It skipped the agrarian phase completely and went on into a modern urbanized economy.

If you analyze the industries on the Far West Coast now, you can see that they tend to be high-technology industries, using the newest kind of plants, equipment, knowledge and so forth, and paying high wages. It is the high wages —not the climate—which keeps bringing people into the West.

The tremendous East-West migration has clearly had an effect upon urbanization. The two most urbanized areas today are the Middle Atlantic, on the one hand—the old industrial area— and, on the other hand, the Pacific Coast, the most recently settled area, which means that the Pacific Coast has accomplished its urban industrial revolution in a fraction of the time that it took the Eastern Coast to accomplish it. As a consequence, many of the cities in the western area were built after the automobile age. They give us a glimpse of the wave of the future if things are permitted to go as modern technology dictates. I suppose that wave of the future is best represented by Los Angeles. In that city they probably now have more miles of freeway per citizen —they certainly have more cars per family—than any other urbanized area in the United States. I find very few people who like it.

Urbanization in the United States, if you take the nation as a whole, not the western regions that I have been talking about, reached its fastest pace in the previous century. If you take the propor-

tion that is urban and analyze the percentage by which it rises each decade, the average rise per decade from 1820 to 1870, which was the most rapid period of urbanization, was 29.3 per cent. From 1900 to 1960 the average rise in the proportion was only 9.1 per cent, or less than a third what it was earlier. So the great wave of urbanization in this country occurred a long time ago.

This is only natural. We are measuring urbanization by the proportion living in towns or cities. One gets much the same curve by taking the proportion of the population in places of 100,000 or over as by taking simply the proportion urban. As the saturation point is reached, as most of the population is already living in cities, there are fewer and fewer other people to draw from to furnish increments to the cities. The percentage increase in the proportion urban is bound eventually to taper off. It yields what we call a logistic-type curve, which eventually flattens out. Our cities, however, are still growing, and growing rapidly. This growth is not due to rural-urban migration any more, but to natural increase. From here on out, you can expect that most of the growth in the urban population—in fact, the overwhelming bulk of it—is going to be just a function of the rapidity of growth of the national population. By now we have a high degree of urbanization. In 1960, for example, there were nearly 96 million people living in the urbanized areas that the Census Bureau delimits. This did not include all of the urban population, because there is some urban population outside of the urbanized areas. Nevertheless, 53.4 per cent of the population in 1960 was living in the urbanized areas. These areas occupied a territorial expanse that was only 0.71 per cent of the total land area of the United States.

I find it ironic that we in the United States often talk about the heavy population densities in India, Egypt, Java, Japan and so forth, when *we* are living at actual effective population densities that would make these people cringe. If you speak not of human density but of the number of automobiles per square mile, ours is the most densely settled country in the world. This is especially true when you realize that most of the automobiles are housed in the urbanized 0.71 per cent of the territory of the United States. Anybody who pays storage bills in Manhattan will soon discover that our auto density is high.

It is difficult to determine where the saturation point will be reached in the process of urbanization in the United States. I suppose we shall eventually reach the point that seems to have been reached in England, where the big ones begin to eat up the little ones. In this situation it is not the rural people but the smaller urban centers that are disappearing. The latter are being engulfed by the expanding large urbanized areas, or else, if remote from those large areas, they are being abandoned.

It would be very difficult to have continued urbanization of the population, in the sense of their living in big cities, if they continued to pile into the same old boundaries of those cities. You can see what would have happened in New York City if all of the population that lives in the outlying areas of the New York metropolitan area had crowded into the city over the decades, instead of living out in the suburbs. Manhattan, for example, would be even more of an impossible place than it already is. Something has been occurring which I find everybody has noticed but few have been able to define or analyze clearly. It is called by various names: suburbanization, metropolitan deconcentration, decentralization, metropolitan dispersion, centrifugal urban expansion, fringe development, and so forth.

Whatever is meant, this movement is not simply an expansion of the territory occupied by an urban aggregate. Everybody can see that the edges of our urban aggregates are moving out. But they are almost bound to move out as they grow in population. Where else could the people go? If you continuously emit sand from one spout, the pile will grow both upward and outward. Similarly, as cities grow in population, as they are doing and will continue to do in this country, their boundaries will inevitably expand. Surely this is not what is meant by urban deconcentration. There has always been expansion of cities beyond their boundaries. Even the medieval cities kept building beyond the wall to get more space for the expanded body of citizens.

As the phrase "suburban movement" is used today, there are three connotations that imply that it is something more than the normal expansion of city territory as the city population grows. There is, first, the implication that the suburbs have developed particularly in the last few decades and that they are therefore a recent phenomenon, whereas the mere expansion of cities at their edges is an old phenomenon. Second, there is the notion that although suburbs are appearing at great distance from the central city, they are composed heavily of people who work in the central city. For this reason they are sometimes called dormitory or bedroom towns, or residential suburbs. The journey to work has become a problem in modern society in consequence. There is, finally, the characterization of the suburbs as low-density areas of settlement. Perhaps the term that carries all of the three implications better than any other is "urban fringe." And it is of interest that it is precisely the urban fringe, the farthest-out zone of the urbanized area, which has exhibited the largest percentage increase in population.

It is possible to find an operational definition of metropolitan deconcentration which will take care of the elements of recency, commutation and low density. This definition is as follows: Urban deconcentration is occurring when the city's territory is growing at a more rapid rate than its population. Concentration is occurring when the opposite is occurring. I am obviously not referring to the city in its political sense, but in its ecological sense—that is, the actual urban aggregate and its expansion. If the territory is growing faster than the population, the city is deconcentrating; if the opposite is true, it is concentrating.

I have tried to examine such deconcentration with reference to two or three cities—unfortunately, not in the United States, because I could not get the data. I found that, according to my operational definition, London had been deconcentrating ever since 1811, but that the movement accelerated and became very rapid after 1921. With Britain's population hardly growing at all, the population of the London urbanized area absolutely declined between 1939 and 1957, but the territory covered by this area expanded. This would appear to be the condition reached when an economy attains a very advanced state. In London, as in the United States, the population was diffusing so rapidly that it was penetrating far into the surrounding rural zone. Such interpenetration of urban with rural modes of settlement

and exploitation makes it difficult to measure just where the urban aggregate extends to.

Another kind of deconcentration, which I have called internal deconcentration, occurs when the different zones within the urban aggregate become more equal in population density. As most of us know, the central part of our cities either has been growing slowly or has been declining in population. Now, if the total population remained the same and the boundaries remained the same, this would mean that people near the center had been moving into other bands, the consequence being an equalization of density across the different bands of the city. This type of deconcentration seems to have been occurring along with the other kind. London has reached the point where, in 1957, the average person lived about seven miles from the center. This was, as nearly as we can calculate, more than four times what it was in 1831.

What explains this deconcentration? People often offer a psychological interpretation to the effect that city-dwellers like green scenery and open spaces. This seems to be absolutely true, but it is of no value in explaining urban deconcentration, because the latter is a *recent* phenomenon. The truth is that our cities now are better places to live in than they were back in, say, the post-medieval period. Since at that time they were awful dumps, you would think that the urge to get out was even greater then than it would be now. People have always liked to be in open spaces, to see greenery; and to have some distance between themselves and their neighbors.

The next most common explanation of urban deconcentration is better transportation. But the effect of the first improvements in city transport was to concentrate people, not to spread them. The early rapid transit developments involved such heavy capitalization that they could be put only in areas where there was going to be dense population. In 1925, in four Boroughs of New York City, 91 per cent of the population was concentrated in the 40 per cent of the area which fell within a half-mile of the rapid transit lines. After the rapid transit lines were laid down, residences were concentrated near them because once the passengers got off, they could only walk, and they would not walk a great distance.

It was not until the automobile that improvements in transportation really facilitated urban deconcentration. This began around the period 1915 to 1920. The automobile, both as a private family vehicle and and as a bus for public transportation, gave a marvelously increased flexibility. It allowed the transportation network to be adapted to almost any residential pattern. Instead of location being determined almost completely by the transport system, the latter came to be determined by the people's preferences for living.

There were other factors that are generally ignored. One of them was the reduction in the hours of work. The reduction in hours of work was not only impressive from an over-all point of view, but also it tended to be selective: It was Saturday that tended to be dropped. The breadwinner who went into the central city had to go in now only five days a week instead of six. In a sense we have not really reduced the hours of work of the metropolitan resident, we have simply changed how he uses his hours. He now spends, say, an hour getting to work and an hour coming back, and his work week has been reduced two hours per day at the office. The result is that the week's work remains exactly what it was, in terms of total hours.

Perhaps this is one reason why the life-expectancy of females has been moving ahead faster than the life-expectancy of males. It is the breadwinner who goes into the city to work. Most of the people in the suburbs do not commute to the central city. In fact, only a very small fraction of them commute to the central city; and of that small fraction, overwhelmingly the commuters are the male breadwinners, on whom the brunt of the whole system necessarily falls.

As mentioned at the start, two abiding conditions under which the geographical shifts of our people have been occurring are the continued growth of the nation's total population and the continued increase in our level of living. Accordingly, in order to understand our urban deconcentration, you have to look at all of the segments of our lives; not merely at transportation to work, not merely at reduction in working hours, but also at other aspects of our increasingly efficient technology. For instance, one should look at the communications industry. If you live in the suburbs, your telephone works as well as it does in the city. You get the same TV programs, the same radio programs, as instantly as anybody in the central city does; usually, the recent movie comes out to the suburbs, sometimes even faster than it comes to the center of the city. Thus, you pay no penalty for living in the suburbs. The morning paper gets there before breakfast, just as it does in the center of the city. Due to our modern instantaneous communication, you are not isolated.

As for the social concomitants and

consequences of urban deconcentration, I must confess that I am speculating. This is a wide-open field. The "social consequences" of something always invite a speculative frame of mind and unwillingness to look for hard evidence. There is a reason for this: The hard evidence is usually extremely difficult to find. So anyone who differs is as much entitled to his opinion as I am to mine.

Let us begin with the family. One possibility is that the spread of city inhabitants to the surrounding suburban and fringe areas of the urbanized aggregates has aided the baby boom, and hence facilitated the population growth that is in part itself behind the expansion of these populations. One of the motives people have in mind for moving out to the suburbs is to find better places to rear children. There is more space in the suburbs for children to play and utilize their gadgets. Having moved out to the suburbs, the parents have less resistance than they would otherwise have to bearing more children. So there may be a stimulant to the birth rate in the very fact of suburban residence.

It is also possible to maintain that there has been a tendency for suburban living to pull the nuclear family apart. I realize this is heresy, because suburbs we regard as good things; the family is a good thing, and so, by the logic of social discourse, a good thing can never cause a bad thing, the tearing apart of the family.

But, as the work-place is moved farther from the home, as increased suburbanization tends to do, the husband's and the wife's worlds are further apart, both geographically and socially. Thus is explained the numerous articles in popular magazines about how the wife, who is living deep in the suburbs, is to cope with the secretary, who sees the husband all during the day.

The situation affects the children, too. Children in the suburbs presumably see their father less. They have only female models, the mother and the teachers in school all being females. This is particularly hard on the boys who have no male model after whom they can pattern themselves. They are unacquainted with that specific aspect of maleness which is the occupational pursuit of the father.

The situation may tend—and notice, I couch this in the subjunctive mood because I do not know for sure— to lead to over-intense but ineffective mother care. It is a peculiar thing, this mixture of extreme permissiveness and intense concern on the part of American parents. We let children do anything they want, and worry about everything they do. The mystery to me is how the children survive it; they manage to in most cases, but some of them come through only as psychic cripples.

The situation is one in which particularly the males could be expected to rebel against female domination. One form that the rebellion may take is peer group allegiance. Suburbs tend to be differentiated, as you know. There are wealthy suburbs, where, for the most part, men who have made the grade live, and they are not bothered with many young children around. Then there are the other, child-oriented suburbs, where the children are most in evidence. And here, of course, it is easy for the children to get together; in fact, they are encouraged to get together, because it is considered good child-rearing practice to have the children get along with their peers and see a lot of them. We are now acquainted with what David Riesman and others have pointed out as the emphasis on the peer-group in American life, in which the main interest of the youngster is in conforming to the group's expectations. These expectations are somewhat different from what adult expectations would be. Observers have noted a kind of anti-learning or anti-effort bias in these groups. Intellectual endeavor is identified with the alien and inimical adult world. Further, there is an unwillingness to do anything that makes one look queer. It has been discovered with some trepidation that the notion of "queer" on the part of our adolescents includes "odd-balls" like scientists, and this is in a society worried about the scarcity of highly trained manpower.

Shifting from these speculations concerning the family to a related subject, we can ask what the effects of urban deconcentration have been for work and leisure. One effect has been that people now draw a sharper distinction between work and non-work. The two have come to be separated in space. One works in the city or in an "industrial park" or other center; one spends one's leisure in the residential suburb. One works with one group and plays cards with another group. The work day is one thing, the non-work part of the day is something else. The work part is associated with pay, the other part with non-pay. We have had, in a sense, a redefinition of work and play.

The movement to the suburbs has accelerated one aspect of this new set of definitions by facilitating the "do-it-yourself" movement. Here, I think. the absurdity of the notion of work versus leisure begins to come to the fore. We notice that do-it-yourself activity required space. This requirement is inherent in certain kinds of do-it-yourself, like gardening; but other kinds require

space because they involve equipment. You have to have a place to put the power-saw, the power-sander, the power-drill, the power-grinder and the power-mower. The necessary space cannot be obtained in the city but only in the low-density suburbs. The movement to low-density areas on the outer edges of the metropolis is thus one of the stimulants to do-it-yourself, and do-it-yourself is one of the stimulants to the outward movement.

Do-it-yourself, including house-painting, plumbing, electrical repairs, toy manufacturing, tree-trimming, planting, lawn-maintenance, etc., embraces activities which, for the most part, we used to hire a specialist to come in and do. The head of the house now attempts to do them himself; it takes him three or four times as long as the specialist would take, and he is therefore working for very low wages. But still, the outside wages are so high that he cannot hire it done. Do-it-yourself is unpaid work and it is the obverse side of the reduction in paid-work-hours and the increase in paid-work wages.

We hear much about the "decline" of the center of cities, the central business district in particular. I find it extremely difficult, however, to get people to exactly pinpoint the problem. What is the trouble with the central part of cities? Is it the loss of residential population or the failure of the residential population to grow? Surely this is not a problem, for these places are too densely settled already. It is the solution of a problem to get people out of the crowded central cities and into less crowded suburbs.

Perhaps the worry is one that people often hesitate to talk about, especially in public and for the newspapers, namely, not so much a reduction in the proportion of people in the central city as a dramatic shift in the character of the population living there. To put it simply, the degree to which the central city maintains its residential population today is largely a function of how rapidly it brings in low-income migrants to replace the middle-class people who are leaving for the suburbs. Inevitably the economic and cultural level of the population at the center is lowered. Since the central city is usually a political entity, too, this has consequences for municipal finances, educational institutions, welfare work and so forth. It is in part the low-income Negroes, many from the South, who have gone to the central cities in great abundance and whose increase there represents not only a lowered economic level for central-city residents but a source of racial friction as well. The process has a spiral character. The more that low-income groups move into the central city, the more will higher-income groups want to move out.

THE CITY AS A SOCIAL ORGANISM
Leo F. Schnore

In his discussion of the emergence of the first urban areas, Lewis Mumford speaks of "little communal village cells, undifferentiated and uncomplicated, every part performing equally every function, turned into complex structures, organized on an axiate principle, with differentiated tissues and specialized organisms, and with one part, the central nervous system, thinking for and directing the whole."[1] This is the image of the city as a social organism.

What is the justification for such a view? We might begin with some specification of basic terms — "city," "social," and "organism." The term "city," of course, has many meanings, but the most common conception is legal or political; that is, the city is regarded as a kind of corporate entity possessing certain delegated powers. Thus, Eric E. Lampard quite properly observes that "city is the name given to certain urban communities in English-speaking countries by virtue of some legal or conven-

tional distinction."[2] For our purposes, however, such a conception is unduly restrictive.

We are interested in cities around the world, not just in English-speaking countries; and we are interested in cities of many forms, from the earliest urban islands that rose above the seas of agricultural villages, through city-states, through preindustrial and post-industrial cities to the Megalopolis of today. Thus, I think it is well to keep a certain looseness in our conceptions of the city, for the city is many things — political, economic and social, historical and geographic, physical, and even psychological. For present purposes, however, we can think of "city" as referring to a particular type of community — the urban community — a large, densely settled community devoted to nonagricultural activities.

Next, we will have to consider what "social" might mean. How shall we understand this term? It happens that the literature in sociology exhibits a very interesting tension or ambivalence between two fundamentally different

Reprinted, with permission of author and publisher, from *Urban Affairs Quarterly*, 1, No. 3, March, 1966, 58-69, copyright Sage Publications, Inc.

[1]Lewis Mumford. *The City in History* (New York: Harcourt, Brace & World, 1961), p. 34.

[2]Eric E. Lampard, "The City," an article prepared for a *Encyclopaedia Britannica*.

views. In the first view, "social" has reference to what we shall call concensus—an explicit or implicit understanding based on some kind of exchange of meaning within a shared frame of reference or universe of discourse. This view takes man's capacity for symbolic communication of ideas as central, focussing upon mental interpenetration, and a meeting of minds is seen as the critical feature of human conduct. Thus the city, along with such social forms as family and society, is regarded as one expression of a uniquely human capacity for meaningful communication.[3] This view is unquestionably valuable. It points to an aspect or facet of city life that is worthy of study in its own right. Yet, an exclusive emphasis upon consensus misses a more fundamental sense in which the term "social" has a great deal of meaning—a sense that permits us to speak of infrahuman social animals such as the so-called social insects. Such animals may be able to communicate rudimentary "ideas," but they are certainly limited by genetically determined characteristics to exchanges far less complex than those made by human beings.[4]

This second view of "social" stresses symbiosis or interdependence, whether or not it is mediated by the use of symbols. The relevance of such a view to any examination of the city becomes clear when one reminds himself that the city is simply not a self-sufficient or wholly independent entity. Rather, it is dependent—dependent on other areas such as rural areas for food and fiber and (through most of history) for men, or migrants to the cities. When we say that the city is dependent on other areas, whether we are thinking of rural areas or of other cities, we understand it to mean interdependent—especially in an economic sense. Cities offer things in return for still other things received by cities, whether these "things" are tangible goods or intangible services. The city is caught up in a kind of web of exchange relationships, supplying goods and services of a wide variety, including, most importantly, direction, control, integration, and coordination.[5]

All of these things are quite evident on the external side, for the interdependence of the city with other areas is obvious. The internal counterpart is somewhat less obvious. But, interdependence does exist *within* cities as well as *between* cities and other places, especially in the contemporary world. There is a territorial or geographic division of labor between the sub-areas making up the city. Most broadly, the division is between homes and workplaces, producing and consuming areas, between which there is a continuous flow of commodities, information, and people. It is exemplified by the stream of commuters between home and work. On a finer grain, there is also a division between areas devoted to different land uses—industrial, commercial, and recreational. From the standpoint of interdependence, then, the city is a "social" entity *par excellence,* for it displays both internal and external forms of symbiosis. Simulataneously, it reveals itself as an expression of symbolic communication between men.

It happens that these two faces of the city, the symbiotic and the consensual, were probably most clearly perceived in the 1920's by a sociologist

[3]Anselm Strauss, *Images of the American City* (New York: The Free Press, 1961).

[4]Martin Lindauer, *Communication Among Social Bees* (Cambridge: Harvard University Press, 1961).

[5]C. J. Galpin, *The Social Anatomy of an Agricultural Community* (Madison: University of Wisconsin Agricultural Experiment Station, May, 1915), "Research Bulletin No. 34."

at the University of Chicago, Robert E. Park. Park's thinking laid the groundwork for a singularly creative series of works by a group that came to be called the "Chicago School" of urban sociology. Park himself was a newspaperman before he was a sociologist, and he carried on a lifelong love affair with the city. In fact, he liked nothing better than to roam the alleys of Chicago and other cities, exploring backyards and observing cities from such vantage points as the lobbies of second-rate hotels. This was his style of work. And this is how he achieved his insight, for out of this habit of observation of city life and city ways, Park came to see that the city manifests a high degree of order and a remarkable level of organization *without* a perfect and somehow all-enveloping consensus. That is, the city was seen as an interdependent entity functioning quite effectively in the face of its inhabitants' indifference to and ignorance of the system as a whole. The residents of the city carried on their daily rounds and lived out their lives in their own small worlds, largely unaware of the larger unity of the city. At the same time, the city was exhibiting a life of its own.[6] This leads us quite naturally to the idea of the city as a so-called organism.

The notion of the community or the society as an "organism" is very old. The idea was especially prominent in the late nineteenth century, when biological reasoning, evolutionary and organismic, was in vogue. It probably reached its fullest and most detailed expression in the writings of Herbert Spencer, a British philosopher and sociologist. It has to be added that this mode of reasoning has since been virtu-

ally abandoned and, in the minds of many people, it has been thoroughly discredited. The historian Crane Brinton, for example, has asked, "Who now reads Spencer?" His question has been repeated by sociologists and others.[7] Without entering into a debate on the merits and demerits of analogous reasoning, without listing anew all of its uncritical uses, and without enumerating all the questionable purposes for which this particular analogy has been used, let us consider some of the ways in which the city may be considered *like,* though not identical to, an organism.

This approach is one way of bringing out the city's unit character, and a way of stressing the interdependence of its parts. In the words of Amos Hawley, a sociologist:

> This community has often been likened to the human individual organism. So intimate and so necessary are the interrelations of its parts, it has been pointed out, that any influence felt at one point is almost immediately transmitted throughout. Further, not only is the community a more or less self-sufficient entity, having inherent in it the principle of its own life process; it has also a growth or natural history with well-defined stages of youth, maturity, and senescence. It is therefore a whole which is something different from the sum of its parts, possessing powers and potentialities not present in any of its components. If not an organism, it is at least a super-organism.[8]

This quotation sketches the main

---

[6]Robert E. Park, "The City: Suggestions for the Investigation of Human Behavior in the Urban Environment," *American Journal of Sociology,* 20 (March, 1916), pp. 577-612.

[7]Crane Brinton, *English Political Thought in the Nineteenth Century* (London: Ernest Benn, 1949); quoted in Talcott Parsons, *The Structure of Social Action* (New York: The Free Press, 1949), p. 3.

[8]Amos H. Hawley, *Human Ecology: A Theory of Community Structure* (New York: Ronald Press, 1950), p. 50.

themes of organismic thinking about the community, and despite the questionable remark about the self-sufficiency of communities, the passage is a valuable summary of the organismic view.

I would like to underscore two points about the city as an organism. First, the parts, the individual human beings making up the city, can be regarded as replaceable and interchangeable. They are very much like cells and, as in the organism, cells may come and go and the organism itself may survive. One might ask if this is radically different from the fact that the city may live on, while people come and go. Secondly, the city may grow and there are young, middle-aged, and old cities. Cities are founded, or born. There are periods of rapid growth, as in "boom towns." Cities live and die. There are "ghost towns," or dead cities.

If all this seems a bit fanciful, or as simply playing games with words, I would remind you that a reversal of the procedure is frequently used. In other words, a "social-system analogy" is often employed in order to say something about individual organism. Communication systems, for example, are likened to the nervous system, with wires as ganglia, trunk lines as the spinal cord, etc. Similarly, transportation systems are likened to the circulatory system, with roads representing veins and arteries. The city is compared to the brain and the heart. Consider the following discussion of the "nervous system" of the higher organisms in a popular encyclopaedia:

> In the "division of labor" characteristic of multicellular animals, a nervous system has developed as a group of tissues and structures that function to regulate the activities of the body.... The nervous system

may be compared to an extensive communications system. It transmits messages (impulses) from sense organs (receivers) to a central switchboard (the brain).... From the brain or lower centers the impulses are transmitted to the proper regions or organs in such a way that an action appropriate to the stimulus is initiated.[9]

If one compares this passage with Mumford's idea quoted earlier, ones sees that the analogy can be turned in either direction.

These considerations lead us to some observations concerning the internal aspects of the cities. Think first about some very simple demographic attributes, or population characteristics, such as the city's size and rate of growth. Without a detailed review of the evidence, one may assert that some of the most imaginative contemporary urban research in sociology, economics, and geography consists of spelling out the implications of variations in growth rates among cities or of identifying the concomitants of differences in size.[10]

Fast and slow growing cities are different structurally, whether regarded from economic, social, or political points of view. Large and small cities are also dissimilar, organizationally speaking. Size operates as a kind of limit upon complexity of organization. Large places are at least potentially more heterogeneous and more complex. Spencer himself observed that "it is a characteristic of social bodies, as of living bodies, that while they increase

[9]Alden Raisbeck, "Nervous System," in *The American Peoples Encyclopedia* (Chicago: The Spencer Press, 1954), Volume 14, p. 466.

[10]Otis Dudley Duncan and Albert J. Reiss, Jr., *Social Characteristics of Urban and Rural Communities, 1950* (New York: John Wiley and Sons, 1956).

in size, they increase in structure.... The social aggregate, homogeneous when minute, habitually gains in hetrogeneity along with each increment of growth; and to reach great size must acquire great complexity."[11] While his language is archaic, Spencer's thought is quite modern, at least in the sense that these problems are still being explored today. These words—complexity, heterogeneity, and homogeneity—are essentially structural or organizational terms.

What do we know about the structural characteristics of cities? We are coming to know a great deal about the internal social and economic organization of cities. In part, the ease of acquiring this knowledge stems from a convenient fact—that some structural features are very clearly represented in the spatial arrangement of parts, the way things are distributed in space. Space acts as a kind of mirror, reflecting structural patterns. Recall our earlier reference to the city as composed of homes and workplaces. There are areas devoted to residential uses and there are others given over to employment or productive uses. You can regard these as multicellular parts or "organs," bound together by flows of every description. In the organism, there are flows of nutrients, blood, and impulses of different kinds constantly being transmitted. In the community, there are flows of commodities, information, and individual persons.

We are also coming to know a great deal about why certain "organs" are located where they are in cities. For example, we are learning why "central offices" are truly central, why manufacturing plants of one type tend to be bound to the city core, while other types tend to move toward the periphery; why there should be selective decentralization of services; and why retailers of different goods take up different locations. We are also beginning to understand why certain units are segregated with others like themselves, as in manufacturing areas and financial districts, as well as why some highly dissimilar units are clustered together, functionally and spatially linked, as in the case of flower shops clustering around hospitals.

This kind of knowledge comes from observations that are very much like those of a laboratory technician examining tissue in a microscopic slide. This represents a static or cross-sectional view. We are also gaining new knowledge in longitudinal or historical terms. For example, we are learning how certain technological eras have left "scar tissue" in cities of a certain age, such as in pre-automobile cities. The street pattern and many of the other contemporary features of cities are residues of the past.[12] We are also beginning to find regularities in the changing shapes of cities.

We know least about a process that might be called "cellular turnover." That is, we don't know much about the appearance and disappearance of households and firms, the entry and exit of individual cells. We have imperfect knowledge, for example, of the absorption and assimilation of immigrants. We know very little about the general impact of the city on the individual. We also know very little about "social selection," the sifting and sorting that goes on, distributing people between occu-

[11]Herbert Spencer, *Principles of Sociology* (New York and London: D. Appleton and Co., 1920 edition), Volume I, Part II, pp. 449 and 471.

[12]Edgar M. Hoover and Raymond Vernon, *The Anatomy of a Metropolis* (Cambridge: Harvard University Press, 1959).

pations and industries, and distributing families through space.

We know a little about residential segregation according to socioeconomic status, and there is a great deal of interest in segregation according to race or color; but research hasn't been pursued to the point that we can speak of these things in any knowledgeable manner.[13] We can't say much about the social-psychological aspects of these problems. One might ask whether or not there is a distinctively urban personality. We have to say we don't know, though we do have a whole family of hypotheses that have been in the literature at least since the publication of a very influential essay by another Chicago sociologist, Louis Wirth, regarding "urbanism as a way of life."[14] In the conventional textbook treatment of this subject, in urban sociology and elsewhere, many of the ideas which Wirth expressed in tentative and hypothetical form have been taken as known facts. We know far less about "urbanism" — the individual in the city setting — than we do about "urbanization," or population concentration. We know a fair amount about the massing of people in cities from a demographic standpoint. We know quite a bit about urban structure, but we have very little in the way of a social psychology of urban life. I should also add that we know more about all of these things in the West than we do for cities in the rest of the world, and we know more about the present than we do about the past.[15]

Though it is being reduced, there is still a kind of cultural bias in our thinking about cities, and I regret to say that there is a kind of historical bias still present in the urban literature, despite the efforts of many historians and others interested in the past. I would submit that the present challenge is to learn more about cities or urban communities and to learn more about societies — both urban and urbanizing socities. We do know enough to appreciate the importance of context. We know of important differences in those societies in which city dwellers are in the majority, as opposed to those in which city dwellers form a small but growing minority.

This matter of context is important. Within cities there are important differences depending on the larger societal setting. For example, preindustrial cities are notably more "segmented," made up of highly similar parts which remain relatively independent of each other. Many cities of Asia and Africa consist of subcommunities which are physically separated from each other by walls and connected only by gates, but which are very much like each other in form and content, containing the same kind of trade outlets and services.[16] This is in contrast to the closely linked, highly differentiated, yet interdependent form of city in the industrial West. In the United States it is useful to think of the urban community as composed of

[13]Otis Dudley Duncan and Beverly Duncan, "Residential Distribution and Occupational Stratification," *American Journal of Sociology*, 60 (March, 1955), pp. 493-503; Leo F. Schnore, *The Urban Scene: Human Ecology and Demography* (New York: The Free Press, 1965), Part 4; Stanley Lieberson, *Ethnic Patterns in American Cities* (New York: The Free Press, 1963); Karl E. Taeuber and Alma F. Taeuber, *Negroes in Cities* (Chicago: Aldine, 1965).

[14]Louis Wirth, "Urbanism as a Way of Life," *American Journal of Sociology*, 44 (July, 1938), pp. 1-26.

[15]Eric E. Lampard and Leo F. Schnore, "Urbanization Problems: Some Historical and Comparative Considerations," in *Research Needs for Development Assistance Programs* (Washington, D.C.: The Brookings Institution, August, 1961); Philip M. Hauser and Leo F. Schnore (editors), *The Study of Urbanization* (New York: John Wiley, 1965).

[16]Gideon Sjoberg, *The Preindustrial City: Past and Present* (New York: The Free Press, 1960).

formerly quasi-independent cities, arranged like a sun and its planets, with a large metropolis surrounded by smaller urban subcenters. It is a community composed of legally distinct cities. In contrast, the segmented type is a city (a legal entity) composed of communities. These social segments or subunits are the true communities in many parts of Asia and Africa.

So much for the internal side. I have stressed the importance of context and I have emphasized the need for understanding cities that are found in different contexts. Externally, too, cities stand in different relations to the outside world. Many entrepôt cities in underdeveloped areas emerging from colonialism actually have closer ties to the cities in Europe and America than to their own hinterlands.[17] In contrast, our cities are intimately linked to rural areas, as well as to other cities, at home and abroad. In a society like our own, heavily urbanized and industrialized, it becomes hard to distinguish the urban from the rural. The diffusion of culture via the mass media has apparently led to a kind of homogeneity that is the counterpart of the heterogeneity we have been discussing.[18]

One cannot overstate the importance of context. To speak of context is only to remind ourselves that any understanding of the nature of an organism, even so complex an organism as the city, requires attention to its environment. We might ask ourselves this question: What is the most salient aspect of the city's environment? After looking at the historical and comparative evidence that is available, I have been persuaded that the critical feature is the growth of the human species itself. The West has already passed through its rapid growth stage. It is no coincidence to find that the period of most rapid city growth in England and Wales was between 1811 and 1851, when Britain was achieving an unprecedented mastery over a far-flung environment. In the United States, the period of most rapid city growth was between 1860 and 1890; in Germany it was between 1870 and 1910. What about the rest of the world? The most rapid growth in Egypt has been since 1920, in Mexico since 1921, and in India since 1941.[19] These periods correspond very interestingly to the periods of tremendous national population growth in these underdeveloped lands.

As a consequence, there are very striking differentials in city growth around the world today. The cities in the West are growing relatively slowly, while those in the developing areas, themselves more numerous than Western cities, are manifesting explosive growth. Calcutta is an interesting case, because its growth has meant that roughly 650,000 of its inhabitants are "street-sleepers," living on the sidewalks or in the railroad stations. Housing has not kept up with population growth. Calcutta is already the tenth largest city in the world, with a population of 4.5 million. But projections of its current rate of growth would yield a population of between 35 and 36 million people by the year 2000. It happens that if one took such a population and gave it the density of New York City, he would have a city that would envelop an area

[17]Hauser and Schnore, op. cit.
[18]Walter Firey, Charles P. Loomis, and J. Allan Beegle, "The Fusion of Urban and Rural," in Jean Labatut and Wheaton J. Lane (editors), *Highways in Our National Life* (Princeton: Princeton University Press, 1950), pp. 154-163.

[19]Kingsley Davis, "The Origin and Growth of Urbanization in the World," *American Journal of Sociology*, 60 (March, 1955), pp. 429-437; Jack P. Gibbs and Leo F. Schnore, "Metropolitan Growth: An International Study," *American Journal of Sociology*, 66 (September, 1960), pp. 160-170.

larger than the entire state of Rhode Island. One may ask if this is really possible. Actually, it may well be impossible, but these figures are really designed to illustrate the magnitude of current growth, the enormous speed of increase in Calcutta and other cities in the underdeveloped areas of the world.

To take another case, there is reason to believe that twenty million people left rural areas to go to the cities of China between 1949 and 1956. This number happens to be nearly equal to the combined population of the Benelux countries, i.e., Belgium, Netherlands, and Luxembourg. Enormous numbers were thus involved in the rural-urban stream. In roughly the same period the cities of China were growing very rapidly.[20]

Such facts underscore the importance of both national growth and world population growth. Consider the difference between the births and deaths that are occurring, i.e., the "natural increase" of world population. At current rates, something like 6,000 persons are added each hour, or around 144,000 persons per day; this is a larger number than the population of Madison, Wisconsin. The world is gaining 4,320,000 people per month, a number larger than the current population of the entire state of Wisconsin. The world is increasing by 52 million people per year; this is roughly the size of the United Kingdom — England, Wales, Scotland, and Northern Ireland.

The emerging picture is one of an ever-more-crowded world, and one finds many expressions of concern about the implications of this "population explosion." It is useful to think for a moment about whether this increasingly crowded world will mean increasingly crowded cities. The answer is clearly in the affirmative. The world is not only growing in terms of human numbers, but these numbers are being more compactly arranged. This holds true for urban communities and for the world as a whole. Cities are multiplying, they are growing larger in area and in population size, and they are containing progressively larger proportions of mankind in every major country throughout the world.

Very generally, with respect to the context of urbanization today, the critical fact is the sheer growth of both urban and nonurban communities. Population increases are being registered not only within cities, but within rural areas, with this latter increase indirectly providing the major source of city growth — rural-urban migration. To state the matter somewhat differently, the most impressive thing about contemporary urbanization is the fantastic proliferation and multiplication of human *and* social organisms.

You may not find the organismic analogy very helpful, but the principal facts that we have been considering remain the same. We should be aware of our growing world and of the fact that it is an increasingly urbanized world. If only to demonstrate that even now someone does read Herbert Spencer, I shall close by adopting as my own the words that he wrote in 1876 in defense of the organismic analogy. As he said, "I have used the analogies elaborated but as a scaffolding to help in building up a coherent body of sociological inductions. Let us take away the scaffolding; the inductions will stand by themselves."[21]

[20]"The World's Great Cities," *Population Bulletin,* 16 (September, 1960), pp. 109-131.

[21]Spencer, *op. cit.,* pp. 592-593.

SLUMS AND SOCIAL INSECURITY
Alvin L. Schorr

How the Poor Are Housed

In arguments about the adequacy of public relief, occasionally someone is heard to say: "But where are these people who are in such difficulty? After all, no one starves in the United States." It is approximately as ambiguous to say that everyone in the United States is, after all, under a roof. Some are mal-nourished, as some are malhoused. In order to examine the question how families get under a roof, it will be useful to visualize the income that they require.

Analysis by Warren Jay Vinton of income and new housing in the years 1947 to 1958 shows that it was, on the whole, those families with over $6,000 a year[1] who were served. Families with less than $6,000 account for 88 percent of the substandard housing in the country, suggesting that they are not served very well by existing housing either. Many have adequate housing, espe-

Reprinted, with permission of author and U. S. Government Printing Office.

[1]Dollar figures used in this paragraph are for years from 1956 to 1959. They are not adjusted here, as they are being used to establish the magnitude of income that is necessary rather than a precise amount.

cially if they are close to $6,000 income or if the income supports one or two people rather than four or five. But it seems clear that income of at least $6,000 is required to assure adequate family housing (235) A similar analysis brings Joseph P. McMurray to the conclusion that, in standard metropolitan areas, an income of $5,000 a year is required to rent or purchase decent housing. In smaller communities, an income of $4,000 is required. (145) That McMurray's estimate may be on the conservative side is suggested by the city worker's family budget of the Bureau of Labor Statistics. Designed to establish an amount necessary to maintain a family of four at "a level of adequate living," the total budget in 20 large cities ranges from $5,370 (Houston) to $6,567 (Chicago). The amount needed for rent and utilities ranges from $871 (Scranton) to $1,386 (Chicago). (125) It is evident that the family to which we are addressing our attention, with income equivalent to $2,500 or less for a family of four, will have to make adjustments of some kind in their housing expenditures.

How do poor families pay for housing? The question has dimensions that are private and public. As a private matter, the question is answerable in terms of budget management and family arrangements. As a public matter, one answers in terms of specific public programs or of the concept that housing filters down to the poor as those who are better off move on to better housing. All national programs intended to sustain income and insure against such risks as old age are, in a certain sense, devices to provide housing (et cetera) to those who might otherwise be poor. However, most of these programs place in the beneficiary's hand money which he has, in one manner or another, earned. He is in the same situation as any wage earner, so far as housing is concerned. (If his benefits are inadequate, he is in the same situation as other poor people.) Two national programs, public assistance and public housing, incorporate a means test and intervene directly in the housing of the poor. They will merit special attention when we come to the public dimension of the provision of housing to the poor.

The Private Dimension

The poor pay for housing, first, in its poor quality. Reflection will show that this is a theme that lies just under the surface of most of our discussion. Whether they own or rent, it is the poor families who tend to occupy the country's substandard housing. In 1956 half of those with income less than $2,000 lived in housing that was dilapidated or lacked plumbing. (226)

This is a rough measure. We have not taken into account size of family. Moreover, current income counts several kinds of people as if they were the same: the rich man who has taken a temporary loss, the retired man who once had more income, and the man who is chronically poor. The first man is likely to be able to spend out of savings and conceivably the retired man too, but hardly the man who has never had a decent income. Nevertheless, the rough measure makes it clear that some who are poor acquire standard housing. They do not acquire it by accident. Analysis of the Chicago population shows that the poor in standard dwellings "typically" pay more rent than those in substandard dwellings. (65, p. 147) Even those who do not manage standard housing make sacrifices for the quality that they do achieve.

One step that poor families take is to allocate a high percentage of their income to housing. We have already noted a tendency for those who relocate from cleared areas to spend more for improved housing. In 1956 the great majority of families with incomes under $2,000 spent 30 percent or more of their income on rent. On the other hand, of families with incomes between $8,000 and $10,000 the great majority spent less than 15 percent. (226) We have suggested that current income is not always a good indication of a family's financial circumstances. However, relating the amount a family spends to the cost of its housing gives a similar picture. In 1950 urban families with incomes under $1,000 a year spent 26 percent of their total outlay for housing. Families from $1,000 to $2,000 spent 22 percent; from $2,000 to $3,000, 18 percent; and so on. (231 table 1-2)

What would a suitable yardstick be? For most cities the BLS city worker's family budget allocates to housing something less than 20 percent of the total.[2] (125) Moreover, the BLS budget

[2]One city, 15 percent; 2 cities, 16 percent; 6 cities, 17 percent; 4 cities, 19 percent; 5 cities, 20 percent; and 2 cities, 21 percent. The BLS budget includes the cost of rent and heat. The

totals are over twice as high as the level of poverty. One would assume that if, out of incomes already lower than adequate, more than 20 percent is allocated to housing, increased deprivation will be felt in other areas of the budget. A depression study in Stockton, England, concluded that higher rents had led to malnutrition. A study reported by Elizabeth Wood came to a more refined conclusion. The study addressed itself to the question, "Can a family pay one-third of its income for rent and yet have enough left to nourish the family?" The conclusion: ". . . under such conditions fathers and children were sufficiently well-nourished, but mothers tended to be undernourished." (265) The same point is made in reverse by a District of Columbia study of 81 families living in public housing who presented rent payment problems. Of the families who presented rent problems, "28 percent had spent their rent money for clothing and other unmet needs of their children."[3] (58, p. 6)

One possibility is clear—to pay for adequate shelter by settling for inadequate food and clothing. In many cases, the family must be governed not by a deliberate choice to favor housing but by the way inadequate money gets spent. Under sustained pressure, costs that are fixed and regular are met and those that seem stretchable or postponable—food, clothing, recreation, medical care—are not met. In any case, the consequences of spending more than 20 percent for housing do not seem

1956 National Housing Inventory figures above and the 1950 figures based on the Survey of Consumer Expenditures also represent the "gross" cost of housing.
[3] 21 percent had failed to receive support money due them; 18 percent presented budget management problems; 33 percent failed for miscellaneous reasons.

healthy. It is anybody's guess how much lower than 20 percent a rule of thumb for poor families ought to be. Certainly, so far as public decisions are concerned, 20 percent should be regarded as a maximum rather than an average housing expenditure for poor families.

Income for income, naturally, the pressure to make some adjustment to housing needs is felt most by large families. If figures can reflect a sense of strain, perhaps those that follow suggest the financial pressure that builds up in the budget management of a large, low-income family. The table is based on the rents paid by families of varying size before and after relocation. The report covers 1,373 families in 9 cities that did not substantially assist with relocation;

AVERAGE MONTHLY RENTALS BEFORE AND AFTER RELOCATION
[By family size, 9 cities, 1955-58]

Number of persons in family	Rent before relocation	Rent after relocation	Rent increase
2	$30.35	$34.81	$4.46
3	32.35	36.23	3.88
4	34.45	37.96	3.51
5	36.50	39.07	2.57

rentals reported for 5 cities that did assist show a similar pattern. (190) Does it force these data to suggest that these small but consistent differences indicate the degree to which any increased cost must be resisted? Relocation means that all the families must pay more. The larger the family, the less, by a matter of pennies, it can accede to the pressure for higher cost.

What steps do the large families take? Reviewing the 1950 Survey of Consumer Expenditures, Louis Winnick concludes about the average large family: "They obtain more housing space and, at the same time, maintain or even increase the budgets devoted to other consumer goods." (262, p. 34)

However, poor large families are not able to bring this off. They spend more in total for food and for clothing. To balance the increase, they spend less in total for housing, household operation, and medical care. (*231, table 2-2*) (This confirms a conclusion we had already reached.) How do the higher income families manage to maintain their spending for other items while obtaining more space? Apparently they do it by sacrificing the physical quality of the housing. (We have seen that poor families are familiar with this tactic too.) So far as ownership is concerned, for example, small families tend to have houses that are worth more, compared to their incomes, than large families. (*226*) Thus, relative values are lower for the larger families despite the fact that they have more space. Larger families generally try to gain some advantage by purchasing rather than renting (*262*), but lower incomes tend to close off this possibility. Poor large families do not, like other large families, show a markedly higher tendency to own than smaller families.

To return to speaking of poor families in general, an additional strategy has now been suggested. Any family, large or small, may think of purchase as a way to secure more housing for its money.[4] Obviously, however, low income restricts the opportunity to buy. Almost 60 percent of the dwellings in metropolitan areas are now owned by the families in them. But in the lowest fifth of the income distribution, in Chicago, 20 percent of the families owned homes. (*65*) Of urban families receiving aid to families with dependent children, predominantly with incomes under $2,000 a year, 17 percent own homes. (*53*) For

those families that manage it, buying a house involves them in the same tactic as committing a high percentage of income to housing. When a poor family buys a house, it is almost always valued at three times or more the family's income. By contrast, families with incomes over $6,000 tend to pay 1.5 to 2 times their income.[5] (*226*) Further, buying reduces the flexibility with which a family can meet other contingencies — illness, unemployment, and so forth.

The purchase of housing, though it is not usually thought of in the same terms, is a form of going into debt. Poor families may not receive more short-term credit than families with more income (because it will be refused), but the struggle to buy on credit or borrow money is an everyday fact of life. Borrowed money may be applied directly to rent or it may buy clothing because clothing money went for rent — the effect is the same. The use of credit to pay for housing produces the problems that have just been noted — a future commitment to sacrifice something tomorrow to pay for today's housing and limited flexibility in the face of emer-

[5]These observations are based on the relation of current income to value, and may be somewhat influenced by families who had purchased homes some time before and whose incomes had declined. However, figures taken at the point of purchase of FHA-insured homes show a similar trend. In 1959 those with incomes under $3,600 bought new homes valued at over 3 times their income or existing homes valued at 2.5 times their income. The ratio of value to income in 1959 shows a steady fall as family income rises. (*145, table 8*)

The values cited in relation to income may understate the poor family's disadvantage in buying a house. If a family with larger income has made a larger downpayment, their monthly payment is reduced even more. Moreover, the owner with more income is likely to secure better lending terms. Some low-income families, at the other extreme, find themselves buying under lease-purchase, with inflated monthly payments and very little chance indeed of eventually obtaining title to the property.

[4]The question of ownership versus rental is not determined simply on financial grounds.

gencies. Moreover, the poor family pays a premium for credit. A study of the buying patterns of families in several public housing projects notes some of the problems associated with credit:

> Because of their poor credit potential, many of these families are restricted in where they can shop for durables. . . . They do not shop in department stores and discount houses. Instead they depend upon chain stores, neighborhood merchants and door-to-door peddlers — in short, merchants who are prepared to extend credit to poor risks. The dependence upon such credit means that they pay high prices for appliances.
>
>   . . . Because of their poor education and relatively young age, and because many are recent migrants to the city, they tend to be naive shoppers, vulnerable to the lure of "easy credit". . . . Perhaps as many as a third of the families have suffered at the hands of unscrupulous salesmen. (33, pp. 197-198)

The strategies that are open to poor families are not limited to trying to shift about small sums of money. Analysis of the living arrangements of the aged in the United States indicates that, when help for the old person is needed, the poor tend to pool living arrangements. The plight of the poor "is so difficult that they must select the most efficient way of sharing, which is living together." (210, pp. 9-10) An attempt to understand crowding among Negroes in Chicago produces a somewhat similar observation:

> Doubling-up of families and sharing the dwelling with non-relatives probably account for the relatively large household size in the non-white population; and such doubling-up and sharing of dwellings are

themselves probably means by which nonwhites pool incomes in order to compete for housing. (65, pp. 209-210)

Smaller studies produce supporting evidence. (112) In sum, one tactic for providing housing is to share space beyond the immediate family and to pool available money.

On the other hand, apparently there is a point of surrender, when adequate housing comes to seem impossible and families break apart. Studying a group of families who were being required to relocate, the Department of Public Welfare of the District of Columbia reported:

> . . . We found some who had already accepted separation as a partial answer. Other families were on the verge of breaking up when it appeared that it would no longer be possible to maintain a common home. (59)

This strategy, if one can call it that, has been of special concern to child welfare agencies. Of 11,500 children in foster care in New York City at one point, 750 could have gone home "at once" if adequate low-cost housing had been available. ". . . 112 children might not have been placed at all had adequate housing with supportive services been available at the point of placement." (63, p. 5) A study of women committed to the New Jersey Reformatory for Women on charges of child neglect found that close to 50 percent "had been living in housing that could only be described as dangerous and not fit for human habitation. . . . Mother after mother described the feeling of discouragement and frustration that came after hours of house-hunting with no success." Says this study in conclusion:

> Grossly inadequate housing was a serious problem to more than

60 percent of these families. This factor was particularly pertinent to the large family groups. A community that cannot provide decent housing and does not exercise adequate control to protect families from exploitation and from living in dangerous situations certainly runs the risk of increasing the neglect problem. (95, p. 56)

The figures vary from study to study (122, 141, 148), but all make a similar point. Despite a national policy that is, perhaps, 50 years old,[6] economic need is still an effective force in separating children from their families. Chief among the specific mechanisms that operate in financial need is inability to find adequate housing.

Obviously, families also seek in a variety of ways to *improve* their income. One device that has consequences for family arrangements is to send an additional member of the family to work. Of the group of families cited earlier who left public housing to purchase homes, 7 percent had originally had more than one member of the family working. When interviewed in their own homes not long afterward, 32 percent had more than one worker. (23) The rate at which married women work appears to confirm this finding. On the whole, women tend not to work when they have preschool children in the home. But couples with less than $2,000 income show a marked tendency for the wife to work, if they have preschool children and if they do

not. (209) Presumably the wife's income is the only income or it is a necessary supplement to bring family income even to this low level.

As a private matter, then, poor families get and apply money wherever they can. They use a variety of strategies, some because they come to hand and some in which there is a measure of choice. An aged widow will make different adjustments from a young father, for example. But few of the deliberate choices that are open seem attractive. Families can go without standard housing. They can borrow from food to pay housing. Few who are poor will have saved money; those who have, can use it. They can struggle to buy on credit or to borrow. They can try to buy instead of rent. Those who manage to bring this off may make out better in the end. Others will face additional difficulty because they are borrowing from other budget items and are leaving themselves less room to maneuver in the next emergency. They can extend the size of their households, trading crowdedness and tension for shelter and a measure of financial flexibility. Families can break up or at least give up children. Throughout, they can seek ways to improve their income. Some poor families try all of these. For some but not for others, purchasing a house and sending additional members to work, when they are possible, are constructive steps. For the rest of it, the avenues that are open go around in a tight little circle, enmeshing families deeper and deeper in deprivation.

[6]Among the conclusions of the White House Conference on Children in 1909: "Home life is the highest and finest product of civilization. It is the great molding force of mind and of character. Children should not be deprived of it except for urgent and compelling reasons.... Except in unusual circumstances, the home should not be broken up for reasons of poverty, but only for considerations of inefficiency or immorality." (180, pp. 9-10)

The Public Dimension

Broadly speaking, the first line of action in providing housing to those who are poor lies in the normal operation of the economy, stimulated and secured by the Federal insurance programs. Clearly, there have been gains in housing poor families that result from the operation of economic forces not directly concerned with them. The number of substandard units in the country has declined steadily in the past two decades, though the total housing inventory has increased by over 50 percent.[7] On the other hand, substandard housing or crowding is still the common and not the exceptional fate of 32 million Americans who live in modern poverty. The normal operation of the economy is not dealing adequately with the housing of the poor while it deals with them incidentally.

We have already observed that new housing does not flow to families with less than $5,000 or $6,000 income, much less to those with half that income. But it is held by some (247) that if the total housing supply increases, some units will be released to "filter down" to poor families. Why has filtration not worked to more substantial effect? Three kinds of factors appear to interfere with filtrations as a method of providing housing to poor families.

First, filtration requires that the real estate market operate in a situation of stable demand and continuing supply, without impediment. We face a situation, however, in which the total population surges upward and inwards to our cities. To add to the pressure, the postwar babies should, by 1965 to 1975, be marrying and establishing new households at a high rate. In regard to supply, it has been pointed out that in those times or areas where there is a sufficient

surplus of housing to produce rapid filtration, the surplus itself acts as a check on further building. (144) Besides, rehabilitation makes properties desirable again for higher income tenancy. Clearance for highways and public buildings reduces the stock of housing available to low-income families. Even urban renewal tends to demolish more units than are produced to replace them.[8] Finally, the real estate market does not operate unimpeded. Segregation is the notorious barrier to free movement of property, but there are other barriers as well. For example, a surplus of housing in one city with high unemployment will not induce filtration in another city with a housing shortage. Thus housing demand is not stable but rising, supply is not continuing but apt to be braked by a surplus, and there are impediments to the free operation of the housing market.

Second, though housing may become less desirable over time, compared to what is currently available, it does not necessarily become cheaper. The price of housing that is released depends upon competition; where even substandard housing is in short supply the price will not drop. (184) For example, the median rent (in real dollars) in the lower East Side of New York City actually rose over a long period of time. Yet the housing had clearly declined in a scale of values relating it to other housing. (72, pp. 50-51) Thus, though filtering down may occur in some senses of the term and though one may see housing obviously undergoing transi-

---

[7]Standards of housing do not remain static over 20 years, any more than other consumption standards. Whether the housing of those who are poor has improved at the same rate as general standards of housing is not evaluated here.

[8]By Dec. 31, 1961, 178,000 dwelling units had been demolished and ground broken for 46,000 new units. (109) The disparity is not an accident of the initial phase. Counting on much faster progress, Leo Grebler had estimated that demolition of 67 million units from 1951 to 1960 might generate new construction of only 4 or 5 million units. (90)

tion in quality and tenancy, the process does not necessarily serve the family whose real income remains below the $2,500 level.

Third and finally, as we have indicated, housing that is sold, converted, and put to uses for which it was not initially designed exacts a nonmonetary price from the families who live in it. If housing is substandard, families pay the cost of design that does not lend itself to their purposes and of dilapidation and crowding. Even standard housing may be ill-designed for families who occupy it because they must, rather than because it is suitable. Moreover, filtration means that the poor must live where the middle class lived under different circumstances; that is, before the development of travel by auto, when unskilled jobs were all in the center of the city, and when services of good quality were available in the neighborhood. Thus, for some, filtration may provide shelter, but it does not provide what we seek—housing that affords the optimum opportunity for escaping from poverty.

Public housing and public assistance, in different ways, address themselves directly to the housing needs of poor families. How do they serve?

Public Housing. Public housing is not a single program, historically; it is a single vessel that has been used for diverse public purposes. In the 1930's, public housing was intended for families who voluntarily sought to improve their housing but could not afford private rentals. This group was not regarded as dependent. Indeed, some housing authorities limited the number of public assistance recipients they would accept and others would not admit any. (232) In the 1940's, the program was redirected to provide housing for war workers. Following the Housing Act of 1949, public housing was oriented again to poor families — with a difference. Partly because postwar amendments gave priority to families having the most urgent housing need, to the aged, and to those displaced by urban renewal, this third generation in public housing contains a high concentration of depressed, untutored, and dependent families.

It would be misleading to speak of the development of the program as if all the crucial changes were made by Congress. If public housing is the vessel, perhaps Congress is the vintner, but one must ask about the grape and the palate of the taster. The recipe for populating a city, of which we have spoken, concentrates Negroes in public housing as in slums. Segregation is not entirely new, of course, but since 1954 it has become a more open insult. To the extent that public housing found its sites chiefly in land cleared for renewal, large areas were devoted exclusively to public housing (St. Louis is an example). To the extent that the growing suburbs successfully resisted public housing, they confined it to the city core. Meanwhile, as between 1935 and 1960, there was a greater proportion of Americans who had never experienced poverty personally or were trying to forget it. They contributed to a more critical, if not pious, public view of public housing. Thus, a conjunction of social and economic trends leads to the setting apart of families in public housing.

As is so often the case, internal problems of policy and administration aggravate a difficult situation. Authorities have been widely criticized for poor housing design—too much standardization, too high densities, lack of imagination, and disregard of informal social patterns. The Commissioner of Public Housing took note of the criticism in a letter to local authorities.

> What the localities need [she said in part] is a loosening of regulations by Washington, and that we will do. There are so many regulations about square footage and the space between buildings, for example, that the result is the same housing in Maine and in southern California. (164)

Housing that was tending to be concentrated in terms of people had taken on, as well, an institutional appearance. Further, tenants must leave public housing if their income exceeds a permissible maximum.[9] In effect, those families must leave who achieve at least limited success and who might provide variety and leadership in the housing developments. The struggle of housing authorities to find remedies may itself create a problem. As a number of tenants have the most primitive understanding of housing, regulations and penalties proliferate: Windows must be shut in the winter...a fine if drains are plugged without good reason...eviction for an illegitimate pregnancy...and so forth. Some tenants find this to be precisely a confirmation of their greatest anxiety, that they were being offered decent housing in exchange for their independence. The stage is set for mutual suspicion between tenant and manager, with relationships inside a housing development diverging increasingly from those that are typical in private housing.[10]

[9]The Housing Act of 1961 permits local housing authorities to retain over-income families for a limited period if it can be shown that standard private housing is not available to them.

[10]A study of management policies in public housing concludes that "...the imposing of nu-

The alteration in its population also leads to a financial problem for public housing. Tenants' income (in constant dollars) has remained level in the past decade (106), but each year the tenants' income falls further below the median for the country. That is, in 1955 the median net income of families admitted to public housing was 46.5 percent of the median income of all families in the United States. In 1961, it was less than 40 percent. (215) Consequently, the rents that may be collected from tenants do not rise as rapidly as maintenance costs. Between 1950 and 1958 monthly receipts from rent increased by 25 percent (from $28.93 to $36.50 per unit per month), but expenditures increased by 52 percent (from $21.32 to $32.50). Not unexpectedly, then, the Federal contribution to local housing authorities has been moving steadily toward its permissible maximum. (235) With the overall Federal contribution reaching 87 percent of the maximum in fiscal year 1961, some local housing authorities would find themselves still with substantial leeway and others with rather little.

Public housing is faced with grave problems which go to the heart of its ability to remain solvent and shape the kind of housing, in the sense of total social and physical environment, that it is able to provide.[11] What are the consequences for tenants? The first and per-

merous controls on tenant behavior has tended to intensify the misunderstandings which arise between tenants and managers." (65a)

[11]Not all of the problems have been touched on here. For a careful description of policy and financial developments, see the "working paper" by Warren Jay Vinton for the Conference of Housing the Economically and Socially Disadvantaged Groups in the Population. (235) For a development of the meaning of the change in tenant population, see "Public Housing and Mrs. McGee." (266)

haps the most serious consequence is that public housing is not available to more than a small proportion of the low-income families. Though the Housing Act of 1949 authorized 810,000 units, that authorization is as yet far from exhausted. There are in all something over half a million units – roughly 1 percent of the housing supply. If public housing were limited to the lowest incomes, with current resources it could house 2 million of the 32 million we have defined as poor. As it reaches above the very lowest incomes, it houses even a smaller percentage of the poor than these figures indicate. Consequently there are waiting lists of people eligible for public housing. In the District of Columbia, the number of families awaiting admission has at times exceeded the total number of housing units. (238)

Since public housing must look to its receipts, it tends to exclude families with the lowest incomes who cannot pay minimum rents. (173) That is, the bulk of families entering public housing have incomes under $4,000 a year. Among the families having less than $4,000, in the total population roughly one in four has under $1,500 income. But only one in eight of those who move into public housing has less than $1,500.[12] Families may be excluded as undesirable, too. Though such exclusions would doubtless diminish if there were more public housing, they represent an effort to maintain a degree of acceptability among tenants. On the other hand, when careful study was made of 82 families excluded as undesirables in New York City, the deci-

sion was reversed for 33 of the families. (44) Other reviews have produced higher percentages of reversal. In addition to the limited capacity of the program, we have already noted that many presumably eligible families are not willing to live in public housing. Their reluctance must arise, to some degree, from the program's current difficulties, but it also represents a feeling about living in a managed – particularly, in a Government-managed – community. As early as 1946, a local study reported that only a third of those eligible were willing to live in public housing. (146) In sum, public housing is limited by its quantity, its fixity upon the middle range of low incomes, and by management and tenant views of acceptability.

Americans are often more attentive to the tempo and direction of a trend than to the underlying facts. Because we are preoccupied with the problems and movement of public housing, we may conceivably overlook the function it is performing. When they are asked, the majority of families who live in public housing say that they like it. They appreciate its facilities; their general morale is higher than it was in substandard housing. (12, 219, 253) One must, of course, take into account that those who would object most to public housing never enter it, or they leave.[13] Nevertheless, for those who take up tenancy, public housing represents a considerable improvement in physical surroundings. Moreover, the aspects of the environment which are offensive to some families may be secondary or even functional for others. Kurt W. Back finds that two types of people move into public

[12]Perhaps half of the families with less than $1,500 income who move into public housing are public assistance recipients. The non-recipient with very low income is therefore represented in a very small proportion indeed.

[13]The rate of moveouts, though it signals difficulty in some places, is not strikingly high compared with general population mobility. It is lower overall than the moveout rate for rental housing insured by FHA. (23)

housing, those who seek to use it as a vehicle for change and those who see it as an end in itself. Of the latter, he writes:

> In general, the tenants form the weaker and more vulnerable part of the [public housing] population. They have less income, less secure income, and are more likely to represent broken homes. In a very real way they need the protection afforded by government action, and many of them received some government aid. These people apparently look on government housing as a type of institutional support, which they need. (12, p. 102)

Thus, public housing performs at least acceptably for those poor families who see it as an improved, somewhat protected environment. Presumably, it offers their children a better start than

PERCENTAGE OF 3- AND 4-PERSON FAMILIES IN TOTAL POPULATION AND MOVING INTO PUBLIC HOUSING, 1960

Income for year	Percentage of total population	Percentage of all families moving into public housing
Under $1,500	5.8	11.7
$1,500 to $4,000......	18.7	83.7835

Sources: *Current Population Reports* (224), table 5, and *Families Moving Into Low-Rent Housing Calendar Year 1960* (107), table 6.

they might otherwise have had. Analysis of turnover statistics suggests that others use public housing as a way station to improved housing. (23) In this sense, too, public housing serves the prevention of poverty.

Thus, strictly managed housing may suit one family — or at least not trouble it — and trouble others very much. Public housing is pressed, if it is going to serve families with any precision, to define its objectives and to alter

policies to further these objectives. At least three choices are open: (1) A real estate operation for the respectable poor — the purely poor. (2) A rehabilitative program for the seriously dependent and troubled poor. (3) A greatly enlarged and altered program, at least in part deinstitutionalized, with a variety of kinds of housing opportunities. In the absence of a settled decision to seek the third course and of the legislation that would make it possible, local housing authorities are moving slowly, in most cases with pronounced reluctance, toward rehabilitative programs.[14] Under present circumstances the families who are entering public housing make such a course inevitable. Not only are the families isolated and segregated; increasing numbers are aged, many receive public assistance, and many are in broken families. They cannot be abandoned to their problems; they must be served. Moreover, when they are not served, buildings deteriorate, delinquencies occur, and deprived youngsters grow into disabled adults. It becomes plain that neglect is expensive.

✿　✿　✿

Can Poor Families Be Housed?

If one reflects upon the ways in which poor families pay for housing in their private lives and upon the ways in which public policies assist them, it is possible to perceive a discrepancy. The

[14]At one extreme, a rehabilitative program suggests therapeutic housing communities, planned to protect and teach families. Tried in a number of European countries, these smack of regimentation to Americans. (9, 214) Though it may seem inconsistent with observations about management tendencies, distaste for excessive management responsibility is probably one factor that leads local authorities to resist the rehabilitative trend.

private and the public dimensions are out of balance. Poor people pay for housing as a total effort, out of their food and out of the fabric of their lives together. The effects of the struggle are experienced without Sabbath and without holiday. But public efforts to assist them are directed only to a minority. Out of those who are reached, many are helped meagerly, subject to conditions that may be relevant, irrelevant, or even self-defeating.

In public efforts to provide housing we have so far relied chiefly upon stimulation and subsidy of private industry. The results, for those with incomes over $5,000 or $6,000, have been respectable. Recent legislation attempts to extend the impact of such activity to lower incomes. The problem has so far appeared to be one of interesting builders and developers in such a market. It appears likely that some gains will be made. But it must be evident that the problem of the poor will not be met in this manner. We have referred to the reasons; they require only to be brought together.

First, though special incentives for low-income building and contraction of demand in the middle-income market may lead to more builder interest in low-cost housing than heretofore, it is unlikely that interest will reach down to the families with $2,500 incomes. High risks, limited profits, and other difficulties that have discouraged business from building for families with $5,000 incomes will seem insuperable at half those incomes.

Second, it is not unreasonable that builders and banks should take pause. A family of four with less than $2,500 income is not able to buy a house or pay a rent that provides a profit on it, no matter how low the interest rate on the mortgage. The family's income is not adequate to its need for food, clothing, and other necessary items — even if it were paying no rent at all.

Third, inducing low-income families to pay 25 or 30 percent of their incomes carries a heavy risk of its own and is not sound public policy. The housing that is bought at the expense of food or medical care is dearly bought.

❊　❊　❊

References

(Page numbers are provided for articles and direct quotations [This list has been abridged])

9. Aronov, Edward, "European Approaches to 'Problem Families' Reviewed, Analyzed," *Journal of Housing,* vol. 14, No. 4, April 1957, pp. 121-123.

12. Back, Kurt W., *Slums, Projects and People: Social Psychological Problems of Relocation in Puerto Rico,* Duke University Press, Durham, N. C., 1962.

23. Bloomberg, Lawrence N., *Mobility and Motivations,* Housing and Home Finance Agency, Public Housing Administration, Washington, D.C., April 1958.

33. Caplovitz, David, with the assistance of Louis Lieberman, *The Consumer Behavior of Low-Income Families,* Columbia University Bureau of Applied Social Research, New York, September 1961, mimeographed.

44. Community Service Society of New York, Committee on Housing, *Not Without Hope,* a Report and Recommendations on Family Relocation, March 1958.

53. Data were provided by a study of Aid to Families with Needy Children

performed by the Institute for Research in Social Science, University of North Carolina, for the American Public Welfare Association.

58. Department of Public Welfare, Public Assistance Division, "Five Years of Cooperative Effort by the National Capital Housing Authority and the Public Assistance Division, 1956-1961," Washington, D.C., mimeographed, p. 6.

59. ———, "Report of the Advisory Committee of the Service to Displaced Families to the Director of Public Welfare at the Expiration of the Six Month's Trial Period," Mar. 21, 1960, to Sept. 20, 1960, Washington, D.C., Nov. 1, 1960, mimeographed.

63. Dumpson, James R., "The Economy of Adequate Service," *Child Welfare*, vol. XXXIX, No. 10, December 1960, pp. 1-6.

65a. Dunham, H. Warren, and Grundstein, Nathan D., "The Impact of a Confusion of Social Objectives on Public Housing: A Preliminary Analysis" *Marriage and Family Living*, vol. XVII, No. 2, May 1955, pp. 103-112.

72. Fisher, Ernest M., and Winnick, Louis, "A Reformulation of the 'Filtering' Concept," *Journal of Social Issues*, vol. VII, Nos. 1 and 2, 1951, pp. 47-48.

90. Grebler, Leo, "Urban Redevelopment as an Outlet for Capital Investment," *Land Economics*, vol. XXIX, No. 4, November 1953, pp. 358-361.

95. Hancock, Claire R., *A Study of Protective Services and the Problem of Neglect of Children in New Jersey*, 1958. Report of project sponsored by the New Jersey State Board of Child Welfare, Department of Institutions and Agencies, conducted June 1957-January 1958.

106. Housing and Home Finance Agency, Public Housing Administration, *Families in Low-Rent Projects—Families Re-examined During Calendar Year 1960 for Continued Occupancy*, Washington, D.C., August 1961.

107. ———, ———, *Families Moving Into Low-Rent Housing, Calendar Year 1960*, Washington, D.C., October 1961.

109. Housing and Home Finance Agency, Urban Renewal Administration, unpublished data for December 1961.

112. Huber, Gizella, *Economic Indicators of Family and Child Dependency in the District of Columbia*, Health and Welfare Council Committee on Junior Village, Washington, D.C., November 1958, mimeographed.

122. Junior Village Committee, *What Price Dependency?*, D.C. Health and Welfare Council, Washington, D.C., 1959.

125. Lamale, Helen H., and Stotz, Margaret S., "The Interim City Worker's Family Budget," *Monthly Labor Review*, vol. 83, No. 8, August 1960, pp. 785-808.

141. Maas, Henry S., and Engler, Richard E., Jr., *Children in Need of Parents*, Columbia University Press, New York, 1959.

144. McFarland, M. Carter, *The Challenge of Urban Renewal*, Urban Land Institute—Technical Bulletin No. 32, December 1958, 44 pp.

145. McMurray, Joseph P., *Ways and Means of Providing Housing for Families Unable to Afford Rentals or Mortgage Payments Necessary for Adequate Private Housing*, National Association of Home Builders, Washington, D.C., Dec. 30, 1960.

146. Merton, Robert K., "The Social Psychology of Housing," *Current Trends in Social Psychology*, Wayne

Dennis, et al., 1948, University of Pittsburgh Press, Pennsylvania, pp. 163-217.

148. Michel, Andrée V., "Kinship Relations and Relationships of Proximity in French Working-Class Households," in *A Modern Introduction to the Family*, ed. by Norman W. Bell and Ezra F. Vogel, The Free Press of Glencoe, Ill., 1960, pp. 287-294.

164. *New York Times*, "New Ideas Sought in Public Housing," Nov. 26, 1961.

173. Philadelphia Housing Association, "Relocation—The Human Side of Urban Renewal," *Issues*, November 1958, Pennsylvania.

180. *Proceedings of the Conference on the Care of Dependent Children*, held in Washington, D.C., Jan. 25-26, 1909. Senate Document No. 721, 60th Cong., 2d sess., Government Printing Office, Washington, D.C., 1909.

184. Ratcliff, Richard U., *Urban Land Economics*, McGraw-Hill, New York, 1949.

190. Reynolds, Harry W., Jr., "The Human Element in Urban Renewal," *Public Welfare*, vol. 19, No. 2, April 1961, pp. 71-73, and 82.

209. Schiffman, Jacob, "Marital and Family Characteristics of Workers, March 1960," Monthly Labor Review, April 1961, pp. 1-10. U.S. Department of Labor *Special Labor Force Report No. 13*.

210. Schorr, Alvin L., *Filial Responsibility in the Modern American Family*, U.S. Government Printing Office, Washington, D.C., 1960.

215. Silverman, Abner D., Paper delivered and discussed by Herman D. Hillman, Director, New York Regional Office, Public Housing Administration at the Conference on Individualized Services, National Social Welfare Assembly, in New York on Oct. 27, 1961.

219. Social Planning Council of St. Louis and St. Louis County, Research Bureau, *Public Housing Residents and Welfare Services*, Missouri, August 1955.

224. U.S. Department of Commerce, Bureau of the Census, "Income of Families and Persons in the United States: 1960," *Current Population Reports*, Series P-60, No. 37, Jan. 17, 1962, Washington, D.C.

226. ———, ———, *1956 National Housing Inventory—Characteristics of the 1956 Inventory*, vol. III, pt. 1, Washington, D.C., 1959.

231. U.S. Department of Labor, Bureau of Labor Statistics, *Study of Consumer Expenditures Incomes and Savings*, Statistical Tables, Urban U.S.—1950, vol. XVIII, University of Pennsylvania (Philadelphia), 1957.

232. U.S. Housing Authority in cooperation with the Social Security Board, *Housing and Welfare*, Federal Works Agency, Washington, D.C., May 1940.

235. Vinton, Warren Jay, "Working Paper," in *Interim Report on Housing the Economically and Socially Disadvantaged Groups in the Population*. Proceedings and working papers of Conference sponsored by the Metropolitan Housing and Planning Council of Chicago in cooperation with Action, Inc., New York, Feb. 26-27, 1960.

238. Washington Housing Association, "7,973 D.C. Families Waiting for Public Housing—Largest Number Since World War II," Letter to the Members, No. 47, July 1961.

253. Wilner, Daniel M., et al., *The Housing Environment and Family Life*, ch. XVII, "Summary and Conclusions," July 1960, processed.

259. Wilner, D. M.; Walkley, R. P.; Pinkerton, T.; and Tayback, M., *The Housing Environment and Family Life: A Longitudinal Study of the Effects of Housing on Morbidity and Mental Health,* The Johns Hopkins Press, Baltimore, Md., 1962.

262. Winnick, Louis, "Economic Constraints," ch. 1 and 2 of *Housing Choices and Housing Constraints,* ed. by Nelson N. Foote, Janet Abu-Lughod, Mary Mix Foley, and Louis Winnick, McGraw-Hill, New York, 1960.

265. Wood, Elizabeth, "Knowledge Needed for Adequate Programs of Public and Private Housing," *Needed Urban and Metropolitan Research,* ed. by Donald J. Bogue, Scripps Foundation and Miami University Press, Oxford, Ohio, 1953, pp. 51-55.

266. ———, "Public Housing and Mrs. McGee," *Journal of Housing,* vol. 13, No. 11, December 1956, pp. 424-427.

A THEORY OF WHY SKID ROW EXISTS
Donald J. Bogue

A Social Psychological Explanation of Skid Row

A scientifically valid and complete statement of causation should fulfill three requirements:

1. It must prove that the causal force antedated the effect. This is a necessary requirement, but alone it is not sufficient to constitute causation.

2. A relevant connection between the causal force and the effect must be established in the form of an hypothesis.

3. A mechanism by which the hypothesized causal influence is exerted must be postulated, observed, and established.

The data available for the present study permit only the first two of these steps to be attempted.

The social psychological approach, when applied to the present study, seeks to explain why individuals react to their social situation in such a way that they arrive on Skid Row. For possible causal forces it searches the personality and personal history of each man.

Reprinted, with permission of author and publisher, from Chapter 19 of Donald J. Bogue, *Skid Row in American Cities,* Community and Family Study Center, University of Chicago, 1963.

The second requirement is the formulation of hypotheses. A list was drawn up that contained twenty different conditions that might have helped to "cause" an individual man to come to Skid Row. The coders were instructed to search each man's entire interview, including the information and ratings of the interviewer, to determine whether each one of these factors was or was not present. Table 19-1 summarizes the results. The hypothesized forces which were noted by the coders as acting on the men before they arrived on Skid Row are as follows, in order of frequency:

As the last two lines of the table indicate, one or more of these causes appeared to be operating in all but about 3 percent of the cases. For the average homeless man, three causes appeared to be operating in combination. The table shows these to be the major causes:

1. *Economic Hardship.*—Heading this list are the hard facts of economic life. Our system seems to create a residue of chronic (though not necessarily culpable) losers, and Skid Row is the home of many of this group. Individual

men gravitate to Skid Row far more frequently because of irregular employment, unemployment, and low income, than because of alcoholism.

2. *Poor Mental Health.* — Deep personal maladjustment and disorganization emerge clearly as a second major "cause" of being on Skid Row. Alcoholism, marital discord, wanderlust, and emotional instability each affect from 20 to almost 40 percent of Skid Row men. Almost all Skid Row men have at least one of these symptoms of personal maladjustment. Coming to Skid Row is clearly a response of persons who are emotionally disturbed.

3. *Poor Social Adjustment.* — Many of the Skid Row men are "marginal men" torn by conflicting cultures or religious beliefs. Others are victims of social pressures and circumstances which made it difficult for them to make a normal social adjustment.

4. *Poor Physical Health, Physical Disability, and Limited Intellectual Ability.* — These constitute a smaller yet substantial group of forces.

Thus, from a social psychological point of view the individual person who comes to Skid Row does so either because he is a victim of economic circumstance, because he is physically handicapped, or because he is psychologically or sociologically "abnormal."

In making this generalization, it is important to underscore the concept of abnormality. Many persons who deal with Skid Row men and alcoholism persist in using the terms "immature" or "incompletely socialized" in speaking of the Skid Row men, as if their development had been normal up to a point and was simply suspended. The data from this study, however, reveal that from early boyhood the course of socialization of many Skid Row men was unusual or deviant. The many cases of violent temper, lack of career plans, lack of usual heterosexual interests, participation in delinquency gangs, and social withdrawal demonstrated this to be true. This does not mean that homeless men are vicious or psychotic, or that they are incurable. In fact, most seem to be almost pathetically harmless. However, these factors suggest that current homelessness is an essential part of their life adjustment. The truck driver who lives as a semi-isolate in a cubicle, minds his own business, drinks a few beers nightly with his friends, and patronizes a prostitute once in a while, is clearly deviant but not necessarily disorganized or psychologically immature.

It should not be overlooked that a majority of these men come from normal and urban homes where there apparently was little conflict or emotional stress, and most of the men feel no emotional tension with respect to the home situation. Their abnormality apparently results from mistakes in child-rearing or from contact with models of deviant behavior.

A Sociological Explanation of Skid Row

The social psychological approach apparently is able to give several major reasons for individuals' consenting to live on Skid Row. The sociological explanation deals with why and how individuals of the type described above get sorted out of the total population, are collected, and become lodged in a particular neighborhood of the city. From a sociological viewpoint, the major generalization is: Skid Rows exist to provide continued survival for familyless victims of society's unsolved social problems while these persons are in the terminal

	Percent of all homeless men		
	Total	Heavy drinkers, alcoholic derelicts	Teetotalers, light drinkers
Irregular employment or unemployment (not due to drinking)	42	28	49
Chronic alcoholism, problem drinking	38	85	9
Marital discord...	28	41	19
Low standard (level) of living	27	23	33
Social maladjustment	26	35	22
Wanderlust, restlessness	25	39	17
Emotional instability	20	37	10
Discontinuance of family (death of wife or parent)	16	14	15
Poor health, impairment of eyesight.................................	10	6	15
Cultural conflict because of ethnic, religious background............	10	2	15
Conflict with relatives other than wife	8	10	7
Poverty as a child...	8	6	10
Physical handicaps..	7	3	10
Failure in realizing ambitions	6	8	6
Poverty in old age, too old to work, limited income, not a heavy drinker..	6	1	12
Extreme egocentricity (self-centered)	6	7	7
Criminal record	5	6	4
Borderline intelligence	3	2	4
Laziness..	2	3	2
Orphanhood	2	2	2
None of the above: evaluation impossible	3	0	4
Average number of causes per homeless man	3.0	3.6	2.7

phase of their affliction and after society at large has abandoned all hope for them and has ceased to try to rehabilitate them.

The average citizen has a great deal of security against misfortune. If he gets ill (either mentally or physically), or if he shows tendencies to uncontrolled drinking, he is sustained first by members of his immediate family. They not only care for him but will try to assemble enough money for treatment. When the resources of the immediate family are exhausted, more distant relatives often lend a hand. Many employers are lenient and will assist a person in solving his personal problems. If the family belongs to a church, they can get counsel and aid there. If all of these fail, public and private welfare institutions enter the field. But when the resources of these agencies are exhausted there is only one place left—Skid Row. Thus, any average

citizen could be forced onto Skid Row as a result of a series of misfortunes. The citizen with below-average resources can be forced onto Skid Row with only moderate misfortune. Skid Row contains the only institutions in urban community that continue to care and hope for the individual when all other resources have been exhausted.

No matter how old or disabled a man is, no matter what evil he has committed, and no matter how sodden a drunk he has become, on Skid Row he can continue to exist and even find hope and help toward his rehabilitation.

But this help and hope are provided by special groups which themselves are only marginal to the larger community organization, or are highly specialized offshoots of those organizations. Like the people they serve, the Skid Row institutions are "out of bounds" for most citizens. The Salvation Army

TABLE 19-1
CODERS' RATINGS OF CONDITIONS THAT EXISTED PRIOR TO THE MEN'S ARRIVAL ON SKID ROW

Condition	All homeless men	Marital status			Drinking classification		
		Single	Separated and divorced	Widowed	Teetotalers, light drinkers	Moderate drinkers	Heavy drinkers, derelicts
Total	100.0	100.0	100.0	100.0	100.0	100.0	100.0
Chronic drinking	37.8	30.7	49.6	19.7	9.3*	25.6	84.7
Irregular employment (not due to drinking).	42.3	45.4	40.9	43.3	48.7	50.7	27.5
Marital discord	28.1	...	62.6	1.7	19.3	26.6	40.9
Conflict with relatives other than wife....	8.4	10.9	7.2	5.1	7.2	8.4	10.2
Low standard of living	26.9	34.1	22.4	20.2	33.2	20.6	23.2
Poverty as a child	8.1	8.6	7.1	10.1	10.4	7.4	5.6
Orphanhood	1.7	3.0	1.1	...	2.2	1.2	1.6
Physical handicaps	6.6	4.7	7.2	11.8	10.4	4.8	3.1
Poor health, eyes	10.5	7.3	9.9	27.0	14.7	8.6	6.3
Wanderlust, restlessness	25.0	30.4	22.6	14.6	16.7	21.1	39.0
Laziness	2.2	4.1	0.9	...	1.5	1.9	3.2
Borderline intelligence	3.3	6.2	4.3	...	4.2	2.9	2.5
Criminal record	5.4	3.4	7.2	6.7	3.8	7.7	5.7
Emotional stability	20.5	15.0	29.1	9.6	9.6	17.7	37.2
Social maladjustment	26.2	29.1	28.0	9.6	21.6	22.2	35.4
Egocentricity	6.1	8.0	4.7	5.1	6.6	3.6	7.2
Failure in realizing his ambitions	6.3	6.8	7.2	1.7	6.3	4.3	7.7
Cultural conflict because of ethnic, religious background	9.7	13.8	5.7	9.0	15.4	9.3	2.3
Discontinuation of respondent's family, wife, or parent	15.6	18.6	5.8	47.8	15.1	19.1	13.5
Respondent too old to work, small or limited income, no family not a heavy drinker	6.2	5.7	2.6	25.3	12.0	2.9	1.1
Unable to evaluate	3.4	3.6	1.7	1.7	3.5	7.2	0.4

*Includes men who at one time drank heavily but because of age, finances, health, etc. are no longer heavy drinkers; may have been on Skid Row for some time; drinking problem at time they came.

and other missions are at the same time admired and looked down upon for catering to hopeless cases. Their efforts in behalf of Skid Row men are considered to be voluntary acts of pity above and beyond the call of customary social duty.

In short, Skid Row exists because the working of social processes in our contemporary civilization creates certain types of circumstances for which society at large accepts minimal responsibility. The persons involved represent problems for which a solution has not been found. A recent book on Skid Row characterized it as a community of hopeless ego-less men who despaired of ever getting back to conventional community life. The results of the preceding chapter indicate that this is not at all correct in a majority of cases. It is society at large, rather than the homeless men, which has given up hope.

Rather than create a coherent program of help and rehabilitation, society temporizes by quarantining the men in a particular section where they may be watched over and kept under control by police. Here they may stay until they are reached by one of the mission programs, recover without treatment, or die. From a sociological viewpoint, Skid Row is a combination poor farm and asylum with freedom of movement where the "patients" are all regarded as incurable and hence are fed, clothed, and housed but not given curative treatment.

Another socio-economic theory explains that Skid Row plays an important economic function. This certainly is no longer true; Skid Row is a severe economic liability, both in terms of excess of cost over return and in terms of lost opportunities for other uses of the facilities.

The research materials presented here suggest that the public view of the incurable Skid Row man is incorrect.

Every major category of Skid Row resident was found to have possibilities for rehabilitation. Instead of being hopeless incurables, Skid Row men gave much evidence that a well-designed program could restore a great many of them to self-support at a much more tolerable level of life and could greatly improve the adjustment of almost all. Whether or not to embark upon such a program is a decision that lies outside the scope of scientific research. However, the research findings indicate that if the public wishes it, the Skid Row neighborhood may be dissolved without undesirable side effects.

PART IV

DEVIANT BEHAVIOR

7

ADULT CRIME AND JUVENILE DELINQUENCY

Defining Adult Criminal Behavior

The term *crime* means an offense against the public order. To an American lawyer, a crime is any

> act or omission prohibited by public law for the protection of the public, and made punishable by the state in a judicial proceeding in its own name. It is a public wrong, as distinguished from a mere private wrong or civil injury to an individual.[1]

A criminal is thus an individual who has been judicially defined as such by the courts. A person who is suspected, arrested, arraigned, indicted or tried in a criminal court is *not* a criminal. Strictly speaking, information about crimes 'known to the police' and reported in the Federal Bureau of Investigation *Uniform Crime Reports*, is not information about criminal behavior. Neither are data about arrests. These are sources of information for social research, as are reports from persons about their undetected but unlawful conduct, or reports from alleged victims

of alleged crimes. But the most fundamental political ethic of the United States prescribes authentic innocence to all who are not authoritatively judged to be guilty.

Explore this legal definition of crime further. If an adult American kills another adult American, and if this act is proved beyond reasonable doubt in court, the killer is not a murderer or a criminal. Proof must be advanced that the killer killed *intentionally*.[2] A child or a mentally ill person, for example, is incapable of intent of this kind under the law.

A crime is a violation of a *criminal* law. American laws represent a crystallization of the informal standards of conduct that regulates social activities. Informal standards build up within communities. Only certain features of them are embodied in the formalized codes of law of states. Indeed, community standards may oppose the statutes of the state.[3]

---

[1] *A Treatise on the Law of Crimes,* Chicago: Callaghan, Callaghan, and Company, 1952, 99. 1-13.

[2] There are exceptions to this, as when the person has killed someone unintentionally in the course of a robbery or burglary.

[3] Various legal systems within the United States depend upon different sources of prescription. The common law, for example, which arose originally out of customs, usage and precedent, is

The range of American law, furthermore, is much broader than the range of criminal law. Legal rights and obligations in this country are organized, first, around the rights of individuals; around the protection of individual interests, including security, reputation, ownership, and occupation. Second, legal rights and obligations arise from contracts between persons. These legal systems have *no* direct bearing on criminal law. Among other types of laws, criminal laws are those designed to preserve the *public* order, or interest.

American criminal laws are changed frequently. A survey made in 1931 found that three fourths of the inmates of federal prisons in that year were serving sentences for crimes that had not been defined as crimes a few years earlier! Most of them had violated one or another of the laws embodied in the Prohibition Act. Statutory criminal law in America is additive: few laws are repealed or otherwise eliminated, while new ones are added each decade.

Criminal law covers but a small portion of the ever-extending, ever more vigorously implemented network of laws that are erected in the United States. Some extensions of criminal law amount to responses to technological changes. They spring from codes of conduct essential for regulating highway traffic, for example. They build up around the food and drug industries, and advertising—all new technologies.

Civil and administrative law change most rapidly. It is in the non-criminal domain that most vigorous modification and most energetic violation of the law are exhibited. Illegal activities

now expressed in the written form of court decisions. Statutory law embodies the acts of legislatures. Finally, these are subordinate to laws derived from the Constitution. Of the three sources, only statutory laws change rapidly.

in banking, the stock exchange, taxation, trade arrangements, labor and professional practices and forms of organization, patent thefts, conspiracies and black and gray marketing, are examples of violations of civil and administrative laws which are *not* defined as criminal.

These legal distinctions seem arbitrary and empirically immaterial to some sociologists. Criminal law in New Hampshire covers the individual act of passing a bad check, and the state penitentiary contains many semi-literate woodsmen, called 'woodchucks,' who are incarcerated for two or more years for conviction of breaking this law. A corporate financial manipulation in the same state may involve equivalent conduct, but it will not be defined as a criminal matter regardless of the difference in fiscal loss. Definitions of crime that do not reflect the definitions under the law merely extend intellectual disorder, however.

In civil, as opposed to criminal, law, a violation is an official judgement that one individual has invaded the interests of another individual. The interests of the public are not directly involved. In a *civil* court action under civil law, an individual may sue another for damage or violation of his rights. In a criminal court action, however, the victim's personal damage may have to be compensated for by the violator, but the criminal court will also penalize the violator for damaging the interests of the state. *It is this penalty, the one levied against the criminal for his act against the state, which is central to the concept of crime.*

We said earlier that crimes were certain acts that were subject to punishments as violations of state laws. Crimes are specified acts and they are acts considered to apply to all persons, regardless of differences in status.

In the ancient language of common law, a crime is a public wrong. A crime in this cultural heritage is thus an act that damages the public interest. It is conduct that offends the public order.

The three broad classes of crimes inform us at once of this reciprocal relation between deviant behavior and the threat to, or disruption of, the ongoing system of social relations. The first class is *treason*. Under American law, treason consists of levying war against the United States, or giving loyalty, aid, or comfort to enemies of the state. In the source of our law in English common law, this was called high treason.

The second (and, in practice) major class of crimes is the *felony*. This class includes murder, certain types of manslaughter, rape, sodomy, robbery, larceny, arson, burglary, and acts which violate federal and state statutes that extend the range of this class.

The third general class, the *misdemeanor,* is a miscellany. It includes all violations of statutorily defined criminal laws that are not classified as treasons or felonies. Examples include forgery, perjury, and conspiracy to subvert justice.

Crime as a Social Problem

We may now rebuild a definition. A crime is an act that intentionally impairs or threatens to impair the social order, as this is defined by the state, or the rights for safe and proper conduct of other persons which are defined as due the protection of the state. Crime is a social problem, then, by the nature of this conception and by the manner in which agents of the state move to control it or correct its effect through the symbolism of punishment.

There are legalisms involved in this conception of crime as a social problem. These make the conception incomplete for social scientific analysis.

For example, the institutions (and their agents) that define the rules about crime, enforce them, and act out the penalties involved in determination of violations, could work against the survival of the society, or against the preservation of the safety and rights of members within it.

Furthermore, the fit between the well-being of the society and the enforcement and adjudication of the criminal law can be poor. For example, laws arise out of conflict. Some persons deviate from informal codes of conduct. Others struggle against deviance and, through success in influencing the court or the legislature, formalize their conception of particular codes. The resulting criminal statute represents the success of one group over others in securing formal sanctions for their version of informal standards of behavior. Where laws result from this process of conflict, their enforcement often stimulates further conflict.

Crime is a social problem in contemporary America for a different reason, as well: Crime is an institution. As such, it provides a script and roles for a cast of characters that goes well beyond the criminal. The definitions are acted upon through agents of the state. The drama of punishment is integral to the legal institution of crime, for example. Other dramatized scenes include arrest, detention, trial, conviction, and incarceration.

The manifest intent of the drama is obviously *protection* of the public interest. Some kind of rebalancing of the ongoing order; some strategy that seems corrective for both the community and the criminal, in the twin sense of redress and rehabilitation, is needed. If the strategy fails seriously, however, the entire organization of criminal justice becomes problematic.

So far we have said crime is a social problem because criminal behavior violates important values and harms or threatens persons and societal institutions. We have reminded ourselves that crime is a problem when law and the agencies of justice are maladapted to the interests of the whole society. And, equally deep problems emerge if the legal strategies fail to protect the public or to correct the criminal.

To these we now add the problem of domestic *warfare* between society and its career criminals. As police protections evolve technologically and organizationally, criminal agents devise ever more impressive counterforces. As with other forms of warfare, this conflict can put the system as a whole in jeopardy. It can endanger the innocent and uninvolved; it can generate forms of state authority which themselves threaten the lawfulness of the community. Also, when the conflict between police and some criminals becomes a matter of warfare, the public often comes to see *all* criminals as enemies. This makes justice and correction more difficult to achieve.

There are also immediate social costs involved in a criminal conviction which produce serious problems. Impoverishment and degradation of kin and other dependents; destruction of self; and demoralization of the intimate groups surrounding the criminal are illustrative of the effects of prosecution and conviction.

The problem-generating contingencies surrounding criminal justice can be extended indefinitely. There is the fit between community codes and the criminal code of the state, the quality of the justice which is adminis-

tered, the problem of protecting the public order, and correcting the wrong when means for doing so are ill understood and unpopular.

In addition, human and procedural errors cumulate around this pressing social problem. For example, a victim may not report a real crime or may report incorrectly. Of crimes known to the police, the error factor is so large that fewer than one out of three offenses are likely to be 'cleared by arrest.' And, where arrests are made, they are sometimes made upon the wrong person. Among those who are charged by the police, only one third are prosecuted. Only one fourth of this fraction are convicted. It thus appears that less than one in 20 crimes known to the police finally lead to a penal institution.[4]

This inventory of errors suggests a pattern of demoralization, frustration, and aggression among agents of justice; and a pattern of injustice toward persons suffering mistaken arrest, false charges, or failure of access to trial to have their reputations cleared.

Within the local community and, on occasion, in the nation as a whole, the frailties of the system of criminal justice become problematic when criminal offenders cannot be located, arrested, arraigned, indicted, or tried. Public frustration, when intense, presses the agents of justice toward hasty enforcement and administration, which increases the chances of injustice. These patterns are understandably the subject of enormous dramatic interest. The interplay between conduct, social control, and symbolic revenge, is a repertory theater of dramas that deplore, under-

[4]Courtland C. Van Vechten, "Differential Criminal Case Mortality in Selected Jurisdictions," *American Sociological Review*, Vol. 7, 1942, pp. 833-839.

stand, or celebrate the human condition.

Functions of Adult Crime

A great sociologist and criminologist, Emile Durkheim, made it plain long ago that the existence of crime is societally normal. He made it equally plain that crime is not merely "An inevitable, although regrettable phenomenon ... it is a factor in public health, an integral part of healthy societies."[5] Crime, like other forms of deviant behavior, is inevitable because individuals differ in character, which is manifested in behavior, and because extreme features of these differences are reacted to by groups which erect limits upon the differences they are willing to allow. A society without crime is inconceivable. It presumes a greater *uniformity* among persons than knowledge and experience lead us to predict.

In what sense is crime "a factor in public health?" What Durkheim meant was that no form of social organization remains sound indefinitely. Survival depends upon the ability of a society to change to meet changing conditions. Rules of conduct, a keystone of social organization, can become so rigid as to resist essential changes through proper conduct. Rules, in fact, often change *only* through acts that violate them. This may be intentional (as in the sit-in demonstrations of civil rights advocates in the South) or it may be the effect of a criminal act motivated by quite different imperatives.

Crime is sometimes functional, then. The law and its procedures depend upon crimes for their expression, reinforcement, and, most of all, for their revision. New moral codes and, eventually, new laws are often fostered by behavior defined as criminal under existing codes. This is one obvious 'lesson' of Western civilization's greatest culture heroes, from Socrates to Martin Luther.

Sociologists call this a functional notion of crime. If the functional premise is true, then the criminal is neither nonsocial nor anti-social. "Crime," said Durkheim, "must no longer be conceived an evil that cannot be too much suppressed."

Is Crime on the Increase?

Criminal laws differ from state to state in America. The local informal standards of conduct underlying them vary even more widely. Crime is an official designation about conduct. Each criminal offense is judged against the law, yet the judgment itself is a process. Therefore, the actuality of a crime is decided upon in the course of court action; the behavior of the defendant is but one element in the structure of this process.

This situation is complicated further by the fact that *no* reliable system of statistical reporting about crime exists in the United States. This is inevitable, given the great variation in local norms, enforcement, and administration of the laws.[6]

[5]*Rules of Sociological Method,* Eighth Edition, edited by George E. G. Gatlin, Glencoe, Illinois: The Free Press, 1950, p. 66.

[6]A sound knowledge of the comparative statistics of crime, which would require equating acts across different societies, would allow us to decide whether the United States has 'more' criminality than we would expect from empirical comparisons with other countries. This is not possible at present.

"To develop an adequate science of crimi-

If American criminal laws change year by year, and if enforcement and administration of the laws are variable, then it is true that changes in rates of crime reflect much more than an increase or decrease in criminal activity, and more than changes in related social conditions such as employment and war.

The statistics about criminal behavior in the United States are very unreliable. Thus, the correlations between crime rates and other indicators of social behavior and status are also unreliable. The correlates, moreover, are not sound indicators of the social causes of criminal behavior. Not only are they subject to great error as measures; they are spurious in substance. A correlate is a statement of association, not causation. Also, correlates themselves are statements about the classes of persons most likely to be arrested, tried, convicted, or punished; but these may not be the same classes of persons who commit crimes most frequently.

For example, many violations of the criminal law go undetected. In one survey of American adults, 26 per cent of the men respondents reported they had committed automobile theft, 17 per cent said they had committed burglary,

13 per cent grand larceny, and 11 per cent robbery. Sixty-four per cent of the men and 29 per cent of the women reported committing at least one felony. No one in the sample had been convicted as a criminal.[7]

Many commercial, corporate, and professional practices involve serious violations of laws which could be prosecuted as criminal acts. Because of the status of the persons involved, these violations are handled in administrative and civil court actions.[8] These do not get recorded as part of indexes of crime rates in the United States.

Volume of Reported Crimes

Some types of offenses are consistently defined under criminal law. These give some basis for analysis of the crime rate. Murder (excluding justifiable homicide and accidental deaths and attempted murders, and negligent manslaughter) is one such serious felony. Even here, criminal homicide is an act defined in the course of variable legal processes.

Murder rates have moved *downward* in the United States for three decades. The rate in 1933, the peak of the Great Depression, was 7.1 per 100 thousand urban population. Except for slight increases in the late war years, this urban rate decreased to 5.1 in 1960 and 4.9 in 1962.[9]

nology, more comparative studies are needed, using theories and procedures derived from one society and applied as precisely as possible to another. A really universal generalization requires the repetition of similar studies by different persons in a similar way on samples differing in time and place ... Any attempt at any international science of criminology may prove impossible at this time, however, because of the widely divergent conceptions of the nature of human behavior." (Marshall Clinard, "Criminological Research," Chapter 23 in *Sociology Today*, edited by Robert K. Merton, et al., New York: Basic Books, 1959, pp. 534-535.)

The same logic applies to domestic historical comparisons.

[7]J. S. Wallerstein and C. J. Wyle, "Our Law-Abiding Law-Breakers," *Probation*, Vol. 25, March-April, 1947, pp. 107-112.

[8]Edwin H. Sutherland, "Crime and Business," *Annals of the American Academy of Political and Social Science*, Vol. 217, September, 1941, pp. 111-118.

[9]*Uniform Crime Reports*, Annual Bulletins of the Federal Bureau of Investigation, Washington, D.C. There are many reasons why these and all other available indices are highly unreliable.

Among other reported felonies against persons, national trends were generally downward from 1933 to 1943, then upward to 1946, and again downward from 1947 to 1962. Only reported crimes of forcible rape and of aggravated assault reveal a contrary, persistent upswing over the past 20 years, and these two crimes are subject to special variations in definition and reporting.

We note that any attempt to gauge changes in crime rates for the United States on the basis of reported crimes against persons is seriously misleading. Reported *crimes against persons* amount to not more than 5 per cent of all reported crime annually. Frequencies are so low that small changes affect statements of rates excessively.

Crimes against property make up the great bulk of criminal behavior as it is reported to the police, and as reflected in rates of arrest, trial, and conviction. Among such crimes, burglary accounts for about 40 per cent of all major reported crimes. Larcenies involving thefts of money or goods worth $50 or more account for 25 per cent; and auto thefts for 17 per cent. In 1960, burglary, larceny and auto theft amounted to 87 per cent of all major crimes reported. These three types of crime against property have become about one and a half times as common as they were in 1938. It is this increase that

Many crimes are not discovered. Others are known but not reported. Biases in local reporting distort the uniformity severely. Official statistics of all kinds concerning crime are not subject to sound knowledge about statistical errors in variation. Rates for some crimes are not routinely recorded or compiled. In the instance of delinquency, great variations in definition complicate reliability even further. See Donald R. Cressey, "The State of Criminal Statistics," *National Probation and Parole Association Journal*, Vol. 3, 1957, pp. 230-241.

underlies most of the sounding of crime rate alarms in urban newspapers.

Who Gets Arrested?

The best criminal statistics are those on crimes reported to local police. These are so unreliable that "the volume of crime in time and place cannot be assayed."[10] Information about arrests is more reliable in some ways, but in other ways it is a less valid indicator of the meaning of crime.

For example, Reckless has estimated that from 75 per cent to 85 per cent of all crimes against persons which are reported are "cleared by arrest." This does not mean that the actual violators were arrested or that the person arrested will be tried, or convicted, or sentenced. When we turn to reported crimes against property, which comprise roughly 95 per cent of all reported offenses, the per cent "cleared by arrest" declines to 25 to 40 per cent, depending upon type of offense.

We can learn several important things from the study of who gets arrested, however. There are some social correlates of arrest that are *so* strong, positive, and consistent over the years as to supply us with rather loud and clear signals. Among these, age, sex, race, place of residence, and socio-economic status are noteworthy.

For any year since 1933, the bulk of arrests for crimes against property were made among youths and young adults under 25 years of age. Two thirds of all arrests for robbery, for example, were arrests of persons under 25 in 1960. Over 77 per cent of all arrests for

[10]Walter Reckless, *The Crime Problem*, 3rd ed., New York: Appleton-Century-Crofts, 1961, p. 12.

burglary, 87 per cent for auto theft, and 70 for larceny, were arrests of persons under 25 in the same year.

Students of criminal delinquency tend to identify the years between nine and 12 as the origin in time of most individual cases of persistent unlawful conduct. Official arrest statistics lead one to emphasize the years from 18 to 24, but various survey and clinical studies suggest that this is a surface record of a patterned relation to the law and the local police that begins, for many who are arrested, in early adolescence.

If Americans who are arrested for crimes are three times as likely to be under 25 years as to be older, those who get arrested are generally ten times as likely to be men than women. Racially, the number of arrests of Negroes occurs at about three times the number of arrests of whites. Arrest rates in large central cities exceed rates in smaller communities and the rural hinterland by two to eight times, depending upon the type of offense. And the odds are three to one that the arrestee will have low, rather than middle or high occupational and income status.

Implications of Arrest Rate Correlates

The difference in arrest rates by sex, age, race, place of residence, and socio-economic status are thus great. They are found consistently; and they are paralleled by who gets tried, convicted and imprisoned. Here we have the clues to an explanation of the social sources of crime.

If there is a pattern, no criminologist or sociologist has articulated it satisfactorily to date, although the correlations have been well identified for decades. The main contribution of this knowledge is to limit our readiness to accept any one interpretation of crime causation.

For example, poverty has long been a tempting explanation. Yet, the correlates lead us to reject an explanation in terms of poverty. Impoverished women are as common in the population as impoverished men, yet neither poor nor wealthy women are arrested even half as frequently as men. The poverty notion also fails to explain rural-urban differences.

Crime Causation

Thus, a good explanation of criminal behavior will account for variations in rates of arrest (as these are roughly consistent with rates of conviction and penalization). The example of the poverty hypothesis makes the point that no single factor will explain crime. Even a diversity of factors may not be helpful if they cannot be interrelated logically into a guiding idea; that is, a theoretical proposition.

Three partial theories have received the serious attention of American sociologists. Foremost among these is the partial theory of *differential association*.[11] This theory is at once situational and developmental. It states that persons increase their chances of becoming criminals to the extent that their association with criminal behavior patterns exceeds their association with anticriminal behavior patterns.

This means more than that contact with criminals will induce criminality. Indeed, it provides a basis for contradicting this common sense impression: even career criminals expose their children to anticriminal patterns of be-

[11]Edwin H. Sutherland and Donald R. Cressey, *Principles of Criminology*, 6th edition, Philadelphia: Lippincott, 1960.

havior. The principle of differential association, while grounded in the premise that criminal behavior develops through social learning in small groups of families and peers, extends to the larger scene through the idea of *differential social organization*. Higher arrest and conviction rates in densely populated cities, for instance, are explained in terms of increased exposure to criminal patterns and to opportunities for violation of the law.

The partial theories of two other criminologists are analogous to the theory of differential association and social organization. As they have so much in common with one another, we have lumped them together. These are the ideas of Thorsten Sellin and Donald R. Taft, which we refer to broadly as the principle of *culture conflict*.[12]

Under the principle of culture conflict, criminal behavior is understood in roughly the same sense that Sutherland treated it, but emphasis is put on the contradictory content of rules within groups in the larger society, rather than upon the process of learning that leads to criminal behavior. Sellin offers an example:

> A Sicilian father in New Jersey killed the sixteen-year-old seducer of his daughter, expressing surpise at his arrest since he had merely defended his family honor in a traditional way.[13]

A vivid illustration from another source enlarges the pertinence of the principle:

> For our next case we go to a city of the Southwest . . . A man was accused of threatening to whip a lawyer in an arguement after the two had been involved in a slight car accident. He was also reputed to have threatened to assault the lawyer's wife. Charged with the offense in court, the man was given a two-year jail sentence and fined $2,000. His bail was set at $10,000, which the lawyer offered to pay for a chance to kill him. As the judge assessed the penalty, he stated from the bench that, if he had been in the lawyer's place, he would have killed the man. Later, realizing that this statement was injudicious, he remanded the sentence. The defendant was a Negro.[14]

Taft extends culture conflict to crime rate differentials between nations. In the 1930s, Taft's empirical research led him to the discovery that the immigrants from southern and eastern Europe to the United States had a commitment rate to prisons that was 87 per cent higher than that for immigrants from northern and western Europe. His finding held at that time for differences in rates between children of immigrants from the two parts of Europe. More recently, Taft turned this interpretation toward American, as compared with other modern societies. He interprets our materialistic, competitive, national culture to be "criminogenic," as compared to others.

Robert K. Merton has fused themes from these and other theories of deviant behavior into an even more general proposition. He maintains that when great value is put upon various types of success within a society (e.g., economic or material and occupational), and when legitimate ways of gaining success are

[12]Thorsten Sellin, *Culture Conflict and Crime*, New York: Social Science Research Council, 1938; and Donald R. Taft, *Criminology*, 3rd edition, New York: Macmillan.
[13]Sellin, *op. cit.*, p. 68.

[14]Austin L. Porterfield and Robert H. Talbert, *Mid-Century Crime In Our Culture*, Fort Worth, Texas: Leo Potishman Foundation, 1954, p. 41.

highly restricted for most people, some of these people will choose unlawful means of securing success.[15]

Merton's partial theory proposes that the success themes of the mainstream of American culture influence Americans who seek to partake of this mainstream to achieve wealth and occupational recognition. Since the means to these ends are denied to most members of most lower class groups, conflict ensues. Criminal behavior is the form the conflict takes when individuals are neither rejecting the values, nor overly conforming to them, nor produce countervalues. Criminal deviance occurs when persons seek the ends of success through illegal means.

These partial theories make sense out of differences in arrest and conviction rates. Merton's ideas may be most powerful, in that they offer an explanation of why certain conflicts lead to criminal, as opposed to other forms of deviant behavior such as passive withdrawal or excessive conformity. Each partial theory contributes to understanding why young adult males, Negroes, central city dwellers, lower class occupational groups, and some other ethnic minority groups, are overrepresented in the criminal population.[16]

Organized Crime

Useful as these theories of crime causation are in explaining variations in groups of criminal offenders, they are more pertinent to a larger, more problematic aspect of American crime: crime as a career.[17]

Theories of differential association, culture conflict, and relative deprivation are most helpful in supplying some understanding of crime as a way of life. The bulk of American crime is organized institutionally. Criminal activity constitutes one, and probably several different, subsocieties within the nation, which recruit personnel, build careers upon programs of training and advancement, and compete with other 'firms' in the same line of business for improved dollar profits. Each subsociety builds up around a cluster of illegal ventures; it occupies a regional or a community territory, has a set of informal standards of conduct, a division of labor and a system of social ranks and rewards.

When Americans think of organized crime, they think of Murder, Incorporated, the Mafia, or (since the 1963 Senate testimony of Joe Valachi) of the alleged Cosa Nostra. In fact, these are but glamorous, more secretive variations upon a much vaster network of criminal enterprises. It is to these diverse enterprises that young men are recruited. For crime in America is an "institution organized for real rather than imaginary war. And like real war, it exacts a heavy toll of its adherents and enthusiasts. Like sport, too, it is a way of life for the young."[18]

[15]Robert K. Merton, *Social Theory and Social Structure*, rev. edition, Chicago: Free Press, 1957, pp. 161-194.

[16]None of the partial theories offers a principle of the developmental and other psychological conditions under which the theoretical process operates upon some but not all members of each social category. All of them inform us of the ways in which criminal behavior is generated from quite ordinary, that is, nonevil, ingredients in the structure of American society.

[17]This section has emphasized that official statistics are unreliable and invalid. The reader should remember that causal explanations, when applied to such statistics, presuppose that offenders have been authentically distinguished from nonoffenders; that criminals, for instance, engage in burglary and larceny, while law-abiding citizens do not. We do not know that this is the case, and we have cited one among several studies that suggest that *most* Americans probably employ some illegal means to culturally approved ends.

[18]Frank Tannenbaum, *Crime and the Community*, New York: Ginn and Co., 1938, p. 116.

Gambling, narcotics and prostitution are the best organized, vastest criminal enterprises. Since the Prohibition era, gambling has matured into one of the nation's largest industries. Gamblers, legal and illegal, do a business totalling $20 to $30 billion a year, according to the Kefauver Committee report.

Each of these large enterprises also generates criminal activity at lower, more localized levels. For example, consider the pattern for juvenile gangs. Some are at first occasionally delinquent, but then adapt to the use of narcotics. The adolescent member of an occasionally deliquent gang may join with the gang in experimenting with nonnarcotic drugs and, later, with narcotics. For complicated psychosocial reasons, the members of certain types of adolescent urban gangs thus become addicted. The source of illegal narcotics is controlled by the larger, more efficient international firms. As monopolies, these firms can charge extreme prices to addicts.

The pressure for money to support addiction involves the addicted members of the gang in intensified delinquent activities. The addict's life becomes organized around crime to maintain his supply, and around evasion of the police. In this double bind, a *group* of addicts can not develop an enterprising criminal firm of their own. They settle for larceny, burglary, and petty robberies.[19]

The criminal activity against property by groups of young addicts is initially unorganized. But it often becomes integrated with networks of criminal enterprise designed to cut risks, improve the transmission of stolen

[19]Contrary to popular impression, evidence suggests that young addicts do not engage in violent or other crimes against persons, but rather specialize in money-generating theft.

goods, and increase profits. Ultimately, the addict is exploited by organized crime. The point of importance here is that some criminal activities are generated from youthful narcotic addition. The New York City police claim that 25 per cent of the reported crime in their city is generated in this one way, and the Chicago Police Department has reported similar conclusions.

The addict who is drawn into crime is but one example of the genesis of the *criminal career*. Most criminologists distinguish between noncareer offenders (who include most persons convicted of aggravated assault, murder, statutory rape, embezzlement, and forgery) and career criminals, whose lives are progressively involved in more complex and more serious offenses.

The career offender originates characteristically in the urban youth gang. Here, specialization builds up around burglary, larceny, auto theft, or robbery. Those who survive the early risks, who prove themselves during brief stays in reformatories and through loyalty and diligence in their work, are absorbed into one of the adult criminal enterprises of prostitution, drugs, gambling, racketeering, or their 'small merchant' equivalents in auto parts, counterfeiting, safecracking, confidence games, or professional shoplifting. It is in the realm of big organized crime and career criminality that the principles of differential association, culture conflict, and the choice of illegitimate routes to success have relevance to understanding a major national social problem.

Treatment of the Offender

But the *genesis* of criminal behavior does not help much in explaining how criminals are treated by the state and informally by the society. Criminology and penology overlap, but the former takes us only a short distance into the latter. And it may well be the case that the best theory of crime will come not from studies of crime and its causation but from studies in penology; in how society *responds* to crime.

Persons convicted of crime in the United States are not necessarily sent to a penal institution. They may be fined, placed on probation, or pardoned. Imprisonment, however, is the most common penalty for a criminal conviction.[20]

In its modern guise, incarceration in a total institution is a peculiarly American cultural development. The Walnut Street Prison, built in Philadelphia in 1790 in response to Quaker humanitarianism, is the prototype from which most of the world's modern penal institutions took their form. The prison is the result of reform efforts to reduce the broad use of capital punishment and brutal maiming of offenders by substituting secure incarceration.

Because of the size, cost, and the limitations inherent in imprisonment, the entire system is a failure. State and federal prisons house between 200 and 220 thousand inmates a year, at a cost in capital equipment, personnel, and operations of hundreds of millions of dollars. Such an investment by the society should yield some 'returns' in terms of the goals of security and correction.

We can dispense swiftly with the notion that there are significant returns, while noting that many other social functions, including revenge, scape-goating and a myth of security, may be well served by the penal system. First, prisons are supposed to deter citizens from criminal behavior. This possibility is undermined in many ways.[21] The threat of punishment is but one minor factor in the forces surrounding the genesis of crime. It is a factor which deters, if at all, only in the case of occasional or noncareer type offenses.

Imprisonment does not protect the society from the criminal. It is a temporary incapacitation which as frequently increases the future dangerousness of the offender through isolation, incubation with hardened offenders, and post-prison stigmatization. Moreover, most serious and dangerous offenders are not in prison in the first place, so that prisons offer protection against the wrong persons.

Prisons are also ostensibly designed to rehabilitate offenders. In spite of efforts toward this end, the separation of persons from participation in the real community; the type of social organization that develops among caged and otherwise stigmatized men; the style of social relation that inheres between guards and the inmates; and the extreme social distance the open society places between its members and the walled prison—all conspire to defeat the attempt at rehabilitation.

It may be impossible to educate men and women toward autonomy and responsibility when one is also charged with complete control over their custody. The rate of previous incarceration is partial proof of this contention. For the nation as a whole, about one in two prison inmates is in prison for at least a second stay. The author agrees

[20]In 1960 in the United States, there were altogether about 4,230 prisons, ranging from state and federal prisons, to prison camps, workhouses and farms, municipal jails and the like. In addition, there were 177 juvenile 'correctional' institutions, designed along similar but usually less secure or incarcerative lines.

[21]Paul W. Tappan, "Objectives and Methods in Correction," in Paul W. Tappan, editor, *Contemporary Correction*, New York: McGraw Hill, 1951, pp. 8-9.

with Tannenbaum, who concluded in 1938:

> If we wished to make a criminal out of anyone, no better method could be devised than to dramatize and herald his activities in the way we are doing. It not only conditions him toward an estimate of himself; it sets the attitude of his fellows and forms...a basis of judgment that makes change on his part proportionately more difficult ... No more self-defeating device could be discovered than the one society has developed in dealing with the criminal.[22]

Prisons may function for an entirely different reason; namely, symbolic integration of the public:

> The prison is expected to restore society to the state of equilibrium and harmony it was in before the crime was committed. "Undesirables," "deviants," "non-conformists," and "outlaws" ... are segregated behind walls so that they cannot disrupt society's peace and harmony at least during a specified period.[23]

There is, in other words, the possibility that prisons, like other schemes of institutional segregation, enhance social solidarity in the open society. Cressey points out that we do not *know* whether prisons are inefficient or efficient means of supplying this solidarity. Nor do we take many steps to find out. Not one half of one per cent of the annual national investment in prisons — state, federal, county and municipal — is spent in obtaining answers about the real functions of imprisonment and their relative efficacy.

[22]Tannenbaum, *op. cit.*, p. 477.
[23]Donald R. Cressey, in Robert K. Merton, et al., editors, *Contemporary Social Problems, op. cit.*, p. 70.

Evolving Alternatives: Probation and Parole

Probation is one alternative to imprisonment that has developed steadily since the turn of the century, especially in application to juveniles. Probation is intended to prevent imprisonment by supervising the conduct of the offender, however directly or indirectly. The mechanism involves suspension of sentence for the adult offender. Some states have statutes that limit the court's power to grant probation to cases of misdemeanors, or minor crimes. Generally, the practice becomes more common and flexible each decade, with corresponding increases in provision of legal and social services to courts to make control of the probated offender more effective and even rehabilitative.

Within the limits of adequate services and resources for individual diagnosis and attention, probation is a protective as well as rehabilitative device. It has come to be employed more widely in the United States than in nearly any other country in the world, since it originated in 1841 in Massachusetts. Its evolution as a procedure for adult criminals has been hampered by lack of public support in most local jurisdictions, but today most large municipal courts and federal courts have probation services. For juvenile offenders, probation has become, through evolution of special juvenile courts with broad discretionary powers, the common instrument of state control.[24]

Most adult offenders still go to prison upon conviction, but extension of the probation scheme is highly probable. Again, social research and systematic evaluation of results can contribute powerfully to procedures of

[24]N. S. Timasheff, *One Hundred Years of Probation, 1841-1941*, New York: Fordham University Press, 1942.

selection and rehabilitation and control.

Parole is a similar, evolving practice. It is employed, however, after the offender has served part of his sentence in a prison. If paroled, an offender enters the open community under various restrictions upon his liberty. These restrictions are set by a state authority and are implemented by parole officers who represent the state but also work on behalf of the offender.

Failure of parole is more common than failure of probation. Greater risks are taken in parole. The crimes of the prospective parolees are more serious, the offender has already been stigmatized by penal incarceration (however temporary), and the decision process leading up to parole contains greater error in view of the time and distance between the initial trial and parole. Probation systems may assess the potentials of the offender more directly. In addition, the administrative machinery for regulating parole is incomplete and poorly coordinated across jurisdictions.

Regardless of these failures, parole, like probation, has rehabilitative potentials which no institutional arrangement can match. Parole removes the offender from excessive association with a community of offenders. It constrains him toward a new participation in the law-abiding community. Its ultimate success as a system of crime control in fact depends mostly upon the response the open community makes to the paroled individual.

Juvenile Delinquency

Juvenile delinquency cannot be defined through logical extension of our definition of criminal behavior to persons under some age (usually 18) specified by the state. Delinquency does mean the violation of a law by a juvenile, but the nature of the violation and the law is more diffuse.

Many more modes of conduct are contained within the codes defining delinquency. The civil liberties, including due process, generally accorded adults are not always applied to juvenile defendants, although certain other forms of court protection are accorded. Most of the common forms of arraignment, indictment, trail and sentencing, as well as forms of penalty, differ greatly.

In many states, a youth may be judged delinquent for engaging in "indecent conduct," as that is assessed by the juvenile court; for drinking; for smoking cigarettes near public places; for running away from home; and for using "vile, obscene or vulgar speech in public" (again, as these are assessed by the court). In many states, cases of juvenile neglect and dependency get interwoven with misconduct, so that the application of the law is not to the issue of judging a charge of criminal conduct, but is rather a study of the particulars of the youth's life situation.

Juvenile Delinquency as a Social Problem

Until this century, children and youth in the United States were subject to the criminal laws of their state, or they were beyond the law. Today, children and youth are protected from harshly undifferentiated application of criminal codes, but in being protected from criminal status, they have become subject to the discretion of the court. The old function of the law and its operation in court was achievement of criminal justice. The new function is to serve the best interest of the child, and, where necessary, to reconstruct the life, and life situation of the child. The irony is that the old set of cruelties were replaced by injustices and ambiguities in functioning.

Many children and youth today are not clearly arrested. They 'come to the attention of the court.' They are not indicted and tried; instead, the court holds a 'hearing.' They are not convicted, but rather 'adjudicated to the status of a deliquent child.' They are not sentenced to prison, but are 'committed to a school.' Or, they are put on indefinite probation, subject to the regulation of the court or a social agency until they become 21 years of age.

The intent is benevolent discipline and guidance. Depending upon the offense, the quality of the court and supporting agencies, and the response communities make to the status of the delinquent, the result may be a help or a further poisoning of a youth's relation to legitimate authority and reinforcement of his disposition toward a criminal career. The uncertainties involved in defining juvenile delinquency and the variable outcomes of legal action upon youths in this society therefore suggest that juvenile delinquency is a major social problem to the extent that *it implies social disorganization in the control relations that regulate behavior between age groups.* A conflict that is so common in human societies is, in contemporary America, poorly mediated under the law.

If we penetrate the confusion and concentrate on hard-core or serious and progressive delinquent behavior, we must regard juvenile delinquency as a major national social problem for the same reasons we advanced about adult offenders. Career delinquency, by which we mean the early stages in the developmental pattern described earlier, damages or threatens to impair the social order. It may disorganize a community by destroying the security of persons and property.[25] Extensive career delinquency can require undue diversions of revenues and manpower into protective, preventive, detective and punitive counterforces.

There is no distinction, in other words, between adult crime and hard-core career delinquency as social problems. There are reasons, however, why delinquency can be regarded as more problematic. For one, delinquency and legal and public action against it is a form of warfare that has higher social stakes. Changing the metaphor, serious and progressive delinquency is a breeding ground where many or few lifetime adult criminals will mature, depending upon the outcomes of each annual conflict.

For another, serious delinquency is a companionate activity. It is learned in and develops out of youth groups. The criminal behavior patterns of these groups can be contagious. They can absorb increasing numbers of youths in each upcoming age group. Moreover, they endanger the conditions under which nondelinquent youths in the same neighborhoods grow toward adulthood, for many delinquent groups attempt to control their territories and govern all youths within them.

Juvenile delinquency may be somewhat unique as a social problem in yet other ways. For example, it provides a scapegoat for adult policy problems. Children and youth are targets for the projected, displaced failures of adults. Youth may also be exploited to communicate conflict and disapproval between adult groups who cannot openly

[25]Some forms may also contribute to changing the rules that presumably govern such security, in the way that Durkheim suggested about crime in general.

condemn different ethnic, social and economic groups in their midst.

Also, juvenile delinquency is a social register of *past* disorganization. Rates of juvenile offenses are highest after major wars. Children reared under the strains, tensions, often conflicts and deprivations characteristic of a nation at war, mature into adolescents with special problems. When these are acted out publicly, they are a reminder of family and community failures in a most vital function: the proper rearing of the young.

In the same sense, serious, progressive delinquency (and some times even occasional misconduct) presents to many American adults a peculiar challenge. They expect to be able to shape and form the conduct of the young. They expect to control the quality of behavior in the the young much as they control the nonhuman environment. Extensive delinquency is thus a statement about limits on social controls, which many Americans believe should work better on youths than upon themselves.

Some social critics have also interpreted delinquency as a commentary upon the absence of relevant goals in the adult society. Where Merton's theory emphasizes deprivation by lack of access to goals, others, like Paul Goodman in *Growing Up Absurd,* view youthful conduct as a response to a society lacking less in legitimate means than in worthwhile ends.

Delinquency Rates

The problems that plague the measurement of adult crime also plague the measurement of juvenile delinquency. They are intensified, however, by weaker definitions; greater variability between communities in what is han-

dled in the courts; by the protective confidence that surrounds children and youth in their movement through the police, courts and other agencies; by differences in the disposition of cases; and by even less effective recording systems than obtain for adult offenders. The volume of delinquency, even more than is the case for adult crime, cannot be assayed.

If one follows the two main sources of official reporting, the Federal Bureau of Investigation and the Children's Bureau of the Department of Health, Education and Welfare, it is clear that the rate of arrests of juveniles increased generally from 1 youth per 100 in the 1930s, to roughly 2 youths in every 100 by 1960. Most reports of increasing delinquency derive from this change. This seems to be an alarming rise of 100 per cent!

If the comparison is made with a longer dateline, this 'alarming' increase vanishes. Two careful analyses by sociologists of community-specific statistics reveal that the delinquency rate in the 1950s was lower than the rates for the years 1900 to 1910, and for 1915-25.[26]

From 70 to 75 per cent of all official delinquency in any year since World War II has involved one or more of these types of offenses: theft, vandalism, assault or other injury to persons, and truancy. Among these, the great bulk is concentrated in theft. By far the most common offense is auto theft, a crime that has increased in frequency in many western European nations in the last fifteen years. Two thirds of all arrests for

[26]Negley K. Teeters and David Matza, "The Extent of Delinquency in the United States," *The Journal of Negro Education*, Vol. 28, 1959, pp. 205-211; and unpublished Chicago study by Henry D. McKay, reported on by Donald R. Cressey, *Contemporary Social Problems, op. cit.,* p. 84.

auto theft in the United States are made against juveniles. All but a small fraction of these are cases of 'joyriding,' where youths have stolen a car to ride around in but not to keep or sell.

Correlates of Delinquency

Official statistics on delinquency lead us to identify the same main correlates we were led to with adult offenders. In order of importance, American delinquents are more likely than chance to be boys, to be from ethnic minority groups, to come from densely populated central cities, and to come from families with low socio-economic status.

Groups who are over-represented among adult offenders are of course over-represented in the same manner among juvenile delinquents; for the correlates come from statistics on police action and court records; and we know that most juveniles detained by the police are in the older, 16- to 17-year-old, group which would most closely parallel the group of young adult male offenders.

Thus, we are again led to apply the principles of differential association, culture conflict, differential social organization, and, through relative deprivation, to expect a response of illegal efforts toward wealth and group status. We need only to give added emphasis to the group matrix out of which career delinquency develops, and we would appear to have a general explanatory account.

While the principles are of great help, they fail to account for some different empirical findings. For example, in recent years sociologists have studied self-reported, illegal misconduct among youths from 11 to 17 years of age. They have found that youths give

fairly reliable and crudely valid answers to confidential questions about their own misconduct.

In other words, until recently our theories about delinquency as well as crime have been founded on dubious comparisons between offenders and the general population. Suppose, however, that the only difference between delinquents and other youths was that the former consist of detected, detained, and otherwise officially labelled youths!

There are technical problems, as well as issues of validity, in self-report studies of delinquency. But there is a general consistency among their results. For example, a comparison of self-reports from two junior high school student bodies in a midwestern city, one Negro and the other white, revealed that theft and vandalism were slightly more common among the whites than among the Negroes. None of the racial differences was substantial statistically, however.

Generally similar types and frequencies of misconduct have been found in rural farm, rural nonfarm, small urban, industrial, and suburban communities. Differences in types and frequencies of misconduct between social and economic status groups, based on parents' educations and occupations, have been found to be slight or negligible.[27]

The same studies have investigated but found no evidence to support hypotheses derived from Merton's theory. The theory suggests that youths who engage in serious misconduct should also exhibit more intense or more frequent feelings of deprivation and of

[27]For an example of this research development, see Robert A. Dentler and Lawrence J. Monroe, "Social Correlates of Early Adolescent Theft," *American Sociological Review*, Vol. 25, October, 1961, pp. 733-743.

alienation from the mainstream of the society. Yet attitudes as measured in questionnaires and interviews do not differ on this theoretically important dimension. Nor are there important observed differences between the self-reports of youths who engage in hidden theft, vandalism, truancy, or aggressive acts, on matters of attitudes toward parents.[28]

Suppose that a fixed proportion of youths in any community exhibit occasional offensive misconduct. Suppose these youths receive differential attention from the police, the courts, and social agencies. Those who carry status disadvantages will be most stigmatized by detection, detention, and treatment. Those with status advantages will be detected less frequently. When they are 'caught,' greater care will be taken to avoid stigma. Both types of community response could be well intentioned, but one of them would be conducive to a career in crime.

A self-report project led one sociologist to theorize that the common forms of adolescent misconduct (joyriding, theft, drinking) are *hedonic* (pleasure-giving) activities that are emphasized more by some youths than by others, for personal developmental reasons. Hedonic activities can become self-reinforcing and, as they multiply, they must be intensified in depth and form to continue to produce pleasure. Along this path of behavior, he argues, the community sets restrictions, traps, and penalties. These restrain and detect some youths more effectively than others. Among those who are caught, some will find public exposure and disapproval again reinforcing of the hedonic pattern.

This we shall call a principle of *developmental contingencies*. It receives support from research in the self-report tradition. It is also supported by research on the careers of youths who get in trouble but who somehow mature into law-abiding citizens like the rest of the unimprisoned community.

One of these studies attends to the most deeply conditioned and trapped of all types of offenders, the narcotic addict. The tentative conclusion reached in this study states that:[29]

"Maturing out of addiction is the name we can give to the process by which the addict stops taking drugs, as the problems for which he originally began taking drugs become less salient and less urgent, if our hypothesis is correct. It is as if, metaphorically speaking, the addicts' inner fires have become banked by their thirties."

This parallels the results of longitudinal and case studies of groups of delinquents. Delinquents who are not severely penalized under the law, or are not casualties in criminal warfare, tend to marry, have children, find a job, and settle into the role of lawful citizen. The crucial years for the urban gang delinquent are those from 17 to perhaps 25. *If this period is bridged, the delinquent will tend to outgrow his gang and his delinquent activities.*

Delinquency Control

The *intent* of all work with and around the milieus of juvenile delin-

[28]This is true for the studies of younger adolescents, but 16- and 17-year-olds who are self-reported delinquents are more apt to be rejecting of their parents. See F. Ivan Nye, *Delinquency and the Family*, New York, John Wiley, 1958.

[29]Charles Winick, "Maturing Out of Narcotic Addiction," *Bulletin on Narcotics*, Vol. XIV, No.1, January-March, 1962, p. 5.

quents is preventive. There is little point in distinguishing between community prevention programs, institutional treatment, and rehabilitation. The outcomes may differ, but all are attempts to prevent the advent and recurrence of offenses against the public order.

As with adult offenders, but to an even greater extent, control and correction are major social problems in contemporary America. *What is tried does not work.* When it does work to some extent, we are unable to determine from evaluation research just what it is that is producing success.

If we are unable to predict which children out of a particular group will become delinquent, we are in no position to design effective controls. Since delinquency is a two-edged event—a pattern of misconduct and a pattern of action by agents of the state and the community—efforts at control must involve both. In short, authentic programs of prevention require effective techniques for reordering the social structure, at least locally. It has often happened, for example, that the pattern of behavior in a neighborhood has gone unchanged but that police and court practices have changed, leading to a spurious conclusion that delinquency rates have changed.

Concluding Notes

Adult crime and juvenile delinquency are senstive forms of deviant behavior. Crime and delinquency rates may not be increasing at some alarming rate, but they have not been reduced, either, during this century. Their treatment in this chapter has been complicated.

This chapter has indicated that American social controls over crime and delinquency are subject to deep, disabling internal disorganization. Laws are not effectively or impartially enforced. They change more rapidly than the informal standards that give rise to the law, without in turn modifying some of the standards themselves.

Arrestees and suspects are perceived as criminals, yet the bulwark of the law is specific in prohibiting such interpretation. Many citizens violate the law, but few are detected, and far fewer are effectively prosecuted. Others are arrested and arraigned but never tried. The bases for deciding penalties are highly variable. The penalties employed do not deter crime, protect the community, or correct the offender. If they do, we have no sound evidence of such. Many aspects of social control (especially the stigmatizing process with juveniles) intensify the likelihood of recurrent criminality.

However, many falsehoods, prejudices, and misimpressions have been eliminated through psychological and social research and practice in criminology and penology. We have dispensed with talk about demons. We have outgrown simple notions about physical stigmata as evidence of criminality.

The adult offenders and delinquents we have considered, however abstractly, have not been discussed as mentally defective, retarded, psychopathic, psychotic, or psychoneurotic (though we are sure there are as many emotional disturbances among criminals as among lawabiders). We have rejected single-factor theories such as poverty, the broken home, or miserable family relations.

This list inventories the favorite hunches of students of crime and delinquency as they have reported upon them in this country and Europe for more than 200 years. If we have something new, it is an intellectual basis for rejecting simple physical, mental, moral, and economic or social hypotheses which separate criminals and delinquents from human beings. There is nothing radically new. Each modern interpretation and analysis, however rigorous, partakes of older notions. But the social scientific study of deviant behavior, particularly of crime and delinquency, has developed to where we can list what we are sure is false. This is the beginning of a science.

We have also avoided interpreting crime as a clear, simple, or objective index of American social disorganization. We pointed, in discussing delinquency, to ways in which youthful offenders, and the public response made to them, impinge upon the social order. But we refused to maintain that the volume or character of crime in a society is a clear measure of its integration, maintenance, or survival prospects. Of course, social disorganization and criminal deviance interact profoundly, yet they are more than just analytically distinct. Each constitutes a partially independent pattern of social relations and personal conduct.

The United States contains an organized public that battles against, punishes, and nurtures, with fascinated care, the flourishing subsocieties of crime and delinquency. That it does this, however, does not give evidence that the criminal pattern is antithetical to a durable national existence.

We have offered a glimpse of evolving, improving systems of probation, parole, and delinquency prevention efforts. To these we should add a growing technology of law enforcement, and the increasing uniformity of criminal codes and court procedures among the states. An improved sytem of social controls is in the making.

References

Abrahamsen, David, *Crime and the human mind.* N.Y.: Columbia University Press, 1944.

Aichhorn, August, *Wayward youth.* N.Y.: Viking, 1935.

Alexander, Franz, and Hugh Staub, *The criminal, the judge, and the public,* rev. ed. Glencoe: The Free Press, 1956.

American Academy of Polical and Social Sciences. *Combating organized crime.* Philadelphia, Pa.: 1963.

Andry, R. G., *The short-term prisoner.* South Hackensack, New Jersey: Rothman, 1963.

Ausubel, David P., *Drug addiction: physiological, psychological, and sociological aspects.* N.Y.: Random House, 1958.

Barnes, Harry E., and Negley K. Teeters, *New horizons in criminology,* 3d. ed. N.Y.: Prentice-Hall, 1959.

Barron, Milton L., *The juvenile in delinquent society.* N.Y.: Knopf, 1956.

Bensing, Robert C., and Oliver Schroeder, Jr., *Homicide in an urban community.* Springfield: C. C. Thomas, 1960.

Bergler, Edmund, *The psychology of gambling.* N.Y.: Hill & Wang, 1957.

Bergler, E. and A. M. Meerlov, *Justice and injustice.* New York: Grune, 1963.

Bok, Curtis, *Star wormwood.* N.Y.: Knopf, 1949.

Bordua, David J., *Sociological theories and their implications for juvenile delinquency.* Washington: Dept. of Health, Education & Welfare, 1960.

Burchill, G. W. *Work-study programs*

for alienated youth. Chicago: Science Research Ass., Inc., 1962.

Clemmer, Donald, *The prison community.* N.Y.: Rinehart, 1958.

Clinard, M. B., *Sociology of deviant behavior.* rev. ed. New York: Holt, 1963.

Cloward, Richard A., and Lloyd E. Ohlin, *Delinquency and opportunity: a theory of delinquent gangs.* Glencoe: The Free Press, 1960.

Cohen, Albert K., *Delinquent boys: the culture of the gang.* Glencoe: The Free Press, 1955.

Cressey, Donald R., *Other people's money: a study in the social psychology of embezzlement.* Glencoe: The Free Press, 1953.

Day, Frank D. *Criminal law and society.* Springfield, Illinois: Charles C. Thomas, 1964.

Dressler, David, *Practice and theory of probation and parole.* N.Y.: Columbia University Press, 1959.

Greenwald, Harold, *The call girl.* N.Y.: Ballantine, 1958.

Grosser, George, ed., *Theoretical studies in the social organization of the prison.* N.Y.: Social Science Research Council, 1960.

Gibney, Frank, *The operators.* N.Y.: Harper, 1960.

Hakeem, Michael, "A critique of the psychiatric approach to crime and correction." *Law & Contemporary Problems,* 33 (Autumn 1958), 650-682.

Henry, Andrew F., and James F. Short, Jr., *Suicide and homicide.* Glencoe: The Free Press, 1954.

Ives, George, *A history of penal methods.* London: Paul, 1914.

Jaspan, Norman, and Hillel Black, *The thief in the white collar.* Philadelphia: Lippincott, 1960.

Kefauver, Estes, *Crime in America.* N.Y.: Doubleday, 1951.

Kennedy, J. P. and D. G. Pursuit. *Police work with juveniles.* Springfield, Ill.: Thomas, C. C., 1962.

Laurence, John, *A history of capital punishment.* N.Y.: Citadel, 1960.

Lindesmith, Alfred R., *Opiate addiction.* Bloomington: Principia, 1952.

Lowenthal, Max, *The federal bureau of investigation.* N.Y.: Sloane, 1950.

McCord, William, and Joan McCord, *Origins of crime: a new evaluation of the Cambridge-Somerville youth study.* N.Y.: Columbia University Press, 1959.

Merton, Robert K., *Social theory and social structure,* rev. ed. Glencoe: The Free Press, 1957.

National Conference of Superintendents of Training Schools and Reformatories. *Institutional rehabilitation of delinquent youth.* Albany, New York: Delmar, 1962.

Porterfield, Austin L., *Youth in trouble.* Austin: Potishman Foundation, 1946.

Powers, Edwin, and Helen Witmer, *An experiment in the prevention of delinquency.* N.Y.: Columbia University Press, 1951.

Pritchard, J. L. *A history of capital punishment.* New York: Citadel, 1963.

Rice, Robert, *The business of crime.* N.Y.: Farrar, 1956.

Rosenheim, M. K., ed., *Justice for the child.* New York: Free Press, 1962.

Rovere, Richard H., "The invasion of privacy: technology and the claims of community," *Amer. Scholar,* 27 (August 1958), 413-421.

Scarpitti, Frank R., Ellen Murray, Simon Dinitz, and Walter C. Reckless, "The good boy in a high delinquency area: four years later," *Amer. Soc. Rev.,* 25 (August 1960), 555-558.

Schuessler, Karl F., "The deterrent influence of the death penalty," *The Annals,* 284 (November 1952), 54-62.

Shaw, Clifford, *Natural history of a*

delinquent career. Chicago: University of Chicago Press, 1931.

Southwestern Law Enforcement Institute. *Law enforcement and the juvenile offender.* Springfield, Ill.: Thomas, C. C., 1963.

Sutherland, Edwin H., *White collar crime*. N.Y.: Holt, 1961.

Sykes, Gresham, *Crime and society*. N.Y.: Random House, 1956.

Sykes, Gresham. *The society of captives*. Princeton: Princeton University Press, 1958.

Tannenbaum, Frank, *Crime and the community*. Boston: Ginn, 1938.

Tappan, Paul W., *Crime, justice and correction*. N.Y.: McGraw-Hill, 1960.

Teeters, Negley K., *The cradle of the penitentiary*. Philadelphia: Pennsylvania Prison Society, 1955.

Thrasher, Frederick M., *The gang*. Chicago: University of Chicago Press, 1927.

Trese, L. J. *101 delinquent girls*. Notre Dame, Indiana: Fides (U.S.), 1962.

Turkus, Burton B. and Sid Feder, *Murder, Inc.* N.Y.: Farrer, 1951.

Vedder, C. B. *Juvenile offenders*. Springfield, Ill.: Thomas, C. C. 1963.

Weeks, H. Ashley, *Youthful offenders at Highfields*. Ann Arbor: University of Michigan Press, 1958.

Whitehead, Don *The FBI story*. N.Y.: Random House, 1956.

Whyte, William F., *Street corner society*. Chicago: University of Chicago Press, 1955.

Wolff, Kurt, ed., *The sociology of Georg Simmel*. Glencoe: The Free Press, 1950.

CRIME AND THE COMMUNITY: POINT OF VIEW
Frank Tannenbaum

1. The Search for a Scapegoat

Criminology has been the happy hunting ground for all kinds of theories. The dramatic quality of criminal behavior has challenged attention and called forth explanation. Its very deviations from the accepted and approved have required elucidation and judgment. The community has ever had to do something about the criminal, and theory served as a justification of social policy as well as an interpretation of its genesis.

From age to age the conduct of society toward the criminal has differed in accordance with the underlying assumption of the prevailing theory. The outstanding characteristic of all criminological discussion has been the assumption that there was a qualitative difference between the nature of the criminal and that of the noncriminal. This probably was inevitable; to find the unsocial and the social identical in nature was to strain all the evidence. All things done despite being forbidden and condemned were done by the unsocial or criminal.

Crime and the Community. Ginn and Company, 1938, New York, Chapter 19; footnotes have been renumbered. Reprinted through courtesy of Blaisdell Publishing Co., a division of Ginn and Company, and of the author.

They were addicted to the vice which the virtuous shunned. The criminal or unsocial committed theft, robbery, arson, murder; they showed regard for neither God nor man. The conduct of these deviates illustrated the perversity of their beings.

This contrast was sharpened by the prepossession of social theorists with the overshadowing conflict between absolute good and absolute evil. This battle, personified by God on one side and the Devil on the other, made the distinction clear and judgment easy. Regardless of the changes that criminological theory has undergone, this underlying contrast has persisted under one or another cover, under one or another disguise. The terminology has changed, but the original idea has persisted. "Good" may have become translated into "normal," and "evil" may have come to be described as "abnormal" in one of its many current variants, but, after all, the change in fundamental attitude is not great. The contrast in absolutes still pervades the air of criminological discussion.

During the Middle Ages the notion that evil action was proof of possession by the Evil One seemed both obvious and consistent with the entire accepted view of the world and its ways, and was descriptive of the motives of human conduct. This belief has long persisted, and even today it has not entirely disappeared from the common judgment of ordinary folk when they condemn the evil-doer. In fact the idea of possession found its way into the North Carolina State Constitution as late as 1862. "To know the right but still the wrong to pursue proceeds from a perverse will brought about by the seductions of the evil one." The "Rationalism" of the seventeenth and eighteenth centuries, their belief in reason, their notions of equality, their rejection of theological theories of causation as a means of explaining human conduct, led them to describe evil-doing in terms of choice rather in terms of "possession" or "seduction" by the evil one. All men were assumed to be both reasonable and wise about their own interests, and if one chose to do evil it was because of the pleasure it would bring him. Evil-doing became evil choice for the sake of the pleasure it provided. Like the earlier doctrine, the explanation was consistent with a current view of the universe.

This theory from the period of the French Revolution, generally identified for criminology with the name of the Italian criminologist, Beccaria, has had a profound influence upon both law and practice in dealing with the criminal.

> Our substantive criminal law is based upon a theory of punishing the vicious will. It postulates a free moral agent, confronted with a choice between doing right and doing wrong, and choosing freely to do wrong.[1]

As it affected children and the insane

this view broke down, but its influence upon our legal system has been very great indeed.

The development of modern science, the growing practice of measurement, the science of statistics, the development of the theory of evolution, and especially the growth of the sciences of anthropology and psychology have sharply influenced criminological discussion.

The controversies which these new additions to social theory have aroused have dealt, in criminology, mainly with *how* the good were to be distinguished from the evil. "Possession" and "seduction" had given way to the "rational" choice to do evil. This in turn was to give way to a series of other explanations. The Positive School of Criminology, so called as distinguished from the Classical (which is the name given to the theories that arose out of the French Revolution), found the evidence of the distinction between the good and the evil in the physical characteristics of the criminal. Lombroso, who is the recognized father of the Positive School of Criminology, has had a wide and persistent influence upon attitudes toward the criminal. His view has been described as "the proposition that a man's mode of feeling and the actual conduct of his life are in turn determined by and find expression in his physical constitution,"[2] and that these constitutions were so variable that the "assassins, ravishers, incendiaries, and thieves could be distinguished according to physical characteristics not only from the general population, but also from each other."[3] The various constitu-

[1]Roscoe Pound, *Criminal Justice in America,* pp. 33-34. New York, 1930; footnotes have been renumbered.

[2]Hans Kurella, *Cesare Lombroso, A Modern Man of Science,* p. 18. London, 1911.
[3]Morris Ploscowe, "Some Causative Factors in Criminality," National Commission on Law Observance and Enforcement, No. 13, *Report on*

tions were in a measure anthropological throwbacks:

> Such a man as this is a reversion to an old type savage, and was born by accident in the wrong century. He would have had a sufficient scope for his bloodthirsty propensities and been in harmony with his environment in a barbaric age or at the present day in certain parts of Africa.[4]

These throwbacks were differentiated by projecting ears, thin beard, insensitiveness to pain, projecting frontal eminences, large jaws, square and protruding chin, and a number of other items. For our purpose here it is sufficient to point out that the proof of criminality now became a matter of external evidence. It seems incredible, although it is true, that in 1890 Havelock Ellis said in his book on the criminal, "The greater number of tattooed criminals are naturally found among recidivists and instinctive criminals, especially those who have committed crimes against the person,"[5] as if being tattooed were one of the evidences of criminality in addition to purely physical deformities. The fact that this adduced knowledge about the criminal is merely a proof of a somewhat naive anthropology and physiology as well as an uninformed description of primitive people is beside the point. The fact that it had wide acceptance and the remnants of it are still to be seen in circles seriously dedicated to the study of the criminal is important.

The development of psychology on one hand, and the annihilating attack upon the naïve "morphological" theories of the Lombrosian school by Goring on the other hand, shifted the ground once more from external to internal evidence of criminality. In the meantime the general sophistication had reduced "the devil" and "possession" to a series of concepts that served the old purpose under a new name or names. The new way of identifying criminality was now more fully aided by a statistical technique almost as naïve as the older morphological and anthropological technique had been. Instead of measuring heads, ears, nose and arm length, it now became the rule to measure intelligence. Apart from the fact that a definition of "intelligence" was no more easily formulated than one of "possession," the game of classifying criminals according to psychological terminology went merrily on for a number of years. It has since been shown that, whatever "intelligence" is, it has no demonstrated relationship to crime, and it has also been shown that the "intelligence" testers seem to test their particular techniques against each other rather than the thing they are testing. But the fact remains that the proof adduced was used to "identify the criminal" in terms as naïve and full of faith as those of the older evidence, as, for example, when Dr. Henry H. Goddard said, "It is no longer to be denied that the greatest single cause of delinquency and crime is low-grade mentality, much of it within the limits of feeblemindedness."[6] Criticisms of this view since about 1915 have reduced its pretensions, but have not entirely eliminated its hold upon either theorists or practitioners in their dealing with the criminal.

the Causes of Crime, Vol. I, p. 21. Washington, D.C., 1931.

[4]Philip Archibald Parsons, Crime and the Criminal, p. 41 (quoting Hack Tuke, Case of Congenital Moral Defect). New York, 1926.

[5]Havelock Ellis, The Criminal, p. 194. London, Fifth edition, 1910.

[6]Henry H. Goddard, Human Efficiency and Levels of Intelligence, p. 73. Princeton, 1920.

Under the influence of recent psychological thought a new body of theories was developed to describe not the mental but the emotional deficiency of the criminal. A new series of tests and devices were brought into play to show that the criminal was not normal. The difference between the older concepts of "good" and "evil" has now become one between "normal" and "abnormal," and the insistence that the criminal must exhibit the evidence of his shortcomings has been shifted from intellectual to psychiatric phenomena.

We are not concerned here with a review of criminological theory. It is sufficient to say here that the theories advanced by the endocrinologists who have asserted that criminals "are either of subnormal mentality or of faulty mental or nervous constitution,"[7] or of the eugenists who claim that eugenics "supplies the most effective and permanent solution to the problems ... of combating disease, disability, defectiveness, degeneracy, delinquency, vice and crime,"[8] have no greater validity than the theories they attempt to supersede.

The criminological theorist has tended to set off the criminal from the rest of the population in terms that would make the difference qualitative.[9] These attitudes have something of absolutism, and their imputation to the man of the physical or psychological deficiency that shows how he is distinguished from his fellows has something of the definiteness and inevitableness of the theories of damnation and predestination. The impact of the idea of "law" in the physical sciences has in this branch of the social sciences led to a crude assumption of definiteness, separateness, difference, in terms so absolute as to be final. The imputation of physical or psychic abnormality has this crude "scientific" basis, that it derives from measurement, testing, calculation. It permits the use of statistical tables and mathematical formulae. The fact that the qualities measured are intangible, that the traits examined may be irrelevant, has not prevented the process from finding wide acceptance and considerable acclaim, and in some instances even legislative sanction.

The issue here, however, is not the adequacy of the method but rather the fact that all through criminological theory has run the notion of good and bad in the older days and "normal" and "abnormal" in the current period. In each period the criminal has been set off from his fellows. This was indicated by Professor Root when he said:

> None is so repentant a sinner as to share the blame with the criminal. If we can localize the blame in the individual we can exact vengeance with precision and satisfaction. The more we can make it appear that all the causes for delinquency have their origin within the individual victim the more we may feel self-elation, the less danger there is of negative self-feeling. Writers of melodramas know this full well. The villain, in order to make us get the full satisfaction out of our positive self-feeling, must be bad with everyone else on the stage oozing goodness from every pore. He must be bad in spite of us; it is highly disconcerting to have him one of us.[10]

[7]Max G. Schlapp and Edward H. Smith, *The New Criminology*, p. 119. New York, 1928.

[8]Report of the President of the American Eugenics Society, June 26, 1926, P. 18.

[9]The environmentalist school does not fall within this classification.

[10]William T. Root, Jr., A *Psychological and Educational Survey of 1916 Prisoners in the Western Penitentiary of Pennsylvania*, p. 10. 1927.

The underlying causes may be deeper than that: they may lie in the inability to accept deviation from the "normal." The projection of the idea of normal or good is merely the passing of a moral judgment upon our own habits and way of life. The deviate who is a communist, a pacifist, a crank, a criminal, challenges our scheme of habits, institutions, and values. And unless we exclude him and set him apart from the group, the whole structure of our orderly life goes to pieces. It is not that we do not wish to be identified with him: we cannot be identified with him and keep our own world from being shattered about us. The question of values is fundamental. Just because we appreciate the habits, ways, and institutions by which we live, we seem driven to defame and annihilate those activities and individuals whose behavior challenges and repudiates all we live by. Under these circumstances the theories of the criminologists are understandable. They have imputed an evil nature to the evil-doer, whatever the terms upon which that nature was postulated — possession by the devil, deliberate evil-doing, physical stigmata, intellectual inferiority, emotional instability, poor inheritance, glandular unbalance. In each case we had a good explanation for the "unsocial" behavior of the individual, and it left unchallenged our institutional set-up, both theoretic and practical.

2. The Meaning of Behavior

In each case these theories rest upon the individual criminal, almost as if he were living in a vacuum and his nature were full-blown from the beginning. Even the mildest of the current theories assumes that the criminal is an unsocial creature because he cannot "adjust" to society. Parsons represents this point of view when he says that the findings "seem to indicate that the bulk of crime is committed by persons who are unable to adjust themselves to society with a sufficient degree of success to meet the requirements of the law."[11] The facts seem to point to just the opposite conclusion. The criminal is a social human being, he is adjusted, he is not necessarily any of the things that have been imputed to him. Instead of being unadjusted he may be quite adjusted to his group, and instead of being "unsocial" he may show all of the characteristics we identify as social in members of other groups. The New York Crime Commission says, "He is adjusted to his own social group and violently objects to any social therapy that would make him maladjusted to it."[12]

Crime is a maladjustment that arises out of the conflict between a group and the community at large. The issue involved is not whether an individual is maladjusted to society, but the fact that his adjustment to a special group makes him maladjusted to the large society because the group he fits into is at war with society.

The difficulty with the older theory is that it assumed that crime was largely an individual matter and could be dealt with when the individual was dealt with. Instead, most delinquencies are committed in groups; most criminals live in, operate with, and are supported by groups. We must face the question of how that group grew up into a conflict group and of how the individual became adjusted to that group rather than to

[11]Parsons, op. cit., p. 46.
[12]State of New York. Report of the Crime Commission, 1930. Legislative Document (1930) No. 98, p. 243.

some other group in society. The study of the individual in terms of his special physical or psychical idiosyncrasies would have as much bearing on the question why he became a member of a criminal group as it would on the question why he joined the Ku Klux Klan, was a member of a lynching bee, joined the I.W.W., became a member of the Communist or Socialist party, joined the Seventh Day Adventists or the Catholic Church, took to vegetarianism, or became a loyal Republican. The point is that a person's peculiar physical or psychic characteristcs may have little bearing on the group with which he is in adjustment.

The question is not how a criminal is distinguished in his nature from a non-criminal, but how he happened to be drawn into a criminal group and why that criminal group developed that peculiar position of conflict with the rest of society. The important facts, therefore, are to be sought in his behavior history.

Criminal behavior originates as part of the random movement of children in a world of adults, a world with attitudes and organized institutions that stamp and define the activities of little children. The career of the criminal is a selective process of growth within that environment, and the adult criminal is the product and summation of a series of continued activities and experience. The adult criminal is usually the delinquent child grown up.

The delinquent child is all too frequently "the truant of yesterday."[13] The truant is the school child who found extra-curricular activities more appealing and less burdensome than curricular ones. The step from the child who is a behavior problem in school to the truant is a natural one; so, too, is the step from truancy to delinquency, and that from delinquency to crime. In the growth of his career is to be found the important agency of the gang. But "the majority of gangs develop from the spontaneous play-group."[14]

[13]State of New York. Report of the Crime Commision, 1930. Legislative Document (1927) No. 94, p. 285.
[14]Frederic M. Thrasher, *The Gang*, p. 29. Chicago, 1927.

CRIME AS AN AMERICAN WAY OF LIFE
Daniel Bell

In the 1890's, The Reverend Dr. Charles Parkhurst, shocked at the open police protection afforded New York's bordellos, demanded a state inquiry. In the Lexow investigation that followed, the young and dashing William Travers Jerome staged a set of public hearings that created sensation after sensation. He badgered "Clubber" Williams, First Inspector of the Police Department, to account for wealth and property far greater than could have been saved on his salary; it was earned, the Clubber explained laconically, through land speculation "in Japan." Heavy-set Captain Schmittberger, the "collector" for the "Tenderloin precincts" — Broadway's fabulous concentration of hotels, theaters, restaurants, gaming houses, and saloons — related in detail how protection money was distributed among the police force. Crooks, policemen, public officials, businessmen, all paraded across the stage, each adding his chapter to a sordid story of corruption and crime. The upshot of these revelations was reform — the election of William L. Strong, a stalwart business-

man, as mayor, and the naming of Theodore Roosevelt as police commissioner.

It did not last, of course, just as previous reform victories had not lasted. Yet the ritual drama was re-enacted. Twenty years ago the Seabury investigation in New York uncovered the tin-box brigade and the thirty-three little MacQuades. Jimmy Walker was ousted as mayor and in came Fiorello La Guardia. Tom Dewey became district attorney, broke the industrial rackets, sent Lucky Luciano to jail and went to the Governor's chair in Albany. Then reform was again swallowed up in the insatiable maw of corruption until Kefauver and the young and dashing Rudolph Halley threw a new beam of light into the seemingly bottomless pit.

How explain this repetitious cycle? Obviously the simple moralistic distinction between "good guys" and "bad guys," so deep at the root of the reform impulse, bears little relation to the role of organized crime in American society. What, then, does?

II

Americans have had an extraordinary talent for compromise in politics

Reprinted, by permission of the author and The Antioch Press, from "Crime as an American Way of Life," The Antioch Review (June, 1953), 13:131-154, copyright 1953 by The Antioch Press.

and extremism in morality. The most shameless political deals (and "steals") have been rationalized as expedient and realistically necessary. Yet in no other country have there been such spectacular attempts to curb human appetites and brand them as illicit, and nowhere else such glaring failures. From the start America was at one and the same time a frontier community where "everything goes," and the fair country of the Blue Laws. At the turn of the century the cleavage developed between the Big City and the small-town conscience. Crime as a growing business was fed by the revenues from prostitution, liquor and gambling that a wide-open urban society encouraged and which a middle-class Protestant ethos tried to suppress with a ferocity unmatched in any other civilized country. Catholic cultures rarely have imposed such restrictions, and have rarely suffered such excesses. Even in prim and proper Anglican England, prostitution is a commonplace of Piccadilly night life, and gambling one of the largest and most popular industries. In America the enforcement of public morals has been a continuing feature of our history.

Some truth may lie in Svend Ranulf's generalization that moral indignation is a peculiar fact of middle-class psychology and represents a disguised form of repressed envy. The larger truth lies perhaps in the brawling nature of American development and the social character of Crime. Crime, in many ways, is a Coney Island mirror, caricaturing the morals and manners of a society. The jungle quality of the American business community, particularly at the turn of the century, was reflected in the mode of "business" practiced by the coarse gangster elements, most of them from new immigrant families, who were "getting ahead," just as Horatio Alger

had urged. In the older, Protestant tradition the intense acquisitiveness, such as that of Daniel Drew, was rationalized by a compulsive moral fervor. But the formal obeisance of the ruthless business in the workaday world to the church-going pieties of the Sabbath was one that the gangster could not make. Moreover, for the young criminal, hunting in the asphalt jungle of the crowded city, it was not the businessman with his wily manipulation of numbers but the "man with the gun" who was the American hero. "No amount of commercial prosperity," once wrote Teddy Roosevelt, "can supply the lack of the heroic virtues." The American was "the hunter, cowboy, frontiersman, the soldier, the naval hero." And in the crowded slums, the gangster. He was a man with a gun, acquiring by personal merit what was denied to him by complex orderings of a stratified society. And the duel with the law was the morality play *par excellence*: the gangster, with whom rides our own illicit desires, and the prosecutor, representing final judgment and the force of the law.

Yet all this was acted out in a wider context. The desires satisfied in extra-legal fashion were more than a hunger for the "forbidden fruits" of conventional morality. They also involved, in the complex and ever shifting structure of group, class and ethnic stratification, which is the warp and woof of America's "open" society, such "normal" goals as independence through a business of one's own, and such "moral" aspirations as the desire for social advancement and social prestige. For crime, in the language of the sociologists, has a "functional" role in the society, and the urban racket—the illicit activity organized for a continuing profit rather than individual illegal acts—is one of the queer ladders of social mobility in American life. Indeed, it is not too much to say that the whole question of organized crime in America cannot be understood unless one appreciates (1) the distinctive role of organized gambling as a function of a mass consumption economy; (2) the specific role of various immigrant groups as they one after another became involved in marginal business and crime; and (3) the relation of crime to the changing character of the urban political machines.

III

As a society changes, so does, in lagging fashion, its type of crime. As American society became more "organized," as the American businessman became more "civilized" and less "buccaneering," so did the American racketeer. And just as there were important changes in the structure of business enterprise, so the "institutionalized" criminal enterprise was transformed too.

In the America of the last fifty years the main drift of society has been toward the rationalization of industry, the domestication of the crude self-made captain of industry into the respectable man of manners, and the emergence of a mass-consumption economy. The most significant transformation in the field of "institutionalized" crime was the increasing relative importance of gambling as against other kinds of illegal activity. And, as a multi-billion-dollar business, gambling underwent a transition parallel to the changes in American enterprise as a whole. This parallel was exemplified in many ways: in gambling's industrial organization (e.g., the growth of a complex technology such as the national racing wire service and the minimization of risks by such tech-

niques as lay-off betting); in its respectability, as was evidenced in the opening of smart and popular gambling casinos in resort towns and in "satellite" adjuncts to metropolitan areas; in its functional role in a mass-consumption economy (for sheer volume of money changing hands, nothing has ever surpassed this feverish activity of fifty million American adults); in the social acceptance of the gamblers in the important status world of sport and entertainment, i.e., "café society."

In seeking to "legitimize" itself, gambling had quite often actually become a force against older and more vicious forms of illegal activity. In 1946, for example, when a Chicago mobster, Pat Manno, went down to Dallas, Texas, to take over gambling in the area for the Accardo-Guzik combine, he reassured the sheriff as to his intent as follows: "Something I'm against, that's dope peddlers, pickpockets, hired killers. That's one thing I can't stomach, and that's one thing the fellows up there — the group won't stand for, things like that. They discourage it, they even go to headquarters and ask them why they don't do something about it."

Jimmy Cannon once reported that when the gambling raids started in Chicago, the "combine" protested that, in upsetting existing stable relations, the police were only opening the way for ambitious young punks and hoodlums to start trouble. Nor is there today, as there was twenty or even forty years ago, prostitution of major organized scope in the United States. Aside from the fact that manners and morals have changed, prostitution *as an industry* doesn't pay as well as gambling. Besides, its existence threatened the tacit moral acceptance and quasi-respectability that gamblers and gambling have secured in the American way of life. It was, as any operator in the field might tell you, "bad for business."

The criminal world of the last decade, its tone set by the captains of the gambling industry, is in startling contrast to the state of affairs. in the two decades before. If a Kefauver report had been written then, the main "names" would have been Lepke and Gurrah, Dutch Schultz, Jack "Legs" Diamond, Lucky Luciano, and, reaching back a little further, Arnold Rothstein, the czar of the underworld. These men (with the exception of Luciano, who was involved in narcotics and prostitution) were in the main industrial racketeers. Rothstein, it is true, had a larger function: he was, as Frank Costello became later, the financier of the underworld—the pioneer big businessman of crime, who, understanding the logic of coordination, sought to *organize* crime as a source of regular income. His main interest in this direction was in industrial racketeering, and his entry was through labor disputes. At one time, employers in the garment trades hired Legs Diamond and his sluggers to break strikes, and the Communists, then in control of the cloakmakers union, hired one Little Orgie to protect the pickets and beat up the scabs; only later did both sides learn that Legs Diamond and Little Orgie were working for the same man, Rothstein.

Rothstein's chief successors, Lepke Buchalter and Gurrah Shapiro, were able, in the early '30's, to dominate sections of the men's and women's clothing industries, of painting, fur dressing, flour trucking, and other fields. In a highly chaotic and cut-throat industry such as clothing, the racketeer, paradoxically, played a stabilizing role by regulating competition and fixing prices. When the NRA came in and assumed this function, the businessman

found that what had once been a quasi-economic service was now pure extortion, and he began to demand police action. In other types of racketeering, such as the trucking of perishable foods and water-front loading, where the racketeers entrenched themselves as middlemen—taking up, by default, a service that neither shippers nor truckers wanted to assume—a pattern of accommodation was roughly worked out and the rackets assumed a quasi-legal veneer. On the water-front, old-time **racketeers perform the necessary func**tion of loading—but at an exorbitant price, and this monopoly was recognized by both the union and the shippers, and tacitly by government. (See my case study "The Last of the Business Rackets," in the June, 1951 issue of *Fortune.*)

But in the last decade and a half, industrial racketeering has not offered much in the way of opportunity. *Like American capitalism itself, crime shifted its emphasis from production to consumption.* The focus of crime became the direct exploitation of the citizen as consumer, largely through gambling. And while the protection of these huge revenues was inextricably linked to politics, the relation between gambling and "the mobs" became more complicated.

IV

Although it never showed up in the gross national product, gambling in the last decade was one of the largest industries in the United States. The Kefauver Committee estimated it as a twenty-billion-dollar business. This figure has been picked up and widely quoted, but in truth no one knows what the gambling "turnover" and "take" actually is, nor how much is bet legally (pari-mutuel, etc.) and how much illegally. In fact, the figure cited by the committee was arbitrary and arrived at quite sloppily. As one staff member said: "We had no real idea of the money spent. . . . The California crime commission said twelve billion. Virgil Peterson of Chicago estimated thirty billion. We picked twenty billion as a balance between the two."

If comprehensive data are not available, we do know, from specific instances, the magnitude of many of the operations. Some indications can be seen from these items culled at random:

— James Carroll and M & G syndicate did a 20-million-dollar annual business in St. Louis. This was one of the two large books in the city.

— The S & G syndicate in Miami did a 26-million-dollar volume yearly; the total for all books in the Florida resort reached 40 millions.

— Slot machines were present in 69,786 establishments in 1951 (each paid $100 for a license to the Bureau of Internal Revenue); the usual average is three machines to a license, which would add up to 210,000 slot machines in operation in the United States. In legalized areas, where the betting is higher and more regular, the average gross "take" per machine is $50 a week.

— The largest policy wheel (i.e., "numbers") in Chicago's "Black Belt" reported taxable net profits for the four-year period from 1946 through 1949, after sizable deductions for "overhead," of $3,656,968. One of the large "white" wheels reported in 1947 a gross income of $2,317,000 and a net profit of $205,000. One CIO official estimated that perhaps 15 per cent of his union's lower echelon officials are involved in the numbers racket (a steward, free to

roam a plant, is in a perfect situation for organizing bets).

If one considers the amount of betting on sports alone — an estimated six billion on baseball, a billion on football pools, another billion on basketball, six billion on horse racing — then Elmo Roper's judgment that "only the food, steel, auto, chemical, and machine-tool industries have a greater volume of business" does not seem too far-fetched.

While gambling has long flourished in the United States, the influx of the big mobsters into the industry — and its expansion — started in the '30's when repeal of Prohibition forced them to look about for new avenues of enterprise. Gambling, which had begun to flower under the nourishment of rising incomes, was the most lucrative field in sight. To a large extent the shift from bootlegging to gambling was a mere transfer of business operations. In the East, Frank Costello went into slot machines and the operation of a number of ritzy gambling casinos. He also became the "banker" for the Erickson "book," which "laid off" bets for other bookies. Joe Adonis, similarly, opened up a number of casinos, principally in New Jersey. Across the country, many other mobsters went into bookmaking. As other rackets diminished, and gambling, particularly horse-race betting, flourished in the '40's, a struggle erupted over the control of racing information.

Horse-race betting requires a peculiar industrial organization. The essential component is time. A bookie can operate only if he can get information on odds up to the very last minute before the race, so that he can "hedge" or "lay off" bets. With racing going on simultaneously on many tracks throughout the country, this information has to be obtained speedily and accurately. Thus, the racing wire is the nerve ganglion of race betting.

The racing-wire news service got started in the '20's through the genius of the late Moe Annenberg, who had made a fearful reputation for himself as Hearst's circulation manager in the rough-and-tumble Chicago newspaper wars. Annenberg conceived the idea of a telegraphic news service which would gather information from tracks and shoot it immediately to scratch sheets, horse parlors, and bookie joints. In some instances, track owners gave Annenberg the rights to send news from tracks; more often, the news was simply "stolen" by crews operating inside or near the tracks. So efficient did this news distribution system become, that in 1942, when a plane knocked out a vital telegraph circuit which served an Air Force field as well as the gamblers, the Continental Press managed to get its racing wire service for gamblers resumed in fifteen minutes, while it took the Fourth Army, which was responsible for the defense of the entire West Coast, something like three hours.

Annenberg built up a nationwide racing information chain that not only distributed wire news but controlled sub-outlets as well. In 1939, harassed by the Internal Revenue Bureau on income tax, and chivvied by the Justice Department for "monopolistic" control of the wire service, the tired and aging Annenberg simple walked out of the business. He did not sell his interest, or even seek to salvage some profit; he simply gave up. Yet, like any established and thriving institution, the enterprise continued, though on a decentralized basis. James Ragen, Annenberg's operations manager, and likewise a veteran of the old Chicago circulation wars, took over the national wire service through a

dummy friend and renamed it the Continental Press Service.

The salient fact is that in the operation of the Annenberg and Ragen wire service, formally illegal as many of its subsidiary operations may have been (i.e., in "stealing" news, supplying information to bookies, etc.) gangsters played no part. It was a business, illicit, true, but primarily a business. The distinction between gamblers and gangsters, as we shall see, is a relevant one.

In 1946, the Chicago mob, whose main interest was in bookmaking rather than gambling casinos, began to move in on the wire monopoly. Following repeal, the Capone lieutenants had turned, like Lepke, to labor racketeering. Murray ("The Camel") Humphries muscled in on the teamsters, the operating engineers, and the cleaning-and-dyeing, laundry, and linen-supply industries. Through a small-time punk, Willie Bioff, and union official George Browne, Capone's chief successors, Frank ("The Enforcer") Nitti and Paul Ricca, came into control of the motion-picture union and proceeded to shake down the movie industry for fabulous sums in order to "avert strikes." In 1943, when the government moved in and smashed the industrial rackets, the remaining big shots, Charley Fischetti, Jake Guzik, and Tony Accardo decided to concentrate on gambling, and in particular began a drive to take over the racing wire.

In Chicago, the Guzik-Accardo gang, controlling a sub-distributor of the racing news service, began tapping Continental's wires. In Los Angeles, the head of the local distribution agency for Continental was beaten up by hoodlums working for Mickey Cohen and Joe Sica. Out of the blue appeared a new and competitive nationwide racing information and distribution service, known as

Trans-American Publishing, the money for which was advanced by the Chicago mobs and Bugsy Siegel, who, at the time, held a monopoly of the bookmaking and wire-news service in Las Vegas. Many books pulled out of Continental and bought information from the new outfit, many hedged by buying from both. At the end of a year, however, the Capone mob's wire had lost about $200,000. Ragen felt that violence would erupt and went to the Cook County district attorney and told him that his life had been threatened by his rivals. Ragen knew his competitors. In June 1946 he was killed by a blast from a shotgun.

Thereafter, the Capone mob abandoned Trans-American and got a "piece" of Continental. Through their new control of the national racing-wire monopoly, the Capone mob began to muscle in on the lucrative Miami gambling business run by the so-called S & G syndicate. For a long time S & G's monopoly over bookmaking had been so complete that when New York gambler Frank Erickson bought a three month's bookmaking concession at the expensive Roney Plaza Hotel, for $45,000, the local police, in a highly publicized raid, swooped down on the hotel; the next year the Roney Plaza was again using local talent. The Capone group, however, was tougher. They demanded an interest in Miami bookmaking, and, when refused, began organizing a syndicate of their own, persuading some bookies at the big hotels to join them. Florida Governor Warren's crime investigator appeared—a friend, it seemed, of old Chicago dog-track operator William Johnston, who had contributed $100,000 to the Governor's campaign fund—and began raiding bookie points, but only those that were affiliated with S & G. Then S & G, which had been buying its racing news from the local

distributor of Continental Press, found its service abruptly shut off. For a few days the syndicate sought to bootleg information from New Orleans, but found itself limping along. After ten days' war of attrition, the five S & G partners found themselves with a sixth partner, who, for a token "investment" of $20,000 entered a Miami business that grossed $26,000,000 in one year.

V

While Americans made gambling illegal, they did not in their hearts think of it as wicked—even the churches benefited from the bingo and lottery crazes. So they gambled—and gamblers flourished. Against this open canvas, the indignant tones of Senator Wiley and the shocked righteousness of Senator Tobey during the Kefauver investigation rang oddly. Yet it was probably this very tone of surprise that gave the activity of the Kefauver Committee its piquant quality. Here were some Senators who seemingly did not know the facts of life, as most Americans did. Here, in the person of Senator Tobey, was the old New England Puritan conscience poking around in industrial America, in a world it had made but never seen. Here was old-fashioned moral indignation, at a time when cynicism was rampant in public life.

Commendable as such moralistic fervor was, it did not make for intelligent discrimination of fact. Throughout the Kefauver hearings, for example, there ran the presumption that all gamblers, were invariably gangsters. This was true of Chicago's Accardo-Guzik combine, which in the past had its fingers in many kinds of rackets. It was not nearly so true of many of the large gamblers in America, most of whom had the feeling that they were satisfying a basic American urge for sport and looked upon their calling with no greater sense of guilt than did many bootleggers. After all, Sherman Billingsley did start out as a speak-easy proprietor, as did the Kreindlers of the "21" Club; and today the Stork Club and the former Jack and Charlie's are the most fashionable night and dining spots in America (one prominent patron of the Stork Club: J. Edgar Hoover).

The S & G syndicate in Miami, for example (led by Harold Salvey, Jules Levitt, Charles Friedman, Sam Cohen, and Edward [Eddie Luckey] Rosenbaum) was simply a master pool of some two hundred bookies that arranged for telephone service, handled "protection," acted as bankers for those who needed ready cash on hard-hit books, and, in short, functioned somewhat analogously to the large factoring corporations in the textile field or the credit companies in the auto industry. Yet to Kefauver, these S & G men were "slippery and arrogant characters. . . . Salvey, for instance, was an old-time bookie who told us he had done nothing except engage in bookmaking or finance other bookmakers for twenty years." When, as a result of committee publicity and the newly found purity of the Miami police, the S & G syndicate went out of business, it was, as the combine's lawyer told Kefauver, because the "boys" were weary of being painted "the worst monsters in the world." "It is true," Cohen acknowledged, "that they had been law violators." But they had never done anything worse than gambling, and "to fight the world isn't worth it."

Most intriguing of all were the opinions of James J. Carroll, the St. Louis "betting commissioner," who for years had been widely quoted on the sports pages of the country as setting odds on the Kentucky Derby winter book and the baseball pennant races. Senator Wiley, speaking like the prosecutor in Camus's novel, *The Stranger,* became the voice of official morality:

Senator Wiley: Have you any children?

Mr. Carroll: Yes, I have a boy.

Senator Wiley: How old is he?

Mr. Carroll: Thirty-three.

Senator Wiley: Does he gamble?

Mr. Carroll: No.

Senator Wiley: Would you like to see him grow up and become a gambler, either professional or amateur?

Mr. Carroll: No . . .

Senator Wiley: All right. Is your son interested in your business?

Mr. Carroll: No, he is a manufacturer.

Senator Wiley: Why do you not get him into the business?

Mr. Carroll: Well, psychologically a great many people are unsuited for gambling.

Retreating from this gambit, the Senator sought to pin Carroll down on his contributions to political campaigns:

Senator Wiley: Now this morning I asked you whether you contributed any money for political candidates or parties, and you said no more than $200 at any one time. I presume that does not indicate the total of your contributions in any one campaign, does it?

Mr. Carroll: Well, it might, might not, Senator. I have been an "againster" in many instances. I am a reader of *The Nation* for fifty years and they have advertisements calling for contributions for different candidates, different cause. . . . They carried an advertisement for George Norris; I contributed, I think, to that, and to the elder La Follette.

Carroll, who admitted to having

been in the betting business since 1899, was the sophisticated—but not immoral!—counterpoint to moralist Wiley. Here was man without the stigmata of the underworld or underground; he was worldy, cynical of official rhetoric, jaundiced about people's motives, he was—an "againster" who believed that "all gambling legislation originates or stems from some group or some individual seeking special interests for himself or his cause."

Asked why people gamble, Carroll distilled his experiences of fifty years with a remark that deserves a place in American social history: "I really don't know how to answer the question," he said. "I think gambling is a biological necessity for certain types. I think it is the quality that gives substance to their daydreams."

In a sense, the entire Kefauver materials, unintentionally, seem to document that remark. For what the Committee revealed time and time again was a picture of gambling as a basic institution in American life, flourishing openly and accepted widely. In many of the small towns, the gambling joint is as open as a liquor establishment. The town of Havana, in Mason County, Illinois, felt miffed when Governor Adlai Stevenson intervened against local gambling. In 1950, the town had raised $15,000 of its $50,000 budget by making friendly raids on the gambling houses every month and having the owners pay fines. "With the gambling fines cut off," grumbled Mayor Clarence Chester, "the next year is going to be tough."

Apart from the gamblers, there were the mobsters. But what Senator Kefauver and company failed to understand was that the mobsters, like the gamblers, and like the entire gangdom generally, were seeking to become quasi-respectable and establish a place for themselves in American life. For the mobsters, by and large, had immigrant roots, and crime, as the pattern showed, was a route of social ascent and place in American life.

VI

The mobsters were able, where they wished, to "muscle in" on the gambling business because the established gamblers were wholly vulnerable, not being able to call on the law for protection. The Senators, however, refusing to make any distinction between a gambler and a gangster, found it convenient to talk loosely of a nationwide conspiracy of "illegal" elements. Senator Kefauver asserted that a "nationwide crime syndicate does exist in the United States, despite the protestations of a strangely assorted company of criminals, self-serving politicians, plain blind fools, and others who may be honestly misguided, that there is no such combine." The Senate Committee report states the matter more dogmatically: "There is a nationwide crime syndicate known as the Mafia.... Its leaders are usually found in control of the most lucrative rackets in their cities. There are indications of a centralized direction and control of these rackets.... The Mafia is the cement that helps to bind the Costello-Adonis-Lansky syndicate of New York and the Accardo-Guzik-Fischetti syndicate of Chicago.... These groups have kept in touch with Luciano since his deportation from the country."

Unfortunately for a good story—and the existence of the Mafia would be a whale of a story—neither the Senate Crime Committee in its testimony, nor Kefauver in his book, presented any real evidence that the Mafia exists as a functioning organization. One finds police officials asserting before the Kefauver committee their *belief* in the Mafia; the Narcotics Bureau *thinks* that a worldwide dope ring allegedly run by Luciano is part of the Mafia; but the only other "evidence" presented— aside from the incredulous responses both of Senator Kefauver and Rudolph Halley when nearly all the Italian gangsters asserted that they didn't know about the Mafia—is that certain crimes bear "the earmarks of the Mafia."

The legend of the Mafia has been fostered in recent years largely by the peephole writing team of Jack Lait and Lee Mortimer. In their *Chicago Confidential,* they rattled off a series of names and titles that made the organization sound like a rival to an Amos and Andy Kingfish society. Few serious reporters, however, give it much credence. Burton Turkus, the Brooklyn prosecutor who broke up the "Murder, Inc." ring, denies the existence of the Mafia. Nor could Senator Kefauver even make out much of a case for his picture of a national crime syndicate. He is forced to admit that "as it exists today [it] is an elusive and furtive but nonetheless tangible thing," and that "its organization and machinations are not always easy to pinpoint." His "evidence" that many gangsters congregate at certain times of the year in such places as Hot Springs, Arkansas, in itself does not prove much; people "in the trade" usually do, and as the loquacious late Willie Moretti of New Jersey said, in explaining how he had met the late Al Capone at a race track, "Listen, well-charactered people you don't need introductions to; you just meet automatically."

Why did the Senate Crime Committee plump so hard for its theory of the Mafia and a national crime syndicate? In part, they may have been misled by their own hearsay. The Senate Committee was not in the position to do original research, and its staff, both legal and investigative, was incredibly small. Senator Kefauver had begun the investigation with the attitude that with so much smoke there must be a raging fire. But smoke can also mean a smoke screen. Mob activities is a field in which busy gossip and exaggeration flourish even more readily than in a radical political sect.

There is, as well, in the American temper, a feeling that "somewhere," "somebody" is pulling all the complicated strings to which this jumbled world dances. In politics the labor image is "Wall Street," or "Big Business"; while the business stereotype was the "New Dealers." In the field of crime, the side-of-the-mouth low-down was "Costello."

The salient reason, perhaps, why the Kefauver Committee was taken in by its own myth of an omnipotent Mafia and a despotic Costello was its failure to assimilate and understand three of the more relevant sociological facts about institutionalized crime in its relation to the political life of large urban communities in America, namely: (1) the rise of the American Italian community, as part of the inevitable process of ethnic succession, to positions of importance in politics, a process that has been occurring independently but almost simultaneously in most cities with large Italian constituencies—New York, Chicago, Kansas City, Los Angeles; (2) the fact that there are individual Italians who play prominent, often leading roles today in gambling and in the mobs; and (3) the fact that Italian gamblers and mobsters often possessed "status" within the Italian community itself and a "pull" in city politics.[1] These three items are indeed related—but not so as to form a "plot."

VII

The Italian community has achieved wealth and political influence much later and in a harder way than previous immigrant groups. Early Jewish wealth, that of the German Jews of the late nineteenth century, was made largely in banking and merchandising. To that extent, the dominant group in the Jewish community was outside of, and independent of, the urban political machines. Later Jewish wealth, among the East European immigrants, was built in the garment trades, though with some involvement with the Jewish gangster, who was typically an industrial racketeer (Arnold Rothstein, Lepke and Gurrah, etc.). Among Jewish lawyers, a small minority, such as the "Tammany lawyer" (like the protagonist of Sam Ornitz's *Haunch, Paunch and Jowl*) rose through politics and occasionally touched the fringes of crime. Most of the Jewish lawyers, by and large the communal leaders,

[1]Toward the end of his hearings, Senator Kefauver read a telegram from an indignant citizen of Italian descent, protesting against the impression the committee had created that organized crime in America was a distinctly Italian enterprise. The Senator took the occasion to state the obvious: that there are racketeers who are Italian does not mean that Italians are racketeers. However, it may be argued that to the extent the Kefauver Committee fell for the line about crime in America being organized and controlled by the Mafia, it did foster such a misunderstanding. Perhaps this is also the place to point out that insofar as the relation of ethnic groups and ethnic problems to illicit and quasi-legal activities is piously ignored, the field is left open to the kind of vicious sensationalism practiced by Mortimer and Lait.

climbed rapidly, however, in the opportunities that established and legitimate Jewish wealth provided. Irish immigrant wealth in the northern urban centers, concentrated largely in construction, trucking and the waterfront, has, to a substantial extent, been wealth accumulated in and through political alliance, e.g. favoritism in city contracts.[2] Control of the politics of the city thus has been crucial for the continuance of Irish political wealth. This alliance of Irish immigrant wealth and politics has been reciprocal; many noted Irish political figures lent their names as important window-dressing for business corporations (Al Smith, for example, who helped formed the U.S. Trucking Corporation, whose executive head for many years was William J. McCormack, the alleged "Mr. Big" of the New York waterfront) while Irish businessmen have lent their wealth to further the careers of Irish politicians. Irish mobsters have rarely achieved status in the Irish community, but have served as integral arms of the politicians, as strong-arm men on election day.

The Italians found the more obvious big city paths from rags to riches pre-empted. In part this was due to the character of the early Italian immigration. Most of them were unskilled and from rural stock. Jacob Riis could remark in the '90's, "the Italian comes in at the bottom and stays there." These dispossessed agricultural laborers found jobs as ditch-diggers, on the railroads as section hands, along the docks, in the

[2]A fact which should occasion little shock if one recalls that in the nineteenth century American railroads virtually stole 190,000,000 acres of land by bribing Congressmen, and that more recently such scandals as the Teapot Dome oil grabs during the Harding administration, consummated, as the Supreme Court said, "by means of conspiracy, fraud and bribery," reached to the very doors of the White House.

service occupations, as shoemakers, barbers, garment workers, and stayed there. Many were fleeced by the "padrone" system, a few achieved wealth from truck farming, wine growing, and marketing produce; but this "marginal wealth" was not the source of coherent and stable political power. Signficantly, although the number of Italians in the U.S. is about a third as high as the number of Irish, and of the 30,000,000 Catholic communicants in the United States, about half are of Irish descent and a sixth of Italian, there is not one Italian bishop among the hundred Catholic bishops in this country, or one Italian archbishop among the 21 archbishops. The Irish have a virtual monopoly. This is a factor related to the politics of the American church; but the condition also is possible because there is not significant or sufficient wealth among Italian Americans to force some parity.

The children of the immigrants, the second and third generation, became wise in the ways of the urban slums. Excluded from the political ladder—in the early '30's there were almost no Italians on the city payroll in top jobs, nor in books of the period can one find discussion of Italian political leaders— finding few open routes to wealth, some turned to illicit ways. In the children's court statistics of the 1930's, the largest group of delinquents were the Italian; nor were there any Italian communal or social agencies to cope with these problems. Yet it was, oddly enough, the quondam racketeer, seeking to become respectable, who provided one of the major supports for the drive to win a political voice for Italians in the power structure of the urban political machines.

This rise of the Italian political bloc was connected, at least in the major northern urban centers, to another important development which tended to make the traditional relation between the politician and the protected or tolerated illicit operator more close than it had been in the past. This is the fact that the urban political machines had to evolve new forms of fund-raising since the big business contributions, which once went heavily into municipal politics, now—with the shift in the locus of power—go largely into national affairs. (The ensuing corruption in national politics, as recent Congressional investigations show, is no petty matter; the scruples of businessmen do not seem much superior to those of the gamblers.) One way urban political machines raised their money resembled that of the large corporations which are no longer dependent on Wall Street: by self-financing—that is, by "taxing" the large number of municipal employees who bargain collectively with City Hall for their wage increases. So the firemen's union contributed money to O'Dwyer's campaign.

A second method was taxing the gamblers. The classic example, as *Life* reported, was Jersey City, where a top lieutenant of the Hague machine spent his full time screening applicants for unoffficial bookmaking licenses. If found acceptable, the applicant was given a "location," usually the house or store of a loyal precinct worker, who kicked into the machine treasury a high proportion of the large rent exacted. The one thousand bookies and their one thousand landlords in Jersey City formed the hard core of the political machine that sweated and bled to get out the votes for Hague.

A third source for the financing of these machines was the new, and often illegally earned, Italian wealth. This is well illustrated by the career of Costello and his emergence as a political power in New York. Here the ruling motive has been the search for an entrée —for oneself and one's ethnic group— into the ruling circles of the big city.

Frank Costello made his money originally in bootlegging. After repeal, his big break came when Huey Long, desperate for ready cash to fight the old-line political machines, invited Costello to install slot machines in Louisiana. Costello did, and he flourished. Together with Dandy Phil Kastel, he also opened the Beverly Club, an elegant gambling establishment just outside New Orleans, at which have appeared some of the top entertainers in America. Subsequently, Costello invested his money in New York real estate (including 79 Wall Street, which he later sold), the Copacabana night club, and a leading brand of Scotch whiskey.

Costello's political opportunity came when a money-hungry Tammany, starved by lack of patronage from Roosevelt and La Guardia, turned to him for financial support. The Italian community in New York has for years nursed a grievance against the Irish and, to a lesser extent, the Jewish political groups for monopolizing political power. They complained about the lack of judicial jobs, the small number—usually one—of Italian Congressmen, the lack of representation on the state tickets. But the Italians lacked the means to make their ambitions a reality. Although they formed a large voting bloc, there was rarely sufficient wealth to finance political clubs. Italian immigrants, largely poor peasants from Southern Italy and Sicily, lacked the mercantile experience of the Jews, and the political experience gained in the seventy-five-year history of Irish immigration.

During the Prohibition years, the Italian racketeers had made certain political contacts in order to gain protec-tion. Costello, always the compromiser and fixer rather than the muscle-man, was the first to establish relations with Jimmy Hines, the powerful leader of the West Side in Tammany Hall. But his rival, Lucky Luciano, suspicious of the Irish, and seeking more direct power, backed and elected Al Marinelli for district leader on the Lower West Side. Marinelli in 1932 was the only Italian leader inside Tammany Hall. Later, he was joined by Dr. Paul Sarubbi, a partner of Johnny Torrio in a large, legitimate liquor concern. Certainly, Costello and Luciano represented no "unified" move by the Italians as a whole for power; within the Italian community there are as many divisions as in any other group. What is significant is that different Italians, for different reasons, and in various fashions, were achieving influence for the first time. Marinelli became county clerk of New York and a leading power in Tammany. In 1937, after being blasted by Tom Dewey, then running for district attorney, as a "political ally of thieves . . . and big-shot racketeers," Marinelli was removed from office by Governor Lehman. The subsequent conviction by Dewey of Luciano and Hines, and the election of La Guardia, left most of the Tammany clubs financially weak and foundering. This was the moment Costello made his move. In a few years, by judicious financing, he controlled a block of "Italian" leaders in the Hall—as well as some Irish on the upper West Side, and some Jewish leaders on the East Side— and was able to influence the selection of a number of Italian judges. The most notable incident, revealed by a wire tap on Costello's phone, was the "Thank you, Francisco" call in 1943 by Supreme Court nominee Thomas Aurelio, who gave Costello full credit for his nomination.

It was not only Tammany that was eager to accept campaign contributions from newly rich Italians, even though some of these *nouveaux riches* had "arrived" through bootlegging and gambling. Fiorello La Guardia, the wiliest mind that Melting Pot politics has ever produced, understood in the early '30's where much of his covert support came from. (So, too, did Vito Marcantonio, an apt pupil of the master: Marcantonio has consistently made deals with Italian leaders of Tammany Hall — in 1943 he supported Aurelio, and refused to repudiate him even when the Democratic Party formally did.) Joe Adonis, who had built a political following during the late '20's, when he ran a popular speakeasy, aided La Guardia financially to a considerable extent in 1933. "The Democrats haven't recognized the Italians," Adonis told a friend. "There is no reason for the Italians to support anybody but La Guardia; the Jews have played ball with the Democrats and haven't gotten much out of it. They know it now. They will vote for La Guardia. So will the Italians."

Adonis played his cards shrewdly. He supported La Guardia, but also a number of Democrats for local and judicial posts, and became a power in the Brooklyn area. His restaurant was frequented by Kenny Sutherland, the Coney Island Democratic leader; Irwin Steingut, the Democratic minority leader in Albany; Anthony DiGiovanni, later a Councilman; William O'Dwyer, and Jim Moran. But, in 1937, Adonis made the mistake of supporting Royal Copeland against La Guardia, and the irate Fiorello finally drove Adonis out of New York.[3]

[3]Adonis, and associate Willie Moretti, moved across the river to Bergen County, New Jersey, where, together with the quondam racketeer Abner "Longie" Zwillman, he became one of the political powers in the state. Gambling flourished in Bergen County for almost a decade but after the

La Guardia later turned his ire against Costello, too. Yet Costello survived and reached the peak of his influence in 1942, when he was instrumental in electing Michael Kennedy leader of Tammany Hall. Despite the Aurelio fiasco, which first brought Costello into notoriety, he still had sufficient power in the Hall to swing votes for Hugo Rogers as Tammany leader in 1945, and had a tight grip on some districts as late as 1948. In those years many a Tammany leader came hat in hand to Costello's apartment, or sought him out on the golf links, to obtain the nomination for a judicial post.

During this period, other Italian political leaders were also coming to the fore. Generoso Pope, whose Colonial Sand and Stone Company began to prosper through political contacts, became an important political figure, especially when his purchase of the two largest Italian-language dailies (later merged into one), and of a radio station, gave him almost a monopoly of channels to Italian-speaking opinion of the city. Through Generoso Pope, and through Costello, the Italians became a major political force in New York.

That the urban machines, largely Democratic, have financed their heavy campaign costs in this fashion rather than having to turn to the "moneyed interests," explains in some part why these machines were able, in part, to support the New and Fair Deals without suffering the pressures they might have been subjected to had their source of money supply been the business groups. Although he has never publicly revealed his political convictions, it is

Kefauver investigation the state was forced to act. A special inquiry in 1953 headed by Nelson Stamler, revealed that Moretti had paid $286,000 to an aide of Governor Driscoll for "protection" and that the Republican state committee had accepted a $25,000 "loan" from gambler Joseph Bozzo, an associate of Zwillman.

likely that Frank Costello was a fervent admirer of Franklin D. Roosevelt and his efforts to aid the common man. The basic measures of the New Deal, which most Americans today agree were necessary for the public good, would not have been possible without the support of the "corrupt" big-city machines.

VIII

There is little question that men of Italian origin appeared in most of the leading roles in the high drama of gambling and mobs, just as twenty years ago the children of East European Jews were the most prominent figures in organized crime, and before that individuals of Irish descent were similarly prominent. To some extent statistical accident and the tendency of newspapers to emphasize the few sensational figures gives a greater illusion about the domination of illicit activities by a single ethnic group than all the facts warrant. In many cities, particularly in the South and on the West Coast, the mob and gambling fraternity consisted of many other groups, and often, predominantly, native white Protestants. Yet it is clear that in the major northern urban centers there was a distinct ethnic sequence in the modes of obtaining illicit wealth, and that uniquely in the case of the recent Italian elements, the former bootleggers and gamblers provided considerable leverage for the growth of political influence as well. A substantial number of Italian judges sitting on the bench in New York today are indebted in one fashion or another to Costello; so too are many Italian district leaders — as well as some Jewish and Irish politicians. And the motive in establishing Italian political prestige in New York was generous rather than scheming for personal advantage. For Costello it was largely a case of ethnic pride. As in earlier American eras, organized illegality became a stepladder of social ascent.

To the world at large, the news and pictures of Frank Sinatra, for example, mingling with former Italian mobsters could come somewhat as a shock. Yet to Sinatra, and to many Italians, these were men who had grown up in their neighborhoods, and who were, in some instances, bywords in the community for their helpfulness and their charities. The early Italian gangsters were hoodlums — rough, unlettered, and young (Al Capone was only twenty-nine at the height of his power). Those who survived learned to adapt. By now they are men of middle age or older. They learned to dress conservatively. Their homes are in respectable suburbs. They sent their children to good schools and had sought to avoid publicity.[4] Costello even went to a psychiatrist in his efforts to overcome a painful feeling of inferiority in the world of manners.

As happens with all "new" money in American society, the rough and ready contractors, the construction people, trucking entrepreneurs, as well as racketeers, polished up their manners and sought recognition and respectability in their own ethnic as well as in the general community. The "shanty" Irish became the "lace curtain" Irish, and then moved out for wider recognition.[5]

[4]Except at times by being overly neighborly, like Tony Accardo, who, at Yuletide 1949, in his elegant River Forest home, decorated a 40-foot tree on his lawn and beneath it set a wooden Santa and reindeer, while around the yard, on tracks, electrically operated skating figures zipped merrily around while a loud speaker poured out Christmas carols. The next Christmas, the Accardo lawn was darkened; Tony was on the lam from Kefauver.

[5]The role of ethnic pride in corralling minority group votes is one of the oldest pieces of wisdom in American politics; but what is more remarkable is the persistence of this identification through second and third generation descendants,

Sometimes acceptance came first in established "American" society, and this was a certificate for later recognition by the ethnic community, a process well illustrated by the belated acceptance in established Negro society of such figures as Sugar Ray Robinson and Joe Louis, as well as leading popular entertainers.

Yet, after all, the foundation of many a distinguished older American fortune was laid by sharp practices and morally reprehensible methods. The pioneers of American capitalism were not graduated from Harvard's School of Business Administration. The early settlers and founding fathers, as well as those who "won the west" and built up cattle, mining and other fortunes, often did so by shady speculations and a not inconsiderable amount of violence. They ignored, circumvented or stretched the law when it stood in the way of America's destiny, and their own — or, were themselves the law when it served their purposes. This has not prevented them and their descendants from feeling proper moral outrage when under the changed circumstances of the crowded urban environments later comers pursued equally ruthless tactics.

IX

Ironically, the social development which made possible the rise to political influence sounds, too, the knell of the Italian gangster. For it is the growing number of Italians with professional training and legitimate business success that both prompts and permits the Italian group to wield increasing political influence; and increasingly it is the professionals and businessmen who provide models for Italian youth today, models that hardly existed twenty years ago. Ironically, the headlines and exposés of "crime" of the Italian "gangsters" came years after the fact. Many of the top "crime" figures long ago had forsworn violence, and even their income, in large part, was derived from legitimate investments (real estate in the case of Costello, motor haulage and auto dealer franchises in the case of Adonis) or from such quasi-legitimate but socially respectable sources as gambling casinos. Hence society's "retribution" in the jail sentences for Costello and Adonis was little more than a trumped-up morality that disguised a social hypocrisy.

Apart from these considerations, what of the larger context of crime and the American way of life? The passing of the Fair Deal signalizes, oddly, the passing of an older pattern of illicit activities. The gambling fever of the past decade and a half was part of the flush and exuberance of rising incomes, and was characteristic largely of new upper-middle class rich having a first fling at conspicuous consumption. This upper-middle class rich, a significant new stratum in American life (not rich in the nineteenth century sense of enormous wealth, but largely middle-sized businessmen and entrepreneurs of the service and luxury trades — the "tertiary economy" in Colin Clark's phrase — who by the tax laws have achieved sizable incomes often much higher than the managers of the super-giant corpora-

a fact which, as Samuel Lubell noted in his *Future of American Politics,* was one of the explanatory keys to political behavior in recent elections. Although the Irish bloc as a solid Democratic bloc is beginning to crack, particularly as middle-class status impels individuals to identify more strongly with the G.O.P., the nomination in Massachusetts of Jack Kennedy for the United States Senate created a tremendous solidarity among Irish voters and Kennedy was elected over Lodge although Eisenhower swept the state.

tions) were the chief patrons of the munificent gambling casinos. During the war decade when travel was difficult, gambling and the lush resorts provided important outlets for this social class. Now they are settling down, learning about Europe and culture. The petty gambling, the betting and bingo which relieve the tedium of small town life, or the expectation among the urban slum dwellers of winning a sizable sum by a "lucky number" or a "lucky horse" goes on. To quote Bernard Baruch: "You can't stop people from gambling on horses. And why should you prohibit a man from backing his own judgment? It's another form of personal initiative." But the lush profits are passing from gambling, as the costs of coordination rise. And in the future it is likely that gambling, like prostitution, winning tacit acceptance as a necessary fact, will continue on a decentralized, small entrepreneur basis.

But passing, too, is a political pattern, the system of political "bosses" which in its reciprocal relation provided "protection" for and was fed from crime. The collapse of the "boss" system was a product of the Roosevelt era. Twenty years ago Jim Farley's task was simple; he had to work only on some key state bosses. Now there is no longer such an animal. New Jersey Democracy was once ruled by Frank Hague; now there are five or six men each top dog, for the moment, in his part of the state or faction of the party. Within the urban centers, the old Irish-dominated political machines in New York, Boston, Newark, and Chicago have fallen apart. The decentralization of the metropolitan centers, the growth of suburbs and satellite towns, the break-up of the old ecological patterns of slum and transient belts, the rise of functional groups, the increasing middle-class character of American life, all contribute to this decline.

With the rationalization and absorption of some illicit activities into the structure of the economy, the passing of an older generation that had established a hegemony over crime, the general rise of minority groups to social position, and the break-up of the urban boss system, the pattern of crime we have discussed is passing as well. Crime, of course, remains as long as passion and the desire for gain remain. But big, organized city crime, as we have known it for the past seventy-five years, was based on more than these universal motives. It was based on certain characteristics of the American economy, American ethnic groups, and American politics. The changes in all these areas means that it too, in the form we have known it, is at an end.

NARCOTICS AND THE LAW
William Butler Eldridge

What is myth and what is fact in the voluminous literature on the nature of narcotic addiction and the character of the narcotic addict? Very few of the frequently announced categoricals can be supported or refuted by the kind of conclusive, concrete evidence which eliminates the possibility of divergence of opinion. When subjected to careful scrutiny, however, most of these over-simplified generalizations will fall in the face of evidence that narcotic addiction is as individual in its etiology, psychology, and result as are the personalities involved. Some charges against the evils allegedly embodied in narcotic addiction, while true, are in reality charges against the iniquity of criminals who prey upon the need of the addict. Such considerations are important, but they should be dealt with as problems in the larger context of organized crime rather than as problems peculiar to, and intrinsic in, the use of narcotics. It is important to evaluate all of these charges dispassionately in order to appreciate the actual and total social challenge presented by narcotic addiction in the United States today.

The discussion which follows attempts to deal with the accuracy of widely disseminated categorical statements concerning drug addiction. It is recognized that case histories or incomplete data may be found to support almost any statement, but it is not recognized that non-typical occurrences, even when very serious, warrant making such occurrences the basis of statements apparently describing characteristic results of drug addiction. Such practice, always intellectually dishonest, is particularly reprehensible where it provides the basis for unreasoned persecution of individuals.

The use of certain drugs, notably cocaine, under certain circumstances may produce some of the results dealt with below, but cocaine use is no longer of great significance in the United States. It is the opiates and their synthetics which constitute the prime problem in this country.[5] In the following

[5]Excluding marijuana, more than 90% of the narcotics seized at ports and borders and within the United States in 1959 were opiates. U.S. TREASURY DEPARTMENT, BUREAU OF NARCOTICS, TRAFFIC IN OPIUM AND OTHER DANGEROUS DRUGS, Table 6 (1960). The total weight of marijuana seized was much larger than the weight of the other narcotics, but the comparative weights are not significant. The importance of marijuana in

discussion of the alleged effects of narcotics use, if the effect is not one attributable to the opiates, the implication that such effects are the general results of the use of narcotics is considered unwarranted.

Narcotics Ravage the Human Body

One of the most popular and understandable images of the narcotic addict is the physical wreckage of a human body debilitated by opiate misuse. The following description from a police journal is illustrative of the source of such an image:

> To be a confirmed drug addict is to be one of the walking dead.... The teeth have rotted out; the appetite is lost and the stomach and intestines don't function properly. The gall bladder becomes inflamed; eyes and skin turn a bilious yellow. In some cases the membranes of the nose turn a flaming red; the partition separating the nostrils is eaten away—breathing is

difficult. Oxygen in the blood decreases; bronchitis and tuberculosis develop. Good traits of character disappear and bad ones emerge. Sex organs become affected. Veins collapse and livid purplish scars remain. Boils and abscesses plague the skin; gnawing pain racks the body. Nerves snap; vicious twitching develops. Imaginary and fantastic fears blight the mind and sometimes complete insanity results. Often times, too, death comes—much too early in life.... Such is the torment of being a drug addict; such is the plague of being one of the walking dead.[6]

The medical profession, however, has found little cause for alarm in the physiological symptoms of narcotic addiction. In fact, the difficulty often arises that cases go unrecognized except by doctors trained in treatment of drug addiction and alerted to the necessity of careful examination to detect them.[7] Even then it may not be an easy task without sophisticated testing methods.

> There are few pathognomonic physical characteristics by which the opiate addict can be recognized as such. Scars and abscesses which result from intravenous injections of opiates are among the few helpful overt diagnostic characteristics. The cocaine or Benzedrine addict may show pupil dilation, tachycardia, tremulousness. It is difficult to recognize a marijuana smoker, although he sometimes

---

the general narcotics problem is a subject of considerable controversy, but the potency of the drug and the manner of its use in the United States indicate that probably its most serious aspect is in leading the user toward addiction to the more potent opiates. See Pescor, *The Problem of Narcotic Drug Addiction*, 43 J. Crim. L., C. & P.S. 471, 473-74 (Nov.-Dec., 1952); Nyswander, The Drug Addict as a Patient 29-31 (1956). Some writers consider that even this aspect of marijuana use is exaggerated and that marijuana is relatively unimportant. Bowman, *Some Problems in Addiction*, in Hoch & Zubin (eds.), Problems of Addiction and Habituation 164 (1958); *contra*, Murtagh & Harris, Who Walk in Shadow 71-72 (1959); Anslinger & Tompkins, The Traffic in Narcotics 18-26 (1953). While marijuana is supposed to be the narcotic most widely used by young people, an extensive study among young drug users in Chicago showed that 90% used heroin. Illinois Institute for Juvenile Research and the Chicago Area Project, Drug Addiction Among Young Persons in Chicago 5 (1953).

[6]*The Scourge of Narcotics*, Spring 3100 at 7 (Dec. 1958) quoted by Richard Kuh, *Dealing with Narcotics Addiction*, Part One, The New York Law Journal, June 8, 1960, p. 4, col. 1, in which Mr. Kuh, who is Administrative Assistant to the New York County District Attorney, urges a program of compulsory hospitalization for drug addicts.

[7]Bobbitt, *The Drug Addiction Problem*, 14 Am. J. Med. 538 (May 5, 1953).

has a characteristic facial flush. Opiates may be detected by analysis of an addict's urine for as much as ten days after the drug was last used. There may be emaciation from lack of food, both because opiates often diminish the appetite and because the addict's money is being used to buy drugs. *Little or no evidence exists to show that the continued use of any opiates causes permanent changes in the brain or central nervous system, or that it causes any changes except the body's greater tolerance of the drug. There is no conclusive evidence on opiates' effect on life-span, although they have been said to shorten life.*[8] (Emphasis added.)

Despite the palpable disagreement of the two preceding statements, the terms of the first cannot be labeled absolutely false, and therein lies its treacherous nature. Most of the symptoms attributed to the "confirmed drug addict" may be found singly in cases of abuse of various drugs. Some of the symptoms may result from *withdrawing the drug,* but not from the drug itself. Prolonged cocaine sniffing may produce inflamed nostrils or a perforated nasal septum. Veins may collapse and abscesses appear, but these are the results of unsterile equipment, impure drugs, and improper methods of injection, not of the drug itself. There may be a diminution of sexual drive or activity, but no permanent organic damage. Each symptom described probably has as its basis cases where such a result was

attributed to prolonged narcotics use, but to make a composite of all those symptoms and offer it as the prototype of the confirmed drug addict is, to put it most charitably, misleading. The latter evaluation of the physiological effect of drug addiction is so universally held by experts in this field[9] that any serious inquirer could not fail to appreciate the inaccuracy of the lurid picture painted by the material first quoted.

Narcotics Destroy Morality

It is often asserted that addiction to narcotics destroys the moral fiber of the addict, that his character deteriorates and his habits become evil.[10] This is a particularly difficult indictment to assay because it seldom has a point of reference. It may well be that many drug addicts display a morality which alarms the law enforcement officer or the social worker, but in assessing the role of a drug addiction as a contributor to that morality, other factors are often overlooked which appear to be far more important determinants.

The addict in the United States usually comes from the area characterized by the lowest incomes, the lowest educational level, and the lowest social status.[11]

[8]Winick, *Narcotics Addiction and Its Treatment,* 22 LAW & CONTEMP, PROB. 9, 13 (Winter 1957). For a readable discussion of the physiological results of addiction see NYSWANDER, *op. cit. supra* note 5, at 29-30. See also JOINT COMMITTEE OF THE AMERICAN BAR ASSOCIATION AND THE AMERICAN MEDICAL ASSOCIATION ON NARCOTIC DRUGS, DRUG ADDICTION: CRIME OR DISEASE? 45-50 (Interim and Final Reports, 1961).

[9]See INTERDEPARTMENTAL COMMITTEE ON NARCOTICS, REPORT TO THE PRESIDENT OF THE UNITED STATES 4 (January 1961).
[10]See quoted material accompanying note 6 *supra.*
[11]See Clausen, *Social and Psychological Factors in Narcotic Addiction,* 22 LAW & CONTEMP. PROB. 34 (Winter 1957) and sources cited therein. See also Hoch & Zubin, *op. cit. supra* note 5, at 2-3. Recent statistical compilations show a marked over-representation of Negro and Puerto Rican minorities in metropolitan areas. *Hearings Before the Subcommittee of the Committee on Appropriations of the House of Representatives,* 86th Cong., 2d Sess. 140 (Jan. 26, 1960). It is interesting to note, however, that studies made twenty years

The picture of the delinquent subculture found within the urban slum has been drawn many times. Perhaps less familiar is the fact that the law-abiding and morally responsible citizens of such areas also tend to share many beliefs and attitudes which are different from those held in the larger middle-class society. Middle-class Americans often find it difficult to realize that the goals to which they aspire and the values which they take for granted do not entirely pervade the population. Socioeconomic status is significant not merely in terms of the physical style of life that can be maintained and the security from want that is offered by a stable and adequate income; it is also reflected in the approach one takes to pleasure and to pain. The lower-class pattern of life, for example, puts a high premium on immediate physical gratification, on free expression of aggression, on spending, and sharing. Cleanliness, respect for property, sexual control, educational achievement—all highly valued by middle-class Americans—are of less importance to the lower-class family or are phrased differently....

...The child growing up amid the disorganization of an urban slum has available neither the models upon which to pattern himself nor the assurance that being "good" will pay off. Indeed, he is likely to hear and see that "everybody has his racket" and to learn in life that this applies to the representatives of law and order as well as to underworld groups.[12]

Excluding the participation in crimes to produce money for drugs, which will discussed later, little evidence has been adduced to show that the morality of the drug addict undergoes a significant modification as a result of his drug use. It would appear, rather, that the addict, in arousing middle-class emotion by his drug use, brings the mores of his subculture into question. Rather than deal with the question of the morality of lower-class patterns, the middle-class arbiters of the moral ethic label them a result of degenerate narcotics use.

Narcotic Addicts Are a Sexual Menace

Any assertion that sexual violence is a general or predictable result of narcotic addiction is untrue. This myth developed during the time when cocaine addiction was more extensive than at present. Cocaine can produce such a relief from inhibition, coupled with exhilaration, that the user may commit some violent act, possibly sexual, that he would not commit while free of the influence.[13] Despite the fact that cocaine has ceased to be a problem in the United States,[14] the myth of the sexual menace from the "dope fiend" has been kept alive by suggestive refer-

ago showed an entirely different ethnic representation. DAI, OPIUM ADDICTION IN CHICAGO (1937). Yet recent studies indicate that the same geographic parts of the city are producing the addicts who happen at present to be largely Negroes and Puerto Ricans. ILLINOIS INSTITUTE FOR JUVENILE RESEARCH AND THE CHICAGO AREA PROJECT, REPORT OF THE CHICAGO NARCOTICS SURVEY 44 (1953). The implication of the effect of environmental factors on the use of narcotics seems inescapable. For comparable statistics relating to treated juvenile addicts in New York City see COLUMBIA UNIVERSITY SCHOOL OF PUBLIC HEALTH AND ADMINISTRATIVE MEDICINE, A FOLLOW-UP STUDY OF TREATED ADOLESCENT NARCOTICS USERS (Ray E. Trussell, M.D., ed.), Chapter 11 (1959). [Hereinafter referred to as TRUSSELL REPORT.]

[12]Clausen, supra note 11, at 42.
[13]TERRY & PELLENS, THE OPIUM PROBLEM 271, 505 (1928).
[14]Anslinger & Tompkins, op. cit. supra note 5, at 281.

ences to "dope parties" and "vicious crimes" which are readily translated by popular imagination into orgiastic sprees following the use of drugs. The truth of the matter is that the opiates depress the sexual appetite, thus actually diminishing the probability of sexual crimes being committed by addicts.[15]

Statistics, medical and psychiatric observation, and police experience all demonstrate that there is a great deal of anti-social activity on the part of narcotic addicts. This does not answer the question, however, as to how much of this activity may be attributed to the drug use alone. The historical evidence just as clearly demonstrates that in the era before the advent of repressive laws, anti-social conduct was not a characteristic of the opium addict.[16] In fact, the very nature of the opiates would seem to give the lie to arguments that the drug produces aggressive anti-social behavior. Opiates are depressants which lull the user into a state of euphoria where everything is "right."

> The euphoria of the addict is a feeling of temporary well-being, induced by the drug's suppression of discomfort or pain. The addict's "high" is a feeling of aloofness from current situations and a postponement of decisions or urgencies. The drug *is* the decision. It provides a feeling of security and self-sufficiency. It temporarily helps to establish self-confidence and quell any disturbing aggressive-

ness. The drug itself is so fulfilling that it becomes the center of the user's life.[17]

Still leaving aside the question of the addict's crimes to secure money, nothing has been shown to demonstrate that the use of opiates generally produces, in and of itself, serious dangers to the physical well-being of the addict or the social well-being of the community. There is assuredly cause for concern in the euphoric effect of opiates which cause the addict to experience a false sense of security, self-sufficiency, and the rightness of things, when the very opposite may be the actuality. The question is not, however, peculiar to opiate use. Alcohol presents a similar problem of greater magnitude,[18] as do the barbiturates and tranquilizers.[19] It is not intended to suggest that we should ignore the social problems implicit in narcotics use because we ignore them elsewhere, but only that the problem should be recognized for what it is, free of unfounded hysteria.

Drug Use Makes Weak, Ineffective Members of Society

Again the shortcomings of the majority of addicts are singled out for criticism in a context which suggests that drug use is the responsible factor. The problem is not so simple. The potential strength and effectiveness of the addict should be measured against his own capabilities or those of the subculture from which he comes, rather than against society's ideal. It appears far more likely that the addict responds to

[15]Pescor, *The Problem of Narcotic Drug Addiction*, 43 J. CRIM. L., C. & P.S. 471, 476; TRUSSELL REPORT 117-21; Wikler and Rasor, *Psychiatric Aspects of Drug Addiction*, 14 AM. J. MED. 567-68 (May 1953).

[16]Kolb, *Let's Stop This Narcotics Hysteria*, Saturday Evening Post, July 28, 1956, p. 19. For an extensive digest of the material relating to the characteristics of the addict population before 1925, see TERRY & PELLENS, *op. cit. supra* note 13, at 1-53.

[17]Winick, *Narcotics Addiction and Its Treatment*, 22 LAW & CONTEMP. PROB. 9, 14 (Winter 1957).

[18]Kolb, *supra* note 16.

[19]Winick, *supra* note 17, at 9, 11.

his weakness and ineffectiveness by using drugs rather than the reverse.

The cause of addiction is not drugs but human weakness. Addiction usually is a symptom of a personality maladjustment rather than a disease in its own right. The psychiatric conditions which underlie drug addiction are chiefly the neuroses and the character disorders.... They (neurotic patients) include nervous, tense individuals with a great deal of anxiety and many somatic complaints; compulsive neurotics; persons with conversion hysteria—strange paralyses, anesthesias, etc. Individuals with character disorders were formerly termed psychopaths. Usually they are irresponsible, selfish, immature, thrill-seeking individuals who are constantly in trouble—the type of person who acts first and thinks afterwards. The majority of addicts do not fall clearly into either the neurotic or character disorder groups but have characteristics of both classes.[20]

Thus it appears that addiction merely represents a way in which some people suffering from neuroses and character disorders react to their problems. Many people who are not addicts experience these psychiatric difficulties from time to time in their lives. The fact that some choose to resolve their difficulties by resorting to drugs is probably due to a great many circumstances,[21] not the least of which is the social attitude of their own respective communities.

[20]Isbell, What to Know about Drug Addiction 2 (Public Health Service Publication No. 94, 1951).

[21]Wikler, Opiate Addiction 5 (1953). Whether or not an individual will use drugs "appears to depend on other factors—the availability of the drugs, suggestion by associates, legal restrictions, painful illnesses, attitude of social groups, etc., as well as the state of the individual's own internalized controls."

The types (of personalities) most commonly found included the passive dependent individuals with weak ego strength who have never made a satisfactory adjustment to the exigencies of everyday living.... Drugs simplify their struggle and appear to aid their adjustment.

Certain social factors appear influential in determining addiction. The addict with a dependent personality structure may come from a social group in which addiction is acceptable and differs only in terms of his use of narcotics from the dependent personality who comes from a cultural subgroup in which addiction is taboo but "neurotic" complaints in one guise or another are commonplace and allowed. The ill-defined back aches and "liver and stomach troubles" are but verbal adaptations to basic neurotic problems for which drugs also provide unfortunate solutions.[22]

The generalization that addicts are the weak, ineffective members of society has a dual vice. First, there is a suggestion implicit in the statement that there is something unique about the weakness or ineffectiveness when these qualities are demonstrated by an addict. Such a suggestion is highly misleading. Second, there is an inference that the use of drugs is the causal factor of the infirmities observed. Actually the reverse would appear to be true, namely, that the addict uses drugs as an attempted method of adjustment. What the actual effect of the drug will be again depends upon the individuality of the user.

The effects of opiate use on the individual as a member of

[22]Chapman, *Management and Treatment of Drug Addiction* 9 J. Chronic Diseases 315, 319 (March 1959).

society are determined in part by the strength of competing motivations. The gratification of "primary" needs by the simple expedient of using opiate drugs may have disastrous social consequences if the individual's productivity has been determined largely through necessity of satisfying his own hunger and sexual urges. Such individuals will give up such responsibilities for others as they have assumed and find, in opiates, the means of pursuing a hedonistic and narcissistic existence of no value to society. While this result is very commonly observed, there are credible reports of some individuals who are unable to function effectively in their work without the use of opiates because of "emotional" problems which appear to be satisfied by the drugs. Usually such persons are highly skilled professional people whose strongest motivations appear to spring from needs for high social esteem. They readily admit that opiates depress their sexual urges, but point out that these have been handled ineffectively by them in the past, and the absence of sexual relations is welcomed by both the husband and wife. However, the social stigma which the use of opiates entails, and the necessity for increasing the dose progressively soon raise serious problems.[23]

What would our hypothetical maladjusted individual do if he did not turn to drug use? He would find some other means of coping with his problem which might be either more or less alarming to society than his addiction. He might turn to the bariturates or alchohol as a substitute for drugs. He might seek gratification by "acting out" his maladjustment through open expres-

[23]WIKLER, *op. cit. supra* note 21, at 57.

sions of hostility, sexual aggressiveness, exhibitionism. The significant point is that many of the ills attributed to narcotics use would exist with or without illegal addiction. Drug use simply represents the attempt of certain persons to deal with the problems confronting them because of their individual personality structure or the social structure of their communities. It may well be that drugs are a socially undesirable solution to the individual's problems, but, if so, our effort should be directed toward finding a solution that is acceptable.

Narcotic Addicts Are Criminals

Except for the medical addict who receives a licit supply of drugs to relieve severe pain, it is inescapably true that narcotic addicts are criminals, since possession of narcotics is uniformly prohibited[24] and addiction itself made a crime in some jurisdictions.[25] The allegation of criminality of addicts is usually presented, however, as a characteristic of all drug users apart from such offenses as addiction, possession, or even stealing to get money for drugs.[26] Depending upon the approach of the person making the statements, it may be alleged that the criminal record precedes the addiction[27] or that it comes as a result of the addiction.[28] The experi-

[24]See Appendix B, p. 149 *infra* [omitted].
[25]*Ibid.*
[26]"The ranks of both addicted and non-addicted drug peddlers are filled with persons dedicated to a life of lawlessness, and the arrest and incarceration of these people on narcotics charges has incidentally protected the public from the depredations of thieves, robbers, and other vicious criminals engaged in organized crime." ANSLINGER & TOMPKINS, *op. cit. supra* note 5, at 272.
[27]ANSLINGER & TOMPKINS, *op. cit. supra* note 5, at 267-78.
[28]LINDESMITH, OPIATE ADDICTION 172 (1947).

ence of police[29] as well as the admissions of drug addicts[30] leaves little doubt that addicts indulge in a wide variety of predatory crime to produce money with which to support their addiction. Evidence obtained in governmental investigations indicates that the range of cost may vary considerably,[31] but considering the educational and income status of the group from which most addicts are drawn, it is always a cost clearly beyond the earning power of most of them.[32] Again we are presented with a subject which should be the concern of the community, namely, the danger inherent in the use of a substance which produces such a desire that crimes are committed to secure it. However, the consideration of this problem should be made in an appropriate context. The addict is drawn from a subculture which does not have the same respect for property as a larger middle-class segment of American society.[33] Thus, in trying to appreciate the intensity of the compulsion which drives addicts to crime to secure money, one must first appreciate that in less compulsive situations, the addict or non-addict from a lower-class subculture will probably not exercise the personal restraint expected by the majority of society.

A great deal of evidence has been marshaled to demonstrate the extensive non-narcotic criminal activity of the addicts before their first arrest on a narcotics charge.[34] From this it is often claimed that the persons who become involved in the "evil" of narcotics are simply manifesting another facet of their anti-social character and behavior and are antipathetic to socially acceptable ideas of law and morality long before addiction.[35]

There arises immediately the question of the validity of the data on which these assertions are based. It is obvious that the first narcotics arrest is not coincidental in time with the first narcotics use. Criminal activity before this time may well have been in support of a yet-undetected habit. In determining the extent to which prior criminal activity is truly unrelated to narcotics use, the starting point must be the time when the offender *first used* narcotics. That information must, in most cases, be obtained from the addict. If the addict believes that more sympathy for his present difficulty will be engendered if he indicates a recent acquaintance with narcotics, that is probably the information he will supply. If his judgment indicates the reverse, it is reasonable to assume that long use will be stated.

[29]Finestone, *Narcotics and Criminality*, 22 LAW & CONTEMP. PROB. 69, Table II, at 71 (Winter 1957).

[30]*Hearings Before the Special Senate Committee to Investigate Organized Crime in Interstate Commerce*, 82d Cong., 1st Sess., pt. 14 *passim* (1951). [Hereinafter referred to as *Crime Committee Hearings*.]

[31]*Ibid.* The price ranged from $3 to $80 per day. *Id.* at 81, 296.

[32]TRUSSELL REPORT, 51-79.

[33]See quoted material accompanying note 12, *supra.*

[34]STATE DEP'T OF JUSTICE, BUREAU OF CRIMINAL STATISTICS, NARCOTICS ARRESTS IN CALIFORNIA, July 1, 1959-June 30, 1960 at 9, Table 8, Chart IV (Dec. 5, 1960); TRUSSELL REPORT 28-29, 43-50.

[35]U.S. TREASURY DEP'T, BUREAU OF NARCOTICS, TRAFFIC IN OPIUM AND OTHER DANGEROUS DRUGS 6-7 (1960). *But see* U. S. TREASURY DEP'T., BUREAU OF NARCOTICS, MEMORANDUM REGARDING NARCOTIC CLINICS, THEIR HISTORY AND HAZARDS 6 (1938) quoted by King, *The Narcotics Bureau and the Harrison Act: Jailing the Healers and the Sick*, 62 YALE L. J. 736, 738, at note 13 (1953): "Under these conditions [legalized opium smoking in Formosa] the only attributable cause for greater criminality among narcotic addicts than non-addicts is the direct effect of the use of narcotics upon the character of the user.... It is because drug addiction causes a relentless destruction of character and releases criminal tendencies."

Assuming for the moment that all the studies have been successful in determining accurately the point at which addiction occurred, and that a number of narcotic addicts have had a record of criminal activity before becoming addicted, the significance of that fact must still be determined. The fact that addicts have criminal records proves no more about the causal role of drug addiction than the fact that underprivileged persons have criminal records proves about the causal role of poverty and deprivation. The factors discussed in the previous section must be understood and weighed carefully in either situation.

Any appreciation of the relationship between addiction and crime must also take into account the legal structure in this country which has forced narcotics traffic into the underworld. There is a considerable body of expert opinion to the effect that there are psychological factors which create "proneness toward addiction," and that this proneness is present in all classes of people in all walks of life.[36] In the United States, the law and public opinion have labeled the narcotic addict a criminal, and have forced all transactions in narcotics into a criminal setting. Therefore, many of the people who by virtue of personality and character disorders would be prime targets for addiction are deterred because they are not identified with the world of crime. Without such an identity, it is extremely difficult to obtain drugs in this country. An unknown, respectable-looking, white-collared clerk does not just walk into the drug-selling area of New York's East Harlem or Chicago's Southside and pick up a "deck" of heroin because he heard that it might

relieve the anxieties he is experiencing. It is quite possible that the only real relation between prior criminal activity and drug addiction in this country is that only those who are known in criminal circles can readily obtain drugs. There is one exception: persons in the medical and paramedical professions also have ready access to narcotics. The logic of the argument that access determines the class of the user is borne out by the fact that, as compared with the general population, the rate of addiction is thirty times higher for people in these professions.[37] Under the British system, where drug addiction is not regarded as a correlative of criminal activity, there is practically no evidence of any relationship between addiction and crime.[38] Further, before the legal suppression of narcotics sales in the United States, addiction was commonly found among the higher social strata.[39] Only after the traffic became illegal did addiction become allied with crime.

These observations are not intended to militate against control of narcotic drugs, since the controls, under the conditions hypothesized, are keeping many people from beginning narcotics use. It is, however, important to realize the significance of the criminal records of narcotic addicts for what it is. When that significance has been clearly understood and appreciated, it will be possible to make a social judgment as to the justifiability of ostracizing narcotics users by criminal sanction in order to dissuade a portion of the populace from indulging in narcotic drugs.

[37]NEW YORK CITY YOUTH BOARD, IN-SERVICE DEPARTMENT, REPORT OF THREE-DAY CONFERENCE ON NARCOTIC ADDICTION AND THE TEENAGER 16-17 (October 1959).

[38]Schur, *British Narcotics Policies*, 51 J. CRIM. L., C. & P.S. 619, 622-24 (Mar.-Apr. 1961).

[39]TERRY & PELLENS, *op. cit. supra* note 13, at 1-53.

[36]DEUTSCH, WHAT WE CAN DO ABOUT THE DRUG MENACE 12-13 (Public Affairs Pamphlet No. 186, 1952).

Addiction Is Contagious

The charge that addiction is contagious is perhaps one of the most effective weapons of those who wish to perpetuate the social anathema of drug use. The evidence is overwhelming that addiction has the spreading character of a contagious disease. Most addicts state that they began using drugs by associating with others who used drugs.[40] Such initiation is similar to the way most people learn to smoke or drink, but unfortunately the public is led to believe that there is a deliberate effort on the part of addicts and peddlers to recruit new users.

> It is also widely believed that addicts have a positive mania for making new addicts on the assumption that "misery loves company." It is true that addiction is spread by addicts — that's what makes it a highly dangerous contagion — but the manner of spread is usually a casual one. Often an addict shows great reluctance in "breaking in" a neophyte.[41]

The testimony of addicts before a Senate investigating committee also indicated that very few addicts are introduced to drugs by peddlers who offer initial doses free in order to trap the adventurous and unwary into addiction. Some of the addicts adverted to known cases where persons were introduced to drugs by peddlers, but the common method was through associates.[42]

Again the true situation presents a grim problem. The contagious character of addiction is an aspect of the problem which must be kept in the forefront of awareness when any attempt at solution is considered or undertaken. It is equally important, however, to remove the impression that the narcotic addict is gleefully seducing the flower of American youth into drug use as a fiendish vengeance against a society which refuses to permit his own indulgences. The problems apparent in the true nature of the spread of addiction are not less serious than those which would be presented by a diligently proselyting addict population. Indeed, the actual mechanics of addiction spread are probably more dangerous since the cause lies not within the relatively small body of addicts but in the much larger cultural subgroup from which addicts come. The efforts of a concerned public should be directed toward erasing the class values which applaud anti-social behavior in certain strata of the social structure. Considering the demonstrated effect of social acceptance on the likelihood of addiction, it would appear that therein lies the fertile soil favoring spread of addiction through association.

Once an Addict, Always an Addict

It is almost unavoidable that we should find a very confused public when the statements of professional people concerned with drug addiction are completely beyond reconciliation. Almost all drug addicts, we are told, want to get off and remain off drugs.[43] Any opiate addict can be treated successfully except those with an incurable malady or the infirm, says a government agent.[44] Still, the rate of relapse is 90 percent or better, argues a critic of intramural treatment.[45] The sad and

[40]*Crime Committee Hearings.*
[41]DEUTSCH, *op. cit. supra* note 36, at 12.
[42]*Crime Committee Hearings.*

[43]MAURER & VOGEL, NARCOTICS AND NARCOTIC ADDICTION 163 (1954).
[44]Treas. Reg. 35, Art. 117 (1919).
[45]Berger, *Dealing With Drug Addiction, A Reply to Mr. Kuh,* in U.S. TREASURY DEP'T,

unfortunate truth is that there is not enough known about what happens to drug addicts after treatment to evaluate accurately either the treatment procedures being followed or the true nature of addiction. It is known that many addicts are curable, but figures on the rate of success are almost totally lacking.

Of the more than seventeen thousand patients admitted to the United States Public Health Service Hospital at Lexington, Kentucky, from 1935 to 1955, 64 percent never returned, 22 percent returned once, 6 percent returned twice, and the remaining 8 percent returned three or more times.[46] It is not claimed, however, that anything like 64 percent of the patients have abstained from the use of narcotics after release from Lexington; the more frequently quoted figure being about 25 percent.[47] Results in the treatment of adolescent addicts at Riverside Hospital in New York City have been less encouraging,[48] probably due to difficulties in the treatment of adolescents which do not apply to the treatment of more mature addicts.[49]

Pescor's study of patients released from Lexington is interesting but far from conclusive or all-revealing. Four methods were utilized in following the progress of dischargees: (1) information secured from patients who returned to the hospital; (2) information secured from the Federal Bureau of Investigation when any former patient is arrested and the arresting agency requests a fingerprint identification; (3) information secured from probation officers on prisoner patients who are still under supervision; and (4) information secured from replies to letters of inquiry addressed to patients or their relatives, such letters assuring absolute confidence. Of the patients on whom information was secured, 74.7 percent had relapsed and 25.3 percent had abstained. Of the total patients discharged, 39.9 percent were *known* to have relapsed and 13.5 percent were *known* to have abstained.

The methods were admittedly crude. The danger in the first two methods is that they are heavily weighted toward identifying the relapsed addict. Information from probation officers reveals relapses and abstentions, but only those occurring during the somewhat coercive period of probation. The fourth method depends solely upon the voluntary cooperation of former patients. The study did not attempt to project the percentages of known relapse and abstention to cover the remaining patients on whom no information was received. Such a projection would be unwarranted considering the methods used in securing the information. In view of the illegal status of drug addiction, it is likely that a large percentage of the relapsed patients were discovered.[50] Conversely, it is likely that the abstention percentage of the patients whose subsequent history was unknown would be relatively high.

Unfortunately, the study has be-

BUREAU OF NARCOTICS, CONTROL AND REHABILITATION OF THE NARCOTIC ADDICT 13 (1961).

[46]Lowry, *Hospital Treatment of the Narcotic Addict*, 20 FEDERAL PROBATION 42, 50 (December 1956).

[47]PESCOR, FOLLOW-UP STUDY OF TREATED NARCOTIC DRUG ADDICTS (Supplement No. 170 to Public Health Reports, 1943).

[48]TRUSSELL REPORT.

[49]Ausubel, *Dealing With Drug Addiction, A Defense of the Kuh Plan*, in U.S. TREASURY DEP'T, BUREAU OF NARCOTICS, CONTROL AND REHABILITATION OF THE NARCOTIC ADDICT 25 (1961).

[50]Interviews with federal and local enforcement officials indicated a consistent conviction that habitual use of illicit narcotics over a period of two years would bring almost all such users to the attention of the police.

come the basis for statements about the success of Lexington by critics and defenders who accept the figures as a total picture. Critics, if they cite any authority, will say that the hospital succeeds in only 13 percent of its cases. In less formal discussion or writing, critics will inch up the relapse figures without stating a source.[51] Even the defenders of Lexington utilize the 25 percent known abstentions as the measure of success.[52] Neither is accurate. Both are misleading unless qualified by the technique of investigation. The same criticism is true of references to the studies made of Riverside Hospital.[53]

It is almost incredible that legislatures and administrative agencies, willing to appropriate huge sums of money for enforcement and hospital activities connected with the drug problem, have not seen the necessity for full and complete study of the progress of treated addicts.[54] It is strongly asserted by the Federal Bureau of Narcotics that institu-

tional treatment is the only proper method of treating drug addicts.[55] This pronouncement, while originally based upon qualified medical consensus, and still supported by many addiction specialists,[56] has never been subjected to the searching evaluation which could result from a thorough follow-up study of treated addicts. Such a study is imperative in the light of present knowledge.

Relapse should be recognized as a predictable symptom of addiction. The nature of relapse is not so thoroughly understood as to permit its characterization as definitely psychological, sociological, or pharmacological,[57] but whatever its nature, it should be accepted in the same way in which relapse is accepted in many chronic diseases. Success should not depend upon whether a former drug user goes to his grave abstaining from drugs, but upon the length of time and the conditions under which treatment has enabled him to function successfully without drugs. It is not enough to remove the patient from drug use if thereafter he suffers intensely from emotional disturbance, maladjustment, and disorientation from his social community. Substitution of one illness for another hardly seems to merit the term "cure." Similarly, a physician who treats an addict who

[51]"The relapse rate at the federal hospitals is known to be in excess of 90%, and if complete figures could be obtained, is probably even higher. 95% is a conservative estimate." Berger, *supra* note 45, at 14.

[52]Ausubel, *supra* note 49.

[53]The TRUSSELL REPORT made use of most of the same sources of information in following up patients treated at Riverside. Only a small percentage remained unknown in this study. It should be noted, however, that the "two per cent success" figure often attributed to the TRUSSELL REPORT findings really relates to the number of patients who had no further difficulty with their communities. Dr. Trussell and his associates were concerned with the overall rehabilitation of Riverside patients. Consequently, any instance indicating that the patient was not adjusting to society was regarded as a "failure" whether or not narcotics were involved.

[54]Financial support has recently been received by the personnel at Lexington for a detailed follow-up study on the approximately 1,000 former patients living in Kentucky. When it is completed, considerable caution should be exercised in applying the findings to the national scene. The study should, however, be very valuable in developing follow-up techniques.

[55]U.S. TREASURY DEP'T, BUREAU OF NARCOTICS, CONTROL AND REHABILITATION OF THE NARCOTIC ADDICT, *Foreword* (1961).

[56]The present policies of the Federal Bureau of Narcotics appear to have been inherited from its predecessor, the Federal Narcotics Control Board. The stand of the American Medical Association in 1924, that ambulatory treatment was inadvisable, is most frequently cited in support of this view. However, the medical profession has shown some dissatisfaction of late with the 1924 statement. See American Medical Association, Council on Mental Health, *Report on Narcotic Addiction* 165 J.A.M.A. 1707 (Nov. 30, 1957).

[57]NYSWANDER, THE DRUG ADDICT AS A PATIENT 54-55 (1956).

subsequently remains abstinent for ten, five, or even three years, hardly deserves to have his efforts labeled a "failure."

Unfortunately, among those who have become interested (in the opium problem) from a professional, legislative, administrative, sociologic, commercial, or other point of view, there has been an almost continuous controversy as to practically every phase of the narcotic situation, with the result that all the way from the causes on through development, course, and treatment of the condition, to say nothing of its underlying nature and methods of control, there has been a lack of unanimity of opinion. These differences have been expressed in reports of scientific research, textbooks on medicine, legislative acts, judicial opinions, and administrative procedures — in general, in the opinions and efforts of all who, from one motive or another, have appeared to seek a solution.

In view of the importance of the problem it is astonishing that little specific information on even the main features of this condition is available in any one place. In general, students and writers appear to have approached the subject from only a limited experience — with too meagre a basis of fact — and to have emphasized unduly one or another feature to the total exclusion of related data. This tendency quite naturally may have led the more or less casual reader as well as possibly legislators, administrators, and others officially or professionally connected with the individuals involved, to prejudicial attitudes and unwarranted generalizations.[58]

The words are those of Dr. Charles Terry in 1928. Despite his, and other dedicated efforts, there has been little change.

[58]TERRY & PELLENS, THE OPIUM PROBLEM, Intro. at xiii-xiv (1928).

MENTAL DISORDERS AND ILLNESS

A Social Problem?

In western society, a person who is ill is expected to behave in a certain way and to enjoy privileges not given to him when he is well. The ill person must stop working, or at least reduce his share of work. He rests, he is quiet, he is attended to with *apparent* special consideration and kindness. (We say apparent because the forms are by no means always experienced as considerate or kind by the ill person himself.)

Those around the ill person expect him to work at getting well. Or they expect him to accept the limitations of his illness as a form of social as well as physical dependence upon them. The person plays out a story in which he is ill for a time and then recovers, although the drama may be re-enacted. Or, he plays out a narrative in which he becomes ill and remains dependent on the care of others for a lifetime. Or, as we say, the illness may 'prove fatal.'

Death following illness represents the only clear condition. The cause of death and its definition through medical diagnosis varies from decade to decade. Most Americans who died in 1900 died from influenza, pneumonia, tuberculo-sis, gastroenteritis, and diseases of the heart, in that order of frequency. Most of those who died in 1958 did so from diseases of the heart, cancer, vascular lesions of the central nervous system, and accidents in the home or on the highways.

Chronic illness is less well specified by modern medicine. About 15 out of every 100 civilian Americans not in jail or hospital or other custodial institution, suffered from chronic medical limitations in movement or activity. Most of them were mobile but unable to work full time or at all, to keep house, or to attend school.[1] The list of the most common forms of chronic illness is headed by arthritis, rheumatism, chronic sinusitis, asthma, hay fever, deafness, and heart conditions.

Or, take the case of the illness from which the person recovers. Most Americans are sick enough at some time each year to take to their beds or to restrict their activities severely for a day or two, or even a week or two. Most acute but temporary illnesses involve

[1] *Health and Vital Statistics for the United States, Summary,* Public Health Service Publication No. 600, U.S. Government Printing Office, 1960, pp. 30-31.

the common cold, which was reported in 1959 by an estimated 115 out of 171 million civilian Americans; respiratory ailments; injuries; and, well down the list, infectious and parasitic diseases.

An illness, whether terminal, chronic, or temporarily acute, is something that Americans tend increasingly to take to a hospital. There are other appropriate settings, of course, such as the outpatient clinic, the doctor's office, and one's home, but hospitalization is a meaningful if partial indicator of the forms and prevalence of illness in American society.

Americans entered hospitals of all types *other than mental and tubercular* at the rate of 130.5 per thousand in 1959, and they stayed about ten days, on the average. This is a sharp increase over the annual entry rate of 56.3 per thousand in 1931, when the average patient stayed 15.3 days.

Contrast this with the rates of mental hospitalization. In 1959, 2.3 Americans per thousand entered mental hospitals, where they remained for more than two years, on the average. In 1931, the rate of entry was .8 per thousand, and patients remained for more than three years, on the average. Nearly half the hospital beds in the nation are occupied by the mentally ill. The length of stay in mental hospitals has declined, but it remains 70 times longer on the average than hospitalization for other illnesses. Hospitalized mental patient loads therefore accumulate. Most of them are *chronically* ill persons.

Perhaps one in 12 Americans now living will spend some part of his life in a mental hospital. But this prediction should be put against the prediction that ten in 12 Americans will spend some part of his life in a general hospital undergoing treatment for some other

kind of illness or injury. More than 600 thousand persons occupied beds in mental hospitals in 1963, but a much larger number occupied beds for treatment of other illnesses.

Has mental hospitalization of Americans increased? Between 1903 and 1959, patients residing in mental hospitals rose from 242 to 499 per 100 thousand civilian population. This increase is due to social change. Foremost is the national pattern of increasing use of hospitalization for illnesses of all kinds. Next, is the increasing age of the general population. For another, use follows facilities, so that the increase in the number of hospitals, hospital beds, and medical personnel, all stimulate the rate. Finally, the increase reflects the cumulative build-up in the number of mental patients that results from the great length of stay.

The most careful study of whether mental illness has increased over time in America involved analysis of first-admission rates to Massachusetts and New York institutions for the mentally ill during 1840 to 1885, and 1917 to 1940. This research revealed "no long-term increase during the last century in the incidence of the psychoses of early and middle life." The rates by age for first admissions under fifty were found to be "just as high during the last half of the 19th century as they are today."[2]

The Social Problem Reconsidered

The purpose of the previous section was to identify mental illness as one among many forms of illness. Until this century in America and elsewhere, per-

[2]Herbert Goldhamer and Andrew W. Marshall, *Psychoses and Civilization*, New York: The Free Press of Glencoe, 1953, pp. 91-92.

sons suffering from mental disorders were defined not as ill but as evil, or mad, or as possessed of something undesirable and abnormal. Many Americans continue to think of mental disorders in this way. But in the sectors of the social structure where authority over such questions is lodged, and especially in the practicing professions of medicine, law, and the ministry, mental disorders are usually defined as *health* problems today.

We do not regard physical illness as a major social problem, although we may attend to the important economic and social costs involved. The fact that schizophrenic first-admission patients in residence five years or more in state mental hospitals at the end of 1949 had cost the states an estimated $490 million should be compared with the medical costs to the nation of combat disabilities in World War II. If illness, mental or physical, is a universal feature of the human condition which is met more or less well in different societies, why do so many groups regard it as a national social problem?

We are tempted to regard mental illness as a major social problem because, in the words of one sociologist, "It is a puzzling, disruptive phenomenon, a problem whose social aspects are not adequately encompassed within the medical context."[3] This distinction seems to us attractive but spurious. Many serious illnesses are "puzzling, disruptive phenomena." Leukemia, brain damage, cancer, are all socially and psychologically disorganizing not only to the ill person but to larger groups and whole subcommunities.

Asthma, arthritis, and respiratory ailments baffle and upset families, co-workers, employers, even the economy as a whole. Yet no one singles these out as major *social* problems.

Mental disorders which take the form of illness, we shall maintain, are a major national social problem because we are unable, culturally, socially, and technologically, to *exorcise* them. Having defined them as health problems, the elite professions most concerned with mental disorders as illness have been unable to prevent their prevalence, reduce their chronicity, or ameliorate the suffering substantially.

This inability to attack or ameliorate mental illness needs to be documented, for we know that helpful forms of treatment have developed since the turn of the century. Let us illustrate. Warren State Hospital in Warren, Pennsylvania, is an institution with an outstanding record of achievement in the early discharge of patients. In 1914 (when medical psychiatry and clinical psychology were in their infancy), 61 per cent of the Warren State patients diagnosed and admitted as schizophrenic were still patients two years later. In 1947, 44 per cent remained patients two years later. More than 30 years of psychiatric and psychological research, development, and clinical experience, netted an improvement of 17 per cent.

We might reverse the standard and ask about early discharges. About 18 per cent of the Warren State schizophrenics were discharged within six months after admission in 1914, in contrast to 36 per cent in 1947—an 18 per cent improvement.[4]

[3]John A. Clausen, "Mental Disorders," Chapter 3 in Robert K. Merton, et al., *Contemporary Social Problems*, New York: Harcourt, Brace, and World, 1961, p. 130.

[4]*Proceedings of the Second Conference of Mental Hospital Administrators and Statisticians*, National Institute of Mental Health, U.S. Government Printing Office, 1953, Appendix A, Table 8.

One statistician converted similar data from New York State into a cost estimate of savings resulting from 'modern advances' in treating schizophrenia. Modern advances netted a savings of about 1.5 million dollars a year for comparisons based on 1914 versus 1948. The greater life span of aged patients diagnosed as psychotically senile, and the increased life span of persons suffering from syphilitic psychoses, erased this saving, however, by adding a neat 1.5 million dollars to annual costs.[5] *For every patient who was discharged through improved treatment, there was another chronically ill resident who lived an extra ten years.* In noneconomic terms, of course, these are two types of modern medical advance.

Many major physical diseases and impairments have also not been prevented, transformed from chronic into acute but temporary conditions, or ameliorated. But in the world of organic diseases and physical injuries, the overall rate of achievement has proved astonishing by any standard.[6] Where we have not succeeded in coping with organic illness through science and the technology of medicine, we fall back upon centuries of accumulated reliance upon acceptance of the risks of existence.

No such development has occurred following the definition of mental disorders as mental illnesses. The typical mental hospital in America today contains a preponderance of persons diagnosed as schizophrenic. This is not a disease entity, but a classification intended to fit persons diagnosed as ill from "fundamental disturbances in reality relationships, and concept formation, with affective, behavioral, and intellectual disturbances in varying degrees and mixtures."[7] For the nation as a whole, roughly half the patients in mental hospitals are classed as schizophrenic. Moreover, about 70 per cent of them have been in mental hospitals for five years or more.

The *social* problem is thus the frustration that results from confronting a welter of human problems related to disabled mental processes of feeling, thinking, remembering, and perceiving. The social problem arises from defining these processes as subject to medical diagnosis and care, without being able in practice to do much about treatment.

We are in transition from a time when men were either ill from organic causes or were insane, and shunned or locked up as dangerous. During this transition, our hopes have been raised powerfully. If a mental disorder or a psychological disability is an illness, it is a health problem. Health problems are something that western science has been able to prevent, repair, or eliminate. Health problems that are chronic or terminal, western man has learned to expect to endure. Yet with serious mental illness, the redefinition has, for the meanwhile at least, failed. We can neither attack a mental illness effectively nor have we learned culturally how to endure it. The old tactics of shunning and of walling mental disorders away continue to be used, but they are now themselves repugnant.

---

[5]*Ibid.*, pp. 2-3.

[6]Influenza and pneumonia, tuberculosis, and diphtheria, major causes of deaths in 1900, have within 60 years either disappeared from the list of major causes or have dropped to the bottom of the list. The national infant mortality rate in 1935 was 56 deaths per 1,000 live births. By 1960, it had declined to 26 per 1,000. Maternal deaths from deliveries and complications of pregnancy and childbirth declined in the same 25 years from 58 to 10,000 live births to less than 4 per 10,000.

[7]*Mental Disorders, Diagnostic and Statistical Manual*, Washington, D.C., American Psychiatry Association Mental Hospital Service, 1952, p. 26.

Conceptual Problems

All societies have experienced something their members perceived as mental disorder. Ideas and reports of madness and insanity, psychological conflict and malfunctioning, are to be found in early historical documents of ancient Egypt and in the Old Testament. Anthropologists have recorded descriptions supplied them by native informants that reveal awareness of something like mental disorder in most preliterate folk societies.

Everyone may agree, then, that they have experienced directly, heard about, or felt the effects of individual behavior that seems to be the result of extremely *different* thinking, feeling, sensing, or remembering. It is this general, virtually universal association between conduct and mental processes which leads us to refer to some kinds of behavior as mentally disordered.

There are intellectual dilemmas surrounding this common experience, however. How shall we decide which kinds and degrees of *conduct* are to receive this designation? How shall we assess the relation of conduct to mental processes? How do we decide whether a mental disorder is an illness?

People disagree strongly from culture to culture, and from place to place in history, about what behavior deviates from the norm, and about the kinds of deviant behavior presumed to be due to mental processes. When these questions have been answered, people have disagreed about what to do about psychologically based misconduct. Today, we think of these as problems of knowledge. We look to the health professions and their grounding in science for answers. The belief common to educated lay publics is that when enough is known about mental pro-cesses, we will find answers to these questions. For example, we look to medical science to treat all or most disorders as illnesses—to be prevented, cured, or repaired psychiatrically.

Mental disorders are social problems, however, to the extent that much knowledge and practice is not available, or to the extent that men continue to disagree strongly about the very idea itself as well as what to do about behavior that is so defined, regardless of the state of knowledge. To those who regard the problem as a matter of knowing, there is the policy question of what to do about mental disorders *in the meanwhile*. Others think they know; they consider mental disorder a problem of changing cultural norms and the social practices based upon them. Others deny the existence of distinctive mental disorders.

Conventional Medical Model

Johann Weyer, in the middle of the 16th century, was the first physician since the end of the Roman Empire to specialize in mental disorders. He attacked the witchcraft trials of the Inquisition for the failure of church authorities to recognize mental disease when it was present. Weyer is one of the founders of modern psychiatry. His concept of mental disease followed the lines of the intellectual development of *physical* medicine for three centuries after Weyer made his contribution. The glory of physical medicine in this period was the achievement of standards for identifying organic disease: A disease could be distinguished from more fuzzy features by the demonstrable presence of physicochemical changes or abnormalities in the *structure* of the body.

As scientific instruments for detecting structural abnormalities evolved, certain mental diseases and defects were clearly observed, described, and transmitted as a part of the general medical heritage. One such mental disease is paresis, or dementia paralytica. In this disease, a visible infection produced by syphilis can be demonstrated by pointing to observable changes in the structure of tissues and by tracing the path of the infection through the body to the brain. The effects of these changes upon motor behavior, thinking, speech, and social conduct, can then be observed and described as a set of symptoms which are the result of the infection. A person disabled by paresis is thus redefined by the physician as an ill person. In the case of paresis, we have a conventional medical model of the criterion for diagnosing a disorder, and the means by which this diagnosis leads to prescriptions about social as well as technical medical response to the person with the disorder.

Of course, even after the medical scientist achieves this firm basis for defining and treating paresis, conflicts flourish because older ideas are retained by the public and by other professions, religious and legal, which have a stake in regulating the social order. These conflicts may be problematic socially; but if science is widely accepted, these conflicts decline as the new knowledge diffuses.

Change in the Medical Model

Contemporary psychiatry departed from this model beginning with Charcot in France, and Freud in Austria, in the late 19th century. Freud did more than change the low state of knowledge about mental processes. He changed the very criterion against which a person's behavior is defined as mentally disordered. To the criterion of structural abnormality, Freud, following Charcot, added the criterion of *function*. Abnormal mental processes were inferred from knowledge of behavior, which he differentiated in terms of "indicative symptoms." The result is that today, mental illness has become an assignment of the role of the sick person to anyone whose behavior fits the functionally defined criteria for that role.

The effect of this shift from a physicochemical concept of mental disorder, along with changing public interest in health as a value, has been to expand the application of mental disorder to all undesired states of mind and types of behavior. Suicide, murder, crimes against property, accidents, school failures, failures to make a living, divorce, desertion, and even frequent remarriage, have come more and more to be defined as behavioral evidence of mental disorder.

Certain types of mental illness which were once viewed as fitting the older model of disease, moreover, have been re-examined. One in four Americans admitted to a mental hospital today is an older person, classified as suffering from an arteriosclerotic senile psychosis. Here, the old medical logic was that senility, or the deterioration of memory and thought and speech, results from physicochemical change, from progressive hardening of the arteries. New evidence makes it plain that many aged persons have become disabled through loss of work, loss of status, loss of the supporting attentions of friends and kin. Senility is as often and as completely a functional disorder as it is a chemical change.

A similar distinction has been

drawn between alcoholic psychoses and the functional mental disorders associated with alcoholism. In fact, the thrust of the functional concept has been so powerful that two of the three predominant types of presumed organic mental illness — senility and alcoholic psychosis — which make up about one third of all new annual admissions to American mental hospitals, may be primarily functional.

The Freudian concept produced chaos among the old social labels for deviants. A goldbrick or malingerer is now defined as psychoneurotic. Jack the Ripper, in his current guise, is a paranoid schizophrenic. The former traitor or a turncoat may now be categorized as a soldier that we failed as a boy.

Who Is Sick and Who Is Well?

The psychiatric and clinical psychological redefinition of mental disorder and mental illness has produced a major social revolution in America. Neither term is any longer a unified or measureable entity. More people may today be defined as mentally sick, and more may themselves be taking on the role of the ill person, than ever before in national history. If this is true, however, it is also true that the role itself has changed. The role of mental illness no longer protects the person from the charge of self-responsibility. Treatment by the psychiatrist involves increasingly the insistence that the patient take responsibility for getting well. Other persons around the mentally sick person tolerate, yet refuse to *excuse,* behavior on the grounds of mental illness.

As the functional conception takes hold, the number of kinds and degrees of mental disorder expands. In addition to an ever-enlarging castle of psychiatric categories, one discovers closets labelled 'emotionally disturbed,' 'sociopathic,' 'character disordered,' 'functionally retarded,' and so on. A lay diagnostic game builds up, in which all undesirable attitudes and actions are fitted to pseudo-explanatory labels.

The next and perhaps more daring step is to reverse the direction of the revolution and to define mental disorder as the absence of mental health. Consider the criteria for what may ideally be expected of a healthy American adult according to one eminent psychiatrist, Thomas Rennie:

> Independence of action, thought, and standards ... freedom from crippling inferiority and guilt feelings, from excessive egotism, and from competitiveness and unbridled hostility ... concern for others, a respect for differing religions and ethics, an appreciation of one's own liabilities and assets ... the assumption of adult responsibilities (including) the obligation to find and sustain a satisfying job, to recognize the need for play and rest, and to find satisfaction in one's role as an individual in relation to family, social, and civic life ... the establishment and maintenance of a home ... loving and giving to mate and children ... a capacity to accept illness, disappointments, bereavements, even death and all that which is largely beyond our own control (as well as) our own make-up and individuality, the perfection and imperfections of self and others, success and failure, sportsmanship, and the social comparisons we call advice, criticism, and authority ... a philosophy of objectivity about the past and a vision of creative opportunity for the present and

the future . . . the capacity to create and participate in a consensus based on understanding others and on making one's self understood.[8]

Individual conduct is a process. It involves change and is a matter of becoming as opposed to static being. Any functional conception of mental health tends to be couched, like Rennie's, in terms of ideals or potentialities. In this formulation, everyone at some point in time must be mentally disordered. Logically, however, if we are all sick, are we then not all well?

This is the ultimate psycho-logic. For, exclusive of a very small number of persons who are mentally disabled for genetic reasons or because of brain damage, most individuals think, feel, remember, sense and act in abnormal as well as normal ways at different times and under different circumstances of support or life stress. Abnormal and normal components may be thought of as potentialities which emerge in various combinations under varying life situations. The abnormal or disordered tendencies run off one end of an indistinct continuum that shades from disturbance and conflict, to detachment from intelligible contact with reality. Normal tendencies extend along the other end of the same continuum. They range from adequate performance in standard roles, to achievement of diverse ideals of maturity and integration of the sort catalogued by Rennie above. The actual nature of this continuum, if indeed there is one, is not at all well known.

The question, Who is sick and who is well?, is therefore answered this way:

[8]As quoted in Leo Srole, et al., *Mental Health in the Metropolis: The Midtown Manhattan Study*, Vol. 1, New York: McGraw-Hill, 1962, pp. 395-396.

Exclusive of organic disorders, everyone is at once healthy and sick. This answer may be refined by adding interpretive dimensions to behavior. For example, we may assess the *motives* that impel the behavior. A statement from an individual that he is endangered by enemies may be examined for its meaning to the person himself. Another dimension is that of *context:* Is the statement of personal danger appropriate to the circumstances within which it is expressed? We may also consider the *basis of judgment* of the person who responds to the behavior. Certainly, any behavior this complex confounds consistent or dependable evaluation.

Social Structure and Mental Disorder

The previous chapter interpreted criminal behavior and delinquency as socially caused and said that nearly all American adults break the law and that nearly all children and youth misbehave seriously at times, but that few do so frequently, and even fewer are officially judged as criminal or delinquent.

The same proposition holds for illness, whether strictly organic, psychosomatic, or functional. All Americans become ill in different ways at different points in their lives. (In this case only some forms of illness are officially judged as problematic, although all are given special types of consideration.)

Thus, man's relation to his social environment has a major influence upon his conformity to standards of conduct, and upon all aspects of his health. Social psychiatrists believe that failure to adapt to social situations, inability to satisfy personal needs as these are personally conceived, frustration in achieving goals, and the pressure of excessive or conflicting social demands are powerful types of environmental *stress*. Stress is a force that may stimulate, induce, or, at the very least, correlate with illness, regardless of the nature of the disorder.

Environmental stress is transmitted in several ways. For one, different persons tolerate different kinds and amounts of stress because they are differently constituted. For another, different persons experience environmental stress in different ways. And, stress is transmitted through the group relations that surround different individuals in different ways. As a social role, illness itself is just such a group support, for example. The way illness stands between the individual and his disorder varies across different groups.

Just as some individuals and some groups may be more prone to learn criminal patterns of behavior than were others, so the sociologist's attention in studying mental illness is caught by the fact that mental disorders, and their official expression as types of defined mental illness, are more likely to be experienced by some groups than by others. The gross group dimensions in the case of crime and delinquency are sex, age, ethnic group, and social class. So in the case of mental disorders and mental illness, we expect social correlates.[9] Environmental stress is what

[9]This is precisely the case as it has been documented in sociological and ecological studies of the incidence of disorders in the American population at large, of rates of first admission to mental hospitals (private and public), and of the prevalence of prolonged psychiatric patients. (E. Gartly Jaco, *The Social Epidemiology of Mental Disorders*, New York: Russell Sage Foundation, 1960; Leo Srole, et al., *Mental Health in the Metropolis: The Midtown Manhattan Study*, New York: McGraw-Hill Book Company, 1962; August B. Hollingshead and Frederick C. Redlich, *Local Class and Mental Illness*, New York: John Wiley, 1958; and Arnold M. Rose, editor, *Mental Health*

physicians call *nonspecific* in its effects, however. For example, one sociologist concludes from his study of the ecological correlates of mental disorder, that catatonics (one type of schizophrenia):

> Represent sensitive, self-conscious and timid personalities who find it difficult to come to terms with a type of social life which is terrifically harsh, intensely individualistic, highly competitive, extremely crude, and often violently brutal . . . the character of life only intensifies the tensions and anxieties which already have been developed in these personalities . . . one might say that such communities deny for many persons "adequate breathing space" in growing up . . .[10]

Dunham here relates one mental disorder to the extremely stressful environmental conditions of impoverished slum life, thwarted needs, and other aspects of community disorganization. These conditions work selectively: They induce mental disorder in those who are most vulnerable in their psychological or constitutional makeup.

Surely, it is such an interplay of noxious pressures that induces mental illness. However, these are so like the explanations we advance for many types of criminal and delinquent behavior, marital and family conflict, suicide, and so forth. Environmental stress is related to a host of personal outcomes. It is therefore *nonspecific*.

Perhaps the best survey ever made in the field of mental health involved a representative sample of a white but otherwise heterogeneous Manhattan residential population of 110 thousand

and Mental Disorder: A Sociological Approach, New York: W. W. Norton Co., 1955.

[10]H. Warren Dunham, "Current Status of Ecological Research in Mental Disorder," in Arnold M. Rose, op. cit., p. 174.

persons.[11] From interviews with 1660 residents, psychiatrists concluded that fewer than one in five adults were free enough of the symptoms of mental disorder to be considered well. Nearly six in ten were diagnosed as falling between mildly and moderately disturbed. One in four were estimated to be markedly, severely disordered or mentally incapacitated, but not presently hospitalized.

Among the latter, there were nearly three times as many persons with low as compared with high socio-economic status. This was apparent whether one used the status of parents or the status of the persons in the sample. The main correlates of serious mental ill health in the Manhattan population at large were low income, low educational attainment, and low occupational status, as characteristic of both parents and sick persons themselves.

Another outstanding survey examined the incidence of psychiatric cases by social class in New Haven, Connecticut, compared to estimates of the proportion of adults within each of five social classes. In this study, the criterion was not diagnosis of persons in the population at large but reports from all psychiatrists on persons under treatment for mental illness. About 11 per cent of New Haven's population was classified as part of two top social classes I and II. These groups contained less than 8 per cent of the psychiatric patient population. The two lowest classes contained about 64 per cent of the normal population, and 75 per cent of the psychiatric patient population.[12]

What is nonspecific about this? The same environmental stresses can be as readily identified in theft or homicide, addiction, or suicide, homeless men on skid row, or tuberculosis. Before the notion of social correlates of mental disorder can take us very far, we must establish valid links between elements in the life history of the ill person and elements in his environment. These would require not only a precise conception of each type of mental disorder, but parallel knowledge of the other kinds of deviations and disorders that are possible. We have no such comprehensive grasp of the subject.

With the word 'nonspecific,' one thus comes full circle. The social problem of mental illness rests in the relation between the expectation of being able to treat illness, and the current inability to treat mental illnesses in particular with any high degree of success. A small proportion of cases, perhaps 10 per cent of the whole at any one time, is fairly definite; the remainder present indications that are confused.

Existing classifications of mental disorders are seriously deficient in two respects: they point not to causes or origins but to symptoms; worse than that, the classifications of symptoms often fail to fit real cases. The prediction of what course a particular illness will follow is usually highly unreliable.

If one can neither classify nor predict the outcomes of an illness, the

---

[11]Leo Srole, et al., *Mental Health in the Metropolis*, op. cit.

[12]August B. Hollingshead and Frederick C. Redlich, *Social Class and Mental Illness*, op. cit. Many studies of the characteristics of hospitalized mental patients confirm a strong correlation between status and mental illness. Rates of first admission for mentally disordered men to mental hospitals in Ohio, for example, revealed the following differences: professional, semi-professional, technical and managerial workers entered at a rate of about 20 per 100 thousand employed persons in the state. The rate for farm workers was 81.5, and the rate for unskilled male workers was 202 per 100 thousand. (Robert M. Frumkin, "Occupation and Major Mental Disorders," in Arnold M. Role, *Mental Health and Mental Disorder*, op. cit., p. 143.)

course of treatment is likely to be equally nonspecific. This is the case in general psychiatry, where treatment often proceeds solely through prescription for symptoms, or through trial-and-error exhaustion of the treatment possibilities.

Techniques of Treatment

Therapies used in treatment of mental disorders have become less harmful (if not always a good deal more helpful) in the course of the last 150 years. Medical treatment of the insane early in the 19th century in America included shaving and blistering of the scalp, bleeding, purging of the bowels, chaining and related modes of restraint. On the convenient assumption that psychotics were insensitive to heat or cold, physicians seldom bothered to prescribe heat or clothing for patients housed in subbasement dungeons and mud huts.

French innovations toward 'moral treatment,' which urged loving care, acceptance and relief from external life stresses, diffused to the United States by the 1850s. Yet over the century that followed, bloodletting, dousings with ice water, and torture were replaced by various 'shock' therapies. First came insulin, then Metrazol, and then electroshock. Shock therapies induce severe convulsions or a state of coma, with the result (in some cases) that the pattern of psychotic symptoms is broken up, at least temporarily. In the period from 1940 to 1955, psychosurgery (including prefrontal lobotomy, transorbital lobotomy and others) involving a severing of nerve connections in the brain, became fashionable. With the advent of a variety of ataractic drugs known as tranquilizers, both the shock therapies and psychosurgery diminished. The evidence for their contribution to treatment remains inconclusive.

The tranquilizers do not cure or even treat mental disorders. They *do* reduce the severity of symptoms of aggression, agitation, anxiety, and motility, however. They therefore contribute to the ability of the therapist to provide meaningful attention to the problems of the patient.

Among the therapies, the oldest is psychotherapy—the establishment between therapist and patient of a type of social relation that either helps both to work toward and to dislodge the root of the disorder, or improves the ability of the patient to cope with his mental processes and conduct, or both. Psychotherapy, at best, offers improved communication under protective conditions. This is for some human problems sufficient to stimulate reconstruction and redirection of feelings, thoughts and conduct. At the very least, psychotherapy provides occasion for encounters between an understanding person and a troubled person and is therefore conducive to feelings of support and hope.

Ironically, psychotherapy has greatest relevance for the most communicative of clients; namely, middle- and upper-class individuals who are *least* vulnerable to psychotic disorders. With few exceptions, psychotherapy is effective among severely disturbed patients chiefly as an investigative or diagnostic procedure. Its triumphs tend to be limited to the treatment of more advantaged, less deeply disordered persons, though dramatic exceptions do occur.

Environmental Strategies

Just as criminal offenders are not rehabilitated by imprisonment, then, mentally ill persons are not treated effectively in the course of hospitalization. And, as the attention of penologists has turned toward the study of the effects of imprisonment per se upon the inmate, so the attention of hospital researchers has begun to focus upon the effects of institutionalization upon the mental patient.

This is more than a crude analogy. Until quite recently in America, serious misbehavior was defined under the law generally as punishable by imprisonment; otherwise the court defined the violator as incapable of distinguishing wrong from right conduct by virtue of mental incapacity or insanity. Mentally ill persons not charged with violating the law are generally processed in the same fashion today.

Only a court of law, for example, has the power to send a person involuntarily to a mental hospital. The court may reach this decision through trial procedures on a charge of criminal offense, or through petition by a lay person who is a close relative or intimate friend of the 'patient.' *It is through petition for involuntary commitment that the large majority of persons are hospitalized today for mental disorders.* Indeed, in many states, prisons, reformatories, schools for the blind, institutions for mental retardates, and mental hospitals are all managed and operated under a single Department of Benevolent and Correctional Institutions, or some equivalent.

Under these conditions, the mental patient is part sick and part prisoner. As a sick person, the patient receives no clearly efficacious treatment. As a prisoner, he serves an indefinite sentence, completed only when he no longer appears to be seriously ill. A hospital environment designed around these re-

quirements is, like a prison, inevitably unsuccessful in the general case.[13]

The large residential mental hospital may supply clean linen, firm mattresses, decent food, programs of recreation and work and education. It may employ trained personnel who are therapeutically oriented; that is, who tend at least overtly to think of the patients as treatable and even recuperative, rather than hopeless. Students of these institutional environments have demonstrated repeatedly that under the best of intentions (physical and programmatic), such places tend to work *against* the well-being, care, and recovery of their inhabitants.

This knowledge has stimulated experiments in modification of the milieu of the mental hospital, both as to program, staff and patient, and patient and community relations. Under the labels of milieu therapy, therapeutic community, intrusive therapy, attitude therapy, and the like, psychiatrists and psychologists have experimented fruitfully with changes in the social organization of the mental hospital. The experiments demonstrate that the behavior setting of the hospital influences profoundly, for better as well as for worse, the prospects of improvement in the condition of patients. Settings, when reorganized thoughtfully, have therapeutic effects more powerful than any known forms of individual organic or psychological therapy. Reorganization presumes, however, that changes in the entire political, fiscal, and professional superstructure of hospitals can be introduced and

[13]Ivan Belknap, *Human Problems of a State Mental Hospital*, New York: McGraw-Hill, 1956. Erving Goffman, *Asylums*, New York: Doubleday and Co., Anchor Books, 1961; and Jules Henry, "The Formal Social Structure of a Psychiatric Hospital," *Psychiatry*, 1954, 17, 139-151.

maintained under more than limited experimental conditions.

Milieu therapy leads one logically to concern with the relation of the patient and his hospital to the community at large. If the condition of the patient improves and his legal status as an involuntary resident is removed, there remains the question of adjustment of home and family, to the world of neighbors, of work and peers. A majority of mental hospitals today send patients home on trial visits before releasing them indefinitely. Other hospitals have developed outpatient treatment programs which allow patients to live and work in the open community but under the protection of clinical support.

Summary of Point of View

The perspective of this chapter is that mental disorders, like other forms of deviant behavior, are intrinsic to society and the human condition. It has been argued that the record of every society reveals the presence of problems of abnormal psychological behavior, and that *all* individuals experience some degree of mental disorder at times in their lives. Finally, this chapter has suggested how individual problems are associated, however non-specifically, with the social structure as conceptualized in environmental stress.

We have pointed to *mental illness,* as against disorder, as the true social problem; and we have argued that mental illness is intensely problematic in contemporary America for several related reasons. First, Americans have made an illness of mental disorder without *knowing* what to do about treating, ameliorating, or preventing, the illness. This is a profoundly frustrating situation

chiefly because of the great expectations aroused by the triumphs of medical science over so many other types of illness.

Secondly, taking on of the role of the mentally ill person is a painful, often stigmatized, and confusing act. It is most often done *involuntarily,* therefore, with resulting damage to self-regard. Third, mental illness is a major national social problem because, in this state of professional as well as public ignorance and personal avoidance, the society responds, not with acceptance and patience, but with institutional incarceration, segregation, and posthospital fear or indifference.

As with crime, we may have more to learn about mental illness from study of how others respond to it than from study of its genesis. Mental disorders will persist as long as men and societies persist, though there is *no evidence* that such problems grow more or less frequent as civilization grows more complex. Their expression as illnesses may well change drastically, however, as psychiatry matures as both an art and a science. In a nation where scientific knowledge commands respect and affects practice and policy, Americans may learn how to respond therapeutically toward themselves and their fellows.

References

Appleby, L., Proano, A., and Perry, R. "Theoretical vs. empirical treatment models: An exploratory investigation." In L. Appleby, J. Scher, and J. Cumming (Eds.), *Chronic schizophrenia: Explorations in theory and treatment.* Glencoe, Ill.: The Free Press, 1960, pp. 226-247.

Barber, B. Resistance by scientists to scientific discovery. *Scientific Manpower*, 1960, *1*, 35-47.

Barton, W. E., Farrell, M. J., Lenehan, Frances, & McLaughlin, W. F. *Impressions of European psychiatry.* Washington D.C.: American Psychiatric Association, 1961.

Belknap, I. *Human problems of a state mental hospital.* New York: McGraw-Hill, 1956.

Bellak, L. (Ed.) *Contemporary European psychiatry.* New York: Grove Press, 1961.

Berne, E. *Transactional analysis in psychotherapy: A systematic individual social psychiatry.* New York: Grove Press, 1961.

Blau, P. *Bureaucracy in modern society.* New York: Random House, 1956.

Bloomberg, W. Must there be two communities in patient care? *Hospitals*, 1960, *34*(15), 35-39.

Bockoven, J. S. Some relationships between cultural attitudes toward individuality and care of the mentally ill: An historical study. In M. Greenblatt, D. J. Levinson, & R. H. Williams (Eds.), *The patient and the mental hospital.* Glencoe, Ill.: Free Press, 1957. Pp. 517-526.

Cantril, H., Ames, A., Hastorf, A., & Ittelson, W. Psychology and scientific research. In F. P. Kilpatrick (Ed.), *Human behavior from the transactional point of view.* Hanover, N.H.: Inst. for Associated Res., 1952. Pp. 195-212.

Carson, R. C. Milieu homogeneity in the treatment of psychiatric inpatients. *Psychiatry*, 1962, *25*, 285-289.

Caudill, W., Redlich, F. C., Gilmore, H. H., & Brody, E. E. Social structure and interaction processes on a psychiatric ward. *Amer. J. Orthopsychiat.*, 1952, *22*, 314-334.

Clausen, John A. "Mental Disorders," in Robert K. Merton and Robert A. Nisbet (Eds.) *Contemporary Social Problems.* New York: Harcourt, Brace, World, Inc., 1961.

Clausen, J. A., & Yarrow, M. Paths to the mental hospital. *J. soc. Issues*, 1955, *11*, 25-32.

Colarelli, N. A re-evaluation of the role of the psychiatric aide. NIMH Research Project, Topeka, Kansas, 1961.

Cumming, Elaine, & Cumming, J. The locus of power in a large mental hospital. *Psychiatry*, 1956, *19*, 361-369.

———, ——— *Closed ranks: An experiment in mental health education.* Cambridge, Mass.: Harvard Univer. Press, 1957.

DeLange, W. H. Conceptions of patient role by patients and staff in a state mental hospital. *Comprehensive Psychiat.*, 1962, *3*, 174-180.

Des Lauriers, A. M. *Reality in schizophrenia.* New York: International Universities Press, 1963.

Dewey, J. *Human nature and conduct.* New York: Holt & Co., 1922.

Dewey, J., & Bentley, A. F. *Knowing and the known.* Boston: Boston Press, 1949.

Doust, J. W. Psychiatry at the crossroads: V. Despite fragmentation of psychiatry and unscientific approaches to research, all hospitals can glean vital information through patient-focused investigations. *Ment. Hosp.*, 1961, *12*(9), 11-16.

Dunham, H. Warren. *Sociological theory and mental disorder.* Detroit: Wayne State University Press, 1958.

Eaton, Joseph W. and Weil, Robert J. *Culture and mental disorders.* New York: The Free Press of Glencoe, 1955.

Eiduson, Bernice T. *Scientists: Their psychological world.* New York: Basic Books, 1962.

Einstein, A., & Infeld, L. *The evolution of physics.* New York: Simon & Schuster, 1942.

Ellsworth, R. The psychiatric aide as an active participant in patient rehabilitation. *Newsletter Res. Psychol.,* 1961, 3(2), 9-13.

———— Personal Communication. Letter dated April 19, 1962.

Etzioni, A. Interpersonal and structural factors in the study of mental hospitals. *Psychiatry,* 1960, 23, 13-22.

Fairweather, G. W. The social psychology of mental illness: An experimental approach. *Newsletter Res. Psychol.,* 1961, 3(2), 3-8. Also see Fairweather, G. W., Simon, R., Gebhard, M. E., Weingarten, E., Holland, J. L., Sanders, R., Stone, G. B., & Reahl, J. E. Relative effectiveness of psychotherapeutic programs: A multicriteria comparison of four programs for three different patient groups. *Psychol. Monogr.,* 1960, 74(5, Whole No. 492). Fairweather, G. W., & Simon, R. A further follow-up comparison of psychotherapeutic programs. *J. consult. Psychol.,* 1963, 24, 186.

Goffman, E. *Asylums: Essays on the social situation of mental patients and other inmates.* New York: Doubleday & Co., Anchor Books, 1961.

Gorman, M. A revolutionary approach to the care of the mentally ill. Paper presented at the Annual Meeting, Ohio Mental Health Federation, Columbus, Ohio, December 1961.

Grinker, R. R., MacGregor, Helen, Selan, Kate, Klein, Annette, & Kohrman, Janet. *Psychiatric social work: A transactional case book.* New York: Basic Books, 1961.

Gurel, L. Restoration of the mentally ill to the world of work: A revised proposal for studies of factors affecting the post-hospital employment of functionally psychotic veterans. Psychiatric Evaluation Project, Working Paper 61-2, Veterans Administration Hospital, Washington D.C., 1961.

Hargreaves, G. R. Current developments in social psychiatry in Britain. In *Symposium on preventive and social psychiatry.* Washington, D.C.: Walter Reed Army Institute of Research, 1957. Pp. 401-408.

Henry, J. The formal social structure of a psychiatric hospital. *Psychiatry,* 1954, 17, 139-151.

Hollingshead, A. B., & Redlich, F. C. *Social class and mental illness: A community study.* New York: Wiley, 1958.

Horney, Karen. *Our inner conflicts,* New York: W. W. Norton & Company, Inc., 1945.

Hyde, R. W. Current developments in social psychiatry in the United States. *In Symposium on preventive and social psychiatry.* Washington D.C.: Walter Reed Army Institute of Research, 1957. Pp. 409-418.

Jackson, J. Methods for comparative studies of mental hospitals. NIMH Research Proposal, Univer. of Kansas, Lawrence, 1961; also see Jackson, J. Toward the comparative study of mental hospitals: Characteristics of the treatment environment. In A. Wessen (Ed.) *The psychiatric hospital as a social system.* New York: Charles Thomas, 1964.

Jahoda, Marie. "Current Concepts of Positive Mental Health," New York: Basic Books, Inc., 1958. Monograph Series, Joint Commission on Mental Illness and Health.

Joint Commission on Mental Illness and Health. *Action for mental health.* New York: Basic Books, 1961.

Jones, M. *The therapeutic community.* New York: Basic Books, 1953.

———— Social rehabilitation with emphasis on work therapy as a form of group therapy, *British J. med. Psychol.*, 1960, *33*, 67-41.

————— Intra and extramural community psychiatry. *Amer. J. Psychiat.*, 1961, *117*, 748-787.

Kahne, M. J. Bureaucratic structure and impersonal experience in mental hospitals. *Psychiatry*, 1959, *22*, 363-376.

Kilpatrick, F. P. (Ed.) *Human behavior from the transactional point of view.* Hanover, New York: Institute for Associated Res., 1952.

Lea, H. C. *Inquisition of the Middle Ages.* New York: MacMillan, 1961.

Leighton, Alexander H., Clausen, John A., and Wilson, Robert N. *Explorations in social psychiatry.* New York: Basic Books, Inc., 1957.

Lewin, K. *Principles of topological psychology.* New York: McGraw-Hill, 1936.

————— *Resolving social conflicts.* New York: Harper, 1948.

————— *Field theory in social science: Selected theoretical papers.* New York: Harper, 1951.

May, R., Angel, E., & Ellenberger, H. (Eds.) *Existence: A new dimension in psychiatry and psychology.* New York: Basic Books, 1958.

Meijering, W. L. Recent developments in social psychiatry in the Netherlands. In *Symposium on preventive and social psychiatry.* Washington D.C.: Walter Reed Army Institute of Research, 1957. Pp. 409-418.

Merton, R. K. Bureaucratic structure and personality. In C. Kluckholm, & H. Murray (Eds.), *Personality in nature, society, and culture.* New York: Alfred A. Knopf, 1950. Pp. 282-291.

Mowrer, O. H. "Sin," the lesser of two evils. *Amer. Psychologist*, 1960, *15*, 301-304.

————— *The crisis in psychiatry and re-ligion.* New Jersey: D. Van Nostrand. 1961.

Meyers, J. K., & Roberts, B. H. *Family and class dynamics in mental illness.* New York: Wiley, 1959.

Nosow, S., & Form, W. H. (Eds.) *Man, work, and society.* New York: Basic Books, 1961.

Pratt, S. Of myth and models: An agonizing reappraisal. Paper read at American Psychological Association, New York, September 1961.

Pratt, S., & Delange, W. The ("theragnostic") admission-therapy group: Treatment of choice at a state hospital. *Ment. Hosp.*, 1963, *14*, 222-224.

Pratt, S., & Tooley, J. How differing concepts of the nature of *psychological disorders* lead to differing practices in the hospital, the clinic, and the community. Paper read at the American Psychological Association, St. Louis, September 1962.

————— , ————— *Contract* psychology and the actualizing transactional-field. *Int. J. soc. Psychiat.*, 1964, spec. ed. no. 1, 51-69.

Pratt, S., Reed, P., & Arnold, R. Widening the treatment field. *Ment. Hosp.*, 1960, *11*(9), 25-26.

Pratt, S., Tooley, J., DeLange, W., et al. *Alice in blunderland: The psychologist in the mental hospital.* Unpublished monograph, 1964.

Pratt, S., Scott, G., Treesh, E., Khanna, J., Lesher, T., Khanna, Prabha, Gardiner, G., & Wright, W. *The mental hospital and the treatment-field.* Monograph, Supplement no. 8, *J. Psychol. Stud.*, 1960, *11*. Also published in *Research on the psychiatric hospital as a social system.* Third Annual Conference, Social Science Institute, Washington University, St. Louis, 1961, pp. 53-122.

Proceedings of the Twelfth Mental

Hospital Institute. *Ment. Hosp.*, 1960, *11*(8).

Rapoport, R. N. *Community as doctor: New perspectives on a therapeutic community.* Springfield, Ill.: Charles C. Thomas, 1961.

Rose, Arnold (Ed.) *Mental Health and Mental Disorder.* New York: W. W. Norton & Company, Inc., 1955.

Ruesch, J. Psychiatry and the challenge of communication. *Psychiatry,* 1954, *17*, 1-18.

Ruesch, J., & Bateson, G. Structure and process in social relations. *Psychiatry,* 1949, *12*, 105-124.

———, ——— *Communications: The social matrix of psychiatry.* New York: Norton, 1951.

Russell, B. *Selected papers.* New York: Modern Library, 1961.

Sanders, R., & Weinman, B. The psychosocial treatment of the chronic mental patient: A rationale. Paper read at American Psychological Association, Cincinnati, Ohio, September 1959.

———, ——— Social interaction therapy and psychiatric adjustment. Paper read at American Psychological Association, New York, September 1961.

Sanders, R., Fitzgerald, B. J., Hobkirk, Janice, Smith, A., Smith, R. S., & Weinman, B. Social rehabilitation of the chronic mental patient. Third NIMH Interim Report, Philadelphia State Hospital, Philadelphia, Pa., 1960.

Schwartz, M., & Schwartz, Charlotte, G. *Social approaches to mental patient care.* New York: Columbia University Press, 1964.

Solomon, D. N. Professional persons in bureaucratic organizations. In *Symposium on preventive and social psychiatry.* Washington D.C.: Walter Reed Army Institute of Research, 1957. Pp. 253-266.

Sullivan, H. S. *Conceptions of modern psychiatry.* Washington: W. A. White Psychiat. Found., 1947.

Szasz, T. S. *The myth of mental illness.* New York: Harper & Brothers, 1961.

Tooley, J., & Pratt, S. A mixed-model cookbook. *Cont. Psychol.,* 1963, *8*, 30.

Umbarger, C. C., Dalsimer, J. S., Morrison, A. P., & Breggin, P. R. *College students in a mental hospital: An account of organized social contacts between college volunteers and mental patients in a hospital community.* New York: Grune & Stratton, 1962.

Veblen, T. *The theory of the leisure class.* New York: Macmillan Co., 1899.

Vitale, J. H. Mental hospital therapy: A review and integration. Unpublished manuscript, 1961. (a)

Vitale, J. H. The therapeutic community: A review article. In *The psychiatric hospital as a social system.* Third Annual Conference, Social Science Institute, Washington University, St. Louis, 1961, pp. 28-52. (b)

Wayne, G. J. Work therapy in the Soviet Union. *Ment. Hosp.,* 1961, *12*(8), 20-23.

Weinberg, S. Kirson. *Society and Personality Disorders,* Englewood Cliffs, N. J., Prentice-Hall, Inc. 1952.

THE URGE TO CLASSIFY

Karl Menninger, Martin Mayman and Paul Pruyser

The Trend From Pluralism And Ontology To Monism

* * *

In each generation since Paracelsus, there have been a few who caught a glimpse of mental illness as a process in flux rather than as a motley collection of bizarre entities. We propose to follow these visionary predecessors, abandoning the old names and listings, not because some of them do not have a certain usefulness in communication but because they are based on obsolete concepts of the human personality and of the vicissitudes which have been called illness.

Many classical designations were of course practical, administrative descriptions rather than scientific concepts. But it is always difficult to free ourselves from the misleading implications that become attached to labels, not necessarily put there by their originators, but often added gradually by their users. This is true even when the old label is replaced with a new model or the con-

cept revised. Here the principle of psychological inertia seems to act.

"Nothing seems to be more refractory and more resistant," wrote Riese, "than the ontological* view of disease. While it was true that nobody believed any longer in spirits and demons as invaders of the diseased individual, very few resisted (and still resist) the temptation of isolating in their thought the disease from the individual himself. Ontology, an offspring of magic and demoniacal medicine, reappeared in the new shape of disease entities."[1]

The notion that there were disease entities which could be discovered and defined and delimited and confirmed by various tests—this notion set psychiatrists off on one kind of wild-goose chase. One name after another was

*"Ontology" is a word with somewhat shifting meanings. As here used it implies the notion that a disease is a real and special thing—not a state of being or a state of the organism or a phase of existence or an aspect of functioning or a reaction of the organism but a thing in itself, a concretely demonstrable invasion by some alien force or substance or entity.

[1]Riese, Walther: "An Outline of a History of Ideas in Pseudo Therapy." *Bull. Hist. Med.* 25:442-456, 1951.

applied to the special proprietary delimitations of some highly articulate or compulsive describer. A hundred names have been applied throughout the ages to the same syndrome; what was called by one generation "hebephrenia," "catatonia," or "onirical delirium" was called by the following generation "dementia praecox" and by the next generation of psychiatrists "schizophrenia." Some of us hope that this generation will solve its name-calling problem by substituting for these appellations the categorical term "mental illness." The failure to recognize the essential characteristics of mental illness persisted in spite of a succession of categorical name changes. "Possession" (demonologic) became "bewitchery," "bewitchery" became "madness," "madness" became "lunacy," "lunacy" became "insanity," "insanity" became "psychosis," a word many of us feel to be no more scientific than the word "bewitched."*

During the second half of the nineteenth century the discoveries of bacteriology, pathological anatomy, and genetics seemed to bring irrefutable confirmation of Trousseau's famous declaration: "The principle of specificity dominates all medicine."[2] The unitary concept of mental illness seemed to be forgotten.

The Unitary Concept

But even while the systematists were elaborating their hundreds and even thousands of orders, classes, genera, and species of mental illness some colleagues strove for simplification and consistency.

Heinrich Neumann was the most outspoken and definite of them all. He felt and declared (in his textbook of 1859) that psychiatric classifications of all kinds were not only artificial and illusory, but directly dangerous. "Rather no classification," he said, "than a false one. The lack of any classification at least leaves free space for investigation, whereas a false classification leads directly into errors!... Diagnosis is not simply the designation of a group of symptoms but the key to the comprehension of the case.... We [i.e., I] consider any classification of mental illness to be artificial, and therefore unsatisfactory, [and] we do not believe that one can make progress in psychiatry until one has resolved to throw overboard all classifications and declare with us: *there is only one kind of mental illness....*"[3]

Neumann, like the present writers, conceived of a progressive and developmental tendency in mental illness; a first stage of sleeplessness, hypersensitiveness, inattention, and allied symptoms might (or might not) proceed to successive and more severe stages, perhaps on to *Verwirrtheit* (confusion) or even to *Blödsinn* (dementia). But these, he emphasized, were different stages, not different things.

---

*If a patient is poor, said Janet with tongue in cheek, he is committed to a public hospital as "psychotic"; if he can afford the luxury of a private sanitarium, he is put there with the diagnosis of "neurasthenia"; if he is wealthy enough to be isolated in his own home under constant watch of nurses and physicians he is simply an indisposed "eccentric." (Janet, Pierre. *La Force el la faiblesse psychologiques.* Paris: Maloine, 1932.) Janet devoted an entire chapter to a sharp criticism of the current psychiatric classifications. He himself distinguished only two large groups: the organic and the functional. Sometimes, he said, a car stops because the machinery is broken, sometimes because it is out of gasoline. Essentially Janet was a unitarian.

[2]Trousseau, Armand: *Clinique médicale de l'Hôtel-Dieu de Paris,* ed. 5. Paris: Baillière, 1877.

[3]Neumann, Heinrich: *Lehrbuch der Psychiatrie* Erlangen: F. Enke, 1859.

Almost contemporary with Heinrich Neumann was Hughlings Jackson, "the father of British neurology." Jackson was not only a neurologist but, in spite of his modest disavowals, he was also a psychiatrist of deep perception, although his ideas "never became part of the recognized teachings of psychiatry, even in Britain."[4] His great influence upon psychiatry was exerted, as Stengel has shown, through Freud. "The close resemblance between Jackson's and Freud's dynamic theories, which has astonished a number of writers (Jones, Grinker, M. Levin, Ey, Angel, and others), can be understood as the result of Freud's encounter with the ideas of Hughlings Jackson."

Jackson has been thus emphasized by us because as far back as 1874 he proposed two types of classification, one for practical purposes, the other for scientific purposes. "He advocated [says Stengel] the ordering of mental diseases according to the degree of the dissolution of functions, i.e. of regression, similar to what Karl Menninger has recommended more recently...."

This unitary view has been consistently supported in the twentieth century by Henri Ey[5] in a form which has been called Neo-Jacksonianism. Ey regards mental illnesses not as disease entities but as syndromes or "pathological reactions" resulting from a multiplicity of factors. He considers these to be the expression of various degrees of dissolution, in Hughlings Jackson's terms. Llopis[6] also concurs in this con-

cept and has recently contributed a history of the unitary concept.

Concerning a particular syndrome one colleague wrote:

> Much confusion arises from indecision and evasion regarding the name of the syndrome. To my mind, the following designations are more or less synonymous: atypical, prepsychosis, ego deviant, seriously deviant child, infantile anaclitic depression, preschizophrenic, autistic, symbiotic, brain-injured, incipient schizophrenia, pseudo psychosis, pseudo-neurotic psychosis, abnormal child, schizoid personality, impulse-ridden character, and oligophrenia. All are conditions of serious ego disturbance. Indeed, among the large group of nonorganic childhood intellectual retardation or so-called idiopathic mental deficiency, many are also probably symptomatic expressions of early ego maldevelopment.... Nevertheless, I favor the straightforward designation childhood schizophrenia for all these states of ego disorganization, which is the essence of schizophrenia.[7]

Blau's adjective "straightforward" is not quite the *mot juste* unless one takes the position of colleagues in Research in Schizophrenia Endowment. As an example of something really forthright, listen to this from a personal letter from the director, Stanley Dean: "Unfortunately, the public at large is unable to identify [itself] with 'mental illness' as an omnibus term, and since identification seems to be a necessary psychological concomitant to participation, I selected schizophrenia as the most

[4]Stengel, Erwin: "Hughlings Jackson's Influence in Psychiatry." *Brit. J. Psychiat.* 109:348-355, 1963.

[5]Ey, Henri: *Études Psychiatriques*, Vol. 3. Paris: DesClée de Brouwer, 1954.

[6]Llopis, Bartolomé: "La Psicosis unica." *Arch. de Neurobiol.* 17:1-39, 1954.

[7]Blau, Abram: "The Nature of Childhood Schizophrenia." *J. Am. Acad. Child Psychiat.* 1:225-235, 1962.

widely known and most compelling nosological focal point about which to rally public opinion." In other words, "schizophrenia" is used as synonymous with "mental illness." It is clear that we have the same notion, namely, that *severe* mental illness is "schizophrenia" and lesser degrees of mental illness may become greater (i.e., severe) degrees.

This idea that there is but one general category of mental illness is paradoxically corroborated by Szasz, who holds that there is no such thing at all! Mental disease is, he believes, a myth which, like all myths, had certain value and expressed a certain understanding at one time. It was derived by analogy from bodily disorders, long the province of the medical practitioner, and called disease. When the evidences of social and psychological maladjustment in individuals began to come within the purview of physicians, the word "disease" was borrowed for something acually different in nature.[8]

We disagree with Szasz on technical and epistemological grounds. We insist that there are conditions best described as mental illness. But instead of putting so much emphasis on different kinds and clinical pictures of illness, we propose to think of all forms of mental illness as being essentially the same in quality, and differing quantitatively. This is what is meant when we say that all people have mental illness of different degrees at different times, and that sometimes some are much worse, or better. And this is precisely what recent epidemiological studies have demonstrated.

For example, a very careful research project recently completed analyzed the population of a representative

sample of American people living in New York City.[9] The area was roughly 200 blocks; the population roughly 175,000. Of these, only about 32,000 (18.5 per cent) showed no symptoms of mental illness. Over 58 per cent gave evidence of mild to moderate mental illness; 23.4 per cent showed marked or severe mental illness. Bear in mind that all individuals under twenty, that is all children, and all individuals over fifty-nine, that is all older people, and all individuals of African or Puerto Rican origins were excluded from the survey. In other words, no one can say that most of the mentally ill were maladjusted adolescents (although there are plenty of them), or confused seniles, or frustrated Negroes or struggling Puerto Ricans. If the troubled individuals in these groups had also been included, the statistics would no doubt have been even more startling.

Gone forever is the notion that the mentally ill person is an exception. It is now accepted that most people have some degree of mental illness at some time, and many of them have a degree of mental illness most of the time. This really should not surprise anyone, for do not most of us have some physical illness some of the time, and some of us much of the time?

The unitary concept does not dispense with the descriptive designations. These we must have if they can be cast in a form that will not deny the essential unity of the process or obscure the understanding of the adaptation difficulties of the patient. The object of the process of diagnostication is not the collecting and sorting of pretty pebbles

[8]Szasz, Thomas: *The Myth of Mental Illness.* New York: Harper, 1961.

[9]Srole, Leo, et al.: *Mental Health in the Metropolis. The Midtown Manhattan Study.* New York: McGraw-Hill, 1962. Copyright, 1962. Blakiston Div., McGraw-Hill. Used by permission.

(although even this may be of some scientific value in large-scale epidemiological studies). It is, rather, to provide a sound basis for formulating a *treatment* program, a planned ameliorative intervention.

For this purpose current nosologies and diagnostic nomenclature are not only useless but restrictive and obstructive. *This does not mean the discarding of useful terminology or syndrome appellations.* To refer to a constellation of symptoms as constituting a schizophrenic picture is very different from referring to the individual presenting these symptoms as a victim of "schizophrenia" or as being "a schizophrenic." Some *symptoms* are by definition "schizophrenic," but no patient is. The same patient may present another syndrome tomorrow.

* * *

"Unfortunately," comments Norwood, "many physicians ... accepted [Rush's] theory and went about their professional duties imposing the heroic treatments of purging and bleeding ... to reduce 'convulsive action' by a process of 'depletion.' "[10]

Here the weakness was not so much

[10]Rush, Benjamin: "Lectures on the Practice of Physic: In Shyrock, R. H.: *The Development of Modern Medicine.* New York: Knopf, 1947; also, Norwood, W.F.: "Medicine in the Era of the American Revolution." *Int. Rec. Med.* 171:391-407, 1958.

the unitary concept of illness proposed, unsound as that was, but the illogical conclusion regarding the indicated therapy. If our efforts to overhaul the concept of mental illness were to result in some unitary blanket therapy, it would be a most deplorable and paradoxical outcome. But it is unlikely.

But, in proposing such a unifying principle for psychiatric nosography, we shall not forget, either, the advice of Alfred North Whitehead: "Distrust the jaunty assurances with which every age prides itself that it at last has hit upon the ultimate concepts in which all that happens can be formulated. The aim of science is to seek the simplest explanations of complex facts. We are apt to fall into the error of thinking that the facts are simple because simplicity is the goal of our quest. The guiding motto in the life of every natural philosopher should be 'Seek simplicity and distrust it.' "[11]

We shall take this advice — both parts of it. We shall strive for greater simplicity, greater clarity, greater consistency, greater usefulness. But while offering our proposals and formulations for what they may prove to be worth, we shall ourselves not cease to question them nor to listen earnestly to the objections of our critics.

[11]Whitehead, Alfred North: *The Concept of Nature.* New York: Macmillian, 1926.

TRENDS IN MENTAL DISORDER*
Nathan Glazer

The various social sciences, like all disciplines possessing an individual history and a corps of specially trained practitioners, ask their own questions, and answer them in their own way. It is not often that the questions they ask are the layman's questions, or the answers they give ones that would satisfy a layman. When they ask a question which has served for decades as one of the common counters in discussions of modern life, and at the same time answer it—that is news.

It is in just this sense that a slim volume recently published by the Free Press (*Psychosis and Civilization*, by Herbert Goldhamer and Alexander Marshall, 126 pp., $4.00) is news. The question it asks is: is it true that the frequency of mental disorder—specifically, of psychoses—has increased over the past hundred years? We know that enormous changes have occurred in the way we live in these hundred years. Many more of us live in cities, the cities are larger and noisier, we travel greater

*Reprinted with permission of author and publisher, from *Commentary*, 16, December, 1953, 587-590; copyright © 1953 by the American-Jewish Committee. The author acknowledges his debt to research by Herbert Goldhamer and Alexander Marshall.

distances to and from work, are subject in larger measure to the tyranny of the clock and the need to oblige a superior —and in view of all this, it would appear a truism to assert that man, subjected to an increasingly inhuman (or at any rate nonhuman) environment, increasingly breaks down under the strain. And indeed, all around us are huge installations which we know house many thousands of the mentally disordered, and the budgets of state governments groan under the pressure of maintaining them and building more. Surely all this, if not new, is far more characteristic of our present-day lives than of life a hundred years ago. But *are* we sure?

This would seem to be a question on which we cannot achieve certainty. For it does not appear very likely that we could find statistics for the 1840's and 1850's which would enable us to answer such a question. Previous studies had, indeed, not gone back very far —hence it was no surprise to find that some of them had discovered no change in the frequency of mental disease. The one study that went furthest back (to 1881, in Massachusetts) did show a rather large increase.

Goldhamer and Marshall decided to go back even further, and in effect constructed their own statistics on the basis of data from the state of Massachusetts beginning with the year 1840. At that time, there were only three institutions in the state devoted specifically to the insane—a private hospital in Boston, established in 1818 (McLean), the Worcester Hospital, then only eight years old, and the South Boston Hospital, then only one year old. In addition, the insane were received in state and town almshouses and in the prisons.

In view of these limited facilities, could the data on the insane be very complete or reliable? Goldhamer and Marshall argue that they were, and very effectively. Quoting from the early reports of the asylums and their superintendents, they demonstrate, for example, that a very clear distinction was made between the psychotic (then called "lunatics") and the mentally defective (then called "idiots"). The latter were almost entirely excluded from the limited places available in the asylums. In the same way, those suffering from epilepsy without psychosis and alcoholism without psychosis were also clearly demarcated from the psychotic, and for the most part excluded. The detailed descriptions of the disorders from which the lunatics of the 1840's and 1850's suffered indicate clearly that we deal with the very same diseases—even though "mania," "melancholia," "dementia," and "monomania of suspicion" had to make do, in those days, to describe what we currently call "manic-depressive psychosis," "schizophrenia," and "paranoia." The authors carefully exclude the possibilities of error related to the readmission of patients (all of the figures quoted here refer to first admissions), or to the chance that the mentally ill of Massachusetts went out of the state for treatment (not likely, in view of the fact that Massachusetts

then—as now—had facilities for the insane as good or better than any other state in the union), or to the fact that the hospitals of Massachusetts contained out-of-state patients (they did, but the record-keeping was excellent, and these can be excluded).

In short, with a most exemplary and remarkable care and precision, the authors of this study establish rates for the frequency of admission for psychosis in Massachusetts for the years 1840 to 1885, rates that must be very close to the true ones and which in any case will not be easily improved upon.

The rates thus established rise from 41 per 100,000 for 1840-45 to 58 per 100,000 in 1880-84. (This rise is undoubtedly a product of the increase in facilities during the period.) These rates seem at first glance much lower than the rate of admissions in 1940: the 1940 admission rate, applied to a population with the age structure of that of the 1840's, would give a rate today of 85 per 100,000, and applied to the population of the 1880's, 91 per 100,000.

However, when one breaks down these over-all rates of admission to examine the rate for each age group, a remarkable and most meaningful difference in the pattern of admissions appears. The 1940 rate rises rapidly for the ages from ten to about thirty, then is about the same for those aged from thirty to fifty, then begins to rise rapidly again, to become very high for the old. In the 19th century, we find the same rise in the rate of admissions for the young, the same plateau between the ages of thirty and fifty, and then a *drop* in the rate of admissions past the age of fifty. *The differences between the 19th-century period and our own day are created entirely by the large number of admissions for psychoses of those older than fifty today. Up to the age of fifty, the rates a hundred years ago and today are roughly the same.* (As we shall see later, there is a technical reason having to do with change in admissions practices that accounts for the rise in the over-fifty group.)

It seems almost inconceivable that this should be the case. Even if there has been no real increase in the frequency of psychosis, one would expect a great increase in the number of hospitalized psychotics. For, comparing the situation today with that in even as late a year as 1885, we find that facilities are much more plentiful and easily available, that the popular attitude toward hospitalization for mental disease is much more favorable, that nonpsychotic disorders such as alcoholism, idiocy, and even psychoneuroses are increasingly dealt with in mental hospitals.

Yet, no matter what our bases of comparison, the frequency of psychosis in the middle of the 19th century is not less than it is today. The earliest rates on record for Massachusetts, for 1840-44, when, as we have indicated, there were few facilities and those only in existence a few years, exceed, for ages thirty to sixty, those for the state of Maine in 1940. And the admission rates for psychosis in Suffolk County—that is, Boston—were in 1875-79 higher than they were in New York City in 1929-31, for all ages up to fifty-five! Even as early as 1840-45, the Suffolk County rate was higher than the New York City rate for the age group forty to sixty. A comparison of the rates in 1885 and 1930 "reveals that the male 1885 rate for the ... age group 20-40 slightly exceeds that of the contemporary period and that the 1885 female rates for ages 20-50 exceed the corresponding 1930 figures."

Nor do we deal with an exceptional situation when we deal with Massachusetts. The authors carefully consider any factor that might have tended to lead to a higher frequency of mental disease in Massachusetts in the period from 1840 to 1885. Thus, they examine the bearing of the proportion of foreign-born, which was low at the beginning of this period (5 per cent in 1840) but rose rapidly, with the Irish immigration, to become quite high by the end of the period (1860, 21 per cent; 1870, 24 per cent; 1880, 25 per cent). However, this proportion of foreign-born has since been fairly constant (it was also 25 per cent in 1930) and could therefore not have been the cause of a peculiarly high rate of psychosis in the middle of the 19th century.

Nor is it the fact that Massachusetts was, among all the states of the union, particularly prone to mental disorder in the middle of the 19th century. Wherever we can find figures, we will find about as much psychosis—that is to say, admissions to hospitals for psychosis—in the 19th century as in the 20th. Thus, Oneida County, in New York State, had easy access to a state hospital established in Utica in 1843. The rate of admissions from 1843 to 1865 for the age group from thirty to fifty is only slightly below the 1930 New York State rate (adjusted for the rural-urban proportion that prevailed in Oneida County during this period). Perhaps most remarkable of all is the case of Fayette County, Kentucky, which had access to the hospital in Lexington, and for which we have figures from as early as 1824. For the years 1824 to 1842 (at the earlier date, Kentucky was scarcely out of the frontier stage), this county "had [a] higher total admission rate in the central age groups than ... Kentucky ... today."

Even before we begin to try to understand why there should have been as much psychosis in the middle years of the 19th century as there is today, we have to consider how it was physically possible for admissions for psychosis to the few institutions that existed in the 1840's to give a rate, even if only for certain age groups, equal to that of today.

There are a number of factors pointed to by Goldhamer and Marshall that are relevant. The first institutions opened specifically for the insane were established for those who created the worst problems for society—thus, the Worcester Hospital in Massachusetts was specifically limited to the "violent and furious." Those psychoses associated with senility, which are responsible for such a large proportion of the inmates of present-day mental hospitals, were in effect ruled out by this definition, and it was only much later that such persons were taken into hospitals. Idiots and those of subnormal intelligence were also ruled out. In effect, these hospitals were established for persons afflicted with manic-depressive psychosis, paranoia, and some of the forms of schizophrenia. These are diseases which characteristically strike young people and people in the middle years of life. It was such people who filled the new hospitals established in the 30's, 40's, and 50's of the 19th century. The psychoses of senility, which are responsible for the presence of most of the aged in our hospitals, and subnormal intelligence, which is responsible for a large proportion of the young, were both managed within the family. And since families were larger, and their living quarters also larger, there was no great tendency to hospitalize these unfortunates.

Consequently, Goldhamer and Marshall argue that even the great increase which has taken place in the last century in the proportions of old people hospitalized for psychosis is an increase only in hospitalization, not in actual frequency. Sufferers from the psychoses of senility, they argue, quoting contemporary records and the advice of leading doctors of the time, remained at home, and there was little pressure to get them into hospitals.

Similarly, the much smaller increase that has occurred in the numbers of young people (under twenty) hospitalized does not indicate a real increase of psychosis in this group, for a very large proportion of those in this age group today are hospitalized for nonpsychotic conditions.

In other words: even where we see an apparent increase over a hundred years ago in the numbers in our state hospitals today (that is, among those under twenty and over fifty), the increase can be explained by the expansion of facilities.

What are we to conclude from all this? The authors of this study are extremely cautious. All we can conclude, they say, is that there has been no great change in the conditions causing psychosis in this country in the past hundred years. Possibly if we could carry our study back another hundred years we would find a great change; possibly by 1840 those conditions of modern life that people believe lead to mental disorder had already been established. But it is not likely that any statistical studies can carry us back before 1840. It is also possible there has been a great increase in the frequency of neurosis; but this is a difficult matter to test statistically.

Another conclusion, they point out, is compatible with these results: that is, that in psychosis we deal with a condition which is independent of environmental circumstances, a condition dependent on heredity or physiological aberration, which, like some physical diseases, strikes a certain proportion of the population. The authors refer to a recent study of the frequency of psychosis on the Danish island of Bornholm, an island inhabited principally by farmers and fishermen. It turns out that the frequency of psychosis there is roughly what we find in New York State. Were it not for this finding, one might be tempted to suggest that the trauma of leaving one's home and emerging across the ocean had affected Americans in general so deeply that the same proportion of psychosis existed among frontiersmen as among city dwellers. However, the Bornholm study shows us that even where the population has deep roots, we find the same measure of mental disorder as in America.

We do not yet know enough to be able to do more than speculate as to the implications of these findings. We already know enough, however, to lay to rest one of the most popular clichés of our culture, one that we run into again and again in sociological, political, and religious writing, and which has often served as the basis for very lazy conclusions. We may hope that the Goldhamer and Marshall study will be only the first of a series analyzing the records of different countries, and different times.

INNOVATIONS IN MENTAL HOSPITAL CONCEPTS AND PRACTICE

Steve Pratt and Jay Tooley

Mislabeled "Mental Hospitals," What are They?

Who Are the Real Clients of These Institutions?[1] Society makes short shrift of people in trouble and troubled people once they become too troublesome for others. A vast network of prisons stretches across our country supplemented by a secondary vast network of some 500 eleemosynary establishments quaintly mislabeled "hospitals-of-the-mind," in which thousands of citizens, close to a million on any given day, mislabeled "mentally ill," are incarcerated. With just a touch of tautology but quite operationally, many researchers *define* what they label "mental illness"

Reprinted with the permission of the authors. Portions of this material, as an invited paper, were presented as part of the symposium, INNOVATIONS IN CLINICAL PSYCHOLOGY at the Annual Convention of the New York State Psychological Association 13 May 1962.

[1]Throughout we will rigorously replace the misnomer "mental hospital" with such terms as "Institute-For-Living," or just "Institute," or this special use of variably used generic terms, "institution," "establishment," etc. Note the changes: Boston Psychopathic Hospital to Massachusetts Mental Health Center, State Hospital to the Mental Health Institute, Clarinda, Iowa; also, the Institute of Living, Hartford, Connecticut.

as the state of being "hospitalized" in what they metaphorically call a "mental hospital" (Cummings and Cummings, 1957). These establishments from the societal level serve neither much nor well their hapless inmates, but certainly serve with drastic "effectiveness" their *true clients*—the social agencies[2] and gatekeepers of control, correction, and "benevolence"—those who have need to put troublesome people away (Clausen & Yarrow, 1955; Goffman, 1961).

Or for a moment take the establishment mislabeled "mental hospital" as a most strange Kafka-like out-of-this-world madhouse where we see the inmates as troubled people either getting out or getting worse but where the staff can be observed to be psychotic, suffering from, and acting out in terms of blatant though not too well systematized delusions. Delusions that include a schizophrenic language in which figures of speech are taken for real; a

[2]State tables of organization under Boards of Health and/or Social Welfare frequently list a Department of "Benevolent and Correctional Institutions," under which are subsumed prisons, reformatories, schools for the blind, institutes for retardates, "mental hospitals," etc.

language based on *metaphors* conceived, accepted, talked about, and acted upon *as if* things, people, and processes (psychological disorders) were, entirely, exactly what they're not: namely sick patients and disease entities. You wake up as an inmate and whatever your troubles are, though you may have never been healthier or more not-sick in your life — you're told you're *sick* and if you deny it you lack insight and you're seriously sick. In any case you're rendered by the staff into something like (yet unlike) both prisoner and patient. You find you must go along with this crazy prisoner-patient role, knuckle under, say uncle, learn the ropes, and if you've a gift for gab learn the staff's schizophrenic language and how to play their games — ritualistic charades euphemistically titled Admissions, Progress Evaluation, and Discharge Meetings, Diagnostic and Appraisal Staffings, *ad absurdum.*

Institutional Structure: Caste, Class, Segregation and Incarceration. Or again, consider the institution mislabeled "mental hospital": topologically, if not geographically, isolated from community, separated into two closed mutually exclusive social systems; the institute-as-a-community itself, fractionated into conflicted subgroups; inmate-staff dichotomy *caste* system; clinical versus "nonclinical," professional versus "nonprofessional"; inflexible artificial class hierarchies within both staff and inmate subcommunities. *Caste and Class in a Southern Town* transposed to *Caste and Class in a State "Hospital."* In this grotesque anthill the staff are drones involved in tireless routines, overtly to treat and serve the inmates, but covertly operating to maintain the psychotic functional autonomy of professional roles and status, to retain possession of the prerogatives of a misplaced public

mandate. The inmates in turn constitute sociologically the most esoteric leisure class in history. No conceptual innovator has yet written this *Theory of a Leisure Class* — or *caste* (Veblen, 1899). Across the country, these detention institutes are based on the authoritarian bureaucratic medical-surgical-intrapsychic-analytic mixed model; are organized and structured to preclude both *full* participation and non-psychotic participation of staff, inmates and townspeople in meaningful, actualizing and corrective interpersonal transactions.

Where are we as diagnosticians when it comes to delineating and dealing with a few of these problems? Where are the innovators of conceptualization, of trying-out-and-testing research, of practice and programing?

Radical Innovations: Looking Backward and Sidewise Simultaneously

(Some concepts and their derivative "corrective" models).[3] Back to radical innovations. These could be looked at as having been or being good or bad, positive or negative, horrendous or hopeful. Also one could consider any number of categories of innovations. We'll arbitrarily choose three: (1) innovations in conceptualization, (2) innovations in investigative, demonstrative, or evaluative research, (3) innovations in application, practice, or programing.

How one loads the regression equation of individual and/or cultural determinants will depend on one's theory of the role of the individual in history-

[3]For further discussion of concepts and their derivative institutional models, refer to "Of Myth and Models: An Agonizing Reappraisal" (Pratt, 1961) and "How Differing Concepts of the Nature of *Psychological Disorders* Lead to Differing Practices in the Hospital, the Clinic, and the Community" (Pratt & Tooley, 1962).

making. We'll leave this chicken or the egg, conceptualizer versus *Zeitgeist* question up to personal bias. Let's take an oversimplified, quick, backward glance.

The 14th century concept of psychological disorder as *involuntary* possession by the devil and evil spirits first resulted in relatively benign exorcism by prayer, propitiation of father-god figures, and mild penance. This is analogous to the modern "mental illness" misconception of psychological disorders as involuntary possession by some alleged disease entity or hypostatized intrapsychic agent or entelechy. This concept, thanks to a maiden, Dymphna, with an overdetermined abience for incest, was conducive to the Gheel-community approach that was operationally several thousand years ahead of our present state of reverse. None of our contemporary innovations are quite this radical; not much of a tranquilizer for those equating history with progress.

The 15th century brought the Inquisition and the concept of personal culpability for psychological disorders, still seen as possession by Satan but through guilt of voluntary consort—a persuasive introduction of the concept of individual responsibility that is staging a modern comeback via Mowrer's (1960, 1961) "sin versus sickness" and the existentialist "responsibility of choice" (May, 1958). Enthusiastic Inquisitionists applied an earlier form of operant conditioning with schedules of reinforcement by submersion, the screws, the stretches and more drastic physiotherapy interventions culminating in one trial extinction at the stake (Lea, 1961).

Under the impetus of the humanistic egalitarian climate of the American (1775-1783) and particularly the French (1789-1799) Revolutions, the concept of treating the psychologically disordered as human beings was actualized in 1792 by Pinel's dramatic chain-chopping at Bicêtre; those inhospitable dungeons probably rivaled our modern so-called "mental hospitals" in making troubled people mad.

This liberal humanistic value system concept of man carried over in England and the States as the "moral" (meaning psychological with transcendentalist overtones) "treatment" approach (circa 1820-1860); its innovators were enlightened, philosophically and politically sophisticated men, from Benjamin Rush and the Tuke family to Samuel Woodward, Eli Todd, Luther Bell, Isaac Ray, et al. The small *retreat* or *asylum* developed around this concept, was based on respect for the person, encouragement of self-respect and self-reliance; the corrective medium being ego-enhancing interpersonal transactions incident to productive activities, work, play, arts and crafts. Bockoven (1956, 1957) has done a brilliant and scholarly job of bringing to life this brief but far-ahead-of-us period. This radical innovation was *done in* because its sustaining concept was *done in* by the growth of the Industrial Revolution, dehumanization of the foreign worker, and take-over by 19th century scientism with its mechanistic physicalism.

This is one of the most graphic and tragic examples provided by history of the ironic fact that nothing blocks scientific or social progress more than the substantive concepts, theories, and models, held by scientists themselves at any given point in history (Barber, 1960; Eiduson, 1962; Kilpatrick, 1952; Russell, 1961):

> ... organized medical science, in step with early 19th century "objective" physical scientism, and exercised over re-

ports of brain lesions, declared that "insanity" was entirely due to disease of the brain.... Distortions of "Social Darwinism" relegated "insanity" to irreversible degenerative brain disease, congenital and hereditary defects reflecting constitutional biological inferiority. The protestant individualism ethic became "rugged individualism" with the eugenicist implication that to treat or save the insane was useless if not immoral (paraphrased from Bockoven, 1957). Thus in brief was born the *custodial* mental hospital model. From then till today, ranging from inadequate (inhuman) custodial or "snake pit" to relatively adequate (humane) custodial, this model has been *modal* (Joint Commission on Mental Illness and Health, 1961)... (Pratt, 1961, p. 6).

The medical-surgical-nursing model found itself partner to another comedy of errors when it was infiltrated with intrapsychic analytic concepts which it had to assimilate or contain. Physicians in name, to their embarrassment, found themselves obligated to make like Freudian *psychologists* (psychiatrists if you prefer) in theory and practice; expected, oddly enough, to employ *psychological* procedures in the correction of *psychological* disorders but still within the dyadic doctor-patient paradigm; again, a "narrow-clinical" approach of "experts" doing specialized things *to* passive-receptive inmates mislabeled "patients."

So-called *social psychiatry* conceptualized corrective transactions in terms of interpersonal relationships dealing the death blow to one-to-one dyadic paradigms whether derived from organic or analytic constructs. Clinical staff of all professions were cast into new roles and operationally, though

never officially, the institutions became *multidisciplinary* organizations. This metamorphosis throws into ultimate strain the monocratic medical line-authority structure which now truly is shot through with the seeds of its own destruction.

Under the impetus of a sociopsychological approach to psychological disorders and the corrective facility, transactional boundaries are inexorably pushed beyond the institution itself into the community. Thus, qualitatively new parameters appear as we move into a variety of offshoots or quasi social psychiatry models: from the *"Institution-as-a-Small Society"* model—intramural organization considered in terms of extramural society (Caudill, Redlich, Gilmore, & Brody, 1952); to the *"Therapeutic-Community"* model—extramural community as model for intramural community (Jones, 1953; Rapoport, 1961); to the *"Open-Door"* (revolving door?) model—toward barrier reduction of intramural-extramural boundaries; and finally to our *"Actualizing-Transactional-Field"* model that's not yet materialized.

Radical Innovations: Contemporary

How can we get the most out of a critical consideration of contemporary innovations? We could say that few really qualify as genotypic or radical. Or we could note that the few that do explicitly challenge, or threaten to comprehensively change status quo, somehow fall ill of a strange sociological malady, then, after such promise, drop dead somewhere between concept, research, and application. Psychologists must ask what germs cause this fatal disease and what can be done to prevent it.

Even a summary of the procedure, findings, and implications of a single current study representing radical innovation (e.g. Ellsworth's "aide" as social-therapist program) would take more space than is allotted. Sheer number of references precludes any kind of representative, much less comprehensive, enumeration of studies. In a recently published and already "out-of-print" monograph (Pratt, Scott, Treesh, Khanna, Lesher, Khanna, Gardiner, & Wright, 1960), we made a preliminary survey of current literature and came up with a *preliminary* bibliography of more than 1200 relevant references.

With apologies then to the many deserving "radicals" unavoidably left out, we'll cite a couple *kinds* of innovation, hoping to trigger interest areas for open inquiry. Again these may involve concepts; demonstration and research; or put-into-practice techniques and programs.

Our Attitude Toward "Attitude Therapy." Never conceptually challenging monocratic medical model or intrapsychic "sick" role, attitude therapy is a monument to faith in the Stanislavsky school of Method Acting and thus, though a creature of traditional psychiatric schools such as the Menninger Foundation, it might still charitably be designated radical. Through an extension of the psychiatrist's role by *prescription* of staff attitude, it operationally does involve so-called "nonexperts," those mislabeled "aides," in ostensibly corrective interactions. But substituting across the board *prescribed* attitudes for natural staff reactions means the inmate faces ten or twenty actors' versions of such ambiguities as: "kind firmness," "matter of fact," "passive" versus "active friendliness," "watchfulness," "indulgence," etc. No one reacts naturally

or realistically, thus, to the extent it's successfully carried out, the staff (from the inmate's standpoint) behaves psychotically. Fortunately in practice the acting doesn't much come off—it succeeds to the extent it fails—and hopefully staff-inmate transactions may be increased.

It's obvious that anyone with a modicum of common sense can spot such shenanigans as nothing but amateur play-acting of less than Oscar quality (Grinker, 1961; Vitale, 1961a). Or as social-therapist, see yourself walking through a ward encountering fifteen inmates; could you execute fifteen shifts in attitudinal role in that many minutes? A fascinating experimental study (Carson, 1962) indicates no congruence between conception of the attitude as prescribed by the psychiatrist and as perceived by ward staff trained over a period of years in its meaning and expression. Furthermore it was found the supposed significant variety of attitudes prescribed boiled down on the semantic differential to two: "friendly persuasive" versus a power-oriented cluster, as in "kind firmness." It can be concluded that "attitude prescription" is not too harmful because it can't be followed and isn't carried out anyway (Ellsworth, 1962).

Conceptualizing the Institution as a "Therapeutic Community." Excellent reviews of the literature on the introduction of the much touted "therapeutic-community" concept within a variety of institutional settings have recently become available (Jones, 1961; Rapoport, 1961; Vitale, 1961b)—Vitale's being the best to date though intended more as a compendium than a critique. The concept having been sufficiently germinal to generate considerable enthusiasm and rather widely scattered adoption

(Barton, Farrell, Lenehan, & McLaughlin, 1961; Bellak, 1961; Hargreaves, 1957; Hyde, 1957; Meijering, 1957), we would like to make a cautionary comment, for others to check and hopefully to disconfirm. We'll do this even though to question, in current institutional circles, whatever the word-symbol "therapeutic community" is supposed to represent is out of the question. As Jay Jackson (1961, p. 5) says, "to be against it is like being for Sin and against Mother." Having observed it in operation under its originator at Salem, Oregon, and recently (1964) at its birthplace, Henderson Hospital, London, we would like to push its possibilities for radical revision of inmate and staff roles but mention again that somehow despite slogans of "democratization," "permissiveness," and "communal living" an autocratic, dear-doctor-Karl type atmosphere still hangs heavy over the whole procedure. And a second look, as it's practiced, raises questions of benevolent paternalism, concealed authoritarianism, pseudo-participation in decision-making and potentialities that somehow can't break through, but remain contained within, the medical-nursing-monocratic structure. You still expect the nurses, if not the psychiatric residents, to jump to attention when the master walks in to take over; "patient conducted" groups are explicitly labeled "the doctor's group" and note the daily staff "post-mortems" (sic), excluding inmates, on these and the other groups.

Conceptualization of Radically New Roles: Staff, Inmate or Client, Community Citizens. Studies in this area, while sometimes conceptualzed within a somewhat narrow frame-of-reference and not overtly challenging

the outer shell of medical monocratic bureaucratic models nevertheless strike (we'll not say bore), directly from within, at the core of the problem. And were they carried out in practice to their logical ends, would certainly culminate in radical total transformation of institutional structure. Unfortunately, vested professional interests wise-up to this threatening possibility (Joint Commission on Mental Illness and Health, 1961, p. 169) before things get out of hand. We'll cite three outstanding current examples, each methodologically relatively rigorous, and conceptually (except for a few theoretical furbelows) simple and tellingly direct.

Ellsworth (1961), in a three-year study recently completed at the Fort Meade, South Dakota Veterans Administration Hospital, tosses out traditional ritualistic professional clinical roles and explicitly has "psychiatric aides" take over as social-therapists, jacking up staff time spent in programed interaction with inmates from 15 to 85 per cent. The proportion of inmates classified as "institutionalized" "hard core schizophrenics" able to stay discharged after 30 months, was increased from 3 to 53 per cent. This research and demonstration required turning over the corrective program from the "experts" to the "aides" (thus no longer anybody's *aides*). The research was completed and final results will soon be reported; will the institution take up these new techniques, or how long till its originator leaves and the program folds up? Why will this occur?[4]

In the Ellsworth Study much of the staff-inmate interaction rationale was based on modifications of so-called

[4]As predicted, he subsequently left and the program folded.

"intrusion therapy" (Des Lauriers, 1955) that has been researched with ward groups at several other institutions; pioneered by Appleby (1961) and currently by Colarelli (1961) both at Kansas State Institutions. How much "intrusion theory" per se adds beyond rationale for special types of increased interpersonal transactions is open to question.

Sanders (1959, 1960) at Philadelphia State Hospital in an extended and elaborately designed research project not only studied the results of increased staff-inmate interaction but assessed the differential effects of three *levels of interaction*. A three year follow-up is being conducted to determine the long-term effects of differing intensities of corrective social-interaction on both status of psychological disorder and social adjustment (Sanders, & Weinman, 1961).

Far more radical than revision in staff roles, per se, or staff-inmate interaction levels, are revisions in inmate roles, which today are characteristically a combination of passive-receptive "sick role" and punitive, prisoner role. In both research and theoretical papers we have described invocation of the "sick role" as the major disaster derived from the medical-monocratic institutional model (DeLange, 1961; Pratt, 1961; Pratt & DeLange, 1962; Pratt & Tooley, 1962; Pratt et al., 1960).

Many of the papers discussing so-called "patient government" programs have unlimited potential in the context of radically revised inmate role, but are not well researched and as practiced are subject to the same kind of criticism as most "therapeutic community" endeavors—they're not what they say they are.

Perhaps the most important and experimentally sound series of research studies involving new group-process roles for inmates is that of Fairweather and his colleagues (1961) begun at Perry Point VA and continuing at Palo Alto VA. Problem-solving, decision-making, initiative, and dependency versus responsibility, were investigated in a variety of institutional situations. Staff members were trained in the system to abandon their own traditionally established role behaviors. Inmate-to-inmate interaction, involving groups of long-time "institutionalized" inmates, superseded staff-inmate interaction. The most radical aspect of the studies deals with corrective programing involving *cohesed task groups* of inmates in which inmate leadership replaces authoritarian staff direction, and staff is relegated to the subordinate role of on-call consultants to inmate group leaders. Significantly, inmate-led groups were found to function more effectively than staff-led groups.

The next phase of this provocative project will attempt to bridge the transitional gap between institution and community through the placement of cohesed task groups in the community. These role conceptualizations, as they apply to the intramural phase of Fairweather's studies, have survived through the research stage. Should we ask now or wait and see what political-social, professional vested interest, and refractory institutional-structure vectors will first contain and then abolish these innovations somewhere between researching and putting into institutional practice? Are we concerned with the parameters that will inexorably preclude fruition of these findings? As a popular TV comedian rhetorically demands, *"Why not?"*

A mountain of material is available on things going on with about-to-be-discharged, recently discharged, or ex-inmates, all of which, while often promising forward steps, represent transitions short of any radical transformation. These activities involve member-employee programs, pre-discharge units, and a variety of community-based programs variously labeled and mislabeled "aftercare clinics," "day hospitals," "night hospitals," "rehabilitation services," "public health nursing services," "foster family care," "halfway houses" (hopefully of good rather than ill repute), "convalescent nursing homes" (where the elderly unwanted can be sent for vegetation and dying), "social clubs," vocational service and training rehabilitation centers including "sheltered workshops." While all such extramural programs should, if anything, overshadow intramural endeavors, they are generally poorly integrated, inadequate to the need, and conceptually in a state of hopeless confusion. They have been critically reviewed elsewhere (Gorman, 1962; Mental Hospital Institute, 1960; Pratt et al., 1960; Schwartz and Schwartz, 1964; Vitale, 1961a).

In terms of new roles for extramural community citizens, related to corrective programing, nothing radical has been introduced with perhaps a few exceptions such as: the college student volunteer program; the investigation and exploitation of *work* within the corrective transactional-field (Gurel, 1961; Jones, 1960; Nosow & Form, 1961; Umbarger, 1960; Wayne, 1961); and the organization of collaborative community-institution planning and action committees composed of staff (inmates conspicuously absent) and citizens representing a wide range of civic organizations, e.g. church, school, veterans, farm cooperatives, BPW, HDU, 4-H, Chamber of Commerce, etc. (Pratt, Reed & Arnold, 1960).

Actualizing Transactional-Field Conceptualization[5]

Corrective interventions to date still primarily fall or are forced within the ubiquitous medical model representing a "narrow clinical" approach essentially limited to the clinical "experts" doing more kinds of things to more kinds of inmates and delegating (via prescription) more of these things to more staff members (as "ancillary," "adjuvant," "paramedical technicians"). On the positive side this has at least brought into the institution a wider multidisciplinary range of clinical *expertise* and has involved in corrective procedures more "nonprofessional" and even some "nonclinical" personnel, e.g. business, engineering, dietary, maintenance, craftsmen, and secretarial.

We want to contrast the narrow clinical-expert approach (however fancied-up with pseudoradical innovations) with what we've called the "actualizing transactional-field approach." Here the basic or irreducible field configuration is conceptualized as a function of the organizational structuring of the sets of person-situation and interpersonal transactions (present or possible) *within* and *between* staff-community, inmate-community, and extramural-

[5]In terms of philosophical, theoretical and methodological sources for our transactional-field approach, we've drawn primarily on the work of Dewey & Bentley (1949; Dewey, 1922); Cantril, Ames, Hastorf & Ittelson (1952); Lewin (1936, 1948, 1951); and Sullivan (1947). This approach developed out of our action-research program and conceptualizations originally presented in *The Mental Hospital and the "Treatment-Field"* (Pratt et al., 1960) and is applied to mislabeled "mental hospitals" reconceptualized as "Institutes-for-Living" in "Contract Psychology and the Actualizing Transactional Field" (Pratt & Tooley, 1964). Both Grinker (1961) and Berne (1961) have employed a transactional treatment paradigm but in an incomplete and reductionistic form (Tooley & Pratt, 1963).

communities (i.e., $ATF = f \dfrac{I_c}{S_c \rightleftarrows E_c}$) The direction is toward *full* staff-inmate-extramural community participation (via radically revised roles) in programing designed (to be tried out and evaluated) to effect correction of psychological disorders, and to facilitate optimal self-actualization.

In this idealized "actualizing trans-actional-field" model the monocratic line-authority form of institutional administration would be replaced by a *multidisciplinary* (social-behavioral sciences), *functionally representative* organization, the executive director and administrative board of which would not be the exclusive representative of any one profession. In a forthcoming monograph, *Alice in Blunderland,* facetiously subtitled *The Psychologist in the "Mental Hospital"* (Pratt, Tooley, De-Lange, 1964), we've delineated in turn happy versus hapless implications, for the role of the psychologist of our "actualizing-field" model versus others. This heuristic model puts in focus, but keeps in proportion, the wider complex of both intramural and extramural determinants. Despite some inroads by conceptualization, research and demonstration having radical implications for role and structure, present institutional goals neither envision, permit, nor plan for *full* identification and involvement of all employees (clinical at *all* levels, and *all* "nonclinical") and of the inmates themselves as conscious participants (as opposed to passive-recipients) in the actualizing transactional program.

In our conception of idealized "Institutes-For-Living," inmates would become the *real clients* of a staff serving as their consultants and technicians; the staff being catalysts facilitating clients' problem-solving and learning from each other in collaboration with extramural communities.

Radical Innovations: Facilitators and Obstructors

Why are contemporary innovations of conceptualization, research and programing so timorous, so half-hearted (more descriptive anatomical metaphors come to mind) and why so rarely implemented or put fully into practice? In terms of radical-genotypic concepts why haven't these institutions been turned upside-down client-staffwise (Belknap, 1956), turned inside-out community-integrationwise, taken out of the hands of the agencies and gatekeepers of detention and control to be turned over to their appropriate clients, the citizens of the communities they purportedly serve?[6]

What historical determinants perpetuate and maintain these monolithic freaks of history with such intransigence —isolated, caste-class, role-ossified, psychotic, iatrogenic niduses? For some

[6]". . . it is the people in the communities and the state as a whole who are actually responsible for the operation of our hospitals.

"State mental hospitals are not run by the superintendents or the psychiatrists. They are the responsibility of the state and its citizens. The state long ago undertook the care of the mentally ill. It hires technical experts—the psychiatrists—to carry out this job. But the responsibility remains with the citizens" (Bloomberg, 1960, p. 36).

"Under our present laws, the responsibility of running mental hospitals rests with the physician. Whether medical or psychiatric training equips one to run a social institution such as a mental hospital in the most effective and therapeutic manner should be a question to be explored rather than an assumption that is taken for granted. *Even if the psychiatrist should continue to play the controlling role in the mental hospital, the public should not permit him to restrict other professions from making their maximum contribution to the restoration of the human condition of mental patients.*" (Joint Commission on Mental Illness and Health, 1961, pp. 191-192, italics ours).

totally inexplicable reason not even the count-them-on-your-fingers few "radical innovators" raise this key question: Why *haven't* some (or at least one!) of these institutions been totally and unrecognizably transformed?

Many stimulating studies deal with these institutions[7] as social systems, exploring their corrective contribution or their contribution to increasing and initiating psychological disorders, driving inmates crazy or crazier. A few such studies deal with organizational structure at the level of the total institution but most are restricted to the special social structure at the so-called ward level. Virtually no studies are aimed at the total institution within cultural-context structure. Only this wider approach could ever possibly bring into view the philosophical, political, socioeconomic, professionalistic, parameters that we have to get at to answer the key question: Why no really radical innovations and what forces obstruct or preclude such innovations?

All of the ward level studies, however imaginative and suggestive, are still contained within, and thus accommodated to, the monocratic medical model. Those that are truly radical in regard to corrective scheme, staff-inmate roles, power-structure and decision-making prerogatives, soon break into open conflict to be quickly "readjusted" or squelched as disturbing to proper "role complementarity" and "institutional equilibrium," usually in the name of medical responsibility. Ward level studies, reductionisticly misconstrue ward microcosm for total institution macrocosm and fail to cope

[7]Several hundred references relevant at the three "levels-of-organization" (i.e. ward, institution, and institutions-in-cultural-context) are available in *The Mental Hospital and the Treatment-Field* (Pratt et al., 1960).

with the institution within its relevant cultural context.

In dealing with the total institutional structure we find "conservative" (reactionary?) theorists using industrial-military bureaucratic models and systems-analysis to rationalize monocratic medical line-authority structure as essential to Parsonian "equilibrium" (Cumming & Cumming, 1956; Henry, 1954). Against this, the painfully few "liberal" theorists (not "radical" because they all stop short of the crux of the matter) argue the partial or total incompatability of the bureaucratic structure model with the goals of this particular kind of institution (Belknap, 1956; Blau, 1956; Etzioni, 1960; Kahne, 1959; Merton, 1950; Solomon, 1957). The currently popular, vehemently espoused, bureaucratic model begs for trenchant criticism in terms of intrinsic characteristics antithetical to, and mutually exclusive of, an actualizing interpersonal transactional-field. The position-derived authority structure, and role-binding specialization, operate through a system of codified rules, with the forced impersonality of "rationally" ordered relationships.

This system is ideal for maintaining an absolute class hierarchy of staff subordination and beneath that of inmate subordination. Spontaneity, self-actualization, democratic peer group process, emergent leadership of inmate or staff— these prerequisites of a corrective transactional program are effectively precluded. Bureaucratic structure inappropriately transforms *secondary* institutional goals of plant efficiency into *primary* goals. Plant efficiency as an end in itself is incongruent with proclaimed goals mislabeled "treatment" or "cure," and antagonistic to appropriate goals of psychosocial actualization through client-client, client-staff, client-community transactions. Vested interests shore up the *status quo* and desperately postpone radical change.

No non sequitur is this simple syllogism if you accept the basic premise: (a) If the medical-monocratic bureaucratic model *fits* the medical-surgical-nursing hospital as sociologists say it *fits* industry and military organizations; and (b) as institutes for dealing with psychological disorders have been mislabeled and "sold" as "mental hospitals'; then *ipso facto*, (c) the medical-monocratic bureaucratic model provides the best possible structure for such institutions. Besides it may be the only structure available in this socioeconomic culture to provide the naked and concealed power arrangements, and authority-derived-from-professional-position, necessary to perpetrate on the public, and perpetuate in practice, such preposterous operations.

Consider some interlocking determinants of obstruction. Both nonmedical psychological *conditions* (disorders) and nonmedical psychosocial corrective *procedures* are redefined by fiat as being *de facto* medical. Content and function are arrogated as medical responsibility and legitimized through legislation of restrictive licensure. Clinical prerogatives are institutionalized within establishments of detention and pseudotreatment. Sanctioned by master-symbols and public mandate, professional vested-interests interlock with society's need for segregation and incarceration of troublesome people — all popularized and santified via propaganda of the mislabeled "mental health" movement; eventuating in the next to the biggest hoax of the 20th century. Can we expect much in the way of radical innovations in this context?

Editor's note: References for this reading are incorporated into the general references for this chapter, pp. 427-431.

A STUDY OF CHILDREN REFERRED FOR RESIDENTIAL TREATMENT IN NEW YORK STATE

Donald A. Bloch, and Majorie L. Behrens,
with Helmut Guttenberg, Frances G. King and Diana Tendler

Background of the Study and the Problem

The Study. Residential treatment is a relatively new addition to the techniques used with children suffering from psychiatric disabilities. It has attracted much professional interest in the United States only over the last ten years or so. Within that time period, however, a small prairie fire of building plans, conferences, professional articles, and the like has swept over the country. Many states and municipalities, hospitals and social agencies, private individuals, and professional organizations have opinions on the subject or plans with regard to it. Interest in this subject has been, and continues to be, high.

Along with this interest, serious questions of public policy and professional practice are being raised. As to public policy, one must consider such things as: the interrelationship of training schools, State mental hospitals, foster

Reprinted with permission, from "A Report to the New York State Interdepartmental Health Resources Board," Albany, New York, 1959, pp. 7-19.

care institutions, and residential treatment facilities; the total pattern of community services to deviant children, both inpatient and outpatient; and finally, the question of auspices and thus the relationships between state, county, and municipality and between public and private agencies. In the field of professional practice we are faced by questions of the nature of milieu therapy, of the role of placement in psychiatric treatment of children, of the indications for it, its techniques, theory, results, and so on.

In response to concerns of this sort, New York State, acting through the Mental Health Commission, engaged in a collaborative venture with three private social agencies; this led to the establishment of three Pilot Residential Treatment Centers—the Pilot Centers as they are known in this report. The centers were: the Astor Home for Children, under the auspices of the Roman Catholic Archdiocese of New York; the Child Care Center of the Children's Aid and Society for the Prevention of Cruelty to Children of Erie County; and the Henry Ittleson Center for Child Research of the Jewish Board of Guardians. The three centers are located, respectively, in Rhinebeck (about 100 miles north of New York City), the city of Buffalo, and the Riverdale section of New York City; they all admitted their first children in late 1952 or early 1953.

The participation of the State in the establishment of these centers was predicated on the assumption that their experience would be used to improve State planning of care for deviant children, particularly those crowding the State hospitals. The program was administratively lodged with the Mental Health Commission (and later with the Interdepartmental Health Resources Board which succeeded the Mental Health Commission) because it was recognized that the problem affected several departments at the State level, notably, Mental Hygiene, Social Welfare, Education, and Health. In early 1955 the senior author of this report became a consultant to the Mental Health Commission to act as coordinator and evaluator of the experience of the centers, as it applied to questions of interest to the State. For approximately a year he regularly made visits to the centers and had the advantage of first-hand knowledge of the experience they were accumulating. Certain uniform reporting systems were established, and data were collected in this way and by direct observation of the daily activities of the centers.

In order to understand the problem in its broader aspects, it seemed necessary to study all children being referred to the centers in addition to that proportion who actually attained admission. We hoped in this way to learn the nature of the problems the residential treatment centers were being asked to cope with and so to facilitate over-all planning. We wished especially to in-

crease our understanding of the relationship of this treatment technique to alternative procedures with seriously disturbed children.

In addition to the children referred to the Pilot Centers, we also studied applicants to three other residential treatment centers and one diagnostic hospital. The other residential treatment centers were Linden Hill, Wiltwyck, and Childville; Kings County Hospital (girls admitted to the children's and adolescents' wards) was the diagnostic hospital. The information was collected principally by means of a 17-page questionnaire and later by a follow-up questionnaire requesting current information about the child. These questionnaires were filled out most often by the agency which had referred the child for residential treatment. The information was then coded and transferred to IBM cards. Analysis was carried out under these principal headings: the characteristics of the children and their families, the community efforts with the children, the way this population was dealt with by the residential treatment centers, and the movement through time and space of the population.

The six centers we studied provided a total of 228 beds; 100 of these were in one institution, Wiltwyck. Most of the children served were boys; only three of the centers admitted girls. Only one institution consistently served adolescent children; the others dealt with 6 to 12 year-olds. According to some definitions, it could be said that they were the only residential treatment centers in New York State. This point will be discussed below.

The Problem. Defined literally, a residential treatment center is an institution for children providing placement plus treatment. This description could, of course, cover such apparently diverse institutions as psychiatric hospitals, training schools, and, in some instances, normal child care institutions. Ordinarily, a residential treatment center is taken to be a small institution of perhaps 20 to 40 beds which provides a therapeutic environment and an abundance of clinical services to the children it treats. Of special note amongst the clinical services are remedial education, psychotherapy, and case work with the children and their families.

The reasons for some of the ambiguities concerning the place of the residential treatment center in the galaxy of in-patient facilites for children may be clarified by a short historical survey of the development of institutions for deviant children generally.

We may start by noting that in regard to both adults and children there were only two classes of institutions for many hundreds of years—alms houses and prisons. At first no distinctions were made between adults and children nor were distinctions made between the socially maladjusted, economically disadvantaged, and mentally ill. The only division was into the criminal and the pauper, and indeed many a prison contained debtor, psychotic, and criminal. The first differentiation concerned children—a sort of junior alms house was established for dependent and neglected children. This was the well-known orphanage of early times, the childrens' home, the congregate care institution or foster care institution of more recent years.

The next major differentiation concerned adults; three principal types of institutions were developed: the poor house, the prison, and the psychiatric hospital. Over the hundred years or so since this development, the poor house has practically disappeared to be re-placed by the out-patient welfare program. The psychiatric hospital during these years has flourished, although very recently the trend has shown signs of reversing itself. This is due to the development of modern therapies and the tendency towards early treatment in the community or in smaller decentralized, open institutions.

So far as children were concerned, two developments of note occurred in the last fifty years, both in the correctional field—a junior prison system came into being, the training schools, and, somewhat later, the first child guidance clinics were established in the context of the juvenile courts. Here matters rested until very recently when a great deal of pressure started to have the State develop a childrens' version of the State hospital system. Thus, remarkably enough, the patterns of development of institutions for deviant children followed almost one hundred years behind that of facilities for adults. One could almost say that for children today there are the alms houses and prisons as there were for adults then, and that we are in the process of developing psychiatric hospital facilities under the auspices of the State as we were for adults a hundred years ago.

It is in this context that the interest in residential treatment develops. The question with which we are concerned is this: What shall be the pattern of in-patient psychiatric facilities for children? Shall the prototype be the large hospital, the remedial treatment center, or what? It is to these questions that the present study has its relevance.

Another contributory stream to the rising tide of interest in residential treatment must be mentioned briefly. This, too, concerns a shift which has gradually been occurring in recent years; we speak of the increasing tendency to regard children as "sick" or "disturbed" rather than dependent or delinquent. Taking delinquency first, it has already been noted that the child guidance clinic had its origin in the Juvenile Court; it is equally true that public and private training schools have pioneered in converting their programs from custodial to therapeutic and that they are, in significant ways, leaders in the development of residential treatment. In a word, both courts and correctional institutions are daily more likely to regard their charges as in need of some form of psychiatric treatment. The same process has been taking place in the foster care field. Most good congregate care institutions accept the fact that placement creates pathology and that some sort of treatment is required for children who must live outside of a family for this reason alone if for no other. Moreover, changing practice in this field speaks strongly for closing large institutions and placing all placeable children in foster homes. As a consequence of this it has been recognized that the hard core unplaceable group is unplaceable precisely because they are in need of some sort of in-patient treatment. Here again is a source of referrals and of interest in relation to residential treatment.

One final point along the same line. The aim of public health is prophylaxis. In regard to mental health this aim has dictated an interest in younger and younger children and an interest in better case finding. The effect in both cases is the same—more young children who are severely disturbed are coming to professional attention. In many instances the child is severely disturbed and, moreover, the family situation and environment generally are antitherapeutic. These cases are often assessed as needing some kind of place-

ment if treatment is to be successfully initiated. For these cases, residential treatment of one kind or another is considered so that another substantial group of applicants for residential treatment is produced.

We have tried in the foregoing material briefly to present those historical trends and changes in current practice which have focussed attention on that particular kind of small, in-patient, psychiatric treatment facility for children known as a residential treatment center. Many of the confusions and ambiguities surrounding this type of treatment facility are related to these origins. Certainly one is impressed with the fact that the whole range of services for deviant children needs to be considered in relationship to each other rather than as separate, isolated entities.

Principal Findings and Impressions

Before presenting a detailed description of the findings of the study, we should like to set forth some of the principal conclusions drawn from our data and the implications of these conclusions.

Two general points stand out. First, as far as residential treatment goes, *the issue is placement.* That is, communities principally look to residential treatment for a solution to the problem of the child who needs placement. In this view of the matter, treatment is a secondary issue. In our study, although less than one-quarter of the children referred to residential treatment centers were admitted, well over 90% were ultimately placed in some kind of institution. For these children the situation had passed a critical point. The forces pushing the child out of the community, the degree of illness, the deterioration of the family, the pathogenic factors in the environment, had overwhelmed the capacity of the community to keep the child living in it. It was only too clear that our cases were referred to residential treatment facilities as the most desirable arrangement, but, if this arrangement were not possible they would be referred again and again until ultimately they would be placed somewhere.

Second, we were impressed throughout the study with the terrible cost levied by the lack of an over-all, unified, consistent plan for providing service to the seriously disturbed child. For the child with relatively minor difficulties, a single service may suffice to correct the problem. The children being considered here have all areas of their lives riddled with pathology and almost always need multiple services which are coordinated with each other. In general, services to these children are provided in discrete packages; agencies are overspecialized and separated from each other by a referral barrier that is often resistive and sometime impervious. School refers to court, court to clinic, clinic to placement agency, and so on. Once admitted to the hospital or treatment center it is difficult or impossible to have the child accepted by an outpatient community agency. Integrated programs of service at the clinical level are literally unheard of.

The following stories of four of the children are representative of the case material covered in this study. They have been chosen, not because of their unusual aspects, but because, in all respects, they are typical of the children in our study population.

Case 1. This case is illustrative of a child whom we placed in our diagnostic category of behavior disorder, whose ulti-

mate disposition was to a training school. Subsequently he was discharged and has been living in his natural home.

Harold was born in 1942. In October of 1953, at the age of 11, he was in a detention home in an upstate county. He is the second born of four children of the same mother and father. Both parents were White and were born in this country. Mother finished two years of high school; father finished eighth grade and was a machinist. According to the record, both parents are alcoholic, and the father was abusive to mother and children. They could not accept agency help for themselves voluntarily. In the description of the home situation, it was noted that "the parents quarrelled, there was much tension in the home, chronic drunkenness and abusiveness". The parents were immature, living conditions were crowded, and the house was in poor repair. In addition, the father had a cardiac condition and a cataract of the eye.

As to the youngster, he "entered kindergarten in a rural community at 6 years of age. For the first two years his adjustment was fairly good. Then, for two years he misbehaved and fought with teachers and children; he twisted a teacher's arm and attacked a child with a knife. Eventually he was excluded from school. In detention he was unable to relate or compete with others, had a short attention span, chattered considerably, had many nervous mannerisms, and talked to himself".

From the detention home he was sent to a medical hospital for diagnosis of abdominal pain, where he became so obstreperous that he had to be transferred to a closed ward. A diagnosis of primary behavior disorder was made and the hospital recommended removal from home and placement in a closed setting.

Before he was finally committed to the State training school, "application was made to six child care institutions or treatment centers, all of whom refused to accept Harold because of his aggressiveness, or, as in the case of . . . State hospital and . . . residential treatment center, he was rejected because there was no space".

Eight months later, in June of 1954, he was committed to a State training school. The last information we have is that he was living in his natural home.

Case 2. To illustrate a slightly different but no less disturbing treatment history, we have the case of Frank, a Jewish youngster, whose diagnosis was of another type. This child was born in 1944 and, at the age of 8, was referred to a residential treatment center specializing in older delinquent children. He had already been seen in two psychiatric hospitals, both of which gave him a diagnosis of childhood schizophrenia.

His principal symptoms were autism, crying spells, and fears; he was unable to dress himself, was clinging, and showed gross motor abnormalities. The Pilot Center to which he was referred could not accept him. On the record there was a notation, "no service given and no knowledge of what happened".

Case 3. Another case is Hope, a little girl born in 1941, the only child of Negro, Protestant parents about whom practically nothing is known. She suffered from depressed and flattened affect, obesity, and precocious heterosexuality She had temporary states of muteness and was withdrawn. Her I.Q. was 84. In 1955, at the age of 14, she was seen by a psychiatrist at a diagnostic hospital who gave her a diagnosis of "schizoid personality with hysterical features and conversion reaction". Four months later she received a diagnosis of mental deficiency with a WISC of 74. She was sent to Letchworth Village, from which she was returned with a diagnosis of "not mentally defective" to the hospital which sent her there in the first place. They, in turn, did another diagnostic workup—the third—and the final disposition was "child returned to Children's Court for planning". At last report, she was in a State training school for girls. "The arrangement is not considered appropriate. Hope was too disturbed to get along in the regular institution program. She is in a special unit but might benefit from intensive treatment of the type a residential treatment center would provide."

Case 4. Jimmy, a White Protestant boy, was born in 1944, the youngest of two children. At that time his father was 59 and his mother was 36. Within two years after his birth the family was known to the Department of Welfare for financial assistance. When he was 4, the Department of Welfare arranged for day care.

The child was diagnosed as "pseudo mentally retarded due to his emotional stress" and is considered by us to be neurotic. He has at various times received the following diagnosis: "personality disorder, immaturity reaction, severe"; "character neurosis"; "not mentally retarded". He is described as being enuretic until age 6, "fearful in peer relationships and requiring an inordinate amount of attention". He is "dependent and shy". He was seen in an educational clinic and was referred for residential treatment. "Recommendation was made for psychotherapy in a therapeutic center. Jimmy has been retested and evaluated three times. He was turned down by one residential treatment center because he was too old, by another because the institution was full, and because of institution group needs and staff limitations. A third center turned him down because he was too old (all of this in 1955 when he was 11), and another because of unsuitable diagnosis and institution group needs. At the age of 13 he was admitted to a school for retarded children.

One of our principal interests was *the characteristics of the children* in our study. The first thing we can say about these youngsters is that they definitely are in need of treatment and, perhaps, treatment plus placement. One test of this is an analysis[1] of a group of our cases who were *not placed at all* up to the time of our follow-up study. This group, which on the face of it seemed best able to maintain itself in the community, and perhaps therefore least disturbed, on more careful examination showed a high proportion of severe pathology. This aspect of the study is especially interesting in that it underscores the point we have made — that placement is the issue. Of the original group of 961 cases referred to the six centers, only 60 cases (6.2%) had *not* been placed in some kind of institution by the time we did our follow-up in January 1957. A second follow-up study of these cases, in December 1958, revealed that 14 of these 60 cases (23%) were placed, lowering the proportion of the children in the total group never placed to a little over 4%. Of those not placed, very few were estimated to have

[1]Done by Mrs. Sophie Grossbard as part of her work toward completion of her Master's degree at the New York School of Social Work.

improved. The inexorable trend toward the institutionalization of these children cannot be overlooked. Even in this small residual 4% group, most were not placed *because facilities were not available,* or because parents refused placement.

As is usual in these matters, the ratio of boys to girls is about five to one. Among the boys, the heaviest concentration is in the 9 to 12 year group; girls are referred at a more even rate per age year. The decrease in referrals at age 13 is an artifact because we did not include applicants to public and private training schools.

As to race, 31% of the children were Negro, 57% White, and 10% Puerto Rican. It is interesting to note that among White Children 34% of those referred were 8 or less. The younger children in the minority groups were not being referred at an equal rate and perhaps were not perceived of as being in need of service until they became behavior problems during the latency years.

The religious distribution of our sample was 35% Catholic, 20% Jewish, and 42% Protestant.

We were forced by the nature of our data, to use a gross diagnostic scheme. Eschewing subtleties, we attempted to place a child in one of three principal diagnostic series — the schizophrenias, the behavior disorders, and the neuroses. We also used the categories of organic brain disease and mental retardation. Our principal finding was *the diagnostic heterogeneity of these cases.* About 23% could be called schizophrenic among the boys, and 34% among the girls; 21% of the boys and 19% of the girls fell in the behavior disorder series; and 18% of the boys and 10% of the girls fell in the neurotic series. Among the boys we felt that 37% were not clearly classifiable on the basis of our data; the same was true for 33% of the girls.

Of considerable importance is the fact that the number of children being referred for residential treatment, and therefore appearing in our study, drops sharply at around the age of 13. The implication, which is borne out by our figures, is that the percept of the child changes drastically once he becomes adolescent. The same child under 13 is felt to be in need of residential treatment; at a later date he is perceived as a candidate for a training school. One is forced to recognize the unity of the "placement", "residential treatment", and "delinquency" problems. This is, of course, just a matter of a definition chasing its own tail. For the most part, there are no residential treatment centers for children over 13 or training schools for children under 13; so fewer children over 13 are referred to residential treatment centers and no children under 13 are referred to training schools. The point is that they are the same youngsters a few years older.

One characteristic of the family which we investigated was the incidence of serious social and psychiatric problems, and for this purpose a scoring technique and a "Multiproblem Family Index" were devised. Each family received a positive score if items indicated serious difficulty in the areas of marriage, parent-child relationship, social pathology, physical illness, mental illness, or financial support. These families turned out to be riddled with pathology. *Only 15% of our families showed no positive information in any of the six problem areas.* Half of them scored positively in three or more of these six problem areas. There was thus an even division of the total number of families into low and high scoring

groups. We should note that a family needs to be in very bad shape in order to score positively in three or more problem areas on a mail questionnaire.

Consolidating the rather meager information we were able to obtain on the socio-economic and cultural status of these families, the largest group among them is American born, poorly educated, and subsisting on a marginal income often supplemented by public assistance funds.

Less than one-quarter of the children have lived only in their natural homes, while 40% have lived in four or more homes or institutions before applying to residential treatment centers. Approximately three-fifths of the children did *not* have a continuous relationship with both natural parents. Of our families, 17% of the parents were not married and another 35% had been married but were now separated by divorce, desertion, or death. Of the greatest importance is the lack of stability of family life for the children in our study. They have experienced changes of location and changes of parental figures far beyond anything which would be remotely conducive to healthy development.

We also studied the *community's efforts with these children.* The importance of *early case finding* is well known in public health and medicine. Three-quarters of our cases were known to an agency before they were 9 years old and one-half of them were known before they were six. These children and their families have been "found" as cases early and often; they have been known to community agencies for a long time (to an *average of six agencies per family and over an average period of 3 to 5 years or about one agency per child per year*); they have received a great deal of diagnostic service (an average of two diagnoses per case); *they have received diagnostic, referral, and placement services and very little else in the way of treatment, such as casework, psychotherapy, or special educational arrangements.* In our study there is little evidence of coordination of services or of continuity of care.

Nor is there any substantial evidence of "accountability", either in a bookkeeping sense or in the sense of responsibility. For example, about half of the children became personally known to agencies sometime *after* their families were known. Although one might expect a canvass of the needs of the total family by social agencies, one finds that, in 50% to 60% of the cases, three to ten years elapse before the child comes to be considered.

Perhaps the most compelling thing to say about the residential treatment centers is that they are unable to admit about 80% of the children who apply to them. There are substantial differences in the rate at which different types of social agencies refer cases to the residential treatment centers. The largest group of children come from public agencies, principally the courts and public welfare placement agencies. Among the private agencies, placement agencies also referred more than any other type. In New York City, for example, courts and placement agencies accounted for 50% of the referrals. It seems clear that a great deal of the pressure that constitutes the "residential treatment problem" comes from the courts and public placement agencies.

We studied the general pattern of applications for residential treatment and found that a tremendous amount of agency effort went into this, for example, the courts and public placement agencies make *from three to five applications per child for most of their*

cases. Diagnostically, as one might expect, there is more referral effort centered on the behavior disorders and the least number of referral efforts for schizophrenic children.

Resources for girls are most seriously limited. Even though three of the centers we studied admitted girls, only four girls or 6.6% of those applying during a one year period, 1955-56, were able to find admission.

There were no significant trends in favor of one or another diagnostic category in regard to admission. The centers, on the whole, seemed almost to take random samples of the population with regard to diagnosis. Indeed, as far as our study goes, the centers could dispense completely with intake procedures, admit children purely on the basis of age and sex, and achieve a population indistinguishable from that currently being treated.

We have also studied the *changes in the child's whereabouts* at varying points in time. Over the years, there is a steady breakup of homes with fewer and fewer children able to live in their natural homes. For example, at the time of first agency contact, 83% of the children were living in their natural homes. By the time they were referred for residential treatment, only 60% were living in their natural homes, and by the time of follow-up, only 30% were living in their natural homes. More and more children are placed, principally in institutions of one kind or another. Eight percent are in institutions to start out with; at follow-up, 58% are institutionalized. As time passes, the trend is heavily in the direction of the State mental hospital and training school. The indications are that the training school will ultimately receive a very large proportion of these children as they move into the adolescent age group.

By the time the children are 15 or 16, 27% of children of these ages are admitted to training schools. While only 9% of the *total* group is in training schools, it is only because the other children are too young. (These figures could be even higher since we scored certain private training schools[2] as residential treatment centers.) In relation to mental hospitals, different processes seem to be at work. Although 15% of the

children were in mental hospitals at time of follow-up, no selection by age is to be found.

While we have not especially been able to demonstrate very tight relationships between diagnosis and outcome, there is unquestionably a strong tendency for the mental hospitals to select schizophrenic children, for the training schools to select those with behavior disorders, and a slight bias of foster homes in favor of the neurotic. Residential treatment centers, on the whole, select evenly from the group referred.

[2]For example, the Hawthorne Cedar Knolls School, Children's Village, etc.

PART V EMERGING SOCIAL PROBLEMS AND POLICY

POPULATION PROBLEMS

Introduction

Every American social problem has a demographic aspect. Each problem is influenced by rates of change in population growth, by size of population, and by population composition, distribution, or quality. Thus, analysis of a social problem requires population analysis.

Population conditions and changes are always either a source, a correlate, or a consequence of special social problems. No population characteristic is in itself problematic, but features of social problems often result directly from rates of change in population relative to other features of a modern society. Substantial changes in rates of birth, death, and migration, for example, often create conflicting social situations which alter social organization, modify or put stresses upon older uses of the environment, and even stimulate or retard technological change. Less abrupt but longer-term population changes often induce changes in social organization. These emerge so gradually and subtly that they are not perceived until strains develop.

Rapid population migration from rural into metropolitan areas in the United States has intensified demands for service facilities; for schools, playgrounds, roads, shopping centers. It has also relocated churches and private accommodations. Equally swift growth of suburban populations has complicated enormously the network of governments that regulate localities.

Some features of deviant behavior result from rates of population growth and from changes in age structure. Juvenile delinquency increased between 1955 and 1960, and it will increase even more drastically between 1960 and 1970, for instance, primarily because of the great increase in the size of the age group between 15 and 19. The rise of official delinquency rates in suburbs may also be little more than a reflection of the redistribution of population from central cities to the suburban fringe. In the same sense, new problems of conduct appear to develop among the aged in America, when these may reflect mainly the great change in the size of the older age group.

No major social problem may be explained solely as a population problem. Yet, modern national population processes and world population conditions must be understood by the student of social problems, for these processes impinge at many points upon disorganization, rates of deviance, and even upon conflicts between values. This chapter attends to several major and illustrative population processes, selecting them for their bearing on American social problems. The first of these is world population growth. The second is the future rate of growth of the American population. A third includes aspects of American population policy.

The World Population Explosion

The great abundance of the human species is a thing of recent origin. Only during the 20th century has the human population of the earth increased at an average rate of more than one per cent a year. The rate of population growth for the world in any year prior to 1900, in fact, never exceeced one half of one per cent. For many centuries, it fluctuated well below even that level. By 1910, the rate of increase reached one per cent. By 1960 it exceeded 2 per cent a year. If the current growth rate of 2 per cent annually were maintained, the present world population of about 3 billion would double to 6 billion before the year 2000.

The rate of world population growth has 'exploded' in this spectacular manner chiefly because of the effects of science and technology upon death rates. Miracle drugs and insecticides have brought lethal infectious diseases under control. Modern systems of transport and irrigation have eliminated wholesale deaths in communities suffering crop failures, drought, and famine, and other natural disasters. At the same time, birth rates in most nations of the world have remained as high as they were under pre-20th century conditions, when most societies were organized to encourage a rate of reproduction that would provide a surplus to guard against early death.

Public health programs, insecticides, and miracle drugs have now been introduced into most countries at fairly modest expense (often at no expense to resident families) and on a vast scale. The direct outcome in all cases has been a marked drop in infant mortality, improvements in general health, and a rise in the average life span of entire national populations. The decline in the death rate produced by medical and technological change is best revealed in communities that enjoyed early benefits. In the city of London, about 42 persons per thousand died each year between 1680 and 1690. Early industrialization and medical improvements reduced this to 35 deaths per thousand by 1750; to 25 per thousand in 1850; and to less than 13 per thousand in 1950. This great decline in the death rate was achieved over 300 years. Some countries like Ceylon, Guatemala, Chile, and Costa Rica have achieved as great a decline within a single decade or two during the last 30 years, thanks to the current efficiency of scientific practices.

Death control through science and technology has spread from the industrially advanced nations of the West to the continents of Asia, Africa, and Latin America. Death control began in the West in the late 17th century; it spread through most of Latin America between 1920 and 1950. The United Nations and foreign aid programs brought it to Asia and Africa after 1946. It is by and large a type of death control that persons and groups of all cultural persuasions welcome vigorously. Its diffusion has proved inexpensive and socially acceptable.

Increased *birth* control in any form has proved far less acceptable in most societies and among some groups within all countries. The world birth rate continues to exceed by far the world death rate. In many societies, the birth rate remains at a biological maximum despite the changing death rate. And, improved health and the inducements of new hope through industrialization sometimes increases the birth rate for a time in societies where it has been below maximum. (By a biological maximum, the student of population means a condition in which mothers of child-bearing age are reproducing about as rapidly as the pace of the birth cycle will allow.)

By birth control, we mean to include the ancient restrictive practices of infanticide, abortion, and sexual taboos — devices groups have used throughout history to restrict their population growth. Under preindustrial conditions, human populations seldom expanded at some biologically maximum rate. Each culture includes standards and practices that tend to balance size of community against food and resource supplies. To natural birth control procedures, we would add such life control devices as abandonment of the sick and the chronically dependent, tribal warfare, marriage restrictions, and migration, to mention a few.

Modern medical science has added to this venerable list a variety of birth control techniques. The most notably efficient among these are contraceptives (mechanical or chemical devices that prevent fertilization), free and painless sterilization, and safe induction of abortion. These, together with the older modes of birth and life control, are employed in most countries of the world. Yet the rate of spread of these control techniques *lags* very significantly behind the rate of decline in deaths.

The experience of India illustrates this vividly. The death rate there dropped from 30 per thousand in 1930 to about 20 per thousand in 1960. Because of this and because of the combined effects of governmental stability and the rise in public hope, the population has grown at a rate of 2.5 per cent a year since about 1950. At this rate, India would expand from 438 million in 1961 to nearly 750 million in 1980.

India, in fact, continues to reveal a high rate of growth despite attempts at population control. As one spokesman puts it,

> We have done something which few governments have had the courage to do. In a highly religious country we have officially adopted the policy of family planning and the government has taken steps to give effect to that policy. I need hardly say that orthodox religions all over the world take up the same unconvincing attitude toward birth control, that it is an interference with the unscrutable ways of God and we must leave it to Him to look after those whom He brings into this world. It is forgotten that every new discovery for combating disease is as much an interference with the limit of life set by Providence.[1]

The Indian government now maintains about 3000 birth control clinics — 25 times the number it sponsored in 1956. Indian public hospitals performed 7,823 sterilizations in 1956; the number grew to 41,091 in 1960. Any parent of at least three children may volunteer for free and painless, yet

[1]M. C. Chagla, "India's Dilemma," *Our Crowded Planet*, Fairfield Osborn, editor, Doubleday, New York: 1962, pp. 161-162.

irrevocable, sterilization by surgery. In some states, volunteers are paid about $6 for participating. Between 1955 and 1963, half a million Indians underwent voluntary sterilization at government expense. The rate of such volunteers is increasing annually, mainly through the effective work of persuaders who themselves have undergone the operation and who testify publically to its harmlessness. (B. L. Raina, Director of the Indian Ministry of Health's Family Planning Unit, reported in 1964 that the average age of men requesting the operation was 37; the average for women, 32. Most parents seeking sterilization already had five offspring. Their average yearly income was less than $260 a family.)

In spite of this costly and culturally difficult government undertaking, following its 1961 census, the government of India projected in its reports to the United Nations an estimated annual population *increase* of 2.4 per cent from 1961 through 1966, and a 2.75 per cent increase through 1976. The official birth control program will not make a substantial contribution to controlling growth until 1980!

Only a handful of nations—Japan, India, Pakistan, Fiji, Singapore, Barbados, Puerto Rico, and China, to name the best known—have similar official policies and programs of birth control. We selected India from among these for illustration chiefly because the program there, while increasingly vigorous, still fail to reduce the current rate of increase. Among the nations engaged seriously in systematic population control, in fact, only Japan reports significant success to date. The Indian case also puts into perspective the situation in the great majority of nations which have *no* birth control programs.

The World Population Projection

The United Nations Department of Economic and Social Affairs is an authoritative source of world population information. Every few years, its experts try to estimate future world population growth. Their estimates have increased constantly since 1951. As better census studies are taken throughout the nations of the world, the revised information is always in the direction of increases, not declines. The experts also tend to err on the side of caution.

The estimate made by the United Nations in 1958 was for a world population of 6.3 billion by the year 2000. This assumed a rate of growth of 1.5 per cent a year over the next 40 years, compared to the current world rate of 2.0 per cent. The estimate thus assumed the spread of birth and other population control policies and programs from the developed to the industrially underdeveloped nations. (It must be understood that this has little to do with the important but parochial issue of religious opposition to so-called artificial birth control techniques. There are *many* means by which a population may reduce its birth rate.)

This projection to the year 2000 is not as helpful as a projection that aims at identifying a period when world population will begin to level off, to balance, to stablize its birth rate in relation to its death rate. Experts have addressed this question. One group foresees a population of nearly 7 billion as representing a fairly balanced level being reached in about 2050. Their guess assumes a very rapid spread of efficient birth control procedures, and a sharp decline in rates of population growth in the industrially developed nations. Their *most optimistic* forecast projects a "long-range, stabilized world population of 7 billion," and a least optimistic forecast of 12 billion by the year 2050.[2]

Overpopulation and Survival

Most specialists agree that the surface and resources of the earth could support more than 7 billion people. The experts agree because they have evidence of what could be produced with existing technology. In the case of food, to support a population twice as great as today's, we would "merely" have "to practice all over the world the techniques now used in developed countries ... fertilizer production and application, plant improvement by plant breeding, and the control of pests."[3]

Other experts say that with the opening of new arable lands and with the application of modern soil feeding technology, the earth will readily support 7 billion persons, even when other available food sources are left only partially developed. In the years from 2000 to 2050, men will raise and consume less meat, but they will not as yet have to turn to cultivating the sea or to chemically synthesized foods. To provide food for 7 billion people requires "mankind as a whole working in single-minded and perhaps even fraternal cooperation ... not enemies split into opposing camps."[4]

The food requirements will be greatest in precisely the most underdeveloped countries. Most of these are currently aligned with neither American nor Soviet political, military, or

[2]Harrison Brown, et al., *The Next Hundred Years,* New York: Viking Press, Compass Books Edition, 1963, pp. 49-51.
[3]Ibid., p. 61.
[4]Fritz Baade, *The Race to the Year 2000,* Garden City: Doubleday, 1962, p. 47.

economic interests. The requirements of people in these countries can be fulfilled during the decades immediately ahead *only* by huge investments of capital and skilled human resources and machinery from already developed countries.

World Overpopulation and the American Dilemma

The world population explosion, even if reduced substantially by industrial and social change and by the diffusion of birth control techniques, is occurring at a pace such that its forward thrust will not be checked until the current world population is at least doubled at some point between the next 50 to 90 years. Obviously, it will make a great difference whether this stabilization occurs sooner or later. But the likely level of balance is 7 billion. A pessimistic projection, assuming no important social changes and little spread of birth control programs, is stabilization at 12 billion.

Resources, industrial and agricultural, *are* available to support this population, only if great cooperative political and economic energies are marshalled to assist underdeveloped areas. *If* the growth continues and the food reserves are potentially available, will men get at them and produce them somehow? If survival is possible, even at mere subsistence levels, will men survive regardless of social and political costs? If they must choose between dependence upon the democracies of the West and the totalitarian patterns of the Soviet Union and China, will they choose ultimately in terms of guarantees for survival, or in terms of political ideologies?

Population growth has occurred and will continue to occur mostly in the countries that can least afford it. The advanced economies of the United States and the Soviet Union probably cannot survive in a future in which the other peoples of the neutral but underdeveloped, high-growth countries around them starve toward desperation. The developed societies probably cannot tolerate the world political instability that would ensue. Nor can they exist without markets for the distribution and consumption of their own products.

One economist has estimated, for example, that for India alone, $12 billion a year for 100 years would have to be invested over and above current levels of investment in order to provide the Indian people with a supply of food, housing and clothing equal to the level currently attained by the citizens of Holland.[5] Moreover, this estimate assumed a perfect stability in the Indian population at its present level, when in fact it may be expected to increase by more than 100 million before 2000! American economic aid to India in 1962 amounted to 528 million dollars.

Clearly, current modes of foreign aid *nowhere* approach the volume or efficiency of impact that would be needed to stimulate great increases in food production and industrial development. The most underdeveloped, fastest-breeding nations, which are now in the politically neutral bloc, can be expected to grow progressively more desperate in their efforts to slow the rate of population increase and, more vitally, to grow economically.

[5]Cited by Bruce Martin Russett, "Some Unpleasant Facts About *Population* Pressures," *America*, November 24, 1962.

America's Own Population Growth and Composition

The world population explosion is thus not a dilemma for the underdeveloped nations alone. The United States may have to contribute ever more substantially to economic and social development in these countries if it expects to protect its own survival in the coming turn into the next century.

At the same time, the United States population has neither checked its own high rate of population increase nor maintained its past level of economic growth. The world population problem is complicated for American society by domestic population problems.

The American population continues to have a high birth rate compared to most European countries. It is less than half that of the birth rate of many Central American and Asian nations, but the irony is that the death rate for the United States is so low that the U.S. rate of annual growth in population remains very high. For example, the United States has a birth rate of 23 per thousand (1962) and a death rate of 9. Indonesia has a birth rate of 43 per thousand and a death rate of 24. The rate of natural increase in the United States is thus 1.4 per cent a year, compared with 1.9 per cent in Indonesia.

At this rate of increase, the United States would double its population by about 2000. This means we would expand within 40 years by perhaps 200 million persons! Using the same rate of annual increase, the American population would tend to level out at a population total of roughly 1 billion by about the year 2050.

The difficulties inherent in this guess are enormous. There are technical and sociological limitations: American demographers are able to estimate death rates, but the rates of economic and attitude change in contemporary American life are so great that accurate, long-term forecasts of average future *birth* rates are impossible to make. The national birth rate has fluctuated between about 30 per thousand in 1915 to less than 19 per thousand in 1935. The present rate is 23. There is no sound basis for predicting a point between these for the future.[6] Demographers cannot project, let alone estimate, for more than 10 to 15 years ahead with any real confidence for a developed and rapidly changing nation.

Even if they could, there exists no principle for setting an *optimum population* limit. A social scientist might define an optimum as that population which will produce the maximum per capita amount of goods with the resources and means of production available to it. A naturalist would think of the optimum in terms of some ideal balance between the environmental preserves shared by a great variety of life species in addition to man. Other thinkers would lead from other value premises. A humanist might use standards of leisure or freedom to pursue the good and the beautiful. Some religionists would emphasize the values of large families. The 'proper limit' on population growth (the optimum population) depends upon what groups value most. In a pluralistic society, these values may conflict sharply.

American Population Imbalance?

Not only may the American population soon grow to excess (by *some* utilitarian standards), but as its net rate of

[6]Conrad Taeuber and Irene B. Taeuber, *The Changing Population of the United States,* New York: John Wiley, 1958, pp. 296-298.

growth continues to be among the highest among the countries of the world, it will also continue to change in composition.

The number of persons *below* working age and thus dependent on others has, since about 1955, begun to exceed the number in the labor force, in terms of rate of increase. In the present decade, for instance, the vast crop of postwar babies is reaching working age. *Three times* as many young adults sought their first jobs in 1963 as sought work in 1953.

In addition, one must note changing rates among older persons. The rate of increase in the number of persons in both the oldest and the youngest age groups from 1950 to 1960 was five times that of persons between 20 and 64. Those under 20 years increased by 35 per cent. Persons over 64 years increased by 32 per cent, compared to 7 per cent for the middle group!

By themselves, these changes mean little. They do not even constitute an *imbalance,* since the shape of a population structure may assume many forms; no one age structure is optimal. Indeed, such changes stimulate new markets, new needs, new demands for service and institutional innovation. We could speak of age imbalance quite reasonably if we had in mind a society based on severe scarcity. The Upper Alaskan Eskimo once had cultural safeguards against an 'excess' of population; for example, aged persons committed what we would call suicide.

We can refer reasonably to population imbalance only in relation to other changing events. If the annual number of qualified youths seeking admission to college increases much faster than the increase of available openings, we have the beginnings of a socially problematic imbalance. If care for the aged is increasingly less available within families, and if the rate of growth in nursing care facilities does not increase, health care of the aged becomes a national social problem. Or, if the rate of increase in care facilities matches the growth rate of numbers of older citizens, a serious national problem may still develop if levels of income among the aging are too low to pay for care. These illustrations are selected for their bearing on the contemporary scene. They are social problems that stem from incompatibility between rates of change in the population structure and changes in rates of supply of services and income.

American Population Policy

Every society maintains a population policy, if by policy we mean a combination of mores and practices as against the set of laws governing demographic processes. Some parts of the policy in the modern case fall under the aegis of the state: Immigration laws control the rate of flow of foreigners into a nation. Divorce and marriage laws affect the fertility rate, household formation rate, and even the infant mortality rate. State bookkeeping regulations affect population, too, as is true of procedures for registering marriages, births, and deaths.

Other parts of a society's population policy are part of custom but not of law. In America, for example, our *customary* population policy has long been that a *high* rate of growth is unequivocally good for business and community development. Of course, important reactions against this are noteworthy. The poor and some ethnic minorities have often been stymied in their efforts to migrate into certain regions and communities; and foreign immigrants have often been

exploited but not socially welcomed as cheap and abundant labor. Many state laws are reinforced by custom: Laws prohibiting abortion and even the open sale of contraceptives, for example, are further supported by customary deep social rejection of unwed mothers and their illegitimate offspring.

Suppose, now, that strong proposals were advanced by various groups to the effect that this nation must stabilize its population; that its world situation and its internal resources required what demographers call a *stationary* population. To achieve this objective, population policies would have to be devised to insure a reduction of the American birth rate by 45 per cent over its 1960 level.

This revision in policy could be implemented democratically. There are enough different methods of birth control to insure that morally acceptable and medically available means are available for all groups. Roman Catholic objections to contraception are not germane to this question. (Except that enough confusion surrounds Catholic policies to make of this at least a short-term delaying force in executing a revised policy of increased birth control.)

The political fact is, however, that no western industrial society has erected deliberately a policy that would control population size or reduce substantially the rate of population growth. There is no precedent for such a development. The laws we have described as parts of a state population policy are laws developed to regulate various aspects of the public welfare. They have not been, with the exception of immigration laws, erected to control population growth. There is, in other words, no explicit legislative population policy in the United States. Implicit policies may be revised through social change, but seldom through political action. It is probably constitutionally feasible that federal and state legislatures might, if their members chose, regulate the rate of population growth. But there is no indication in early or recent history of any precedents (let alone any political quest) for such decisions.

Interest groups concerned with reducing or stabilizing population growth in the United States have instead emphasized sex and parental *education* as means toward influencing implicit national policies. The Planned Parenthood Federation represents this alternative. This group urges careful planning of family life and family size by parents. It advances its claim through information, propaganda, and the clinical provision of health and social services. It is doubtful whether these educational approaches influence even faintly the national level of population growth. Educational influences seldom reach those least able to plan family growth, for example. The poor are not well situated to learn to plan, and the rich are free to rationalize a family of virtually any size.

Americans do have a powerful national consensus about the great importance of reducing the death rate. There are exceptions, as in the situation in 1964 when governors of the three major tobacco growing states opposed an effort in the Congress and the Federal Trade Commission to place a label of warning on packages of cigarettes. But these usually occur where the value of death control is pitted against some other keenly held value, such as net profit. Generally, health research and health care are given maximum attention and preference in both the state and the society.

No equivalent consensus exists about birth control. The sometimes held belief that Roman Catholic policies opposing most techniques of birth control prevent the formation of an explicit set of enacted population controls is as idle a contention as the notion that entire publics may be educated toward rational limitation of family size. Real conflicts of value exist between most American Protestants and most Catholics on this issue, but these conflicts have to do mostly with prejudice and with differences in moral philosophy. They do not bear directly on bargaining about legislation, for no such bargaining is going on.

The American pattern is to project population control questions *outward*. The history of immigration legislation is one of progressive restriction, for example. Outsiders have been kept out, while insiders have not been regulated as to fertility. Eugenics, the discipline that deals with influences that improve the genetic quality of a population, has never been seriously or widely received in the United States. It has narrow medical applications to diagnosis and preparation for special treatment of difficulties in pregnancy and birth and postnatal care. But laws intended to prevent the transmission of presumably undesirable characteristics through sterilization have not only been abandoned in nearly all instances after short trial, but they were *always* directed at peripheral minorities (such as the mentally retarded) in the population, not to the general public.

There are continuing traces of eugenic policies, to be sure. Indigent mothers (most of whom 'happen' to be Negroes) in Fauquier County, Virginia, for example, can be sterilized after the birth of their fourth child. Marriage laws that require medical certification of the absence of venereal disease are also eugenic. But castration of mental defectives and the sterilization of psychotics have been abandoned as totally unwarranted. And eugenicist proposals that 'society' regulate heredity seem generally fantastic in a post-Nazi era.[7]

Many other economic, health, and welfare policies taken together amount *indirectly* to a national population policy, however, both as to birth control and eugenics. For example, programs of social insurance and public assistance enable disadvantaged groups to improve their life chances. Programs which contribute to the elimination of social and economic disadvantage also affect the birth rate. The American Negro population today is increasing at a rate 60 per cent ahead of the white population, yet this higher fertility diminishes as southern rural Negroes have the option of becoming more secure northern urban wage earners. For a short period, as this northward migration occurs, Negroes in the North will exhibit an increased birth rate because their health and medical care is so much better in the cities. Later, as more Negroes have a chance at good education and employment and housing, their birth rate will equal the urban white middle-income birth rate, which is *low*.

In other words, welfare policies that contribute to equal opportunity and the provision of equal services also contribute to reducing the present birth rate of the poor and of depressed ethnic minorities. Their rates move down toward white middle-income levels as better life chances take hold.[8]

[7]We may someday urge eugenic programs upon Asian, African, and Latin American nations, as today American interest groups urge increased birth control abroad without lobbying seriously for this policy domestically, but even missionary eugenics seem unlikely.

[8]The same welfare policies are demographically eugenic: They equalize environmental conditions which otherwise make it impossible to identify authentic *hereditary* factors. Under pres-

American Population Distribution

Questions of population distribution within localities and between regions in the United States are often discussed by experts. No manifest national, regional or local policies about distribution exist, yet decisions are made 'around' the subject every year. For example, the far western states cannot meet water requirements for a population much larger than twice the present load (at least not if only current water sources are considered). Yet, water-use policies in the west today are designed to promote irrigation. A marked shift in economic emphasis from argiculture to industry could divert water resources to household and factory use.

Chapters 5 and 6 of this book document many ways in which people may not be *optimally* distributed in the United States. Rural villages are declining and leaving underemployed, stagnating pools of disadvantaged families. The housing supply in metropolitan areas is unstable, uneven, and in places, gravely inadequate, given the present intra-urban distribution. Yet the idea of an optimum distribution is as questionable as the concept of an optimum population size or rate of growth. It depends for its validity upon the values of diverse interest groups. Kentucky hill people, for example, may be impoverished and unemployed, but in view of their total attachment to their area, we cannot conclude objectively that they *should* be relocated.

In Chapter 2 of this book, we documented ways in which nuclear warfare could threaten all facets of American life. Against the criterion of civil defense, neither the population nor

ent conditions, defective heredity is thoroughly obscured by environmentally caused deprivations and deficiencies.

the industrial apparatus that helps maintain it, nor even the military bases that 'defend' the civilian population by offering a deterrent offensive capability, are rationally distributed. Periodically, there have been federal efforts to redistribute certain industries vital to defense, but these have not been substantial. The nation has not gone so far as to separate military bases and major targets from proximity to metropolitan populations. *No* explicit national population policy exists on issues of distribution, whether on problems of civil and industrial defense or mere improvement in the balance of employment opportunities from area to area.

Immigration Policies

During the first two centuries of settlement of the United States, few restrictions were placed upon free movement in and out of the country. As a steady buildup of the population continued, and as the nation transformed from a rural to an industrial system, competition for occupational advantage intensified. Intergroup hostilities also intensified.

The first important federal legislation set the tone and motive for nearly all subsequent immigration policies. In 1882, Congress suspended the immigration of Chinese laborers for ten years. Selective ethnic *exclusion* became the basis for immigration control. This first act was expanded to include all Asiatics except the Japanese, and was later extended to include them as well. Additional groups were excluded with each new piece of legislation: criminals, illiterates, radicals, the chronically and infectiously diseased, and ultimately, any individual regarded as likely to become a public charge.

As exclusionist restrictions evolved,

the concept of the *quota* was perfected. A 1924 act limited the annual immigration of anyone from any European country to 2 per cent of the number of foreign-born persons of that nationality living here at the time of the 1890 census. The immigration laws of 1929 combined the principle of exclusion with an entry quota based on national origin. The quota fixed proportions on the basis of the proportions of nationality groups in the 1920 census.

Total immigration from Europe was limited to 150,000 a year. Within this, however, the migration from Southern and Eastern European nations was limited to roughly 25,000, while more than 75,000 openings were assigned for England and Ireland. Italians, Greeks, and other Southern and Eastern Europeans were thus excluded from immigrating. Where about three in every four immigrants to the United States between 1901 and 1910 came from these areas, less than one in ten came after 1935. Less than one-fourth of the total quota provided was filled between 1930 and about 1955, as people in the favored nations had no economic or social incentive to emigrate.

Congress modified slightly its 1929 legislation several times in the last 35 years. During World War II and after, restrictions were modified to accommodate refugees and victimized displace persons. Even some of these modifications were discriminatory, however. The Displaced Persons Act of 1948 required that 30 per cent of those let in were to be agriculturalists, and that half of the Germans and Austrians admitted were to be of "German ethnic origin." Altogether less than half a million persons migrated to the United States under this act.

The 1929 law was further modified in 1952, but the McCarran-Walter Act of that year preserved the guiding principles of restriction through quotas by national origin, exclusion, and rigidly absolute ceilings. Not until 1965, when a new act was made into law, were these principles modified significantly. The 1965 act sought to replace the more onerous features of national quotas and exclusion with principles based upon employability, job guarantees, and acceptance of responsibility by already naturalized or native citizens.

The conflict of values implicit in American immigration policies is best manifested at times when foreign troubles stimulate sympathy and aid. When Korea was devastated by war, and again when Hungary was torn by the Budapest Revolt, the American public and its legislators were torn between helping persons in distress and excluding 'undesirable' aliens. The parallel between this conflict and all majority-minority group relations in the United States is striking. In both, there is customarily an emphasis on discriminatory exclusion, except in periods of special military or political *crisis*.

Under peacetime conditions, the important determinant of immigration policy is most often the job market. In spite of general affluence, the question seems to be whether newcomers should be let in who might compete for jobs. Even when paychecks are fat, if job openings are few and especially if opportunities for less skilled employment are limited, then resistance to immigration increases.

For example, South Bend, Indiana, is a city where many automotive factory workers have lost their jobs or have been replaced by plant shutdown and automation. In a major Labor Day speech in that city in the presidential election campaign of 1964, Republic vice-presidential candidate William E. Miller voiced his ticket's opposition to any increases in immigration quotas. He said that, if elected, the Goldwater-Miller administration would "refuse to toy with dangerous programs in the field of tariffs and immigration which could well destroy our labor market. . . . Immigrants need jobs . . . Are you willing to give them yours?" Miller asked his audience of factory workers. The 1965 Act did change policy, but with safeguards against labor competition.

Changes in immigration policy are also influenced by the ethnicity of native and naturalized Americans. Italian-Americans, Polish-Americans, and many other nationality groups are affected by strong ties of family loyalty. They often have kin they want to bring into the United States. They often want to reunite their families on American soil. This fact still exerts strong political force, although it has been dampened by the division of Europe into West and East. Nationality group lobbyists and representatives continue to press for liberalized immigration policies. Their role in passage of the 1965 Act was very substantial. This pressure increases when domestic economic conditions are good and in peacetime. Of course, as generations of Europeans accommodate to the United States, ties with the former homeland and with kin become more dilute; the pressure for change weakens.

An Overview

American life—the physical environment and the local social institutions in particular—has been shaped since the founding of the Colonies by the fact of rapid population change. Since the Civil War, the national population has increased from about 24 million to about 180 million persons. The *rate* of growth declined over each decade from 1890 to 1930 because of immigration restrictions and a gradual, long-term decline in the birth rate. But even this drop in the rate was reversed after 1940, due to an increasing birth rate.

This ever-expanding population, more heterogeneous than any other in modern history, changed location, distributed itself and redistributed itself restlessly, and in the process hacked out of a raw environment a ceaselessly extending string of communities, all in response to the pull of *opportunity*. A society designed around high and rapid in-migration and domestic migration toward opportunity is inevitably a society in which the interrelated units of social life, environment, and technology, are bound to contradict and to strain one another again and again.

Thus, the nearly 17 million immigrants who entered this country in the second half of the 19th century, and the almost 19 million more who entered during the next 30 years, had to crowd into seaboard cities and towns, and into cramped and wretched housing within these communities. Provisions and adjustments were rarely made to accommodate newcomers until long *after* their arrival. Differences in health and living standards, and great differences in death rates between natives and newcomers, reflected this failure to adjust in advance. Yet, sound work and income opportunities were so plentiful that the social problems multiplied by rapid and high in-migration were always mitigated or ignored. The odds for survival were always so good for so many — native and newly arrived alike — that the national eye has historically remained trained on the quest for opportunity, for economic growth, and not upon the quest for the resolution of population problems.

As the flow of immigration from without has been cut off, population problems of community dislocation, change in the age structure, and accommodation to the decline of rural areas and the rise of cities, have become a chief source of domestic issues. The issues are seldom discussed in terms of population, however, for the cultural prescription of this pluralistic society has always been that population growth and change are natural processes, not to be tampered with except as questions of ethics and health under marriage and related laws governing personal relations. If the issue of the national rate of population growth is raised, for example, it is most likely to be displaced: The issue becomes one of helping to control population growth in foreign, developing societies. Or it becomes one of birth control for problematic groups within the national society. Reformers and commentators, for instance, are most often concerned with birth control and family planning among families of the poor.

In lieu of explicit policies about population control, the adjustive approach is taken to problems that ensue from rapid population change. Initially, the growing reserve of children in the national population were directed into the expanding labor force. With the advent of child labor laws, children were directed mainly into full time attendance at school, again under laws of compulsory attendance. In 1900, for example, about 18 out of every 100 children from 10 to 15 years old were in the labor force. In 1950, only 5 per 100 were so employed. Underneath these surface changes, however, the fact of continued, high growth in the youth population persists. No matter how long schooling is extended, new difficulties of fit between a growing youth population and a comparatively static labor force keep cropping up.

Social problems connected with population change stem, then, from relations between population characteristics and processes and other elements in the national society. The changing distribution of the American population, for example, results from changes in the location of opportunities, but these result from changes, not in population, but in technology and the economy. Wars, for instance, cause industries to build up where there were none before. Wars cause industries to shift from one part of the country to another. Technological changes induce the collapse of some industries and the development of others. Populations relocate, families expand and communities grow or decline as a function of these economic and technological changes.

Therefore, with the exception of the pressures induced by world population growth, most population problems are in fact social problems that result from incompatible rates of change in relations between the technology, environmental uses, and social organization of the nation on the one hand, and population changes on the other. These incompatibilities are reflected in dislocations, crowding, mortality differences between ethnic and income groups, and in the decline of communities. We have also suggested that immigration policies represent an excellent case model for social problems based in conflicts of value.

References

Blake, Judith. *Family structure in Jamaica: the social context of reproduction.* Glencoe, Ill.: The Free Press, 1961.

Brown, Harrison. *The challenge of man's future.* New York: Viking Press, 1954.

Burch, Thomas K. "Facts and fallacies about world population growth" — *Catholic World.* March, 1960.

Coale, Ansley J. and Hoover, Edgar M. *Population growth and economic development in low income countries: a case study of India's prospects.* Princeton University Press. 1958.

Cold Spring Harbor Symposium on Quantitative Biology. *Population studies: Animal ecology and demography.* Vol. XXII. Cold Spring Harbor, Long Island, New York: The Biological Laboratory, 1957.

Cook, Robert C. *Human fertility: the modern dilemma.* New York: William Sloane Associates, 1951.

Davis, Kingley, ed. "A crowding hemisphere: population change in the Americas" — *Annals of the American Academy of Political and Social Science.* Vol. 316, March, 1958.

Davis, Kingsley and Blake, Judith. "Social structure and fertility: an analytic framework" — *Economic Development and Cultural Change.* April, 1956.

de Lestapis, S., S. J. *Family planning and modern problems.* New York: Herder and Herder, 1961.

Duke University School of Law. "Population control" — *Law and Contemporary Problems.* Vol. 25, No. 3, Summer 1960, Durham, 1960.

Eldridge, Hope T. *Population policies: a survey of recent developments.* Washington: International Union for the Scientific Study of Population, 1954.

Freedman, Ronald, Whelpton, Pascal K. and Campbell, Arthur A. *Family planning, sterility, and population growth.* New York: McGraw-Hill, 1959.

Guttmacher, Alan F., with Best, Winfield and Jaffe, Frederick S. *The Complete book of birth control.* New York: Ballantine Books, 1961, (paperback).

Hauser, P. M., ed. *Population and world politics.* Glencoe, Ill.: Free Press, 1958.

———— ed. *The population dilemma.* The American Assembly, Columbia University. Englewood Cliffs, N.J.: Prentice-Hall, Inc., 1963.

Hauser, P. M., & Duncan, O. D., eds. *The study of population: An inventory and appraisal.* Chicago: University of Chicago Press, 1959.

Hertzler, J. O. *The crisis in world population.* Lincoln, Nebraska: University of Nebraska Press, 1956.

Hirschman, Albert O. *The strategy of economic development.* New Haven; Yale University Press, 1958.

Hoffman, Paul G. *One hundred countries—one and one-quarter billion people.* Washington, D.C.: Albert and Mary Lasker Foundation.

Jaffe, A. J. *People, jobs and economic development: A case history of Puerto Rico supplemented by recent Mexican experiences.* Glencoe, Ill.: Free Press, 1959.

Meier, Richard L. *Modern science and the human fertility problem.* New York: Wiley, 1959.

Milbank Memorial Fund. *Research in family planning,* Princeton University Press, 1962.

————*Trends and differentials in mortality.* New York: Author, 1956.

Myrdal, Alva. *Nation and family: The Swedish experiment in democratic family and population policy.* London: Kegan Paul, Trench, Trubner, 1945.

National Bureau of Economic Research. Special Conference Series, No. 11. *Demographic and economic change in developed countries.* Princeton, University Press, 1960.

Osborn, Fairfield. *Population: An international dilemma.* New York: Population Council, 1958.

Petersen, William. *Population.* New York: Macmillan, 1961.

Population Reference Bureau: *Population Bulletin* (Published eig..t times a year), 1507 M Street, N.W., Washington, D.C. (NOTE: The Population Reference Bureau, a pioneer in public education on the subject of demography, collects, coordinates, interprets, and publishes in its Bulletin, data on population trends.)

Sauvy, Alfred. *Fertility and survival, population problems from Malthus to Mao-Tse-Tung.* New York: Criterion Books, Inc., 1961.

Sax, Karl. *Standing room only.* Boston: Beacon Press, 1957.

Spengler, J. J., & Duncan, O. D., eds. *Demographic analysis, selected readings.* Glencoe, Ill.: Free Press, 1956. (a)

———— eds. *Population theory and policy, selected readings.* Glencoe, Ill.: Free Press, 1956. (b)

Stycos, J. Mayone. *Family and fertility in Puerto Rico: a study of the lower income group.* New York: Columbia University Press, 1955.

Sulloway, A. W. *Birth control and Catholic policy.* Boston: Beacon Press, 1959.

Taeuber, C., & Taeuber, Irene B. *The changing population of the United States.* New York: Wiley, 1958.

Thompson, Warren. *Population problems.* New York: McGraw Hill, Revised, 1963.

United Nations, Department of Economic and Social Affairs, New York: *The future growth of world population.* 1958.

———— *Demographic yearbook.* Published annually.

_____ Handbook of vital statistics methods, studies in methods, Series F, No. 7, 1955.

_____ Handbook of population census methods, studies in methods, Series F. No. 5, 1954.

_____ Report on the world social situation, with special reference to the problem of balanced social and economic development. New York: United Nations, 1961.

United Nations, Department of Social Affairs, Population Division. The determinants and consequences of population trends (Population Studies No. 17), New York, 1953.

Vogt, William. People: challenge to survival. New York: William Sloane Associates, 1960.

Westoff, C. F., Potter, R. G., Jr., Sage, P. C., & Mishler, E. G. Family growth in metropolitan America. Princeton, N.J.: Princeton University Press, 1961.

Williamson, H. F. and Buttrick, J. A. Economic development, principles and patterns. New York: Prentice-Hall, 1954.

Wrong, Dennis H. Population. New York: Random House, 1956.

DOES OVERPOPULATION MEAN POVERTY
Joseph Marion Jones

I. The "Population Explosion"

What is meant by the "Population Explosion"? It has taken all the vast reaches of time for world population to reach 3 billion. It will take only 35 years to add the next 3 billion if present growth rates remain unchanged. And it will take less than 35 years after that for 6 billion people to double to 12 billion, if present growth rates persist.

Just since World War II the rate at which the population of the world is growing has doubled, increasing from 1 percent to 2 percent a year, and it is expected to go higher.

For every four persons on earth in 1950 there are today five, and ten years hence there will be six.

In 1961, the number of people added to the world's population was equivalent to more than the entire population of France.

Is rapid population growth a new problem? Yes. Population growth at today's rates, and at those projected for the future, is something entirely new

The Facts about Population Growth and Economic Development, Center for International Economic Growth, 1963; reprinted with permission of Planned Parenthood—World Population, and the author.

under the sun. According to the best possible estimates, based upon historical and archeological evidence, it took hundreds of thousands of years for world population to reach about 250 million by the time of Christ, and it took 16 centuries more for that figure to double, to 500 million, population growth being held to an extremely small fraction of 1 percent each year by starvation, disease, and violence. But about 1650 the growth rate began to move up:

In the years	The average annual increase world population was
1650-1750	0.3 percent
1650-1950	0.5 percent
1900-1950	0.9 percent
1930-1940	1.0 percent
1961	2.0 percent

The Mainland China census of 1953 produced a population figure of 583 million, which was 100 million more than had been estimated, but its accuracy is seriously questioned and there is no consensus as to whether the figure is too high or too low. The official Chinese indications of both birth and death rates and of rates of natural in-

THE "POPULATION EXPLOSION"

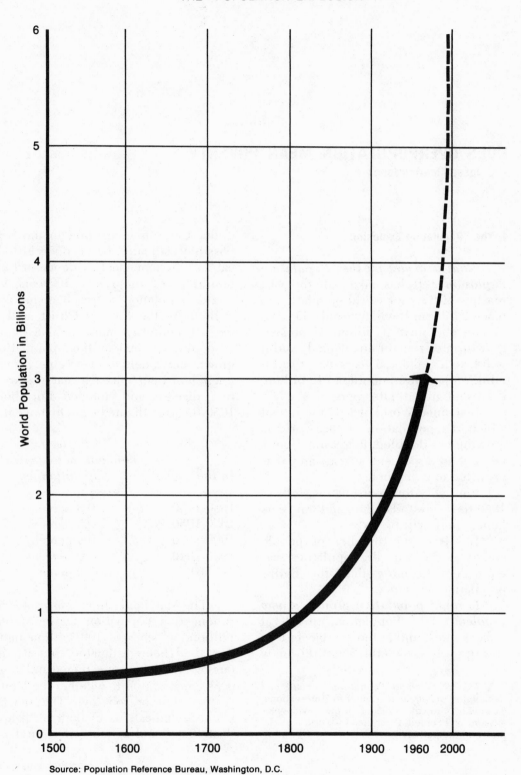

Source: Population Reference Bureau, Washington, D.C.

crease are believed to be far out of line on the low side. The population of Mainland China is believed by a number of experts to total about 690 million today and to be increasing at about 2.3 per cent a year.

In 1961, censuses taken in India and Pakistan revealed populations of 438 million and 95 million, there being 7 million and 4 million more people,

increase of 2.4 percent between 1961 and 1966, 2.8 percent between 1966 and 1971, 2.7 percent between 1971 and 1976. The estimated population increase over the next 15 years is put at 187 million people, which is slightly larger than the entire population of the United States today. Recent studies of the population growth rate in Pakistan indicate an annual figure of 2.5 percent

POPULATION PROJECTIONS TO THE YEAR 2000, FOR THE WORLD, CONTINENTS AND REGIONS
(in millions)

	1950	1960	1970	1975	2000
WORLD TOTAL	2,500	2,920	3,500	3,860	6,280
AFRICA	199	237	294	331	517
Northern Africa	43	53	67	76	147
Middle and Southern Africa	156	185	227	254	370
NORTHERN AMERICA	168	197	225	240	312
LATIN AMERICA	163	206	265	303	592
ASIA (excluding the Asian part of the Soviet Union and Japan)	1,296	1,524	1,870	2,093	3,717
JAPAN AND RYUKYU ISLANDS	84	96	110	117	153
EUROPE (excluding the European part of the Soviet Union)	393	424	457	476	568
Northern and Western Europe	133	140	148	154	180
Central Europe	128	140	151	156	183
Southern Europe	132	144	158	166	206
OCEANIA	13.2	16.3	19.4	21.0	29.3
Australia & New Zealand	10.2	12.7	14.9	16.0	20.8
Pacific Islands	2.9	3.6	4.5	5.0	8.6
SOVIET UNION (Asian and European parts combined)	181	215	254	275	379

Source: United Nations, Department of Economic and Social Affairs: "The Future Growth of World Population" (Population study No. 28), New York, 1958. High estimates are used through 1975 and medium estimates for 2000.

respectively, than had been previously estimated. Following the 1961 census the Government of India, which had been reporting to the United Nations an estimated annual population increase of 1.3 percent, now projects in its Third Five Year Plan an annual population

rather than the 2.0 percent previously reported.

In spite of gaps and inadequacies which still exist, vital statistics are improving, and as they improve they expose even more clearly the gravity of the population crisis.

Why has the rate of world population growth increased so spectacularly in recent years? Chiefly because of the sudden and sharp decline in death rates, without any corresponding decline in other advanced countries. Also, in a number of countries there has been some improvement in food supply. The result has been a drastic decline in infant and child mortality, some im-

DECLINING DEATH RATE

America: Late 1930's—1960   Asia and Africa: 1946—1958-60

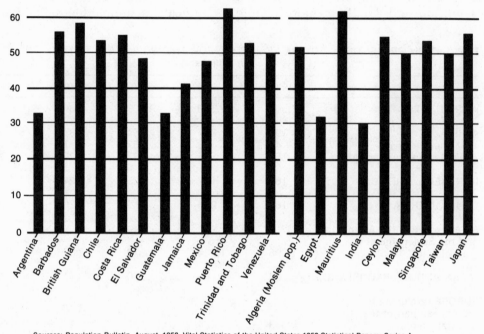

Sources: Population Bulletin, August, 1958. Vital Statistics of the United States 1959.Statistical Papers: Series A, Vol. 13, No. 4, UN, New York. Demographic Yearbooks.

the very high birth rates, in Asia, Africa, and Latin America, where two-thirds of the human race live. The introduction in public health programs, of newly discovered insecticides such as DDT, and antibiotics, vaccines, sulfa compounds, and other "miracle drugs" have brought mass infectious and contagious diseases under varying degrees of control in most underdeveloped countries. These programs are administered at modest expense and on a vast scale, frequently by or with the assistance of technical experts from United Nations organizations, the United States, or

provement in general health, and a sharp rise in the life expectancy of entire populations.

Death rates have been reduced by more than a third in Chile and Costa Rica, and by two-thirds in Puerto Rico, in the last 30 years. And they have been reduced by a third or more in India, Malaya, Ceylon, and Pakistan just since World War II.

"Death control" has thus been introduced into the continents of Asia, Africa, and Latin America. It is popular, relatively inexpensive, requires little initiative on the part of the people, and meets little or no resistance from them. But birth rates are as high as before. The decline in death rates is expected to continue in the underdeveloped countries for many years to come, but there is very little prospect for a decline in birth rates, unless something is done.

Public health programs were introduced into Latin America after World War I, and declines in death rates there began somewhat earlier than in Asia and Africa.

Where are birth rates highest? In which parts of the world is population growing the fastest? Birth rates are highest in the underdeveloped areas of Asia, Africa and Latin America. In those continents live roughly two-thirds of the world's population of 3,000,000,000; and birth rates there average between 40 and 50 per year per thousand people. Birth rates are much lower in Europe

(19 per thousand); the USSR (26); the United States and Canada (25); Australia, New Zealand (23); and Japan (19).

Rates of population increase are also higher in the underdeveloped areas of Asia, Africa, and Latin America (even though death rates there are still relatively high) than in the economically more advanced areas of the world where there are fewer people and where both lower birth rates and comparatively much lower death rates prevail. The figures are: Asia, (not including Japan) 2.3 percent per year; Africa, 1.9 percent; Latin America, 2.5 percent; Europe, 0.8 percent; the United States and Canada, 1.7 percent; the USSR, 1.8 percent; Australia and New Zealand, 1.4 percent; and Japan, 1.0 percent.

There was a sharp rise in birth rates immediately following World War II in many of the developed countries — in

WORLD POPULATION INCREASE BY REGION

	Mid-year Estimate 1950 1959 Population (millions)		1954-1958		
			Birth Rate	Death Rate	Annual Rate of Increase
			(per thousand) (annual average)		(percent)
ASIA (excluding Japan)	1,293	1,529	40[1]	—*	2.3*
AFRICA	198	236	45	26	1.9
Northern	65	78	45	25	2.0
Middle and South	133	158	46	27	1.9
LATIN AMERICA	163	201	41	16	2.5
EUROPE	395	423	19	11	0.8
Northern and Western	133	141	18	11	0.6
Central	128	138	19	11	0.8
Southern	134	144	21	10	0.9
NORTHERN AMERICA	168	197	25	9	1.7**
USSR (Asian and European parts combined)	181	210	26	8	1.8
AUSTRALIA AND NEW ZEALAND	10.2	12	23	9	1.4
JAPAN	83	93	19	8	1.1

Source: United Nations *Demographic Year books* and other United Nations publications; and, Government of India Planning Commission: "Third Five Year Plan".

*United Nations publications show for Asia: Birth rate 40; death rate 22; annual rate of increase, 1.8 percent. However, following the 1961 census of India the Indian Government revised its figures radically and in the Third Five Year Plan it estimated an average annual population growth rate, 1961-1966 of 2.4 percent (instead of 1.3 percent as it had previously reported). Recent studies of population growth in Pakistan indicate a figure of 2.5 percent rather than the reported 2.0 percent. As for Mainland China, the figure frequently used for annual population increase is 2 percent, derived from official releases. However, more recent estimates indicate that the population of Mainland China is around 690 million and growing by 16 million a year, which means an annual increase of 2.3 percent a year. We are therefore taking the liberty of revising accordingly the annual increase figures for Asia in this table.

**The figure for the United States, 1960-61, is 1.6 percent.

Western Europe, North America, Australia and New Zealand—where standards of living are high and where birth control has been long and widely practiced. This was attributable largely to millions of extra marriages and births which had been deferred during the war. This "baby boom" was short-lived in Europe, but the higher rates of population increase have persisted in the United States, Canada, Australia and

creasingly eliminating jobs at a time when millions are being added to the labor force each year. Moreover, these annual entrants into the labor force will increase sharply for the products of the postwar "baby boom" are beginning to hit the labor market.

What are the rates of population growth in the countries of Asia? They vary widely, as shown in the table below. In all Asian countries except

RATES OF ANNUAL POPULATION INCREASE IN CERTAIN COUNTRIES IN ASIA

(Latest available figures) Country	Birth* Rates	Death* Rates	Annual Rate of Natural Increase (percent)*
China (Taiwan)—1960	39.5	6.9	3.3
Malaya—1959	42.2	9.7	3.3
Singapore—1960	37.8	6.2	3.1
Philippines (est. 1953-1959)	—	—	2.6
Ceylon (est. 1953-1959)	47	22	2.5
Thailand (est. 1954-1956)	47	23	2.4
China (Mainland) (est. 1960)	—	—	2.3**
Pakistan (est. 1951-1961)	—	—	2.1***
India (est. 1951-1961)	—	—	2.0***
Indonesia (est. 1954-1956)	43	24	1.9
Japan—1959	17.5	7.4	1.0

Sources: For China (Taiwan), Malaya, Singapore, Philippines, Ceylon, and Japan, United Nations *Demographic Yearbook,* 1960. For Thailand and Indonesia, United Nations Economic Commission for Asia and the Far East: "Population Trends and Related Problems of Economic Development in the ECAFE Region," June 1959. For India and Pakistan, estimates based on 1961 census data. For Mainland China, estimates of a number of leading authorities.
*Birth rates and death rates are in terms of 1000 of the population per year. Rates of natural increase are in percent of total population of the country.
**See Footnote 1 to Table II (omitted).
***These are annual average figures for ten years. They are estimated to be higher now, 1962 (see Footnote 1 to Table II).

New Zealand, where a pattern of earlier marriage and larger families prevails amid prosperous economic conditions. At the present time the land space and the mature expanding economies of these countries accommodate rapid population growth, while permitting increases in average levels of living. Even so, the problem of providing housing, educational and health facilities and other services is a great strain. And in the United States the problem of finding jobs is even more serious. Science and technology have nearly decimated employment in agriculture, and now automation in industry is in-

Japan birth rates are extremely high; death rates vary because of differing economic, social and political conditions and the extent and quality of public health programs. Japan is a case apart, for widespread abortion and birth control have brought about a low birth rate; relatively good economic conditions and public health services have brought about a low death rate; and these together have operated to produce a population increase rate of only 1 percent.

What is the situation in Latin America? In Latin America variations in population increase are also extremely wide. In the temperate zone countries of Argentina and Uruguay where relatively higher standards of living prevail, birth rates are much lower than elsewhere in Latin America. The Central American countries together have the highest rates of increase of any area in the world.

Throughout Latin America there is evidence of a high degree of "death control" but nowhere except in Argentina and Uruguay is there evidence of fertility control. Latin America as a whole has the highest rates of population increase of any region.

less, the rates of population increase are high, as shown in the table below. As public health services and nutritional levels improve, death rates are expected to continue to decline and population growth rates to increase. Thus Africa, like other underdeveloped regions of the earth seeking economic and social progress, has serious population problems.

What accounts for the wide variations among countries?

In Birth Rates? The lower birth rates that prevail in one-third of the world comprising Europe, the USSR, the United States and Canada, Argen-

RATES OF ANNUAL POPULATION INCREASE IN CERTAIN COUNTRIES IN LATIN AMERICA

(Latest available figures) Country	Birth* Rates	Death* Rates	Annual Rate of Natural Increase* (percent)
Dominican Republic (est. 1953-1958)	—	—	3.5
Costa Rica (1959)	42.8	9.0	3.4
Mexico (1960)	45.5	11.4	3.4
Nicaragua (est. 1953-1958)	—	—	3.4
El Salvador (1960)	44.8	10.8	3.4
Guatemala (1960)	50.0	17.9	3.2
Brazil (1961)	—	—	3.1
Venezuela (est. 1953-58)	—	—	3.0
Chile (1959)	35.4	12.5	2.3
Argentina (1960)	22.3	8.1	1.4
Uruguay (est. 1953-1958)	—	—	1.3

Source: For Costa Rica, Mexico, El Salvador, Guatemala, Chile, and Argentina, United Nations *Demographic Yearbook,* 1960. For Brazil, Population Reference Bureau: "Population Profile," April 2, 1962. For others, Department of Statistics, Pan American Union Release 4117a6, No. 700, July 27, 1960.
*Birth and death rates are in terms of 1000 of the population per year. Rates of natural increase are in percent of total population of the country.

What about Africa? Considerably less is written or known about the population problems of Africa than about those of Asia and Latin America, chiefly because vital statistics for most African countries are scarce and unreliable and population density in most African countries is relatively low. But a number of things *are* known: Birth rates are extremely high; infant and child mortality rates are extremely high; malnutrition is endemic, over-all death rates, though lower than in the past and declining, are still high; and neverthe-

tina and Uruguay, Australia and New Zealand, and Japan are the result of some form of family limitation brought about by practices ranging from abortion and contraception to late marriage and celibacy. But of course the exercise of these practices in any particular country (or group of related countries) is the product of history and tradition, social structure and culture, religion, and economics.

For example, late Hellenistic, late Hebraic, and early Christian cultures produced in Western Europe a family unit in which a man was responsible for the support only of his wife and their children (and of immediate relatives without means of support), and it was assumed he would not marry until he was in a position to discharge his responsibilities properly. There was strong social pressure against "improvident marriages." The results were relatively

dren. Historically, where the will to limit families has existed, as for example in Europe, it has prevailed in spite of religious or government opposition and, until relatively recently, with only common sense or folk methods as aids.

In Death Rates? Variations depend for the most part upon the relative effectiveness of different public health

ESTIMATED ANNUAL RATES OF POPULATION INCREASE IN
CERTAIN COUNTRIES IN AFRICA

	Percent	Period Covered
Algeria	3.3	1954-1960
Libya	1.6	1954-1960
Egypt	3.5	1957-1960
Sudan	3.1	1956-1960
Kenya	1.6	1948-1960
Ghana	4.0	1948-1960
Guinea	2.9	1955-1960
Nigeria	2.0	1953-1961
Tanganyika	1.7	1957-1960
Somalia	2.4	1931-1960
Mozambique	1.1	1950-1960
Union of South Africa	2.4	1951-1960

Sources: *Population Index,* January, 1962—Office of Population Research, Princeton University.

late marriages and also, as infant and child mortality declined in the late 18th century and after, family limitation in marriage and a small family pattern.

Asian cultures, on the other hand, produced the "joint family" which included brothers and their wives, and in many cases first cousins, with joint family responsibilities and pooled property and earnings. This system, in turn, gave rise to extremely early marriages and uncontrolled fertility.

These are but indications of the many factors that cause wide variations in birth rates. Full explanations require, for any country or group of related countries, extensive historical and social research and analysis.

Family planning depends upon the *will* of a couple (from whatever motivation) to limit the number of their chil-

services, using the new products of medical research, in controlling mass infectious diseases. Beyond that, they depend upon the quality of medical services in general and their availability to the masses of the people, population density and the availability of cultivatable land, the nutritional adequacy of diets, and conditions of sanitation.

In the Rates of Population Increase? The rate of population increase is the difference between the birth rate and the death rate. One can get various combinations of birth and death rates which produce under extremely different conditions the same rates of population increase. For example, the rate of natural increase in the United States and Indonesia are, 1.6 percent and 1.9 percent respectively, but the United States has a birth rate of 25 per thousand and a death rate of 9, while Indonesia has a birth rate of 43 per thousand and a death rate of 24.

Europe and North America once had high birth rates and high rates of population increase. What happened to change the pattern? Before the middle of the 18th century Europe had high birth rates, high death rates, low life expectancy, and very slow rates of population growth. Beginning around 1750 — in a setting of revolutionary advances in medicine, science and technology, growing industrialization, increasing world development and trade, improvement in transportation, and rising standards of living — there occurred a "demographic transition" of greatest importance. First, the death rate began a slow and steady decline; and then *several generations later*, after the middle of the 19th century, the birth rate began a similar decline, slow at first. During the early decades of this "demographic transition" — before birth rates started declining — population growth was extremely rapid. But then the accelerating decline in the birth rate began to catch up, so that by 1940 Europe had nearly stabilized its population with low death rates, low birth rates, and slow rates of population growth.

A somewhat similar demographic transition occurred in the United States, but with differences. During colonial times the United States had very high fertility but with death rates lower than in Europe; population increase was therefore rapid. But in the latter part of the 18th century death rates began to decline, causing an even more rapid population increase for a generation or so until about 1800 when birth rates began a steady decline. By 1930 the United States, too, had achieved low birth and death rates and a slow rate of population increase. However, the rate of population increase in the United States is now 1.6 percent.

May we not expect that there will be a decline in population growth in underdeveloped countries of Asia, Africa, and Latin America as they become more developed? It is questionable. Even if such a decline should occur, it would probably take place too late to prevent unmanageably large populations, for several reasons:

1. The *transition* in Europe and North America from high to low rates of population growth was *very slow* beginning with small populations in relation to resources and extending over about 150 years.

2. In the early decades of the demographic transition in Europe the decline in birth rates lagged behind declines in death rates for several generations, causing during that period a very rapid increase in the rates of population growth (which nevertheless did not reach one percent until after 1900). Death rates in the underdeveloped countries have in the last fifteen to thirty years plummeted, suddenly and spectacularly, much more so than in the 19th century (and are continuing to decline). If declines in birth rates lag behind for generations, as in Europe, populations will grow so large as to defy all efforts in theory about that economic and social development which might in theory bring about a decline in rates of population growth. Already, according to Mr. Eugene Black, President of the World Bank, "population growth threatens to nullify all our efforts to raise living standards in many of the poorer countries".

Will growing population pressures increase the likelihood of world unrest and war? The expectations among the peoples of many underdeveloped countries for a rapid rise in living levels are building up powerful pressures which can lead to violent internal revolutions (which could not in themselves change the economic situation and which would probably end in totalitarianism), or to external aggression, or to both. Uncontrolled population growth is making it virtually impossible, even with vast amounts of foreign aid and investment, to begin closing the gap between the richer and the poorer nations.

The per capita income in the underdeveloped countries as a whole is about $100; in Western Europe it is about $850; and in the United States it is about $2350. The income gap is thus extremely wide; moreover, it is growing. Whereas in ten years (1951-1960) the people in the underdeveloped countries (not including Mainland China) gained in per capita income only about $10 per person, the people in the United States gained about $225 per person in constant dollars; and in the years 1950-1959 the people living in the European Economic Community gained no less than $275 per person.

High rates of population increase which make it extremely difficult or impossible to raise per capita living standards in many of the underdeveloped countries, are thus feeding fires of violence and war. There can be little prospect of peace or world order so long as present rates of population increase persist. And ultimately there must be either a decrease in birth rates or an increase in death rates.

DEMOGRAPHIC TRENDS AND THEIR SIGNIFICANCE
Ewan Clague

This article deals with demographic trends, which are by no means new to members of the Bureau of Labor Statistics and the Department of Labor. We have been looking at these trends for a long time.

For example, I was engaged in this work in the middle 1930's in the Social Security Board. Then, we were trying to look forward to the year 2000. I later worked with the Bureau of Labor Statistics, where we tried to forecast the outlook for specific occupations, so that we could guide young people in what to study so that they could enter fields with a bright economic future. Incidentally, in my own advice to a youngster, I always emphasize that he first should select what he wants to do, and then only secondarily apply the economic test. I am not worried about anyone who enjoys his work, even if he is in a crowded occupation. However, this gives one example of the use of our projections.

How did we make our projections? Of course, we had to rely on sound,

solid data, not only our conjectures. We always have consulted the profession in every field where we have made a forecast. But we developed some information on the economic outlook, and published this in bulletins issued from time to time, projecting the growth of the labor force by major occupational groups for some years into the future.

James P. Mitchell, then Secretary of Labor, conceived the idea of putting this into a popular pamphlet. Mitchell believed that people would not read a statistical bulletin, but that they could understand a chart book with relatively simple text, even though they might not be able to go through the mathematical formulas that we used in making the projections.

And so, we have a basic bulletin; now we are issuing another edition based on the developments of the last few years. These charts are the basis for the judgments I am expressing in this article.

The census makes four projections for population. I believe that the most likely of these predicts 208 million people in 1970. (Chart 1.) This figure, in my opinion, will be too low, barring an unforeseen cataclysm. I expect a some-

Reprinted, with permission of the author and the Institute of Life Insurance, from *The Changing American Population*, 1962, pp. 11-20.

CHART 1: POPULATION GROWTH 1930-1970

Population Will Increase by 15%, to 208 Million In 1970

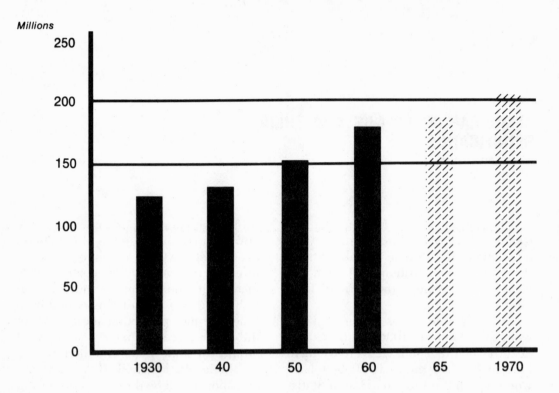

Millions

what larger population in 1970 than 208 million. However, this is the first step in our analysis of the labor force.

A division of the population by age brackets indicates some significant trends. One important population figure is the number of persons reaching age 18 annually. (Chart 2.) In the 1950's, there were approximately 2 million boys and girls reaching this age each year. In 1961, the number was about 2¾ million. This figure will stay the same for the next two years. Then, in a single year, in 1965, it will jump to 3¾ million. Obviously, this is due to the births of 1947. It means that anyone who tries to get into college in 1965 is going to have a difficult time.

There already is an increase in college students. Considering that the colleges are becoming crowded now, it is obvious what a problem the crowding will be in a few years. There is no relief in sight. Nor will there be any relief when we enter the 1970's, for during most of the next decade, the flood of young people will continue at the same level.

The college is one example of a place where there will be great population pressures. High schools are another example. The students who will swell the college population in 1965 now are in first-year high school. The high schools are going to be very crowded in the next few years; and one worries about the quality of the education given to these students. Then, in 1965, there will be the problem of how the colleges will handle the mass.

In addition, there is an increasing pressure on young people to go to college. If we fatten the percentage of high school graduates who go to college (say, up to one-fifth or more of this age group), there will be an even greater pressure on the colleges at that time. We often cite the number of teachers who will be needed in the high schools and colleges, and we emphasize the problem of facilities and equipment, including the question of whether television will help enlarge the teacher-pupil ratio, thereby making it possible for fewer teachers to handle more students.

How will we deal with the increased pressures on colleges? That is one question raised by our population projections. Another, related question is this: Will we educate more of our children in the future?

Our answer is, yes, we will. We estimate that about 6½ million students will go at least part-way through college in the 1960's. (Chart 3.) Twelve million others, we estimate, will complete high school and then quit. There are left about 5½ million young workers who will go part way through high school, and only about 2¼ million who will not go beyond grade school. This is much better than we did in the 1950's; we are educating more of our children.

Because of the increase in education, the typical entrant into the labor force in the 1960's will be at least a high school graduate. Therefore, the workers who do not graduate from high school will not get the better jobs: For this reason, we also stress the fact that about 7 million boys and girls will not finish high school. Most employers will be able to require for all good jobs a minimum of a high school diploma, thereby cutting off the workers at the lower end

CHART 2: YOUNG PERSONS REACHING 18 ANNUALLY 1950 TO 1970

Population Growth Will be Especially Rapid Among Youth Reaching Working Age

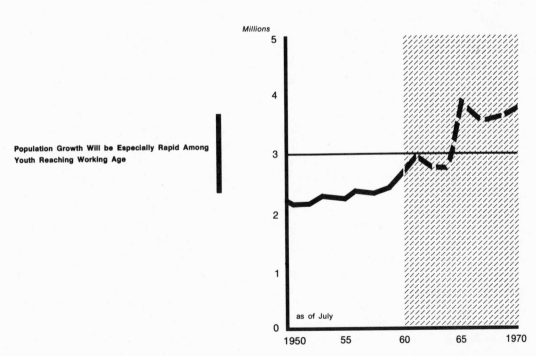

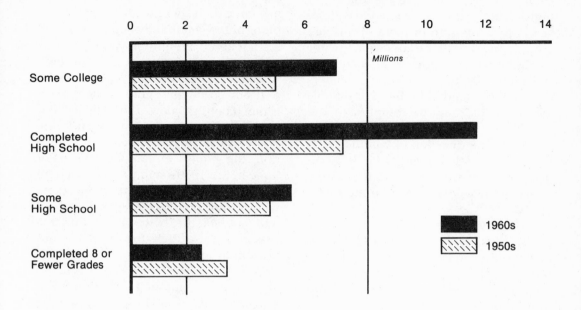

CHART 3: AMOUNT OF SCHOOLING OF NEW YOUNG WORKERS
IN THE 1960s & 1950s

of the scale, and leaving as their only outlet the unskilled and semi-skilled occupations.

Our population projections also deal with changes in the labor force. We estimate that the labor force will jump from some 73½ million in 1960 to some 87 million in 1970. (Chart 4.) We will lose about 15 million of our present labor force through retirement, disability or death. That will leave 58 million of us, and we will pick up 29 million more. Of these, 26 million will be new-entry young people, and 3 million will be adult women entering or re-entering the labor force. We foresee no slackening in the general upward trend in women's employment, a trend which has existed for at least four decades.

I would like to point out that our labor force projections are not based on projections of future birth rates; the workers of 1970 are already here among us. Our only problem in making these projections is estimating how many will die or retire.

Knowing what the present population is, we say that 26 million new young workers will begin their careers in the 1960's. (Chart 5.) In the 1950's, the number was only 19 million.

That is not the net gain in the labor force; it is the young entrants, from which we must subtract the workers who died or retired. The new entrants will number some 2½ million a year—and by 1970, 3 million. For a few years, the annual net gain will be about a million and a quarter to a million and a half. After that, it will be still higher.

One of the reasons why we have had higher unemployment rates recently is that more workers are entering the labor force, and more people are seeking work. A larger supply is likely to produce some leftovers. At any rate, the labor force certainly will grow much more rapidly in the coming decade. And year after year, there will be more job-seekers.

The current population trends are producing an imbalanced labor force. Our labor force has aged during the last decade. There were hardly any more people under age 35 in 1960 than there until about 1967 or 1968, in the end years of the decade. So in the years immediately ahead, this may be a great shortage area.

In brief, we expect almost no gain in prime workers, whom employers normally use, but there will be a further

Chart 4

HERE IS THE LABOR FORCE BALANCE SHEET FOR THE 1960s

	(MILLIONS)
NUMBER OF WORKERS IN 1960	73.6
SUBTRACT: Withdrawals— death, retirement, marriage, childbearing, etc.	—15.5
1960 WORKERS STILL IN LABOR FORCE IN 1970	58.1
ADD: Young entrants	+26.0
Adult women returning to work	+ 3.0
NUMBER OF WORKERS IN 1970	87.1

were in 1950. (Chart 6.) In other words, at the lower end of the age scale, we have had almost no gain. On the other hand, from 1950 to 1960, we added about 2½ million workers in the age group from 35 to 45, plus nearly 6 million over age 45. This means a distinct aging of our labor force.

From now to the 1970's, we will move in another direction. We will add 6½ million to the group *under* age 25. That is due to the flood of young people. For the middle-age group, 25 to 45, almost no change is in sight. The rise of 2 million in this group does not occur

growth of elderly people, 5½ million more than we have now. There will be an increase only in the very old and the very young workers. This will produce imbalance in the labor force. The shadow will grow during the decade, becoming more and more apparent. It will affect the way businessmen will have to manage their work forces. And it also may have a bearing on the kind of unemployment we have and the social problems that will grow out of it.

Another important trend is the ever-increasing number of women entering the labor force. Among teen-agers,

CHART 5: NEW YOUNG WORKERS ENTERING LABOR FORCE ANNUALLY
1950 TO 1970

26 Million Young Workers Will Enter Labor Force During 1960s; 40% More Than in 1950s

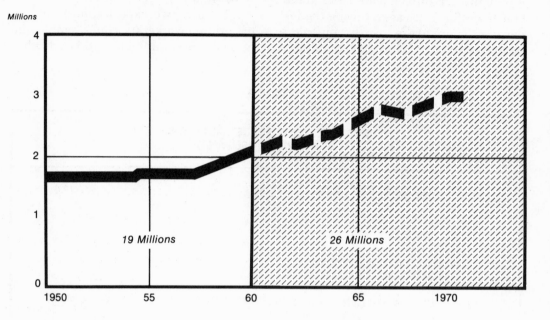

CHART 6: CHANGES IN THE NUMBER OF WORKERS IN EACH AGE GROUP
1950 TO 1960 AND 1960 TO 1970

Labor Force Changes Will Differ Significantly From Those of Past Decade

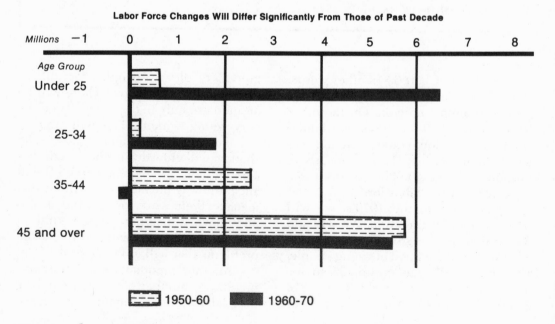

498 Major American Social Problems

about 30 per cent of the girls are in the labor force; among those aged 20-24, about 45 per cent. After this age, women often disappear from the labor force for a period of time. They get married and begin rearing a family. But later, at 35-40-45, large numbers of them return to the labor force.

We guess that by 1970, 55 women out of every 100 (married, widowed, single or divorced) in the age group 45 to 55 will be trying to earn a living. (Chart 7.) Even at age 55 to 65, there will be about 45 in 100. This means a

the year. That is because of a great increase of women and young people working in June, July and August. The number increases again at Christmas, Easter, and at other periods. One of the problems associated with our figures of employment and unemployment is that we are dealing with full-time, year-round workers, who normally work at least 2,000 hours a year, at the same time we are dealing with people who work quite intensively for only a few weeks or a few months, or who work a few hours a day all the year around.

CHART 7: PERCENT OF WOMEN IN EACH AGE GROUP WHO WILL BE IN THE LABOR FORCE IN 1970

A Larger Proportion of Women, Especially Older Women, Will Work

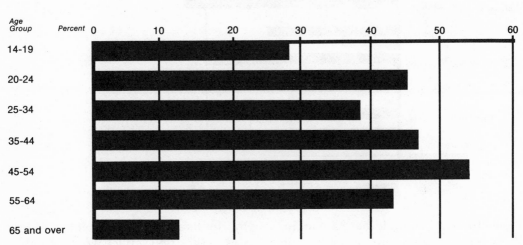

persistent increase in the number of women seeking jobs. We see no end to the trend.

Women are frequently part-time workers. They seem to prefer part-time jobs. Some of them are only occasional or intermittent workers. In a recent year, for example, when about 68 million persons were employed in July, there were no less than 78 million persons who worked some time during

There is a large fringe labor force, which varies month by month.

The occupational outlook also is affected by the distribution of Negroes. Some interesting facts emerge from a classification of Negro and white workers in 1959 by occupations. (Chart 8, p. 500.) Many of the whites are in the professional and technical groups, including proprietors, managers, clerical workers, sales people and skilled workers. But going to the lower occupations, by which I mean the occupations that require less education, the Negroes begin to appear in the semi-skilled group. Here we find a higher proportion of Negroes than of whites. This does not mean that there are fewer white workers

1970 there will be an increase by 40 per cent in professional and technical workers, including laboratory technicians, statistical technicians, and others who supplement the professions. (Chart 9.) This is a tremendous increase.

We estimate that there will be more

CHART 8: OCCUPATIONAL DISTRIBUTION OF NEGRO AND WHITE WORKERS IN 1959

Negro Workers Are Concentrated in Different Occupations Than White Workers

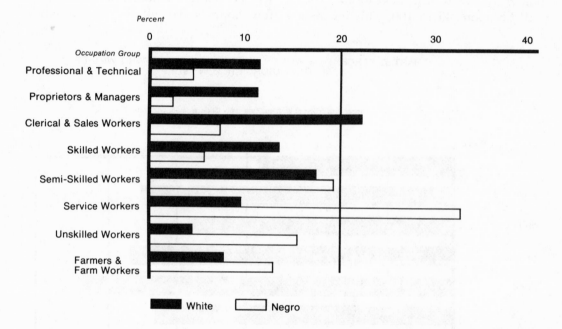

among the semi-skilled; there are more. However, a higher proportion of the Negro than of the white population do semi-skilled work. This is also true among the service and the unskilled workers, and even among the farmers and farm workers.

The preceding describes how the population is composed today. We also have a projection for the future. This may prove to be wrong, but it is our best estimate.

We believe that between 1960 and

proprietors and managers, more clerical, sales, skilled and service workers. There will be a slight decline in the proportion of semi-skilled workers, but no change at all in unskilled workers. Common labor is fading out.

Someday, that decline in farm workers must end. During my working life, from 1910 when I was a boy on a farm in the state of Washington until 1960, we have seen a decline of about 50 per cent in the farm labor force. We had about 11½ million farmers and farm workers in the spring of 1910, when they took the census. I would guess that on a comparable date now, the number would not be more than 5½ million. We have lost some 6 million in the interval.

We think there will be a further decline of another million or so. In fact, we think that the farmers and farm workers will shrink until they constitute no more than about 6 per cent of the entire labor force in 1975. But this trend will not go on indefinitely. Sooner or later, productivity in agriculture will catch up with that in industry and in the services. Then people may leave jobs in

output per worker) is not equal to that in the rest of the economy, and consequently, people still are drifting to the city. The demand for food, the pressures of the population on the food supply, eventually will put an end to that decline. From then on, the farm labor force will remain stable, or actually might increase.

In studying the occupational change that is likely to occur, it is interesting to consider the educational attainments of the different occupational groups. In 1959 among the professional and technical, 75 per cent had some college education, about 20 per

CHART 9: PERCENT CHANGE IN EMPLOYMENT 1960-1970

Job Opportunities Will Increase Fastest in Occupations Requiring Most Education and Training

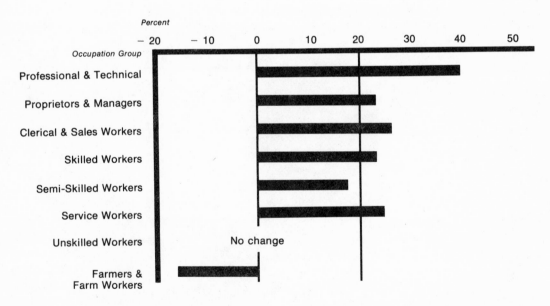

industry and commerce in the city, and move out to the farm to get higher wages. This can happen when farm productivity equals productivity in the rest of the economy. However, as yet, productivity on the farm per worker (the

cent had completed high school, and only 6 per cent did not reach high school graduation. Among proprietors and managers, there is a little more diversification. There were 38 per cent with less than a high school education, but there were 30 per cent with some college. Far different amounts of education were found in the less skilled groups. Only four semi-skilled workers in 100 had any college education. Only 6 per cent of the service workers, 5 per cent of the farm, 3 per cent of the unskilled workers had attended college.

This shows that the occupations that are expanding require more education, and those which are slowing down or declining require less. Obviously, a very important question is: Are our educational institutions expanding to keep up with the requirements of our growing occupations?

10

SOLUTIONS

Introduction

In Chapter 1 of this book we noted that awareness of a major social problem tells us little about whether the problem can be solved, remedied, or even comprehended. Our definition of a social problem did imply that influential groups become concerned about a social problem, most often in the belief that something worth doing can be done about it if only their concern were more widely shared, or if resources were invested toward a solution. Social problems tend to receive public interest to the extent that a belief in their resolution gains currency.[1]

The social problems attended to in this book are in general *unresolvable:* War, poverty, crime cannot be 'done away with,' without also doing away with society, at least as it has operated thus far. This does not mean that these and other major social problems are eternal or untreatable. It means that the possibility of warfare continuing in

some potentially catastrophic form is infinite.[2] It also means that crime may persist indefinitely. Large-scale violence and individual-scale violations of the law are just as probable future events as are peace and conformity.

Poverty, as indicated in the chapter on that problem, is an aspect of the kind of affluence we value and cultivate in America today. It is a 'price' of our present cultural design. Cash benefits, like other more symbolic rewards, could be distributed differently, to be sure. But with each new distribution, some groups might lose where others gained. What then of a transition from a society based on scarce resources to one based on *limitless* abundance? What of an economy in which growth in the national product were so great that a new distribution of income might eliminate poverty without seriously disadvantaging any group? Technologically, these are imaginable alternatives. Sociologically, as we suggested in approaching the root causes of poverty, new kinds of deprivations are inevitable. Of course,

---

[1]To the social scientist, a social problem may be worthy of study for quite different reasons, including the possibility that an unresolvable social problem, if comprehended as such, tells much about the nature of a society.

[2]Nuclear and biological weapons, for one thing, will be with us for the rest of human time. Their invention is irreversible.

new deprivations might prove to be of a socially and personally *less* costly type. Hence the worth of remedial efforts.

For the citizen, however, these seem to be unduly elaborate questions about social problems. Social problems often loom very large and call out for dramatic resolution. The citizen may sway between a defeating fatalism, a deadening belief that nothing can be done, and a susceptibility to authoritarian or stupid attacks upon problems. Often, the citizen asks nothing of the social scientist by way of analyses or solutions to social problems. At other times, he asks far too much. He asks what he would seldom demand of his physician — instant, permanent cure.

The social scientist can be useful to the citizen's effort to launch an attack upon a social problem by offering cumulative knowledge about schemes, tactics, and alternatives that are demonstrably worthless or mad. At best, the social scientist can invent *some* approaches to solutions and he can veto others without recourse to costly or damaging experimentation.

Keeping our citizen in view can be helpful. For he may give up too soon, or he may be overpersuaded that resolution of the problem is achievable, yet he is also engaged in direct encounter with the humanly severe costs and consequences of social problems in their daily unfolding. He may accept widespread poverty as inevitable or hopelessly complex; he may insist upon its elimination overnight. More often, however, he presses toward compromises.

Especially in an industrial and pragmatic culture, most groups that make up the population look ahead toward a partial, sporadic, yet *progressive* mediation of major social problems.[3]

[3]The social organization of a national society evolves, or matures. If people assess the process

Annually, public leaders join issue through party platforms, speeches, and campaign promises with those social problems they view as most pressing in that season. Witness a typical State of the Union Message to the Congress in its emphasis upon two major social problems we have described:

> Most Americans tonight enjoy a good life. But far too many are still trapped in poverty ... Let a just nation throw open to them the city of promise.... To the poor, through doubling the war against poverty this year. To Negro Americans through enforcement of the Civil Rights Law and elimination of barriers to the right to vote.

In this 1965 Message, President Lyndon Johnson referred also to crime:

> Every citizen has the right to feel secure in his home and on the streets of his community. To help control crime, we will recommend programs ... put the best techniques of modern science at their disposal . . . discover the causes of crime and better ways to prevent it.

Here, in the civic language of limited optimism, is the plain assumption that crime is preventable. Note, however, the presidential caution placed in the phrase, "better ways to prevent it."

The Delusion of the Philosopher-King

Social problems *in general* are not resolvable, then, but significant attacks

as coherent and directional, they call the maturation "social progress." Popularly, social progress is societal movement toward desired goals. Sociologically, social progress is an unhelpful concept because it *cannot* be described or identified over the historical long term. The philosophical bases of the idea of progress are questionable, too.

upon some aspects can be devised and implemented. We have also said that this is what citizens are in quest of most of the time: telling blows at points along the frontiers of a few salient problems.

This much is implicit in the very concept of a social problem. The concept of a social problem is negotiable *only* within a culture where the human situation is defined in important degree as a matter of problem-solving behavior. Take this cultural interpretation further. Our conceptions of specific social problems are themselves often neatly balanced. We seek problems we aspire to resolve. We hope (in the Faustian tradition) for the key to power and wisdom. Realization of this hope—success— would distroy the balance; it would induce the despair that can come with successful achievement. If we had no pressing issues to encounter, we should probably have to invent some at once, or disintegrate culturally.

If this is something of our basic design, then we must not be surprised to witness the evolution of *experts,* specialists who cultivate wisdom and don power in the service of resolving or attacking national problems. The American expert on a social problem is much like an updated version of Plato's ideal of the philosopher-king in his Republic. There, the wisest men of greatest knowledge were to be the natural heirs to total power. Sociology, as one modern social scientific discipline, for example, was born out of a similar 18th-century vision by Saint Simon. He envisioned a sociologist who would discover the natural laws of society and of social behavior and who therefore would have the power to *prescribe* public conformity to the inexorable force of these laws.

The utopic vision of the modern expert culminates in the model of the social practitioner as the physician of society.[4] In this model, the decision maker or client is provided with diagnosis, prognosis, and prescription by the social expert. The logic of the model is precisely that of the physician to the public. Citizens are expected only to support those agencies (such as universities) through taxes and good will which improve the ability of experts to diagnose and prescribe. Ultimately, clients may learn to have the good sense to act on the advice of the expert. In the meanwhile, their good sense may need some monitoring, some expert guidance.

None of this disparages the contributions social scientific and administrative experts can and do make in ameliorating social problems. Their work is based firmly on the great, demonstrable value to society of *specialization.* Agents of the Federal Bureau of Investigation can detect, apprehend, account for, and, on occasion, prevent crimes faster and more reliably than perhaps any body of agents of justice in the history of human society. The psychiatrist, the clinical psychologist, and the psychiatric social worker, specializing yet collaborating as they do, are often effective in alleviating the pain of mental disorder, even when the general state of knowledge in their domain is severely limited.

The work of the modern social expert is vindicated. It is justified by the principles of gain through increasing division of labor and of cumulative knowledge gained through scientific inquiry. There are effective recommendations that the traffic engineer and the safety expert can make, for instance, to

---

[4]Richard Korn, "Expert and Polity: Reconciling Wish and Prescription," *Mass Society in Crisis,* Bernard Rosenberg, et al, editors, Macmillan: New York, 1964, p. 578.

community leaders concerned with a spate of auto fatalities. A public treasurer or budget maker can rely, in coping with some problems, more completely upon the advice of an economist specializing in public finance than he can upon his own experience or his ability to guess what his electorate wishes.

Perhaps the greatest recent achievement of the social-scientifically oriented expert in the United States was the introduction of the policy of tax reduction. In 1964, the American government enacted a massive tax cut when its budget was already in deficit. As a result, the Gross National Product grew by an unprecedented total of $40 billion. One of the most significant aspects of this amount is that this is exactly as much as the government's economists predicted by way of growth. Moreover, the growth occurred, as they said it would, in a framework of stable prices, at least until the inflationary forces of the war in Vietnam set in in 1965.

Even where experts induce more social problems than they remedy, there is probably no reversing the trend toward greater specialization and greater public reliance upon the emerging experts. There is no stopping it, at least, without great changes in the culture which shapes the evolution of the social expert and the society which comes to depend upon its controls by virtue of the cultural arrangement. This evolution of experts is an outgrowth of personnel technology; that is, of the application of science to the preparation and supply of *elites*.

What, then, is the 'delusion' involved in our national dependence upon social-scientific and social-technical philosopher kings? The delusion rests in the common belief that expertise must ultimately prevent or eliminate social problems. The delusion lies, too, in the belief that a society is something like an engine; that its parts can be 'tuned up' mechanically to achieve progress or greater harmony. *Society is neither a machine nor a patient.* It cannot be rationally tuned up to work better. Neither can it be operated upon. Experts and the clients they serve cannot solve problems in society in the sense that they can accomplish a trip to the moon. Men cannot *do* things to or for one another in the way they can do things to the materials and events of nature. Men can control other men, of course, but not as objects — at least not for long. Even the mechanics of a tax cut depend upon how investors and other participants in the market economy come to define their confidence in the market.

The Political Core

Experts and the leaders they serve therefore cannot dispense rational or otherwise scientific human services. The premise of a democratic society is that the people rule. The population takes a direct part in distributing the advantages that promise to meet the different wants of citizens. In this condition, the tacks which groups take toward major social problems will depend upon what they want, how they fare under the current distribution of advantages, what they perceive about alternatives, and perhaps most of all, how much each group of citizens *cares* about the question. If the United States were not a democracy; if the rules under which advantages got distributed did not involve key roles for citizens, the process would differ, yet it would still be unmechanical and unscientific. For one thing, public intensity of concern with a problem, affects action, even in rigidly totalitarian societies

In advanced industrial societies, major social problems are transformed regularly into major policy issues. As such, whatever resolution is to be accomplished will be attempted politically. Social problems tend to become policy questions when they reach a certain salience, a certain intensity of public concern. A policy problem is a matter that is dealt with through a process in which various authorized leaders make *decisions* about who should get what, or who should be dealt with and in what manner. The process is political in that it entails the exercise of influence — of control — over the behavior of others by virtue of such factors and resources as authority, intensity of concern, status and money, and sometimes, expertise.[5]

Technological problems (as against social problems) also require action through human organization for their solution. Yet techniques for the manipulation of matter can be worked upon directly, while social problems may prevent action even if special knowledge has been accumulated. People tend to endorse those social facts which in themselves endorse established institutions. Groups may distrust facts that are found by anyone, including their own members, if the facts are inconsistent with group standards. In

[5]We now have the role of the expert in more accurate perspective. Advanced industrial population rely increasingly upon experts to the extent that new sources of influence are opened up when new knowledge about alternatives, appeals, and outcomes of decisions is developed. Even false knowledge, or the pretense of knowledge, may be useful for the short-run exercise of influence. (See Nelson W. Polsby, et al, *Politics and Social Life,* Houghton Mifflin: Boston, 1963, pp. 781-802. Also, Robert A. Dahl, *A Preface to Democratic Theory,* Chicago: University of Chicago Press, 1956.)

short, just as the ability to identify and define a social problem depends upon the values one chooses to apply, so the ability to solve a social problem often depends upon which values one is willing to revise or give new priority.

Our reason for identifying the central contemporary approach to social problems as political may now be clearer. The major ingredients in the ability of humans to solve social problems are decisions and transformations. One can treat a social problem only if transformations in social arrangements are made. (These can sometimes be made through the efforts of individuals to transform aspects of themselves. Indeed, this is often a major value assumption of historical religions: Desired social change can occur chiefly through individual transformations.) Individuals may arrange transactions with others which offer promise of accomplishing a collective transformation. In these activities, individuals make social decisions. They decide to transform existing arrangements, they decide to coalesce and cooperate, to join one group and to leave another. The process is by nature political: To *choose to change* a social policy or practice is to initiate a process of influencing others.

Public and Private Decisions

Decisions to change practices engaged in by the General Electric Corporation may be viewed as political and as having effects upon national social problems. Many material and symbolic rewards are private, and typically consumed by individuals or families. One important feature of private rewards is that any person can consume any one good or not, according to his preferences and his ability to pay. The production and consumption of private goods occurs within a decision process that is in essence political. This process is influential in causing and remedying social problems, as is the public decision process.[6] We shall distinguish between them, however, and speak of *market* processes in the private sphere and *political* processes in the public sphere.

Market transactions and political processes are the main but not the only means for making decisions about coping with social problems. In American society, where many institutions are left free from more than superficial regulation by the government, there are influential factors operating among groups, cooperative, voluntary, and pressure. A market system is a kind of system within which profit-making firms are controlled, and government is a formal regulatory institution for distributing advantages involving public goods. But there are problems that go unattended in either sphere. Therefore, organizations with an in-between status evolve. Pressure groups seek to influence the political decision process. Cooperative agencies work with both firms and governments.

There are severe limits imposed on what the private market can accomplish in remedying social problems. Specifically, the decisions and transactions of firms can make decisions only about goods that are privately produced and privately consumed. Private suppliers

and consumers cannot make choices about defense of the society—for example, about how much should be expended for defense. Nor can sellers and buyers make decisions about the system of justice a society should maintain. Firms cannot judge how the total income of a society should be divided between public and private goods. National defense, police protection, and the setting of standards for the purity of foods and drugs, cannot be offered for sale to individuals.

Similarly, people as consumers cannot decide whether 10 per cent or 12 per cent of the Gross National Product should be devoted to public welfare assistance. The decision about how many goods are to be private and how many public, is itself a public decision. It is achieved politically through government. The government decides how much it will spend. The remainder of the product remains private.

Solving Major Social Problems Through the Federal Government

No matter which of the three main channels for action upon social problems is primary—market, government, or interest group—the events involved are very similar. In order to achieve a decision or to make a change, leaders approach the issue by gathering information; they sort alternatives; they prescribe and invoke rules of conduct; they apply the rules to the situation under question; and they evaluate the success of their new policy.[7]

[6]Note that aluminum is manufactured, animals are butchered, and ores mined by about the same techniques of production in a socialized economy as in a capitalist. The differences between the two types of economies are not technological but organizational. They have to do with who makes decisions about what issues, and on behalf of whom. Under socialism, public authorities produce private as well as public goods, where under capitalism they produce only public goods (in the pure case).

[7]See Harold D. Lasswell and A. Kaplan, *Power and Society*, New Haven: Yale University Press, 1950; and Lasswell, "The Decision Process," pp. 93-105, Nelson Polsby, et al, editors, *Politics and Social Life*, Boston: Houghton Mifflin, 1963.

There are forces which constrain the treatment of major social problems increasingly to the domain of the federal government, however. Some of these considerations have to do with the limits of power held by the market or by interest groups. These limits increase as the scale of a society increases and as the multiple effects of problems intensify.

A national industrial economy, for example, may undergo a depression. Nobody in the society may want a depression, and many business firms would be eager *to pay* to avoid one. The market includes no mechanism for accomplishing this, however. Prosperity cannot be purchased in the market for private goods. A depression ordinarily springs from events within the market, of course, but once a depression emerges it becomes a public event. A depression might correct itself in time; that is, the private market forces that induced it can modify themselves so as to reverse the condition. Yet, if the economy is an extremely interrelated affair, the public it serves may *refuse* to wait out the unfolding of self-correcting forces. And, in such an economy, the *public dangers* to national defense and welfare from a private economic depression may be defined as intolerable.

Issues of economic growth and levels of employment are like the problem of depression. The market system of the United States tends to produce, somewhat on its own and through decisions from within its own province of free enterprise, a characteristic *rate* of annual economic growth. The market system, however, includes no mechanism through which firms choose to increase or decrease this rate. If an increased rate of growth is desired, it must be sought publicly, and the primary channel for decision will be the federal government. This is not to say that agencies of the American government *know* how to increase the rate, although the tax cut described earlier is one promising illustration of intellectual control. Indeed, the decisions that are made may be failures. They may decrease economic growth; they may succeed beyond expectation. But, because there can be no such thing as a private market decision to expand total growth, or to reduce unemployment, these decisions, for better or worse, must be made by political leaders.

This point is so important that another illustration of the limits on the private market domain is in order. Consider radio commercials. These improve the net profits of those firms that use them strategically. They have value to advertisers, to ad men, and to the owners of radio stations. If a way existed, however, many listeners might be willing to *pay* to have commercials eliminated. Some listeners for instance attend loyally to a particular network's news broadcasts. They would give much to be spared the inanity of commercials from that network. Such listeners would in effect buy silence, or the absence of commercials. This is barely possible to achieve, however. It would involve payment for every commercial *not* delivered. Who is to estimate the return to the station of commercials they have thus far not even contracted for?[8]

[8]There are, in addition, innumerable natural monopolies such as gas, electricity, and water industries, in which it would economically be foolish to allow a large number of competing companies, in view of the large capital outlays entailed in establishing these industries and their facilities for distribution power or other services to consumers. Public regulations through government based on political decisions is thus substituted for the market. There are also *partially* public goods such as parks and bridges. These could be developed and operated within the private market, and indeed many things such as

We could multiply the illustrations, but our point is that, as a society matures technologically, environmentally, demographically and organizationally, its functions come to be divided in ever more complicated ways between the private and the public domains. In a previously underdeveloped country like Yugoslavia, the government may take over the development of an industrial-commercial *market* system, and by virtue of authority and planning stimulate market formation more rapidly than would occur naturally. When the market has gained a good foothold, the government may begin to *relax* public ownership and control, in spite of ideological doctrines warning against it, in order to maximize market autonomy and growth. In this instance, a modern industrializing and urbanizing nation may shift from a socialistic economy toward an ever more complicated balance between public and private ownership and control of goods.

In the American system, the private market has developed without much public governmental intervention. Only as the society has become vast and interrelated, has a new balance which involves a substantial increase in federal political control over all aspects of the society, including the economy, come about. The most dramatic shift in the historic balance came after the Great Depression:

> The grim decade of the nineteen-thirties had left a number of legacies to the American people.... The first of these, and the most fundamental, was

the idea that the fortunes of individual Americans are interlocked, that they are 'all in the same boat.' [A second] One was the idea that if individual Americans are in deep trouble, it is the job of the rest of the people, through their government, to come to their aid. The other was that it is their job, again through their government, to see that there is never another Great Depression.[9]

Limits of Government

In a society with a complex balance between the realms of private market and public authority, and especially in a society where the balance is changing, it is never clear *who* is responsible for attacking and alleviating social problems. The American tradition, moreover, includes precedents that work a kind of *devolution* toward federal responsibility. The federal government does not inherit a social problem (with a few well specified exceptions like national defense) until many private and local public recourses have been exhausted. Even when the federal authority intervenes, the country is so huge and its states and communities so diverse that federal programs must depend upon local initiatives for help and local programs of implementation. The arrangement is one in which under all save very tardy time schedules or virtual crises, federal intervention and aid is withheld from efforts to cope with major social problems.

The Johnson Administration's War on Poverty illustrates the historic, if changing, theme of the culture. Before a program could be mounted even in

transit systems and roads have been created in just this manner. When the scope of the operation becomes too enormous, however, or when it proves uncompetitive yet must be maintained because of the great public it serves, a park or a subway or even a railroad may become publically financed and maintained.

[9]Frederick Lewis Allen, *The Big Change*, New York: Harper, 1952. pp. 155-57.

miniature, presidential persuasion was required to assert that poverty is a threat to the nation's welfare and security. Presidents Kennedy and Johnson spent many months arguing the case that some effective steps could be taken, and that it was a governmental obligation to combat poverty as certainly as it is an obligation to protect against civil disorder. Finally, with the fatalism common to public acceptance of poverty, and with the civic conviction that poverty is inevitable, the steps the federal government takes are seldom if ever *sufficient* to cope with the problem.

The rate of change in public policies is — by nature of the decision process, the diverse publics and the distance between the government and the field — permanently incompatible with the rate of change in problems. New techniques of communication, new bodies of expert knowledge, and the maturity that comes from the accumulation of federal experience, suggest that this lag can be reduced somewhat. However, as the scale of the society enlarges and the intimate interrelations between elements continues to grow, social crises occur more rapidly too, making the new governmental efficiency insufficient once again. The agenda of the government, in any event, ordinarily contains issues of domestic social policy only *after* these have become extremely pressing matters in at least several sectors of the population. On issues of nuclear and space technology, the governmental agenda may take shape 'ahead' of the issue. It may play a defining, even innovative, role.

The legitimate authority of government is *coercive*, but this authority will be reserved and persuasion will be applied in all but the most threatening and pathetic of social crises. The 1964 Civil Rights Law contains the basis for coercion, just as the Supreme Court could arrange to demand rapid school desegregation. However, in these instances as with the power of intervention of the Federal Bureau of Investigation in the murders and bombings and church burnings in the Deep South in 1963 and 1964, all federal precedents point away from the use of coercive power save as a very last resort.

The character of limitations on government is revealed in the events that followed the murder of three civil rights workers in Mississippi in June of 1964. After many months of investigating, the FBI submitted its evidence to the Justice Department, which sought indictments against 21 alleged participants in the crime, first from a Grand Jury in Mississippi and second by presenting charges to a federal official, United States Commissioner, Esther Carter, who was appointed locally to her office. Both times, the federal attempt to prosecute was rejected; and a third attempt was initiated only after the evidence obtained had mounted to include increasingly impressive and verified facts.

More revealing is the point that the Justice Department sought indictments, not on a charge of criminal homicide, but on the charge of conspiracy to violate the federal Civil Rights Code. It applied an 1870 statute that provides a maximum penalty of 10 years in prison and up to $5,000 fine. The government cannot file charges of murder. These must come from the state in question, and the State of Mississippi made no arrests in this particular case under a state charge of murder until February, 1965.

The enactment of laws and their promulgation by education and persuasion is a very slow affair when the issues involved are brutality, terror, individual justice and survival. Yet this is an enduring limit upon the exercise of public power in the United States.

Pressure Groups

Under these ambiguous circumstances, and because most people are burdened by the task of looking out for their own interests — very few can spare time for the needs of others — most domestic social problems in America are worked on by special interest groups. Americans organize elaborately to advance and protect their special interests. Their organizations operate by applying persuasion, incentives, and fear to leadership within both the private market system and the government. Advertising, market research, public relations, industrial and commercial espionage, and other techniques exist for the application of pressure upon competing and cooperating private firms. The same techniques are used to press public authorities toward desired actions.

Special interest groups not only promote the wants of their members; they also help to relate government to the public at large. Political parties are crucial to the process of recruiting and electing leaders, but in the United States parties are generally seldom issue-centered. By providing for geographic and demographic representation, parties help insure that sectional interests will be involved in the making of public decisions. But special interest groups rather than parties supply *functional* representation. This means that these groups speak to social and economic issues which may cut across sectional differences. Unions, religious organizations, farm and business interest groups, for example, frequently identify and advance national problems

and policies by pressing for their consideration by Congress.[10]

Interest groups do more than initiate and influence legislation. Laws are but the groundwork of policies. A seemingly crucial law can be neutralized and a trivial law be made crucial by those who execute the law. Implementation is the task of public agencies of administration. It often involves decisions about what a law covers and *how* it is to be applied. There are problems of interpretation that fall short of judicial review. Special interest groups regularly seek to bias the interpretation of administrators in favor of their wants.

Education

Many people believe that education is basic to any attack on a social problem. Efforts to control crime and delinquency depend upon public understanding, but special interest groups take on the task most avidly. For if a climate of opinion hospitable to the group's position can be established, then the work of influencing lawmakers and administrators can be simplified tremendously.

Special interest groups include the professions within which social experts and practitioners reside, of course. Most educating on behalf of programs to reduce mental disorder, for example, is carried out through citizen mental health organizations and professional associations. These groups, composed of prospective clients and their professional helpers, produce public speakers,

[10]See William Kornhauser, *The Politics of Mass Society,* New York: Free Press, 1959, Chapter 3; and V.O. Key, Jr., *Politics, Parties, and Pressure Groups,* New York: Knopf, 1958, 4th edition.

movies, radio and television messages, which urge programs to support, train, and pay more for services in the field of mental health.

Efforts to shape opinion through propaganda are limited in their effects. In spite of years of public education about how mental disorders are illnesses that can be treated by neo-medical specialists, there is evidence that the American public continues to think of mental disorder as a shameful personal stigma. One study showed that about 25 per cent of the adults sampled thought they had psychological problems serious enough to require help, yet less than 14 per cent sought such help. Americans tend to expect that their neighbors will treat the mentally ill with rejection and disapproval. They also think of mental disorders stereotypically as involving dangerous or wild behavior.[11]

Perhaps the most telling indication of the limits upon the influence of public education comes from interest group efforts on civil rights and human relations. For more than a quarter of a century, labor unions, church groups, colleges, Negro protest groups, and minority associations have sponsored workshops, lectures, action research, publications, and professionalization of the field itself. These efforts have contributed, to be sure, to the enactment of state laws against discrimination and to the creation of governmental agencies to administer these laws. Moreover, the growth of civic participation in this educational endeavor is an index of social change.

It is impossible, in spite of the

[11]Gerald Gurin et al, *Americans View Their Mental Health,* New York: Basic Books, 1960. Also, Report of the Joint Commission on Mental Illness and Health, *Action for Mental Health,* New York: Basic Books, 1961.

scope and weight of these efforts, to know whether the total propaganda has had social effects upon the scope and intensity of discrimination. The state civil rights agencies vary tremendously in the relevance and force of their powers. Many of the techniques that characterize this field involve efforts to persuade without the power to coerce. Fact-finding, discussion groups, human relations commissions, have helped to stimulate a climate of public opinion within which equal opportunity for disadvantaged groups has become more acceptable. But little of this effort has had impact except in communities and groups already disposed toward civil rights. We believe that legal action and, in this current decade, non-violent protests and violent rioting have blended to induce more change of greater consequence than all of earlier educative endeavors combined.

Deliberate Action on a Social Problem

We have sketched in the major groups and institutions that participate in coping with major national social problems. We have emphasized the structural limits upon the influence of each element. We have not suggested in this sketch exactly *how* decisions to work on social problems are reached and implemented.

A sociological sketch of the entire process would take too long to develop, but we can point up several essentials of the process here. Perhaps the main proposition is that of a *blending of initiatives.* Special interest groups are only on occasion monolithic. Most members of the American Medical Association may tend to be physicians first, last, and always; but most members of the United Steelworkers of America, or the United States Chamber of Commerce, are also home owners, parents, and church members. Action toward change occurs most often when the general social interest is reflected in the converging of multiple interests of otherwise diverse interest groups. "It is thus multiple memberships in potential groups based on widely held and accepted interests that serve as a balance wheel in a going political system like that of the United States."[12]

A corollary is that this blending must be reinforced by pressure from *within* government, if action is to occur. Staffs of government are not passive agents. They operate from consolidated power; they also accumulate experience and special interests of their own. Through propaganda and education, government departments often seek to prepare the basis for changes in policy and practice. Many government officials are also situated as citizens in professional and other special interest groups, some of which (say, the Air Force Association) have unusual influence in congressional deliberations. Government workers also prepare the documents, do the research, and present the basis upon which many legislative and judicial decisions are reached. When extra-governmental pressures coincide with intra-governmental dispositions, changes in policy and practice are most likely to be accomplished.

A third feature qualifies the way in which deliberate action may be taken, however. A concert of interests and a mutually reinforcing set of shared goals between government staff and pressure groups will often trigger decision, but there are other conditions that also

[12]David B. Truman, *The Governmental Process*, New York: Knopf, 1951, p. 514.

permit of change. One of these occurs when *conflicts of interest* between pressure groups, sectional factions of the society, or governmental staff, deepen and spread toward civil disorder.

If two or more powerful groups are committed very intensely on some issue, the usual process of competition for advantage may break down and become a damaging conflict. In this respect, efforts to cope with social problems can in themselves stimulate new, more disorganizing problems. On occasion, however, government will speed up its decision process and introduce policy changes in order to prevent the spread of conflict.

Social change may be consciously achieved by a fairly small interest group —against the grain of the culture, perhaps, and even against the opposition of larger if less intense interests—if its members are prepared to risk enough, including their status as citizens. Threats of revolution, disobedience, subversion, and treason have, historically, been influential if illegal means of change for the American labor movement, for the achievement of civil liberties, and for securing civil rights.

Concluding Note

Programs to prevent social problems are just now becoming common in the United States. Deliberate efforts to alleviate poverty in the mass, programs to improve and to enforce civil rights, and community programs for reducing delinquency, mental disorders and family conflict, are becoming widespread, though they remain controversial.

Newspaper editorials never instruct engineers how to build bridges, yet they deal every day with social problems.

Some editorial writers, moreover, seem convinced that there is little to learn about social problems beyond the current views of leaders, common sense, and descriptive data. The public has few fixed notions about designing airplanes, while it has deeply fixed views about the causes of and remedies for social problems

This chapter has argued that the solution to social problems does not lie in recourse to social experts. On the other hand, this book has tried to show that many avenues exist for profound and productive participation in the social decisions that lead to prevention and remedy of major social problems. The author wishes to reassert the important contribution that can be made by the social scientifically trained expert. The social scientist carries a valuable catalog of plans that have failed. He is expert on the question of what will most likely not work. He is also vitally helpful on occasion in sorting out the costs and benefits of various alternatives.

Economists have pointed the way toward the production of various goods that are very low in cost and very high in benefits for ameliorating public difficulties. Social insurance through social security payments and benefits and unemployment insurance are perhaps the best proofs of what experts can contribute. The concept of social insurance was extended to include medical care in 1965, for instance. Medical care under an insurance scheme, whether all public or partly private and partly public, probably reveals the lightest limitations conceivable upon freedom of consumer choice. Free education and free mass transit are comparable programs with relatively low costs and very high returns for the population.

But experts cannot go far beyond the existing framework of the community culture, even if their schemes would offer the public what it needs. "An overwhelming sentiment in favor of good health is no assurance that people will rush to support a program that promises health improvement," cautions one anthropologist. "Health, like sin, can be controversial."[13] Nor can the expert resolve the issues of financing a program, administering it, and making it more or less compulsory. In innumerable ways, the expert is but one adjunct to the three-way decision process we have outlined in this chapter. But what he contributes can sometimes be decisive in determining the *effectiveness* of programs. It is this fact that makes the analytical study of contemporary social problems worthwhile.

We have emphasized the political decision process because it is through this channel that programs of prevention rather than amelioration are most likely to take shape. Wide public participation in the quest for ways to prevent social problems, and therefore substantial governmental committment to work on an issue, are integral to the process of social change. When public interest in delinquency is very low, for example, the most that may be achieved is improved means of detection, arrest, adjudication, and formal incarceration. These improvements all presuppose little or no social change, and all occur *after the fact* of the delinquent act. Without preventive effort, the rate of delinquency could remain constant even though technical procedures for catching offenders improved.

When public concern is strong (though not so intense as to prove repressive and punitive, perhaps), the fact

[13]Solon T. Kimball, "An Alabama Town Surveys Its Health Needs," *Health, Culture and Community*, ed. Benjamin Paul, Russell Sage Foundation, New York, 1955, p. 292.

that a dollar spent on prevention goes further than a dollar spent on incarceration begins to be taken seriously.[14] If there is some disposition to invest in this more economical strategy of prevention, the public, having decided politically to take this step, will also experience changes in its own treatment of adolescents.

[14]According to one expert, $25 thousand a year spent on one boy in a correctional institution in New York City would cover intensive casework with 12 families, or recreation programs for 85 children, or salary for a trained youth leader, or a remedial reading teacher. See Kirson Weinberg, *Social Problems In Our Time*, Englewood Cliffs, N.J.: Prentice-Hall, 1960, p. 140.

The awareness that official delinquency is related to attitudes of adults toward children, toward the availability of community facilities for youth, and toward employment of parents, may grow through progressive investment in prevention in a way that cannot occur with a correctional effort. At this juncture, prevention might stimulate social changes in the overall causal conditions underlying deviant behavior. Insofar as many social problems are profoundly interconnected, only efforts at prevention will commit a public to the comprehensive changes that would be necessary to ameliorate the chain of problems.

INDEX

Abrahamsen, David, 378
Abrams, Charles, 177
Abu-Lughod, Janet, 351
Accardo, Tony, 392, 393, 395
Accidents, automobile, 315
Adloff, Richard, quoted, 189
Adonis, Joe, 391, 395, 400, 401 n., 402
AFL–CIO, and migrant workers, 275–76
Africa, 95, 97, 101, 164; cities in, 334–35; estimated annual rates of population increase in, by countries (table), 490; nativity of white populations in (table), 189; population problems in, 468, 485, 487, 489–90; white populations in, 188–89
Age, as aspect of poverty, 113–14, 129
Aged, housing of, 307–08
Agricultural problems, see Rural problems
Agricultural work, see Migrant farm workers, Rural problems
Agricultural work by factory workers, 29
Aichhorn, August, 378
Air pollution, 3–6, 315–16
Alaska, 186
Alexander, Franz, 378
Algeria, 96, 188, 189; population problems of, 486–90
Allen, Frederick Lewis, 243, 510 n.
Allport, Gordon, 177
Almon, Clopper, Jr., 262 n.
Amend, Eleanor A., 37 n.
American Civil War, 56
Ames, A., 430, 451 n.
Amidon, Edna P., 124
Anderson, C. Arnold, 243
Anderson, Nels, 122, 123, 318
Anderson, William A., 32 n., 243
Andry, R. G., 378
Angel, E., 432, 436
Annenberg, Moe, 392
Anslinger, 405 n., 407 n., 410 n.
ANZUS, 99
Appalachia, 136, 241, 262; see also Folk culture
Appleby, L., 429, 450
Area Redevelopment Program, 139
Argentina, 321; population problems in, 486, 489
Arhus University, Denmark, 102
Arizona Cotton Growers' Assn., 289
Arnold, R., 432, 451
Aron, Raymond, 59 n., 67
Aronov, Edward, 348
Aronowitz, Stanley, 152 n.
Arrest, social correlates of, 365–66
Ashmore, Harry S., 177
Asia: population problems in, 483–88, 491; rates of annual population increase in, by countries (table), 488
Astor Home for Children, Rhinebeck, N.Y., 455–56
Augusta, Ga., 236

Aurelio, Thomas, 399, 400
Australia, 143, 181, 182, 184, 190, 321; population problems in, 485, 487–89
Austria, 92, 100, 102
Ausubel, David P., 378, 414 n., 415 n.
Automation, 27–28; and unemployment, 116, 193; proposals for government policy on, 152–62
Avoidance in sociological studies, 38–45

Baade, Fritz, 471 n.
Back, Kurt, 122, 318, 346, 348; quoted, 347
Bahamas, 287
Bain, J. S., 252 n.
Baker, Gordon E., 27 n.
Baldwin, Hanson W., 67
Baldwin, James, quoted, 163, 166 n., 177
Ball, George, quoted, 61
Baltimore, Md., 307
Barbados, 470, 486
Barber, B., 430, 446
Barnes, Harry E., 378
Barnes, John A., 184 n.
Barron, Milton L., 177, 378
Barton, Paul, 179
Barton, W. E., 430, 449
Baruch, Bernard, quoted, 403
Basutoland, 189
Bateson, Gregory, 433
Bauer, R. A., 45
Bayley, Monica, 122
Beale, Calvin L., 200 n.
Beccaria, 382
Bechuanaland, 189
Becker, Howard S., 16
Beegle, Allen J., 244, 258 n., 335 n.
Behrens, Marjorie, quoted, 455–64
Belcher, John C., 244
Belgium, 5, 100, 101, 102
Belknap, Ivan, 428 n., 430, 452, 453
Bell, Daniel, quoted, 387–403
Bell, Luther, 446
Bell, W., 298 n.
Bellak, L., 430, 449
Bendix, Reinhard, 122, 191, 318
Benedict, Murray R., 244
Benedict, Ruth, 260 n.
Benelux, 101; see also Belgium, Luxembourg, Netherlands
Bensing, Robert C., 378
Bensman, Joseph, 245
Benson, Ezra Taft, 293
Bentley, A. F., 430, 451 n.
Benvenuti, B., 244
Berger, 413 n.; quoted, 415 n.
Berger, Monroe, 177
Berger, Victor, 150
Bergler, Edmund, 378
Bernard, Jessie Shirley, 16, 177

Chinese Americans, 183, 218; *see also* Oriental Americans
Cities: as social organisms, 329–36; *see also* Urban problems, Urbanization
Civil War, American, 56
Civil War, Spanish, 60 n.
Clague, Ewan, quoted, 493–502
Clarence, Clyde Ferguson, 177
Clark, Colin, quoted, 402
Clark, Harvey, 170
Clark, Kenneth, 178
Clausen, John A., 406 n., 419 n., 430, 432, 444; quoted, 407
Clay, Ky., 205
Clayton, Horace, 178
Clemmer, Donald, 379
Clinard, Marshall B., 25 n.; quoted, 363–64 n., 379
Clinton, Tenn., 205, 208
Cloward, Richard A., 379
Coale, Ansley J., 480
Cochrane, W. W., 251 n.
Cohen, Albert K., 379
Cohen, Mickey, 392
Cohen, Sam, 394
Cohen, Wilbur J., 123, 131 n.; quoted, 125–40
Colarelli, N., 430, 450
Coleman, James S., 188 n.
College of Europe, Brussels, 102
Colleges, population pressures on, 494–95
Common Market, *see* European Common Market, Latin American Common Market
Commons, John R., 151
Conant, James B., 122
Congo, 60, 66, 96, 97, 185 n.
Conrad, Earl, 179
Cook, Robert C., 480
Cooper, Joseph B., 67
Cooper, Robert L., 178
Copeland, Royal, 400
Cornell University, 309
Coser, Lewis, 225
Costa Rica, 91, 468, 486, 489
Costello, Frank, 390, 391, 395, 396, 398–401, 402
Cox, Oliver Cromwell, 178
Cressey, Donald R., 365 n., 366 n., 374 n., 379; quoted, 371
Crim, J., 405 n., 408 n.
Crime, 12, 125, 359–416; causes of, 366–68, 369; as concomitant of urbanization, 26; definition of, 359–61; functional interpretation of, 363; as an institution, 361–62, 368–69; as normal and inevitable, 363; organized, 368–69, 388–403; penalties for, 369–72; rates of, 374–75, 377; reported volume of, 364–65; as result of nuclear attack, 79–80; as social problem, 361–63; statistics on, unreliability of, 363–64, 365, 368 n.; theories of, 366–68, 376, 381–85; U.S. characteristics and history of, 387–403
Criminal behavior, meaning of, 385–86
Criminal law, 359–61
Cuba, 91–92
Cuban Americans, 175
Cuber, John Frank, 16

Cultural lag, 10, 12, 19–20
Culture conflict theory of crime, 367, 375
Cumming, Elaine, 430, 444, 453
Cumming, J., 429, 430, 444, 453
Cumpston, I. M., 186 n.
Curran, Joe, 276
Cutright, Phillips, quoted, 69–83

Dahl, Robert A., 507 n.
Dai, 407 n.
Dalsimer, J. S., 433
Dandekar, D. P., 221
David, Martin H., 131 n.
Davie, Maurice R., 178
Davies, Ronald, 187 n.
Davis, Allison, 178
Davis, Kingsley, 335 n., 480; quoted, 320–28
Dawson, Howard H., 244
Day, Frank D., 379
Dean, Stanley, quoted, 436–37
Death: causes of, 417, 420 n., (table) 315; rate, decline in, 468, (chart) 486; world variation in, 490
Defense, *see* War
Deficiency, mental, *see* Mental deficiency
De Gaulle, Charles, 90
De Lange, W. H., 430, 432, 450, 452
de Lestapis, S., 480
Delinquency, juvenile, *see* Juvenile delinquency
Demilitarization, *see* Disarmament
Demographic problems, *see* Population problems
Denmark, 100, 102, 122, 142, 277, 443
Dennis, Wayne, 349–50
Dentler, Robert A., 152 n., 375 n.; quoted, 69–83
Desegregation: negotiations on, 222–28; in restaurants, 226; in schools, 205–07, 209–17; white attitudes toward, 205–17, (charts) 209, 213, 214, 215, 216
Des Lauriers, A. M., 430, 450
Detroit, Mich., 235
Deutsch, 412 n., quoted, 413
Deutsch, Morton, 67, 68
Deviant behavior, 8–9, 11, 12, 26; as aspect of poverty, 121; *see also* Crime, Criminal behavior, Juvenile delinquency, Mental illness, Narcotics, Skid Row
Dewey, J., 430, 451 n.
Dewey, Thomas E., 387; quoted, 399
Dexter, Lewis Anthony, quoted, vii, 38–44
Dexter, R. C., 45; quoted, 39
Diamond, Jack "Legs," 390
Diamond, Sigmund, quoted, 141–51
Differential association theory of crime, 366–67, 375
Differential social organization theory of crime, 367, 375
Di Giovanni, Anthony, 400
Dinitz, Simon, 379
Disability, mental, *see* Mental disability
Disability, physical, *see* Physical disability
Disability insurance, 280
Disarmament, 85–98
Discrimination: in housing, 170, 208–10; against nonwhites, 136; and prejudice, 165–66; reli-

gious, 177; in voting rights, 168, 172; *see also* Desegregation, Negroes, Nonwhite population, Nonwhite workers, Segregation

Disorganization, social, 7–8, 11, 12, 19–20; following nuclear attack, 79–80

Dollard, Charles, 178

Dollard, John, 178

Dominican Republic, 60, 489

Douglas, William O., 68

Doust, J. W., 430

Dowdy, George T., Sr., quoted, 275

Drake, St. Clair, 178

Dresden, Germany, 78

Dressler, David, 379

Driscoll, Gov., 400 n.

Drug addiction, *see* Narcotics

Du Bois, W. E. Burghardt, 178

Duhl, Leonard J., 122

Dumpson, James R., 349

Duncan, Beverly, 334 n.

Duncan, Otis Dudley, 27 n., 181 n., 183 n., 244, 332 n., 334 n., 481

Dunham, H. Warren, 309 n., 349, 430; quoted, 425

Dunn, Frederick Sherwood, 67

Du Pont de Nemours & Co., E. I., 236

Durkheim, Émile, 36; quoted, 363

Dutch East Indies, 188; *see also* Indonesia

Dyer, Murray, 67

Earnings of elementary school graduates (table), 132

Eastern Europe, 103

Eaton, Joseph W., 430

Economic aspects of poverty, 106–116, 120–22, 129–32

Education: as aspect of population problems, 30–31, 494–96, 499–502; as aspect of poverty, 114, 129, 131, 132–33, 139; of children of migratory workers, 282–83; farmer attitudes toward, 259–60; and income, 202–04; for leisure, 161–62; as means of increasing employment, 254–55; among nonwhite population, 167, 203; supranational, 102; of young workers in 1960's and 1950's (chart), 496

Egypt: growth of cities in, 335; population problems in, 486, 490

Eiduson, Bernice T., 430, 446

Einstein, A., 431

Eisenhower, Dwight D., 402 n.

Eldridge, Hope T., 480

Eldridge, William Butler, quoted, 404–16

Ellenberger, H., 432

Ellenbogen, Bertram L., 37 n.

Ellender, Allen J., 168

Ellenton, S.C., 236

Elliott, Mabel Agnes, 16

Ellis, Havelock, quoted, 383

Ellsworth, R., 431, 448, 449

Employed persons: by industry and color (table), 194; in nonagricultural industries, by full- or part-time status and color (table), 199; by occupation group and color (table), 195

Employment: change in, 1960–70 (chart), 501; of nonwhites, *see* Nonwhite workers; *see also* Unemployment

England, *see* Great Britain

Engler, Richard E., Jr., 349

Environmental problems, 34–35; *see also* Urban problems

Epstein, Lenore A., 122

Erickson, Frank, 393

Ethnic groups: definitions of, 163–66; *see also* Indians, American; Cuban Americans; French Canadians; Irish Americans; Italian Americans; Japanese Americans; Mexican Americans; Negroes; Nonwhite population; Polish Americans; Puerto Ricans; Spanish Americans

Ethnic relations, 163–77, 181–91; conflict and assimilation in, 188–91; at contact, 182–84; in multiple contacts, 186–88; political and economic aspects of, 184–86; *see also* Race relations

Etzioni, Amitai, quoted, 99–105, 431, 453

European Coal and Steel Community, 91, 101

European Common Market, 90, 100

European University, Florence, 102

Evan, William M., 68

Evans, G., 318

Everett, Hugh, III, 73

Ey, Henri, 436

Fairweather, G. W., 431, 450

Families: with female head, income of (chart), 137; with income below $2,000, percent of (chart), 138

Families, deprived: budget estimates for (table), 111; housing of, 112, 113

Families, poor: budget estimates for (table), 111; characteristics of (charts), 130, 134, (table) 126; housing of, 337–48; income of, 110–13, 129–32, (table) 128

Family breakdown, 12–13, 341–42; as cause of poverty, 113, 114

Family income, median: by color (table), 203; by color and educational attainment (table), 204

Family income, total money, by color (table), 204

Farber, Maurice L., 67

Farley, James, 403

Farm: income, 246–55; ownership, decline in, 232–34; technology, 232, 256–57; workers, *see* Migrant farm workers; *see also* Rural problems

Farmers, subsistence, 256–60

Farrell, M. J., 430, 449

Feder, Sid, 380

Fellsmere Sugar Producers Assn., 276–77

Felony, definition of, 361

Field, R. F., 29 n.

Fiji Islands, 186, 470

Filipino migrant workers, 286, 293

Finestone, 411 n.

Firey, Walter, 28 n., 335 n.

Fischetti, Charley, 392, 395

Fisher, Ernest M., 349

Fisher, Robert Moore, 27 n.

Fitch, Lyle C., quoted, 316–17

Japanese Americans, 167, 176, 182, 187, 218, 477
Jaspan, Norman, 379
Jencks, Christopher, 152 n., 155
Jerome, Harry, 185
Jerome, William Travers, 387
Jersey City, N.J., 398
Jews, American, 167, 175, 397, 399, 400, 401
Johnson, Charles S., 178
Johnson, D. Gale, 248, 249 n.
Johnson, Lyndon B., 510–11; quoted, 125, 504
Johnston, Helen L., 123
Johnston, William, 393
Jones, Joseph Marion, quoted, 483–92
Jones, M., 431, 436, 447, 448, 451
Jones, Victor, 33 n.
Jorgenson, Janet M., 239 n., 241 n., 244
Jungk, Robert, 84; quoted, 83 n.
Juvenile delinquency, 20 n., 42, 125, 371, 372–78; as concomitant of organization, 26; correlates of, 375–76; prevention of, 376–77; rates of, 374–75; as social problem, 372–74; *see also* Gangs, juvenile

Kahn, Herman, 68, 77, 84
Kahne, M. J., 432, 453
Kansas City, 396
Kaplan, A., 508 n.
Kardiner, Abram, 178
Karraher, Cyrus, 292
Kastel, Phil, 399
Kates, Philip, 33 n.
Kaufman, Harold F., 244
Kefauver, Estes, 379, 387, 390, 393, 394, 395, 396, 397 n.; quoted, 394, 395, 396
Keller, Allan, quoted, 269, 272, 283–84
Kennedy, J. P., 379
Kennedy, John F., 88, 207, 402 n., 511; quoted, 312
Kennedy, Michael, 400
Kenya, 490
Kephart, William H., 191
Kern Land Co., 266
Kessler, Matthew A., quoted, 192–204
Key, V. O., Jr., 512 n.
Keyserling, Leon, 109, 110, 114, 122
Khanna, J., 432, 448
Khanna, Prabha, 432, 448
Khrushchev, Nikita, 88, 96
Killian, Lewis M., quoted, 222–28
Kilpatrick, F. P., 430, 432, 446
Kimball, Solon T., 515 n.
King, 411 n.
King, Arden R., 257 n.
King, Frances G., quoted, 455–64
King, Martin Luther, 171, 178
Kinsey, Alfred, 40
Kitsuse, John I., 191
Klein, Annette, 431
Kleist, Col. von, 104 n.
Klineberg, Otto, 68
Kluckhohn, Clyde, 432
Knight, Gov., 285
Knorr, Klaus E., 60 n., 68
Kohrman, Janet, 431

Kolb, 408 n.
Kolb, John Harrison, 244
Kolb, William L., 36
Korea, 60, 66, 96, 478
Korn, Richard, 505 n.
Kornbluh, Joyce L., 269 n., 271 n.
Kornhauser, William, 512 n.
Kraenzel, Carl F., 244
Krótki, Karol Józef, 185 n.
Kuh, Richard, 405 n.
Kuper, Leo, 187 n.
Kurella, Hans, quoted, 382

Labatut, Jean, 335 n.
Labor force: balance sheet for 1960's (chart), 497; nonwhite participation in, 200–02; participation rates, by age, color, and sex (table), 202; projected percentage of women in, 1970 (chart), 499; young workers entering annually (chart), 498
La Guardia, Fiorello, 387, 399, 400
Lait, Jack, 396, 397 n.
Lamale, Helen H., 349
Lampard, Eric E., 334 n.; quoted, 329
Lampman, Robert J., 30 n., 109, 123, 318
Lancaster, Lane W., 244
Landis, Paul Henry, 16, 25 n.
Lane, Wheaton J., 335 n.
Langner, Thomas S., 123–24
Lansky, Meyer, 395
Laos, 60
Larrabee, Eric, 160
Larson, Olaf F., 244
Las Vegas, Nev., 297, 393
Lasswell, Harold D., 508 n.
Latin America, 91, 93, 94, 101–02; population problems in, 485, 487–89; rates of annual population increase in, by countries (table), 489; *see also* Argentina, Brazil, British Guiana, Chile, Costa Rica, Cuba, El Salvador, Guatemala, Mexico, Nicaragua, Venezuela
Latin American Common Market, 101
Laurence, John, 379
Lawrence, Kans., 236
Lea, H. C., 432, 446
League for Industrial Democracy, 281
League of Nations, 95
Leckie, R., 68
Lee, Raymond Lawrence, 16
Lee, Reba, 177
Lehman, Herbert H., 399
Leighton, Alexander H., 432
Lemert, Edwin, 16
Lenehan, Frances, 430, 449
Lesher, T., 432, 448
Leslie, Gerald L., 16
Levin, M., 436
Levine, Louis, 254 n.
Levinson, D. J., 430
Levitt, Jules, 394
Levitt, William, 303
Lewin, K., 432, 451 n.
Lewis, John L., 42
Lewis, Oscar, 123, 318; quoted, 121

Lexington, Ky., U. S. Public Health Service Hospital at, 414–15, 441
Liberia, 185
Libya, 490
Lieberman, Louis, 348
Lieberson, Stanley, 334 n.; quoted, 181–91
Lincoln, Eric C., 178–79
Lind, Andrew W., 179, 181 n., 187, 188 n.
Lindauer, Martin, 330
Lindesmith, Alfred R., 16, 379, 410 n.; quoted, 46–51
Lipset, Seymour M., 122, 191, 318
Little Rock, Ark., 205, 208
Living standard, as aspect of poverty, 108–13
Llopis, Bartolomé, 436
Lodge, Henry Cabot, 402 n.
Lombroso, Cesare, 382
London, 324, 468
Long, Huey, 399
Loomis, Charles P., 244, 258 n,, 335 n.
Los Angeles, Calif., 322, 396; air pollution in, 3–6, 13–14, 315; crime in, 392–93
Louis, Joe, 402
Lowenthal, Max, 379
Lowry, 414 n.
Lubell, Samuel, 402 n.
Luciano, Charles, 380, 390, 396, 399
Luck, James Murray, 123, 318
Luxembourg, 100, 101
Lynching, 14, 177

Maas, Henry S., 349
McCarran-Walter Act, 477–78
McCarthy, Joseph, 42
McCord, Joan, 379
McCord, William, 379
McCormack, William J., 397
McDonagh, Edward C., 16–17, 179
MacDonald, Dwight, 123, 318
MacDonald, Stephen L., 28 n.
McFarland, M. Carter, 349
McGee, Reece, 16
MacGregor, Helen, 431
Mack, Raymond W., 191
McKay, Henry D., 374 n.
McKee, James B., 179
McKenzie, R. D., 33 n., 183 n., 186, 187 n.
McLaughlin, 430, 449
McLean Hospital, Boston, 440
McMurray, Joseph P., 337, 349
McNamara, Robert L., 242 n.; quoted, 55–56
McSweeney, E. S., 289
Mafia, 395–97
Maier, Frank H., 231 n.
Malaya, 186, 486, 488
Malone, Carl C., 244
Malthusian theory, 34–35
Mangus, A. R., 37 n.
Manno, Pat, quoted, 389
Mansfield, Tex., 205
Maoris, 181
Marcantonio, Vito, 400
Marden, Charles F., 179

Marinelli, Al, 399
Markoff, Sol, 282 n.
Marsh, Bernard L., quoted, 314 n.
Marshall, Alexander, 439–43
Marshall, Alfred, 248
Marshall, Andrew W., 418 n.
Martin, H. David, 123
Marvick, Elizabeth Wirth, 36 n.
Massachusetts, mental illness in, 439–42
Massachusetts Bay Colony, laws relating to poor in, 146–49
Maternal death rates, 420 n.; among Negroes, 170
Matthews, M. Taylor, 259 n.
Matza, David, 374 n.
Maurer, 413 n.
Mauritius, 186, 486
May, Edgar, 123
May, R., 432
Mayman, Martin, quoted, 434–38
Meadows, Paul, 37 n.; quoted, 36
Meany, George, 276
Meat and Cannery Workers (AFL–CIO), 276
Meerlov, A. M., 378
Mehl, Paul, 260 n.
Meier, Richard L., 481
Meijering, W. L., 432, 449
Melman, Seymour, 156
Menninger, Karl, 436; quoted, 434–38
Mennonites, 175
Mental deficiency, 38–44
Mental disability, 113, 125, 134; see also Mental illness
Mental hospitals, 419–20, 426 n., 440–43, 444–54; innovations in, 444–54; institutional structure of, 445
Mental illness, 12, 134, 417–64; in children, 455–64; difficulties in classifying, 434–38; functional concept of, 422–23; in Massachusetts, 439–42; in New York City, 425–26, 437, 441; physical concept of, 421–22; problems in defining, 423–24, 426–27; rates of, 437, 439–43; rates of hospitalization for, 418; a social problem, 418–20; and social structure, 424–27; treatment of, 427–29, 444–64; trends in, 439–43
Meredith, James, 11, 208
Merrill, Francis E., 16
Merton, Robert K., 16, 37 n., 79 n., 243, 349, 364 n., 367–68, 374, 375, 379, 419 n., 430, 432, 453; quoted, 371
Metzler, William H., 258 n., 261 n.; quoted, 256–63
Mexican Americans, 167, 175, 181, 190, 239–41, 266, 267; see also Migrant farm workers
Mexico, 5, 187, 268; growth of cities in, 335; population problems in, 486, 489
Meyers, J. K., 432
Miami, Fla., crime in, 393, 394
Michael, Donald N., 152 n.
Michel, Andrée V., 350
Michigan, University of, 131, 132, 133
Midland, Tex., 297
Mighell, Ronald L., 244

elimination of, 158–59; rural, 139, 241–42,
246–55; size and nature of, 127–36; strategy
against, 136–39; *see also* Slums
Powers, Edwin, 379
Pratt, Steve, 432, 433, 445 n., 447, 448, 450,
451, 452, 453 n.; quoted, 444–54
Prejudice, *see* Discrimination
Premature birth, among nonwhites, 134
Price, A. Grenfell, 181 n., 182 n., 184
Price, Donald O., 122
Price system, 106–07, 110
Prince Edward County, Va., 8, 208
Prison system, failure of, 370–71
Pritchard, J. L., 379
Proano, A., 429
Probation and parole, 371–72
Prostitution, 369, 389, 390, 403
Pruyser, Paul, quoted, 434–38
Public housing, 344–48; income of families in,
345–46; percentage of 3- and 4-person fam-
ilies in total population and moving into (ta-
ble), 347
Puerto Ricans, 175, 239, 287, 293, 307; nar-
cotics addiction among, 406–07 n.
Puerto Rico, 268, 279, 470, 486
Pugh, George E., 73
Pursuit, D. G., 379

Quaker Maid Co., 283

Raab, Earl, 17, 179
Race relations, in U.S., 222–28; major events in
(chart), 208; *see also* Desegregation, Discrimi-
nation, Ethnic relations, Negroes, Nonwhite
population, Nonwhite workers, Segregation
Racial minorities, *see* Ethnic groups
Ragen, James, 392
Raina, B. L., 470
Raisbeck, Alden, quoted, 332
Randolph, Vance, 258 n.
Ranulf, Svend, 388
Rapoport, R. N., 433, 447, 448
Rasor, 408 n.
Ratcliff, Richard U., 31 n., 350
Ray, Isaac, 446
Reahl, J. E., 431
Real, James, 68; quoted, 85–98
Reckless, Walter C., 365 n., 379
Reddaway, William B., 30 n.
Redfield, Robert, 258 n.
Redlich, F. C., 123, 425 n., 426 n., 430, 431, 447
Reed, P., 432, 451
Rees, J. Sidney, 104 n.
Reiss, Albert J., Jr., 27 n., 36 n., 332 n.
Religious composition of U.S., effect of nuclear
attack on (chart), 72
Religious discrimination, 177
Rennie, Thomas, 124; quoted, 423–24
Rent, average monthly, before and after relo-
cation of low-income families (table), 339
Reuter, E. B., 181 n., 184
Retardation, mental, *see* Mental deficiency
Reves, E., 68
Reynolds, Harry W., Jr., 350

Reynolds, Q. J., 68
Rhinebeck, N.Y., 455–56
Ricca, Paul, 392
Rice, Robert, 379
Richards, Eugene S., 179
Riese, Walther, quoted, 434
Riesman, David, 156, 160, 326
Riessman, Frank, 154
Riis, Jacob, quoted, 397
Riverside Hospital, New York City, 414–15
Roberts, B. H., 432
Roberts, Stephen, 184 n.
Robinson, Ray, 402
Rogers, Everett M., 239 n., 243 n., 245
Rogers, Hugo, 400
Rogers, Lewis H., 316 n.
Roosevelt, Franklin D., 152, 311, 399, 401
Roosevelt, Theodore, 96, 387; quoted, 388
Root, William T., Jr., quoted, 384
Roper, Elmo, quoted, 391
Rose, Arnold, 17, 179, 425 n., 426 n., 433
Rose, J. Hugh, 31 n.
Rosenbaum, Edward, 394
Rosenberg, Bernard, 17, 505 n.
Rosenheim, M. K., 379
Rothstein, Arnold, 390, 397
Rovere, Richard H., 379
Ruesch, J., 433
Rumney, Jay, 305 n.
Rural problems: area development, 237–39; com-
munity decline, 234–35; decline in farm own-
ership, 232–34; economic adjustment, 260–62;
folk culture, 256–63; government, 242–43;
health, 242; industrialization, 235–37, 242–43,
262–63; migrant workers, 239–41; poverty,
139, 241–43, 246–55; technological changes,
232, 256–57; underemployment, 248–55; vil-
lages, 234–35
Rush, Benjamin, 438 n., 446
Russell, B., 433, 446
Russett, Bruce M., 472 n.
Russia: poverty in, 106; *see also* U.S.S.R.
Russo Bros., 283
Rutgers University, 154 n.
Ruttan, Vernon W., 260–61 n.
Ryder, Norman B., 30 n.

Saenger, Gerhart, 179
Sage, P. C., 482
St. Louis, Mo., 344; crime in, 391
Saint-Simon, Comte de, 505
Salvador, El, 486, 489
Salvation Army, 354–55
Salvey, Harold, 394
Salzburg, Austria, 102
Sanders, R., 431, 433, 450
Sarason, S., 43 n., 44, 45
Sarubbi, Paul, 399
Sauvy, Alfred, 481
Sax, Karl, 481
Scandinavia, 102, 103, 104; *see also* Denmark,
Norway, Sweden
Scarpitti, Frank R., 379
Schelling, Thomas C., 68

79926

DATE DUE

MAR 27 '01			
NOV 3 0 1990			
NOV 14 1992			